James Robinson Planché

A Cyclopädia of Costume

Dictionary of Dress

James Robinson Planché

A Cyclopädia of Costume
Dictionary of Dress

ISBN/EAN: 9783742837646

Manufactured in Europe, USA, Canada, Australia, Japa

Cover: Foto ©Andreas Hilbeck / pixelio.de

Manufactured and distributed by brebook publishing software
(www.brebook.com)

James Robinson Planché

A Cyclopädia of Costume

A

CYCLOPÆDIA OF COSTUME

OR

DICTIONARY of DRESS,

Including Notices of Contemporaneous Fashions on the Continent;

AND

*A General Chronological History of the Costumes of the principal Countries
of Europe, from the Commencement of the Christian Era
to the Accession of George the Third.*

By JAMES ROBINSON PLANCHÉ, ESQ.

SOMERSET HERALD.

IN TWO VOLUMES.

VOL. II.—A GENERAL HISTORY OF COSTUME IN EUROPE.

London:

CHATTO AND WINDUS, PICCADILLY.

1879.

TO

THE PRESIDENT AND MEMBERS

OF

The Royal Academy of Arts,

These Volumes

ARE

RESPECTFULLY INSCRIBED

BY

THEIR OBEDIENT SERVANT,

J. R. PLANCHÉ.

CONTENTS.

CHAPTER IX.

THE EIGHTEENTH CENTURY.

CHAPTER X.

THEATRICAL, ALLEGORICAL, AND FANCIFUL COSTUME.

DIRECTIONS FOR PLACING THE PLATES IN VOL. II.

CHROMOLITHOGRAPHS.

[Those Plates marked with an asterisk (*) have already been placed at the end of the First Volume.]

** The subjects in the Plate of Russian Crowns and Tiaras are wrongly numbered : No. 2 should be No. 3, No. 3 should be No. 4, and No. 5 should be No. 5.

INTRODUCTION TO THE GENERAL HISTORY.

THE History of Costume is an important portion of the History of Civilization; for previously to the invention of the arts of weaving, dyeing, tanning, and working in metal, nothing with any pretension to be called Costume can fairly be considered as existing. At what period and in what part of the world those arts were first practised will probably never be known to man; at all events their origin is at present shrouded in the mist of ages, and Costume startles us by its sudden appearance in full splendour, like Minerva springing completely armed from the brain of Jove.

The earliest written records of which we have knowledge at present, whether sacred or profane, testify that at the time of their composition fine linen, variegated garments, and personal ornaments of gold and silver were not objects of novelty. Warlike nations were also in possession of offensive weapons and defensive armour. Egypt, Assyria, Persia, and India, have illustrated those records by contemporary paintings and sculptures; and modern researches are constantly adding to the priceless treasures which have been from time to time recovered from the long-buried remains of cities, the sepulchral caves, the beds of rivers, and the mounds of battle-fields in the world known to the ancients.

All I propose to attempt in entering on so vast and really inexhaustible a subject is to show how few, after all, have been the important alterations in the apparel and arms of mankind during the period of which we possess any reliable information; and that as History is said to repeat itself, so does Fashion, notwithstanding its apparently interminable transformations.

I do not intend therefore to touch upon pre-historic times or occupy a single page of the number to which I am limited by indulging in what at the best could only be plausible speculation. The sole object of this work is truth as near as it can be arrived at, and the only merit it pretends to is that the pursuit of truth has been assiduously and conscientiously maintained throughout it.

I have insisted on no opinions of my own, and have fairly placed those of others who differ from me beside them, that the impartial reader might form his judgment from the evidence before him.

The plan I have, after much deliberation, decided upon as the most novel and, I think, most instructive arrangement for a general History of Costume, is not to divide it into separate notices of nations or into the successive reigns of their respective sovereigns, which would entail a most undesirable amount of repetition, but by chapters into sections from the commencement of the Christian era, and into centuries from the Norman Conquest, each chapter containing a view of the costume prevailing in the principal countries of the globe at the same period, and illustrating that of one by the other. Glimpses will thus be obtained of the origin and migration of fashions and of the probable date of their introduction to these islands, from the time when their inhabitants were semi-barbarians to the year of grace 1760.

With these preliminary observations I commence the concluding portion of my labours.

CYCLOPÆDIA OF COSTUME.

A GENERAL HISTORY OF COSTUME IN EUROPE.

CHAPTER I.

B.C. 53—A.D. 450.

T the period I have decided to commence my History of Costume, Rome was the mistress of what was then considered the world. The limits of her empire were, under Augustus, bounded by the Euphrates on the east ; the Cataracts of the Nile, the Deserts of Africa, and Mount Atlas, on the south ; the Danube and the Rhine on the north, and the ocean on the west. Our business lies with her power and influence in Europe, which extended certainly before the birth of Christ from the Danube to the Atlantic, from the north of Britain to the Mediterranean.

It is from Rome therefore that we must start on this voyage of discovery, and endeavour to trace the influence of her arts and arms on the surrounding nations, whose inhabitants she, with Chinese ignorance and arrogance, designated Barbarians.

Mr. Strutt has truly observed that the necessary garments of mankind were never many : one adjusted to the body, reaching to the knee or mid-leg, for the men, and to the ankle for the women ; another, ample enough to cover the whole person in inclement weather. These two, with or without some protection for the feet, comprised the whole of the clothing of many millions of human beings in pre-historic times, and under innumerable names have, with very few additions, descended, however altered in form or material, to the present day. The first of these two garments was adopted by the Romans from the Greeks, who called it *kiton*.[1] The Latin name for it was *tunica* (" a tuendo corpore "), familiarized to us as *tunic*, which has within some few past years reappeared in the nomenclature of English costume, both civil and military. It was woollen or linen, according to the season, and originally had sleeves reaching scarcely to the elbow ; but, in the time of the Emperors, to the wrist. Over the tunic patricians wore that specially Roman garment, the toga (from *tego*, to cover), the exact form of which has been an endless subject of controversy. It was sufficiently ample to envelope the whole person when necessary, and to allow a portion to be pulled over the head for protection from the weather. In fact, during the Republic it was the only garment, and may be likened in that particular to the plaid of the Scotch Highlanders (see PLAID), which was wrapped round the body much after a similar fashion.

The plebeians, in lieu of the toga, wore as their outer garment a cloak of rough or coarse material, and of which there were three kinds—viz., the *lacerna*, the *byrrhus*, and the *penula*—each of which had a cowl attached to it to cover the head when required, and nearly resembled each other. Montfaucon, speaking of the byrrhus, describes it as nearly the same thing as the lacerna, and adds,

[1] χιτών.

B 2

"It is also thought that the lacerna took the name of byrrhus from a Greek word signifying something reddish,—(πυῤῥός), it being usually of a red colour."[1] The name of byrrhus was subsequently given to a cowl, or other head-covering, whence the Italian term for a cap, *berretta*, French *birette*. To these must be added a military mantle, the *sagum* or *paludamentum*, which the Romans had borrowed from the Gauls. It was a large open woollen cloak,[2] and originally had sleeves, which were taken from it when it was brought into Italy. In dangerous times it was worn in the city of Rome by all ranks of persons except those of consular dignity. When worn by the general or the chief officers of an army, it was of a scarlet colour with a purple border. It has been sometimes confounded with the *chlamys*, which was principally worn by travellers.[3]

Roman Senator in the toga. From Hope.

Roman Emperor in a military tunic (*paludamentum*), unarmed.

The women were clad in the long tunic, or the *stola*, a similar vestment, reaching to the feet, having a broad fringe or border at the bottom. Of outer garments they had a variety, all borrowed from the Greeks,—the *peplus* or *eanos* (called by them also the *palla* or *amiculum*) ; the *palliolum*, a small cloak or veil ; the *theristrion*, an exceedingly thin summer mantle ; the *chlamys* and the *penula*, which they wore in common with the men ; and several others of which we have the names but no definite description : and still be it remembered, whichsoever was worn, according to season, fashion, or convenience, it formed only one additional article of attire to the tunic or to the stola.

I have said that millions of men and women in these early ages were content with two or three garments of a similar description, whatever their name or the material of which they were composed ; there were, however, other millions whose costume at the same period presented an important addition, so markedly characteristic of a distinct origin that it deserves, I think, more consideration than it seems to have hitherto received. This addition was the clothing of the legs independently and completely down to the feet ; a custom invariably observed by them through all their migrations, unaffected by change of climate or form of government. In brief, the nations of the ancient world might be fairly

---

[1] L'Antiquité expliquée par les Figures, lib. iii. cap. 7.   [2] Suetonius, August. cap. 26.
[3] *Vestis viatoria.* Hence *chlamydatus* was used to express a traveller or foreigner. (Plautus, Pseud. iv. 2, 8.)

divided into two great groups or classes, the trowsered and the untrowsered. Amongst the latter were the Greeks and the Romans, deriving their origin, as it appears to be generally acknowledged, from the bare-legged Egyptians ; while two great branches of the Scythic or Northern Asiatic family, which had overrun Europe and colonized the south of Britain long previous to the Roman invasion, viz. the Kimmerii and the Keltæ, wore the distinguishing close trowsers or loose pantaloons called by them *braca* or *bracha.*[1]

To return to the Romans. The material of the toga was wool, the colour in early ages its own natural hue, a yellowish white, but later the undyed toga was retained by the higher orders ; only inferior persons wearing them of different colours, while candidates for public offices bleached them by an artificial process. In times of mourning, a dark-coloured or black toga was worn, or it was left off altogether. Young men of noble birth wore a white toga edged with a purple border, and called the *toga prætexta,*[2] until they attained the age of fifteen, when they assumed the *toga pura,*[3] without a border. A toga striped with purple throughout, and called the *trabea,* was worn by the knights, and victorious generals in their triumphs were attired in togæ entirely of purple, which were in process of time made of silk and elaborately embroidered with gold. Such were denominated the *toga picta* or *toga palmata.*[4] Varro in Nonius speaks of certain togæ being so transparent that the tunics might be seen through them. There were also watered togæ, called by Pliny *undulatæ vestes.*

Among the ancient Romans the tunic was made of white woollen cloth and without sleeves, which were added to it afterwards, when it was called *chiridota* or *tunica manicata.* In general, the sleeves were loose and short, reaching only to the elbow, but their length and fashion seem to have depended on the fancy of their wearers, and in the time of the Emperors they were lengthened to the wrists and terminated with fringes or borders.[5] After the Romans had, in imitation of the later Greeks, introduced the wearing of two tunics, they used the words *subuculum* and *indusium* to designate the inner one, which, though the prototype of the modern shirt, was also woollen. Augustus is said to have worn in winter no less than four tunics beside the subucula or under-tunic, and all of them woollen.[6] Montfaucon is of opinion that the interior garments of men were rarely if ever made of linen until a late period of the Roman Empire. Young men when they assumed the *toga virilis,* and women when they were married, received from their parents a tunic wrought in a particular manner, called *tunica recta* or *regilla.*[7] The Roman women had several kinds of tunics, which are mentioned by Plautus, but unfortunately without any description. The *impluviata* and the *mendicula* were tunics, but their colour, form, and texture are totally unknown. The *ralla* (which is thought to be the same as the *rara*) and the *spissa* differed much from each other in texture, the first being of a thinner and looser texture than the latter. They had also a tunic called *crocotula,* the diminutive of *crocota,* which was an upper garment in use amongst the Grecian females, and received its name, Montfaucon says, from *crocus,* saffron colour, or from *croca,* the woof of any texture.[8]

The tunic worn by the senators was distinguished by a broad stripe of purple sewed on the breast, and called *latus clavus.* Those who had not arrived at patrician honours wore a narrow stripe of the same colour, and therefore denominated *angusti clavus.* Roman citizens whose means were insufficient to enable them to procure a toga, wore the tunic only, as did also foreigners, slaves, and gladiators.

The belt or girdle was a necessary appendage to the tunic, and was made of various materials

---

[1] Plutarch, in Vit. Alexandri. Pythagoras wore the *braca.* Ælian, Var. Hist. lib. ii. cap. 31.
[2] Tit. Liv. lib. xxxiv. cap. 7. Cicero, Varr. I. Sueton. in Vit. August. cap. 44.
[3] Also called *libera,* because the wearer had become his own master; and *virilis,* having arrived at man's estate. Cicero, Att. v. and xx. ; Ovid, de Trist. lib. iv. ; Persius, Sat. v.
[4] Tit. Liv. lib. x. cap. 7 ; Martial, lib. vii. ep. 1; Pliny, lib. iv. cap. 36.
[5] After the manner of Julius Cæsar, "ad manus fimbriatæ" (Sueton. in Vit. Jul. 45). But it is not quite certain that by *fimbriatæ* we are to understand "fringed." The tunic Suetonius speaks of was the *latus clavus* ; and as Cæsar chose to wear it with long sleeves, it was more probably *bordered* with purple than fringed.
[6] Sueton. in Vit. August. 82.   [7] Pliny, Nat. Hist. lib. viii. cap. 48, sec. 74.
[8] L'Antiquité expliquée par les Figures, lib. i. cap. 11 and 12.

and ornaments, according to the rank or circumstances of the owner. It was not customary with the Romans to wear it at home, but no person appeared abroad without it, and it was thought

Roman Orator in sleeveless tunic.

Roman in sleeved tunic and female in treble vests.

Roman in long-sleeved tunic.

Roman Ladies. From Hope.

effeminate and indecorous to appear uncinctured in the streets. The Roman women, married as well as unmarried, used girdles, which are occasionally concealed by the upper portion of the tunic falling over them.

Of sandals and shoes the Romans had a variety, the greater portion copied from the Greeks;

one sort covering the whole of the foot, and sometimes reaching to the middle of the leg, called *ypodemata* in the Greek, and in the Latin by several names, viz., *calceus, mulleus, pero,* and *phæcasium.* Another kind covered the sole of the foot only, and were made fast to it by thongs of leather or of other materials. These were called by the Greeks *pedila* generally ; but were variously denominated by the Romans *caliga, campagus, solea, baxea, crepida, sandalium,* and *sicyonia.* Occasionally the term *calceus* was applied to all. The *mulleus* was a shoe forbidden to be worn by the common people. Its colour was usually scarlet ; but sometimes it was purple.[1] The *phæcasium* was a thin light shoe worn by the priests at Athens, and also used by the Romans. It was commonly made of white leather, and covered the whole of the foot. The *pero,* a shoe worn by the people of ancient Latium,[2] was made of untanned leather, and in later times worn only by rustics and people of the lowest classes. The *caliga* and the *campagus* were sandals worn by the military. The sole of the former was large, sometimes strengthened with nails, and chiefly appropriated to the common soldiers, while the campagus was the sandal worn by the Emperors and generals of the army. It differed little in form from the caliga ; but the ligatures were more often crossed over the foot and more closely interwoven with each other, producing a resemblance to network. The Emperor Gallienus wore the

Roman Buskins and Sandals.

caligæ ornamented with jewels in preference to the campagi, which he contemptuously described as nothing but nets.[3]

[1] Montfaucon, Antiq. expliq. lib. ii. cap. 4.   [2] Virg. Æn. lib. vii. ver. 690.   [3] Montfaucon, *ut supra.*

The solea, the crepida, and of course the sandalium, were all of them species of sandals fastened about the feet and ankles by fillets or thongs ; but though probably each had its peculiarities, it is, as Mr. Strutt remarks, impossible at this distance of time to ascertain them.

The soleæ, we are told, might not in strict decorum be worn with the toga, and it was considered effeminate to appear with them in the streets of Rome. The Emperor Caligula, however, regardless of this rule, not only wore the soleæ in public, but permitted all who pleased to follow his example.[1]

The baxea was also of the sandal kind, worn originally, according to Arnobius and Tertullian, by the Grecian philosophers, and, as it appears from the former author, manufactured from the leaves of the palm-tree. The baxeæ are noticed by Plautus, but nothing respecting their form is specified.

The sicyonia, Cicero tells us, was used in races, and must therefore have been a very light kind of sandal. Lucian speaks of it as worn with white socks.

There was a shoe or sandal called the *gallica*, being adopted from the Gauls, which was forbidden to be worn with the toga, and to these may be added the *soulpones* worn by the country people,[2] and the shoes with soles of wood (*soleæ ligneæ*) used by the poor.

Two names, "familiar in our mouths as household words," occur in the catalogue of Roman foot gear—the sock and the buskin. The sock (*soccus*) is stated to have been a plain kind of shoe, sufficiently large to receive the foot with the caliga, crepida, or any other sort of shoe upon it.

The buskin (*cothurnus*) was anciently worn by the Phrygians and the Greeks, and derived its reputation from being introduced to the stage by Sophocles in his Tragedies. It was a boot laced up the front of the leg, in some instances covering the toes entirely ; in others a strap passed between the great toe and the toe next to it connected the sole with the upper portion, which met together over the instep, and were from thence laced up the front like the half-boots worn at present. Virgil thus alludes to them as worn by the Tyrian huntresses :

> "Virginibus Tyriis mos est gestare pharetram
> Purpureoque alte suras vincire cothurno."
>   *Æneid*, lib. i. v. 336.

In Rome, as in Phrygia, the cothurnus was worn by both sexes ; but, from the circumstance above mentioned, it has been specially associated with Tragedy. The *soccus* being worn by the comic actors, in like manner became typical of Comedy.

Socks or feet-coverings made of wool or goat's hair, called *udones*, were used by the Romans, but it was considered effeminate for men to wear them. The shoes of the wealthy were not only painted with various colours, but often sumptuously adorned with gold, silver, and precious stones.[3] The Emperor Heliogabalus had his shoes set with diamonds interspersed with other jewels.[4] The Emperor Aurelian disapproved of the painted shoes, which he considered too effeminate for men, and therefore he prohibited the use by them of the *mullei* (which were red), and of white, yellow, and green shoes. The latter he called "ivy-leaf coloured,"—*calcei hederacei*.[5] Sometimes the shoes had turned-up, pointed toes, which were called "bowed shoes," *calcei repandi*,[6]—a fashion evidently derived from the East, and which was subsequently carried to such an extravagance in the Middle Ages. The senators, from the time of Caius Marius, are said to have worn black leathern boots reaching to the middle of the leg, a custom to which Horace is supposed to allude by the words—

> "Nam ut quisque insanus nigris medium impedit crus
> Pellibus."—Lib. i. Sat. 6, v. 27, 28.

Both Greeks and Romans generally went bare-headed, but they had several sorts of head-coverings for special circumstances, the two best known being the *petasus* and the *pilus*. The petasus was a

[1] Sueton. in Vit. Calig. cap. 52.
[2] Pliny, Nat. Hist. lib. xxxvi. cap. 2.
[3] Flav. Vopiscus in Aurelian.
[4] Cicero, de Re Rustica, cap. 59.
[5] Lampridius in Vit. Heliogab.
[6] Cicero, de Nat. Deor. lib. i. cap. 30.

low-crowned hat with a broad brim, which might be profanely likened to the celebrated *membrino* of Don Quixote, originally a barber's basin. It was worn chiefly by travellers, and for that reason it is usually accorded to the figure of Mercury, with the addition of wings. Caligula permitted the people of Rome to wear the petasus at the theatre, to shade their faces from the sun.[1]

The pileus was a woollen cap, worn by the Romans at the public games and at festivals,[2] and by such as had been slaves, after they had obtained their freedom. It was also generally worn by sailors.[3]

There was a head-dress called *infula*, or *mitra*, which was a white woollen *fascia* or riband, or, as some say, white and yellow, which was tied round the head from one temple to the other, and fastened with a knot behind, so that the two ends of the bandage might hang down, one on each side. It appears to have been a ceremonial ornament, and worn only by those persons who sacrificed.[4] The girdle was called *mitra* by the Greeks.

Amongst the most favourite ornaments of the Roman ladies we find ear-rings, necklaces, and bracelets. Their extravagance in the purchase of these articles is commented upon by contemporary writers with a severity not exceeded in after-ages by the censors of the fashions of their time. Pliny says, "They seek for pearls at the bottom of the Red Sea, and search the bowels of the earth for emeralds to decorate their ears." And Seneca tells us that "a single pair was worth the revenue of a large estate," and that some women would wear at their ears "the price of two or three patrimonies,"[5] almost the very words of Taylor the Water-poet, in his condemnation of the fashions of the reign of James I. Ear-rings and bracelets were also worn by some effeminate young men, and finger-rings by both sexes.

We must now turn to the armour of the Romans, derived from the Greeks and the Etruscans. Livy, speaking of Servius Tullius, tells us that "he armed the Romans with the *galea*, the *clypeus*, the *ocrea* or greaves, and the *lorica*, all of brass" ("omnia ex ære"). This was the Etruscan armour, but in later times they substituted steel; for Silius Italicus says, "ferro circumdare pectus."[6] The lorica was a breast-plate, deriving its name, as did the modern cuirass, from its having been originally of leather, and in like manner retaining it when made of metal. It followed the line of the abdomen at the bottom, and seems to have been moulded to the human body. The square aperture for the throat was defended by a pectoral, also of brass; and the shoulders by pieces of the same metal, made to slip over each other.

Some of these abdominal cuirasses were made of gold. One is said to be in the possession of the Count of Erbach, but I could not obtain any information about it when I visited the collection at Erbach. They were also enriched with embossed figures, Gorgons' heads, thunderbolts, &c., and appended to them were several straps or flaps of leather, to which the French have given the name of *lambrequins*. They were fringed at the ends, and sometimes highly ornamented. In the time of Trajan the lorica was shortened and cut straight round above the hips, and, to supply the deficiency in length, two or three overlapping sets of *lambrequins*, as may be seen by the figures of generals on the Trajan Column.

Another sort of lorica was composed of several bands of brass, each wrapping half round the body, and being fastened before and behind, on a leathern or quilted tunic. In the British Museum, some of these brazen bands are preserved, and are about three inches wide. It is to this class of armour, when subsequently made of steel, that the above words of Silius Italicus allude.

These laminated loricæ were very heavy, and their weight was complained of by the soldiery in the time of the Emperor Galba.[7]

Other loricæ were composed of scales or leaves of brass or iron overlapping each other, and called *squamata*.[8] This sort of armour had been adopted by the Romans from the Dacians or Sarmatians by the Emperor Domitian, who, according to Martial, had a lorica made of slices of boars' hoofs stitched

---

[1] Dio. lib. lix. c. 7.
[2] Horace, Epist. i. v. 13; Suet. in Vit. Nero, c. 37.
[3] Montfaucon.　　　　　　　　　　　[4] Ibid.
[5] Vit. Beat. 17.　　　　　　　　　　[6] Lib. vii.
[7] Tacitus, lib. i.　　　　　　　　　　[8] Virg. Æn. xi. 487.

together ;[1] and Plutarch tells us that Lucullus wore a lorica made with pieces of iron, shaped like the scales of a fish.

Roman General.

Abdominal Cuirass with lambrequins.

Roman Emperor, armed.

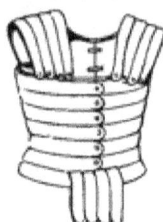

Laminated Lorica.

Lorica squamata.

The Romans had two sorts of helmets, the *galea* and the *cassis*, the former being originally of leather, and the latter of metal ; but the leathern head-piece seems to have fallen into disrepute in the

Helmet with umbril and cheek-pieces.

Helmet of common Soldiery.

Helmets of Generals.

[1] Lib. vii.

days of Camillus, who, according to Polynæus, caused his soldiers to wear light helmets of brass, as a defence against the swords of the Gauls. After this time the terms *galea* and *cassis* were used indifferently. On the top of the helmets of the common soldiery is generally seen a round knot, and those of the infantry were furnished with umbrills and movable cheek-pieces, called *buccula*.

> "Fracta de casside buccula pendens."
>
> Juvenal, Sat. x., v. 134.

The helmets of the generals were of gold, surmounted by crests ornamented with feathers of various colours :

> "Cristaque tegit galea aurea rubri."
>
> Virgil, Æn. ix., v. 49.

"The Roman shield," Mr. Hope remarks, "seems never to have resembled the large, round buckler used by the Greeks, nor the crescent-shaped one peculiar to the Asiatics."[1] Its form was

Roman Shields.

either an oblong square or an oval, a hexagon or an octagon. The cavalry alone wore a circular shield, but of small dimensions, called *parma*.

As offensive weapons, the Romans had a sword of somewhat greater length than that of the Greeks,—in the earlier ages they were of bronze, but at the time of their invasion of Britain they were of steel ; a long spear, of which they never quitted their hold ; and a short javelin, which they used to throw to a distance.[2] They had also in their armies archers and slingers.

The Romans, like all other nations, had peculiar dresses appropriated to peculiar offices and dignities. The Flamens or priests of Jupiter wore a cap or helmet, from its conical form called *apex*, with a ball of cotton wound round the spike.[3] The Salii or priests of Mars, on solemn occasions, danced through the city of Rome clothed in an embroidered tunic, girt with a brazen belt, and over it they wore the *toga prætexta*, or the *trabea*, having on their heads a very high cap, a sword by their side, in their right hand a spear or a rod, and in their left, or depending from the neck, the *ancilia*, one of the shields of Mars.[4]

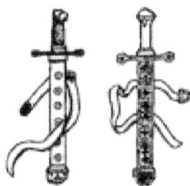

Roman Swords.

The Luperci, or priests of Pan at the Lupercal, wore only a girdle of goat-skin about their waist.

The vestal virgins wore a long white robe, bordered with purple ; their heads were bound with fillets (the *infulæ* and *vittæ*). At their initiation their hair was cut off and buried, but it was permitted to grow again and be worn afterwards.[5]

---

[1] Costume of the Ancients.   [2] Ibid.   [3] Lucan, lib. i. v. 604 ; Virgil, Æn. viii. v. 554.

[4] Dionys. ii. 70 ; Lucan, Pharsal. lib. i. v. 603.   [5] Ovid, Fast. iii. 30 ; Pliny, Nat. Hist. lib. xiv. cap. 44.

Wreaths or crowns were given as rewards of military achievements or other noble deeds. The *corona castrensis*, wrought in imitation of a palisade, was presented to whoever had been the first to penetrate into an enemy's camp ; the *corona muralis*, shaped in the semblance of battlements, to whoever had been the first to scale the walls of a besieged city ; the civic crown, formed of oak leaves, to whoever had saved the life of a citizen ; and the naval crown, composed of the *rostra* or beaks of galleys, to whoever had been the first to board an enemy's vessel.

Julius Cæsar is said to have worn a wreath of laurel to conceal his lack of hair, baldness being accounted a deformity amongst the Romans. In the time of his successors, such as were bald used a kind of peruke, made with false hair upon a skin, and called *capillamentum* or *galericulum*—" crines ficte vel supposite."

The Romans, like the Greeks, commonly wore their hair short, but combed it with great care, and perfumed it. The professors of philosophy let their hair and beards grow, to give themselves an air of gravity. The head-dress of the women in the days of the Republic was exceedingly simple ; but as

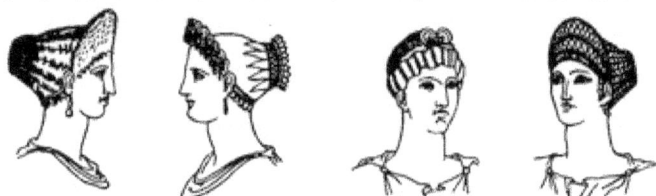

Head-dresses of Roman ladies.

riches and luxury increased, the ladies' toilet was proportionally extended, and obtained the name of "the woman's world,"—*mundus muliebris ;* a title adopted by John Evelyn in the reign of Charles II. for a satirical poem on the female fashions of that period. The ladies of the Roman Empire frizzled and curled their hair in the most elaborate manner, adorning it with ornaments of gold, pearls, and precious stones, garlands of flowers, fillets, and ribbons of various colours. The back-hair was enclosed in a net or caul after the Grecian fashion, enriched sometimes with embroidery, and made so thin that Martial sarcastically called them *bladders*. Slaves, for distinction sake, wore long hair and beards, but when anyone was manumitted he shaved both head and chin, and assumed the woollen cap called the *pileus*. The ancient Romans permitted their beards to grow, until Publius Ticinius Mænas, about 450 years after the building of Rome, brought barbers from Sicily, and first introduced the custom of shaving which prevailed till the time of Hadrian, who, to conceal certain excrescences on his chin, revived the fashion of wearing beards ; but after his decease it was neglected, and shaving was resumed.[1]

The slaves in Rome wore habits nearly resembling the poor people. Their dress, which was always of a darkish colour, consisted of the *exomis* or sleeveless tunic, or the lacerna, with a hood of coarse cloth, and the shoes called *crepida*.[2]

Bulla of gold.

The Roman boys who were sons of noblemen wore a hollow ball of gold, called *bulla*, which hung from the neck upon the breast. The origin of this practice amongst the Romans was, according to Macrobius,[3] the gift of a bulla by Tarquinius Priscus, the conqueror of the Sabines, to his son, who, at fourteen years of age, had killed an enemy with his own hand. The bulla was made hollow for the reception of amulets against envy. A beautiful one was in the exquisite collection of the late Mr. Samuel Rogers. Our engraving is from one in the British Museum. Sons of freedmen or of poor citizens wore the bulla made of leather.[4]

[1] Spart. in Vit. Adrian, cap. 26.
[2] Sat. lib. i. cap. 6.
[3] Aulus Gellius, lib. viii. 12 ; Juven. Sat. iii. 170 and v. 171.
[4] Juven. Sat. v. 165.

Respecting the materials known to the Romans for their ordinary clothing, they appear to have been limited to woollen, linen, and silk. Linen, we learn from He-rodotus, was imported to Greece from Colchis and Egypt. The women used it earlier than the men, and at all times in much greater quan-tities. Pliny,[1] citing a passage from Varro, says it had long been a custom in the family of the Serrani for the women not to wear robes of linen, "which being mentioned as a thing extraordinary," observes Mr. Strutt, "proves that linen garments were used by the Roman ladies in times remote." A vestment of this kind, called *supparum*, was worn by the unmarried Roman females as early as the time of Plautus.[2]

Silk appears to have been unknown to the Romans during the Republic. It is mentioned shortly afterwards, but the use of it was forbidden to the men.[3] Vespasian and his son Titus are said to have worn robes of silk at the time of their triumph,[4] but it is thought that the garments were only embroidered with silk, or that they were made of some stuff with which silk was interwoven ; for Heliogabalus, A.D. 218–222, is described as being the first Emperor who wore a robe of pure silk ;[5] and we learn from Pliny[6] that the silk manufactured in India was esteemed at Rome too thick and close for use. It was therefore unravelled and wrought over again, in the island of Cos, with linen or wool, and made so thin as to be transparent.[7] In the time of the Emperor Aurelian, A.D. 161–180, a vestment of pure silk was estimated at so high a price that he refused to allow his Empress one on that account.[8] The Emperor Justinian, by the agency of two Persian monks, introduced silkworms at Constantinople in the sixth

Roman youth wearing the Bulla.

century,[9] and in the following reign the Sogdoite ambassadors acknowledged that the Romans were not inferior to the natives of China in the education of the insects and the manufacture of silk.[10]

When the arts fell into a total decline, glitter of materials became the sole substitute for beauty of form, and Oriental splendour characteristically denoted the gradual extinction of the Roman Empire in the West.

In this rapid *résumé* of the information which has been collected from the best ancient authori-ties, and commented upon by the most learned modern writers on Roman antiquities, I have confined myself to such points of the subject as I consider may be necessary for the illustration of the Costume of Europe generally, and especially that of the various nations who, under the sway of the Cæsars, naturally adopted the habits and customs of their powerful and more cultivated conquerors.

We have the united testimony of Julius Cæsar, Strabo, and Pomponius Mela, that "the Britons were near and like the Gauls ;" that "in their manners they partly resembled the Gauls ;" that they "fought armed after the Gaulish fashion ;" and that "the inhabitants of Cantium (Kent) were the most civilized of all the Britons, and differed but little in their habits from their continental kinsmen."[11] We also learn from Diodorus Siculus, Strabo, and Pliny, that they had acquired the arts of dressing,

---

[1] Nat. Hist. lib. xix.   [4] Rudens, act i. sc. 2.
[2] Tacitus, Ann. lib. ii. cap. 33.   [5] Josephus, Bell. Jud. lib. vii. cap. 5, sec. 4.
[3] "Vestis holosericus." (Lampridius in Vit. Heliogab. lib. xxxi. 29.)
[4] Nat. Hist. lib. vi. cap. 22.
[5] "Ut translucerent." The Latin authors call such garments *vitreas vestes*. This mixed stuff was first made by the Greeks in the island of Cos, and Horace calls it Coan cloth :

"Cois tibi pœnè videre est ut nudam."

Lib. i. Sat. 2.

[8] Flavius Vopiscus in Aurelian, c. 45.
[9] Pagi assigns this memorable importation to the year 552. (Tom. ii. p. 602.)
[10] Procopius, lib. viii. Gibbon, Decline and Fall, cap. xl.   [11] Julius Cæsar, de Bell. Gall. lib. v.

spinning, dyeing, and weaving wool, and possessed, in common with the Gauls, some valuable secrets in the practice of those arts unknown to other nations. Pliny specially names the herbs they used for colouring purposes, and says they dyed purple, scarlet, and other colours from those alone.[1]

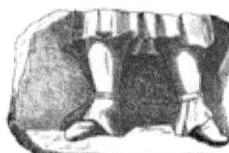

To the Gauls, then, we naturally turn for the illustration of the dress and arms of the Britons ; and the coins, columns, and arches of their conquerors, the Romans, furnish us with numerous examples of them at different periods of the Empire. Their dress denotes their Oriental origin. It consisted of close-fitting pantaloons or loose trowsers (for both are represented) reaching only to the ankles, where they are met by shoes of leather, such as we give examples of below from originals engraved in the work of the Abbé Baudry, 'Puits funéraires du Bernard ;' a body-garment with sleeves, reaching to about the mid-leg, and a mantle. These articles of apparel were called by the Romans *braccæ, gallicæ, tunica*, and *sagum*,

Portion of a bas-relief in the Museum at Narbonne.

from which names are derived the modern French *braies, galoches, tunique,* and *saie.*

Gallo-Roman Slipper.

Gallo-Roman Shoe.

This description perfectly corresponds with that of the Britons, who at the time of the Roman invasion were clad in the *pais* (from *py*, inward ; *ais*, the ribs), which Diodorus calls *kiton*, a tunic ; the *llawdyr*, or loose pantaloons, called by the Romans *brages* and *braccæ ;* the mantle (*saic*, in Keltic), from whence the Latin *sagum ;* and the shoes of untanned leather,—raw cow-hide that had the hair turned outwards, called *esgidiau* (from *æs-cid*, protection from hurt). (See SHOE, Dict. p. 458.)

The engravings next page are from Roman statues of Gauls in the Louvre at Paris, and afford examples of this costume as admirable as they are doubtlessly authentic. On the head of the seated figure is a cap, the peak of which falls forward, as in the representations of Phrygians and Amazonians. The British cap is described by Meyrick as more conical, but he says they had one with a peak, which they termed *penguick* ('Orig. Inhabit. of Brit. Islands,' p. 11.)

Of the several kinds of cloth manufactured in Gaul, one, according to Diodorus and Pliny, was composed of wool dyed of various colours, which being spun into yarn was woven either into stripes or chequers, and of this the Gauls and Britons made their summer garments. This striped or chequered cloth was called *brnach, brycan*, or *breacan ; breac*, in Keltic, signifying anything speckled, spotted, striped, or in any way party-coloured. The cloak or mantle called *sagum*, from the Keltic word *saic*—which, according to Varro, signified a skin or hide, such having been the material which the invention of cloth had superseded—was, in Britain, of one uniform colour, generally either blue or black, while the predominating tint in the chequered tunic and trowsers was red. That in this chequered cloth we see the original *breacan feile*, "the garb of old Gaul," still the national dress of the Scotch Highlanders, there can be no doubt ; and that it was at this time the common habit of every Keltic tribe, though now abandoned by all their descendants except the hardy and unsophisticated Gaelic mountaineers, is admitted, I believe, by every antiquary who has made public his opinion on the subject.

The hair was turned back upon the crown of the head, and fell in long and bushy curls behind. Men of rank amongst the Gauls and Britons shaved the chin, but wore immense tangled moustaches.

---

[1] Hist. Nat. lib. xvi. cap. 8 ; lib. xxii. cap. 26.

Strabo describes those of the inhabitants of Cornwall and the Scilly Islands as hanging down upon their breasts like wings.

Gauls, from statues in the Louvre.

The British and Gaulish women wore a long tunic (the *pais*) reaching to the ankles, and over it a shorter one (the *gwn*), latinized by Varro *guanacum*, whence our modern word *gown*, the sleeves of which reached only to the elbow.   The dress of Boadicea (*Voedugg*, i.e. "the Victorious "), Queen of the Iceni, has been described by Dion Cassius.   She wore a tunic of several colours, all in folds, and over it, fastened by a *fibula* or brooch, a robe of coarse stuff; her light hair fell loosely over her shoulders, and round her neck was a torque of gold.   This necklace, or collar of twisted wires of gold or silver, called *torch* or *dorch* in British, was worn by both sexes in all the Keltic nations, and was peculiarly a symbol of rank and command.   So fond were they of ornaments of this kind that those who could not procure them of these precious metals wore them of brass and iron, of which, Herodian says, "they were not a little vain."

Rings, bracelets, armlets, brooches, and necklaces of gold, silver, brass, beads, and Kimmeridge coal, have been found in undoubtedly Gaulish and British interments.

The priesthood in Britain was divided, we are told, into three orders,—the Druids, the Bards, and the Ovates.

The dress of the Druidical or sacerdotal order was white,—the emblem of holiness, purity, and truth.   The Welsh bard Taliesin calls it the proud white garment which separated the elders from the youth.   Unless by elders we are to understand elders in the church, as in some communities the phrase is used at present, we might infer that white garments were not confined to the priesthood.

The Bards were attired in garments of blue, emblematical of peace.   They were the poets, the historians, and the genealogists of the Keltic nations.   Cynddelw, in his ode on the death of Cadwallon, calls them "wearers of long blue robes."

The Ovates, professing astronomy and medicine, wore green, the symbol of learning, as being the colour of the clothing of nature.   Taliesin makes an Ovate say, "With my robe of bright green possessing a place in the assembly." The disciples of the orders wore variegated dresses of the three colours, white, blue, and green, or, according to another account, blue, green, and red.

Such are, at least, the statements of various learned Welsh archæologists, collected and commented on by Sir Samuel Meyrick, in his 'Costume of the Original Inhabitants of the British Islands,' himself a Welshman and most critical antiquary; but while bound to place them before my readers, I am equally compelled to warn them of the very slender claim they have to authenticity. Taliesin, "chief of the Bards," is said to have flourished in the sixth century; and even granting him so early a date, there is a lapse of five hundred years between the landing of Cæsar and the composition of the poems attributed to the Welsh bard, whilst many of the works relied upon for information on this subject are of the twelfth and thirteenth centuries.[1] The only authority I am aware of for the dress of the Druids is the bas-relief found at Autun, and engraved by Montfaucon. It represents two Druids in long tunica and mantles, colour, of course, not indicated : one crowned with an oaken garland and bearing a sceptre ; the other with a crescent in his hand, one of their sacred symbols. The mantle of the former is fastened on the left shoulder by a portion of it being drawn through a ring, and instances of this fashion are subsequently met with in Anglo-Saxon costume. I believe I was the first to suggest that the annular ornaments resembling bracelets, so constantly discovered both here and on the Continent, and presumed to be merely votive from the circumstance of their being too small to wear on the arm or the wrist, may have been used for that purpose. Of the gold crescents and other articles supposed to be Druidical found in Ireland and in every part of Keltic Europe, numerous examples have been engraved. (See woodcut subjoined and Plate XIX.)

Druidical ornaments and implements.

Bas-relief found at Autun.

Of the weapons and armour of the Gauls we gain a better knowledge from contemporary writers, illustrated by sculpture and specimens exhumed and preserved in national and private collections. Diodorus Siculus says, " Upon their heads they wear helmets of brass, with large appendages for the sake of ostentation, for they have either horns of the same metal joined to them or the shapes of birds and beasts. Some wear hooked thoraces of iron, and others of gold." " Hooked " I consider to mean " linked "—rings or scales hooked together, as both descriptions of armour were worn by the Dacians, Sarmatians, Phrygians, and other Asiatic nations, the Sarmatians using scales made from the hoofs of horses, in lieu of metal. The Romans also had their " lorica hamata." The offensive weapons of the Gauls consisted, according to Diodorus, of a long and broad sword called *spatha*, which they suspended by iron or brazen chains on the right thigh, and darts called *lankia*, whose iron blades were a cubit or more in length, and nearly two hands in breadth. To these Propertius adds a peculiar sort of spear or javelin, which he calls *gesum* :

" Nobilis e tectis fondere gesa rotæ."

[1] See 'Taliesin, or the Bards and Druids of Britain,' by D. W. Nash. 8vo. 1858.

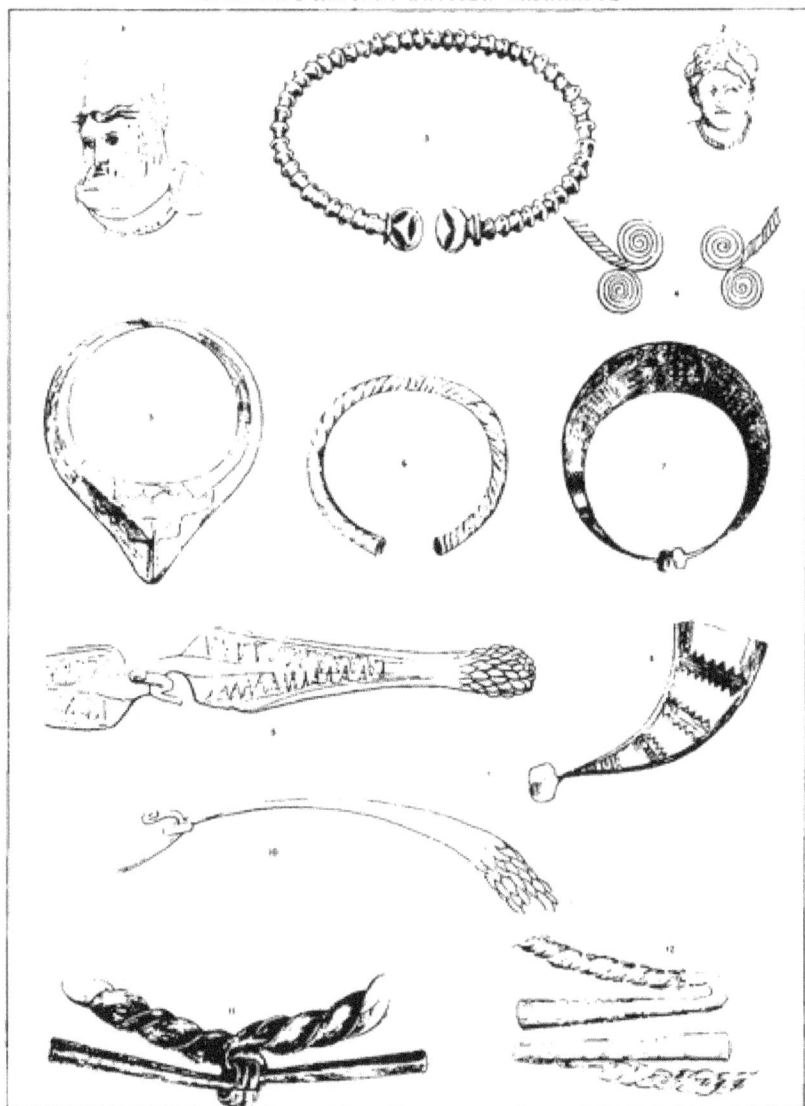

Posidonius mentions, also, a dagger which served them for a knife. I cannot identify in any sculpture these weapons, and they do not apparently correspond with those of the Britons, to whom they are assimilated by Cæsar and Tacitus. The British sword could neither be called long nor broad. It was leaf-shaped, made of mixed metal, and identical with the swords found throughout Keltic Europe and on the northern coast of Africa (see SWORD). It is true that after the Roman occupation there appears to be some authority for presuming that a long, straight, two-handed sword, called by Meyrick a *cleddyv deuddwrn*, the prototype of the claymore of the Scottish Highlander, was in use in the subjugated provinces, but whence derived it is difficult to say, as it is certainly neither Roman nor Phœnician.

Another Gaulish weapon was the *sauwian*, a sort of spear or lance, which is vaguely described as hooked, but has no affinity with the spears or lances of the Britons, designated by Meyrick the *llanawr*, or blade weapon, and the *gwarw-fon* or *gwayw-fon*, the former of which was leaf-shaped like their sword, and made of the same metal, a mixture of copper and tin, whilst the *sauwian* is said to have been all of iron. It is also remarkable that no mention is made of the small bronze axe or hatchet known to antiquaries by the name of *celt*, which has been so much and so long an object of the keenest controversy (see CELT), and is so curiously illustrated in the tomahawk of the North American Indians and the South Sea Islanders.[1] Neither do the shields of the Gauls correspond with

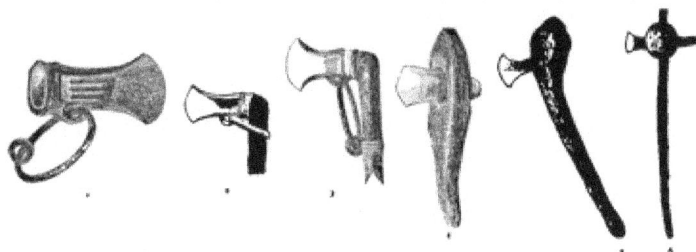

1. Bronze Celt with rings, British Museum; 2 and 3, Mode of hafting; 4, Stone Celt and handle found in co. Tyrone, Ireland; 5, Celt with handle, from Mexico; 6, Celt with handle, from the South Sea Islands.

those of the Britons. The latter were round, or oblong and flat (see SHIELD); the former are represented as oval or sexagonal, and in some instances semi-cylindrical.

We can only reconcile these discrepancies by considering that Britain, by its insular position and remoter distance from Rome, at that period the centre of European civilization, acquired more tardily the knowledge of the arts than their continental kinsfolk, who were not only the immediate neighbours and subjects of the masters of the world, but also in continual communication with the Greek colony at Marseilles, and the Phœnician merchants on the opposite coast of Africa. Of the body armour and helmets of the Gaulish chiefs, some precious relics have been preserved. M. Demmin has engraved a Gallic cuirass in bronze, found in a field near Grenoble, and preserved in the Musée d'Artillerie at Paris; and M. Quicherat a Gaulish casque, found near Falaise, and a highly-ornamented one with

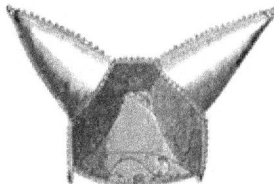

Bronze Head-piece found in the Thames.

cheek-pieces from the borders of the Danube (see next page). A most singular head-piece, resembling an early form of mitre, but called a helmet, was found in the Thames, and is now in the British Museum.

[1] See a paper on this subject, with many other examples, by Mr. George V. Du Noyer, in 'Archæological Journal,' vol. iv. p. 2.

It is of bronze in beaten work, and ornamented with incrustations of cement which resemble enamel. A bronze helmet, either Gaulish or British, corresponding in ornamentation with the peculiar patterns

Ancient Casque with cheek-pieces found near the Danube.   Gaulish Casque found near Falaise.

of that period, was found amongst the armour at Goodrich Court previous to its removal to South Kensington, but when or whence acquired by Sir Samuel Meyrick no record has been found. The fragment of a breastplate, gorget, or pectoral of gold, found at Mold, in Flintshire, is also in the British Museum. It is of pure gold, three feet seven inches in length; and its width in front, where it appears to have been hollowed out to receive the neck, is about eight inches.

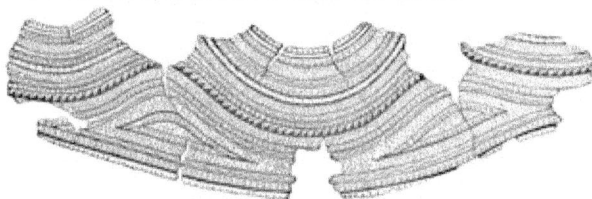

British Breastplate of Gold found at Mold, in Flintshire.

M. Quicherat remarks that these golden breastplates were so thin that they were worn more for ornament than defence, and were probably sewn on to some under-garment, and that the bronze helmets were equally thin, and would require a lining of leather.

Such breastplates and helmets were probably worn only by chieftains, as the Keltic races generally stripped themselves for battle, fighting naked to the waist; and Herodian and Xiphilin, in contradiction to Diodorus, assert that the Gauls did not wear helmets, and they certainly do not appear on the heads of any of the barbarians represented in conflict with the Romans on the arches and columns of the Empire.

I have hitherto spoken of Gaul in general terms; but we must not forget our earliest schoolboy introduction to it, "Gallia omnis est divisa in partes tres," &c., and that those three parts were occupied by the Belgæ, the Kelts or Gauls proper, and the Aquitani, who, though all of the same race, differed from each other in language, institutions, and laws.[1] It is clear that there was also some difference in their dress, for the Aquitani, who were separated from the Gauls by the Garonne, wore whole coloured garments in lieu of the striped or chequered dresses of their kinsmen; while the Belgæ, situated to the east of the rivers Seine and Marne, are described as wearing a short body garment not reaching lower than the waist and the braccæ, but neither the tunic nor the sagum. As the Gauls who were settled in the south of Britain at the time of the Roman invasion are supposed to have been principally of the Belgic branch of the great Keltic family, we must consider them to have been recognized by Cæsar from some national peculiarity in their attire, and I am, therefore, at a loss how to reconcile the account of Diodorus with that of equally credible historians.

I fear that without the corroborative testimony of coeval sculpture or painting little reliance can be placed on descriptions of dress, armour, or weapons by foreign authors situated at a considerable distance from the countries of which they were writing, in days when communication was so difficult, and information confined principally to hearsay. The tales of travellers, I presume, were not more distinguished for accuracy then than subsequently; and, without any intentional desire to depart from the truth, superficial observation or defective memory, added to the perplexing medium of a strange tongue, must almost infallibly lead to error and confusion.

While, therefore, I am bound to place before my readers all that within my knowledge exists on the subject of Costume which can be extracted from works ordinarily cited as authority, I feel equally bound to express my misgivings on certain points, leaving the decision to the unprejudiced judgment of the critical student.

The sculptures to which we are indebted for the costume of the Gauls are, for the most part, of a much later date than the conquest of Britain, and we cannot depend even on them for a faithful representation of the dress and arms of the Belgic colonists of the county of Kent, B.C. 55.

Very meagre and scattered are the notices of those branches of the Kimbri or Kimmerians who had settled in the west of Europe beyond the Aquitani, and were known to Diodorus the Sicilian as the Celtiberians and the Lusitanians. He describes the former as wearing black rough sagas made of coarse wool, and being armed, some with light Gallic shields and others with circular *cyrtræ*,[1] as big as bucklers; that their legs were protected by greaves made of rough hair, and their heads by brazen helmets with red or purple crests. They had two-edged swords of well-tempered steel, and darts of the same metal, their mode of preparing it being to bury plates of iron so long in the earth as was necessary for the rust to consume the weaker part, and therefore used only that portion which was strong and incorruptible. These weapons, he tells us, were so keen that neither shield, helmet, nor bone could withstand them.

It is curious to find the early colonists of Spain celebrated for the tempering of steel, as Toledo became in after-ages famous for its sword-blades, and the question arises in my mind how far we may depend upon the accuracy of the description retailed by Diodorus of the mode by which the Celt-iberians attained such superiority for their weapons. The soil in the neighbourhood of Toledo, watered by the Tagus, contains an iron ore possessing all the most valuable qualities for which steel is distinguished, so that unskilled workmen can and do manufacture these famous weapons by simply roughing them out and leaving them for a few weeks in a trough filled with the river water, to which the ore is undoubtedly indebted for its peculiar properties. It is extremely probable, I submit, that the early colonists discovered this fact, and that the story of burial in the earth is either one of the misrepresentations I have alluded to, or that they effected by those primitive means what their more scientific successors have done by the direct action of the water.

Of their neighbours and kinsfolk, the Lusitanians, the same author says, "They are the most valiant of all the Kimbri. In time of war they carry little targets made of bowel strings, so strong as completely to defend their bodies. They manage them with such dexterity that by whirling them

---

[1] "Illi omnes linguâ, institutis, legibus inter se differunt." (Cæsar, *De Bello Gallico*.)
[1] Lucan says the Spaniards had a *small* shield called *cetra*. (Lib. 1.)

about they avoid or repel every dart thrown at them.   They use hooked (barbed ?) saunians, made all
of iron, and have swords and helmets like those of the Celtiberians."

Eastward of the Belgæ were the Teutones or Germans (Wher-man), the latter name being a

Parthian.

The Trojan Paris.

Phrygian, with coat of ring-mail.

Sarmatian.

Dacian King.

The renowned Nations. From Hope's 'Costumes of the Ancients.'

new one for that people in the time of Tacitus, as he himself informs us.[1]   He describes those
who lived near the Weser as wearing neither helmets nor breastplates, but armed with a spear of
enormous length and an unwieldy buckler, not riveted with iron, of which metal they had little, nor
covered with hides, but formed of osier twigs intertwined or boards daubed over with glaring colours.[2]
The long spears, he tells us, were called *frameæ*.[3]   Swords were seldom seen, or the longer kind of
lances (he has already remarked on the length of the spears) ; and some tribes (the Rugians and the
Limovians, who dwelt on the coast of the Baltic) had short swords and round shields.   The Æstians,
who inhabited what is now called Prussia, used for their principal weapon a club.   A multitude of
darts, scattered (" *missilia spargunt* ") with incredible force, were an additional resource of the infantry.
Gibbon, in a note on this passage, observes that either the historian used a vague expression, or he
meant that they were thrown at random.[4]   Their military dress, when they wore any, was nothing
more than a loose mantle.   In the most inclement weather they were content with the skin of some
animal.   The tribes who dwelt in the most northerly parts clothed themselves in furs.   The women
manufactured for their own use a coarse kind of linen, which they embroidered with purple.

In accordance with Pomponius Mela, Tacitus says the rich wore a garment, not flowing loose, like
those of the Sarmatians and Parthians, but girt close, and showing the shape of every limb.   The
sculpture on the Antonine Column commemorates the victories gained by Marcus Aurelius over
several of the German tribes, wherein they are represented wearing the trowsers (*braccæ*), shoes like
those of the Gauls, tunics also of similar form, and a cloak (the *sagum Germanicum*) fastened on the
shoulder by a *fibula*, and armed with a shield and a short curved sword, supposed by some
antiquaries to be the *seax* of the Anglo-Saxons.   The tribes on the borders of the Rhine wore the
skins of wild beasts without choice or nicety, but those on the shores of the Baltic or Northern Ocean
selected particular beasts, and, having stripped off the fur, ornamented themselves with pieces of the

skins of marine animals unknown to the Romans.[5]   It would
seem, therefore, that like the Britons described by Cæsar, while
certain tribes or classes were clothed in skins, the more noble
and wealthy were attired in that remarkable garb which, as I
have already observed, distinguished at this period one-half of
the world from the other.

The submission of a considerable number of German
tribes to the Romans led to an interchange of fashions
apparently ; for while the Germans, like the Britons, began
to affect the dress and manners of the Romans, a Roman
emperor adopted the sagum of the Germans in like manner,
as another emperor assumed the caracalla of the Gauls.

To the east of the Germans were the Dacians and the
Thracians, differing little in their dress and arms from the
Asiatic nations from which they had branched—the trowsered
races of Europe.   As early as the time of Herodotus they
were similarly armed and attired ; the Thracians wearing
tunics and mantles variously coloured, their legs covered with
Phœnician cloth, and their shoes bound above their ankles.
They were armed with small shields shaped like a half-moon,
javelins, and short daggers.   On their heads they wore
helmets of brass, having ears and horns like an ox, of the
same metal.

Dacian warrior.   From the Trajan Column.

Such helmets were also worn by the Phrygians, by the Greeks, and, according to Diodorus

---

[1] " *Ceterum Germaniæ vocabulum recens.*" (Germ. cap. ii.)   [2] Ibid. cap. vi.
[3] " *Hastas vel ipsorum vocabulo frameas gerunt.*" (Ibid.)   So named, according to Dithmar, from *fríom*, or
priom, the point of a spear.
[4] It is a question, however, whether by *missilia* we are not to consider the author meant missiles generally.
[5] Germ. cap. xvii.

Siculus, by the Belgic Gauls. They were typical of the religion of the country, the horns of the ox or cow being emblematical of the moon; they were a fit accompaniment for the crescent-shaped shield which is seen subsequently in the hands of the Danes. The Trajan Column furnishes us with several examples of Dacian costume scarcely distinguishable from that of the Gauls. Their cavalry are clothed in tight-fitting dresses, entirely covered with scales from the throat to the point of the toes, their horses being similarly protected down to their hoofs (see woodcut previous page). They wore the Phrygian

Battle between the Romans and the Dacians. From the Trajan Column.

bonnet when in civil attire, but their helmets were high skull-caps, differently shaped from the Phrygian, with a spike at the top, cheek-pieces, and a flap to protect the neck. Their arms were bows and arrows and a sickle-shaped sword, the edge on the inner curve like those of the Germans.

The Veneti and the Ligurians, destined to found the great republics of Venice and Genoa, were amongst the latest colonists of Italy, and their origin and migrations have been variously suggested. As little is known of the former for a long time after their settlement as before their arrival, for it is not till four hundred years after the foundation of Rome that we hear of them as a powerful and warlike nation, when the Gauls, at the moment they were about to become masters of the Capitol, were compelled to make a hasty retreat, in consequence of an incursion into their own territories by the Veneti[1] We shall find them, centuries after their absorption into the Roman Empire, in the reign of Augustus, still wearing the Phrygian cap, as their gondoliers do to this day; nay, more, indicating in the official head-dress of the chief of their republic, the Doge, the form of the bonnet we perceive on the head of the Trojan Paris (page 20). All that we learn about the Ligurians is that they wore tunics and belts, and flung over their shoulders, by way of a cloak, the skin of some wild beast.[2] Of the various tribes or hordes which, issuing from "the teeming North," under the names of Goths, Vandals, Huns, Sclavonians, &c., swooped down by turns on Southern and Western Europe, we know little but what is legendary, or rendered doubtful by later investigations, and of that little nothing of importance to our present subject. The raw hides or undressed furs of wild animals cannot rank as

[1] Polybius, xi. 18.   [2] Diodorus Sic. lib. v. c. 2.

costume, and, unlike the Assyrians, the Persians, the Egyptians, the Greeks, and the Romans, they were too ignorant of the arts of painting and sculpture to transmit to us any comprehensible representations of themselves, however armed or attired. With the exception, indeed, of the above-named highly-civilized and luxurious peoples, the same may be said of all the world known to the ancients from the days of Herodotus to the defeat of Attila, A.D. 451.

The natural consequence of the gradual annexation to the Roman Empire of the various nations subjugated by Roman arms, was an assimilation of costume ; and shortly after the perfect establishment of the Roman dominion in Britain by Julius Agricola, A.D. 78, the ancient British habit began to be regarded by the chiefs as a badge of barbarism, and their sons, we are told by Tacitus, affected the Roman dress.[1] The braccæ were abandoned by the Southern and Eastern Britons ; and the Roman tunic reaching to the knee, with the cloak or mantle still called the sagum, which the Romans had adopted from the Gauls, became the general habit of the higher classes.

In the dress of the British females, little if any change took place, as it had originally been nearly the same as that of the Roman women. The coins of Carausius, and the columns of Trajan and Antonine, exhibit the Keltic females in two tunics ; the under one descending to the ankles, and the upper about half-way down the thigh, with loose sleeves extending only to the elbows, like those of the German women described by Tacitus.[2] The upper tunic was sometimes confined by a girdle, and was called in British gun, the guanacum of Varro, and the origin of our word " gown." The hair of both sexes was cut and dressed after the Roman fashion, and constituted one of the most remarkable alterations in the appearance of our Keltic ancestors.

Under the word SHIELD will be found in the Dictionary engravings of two Romano-British shields, evident imitations of the Roman scutum. In his description of the larger one, found in the river Witham, and which till recently was one of the gems in the unrivalled Meyrick Collection, Sir Samuel remarks—" It is impossible to contemplate the artistic portions without feeling convinced that there is a mixture of British ornament, with such resemblance to the elegant designs on Roman work, as would be produced by a people in a state of less civilization."[3]

Whether or no the Britons, during the three centuries of Roman domination, assumed any defensive body armour, in imitation of their masters, we are left to conjecture. In the fourth century they had to contend against repeated descents of the Saxons, and, with the assistance of the Romans under Theodosius, repelled them, but we have no description of the dress or weapons of the British forces.

Of the inhabitants of the remoter parts of Britain at this later period we know nothing appertaining to our subject. The Caledonians and Mæatæ, in the time of Severus, A.D. 193, are represented as naked savages, whose costume consisted of an iron chain round their waists.[4] The Irish, who are described by Tacitus as in his time differing but little from the ancient Britons, evidently received at some remote period colonists from one or more distinct races. "The fact is substantiated by the marked distinction still existing in the persons and complexions of the eastern and midland districts and those of the south-western counties ; the former having the blue eyes and flaxen hair characteristic of all the Scythic and German tribes, and the latter the swarthy cheeks and raven locks that bespeak a more southern origin, and point to Spain as the country from which they had ultimately passed, and Asia Minor or Egypt as the land of their fathers."[5]

In every part of Ireland weapons and ornaments have been found, precisely similar to those discovered in England, and proved to have been worn by the Belgic Gauls and Southern Britons. Undisturbed by the imperial legions, the Irish retained their ancient arms and clothing for centuries after Britain had become a Roman province ; and the truis and braccæ, the cota and the mantle fastened on the breast or shoulder, the torques and bracelets of gold and silver, the swords and battle-axes of mixed copper and tin, and spears and darts headed with the same metal, composed the habits and arms of the Irish chieftains during the Roman occupation of Britain, and down to the period at which the authentic history of Ireland begins.

[1] In Vit. Agric.   [2] De Morib. Germ. c. 17.   [3] Archæologia, vol. xxiii.
[4] Herodian, Xiphilin, Isidore.   [5] Hist. Brit. Cost. chap. xxvi.

I have left to the last part of this section the most delicate question with which I have to deal,—the dress and weapons of the people inhabiting that little mysterious corner in the west of England, who still speak the language they did in the days of Julius Cæsar, proclaim themselves "ancient Britons," and assert, on the authority of their poets, that they are the lineal descendants of that tribe of the Kimmerians, or Kymry, who were led by Hugh Cadarn, or "the strong," from the country of Summer, called "Deffrobani," where Constantinople is, "through the hazy ocean to the island of Britain, when there were no men alive on it, nor anything else but wolves, bears, and oxen with high protuberances." It is, fortunately for me, unnecessary that I should plunge into the interminable controversy respecting the origin of the Welsh, and the date of their first arrival and place of settlement in Britain. All I have to remark is, that the doubt thrown by recent investigations as to the Welsh language being that which was spoken by the Keltic tribes inhabiting the southern portion of the island, and the assertion of the latest editor of Gibbon that there never was an ancient people of any consideration or magnitude that permanently bore the name of Cimbri,[1] added to the fact that no trace is to be found in the notices of Britain by the Greek or Roman writers of any people or tribe settled in the district now called Wales, from which the Welsh can with any probability be supposed to have sprung, deter me from relying upon the illustration of British antiquities by Welsh descriptions and appellations, as confidently as Sir Samuel Meyrick has done. At the same time, I have considered it incumbent upon me, in this as in every other instance, to place before my readers the views and opinions of all writers of acknowledged reputation with whose works I have been fortunate enough to become acquainted. Of the Silures, the Demetæ, and the Ordovices, the only British tribes whom we read of in Ptolemy, Tacitus, or in any of the historians of the period, as occupying, in the time of the Romans, the province afterwards called Cambria or Wales, we have no information of consequence to us in this inquiry, and of the Welsh it will be time enough to speak when we find them mentioned by contemporary authorities.

[1] He observes that it only occurs three times in actual history, with long intervals between. There were three important occasions on which the Celtæ, being hard-pressed, united in a general cymrhi, or gathering of strength; when the league was dissolved, the designation ceased. ('Decline and Fall,' ed. 1867, vol. i. chap. ix. p. 272, footnote.)

CHAPTER II.

A.D. 450—1066.

EARLY at the same time that the Saxons obtained a footing in Britain, their cousins, the Franks, established themselves in Gaul. In 449 three Saxon ships (*cyules* or keels) arrived from Jutland at Ebb's-fleet, in the Isle of Thanet, near Richborough. The leaders are said to have been called Hengist and Horsa, both names signifying a horse and presumably assumed, and, after being employed by the Britons to assist them against the Picts and the Irish, made peace with the former, and, largely reinforced by their countrymen, turned their swords on their former allies, and in 457 established themselves in the county of Kent.[1] In 451 Aetius defeated Attila at or near Cabillonum (Châlons), and saved Gaul from the domination of the Goths, but unconsciously led to the subjection of it by another nomadic race, who had twice invaded it unsuccessfully in the previous century. These were the Franks. A tribe of them, led by a young, enterprising, and valiant chieftain, named Mere-wig, which in their language signified "great or renowned warrior," and was latinized into the more euphonious form of Merovechus or Meroveus,[2] had volunteered or been subsidized by Aetius to fight on the side of their former foes, against the new hordes of barbarians which were swooping down on the expiring Empire of the West. As the price of his services, the valiant Frank took possession of the whole of that portion of Gaul situated between the Seine and the Rhine, having Lutetia (Paris) for its western frontier, and Tournay for its capital. Rome, too enfeebled to resist, silently submitted to the spoliation of her provinces; and at the same time that Merewig established himself in this corner of Gaul, the Vandals captured Carthage, and the West or Visigoths overran Celtiberia.

As the costume of the Belgic Britons receives its best illustration from that of the Gauls, the apparel and armour of the Anglo-Saxons will have much light thrown upon them by an examination of those of the Franks, who inherited from their chief the appellation of Merovingians.

The earliest illuminated Saxon MSS. in the British Museum, on the dates of which we can depend, are the splendid copy of the Gospels known as 'The Durham Book,' having been written by Eadfrid, Bishop of Durham, and illuminated by his successor, Bishop Ethelwold, about the year 720, and a book of grants by King Edgar to the Abbey of Winchester, written in letters of gold in 966. The first, however, contains only representations of the four Evangelists, copied apparently from some of the paintings brought over by early missionaries, and therefore

Adræs. From an Ivory diptych.

[1] Saxon Chron. 12, 13 ; Bede, lib. i. cap. 15 ; Ethelward, p. 833.
[2] "Merovechus à quo cognominati sunt Merovingi." (Sigebert, Chron.) "Meroveus à quo Franci Merovumei appellati sunt." (Roricornis Gesta Francorum.)

affording us no information on the subject of Anglo-Saxon costume, and the second giving us the figure of the king, which, though illustrative of the regal costume of the first half of the tenth century, is of course no authority for anything previously.

Sidonius Apollinaris, a writer of the fifth century, describing the dress of some Franks he saw enter the city of Lyons, in 470, says they were attired in a closely-fitting body garment, terminating above the knees, with exceedingly short sleeves, scarcely covering the shoulders (in point of fact, a tunic), and made of some striped material not specified. Over this they wore a sagum of a greenish colour, with a scarlet border. They were girt with a broad belt, ornamented with metal bosses or studs, and wore their swords suspended on the left side by a baldric crossing their breast. Their thighs and legs were entirely bare, but they had laced boots of undressed leather reaching to the ankles. The tunic of their Regulus Sigismund, who came to marry a daughter of the King of the Burgunds, was of white silk, and his sagum or mantle of vermilion. They shaved the backs of their heads completely, leaving their front hair to grow to a great length, and piling it on the top of their heads, so as to form a knot or toupée. They also shaved their faces closely, leaving only very small whiskers, which they combed continually.

M. Quicherat, who quotes the above passage, expresses his surprise at the description of the naked legs, as the Germans, from the time of Trajan down to that of Constantine, are universally represented on the columns and arches of the Empire clad in the braccæ ; and Agathias, who wrote a century after Sidonius, designates the braccæ of linen or of tanned leather, the principal article of the apparel of the Franks, many of whom wore no other. It is quite probable, though, that the Franks Sidonius saw in 470, had, like the Romanized Britons, adopted the style of dress of the more civilized people they had mingled with. Nor is it quite clear that the Anglo-Saxons at some period had not abandoned the trowsers which so markedly distinguished the barbarians from the Greeks and the Romans. It is difficult for us in these days to suppress a smile at the idea of the progress of civilization being characterised by the disuse of nether garments. Some change, however, must have taken place in their apparel after their conversion to Christianity, at the beginning of the seventh century ; for in the Council of Celchyth, held at the close of the eighth, it was said, " You put on your garments in the manner of Pagans, whom your fathers expelled from the world ; an astonishing thing that you imitate those whose lives you always hated."[1] The practice of tattooing, which Herodotus states to have existed amongst the Scythians and Thracians, and is still considered a badge of nobility or a sign of courage amongst the savage islanders in the South Pacific, was either a national custom of the Saxons, or was adopted by them in imitation of the Britons, who carried it to an excessive extent. Certain it is, however, that the Saxons were forbidden to indulge in it at the end of the eighth century, by a law passed against it in 785 ;[2] and as in those days the object was undoubtedly display, it is highly probable that the legs of those amongst the Franks who wore a short and all but sleeveless tunic were as naked as the arms. Agathias also gives us a very different account of the mode of wearing the hair amongst the Franks of the sixth century. Long hair was the distinguishing characteristic of the Teutonic tribes,[3] and it was a mark, Agathias tells us, of the highest rank amongst the Franks, who, far from shaving any portion of their heads, encouraged the growth and took the greatest care of their locks, which only the nobility and princes of the blood were allowed to wear in flowing ringlets on their shoulders.[4] Again, in distinct contradiction of Sidonius, who speaks of the length of the front hair of the followers of Sigismund, both Agathias and Gregory of Tours inform us that the people were commanded by an express law to cut their hair close round the middle of their forehead.[5] The chin, also, was not shaven, but the beard held in the greatest reverence, and to touch it stood in lieu of a solemn oath. It would waste much time and weary the reader to attempt to reconcile these conflicting accounts, all of which may have some foundation in fact. The shaving of the back of the head was an ancient Aquitanian custom, as we shall have occasion to mention. The Visigoths had overrun Aquitaine during the rule of Hlodowig (Clovis), the grandson of Merewig. They had also occupied the south-eastern portion of Gaul, and

[1] Spelman, Concilia, p. 300.
[2] Tacitus, De Morib. Germ.
[3] "Ad frontem mediam circum tonsor." (Jus Capillitii.)
[4] Wilkins, Concilia, tom. i.
[5] Agathias, lib. i. Gregory of Tours, lib. vi.

established their capital at Toulouse. The Bishop of Clermont admits that there was little difference between the dress of the Franks and the Goths, and the Aquitanian fashion might have been adopted

Sword found in the tomb of Childeric.

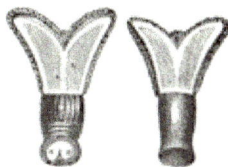

Gold ornaments supposed to represent bees.

by some of the former, as it undoubtedly was subsequently by the Normans. Independently of these considerations, similar alterations have taken place in the dress and habits of other nations, for which no reason has been recorded. Tacitus has accounted for the abandonment of the braccæ by the later Britons; but the Irish, another trowsered tribe, at some unascertained period became bare-legged, and their chieftains are depicted so as late as the reign of Elizabeth. For the costume

of the Merovingian Franks we possess only a few interesting relics. Hilder-rik, or Childeric, as he is more popularly called, son and successor of Merewig, died at Tournay in 481. His tomb was discovered in 1665, and in it were found some portions of purple silk and a quantity of gold thread, his ring, his sword in its sheath, the pommel and ornaments of gold, a spear-head of iron and the blade of a battle-axe (the *francique*) of the same metal, but shapeless from corrosion, and a vast number of small objects of gold, resembling bees, which probably had decorated some portion of his dress or equipment.[1] Montfaucon has engraved the principal relics in his 'Antiquités de la Couronne de France,' and above are copies of those which specially interest us in this inquiry.

The monuments and statues of the Merovingian kings from Clovis[2] (481) to Pepin le bref (752-768), which are engraved in the same work, are of a much later date than has been attributed to them by former antiquaries. Mr. Shaw, who has given us in the first volume of his 'Dress and Decorations' a much more accurate representation of those of Clovis and his Queen Clotilda, was the first to point out that the church of Notre Dame at Corbeil, from the porch of which they were taken, was not built before the close of the eleventh century, and the costume is of the commencement of the following one, corresponding with that of the reign of Henry I. of England. The very fact of a series of statues of kings whose reigns extended altogether for nearly three hundred years

The Emperor Anastasius in the consular habit.

[1] The Emperor Napoleon I. assumed bees for his badge from this circumstance, in place of the discarded fleurs-de-lis of the Bourbons.

[2] Hlodo-wig, latinised Clodovicus, became Clovis in French, while another change in the Latin to Ludovicus was translated into Louis. Hlodo-hilde (brilliant and noble), which was the name of his wife, was in like manner translated into Chlotilda and Clotilde.

having been evidently the work of the same hands, is of itself sufficient evidence in support of
Mr. Shaw's side of the question.

Several passages in historians of the sixth and seventh centuries appear to indicate that the

The Emperor Justinian and his Court.   From a mosaic at Ravenna.

The Empress Theodora and her attendants.   From a mosaic at Ravenna.

Franks had adopted to a considerable extent the dress and ornaments of their allies, the Romans of the Lower Empire, who had themselves assumed those of more Eastern nations. The Frankish kings entitled themselves Augustus, in imitation of the Emperors. They received diplomas from Constantinople, appointing them consuls of Roman Gaul, accompanied by the official robes of a Roman Consul. Gregory of Tours describes the delight of the people at beholding Clovis in the purple tunic and embroidered toga which had been sent to him with his diploma by the Emperor Anastasius; and a diptych of that emperor, representing him in the consular habit, engraved in Labarte's 'Histoire des Arts industriels,' affords us an admirable representation of it (see page 27).

The destruction of the beautiful mosaics which decorated the early churches of France, and in which the successors of Clovis and their wives were represented either as founders or benefactors, has deprived us of the most authentic and precise illustrations of the regal and noble costume of the Merovingian Franks; and we must resort to those of Italy which have been preserved for us, for a view of those dresses and ornaments which, worn at the Court of Constantinople, became the fashion amongst all the various races that had overrun the West of Europe during the first five centuries of the Christian era,—the Gauls, the Goths, the Franks, and the Lombards.

In the 'Revue Archéologique,' 1830, are copies of two mosaics from the originals at St. Vital, Ravenna; one representing the Emperor Justinian, his Court, and the clergy of Ravenna, and the other his wife, the Empress Theodora, and her attendants, said to have been the works of artists about the year 540. From these and other similar authorities we glean some ideas of the prevailing costume of the higher classes on the Continent at the period now under consideration, and also of the earliest appearance of Christian ecclesiastical vestments. (See opposite page.)

A singular mixture of Greek and Asiatic decoration gives a peculiar character to the costume of all classes at this period of the Eastern Empire; and it will be also remarked that while an Oriental taste was gradually increasing, to the obliteration of all the features of ancient Roman classical attire amongst the people in and adjacent to Constantinople, the Franks, and other Scythic or Teutonic

nations occupying the old provinces of Rome, were assuming more and more the dress and habits of the former Empire of the West. Montfaucon has collected and had engraved for his 'Antiquités'

before mentioned, many subjects from statues, illuminated MSS., and other sources, representing the kings of France of the second race, from Pepin to Louis V., "dit le Fainéant," A.D. 986; but no reliance is to be placed on the earlier figures, which have evidently been the work of later times. That of Clotaire or Lothaire, whichever of that name, or at what precise date executed, is at all events interesting as illustrating not only the regal but also the military costume of the Anglo-Saxons. I give it, therefore, under reservation (page 29), calling attention to the square helmets of the two soldiers, a form of headpiece described by Aneurin, a writer who flourished in the sixth century in Britain, and fought, he says, in person against the Saxon invaders at the battle of Cattraeth; at which, he tells us, there were present "three hundred warriors arrayed in gilded armour," "three loricated bands with three commanders distinguished by golden torques," armed with "white sheathed piercers" (daggers?) and wearing "*four-pointed helmets.*" Their principal leader had a projecting shield, was harnessed in "scaly mail," armed with a slaughtering pike, and wore (as a mantle?) the skin of a beast. His long hair flowed down his shoulders, and was adorned when he was unarmed with a wreath of amber beads; round his neck he also wore a golden torque. It is also deserving our notice that the same square helmets must have continued in use amongst the Franks for two hundred years, as they are seen

Frankish Chief, 9th century. From Lacroix, 'Arts somptuaires.'

in the undoubtedly contemporaneous illuminations of the Bible of Charles le Chauve, or the Bald, 840 (see chromolithograph, also woodcut above, in which the four-pointed helmet, the scaly mail, the slaughtering pike, the projecting shield, and the long hair flowing down the back, are all remarkable).

Annexed are examples of the costume of ladies of the time of Charles the Bald, which will be

Frankish Ladies. From the Bible of Charles le Chauve.

found to correspond with that of Anglo-Saxon women, consisting of an under- and a super-tunic, with a mantle, or veil which covers the head. Annexed is a portrait of Charles le Chauve in royal robes, from a Bible preserved in the monastery of St. Calixtus at Rome.

It is with a sigh of relief that I pass from a period of uncertainty, conjecture, and contradiction, to more authentic materials, illustrated by undoubtedly contemporaneous works of art. The Life of Charlemagne, written by his secretary and supposed son-in-law Eginhart, furnishes us with a most precise account of the costume of that celebrated sovereign, and consequently with very valuable information respecting the clothing arts in the eighth century. His civil dress consisted of a shirt, drawers, tunic, stockings, leg-bandages, and shoes. In the winter he added the thorax and the Venetian cloak. The shirt is expressly said to have been made of linen, "camisiam lineam." The drawers were of the same material, "feminalibus lineis." The material of the tunic is not mentioned by Eginhart, but M. Des Carrières, in his 'Epitome of the History of France,' says, without quoting his authority, that it was woollen. It was bound, however, with silk, and ordinarily short, as his biographer assures us that he wore the long tunic but twice in his life. The stockings (*tibialia*) are simply referred to without mention of the material; but the Monk of St. Gall, another writer of his time, describes them as of linen of one colour, but ornamented with precious workmanship: " Tibialia vel coxalia linea quamvis ex eodem colore tamen opere pretiosissimo variata." (Lib. i., cap. 36.) It may be that by "vel coxalia" he means they were the long or *brach hosen* of the Saxons, so called in contradistinction to the short *socca*, as the conjunction *vel* seems to imply the uncertainty of the author under which term, stockings or trowsers, to class them. A mosaic in the church of St. John de Lateran, however, represents him apparently in stockings reaching only to the knees, beneath which they terminate in an ornamental border.

On state occasions Charlemagne wore a jewelled diadem, a tunic interwoven with gold, a mantle fastened with a brooch of gold; his shoes were adorned with gems; his belt was of gold or silver, and the hilt of his sword of gold, ornamented with jewels. M. Quicherat observes that one is so accustomed to see Charlemagne arrayed in imperial vestments that he would not be recognized if a painter or sculptor were to represent him in any other costume, and yet it is historically true that he never wore them in his life. Once, on the occasion of his inauguration in St. Peter's at Rome, he appeared in the dress of a Roman patrician at the urgent solicitation of Pope Leo IV., who only succeeded in persuading him to do so by recalling to him that sixteen years previously, at the request of Adrian, he had presented himself one day to the people in the long tunic, the chlamys, and the calcei of a Roman senator : " Longâ tunicâ et chlamyde amictus et calcea mantis quoque Romano more formatis."

In his reign the Franks had adopted a short variegated or striped cloak, called by the writers of that period "saga Fresonica." Charlemagne, on the contrary, wore what Eginhart calls the Venetian mantle, "sago Veneto amictus," which epithet, it is probable, he used in this instance for Lombardic, as the dress of the Lombards was, according to Paulus Diaconus, precisely that of the Franks and Anglo-Saxons. The Monk of St. Gall gives us the following description of it. It was of a grey or blue colour, quadrangular in form, and so doubled that when placed on the shoulders it hung down as low as the feet before and behind, but on the sides it scarcely reached to the knees. (Lib. i. c. 30.) The figure of this monarch in the mosaic in the church of St. John de Lateran at Rome, before mentioned, is probably the most reliable one as far as his costume is concerned. He is represented in a short tunic terminating above the knees, with a mantle apparently fastened on the right shoulder (though by what means is not visible), and which if not borne up as it is, by his arm on

the left side, would hang down to his feet. It has an ornamental border, the studs in which may be meant either for gold or jewels. Over his shoulders is a collar of flat plates studded, it may be,

with jewels, and of the same pattern as the bands or borders of his leggings before described; his shoes are very indistinctly represented. On his head is a cap rising to a low peak atop, with a border of an indented pattern, and having a circular ornament in front. Another mosaic represents him in a similar costume, with the exception of his legs being bandaged cross-wise in the Anglo-Saxon fashion, which the Monk of St. Gall assures us was also that of the Franks.

I have descanted at some length upon the dress of Charlemagne, because it has been the custom of painters and sculptors for so many years past to portray him in the gorgeous robes of an emperor of the fifteenth century, and crowned with the remarkable diadem which is erroneously appropriated to him, and which is still reverently preserved in the Imperial Treasury at Vienna. It is therefore a duty incumbent upon me to call the attention of artists and costumiers to the above accounts of contemporary authorities, which at least deserve their consideration when about to introduce this famous historical personage in a picture, or to place him on the stage.

I have already quoted the statement of the ancient historian of Lombardy, that the dress of the people who occupied in the sixth century

Charlemagne. From a mosaic in the church of St. John de Laterne.

that part of Italy which still bears the name they had acquired either from their long beards or their long axes[1] was generally similar to that of the Franks and Saxons, being loose and flowing, and consisting chiefly of linen ornamented with broad borders woven or embroidered with various colours; we may therefore fairly conclude that with the exception of some national peculiarities of form, ornamentation, or mode of wearing them, the garments of the principal inhabitants of Europe west of the Rhine and south of the Danube, including the British Islands, were, during the three centuries following the establishment of Saxons in England and the Franks in Gaul, as similar as are at this day those of their descendants, Constantinople setting the fashions of the upper classes as Paris does at present.

I do not know where I could more appropriately introduce the annexed woodcut from an engraving by Willemin ('Monuments inédits') of two figures sculptured in bas-relief on porphyry, in the Place of St. Mark, Venice. Their age is uncertain. Some similar bas-reliefs in the Vatican are ascribed by Agincourt, in his 'Histoire de l'Art,' to the fourth century. Willemin dates these before us "eighth

Bas-relief at Venice.

[1] " Easy submission to authority long accepted the derivation of Longobardi, from the length of their beards. A more judicious criticism has of late deduced it from the long-handled axes that armed them (see Latham's ' Germania of Tacitus,' p. 139). *Barthe*, from *barja*, *barm*, ' to strike,' was an ancient German term for a hatchet or axe (Adelung, 'Wörterbuch '). *Langa barthen* were therefore long axes, which in reduced dimensions have descended to later times as *Aalberds*." (Note to the latest edition of Gibbon's ' Decline and Fall of the Roman Empire.' Lond. 1867, vol. iv. p. 442.)

ANGLO-SAXON MALE AND FEMALE COSTUME. Xᵀᴴ CENTURY.

FROM THE "BOOK OF GENESIS" COTTON COLLECTION, BRITISH MUSEUM (CLAUDIUS B iv)

century," while his editor hesitates to place them later than the sixth. The semi-Roman character of the costume, the eagle heads of the pommels of the swords, considered in conjunction with the Gothic fashion of their caps and shoes, incline me to believe them Lombards of the time of Charlemagne.

To return, therefore, to the Anglo-Saxons, for whose dress and equipments we have no pictorial authority earlier than the latter half of the tenth century. At that period we find the dress of the men consisting of an under-garment of linen, over which in summer was worn a tunic (Ang.-Sax. *roc*) of linen, and in winter one of woollen, with ornamental borders, and having long close sleeves, which sat in wrinkles, or rather rolls, on the fore-arm from the elbow to the wrist. In some instances these rolls are so regular as to present the appearance of a succession of bracelets, and, when painted yellow, may probably be intended to do so, as William of Malmesbury tells us the English at the time of the Conquest were in the habit of *loading* their arms with them;[1] but it is also evident that generally the marks are merely indicative of a long sleeve, wrinkled up and confined by a single bracelet at the wrist, by removing which perhaps the sleeve was pulled out of its folds and drawn over the hand as a substitute for gloves, a fashion of which we find many examples at a later period. The roc, or tunic, was either plain or ornamented round the collar and borders, according to the rank of the wearer; of silk, as was that of Charlemagne, or woven and embroidered with various colours, like those of the Lombards. Over this, again, the warriors and upper classes wore, when abroad or on state occasions, a short cloak (*mantil*), like the Roman *pallium* or Gaulish *sagum*, fastened sometimes on the breast,

Inauguration of King.   From a Greek MS. of the 10th century.

sometimes on one or both shoulders, with brooches or *fibulæ*. It appears that, when once fastened, it might be removed or assumed by merely slipping the head through the space left open for the neck. (See CLOAK, vol. i. p. 99.) Drawers reaching half-way down the thighs, and stockings meeting them,

[1] "Brachia onerati."

are constantly seen in Saxon illuminations, and are alluded to by contemporary writers under the names of *brech* and *hose*. Over these they wore bands of cloth, linen, or leather, terminating a little below the knee, either in close rolls, like the hay-bands of a modern ostler, or crossing each other sandal-wise, as they are worn to this day by the people of the Abruzzi and the Apennines, and in some parts of Russia and Spain. The Saxon name for them was *scanc-beorg*, literally shank or leg guards, and latinized by the writers of that period "fasciolæ crurum." In the ancient Canons the monks were ordered to wear them of linen, to distinguish them from the laity, who wore woollen. (Ducange *in voce* FASCIOLA.) Royal personages are, however, depicted with golden fillets. *Scin hose* (leathern hose) is frequently mentioned in Anglo-Saxon documents. Socks were worn as well as stockings with them; and some have ornamental borders. The Saxon shoe is usually painted black, with an opening down the centre, secured by a thong. Labourers are generally represented bare-legged, but rarely bare-footed. The hair was worn long, and the beards of old men forked. The face, however, was generally shaven. Hats and caps seem to have been rarely worn, except by travellers or in battle. For examples of them, and the details of other articles of attire, the reader will refer to the Dictionary.

As I have previously observed, the only difference in dress between the classes at this period seems to have been in the richness or ornamentation of the material, and the costliness of their personal decorations. The bretwald, or king, was distinguished of course by his crown, and the nobles of his court, the ealdorman and the thegn, as well as the sovereign, wore upon state occasions longer tunics and more ample mantles; but, with these exceptions, the same few articles of apparel appear to have been common to people of all conditions.

The Saxon MS. in the Cottonian Collection marked 'Claudius, B iv.,' supplies us with a good example of a monarch of the tenth century; and another, marked 'Tiberius, C vi.,' of later date, one more sumptuously attired, wearing the remarkably ugly and, we should suppose, uncomfortable square crown seen on the head of King Edgar in the Cottonian MS. Tiberius, A iii. (engraved for the Dictionary, under article CROWN, p. 150), and a variety of which appears on those of the Frankish kings Lothaire and Charles the Bald, centuries previously.[1]

The Saxon monarchs appear to have worn occasionally a jewelled circlet of gold, as Charlemagne is said to have done; *heafod-begh* and *gebeafod-ringe*, head-bracelet or head-ring, being the names

used for the simpler diadem. Similar diadems were worn by princes and nobles of the highest rank. The crown of the Empress Helena, wife of Constantine Chlorus and mother of Constantine the Great, throws considerable light on the form and ornaments of those we see on the heads of early Anglo-Saxon and Norman monarchs.

When a king is represented seated in state upon his throne, he generally bears a sceptre. When he has no sceptre, the place of it is usually supplied by a sheathed sword, held hilt upwards, sceptre fashion; in some instances he is drawn without either, and in others with both, the sceptre in the left hand and the sword in the right. When the sword is not held by the sovereign, it is borne by an officer beside him. In early MSS., the sceptre appears to be simply a staff with a round knob at the top,[2] and the pommel of the sword in some examples terminates in a *fleur-de-lys*, an ornament of Roman design, observable in bronzes, sculpture, and fresco-paintings, and first adopted as a badge by Louis VII., king of France, in the twelfth century. In a MS. of the tenth century, Cotton. Lib., Claudius, B iv., the sceptre of Pharaoh, who is of course represented in Anglo-Saxon costume, is surmounted by a dove. Montfaucon gives, in his 'Antiquités de la Couronne de France,' an engraving from a painting in a Greek MS. of the tenth century, representing the ancient Teutonic ceremony of the inauguration of a king by elevation on a buckler. The king is intended for David, but the costume is Byzantine, as adopted by the Germans of the time of Otho I. (See previous page.)

[1] For other examples, see Plate VI. vol. i. page 150.
[2] That of Louis le Débonnaire, son of Charlemagne, is described by his biographer, Theganus, as "baculum aureum" (cap. xix.).

The military habit in the earlier Saxon times differed little from the civil. Prior to the introduction of body armour, the short linen tunic was preferred by them to all other vestments as the one in which they could most freely wield their weapons, and the only addition to it appears to have been a border of metal at the collar which acted as a pectoral, and is probably alluded to under the name of *breast-beden* or *breast-beorg*, breast-defence or breast-guard. But the word *lorica* occurs in some Saxon authors, and appears to be perfectly synonymous with the coat or shirt of mail, for which the name in Saxon was *gehrynged byrn*. Several examples of it are to be found in the miniatures of MSS. of the tenth and eleventh centuries, not to mention the Bayeux Tapestry, in which Harold, his brothers, and the majority of the English are in mail hauberks similar to the Normans'.

Whether, previously to the adoption of the ringed mail, the Saxons had followed the fashion of the Franks, and imitated the military equipment of the Romans, we have no evidence before us. The soldiers represented in the Frankish drawings of the ninth and tenth centuries are armed, with the exception of the quadrangular form of the helmet, completely in the old classical Roman style. They wear the abdominal cuirass, with its pendant straps or lambrequins, and, but for the above-named peculiarity, would scarcely be distinguished from legionaries of the days of Augustus or Trajan.

Caps or helmets of various descriptions appear on the heads of warriors of the ninth and tenth centuries, some conical, others of the Phrygian form, others with serrated combs or crests. They appear to have been made of leather or felt, sometimes bound or bordered with metal. The leather helmet is continually mentioned by Saxon writers, as is also the *fellen hæt*, a similar head-piece, as the terms "camb on hætte" or "camb on helme" clearly indicate. Metal frames for helmets, as they are supposed to be, have been dug up in various parts of England: one of bronze was found at Leckhampton, in 1844, on the skull of a skeleton, which appears decisive as to its purpose (see woodcut); but there is something about their make that is to me by no means satisfactory. They have not the character of framework intended to strengthen a head-piece. Metal rims, or borders elaborately ornamented, were discovered some few years ago and believed to be portions of head-bands or crowns, and ultimately proved to be hoops of buckets. At any rate, the form does not correspond with any Anglo-Saxon helmet I have seen represented.

Frankish Monarch. From Willemin, 'Monuments inédits.'

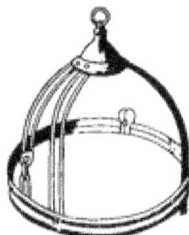

Bronze framework found at Leckhampton.

The Anglo-Saxon shields have been fully described in the Dictionary (p. 453). They seem to have been similar to those of the Franks; but the umbo of one found at Faversham, and considered by Mr. Roach Smith to be *unique*, is sufficiently curious to warrant an engraving of it here. The weapons of the Anglo-Saxons were all of iron, and consisted of long, broad, straight, double-edged swords, daggers, javelins, and long spears. Of the *seax*, supposed to be a curved dagger and their ancient national weapon, I have said all I have to say in the Dictionary. Long-hafted axes, both single and double, called *byl* and *twy-byl*, were used by them with terrible effect in the battle of Hastings, but they do not appear in their illuminations. Ordinary double-bladed axes are, however, occasionally depicted. The battle-axe of the Franks, popularly supposed to have given its name,

F 2

"francisque," to the nation, though much more probably receiving it from them,[1] was of the same description as the single-bladed one of the Saxons. Many specimens have been found on the Con-

Base of an Anglo-Saxon Shield found at Faversham.

tinent, but Mr. Hewitt notices the extreme rarity of the discovery of Saxon examples in England.[2] One form of the axe, exhibiting an elongated blade, has been distinguished as the *taper-axe*. Such was the weapon found in the tomb of Hilperic.

The dress of the Anglo-Saxon females of all ranks consisted of long loose garments reaching to the ground, and named in various documents *tunica*, *gunna*, *cyrtle* or kirtle, and *mentil* or mantle. The first and last articles describe themselves, but the terms *gunna* and *cyrtle* have caused much controversy, from the capricious application of them to different articles of attire. (See Dictionary, under GOWN and KIRTLE.) The sleeves of the tunic reaching in close rolls to

the waist, like those of the men, are generally confined there by a bracelet, or terminate in a rich border, and the mantle hangs down before and behind, covering the whole figure except when looped up by the lifted arms, when it takes a form resembling that of the ancient chasuble of the priesthood. The materials of which the outer garments were made were for the most part woollen cloth, the manufacture of which was carried to very high perfection by the Saxons; and Mr. Strutt says, "I am inclined to think that the fineness of the materials, and the costliness of the workmanship, rather than any particular colour or form of the garments, made the chief distinction of rank among the Anglo-Saxons."[3] Women of the first quality employed much of their time in carding wool, spinning, and working with the needle. Some of them also engaged in the labours of the loom. The four princesses, daughters of Edward the Elder and sisters of Athelstan, are highly celebrated for their skill in spinning, weaving, and embroidery;[4] and Edgitha, the wife of Edward the Confessor, is described as being a perfect mistress of the needle.[5] A foreign writer of the eleventh century records, "The English women excel all others in needlework and in embroidering with gold;"[6] and another, that the Anglo-Saxon ladies were so famous for their skill in the art of embroidery, that the most elegant productions of the needle were called, by way of eminence, *Anglicum opus*, English work.[7] Not only flowers, animals, rings, stars, and every variety of figures, but even historical subjects, were wrought upon cloth with threads of gold and silver, intermixed with silk, worsted, or cotton, of such colours as the nature of the design required, the pattern being first drawn on the cloth either by the lady herself or persons whose profession it was to furnish such designs, as is the case at present. The celebrated Dunstan, when a young man, was considered a proficient in this art, and assisted a lady in designing the subject she desired to embroider in gold upon a sacerdotal vestment.[8]

While on this topic, I will call attention to the peculiarity of the patterns or ornamentation of the dresses of ladies of rank, as they are depicted in drawings and paintings of the period under discussion. The rudeness of some of the originals, the carelessness of copyists, the poor character of the engravings of the time of Montfaucon—all combine to militate against a fair comprehension, not only of the style of decoration, but actually of its nature. What, for instance, are we to consider the oval patches upon the shoulders and on, apparently, the right knee of the female figure in the following woodcut? Are they plates of metal studded with jewels, or pieces of cloth of gold sewn upon the mantle and tunic, and similarly ornamented?[9] The Empress Judith, wife of Louis le Débonnaire, is recorded to have had as much gold plate upon her dress as weighed three pounds. At the same

---

[1] "Secures quas Hispani ab usu Francorum per derivationem *franciscas* vocant." (Isidorus, lib. xviii. c. 8.)

[2] "In the Wilbraham excavations a hundred graves only yielded two axes. In the Fairford researches not one was found in a hundred and twenty graves; and in the many Kentish barrows examined by Lord Londesborough in 1841, not a single specimen was obtained." (Hewitt, 'Ancient Armour and Weapons,' vol. i. p. 45.)

[3] Vol. i. part ii. cap. 6.   [4] Malmesbury, 'De Gestis Rerum Angliæ,' lib. ii. p. 16.   [5] Ibid.

[6] Gesta Guliel. Ducis apud Duchesne.   [7] Gulielm. Pictavinus.   [8] Osbernus, 'De Vita Dunstani.'

[9] "Calliculas, galliculas—signa vestis." (*Vide* Ducange *in voce*.)

time we perceive precisely the same oval-shaped pieces of embroidery in the Chinese costume of the present day, and we know that silk was imported into Europe from India and China as early as the eighth century, while many features in Byzantine costume curiously remind us of that which has for so many centuries been worn by the higher classes in the Celestial Empire.

Nobleman and Noble Lady, 9th century. From Willemin, 'Monuments inédits.'

Another peculiarity in the representation of Saxon or Frankish dresses of the ninth and tenth centuries is the mode in which a band or border appears most inconveniently to confine the legs of the wearer. It can scarcely be merely ill-drawn, because in some instances the compression of the folds of the under-dress is clearly indicated; and in that of the figure of an Anglo-Saxon king, from the Cotton. MS. Claudius, B iv., a portion of the super-tunic passes under the band and reappears below it. (See also woodcut of bishop annexed.)

In the same Cottonian MS. are drawings of personages of distinction in tunics which have broad borders round the bottom and up the sides, which seem to be open to the girdle, giving in some instances the appearance of an apron. (See figure of old man in Plate XX.)

"The tanner's art," Mr. Strutt remarks, "must certainly have been well understood by the Anglo-Saxons, for leather not only formed part of their habits, but was used for a variety of other purposes ; and connected with it was probably the art of dressing the skins of animals with the hair upon them. The garments of the nobility and dignified clergy (such of them, especially, as were appropriated to the winter) were often bordered, and even lined, with furs of various kinds : those of sables of beavers and foxes were the most esteemed ;[1] the inferior sorts were made from the skins of cats and of lambs."

Bishop, 9th century. From Willemin, 'Monuments inédits.'

Of the vestments of the clergy it is now time to speak. It is a subject of great interest, and one which has of late years attracted public attention to a considerable degree. To the late Rev. Wharton B. Marriott we are indebted for a work upon it,[2] remarkable for the extent

[1] "Sabelinas, vel castorinas, vel vulpinas." (Ang. Sacra, vol. ii. p. 299.)   [2] 'Vestiarium Christianum,' 8vo, 1868.

of the research and the lucidity of its exposition. A French writer, M. Didron, is also entitled to our gratitude for the publication of an elaborately illustrated treatise, which, previous to the appearance of Mr. Marriott's volume, was the only text-book on which the critical antiquary could fairly rely.

There appears to have been little, if any, difference between the dress of the laity and that of the clergy during the first four centuries of the Christian Church, and the alteration seems to have gradually taken place more in consequence of the restrictions imposed on the latter than any particular additions to their ordinary clothing. Prohibited by the councils from following the caprices of fashion indulged in by the noble and the wealthy, they were compelled to retain their primitive attire, which was the general dress of the people, and from whom they were originally distinguishable only by the tonsure. That they very unwillingly obeyed the injunctions of the councils, and constantly violated and evaded the laws enacted by them, is proved by the repeated censures and reiterated interdictions contained in the Canons themselves. St. Clement of Alexandria, who died in 220, had so early declared, "As there is a dress proper to soldiers, to sailors, to magistrates, so is there a garb befitting the sobriety of the Christian ;" and the vestments of the Christian ministers were such as were worn by grave and decorous Romans of condition on occasions of State festivals or religious ceremonials ; and that, as we have seen, consisted of the tunic and the toga. In the Council of Celchyth, A.D. 787, the wearing of "tinctured colours of India" and "precious garments"[1] is specially reprobated and forbidden ; and Boniface, the Anglo-Saxon missionary, in his letter to the Archbishop of Canterbury, inveighs against the luxury of dress amongst the clergy, and declares those garments that are adorned with very broad studs and images of worms announce the coming of Antichrist.[2] In the tenth century we find them even endeavouring to conceal the tonsure by letting the surrounding hair grow so long as to fall over it.[3]

Adhelm, Bishop of Sherborne. From MS. in the Lambeth Library.

At the Council of Cloveshoe the nuns were exhorted to pass their time rather in reading books and singing hymns than in working and wearing garments of empty pride in diversified colours.[4]

There is great uncertainty respecting the details of ecclesiastical costume previous to the ninth century ; but the vestments and insignia mentioned in the acts of the Council of Toledo, A.D. 633, are the alb, the planeta (the older name for the chasuble), the orarium or stole, the episcopal ring, and the pastoral staff. From other authorities we hear of the dalmatic and the pallium ; but the dalmatic does not appear to have been used in Spain. In the Canons instituted under the patronage of King Edgar, priests are commanded to wear at the celebration of mass a garment called the *corporale*, in addition to the *subumlem*, under the *alba ;* and it is further insisted upon, that all these garments shall be kept clean and in good order. The corporale, according to Ducange, was a fine white linen cloth, used to cover the sacred elements : but Mr. Strutt says, "The same, I presume, as the camisia or shirt ;" and the context is certainly in favour of his interpretation. *Subumlem* is a word used instead of *subtile*, a vestment appropriated to a sub-deacon. The alb is well known, and has been fully described under that head in the Dictionary.

Another clause expressly commands that no priest shall come into church or chancel without his surplice (ofer-rype in the Saxon).

The *dalmatic*, the *stole*, and *chasuble* are seen in illuminations of the ninth century, and the *maniple* is carried by the priests in the Bible of Charles le Chauve (see chromolithograph). Adhelm,

---

[1] Spelman, Concil. p. 294.   [2] Ibid. p. 241.   [3] Johnson's Canons, sub an. 960.   [4] Spelman, Concil. p. 256.

bishop of Sherborne, is represented, in a MS. in the Lambeth Library (No. 200), in an alb with ornamental borders, and some sort of vestment over it, the character of which is not sufficiently defined to allow of its identification. He is bareheaded. The mitre is the latest of all the ecclesiastical distinctions. For its various forms the reader is referred to the Dictionary *sub voce.*

Earliest form of Chasuble.
Catacombs at Rome.

Earliest form of Dalmatic.
Christian Martyr. Catacombs at Rome.

Youth in the furnace. From Tomb of
Pope Callistus.

Priscilla. From a Cemetery
on the Via Salara Nova.

Calopedas and *subtalares*, as their names import, were species of coverings for the feet, chiefly calculated for warmth, and were much used by the clergy in the performance of their nocturnal duties and in the winter. So likewise were socks, in addition to stockings and drawers. In the Council of Celchyth it was distinctly ordered that no minister of the altar presume to approach it to celebrate mass with naked legs. The pall or pallium, the special distinction of an archbishop as early as the eighth century, has been fully described in the Dictionary (*sub voce*). A mosaic of the age of Pope Leo III. represents him receiving the pallium from St. Peter, who also wears it with the rest of the ecclesiastical vestments, but is bareheaded. (See woodcut, p. 41.)

M. Victor Gay, in an interesting paper published in M. Didron's 'Annales Archéologiques,' tracing the clerical vestments from the classical costume, and more particularly from that worn by the Ascetic philosophers, illustrates his essay by the figures of early Christian martyrs copied from paintings in the Catacombs of Rome, and executed, as it is supposed, in the sixth century. We give them here, showing the earliest form of the dalmatic, with its wide sleeves and purple stripes, reminding us of the *clavus angustus* of the Romans, and also the original form of the chasuble, which had begun to be adopted by the clergy in the fifth century. A curious painting on the tomb of Pope Calixtus, on the Via Appia, representing the three youths in the furnace, affords an example of a tunic, the clavi or *lora* of which do not extend to the bottom of it. (See woodcut, p. 39.)

Mr. Marriott gives several plates in his valuable volume from mosaics and paintings, in which the Saviour and the Apostles are all attired in tunics, with clavi either black or very dark purple. Mr. Marriott mentions one instance in which they are red.

In the sixth century the clergy were enjoined to eschew the fashions of the laity, to disuse all

Adoration of the Magi. From the 'Roma Subterranea' of Aringhi.

gay colours, and to dress with gravity and decorum in a costume by which their holy office might be known. The chasuble, or planeta, as it was then called, which had been previously worn by laymen as well as ecclesiastics, answered to the description of the costume recommended, and was therefore retained by the latter when it was discarded by the former; and St. Augustine alludes to it under its Latin name of *casula*, as the habitual Christian vestment. The dalmatic was adopted by the Christians in the third century, and in the fourth [1] its use was made obligatory by Pope St. Sylvester (A.D. 314-335). It was worn by women as well as by men. Priscilla, an early martyr, is represented in it, in a cemetery on the Via Salara Nova (see woodcut in the preceding page). It is remarkable for having a double stripe of purple round the sleeves. In the 'Roma Subterranea' of Aringhi, two vols. fol., Rome, 1651, is an engraving from a painting in the Cemetery of SS. Marcellinus and Peter, representing the Adoration of the Magi, in which the Virgin and the three kings are all attired in such tunics. Mr. Pugin considers the stole of the priesthood to have been derived from the stripes of the dalmatic; but Mr. Fairholt has engraved the figure of a centurion sacrificing at an altar, copied from a bas-relief at Rome, which shows that something still more like the modern stole was worn by the Romans.

M. Didron, in his 'Iconographie Chrétienne,' has engraved a figure which he describes as that of Pope Paschal I. (817-824), from a mosaic of the ninth century, in the Church of St. Cecilia at Rome, which, Mr. Fairholt (who has engraved it) remarks, "very clearly delineates the form of the ancient stole; while the plainness of the chasuble and dalmatic denotes his humility equally with the *square nimbus*, adopted as less dignified than the circular one usually given to saints and martyrs." [2]

[1] Mr. Fairholt has "sixth," perhaps a typographical error. St. Sylvester I. died in 335. The second of the name was enthroned in 999, and died in 1003.

[2] The same back is placed behind the head of Charlemagne in both the mosaics. He certainly was canonised, but the solidity of the square nimbus in every instance is to me incomprehensible, and, where the head is bent down, absolutely ludicrous.

Centurion sacrificing. From a bas-relief at Rome.

Pope Paschal. From a mosaic.

St. Peter. From a mosaic.

Montfaucon, however, who has given the same figure on the twenty-second plate of his 'Antiquités de la Couronne de France,' tells us it is Pope Leo III., the predecessor of Paschal, to whom, in another mosaic, St. Peter is giving the pallium. I question the band he wears being a stole. Taken in conjunction with the other mosaic I have mentioned, I believe it to be the pallium which Leo is therein receiving from St. Peter, and which it perfectly resembles, and is therefore more worthy of attention, as it differs in form from that archiepiscopal decoration as subsequently represented, being, like the stole itself, a band with fringed ends. See also the engraving from a picture of St. Gregory the Great, in which he is represented, according to the description of Johannes Diaconus in the tenth century, wearing the pallium, "a dextro videlicet humero sub pectore super stomachum circulatim deducto : deinde sursum per sinistrum humerum veniens proprie rectitudine *non per medium corporis sed ex latere pendet*." Mr. Marriott remarks on this passage : "The language of John the Deacon implies that in his own time (tenth century) the form and arrangement of the pallium had undergone a change" (p. 238, note). The stole is seen in the dresses of the clergy in illuminations of the ninth century.

Upon the Arch of Constantine figures are seen wearing a broad ribbon or scarf over their shoulders, like the modern *cordon* of an order of knighthood ; and Mr. Marriott remarks that "the scarf or broad ribbon so worn corresponds in general appearance to the orarium of the earliest ecclesiastical monuments in which this vestment is represented, though in point of arrangement some difference is observable." In the acts of the Council of Toledo before quoted, the orarium is recognised as a distinctly ministerial vestment, to be worn by bishops,

Pope Gregory the Great.

presbyters, and deacons ; the latter, however, to wear it over the left shoulder only. It is important also to state that the term *stole* was never applied to this vestment till the ninth century.

It is in the ninth century also that the figure of a Pope first appears with his head covered. In the 'Chartularum Prumiense'—a MS. partly of the ninth century, partly of later date, in the Stadtbibliotek at Trèves—is a drawing of Pope Nicholas I. (A.D. 858–867) and the Emperor Louis II. (A.D. 843–876). The Pope is attired in alb, dalmatic, stole, and chasuble or planeta, and wears the pallium. On his head is a cap, called a *camelaucium*, according to Florovantes, who, speaking of a coin of Hadrian I., says : "Figura in medio Pontificali habitu et *bireta* quod *camelaucium* ab Anastatio in Constantino, hodie vero *Camaurum* dicitur" (Ant. Pontif. Rom. Dan. p. 37). The first change of head-dress on the coins is early in the tenth century. Describing a coin of Sergius III. (904–911), the same author says : "Sergium III. pontificia veste indutum et mitra ornatum, hic exhibet nummus ut in superioribus nummis Pontificum capita camelaucia tantum tecta visuntur ; quæ res mire favet, eorum sententiæ qui Pontifices serius mitram gestasse arbitrantur." "These

Figures from the Arch of Constantine.

facts," observes Mr. Marriott, "throw back the mitra at Rome itself to a somewhat earlier date than most modern antiquaries have assigned to it." For the earliest form of the tiara "*en éteignoir*," see the following chapter.

Pope Nicholas I. From the 'Chartularum Prumiense.'

Until the separation of the Latin and Greek Churches, the ecclesiastical costume was uniform throughout Christian Europe. That separation took place in the ninth century, the eighth and last General Council having been held at Constantinople, on the 5th of October, 869. The vestments at that time worn in the East were the sticharion, corresponding to the dalmatic of the West ; the phænolion, answering to the planeta or chasuble ; the orarium, a term common to both East and West in respect of the deacon's scarf or stole, but which was known as peritrachelion or epitrachelion, when worn pendent round the neck by bishops or priests ; and the omophorion or pallium, which, as worn by patriarchs, metropolitans, and almost all bishops in the Greek Church, was evidently copied from the imperial or consular ornament of the same name, of which we have given an example at page 27. Such was in point of fact originally but a more important orarium or stole, as it is seen in the Lateran Mosaic and numerous other representations, to be worn "in modum crucis in pectore." (See under STOLE, in Dictionary.) Of these vestments illustrations will be found in our notices of Costume in Russia. I have occupied more space than I can well afford in this attempt to give a clearer notion of the origin and history of Ecclesiastical Costume than the general public could gather from any work not specially dedicated to the subject, or, indeed, from many that are.

At the commencement of the eleventh century, another Scythic race had established itself in France, England, Naples, and Sicily. The Vikings of Scandinavia, known as Danes to the English and as Normans to the French, had made continual descents upon the coasts of our islands, and incursions into the heart of the Empire of the West. Charlemagne had wept at the sight of their ships, and predicted the evils that would befall his dynasty through the inroads of these audacious pirates. As early as the year 911, Charles the Simple, king of France, had given the whole of the province of Neustria between Brittany and the river Ept, with the hand of his daughter, to Rolf or Rollo, the chief of the pagan Norsemen, on condition that he should become a Christian, and engage to live in peace with France, doing homage to its sovereign for what thenceforth became the Duchy of Normandy.

In 1017 the first Danish king of England, Canute or Knut, had ascended the throne of Ethelred the Unready; and before the first half of the century had elapsed, the Normans, under Robert Guiscard, were firmly seated in Apulia.

The civil habits of the Danes, Norwegians, and Normans do not appear to have differed greatly in form from those of the Anglo-Saxons; but from various passages in the Welsh chronicles and the old Danish ballads we gather that the favourite, if not the general colour of the ancient Danish dress was black. Caradoc of Llancarvan repeatedly calls them the "black Danes," and the Chronicles continually allude to them as the "black army." In the Danish ballad of 'Child Dyring' the child is described as riding even to a bridal feast in "black sendell;" and black, bordered with red, is still common amongst the Northern peasantry. Black amongst the pagan Danes had certainly no funereal associations with it. The absence of black in representations of Anglo-Saxon burials is remarkable; and it is well known that the Danes never mourned for the death of even their nearest or dearest relations, and this sombre hue may have been their national colour, their standard being a raven. I observed, in a note on this subject in my 'History of British Costume,' that the Danes being undoubtedly of Scythic origin, it is a curious circumstance that we should find Herodotus mentioning a nation bordering on Scythia who wore no other clothing than black, and whom he therefore calls the Melanchlænians. In addition I would suggest that the inhabitants of the Cassiterides, or Scilly Isles, who are distinguished from the Gauls and Britons by their long black dresses, may have been Scandinavian colonists, allured thither by the commerce in tin, the product of those islands, which was actively carried on by the Romans and the Phœnicians.

Arnold of Lübeck describes the whole nation of Danes as originally wearing the garments of sailors, as befitted men who lived by piracy and inhabited the sea; but that in process of time they became wearers of scarlet, purple, and fine linen. It is probable, therefore, that on their conversion to Christianity they "cast their nighted colour off," and on their establishment in England endeavoured to outshine the Saxons; for it is affirmed by John Wallingford, a writer of the early part of the thirteenth century, that "the Danes were effeminately gay in their dress, combed their hair once a day, bathed once a week, and often changed their attire. By these means they pleased the eyes of the women, and frequently seduced the wives and daughters of the nobility." This account, though not contemporaneous, is verified by many facts that are recorded by other authors and passages in the various sagas which have been preserved to us.

A monument containing the body of Canute was discovered in 1766 by some workmen repairing Winchester Cathedral. The body was remarkably fresh. A wreath or circlet surrounded the head, and bands of gold and silver, which had ornamented a portion of his attire, were found in the tomb. On his finger was a ring in which was a remarkably fine stone, and in one of his hands was a silver penny.[1]

We have no pictorial authority for the female costume of the Danes at this period, if we except what is meant for a representation of the queen of Canute in the register of Hyde Abbey, wherein she is delineated in tunic, mantle, and veil, with a diadem or *half bend*, differing in no respect from the usual habit of Anglo-Saxon or Norman women of royal or noble rank. (See Dictionary, page 101.)

The Danish ballads, the Icelandic and Norwegian sagas, add but little to our information respecting female costume, communicative as they are on that of their sea-kings, and in the poem on Beowulf we are told—

[1] 'Archæologia,' vol. iii. p. 890.

G 2

> "Waltheow came forth,
> The Queen of Hrothgar,
> Mindful of her descent,
> Circled with gold ; "

and in the same poem she is again spoken of as

> " The Queen circled with bracelets : "

also, in another passage,

> " Encircled with gold she went,
> The Queen of the free-like people,
> To sit by her lord."

It is presumable that these allusions are not only to the bracelets which are specified, but to her girdle and her diadem, as in the Danish ballad of 'Ingefred and Gerdrune' mention is made of Ingefred's golden girdle, and she takes a gold ring from her arm to give to the physician.

Of their armour and weapons we possess, as I have intimated, abundant information. By the laws of Gula, said to have been established by Hacon the Good, who died in 963, every possessor of property to the amount of six marks, besides his clothes, was required to furnish himself with a red shield of two boards in thickness, a spear, an axe, and a sword. He who was worth twelve marks was ordered, in addition to the above, to procure a steel cap (*stal hufu*) ; whilst he who had eighteen marks was obliged to have a double red shield, a helmet, a coat of mail (*brynia*), or a tunic of quilted linen or cloth (*panzar*), and all military weapons. In the history of this same King Hacon, who was called "Adelstein's fostra," from having been educated at the court of our English Athelstan, it is said that the king put on a coat of mail (*brynia*), girded round him his sword, called *quærn-bit* (*i.e.* millstone biter), and set on his head his gilded helmet. He took a spear in his hand, and hung his shield by his side.[1] Also, in the description of the battle of Slicklastad, where King Olaf of Norway, called "the Saint," was slain (A.D. 1030), that monarch is described as wearing a golden helmet, a white shield, a golden-hilted and exceedingly sharp sword, and a tunic of ringed mail (" hringa brynio "), the "ringed byrne" of the Saxons. The Danish helmet, like the Saxon, had the nasal which in Scandinavian is called " nef-biorg " (nose-guard).[2] Of the splendour sometimes displayed in the military equipment of the Danes, we have an instance in the attempt of Earl Godwin to appease the anger of Hardicanute. He presented that prince with a magnificent vessel, on board of which were eighty soldiers, armed in coats of gilded mail, their shields enveloped with gold, and their helmets richly gilt, each of them having on either arm two golden bracelets of the weight of sixteen ounces. The hilts of their swords were also of gold, and every man had a Danish axe on his left shoulder, and a spear in his right hand.[3]

The spear, the sword, the bow, and particularly the double-bladed axe, were the offensive weapons of all the Northmen. The Danes were famous for the use of the last, and to shoot well with the bow was a necessary qualification of a Danish warrior.

The short interval between the Danish and Norman Conquests, during which the crown of England reverted to the Saxon line, furnishes us with only two anecdotes of costume worth recording. The first is the general complaint of William of Malmesbury, that in the time of Edward the Confessor the English had transformed themselves into Frenchmen and Normans, adopting not only their strange manner of speech and behaviour, but also the ridiculous and fantastic fashions of wearing shorter tunics and clipping their hair, and shaving their beards, leaving, however, the upper lip still unshorn. They were also guilty of puncturing their skins and loading their arms with golden bracelets. The latter practice is clearly to be traced to the Norsemen ; but the puncturing of the skin was an ancient Keltic custom, and is not alluded to by any of the Norman or Danish contemporary historians. William of Malmesbury was not a contemporary writer, and must have gathered his information either from earlier authors or from oral tradition. The predilection of Edward the Confessor for Norman customs is, however, a fact testified to by nearly every authority ; and the results of it are obvious in the resemblance visible in the general features of the civil and military

---

[1] Kempe Vixer, p. 662.　　　[2] Saga Magn. Bur.　　　[3] Florence of Worcester, 403.

costume of the two countries in the middle of the eleventh century. Even the substitution by Harold II. of leathern armour in his Welsh expeditions may probably have been suggested by his reminiscences of Normandy, as we perceive it worn by personages in the Bayeux Tapestry, and depicted in Anglo-Norman illuminations as late as the thirteenth century.

Branches of the same great Scythic stock, a species of family likeness had always existed between the Saxons, the Danes, and the Normans ; but the residence of the latter on the Continent, in close contiguity to what had become the important kingdom of France, their expeditions to the Mediterranean and intercourse with Italy and the East, had materially improved their character and manners ; and while the Danes continued pirates, and the Saxons, originally the fiercest nation of the predatory North, had sunk into a slothful and unwarlike people, the Normans became distinguished throughout Europe for their military skill, their love of glory, their encouragement of literature, the splendour and propriety of their habiliments, the cleanliness of their persons, and the courtesy of their demeanour.[1] The curious custom of shaving the back of the head, which they had adopted from their Aquitanian neighbours, was almost the only marked distinction of the immediate descendants of Rollo.

In the year 1066 Europe presented a very different aspect to that she wore during the latter years of the Roman Empire. No longer harassed by successive hordes of barbarians, issuing from "the great hive of the North," and driving their predecessors before them to the verge of the ocean, the greater portion of the Continent was at this date occupied by firmly established nations, bearing already the names which they have retained to the present day. On the throne of France was seated Philip I., the fourth sovereign of the house of Capet. Germany was an empire swayed by the sceptre of Henry IV.

Boniface II., duke of Tuscany.

From MS. in the Vatican.

The Countess Matilda.

The Papal States were in existence, and had become the seat of a power greater than that of the Cæsars. The rest of Italy was divided into duchies, marquisates, and republics, the general

[1] Turner's Hist. of the Anglo-Saxons. Hist. of Brit. Costume.

resemblance prevailing in their costume being slightly varied in the South by intercommunion with Greece, Constantinople, and Asia Minor; and in the North by the neighbourhood of France and Germany. A valuable MS. in the Vatican contains a representation of Boniface II., called "the Pious," Duke and Marquis of Tuscany, 1027–1052; and also of his celebrated daughter, "the great Countess" Matilda, 1076–1115. As the latter is represented in the prime of her life, the portraits were probably executed shortly after her accession to the Duchy, and at all events present us with the costume of the nobility of Tuscany in the eleventh century, and its similarity to that of Northern and Western Europe is sufficiently apparent.

The conquests in Spain and Portugal by the Arabs in the eighth century had resulted in the foundation of nearly as many kingdoms as they possessed towns; but Sancho IV. reigned in Aragon, Castile, and Navarre; his brother, Alfonso VI., was King of Leon and the Asturias; and Garcia, his youngest brother, King of Galicia.

Of this period one of the Additional MSS. in the British Museum, numbered 11,695, affords us some most interesting examples of Spanish costume bearing a remarkable resemblance to the dress, both civil and military, of the Saxons and the Normans, and are the earliest of that country I have met with. Mr. Shaw, who has given a plate from it in his 'Dresses and Decorations of the Middle Ages,' remarks : "The style of the drawings in this manuscript is half Saracenic. The elegance of the ornaments contrasts strongly with the unskilful rudeness in the designs of men and animals—a

circumstance which reminds us of the repugnance among the Arabs to drawing men and living things : " by which, I presume, he considered the illuminations to have been the work of Mohammedan artists. To me it appears that the representation, however rude, of human beings and animals, is a fact which proves the direct contrary ; to say nothing of the assurance contained in the MS. itself, that it was executed in the monastery of Silos, in the diocese of Burgos (Old Castile), having been begun under the Abbot Fortunius, carried on after his death by the Abbot Nunnus (Nuñez), and finished in the time of Abbot John, A.D. 1109, thus occupying not less than twenty years in writing and illuminating, undoubtedly by one or more Christian inmates of the monastery. The subject being a commentary of the Apocalypse, is an additional reason for rejecting the idea of a Moorish draughtsman being employed upon it, and accounts for the Saracenic features of the architecture, introduced intentionally to give an Oriental character to the incidents, and copied, as usual, from contemporary examples. The figures of the Jongleurs or Minstrels dancing on some sort of clogs are very curious ; and the ringed hauberks of the warriors, worn over a long tunic, furnish

Jongleurs or Minstrels. From a Spanish MS., 11th century, in the British Museum.

additional evidence in support of my view of the form of those depicted in the Bayeux Tapestry. (See Dictionary, page 265.) I would direct the reader's attention especially to the standard-bearer on horseback, whose hauberk, bordered with scale-work, is cut up before and behind for the convenience of riding, and is so clearly delineated that the divisions cannot possibly be mistaken for breeches. The round shields or targets, in some instances elegantly ornamented, and the trilobed and cinquefoil pommels of the sword-hilts, are interesting. Some of the warriors seem to be armed with two swords. The conical head-piece with its nasal, and the bandaged and studded leggings of the soldiers, correspond so nearly with those of the Normans, the French, and the Germans of the same period, that it would appear that the same style of military equipment had become general throughout Christian Europe before the close of the eleventh century.

Spanish Warriors. From the same MS.

By Christian Europe we must, however, be understood to mean the nations established west of the Carpathians. East of those mountains the great Sclavonic family, of which Russia was destined to become the most important portion, had not embraced Christianity before the end of the tenth century. Vladimir the Great, the first Prince of Russia of that name, was converted *circa* 1000. The Sarmatians, who had acquired the name of Poles, from the Sclavonic word *Pole*, signifying a flat country fit for hunting, received the Gospel according to the Greek Church in 966; but as late as 1386 the Lithuanians and Samogitians were worshippers of fire and adored serpents. Of the costume, civil or military, of these peoples in the eleventh century, we have no description. In the magnificent work recently published at St. Petersburg, entitled 'Les Antiquités de l'Empire de Russie,' the only plate professing to represent the civil dress of the upper classes of the Muscovites previous to the fifteenth century is taken from a very much injured painting forming the frontispiece of a Greek MS. attributed to the year 1073, in which are depicted Sviatoslaf Jarolslavich and family. It is too much defaced for copying, and presents no peculiar feature to distinguish it from the costume of the Lower Empire, except high boots. On one of the gates of the Cathedral of St. Sophia, in Novgorod, men in armour are represented with conical helmets, long shields, and hauberks over tunics; but I will not undertake to affix a date to the work, or decide as to the nationality of the warriors.

CHAPTER III.

TWELFTH CENTURY.

OMMENCING, as in duty bound, with our own country, we have the authority of all the early historians that the Normans and Flemings, who accompanied William I. into England, or flocked over in such numbers after his establishment on the throne, were remarkable for their love of finery, personal decoration, and constant change of fashion. This observation, however, applies, of course, only to the noble and wealthier classes, the commonalty continuing to wear the short tunic, with sleeves to the wrist; the better sort with chausses, and shoes or short boots; and in bad weather, or when travelling, a cloak with a cowl to it, called by the Normans *capa*, and closely resembling the *pœnula* of the Romans. Scarcely any difference, beyond nomenclature, appears between the dress of the Norman women and that of

Anglo-Norman Ladies.

the Saxons. The head-rail becomes a *couvre-chef*, and the tunic a *cote*; but the fashion of the articles is well-nigh unchanged.

The dress of the higher orders seems, from such pictorial authorities as we possess, to have fully justified the censure and satire that were heaped upon it by contemporary writers. The rage for splendour of material and extravagance in form had commenced in the reign of Rufus, who had himself set the example, and both clergy and laity became infected with the love of costly clothing. The long tunic worn on State occasions, and the *interula* or linen vestment worn under it, positively trailed upon the ground; and the sleeves were also of length and breadth sufficient not only to cover the whole hand, but to hang down over it, notwithstanding that gloves were now generally worn by the upper classes. The mantles were made of the finest cloth, and lined with rich furs. One presented by Richard Bloet, Bishop of Lincoln, to King Henry I. was lined with black sables with white spots, and is said to have cost one hundred pounds of the money of that period. With the shorter tunic was worn a shorter cloak, lined also with precious furs, and called a *rheno*. The Phrygian cap was still in favour; but the generality of the middle and poorer classes went bareheaded, or in bad weather covered their heads with the cowl of their capa. Peaked boots and shoes, of an absurd

Anglo-Norman Male Costume. From Cotton MS. Nero, C. iv.

shape, called by the Latin writers *ocrea rostrata*, and said by Ordericus Vitalis to have been invented by Fulk le Rechin, Comte d'Anjou, who was deformed in the foot, was another eccentric and ugly fashion introduced at this time. A variety was called *pigaciæ*. The points of the toes were made like a scorpion's tail, or stuffed out with tow, and caused to curl round like a ram's horn. The latter folly being laid to the charge of a Norman courtier named Robert, obtained for him the *sobriquet* of "Cornadu." Notwithstanding these accounts, there can be little doubt that such boots or shoes were worn long previously, and that the Count and the courtier merely revived a fashion Oriental in its origin, and which has never been entirely abandoned in the East.

M. Quicherat observes: "Enfin les monuments Égyptiens et Étrusques attestent que dès la plus haute antiquité on porta des chaussures munies à leur extrémité d'une sorte de bec, qui se relevait à une hauteur prodigieuse comme un fer de patin;" and states that in the Museum at Berne the foot of a bronze statue of the best period of Roman art has upon it a shoe "à pointe recourbée."[1] The peaked toed boots were strictly forbidden to the clergy.

The extraordinary Aquitanian custom of shaving the back of the head, which had been adopted by the Normans, as described in the Dictionary (page 239), was abandoned by them soon after their establishment in this country; and, with the usual caprice of fashion, they ran into the opposite extreme. As early as 1095 a decree was passed by the Council of Rouen against long hair; but, like the majority of such ordinances, it proved ineffectual. Several amusing anecdotes concerning this fashion are to be found in the writers of the period. (See Dictionary, under HAIR.) Long

[1] 'Histoire de Cost.' p. 156. Such shoes were called by the Romans *calcei rostrati*. (See p. 8 *ante*.)

beards were also the rage. In fact, a passion for increasing to an absurd and inconvenient length every article of attire extended itself from head to foot, in France as well as England, in the first half of the twelfth century, London following the lead of Paris as slavishly then as at the present day.

As the costume of the ancient Britons is best illustrated by that of Gaul, and the dress and arms of the Anglo-Saxons by those of the Franks, so shall we find the civil and military habiliments of the English generally reflecting those of the French throughout the six succeeding centuries, although occasionally some foreign alliance or important event was the cause of the introduction of a particular garment, colour, or weapon. A statue of the Queen of Sheba which formerly stood in the porch of Notre Dame de Corbeil, was exhibited in the Museum of French Monuments as that of the Merovingian Queen Clotilde; those of which I have already spoken as representing the kings and queens of that dynasty in the grand portal of the Cathedral of Chartres were executed about the middle of the twelfth century; and our own contemporary statues of Henry I. and his

French Nobles of the 11th century. From Willemin, 'Monuments inédits.'   Statues of a King and Queen at Corbeil.

queen at Rochester having suffered such injury from time and weather that the details of their costume are all but completely obliterated, we are most fortunate in being able to refer to the better-preserved French sculptures for information respecting the regal costume of the reigns of Henry I. of England and Louis VI. of France.

The kings present no special novelty in their robes of State. They wear the long tunic with capacious sleeves, and an ample mantle with richly-embroidered borders; hair flowing over their shoulders, a jewelled diadem or circlet, and a comely beard. The dress of the queens has a marked character, the body consisting of a sort of corset, tightly fitting the bust, and descending over the hips, where it terminates in front in a curve, with a decorated border; the waist being confined by a belt, ornamented with jewels; independently of which is a girdle below the corset, the ends of which hang down to within a short distance of the bottom of the full-pleated skirt of the under-garment, which M. Quicherat calls a *bliaud, bliaut, bliaus*—a name given by M. Viollet-le-Duc to half-a-dozen widely different dresses (see Dictionary, p. 43), and which may have been a general term for a tunic of any sort, though I am not of that opinion.

Of what material this corset was made we have no description, but its name is conjectured by M. Quicherat to have been *gipe*, the original form of the words *gipon*, *jupe*, *jupon* (see Dictionary, page 317 ; also under JIPOCOAT, page 316), in which case it might occasionally have been of fur, as in the 'Roman de Garin' we read of a " gipe de gris " as being worn with a "bliaut d'or ouvré." In the sculpture, however, it has the appearance of a textile fabric of the most delicate description, or gold or silver tissue, and defines the form exactly.

The representation in Montfaucon of some similar statues at St. Germain des Prés gives an idea of scale-work, but no reliance can be placed on the accuracy of the engraving.

The sleeves of the tunic are of two sorts. In one example they are extremely wide and long, the edges having the appearance of frills (*frissaux*). In another they are tight to the wrists, and have a band of embroidery round the upper part of the arm. Over all is a mantle, which touches the ground when not held up, and is sometimes fastened on one shoulder. It has a richly ornamented border. The hair, parted on the forehead, falls on each side of the head in a long plaited tail, precisely as in the statue of Queen Matilda at Rochester, and the brows are bound by a jewelled diadem. At page 463 of the Dictionary, under the word SLEEVE, will be found examples of the preposterous length of the ladies' sleeves *temp.* Rufus and Henry I. That the fashion existed at the same period in Germany is shown by a copy fortunately made by Engelhardt's 'Herrard von Landsberg,' of an allegorical figure of Pride in the MS. Hortus Deliciarum (1135), destroyed by the bombardment of Strasburg in 1871. The curiously-twisted couvre-chef and the skirt of the tunic are equally elongated to an immoderate extent.

The regal habits of the second half of the twelfth century in England are perfectly presented to us in the effigies of Henry II., Richard I., and their queens, at Fontevraud. We have given a fac-simile of Stothardt's carefully - executed copy of them in a chromolithic plate issued with the Eighth Part of the Dictionary ; and to it we must refer our readers for the pictorial illustration of them. In the Imperial Treasury at Vienna there are preserved several garments of this date, which formed a portion of the coronation robes of the German Emperors, the most interesting of which are two tunics. One, described by M.

Figure of Pride. From the 'Hortus Deliciarum,' 1135.

Quicherat as a *bliaud*, and called Charlemagne's in a work published at Nuremberg in 1790, has an inscription in Latin and Arabic, stating it to have been made at Palermo, in 1181. The other, which from the text of Willemin we learn was also of Arabic workmanship, in the 28th of the Hegira, A.D. 1143, M. Quicherat designates a *chainse*—a term, he tells us, in the oldest French language signifying *chemise*. (See, however, my notice of CHAISEL, in Dictionary, p. 89.) Another tunic of the same character is preserved in the Museum at Munich, traditionally appropriated to the Emperor Henry II. (1002–1024). This M. Quicherat also calls a *bliaud*. Neither of these names is applied to these garments by Dr. Bock, who has given coloured engravings of them in his sumptuous work, 'Kleinodien des heil römischen Reiches deutschen Nation,' from which our subjoined woodcuts are taken ; and the terms "bliaut" and "chainse" for such garments seem to have been confined to France and Norman England.

Tunic in the National Museum at Munich.

Tunic made in Sicily, a.d. 1143.

The costume of the people generally underwent no remarkable change beyond the limitation of the length of the garments and the hair to moderate dimensions. The latter was no longer permitted to fall on the shoulders of the men, or worn in plaited tails by the women. The gipe or corset gave place to a supertunic in the female costume, but in that of the men no important alteration is discernible. A fashion, however, crept into favour during the reign of Henry II., which attained to great extravagance in later times, and was the subject of censure and satire for three centuries. This was the cutting of the edges of the garments into various shapes. However fantastic or (if you will) absurd may have been this fashion, I fail to see the reason that it should have awakened such serious alarm that it was thought necessary to enact laws prohibiting certain classes from adopting it. But for the attempt at suppression, it might have died the natural death of such caprices. As it proved, the statute passed in 1188 against wearing cut or jagged garments was, like the many that succeeded it, utterly disregarded, and the violence of restriction only increased the vogue of the offence.

Tunic made at Palermo, A.D. 1181.

It is remarkable that even the industry of Montfaucon has failed to find an example of this fashion in France previous to the fourteenth century, and M. Quicherat only alludes to its existence during the reign of Philip Augustus as a singular custom which, being adopted by the clergy, came under the consideration of the Council of Montpellier in 1195, when an edict was issued against it.[1] That it was followed in Germany appears from a drawing of this date (copied from Engelhardt's 'Herrard von Landsberg') of two lovers embracing, the edges of the surcoat and mantle of the male personage being cut into lobes or tongues. It was probably but a revival of an old barbaric practice, as the figure of a Romano-Gaulish woman is represented with the edge of her tunic indented.

From Engelhardt's 'Herrard von Landsberg' (Hortus Deliciarum).

It is in the twelfth century that we obtain the earliest information from pictures of the costume of the Republic of Venice, which has always retained a distinctive character. In the church of St. Mark are still to be seen some ancient mosaics representing incidents connected with the translation of the body of St. Mark. The figures from some of these were engraved and published, with descriptions in Italian and Latin, by Cesare Veccellio, a kinsman of the celebrated Titian, at Venice, in 1590.[2] Tradition attributes to that great painter the drawings made for the work; but there is no evidence in support of it, and the story was probably founded on the fact that some of the figures were copied from portraits by him of the nobility of his own time. The dates given in many of the descriptions of costume previous to the sixteenth century are extremely inaccurate. M. Camille Bonnard has included a few of the most interesting of the ancient figures in his collection of 'Costumes Historiques,' by which we find that, as late as 1176, the cap of the Doge had not assumed

[1] " Vers le temps de la croisade de Philippe-Auguste, il y eut une mode qui donna au surcot masculin une grande singularité. L'étoffe était decoupée par le bas en une suite de languettes. Des ecclésiastiques s'étant avisés de faire tailladder leurs robes de cette façon, cela fit scandale. Le Concile de Montpellier y mit ordre en 1195." ('Hist. du Costume en France,' p. 195.)

[2] 'Habiti Antichi e Moderni di tutto il Mondo.'

Doge.　　　　　　Noble Lady and Child.　　　　　　Noble or Senator.

Venetian Costume, 11th century. From mosaics in the Church of St. Mark.

the well-known form which afterwards distinguished it. It was simply a conical cap or bonnet, like that we have seen on the head of Boniface, duke of Tuscany (*vide ante* p. 45), with a jewelled band and a pearl or diamond button on the top (see first figure in the preceding page). The dress of the ladies is that of the twelfth century in Europe generally, but with features evidently characteristic of the costume of the Lower Empire. The bas-reliefs on the tomb of Blanche de Navarre, queen of Sancho III., king of Castile (1157), in the chapel of Santa Maria de Najara, rude as they are, sufficiently show that the female costume in Spain was similar to that in France and England, consisting of a long tunic and mantle, the ornamentation resembling that on the tunic of the French nobleman at page 50 *ante.*

There can be no doubt that the Crusades which commenced in the twelfth century had a considerable effect on the costume, both civil and military, of Western Europe, particularly on the latter. One of the characteristic features of the knightly equipment of the time of Stephen is the length of the tunic, which streams down from beneath the hauberk to the heels, the revival of a Frankish fashion, of Oriental origin. On the Trajan Column some of the Roman auxiliaries are seen attired in

flowing tunics, over which is worn a lorica ; and in a MS. copy of Prudentius, in the National Library at Paris, marked 283, illuminated by Frankish artists, warriors are so represented. (*Vide* also fig. 4, Plate X., from a Cottonian MS., Brit. Mus.) The seal of Richard, Constable of Chester, A.D. 1154, and the great seals of Richard Cœur de Lion, exhibit this peculiarity, while that of King John, A.D. 1199, represents him with the surcoat *over* the hauberk. It has been conjectured that this custom originated with the Crusaders both for the purpose of distinguishing the many different leaders serving under the Cross, and to veil the iron armour, so apt to heat excessively when exposed to the direct rays of the sun. The date of its first appearance in Europe, and the circumstance of the Knights of St. John and of the Temple being so attired in their monumental effigies, are certainly arguments in favour of the supposition, and no fact has been discovered since it was first mentioned by Meyrick that tends to discredit it. The seal of the Constable of Chester also illustrates the fashion of the long-toed shoes noticed in our view of the civil costume. (*Vide* Dictionary, p. 349.) They are alluded to by Anna Comnena, in her 'Alexiad'

German Knight. From a MS. in the Library at Darmstadt.

German Knight. From mural painting on Cathedral of Brunswick.

(lib. v. p. 140), who mentions them as encumbering the dismounted cavalry of the Franks,[1] as she calls the Normans under Bohemund, son of Robert Guiscard. Of the varieties of the body armour at this date I have spoken at length in the Dictionary, under the heads of HAUBERK and MAIL. It is sufficient here to observe that "the ingenuity both of armourers and warriors was naturally in continual exertion to invent such defences for the body as would be proof against all the various weapons invented with equal rapidity for the purposes of destruction, and that consequently alterations and improvements were taking place every day of great importance to the actual wearer, but too minute for delineation then or for distinction now, when time has half obliterated the details

[1] Her words (τως εικλιας εποκμετα) were misinterpreted as referring to spurs. The error is noticed by Gibbon in a note, chapter lvi.

of objects at first but imperfectly represented by the rude artists of this dark but interesting period."[1]

That many a hint was taken from the equipment of the Saracens is extremely probable, and to them I am inclined to attribute the introduction of the wambais or gambeson, and the hauqueton or aketon, both of which stuffed and quilted garments became common in the twelfth century.

Combat between Crusaders and Saracens. From a window formerly on the Church of St. Denis.

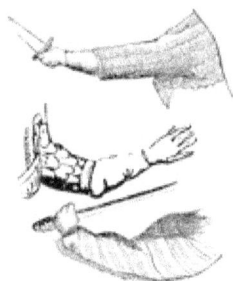

Details of Saracenic Armour from other windows.

The mural paintings on the Cathedral at Brunswick, executed in the reign of Henry the Lion, who died in 1198, present us with figures of warriors in hauberks or tunics composed of scales divided by bands; but whether of metal or leather, it would be hazardous to determine. The windows formerly in the church of St. Denis, painted by order of Abbot Suger about the close of the century, representing several of the principal events in the First Crusade, exhibit some of the Saracenic warriors in tunics which have all the appearance of being wadded and stitched in regular lines or divisions.

[1] Hist. of Brit. Costume, p. 77.

Two or three examples are very similar to that of the knight from Brunswick. They have been engraved by Montfaucon, and a portion of them are copied for this work. Though I cannot vouch for the accuracy of the Rev. Father's pencil, they are well worthy the study of the antiquary.

The helm, which had remained sharply conical during the reigns of Henry I. and Stephen, became cylindrical in the reign of Henry II.; and though in the first seal of Richard I. he is represented in a conical head-piece, yet on his second he is seen with a flat-topped helm, surmounted by a fan-shaped ornament, on the side of which is depicted a lion passant—the earliest appearance, I believe, of anything approaching to a crest in England. (See Plate XI., figs. 1 and 2, for instructive examples of the gradual change of form during the above reigns.) The nasal was retained as late as the reign of Edward I.; but a more complete defence for the face was invented in the twelfth century, consisting of a plate of steel with perforations for seeing and breathing, which was called the aventaile,

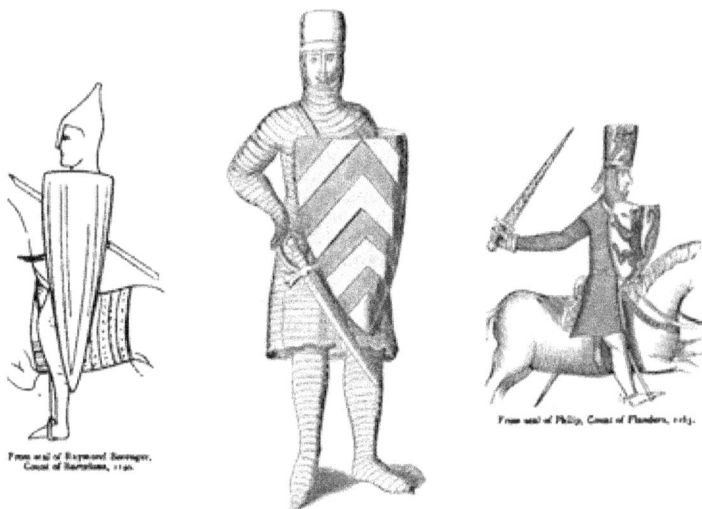

From seal of Raymond Berenger, Count of Barcelona, 1140.

Raoul de Beaumont, founder of the Abbey of Estival in 1110.

From seal of Philip, Count of Flanders, 1163.

removable at pleasure, or a straight bar of iron, connecting the helm with that portion of the mail-hood which passes under the chin (*vide* woodcut annexed). The conical helm is, however, occasionally seen in foreign examples. Two German helms of the close of the twelfth century will be found at page 281 of the Dictionary; see also the figures from the Strasburg MS. at pp. 267 and 268. The seal of Don Raymond Berenger, fourth Count of Barcelona, 1140, presents him to us in a particularly sharp-pointed head-piece, and his kite-shaped shield is of a remarkable length and fashion. Another novelty made its appearance in the second half of the century, originating no doubt in the necessity for distinguishing important personages in that great commingling of troops of all nations in the plains of Palestine. The shield—which, though still retaining its kite or pear-shaped form, was semi-cylindrical—in lieu of displaying some more or less tasteful ornament or rudely-designed figure of a monster which could be likened to nothing in the animal creation, was

VOL. II. I

now carefully gilt, silvered, or painted with a certain colour, on which was depicted an unmistakable, however quaintly drawn, lion, eagle, or other bird or beast, crosses, crescents, stars, and a variety of other objects, natural and artificial,—no longer fantastic and unmeaning devices, to be changed according to the caprice of the moment, but selected and assumed as personal badges, identifying the wearer, by typifying his name, property, or position as clearly as it was possible to do by pictorial representations of synonymous objects or symbols generally recognized as indicating certain sovereignties; such as the eagle of the Roman Empire, the fleur-de-lys of France, the lion of England, which may have been assumed by Henry I., and was certainly borne by Richard Cœur de Lion, &c. In brief, HERALDRY, properly so called, had its birth about the middle of the twelfth century, and before the close of it had become a science, some knowledge of which was an indispensable portion of the education of every gentleman. Our concern with it in this work is limited to its connection with costume, wherein it subsequently became so important and splendid a feature. At the period now under consideration, it was confined to the decoration of the shield and the helm. I have already spoken of the lion on the helm of King Richard. Another example occurs on the cap of the Norman nobleman in the enamelled tablet at Mans. (See chromo-lithograph published with Part V. of this work.) A third is seen on the seal of Philip, Count of Flanders, 1163 (see preceding page). He is represented in a very tall, cylindrical helm, on which is painted a lion rampant as upon his shield.[1] We give the equestrian figure entire, as one proof of the prevalence of the similarity of the military equipment throughout Western Europe at the same period. The height of the helm corresponds with that of the helm of Henry II., as given on his great seal ; and in neither instance is there the slightest indication of a nasal or any sort of defence of the face. Subsequent to that date the varieties of aventailes are well-nigh numberless.

Of the Scotch previous to the fourteenth century, we have little information, and that little appears to be embodied in the couplet of the old song which informs us that the Highlanders

> " Had only got the belted plaid,
> While they [the Lowlanders] were mail-clad men."

The *rynged byrn* of the Saxons, and the improved hauberk of the Normans, soon found their way across the border, but were adopted by the sovereign and the Lowland chiefs alone ; for though the early monarchs of Scotland appear upon their seals in the nasal head-piece and the mascled, ringed, or scaly armour of the Anglo-Normans,[2] we must remember the old story of the Earl of Strathearn, who, at the famous Battle of the Standard in 1138, exclaimed, " I wear no armour, yet they who do will not advance beyond me this day." The seal of Alan Stuart (1190) represents him with a cylindrical helm, and a heater-shaped shield charged with a fess chequée.

Of the costume of the Irish we have more detailed accounts by Giraldus Cambrensis, who describes it from his own personal observation : "The Irish wear their woollen clothes mostly black because the sheep of Ireland are in general of that colour. The dress itself is of a barbarous fashion. They wear moderate close-cowled or hooded mantles (*capatiis*), which spread over their shoulders and reach down to the elbows, composed of small pieces of cloth of different kinds and colours, for the most part sewed together, beneath which woollen fallins (*phalanges*), with breeches and hose in one piece ("brachis caligatis seu caligis brachatis'), and those generally dyed of some colour."[3]

Irish costume, 12th century. From contemporary copy of Giraldus.

---

[1] Olivarius Vredius, ' Sigil. Com. Fland.,' p. 18. The colour of the Flemish lion was black.

[2] Duncan II. (1094–1098) is in trellised hauberk and chausses, conical head-piece with nasal, gonfanon with two points, and kite-shaped shield ; Edgar (1098–1107) in ring mail over long tunic, nasal head-piece, and gonfanon with three points. (*Vide* Descriptive Catalogue of Ancient Scottish Seals, by Henry Laing, Edinburgh, 1850.)

[3] The passage is rather confused : " Variisque colorum generibus panicolorumque plerumque consutis," apparently

An invaluable contemporary MS. of this work, in the library of the late Sir Thomas Phillips, Bart., enabled me to illustrate my 'History of British Costume' by several curious examples of the dress and weapons of the Irish in the reign of Henry II. One figure from it will be found at page 25 of the Dictionary. Others are annexed here (see preceding page).

The harpist, or bard, it will be observed, is attired simply in a long robe, his hair bound with a fillet; but a mantle appears to be thrown over the back of his chair. The scribe has a short jacket, with an indented border, and the truis. The Irish mantle appears upon the shoulders of the warriors, but the mode of fastening it is not visible. There are authorities enough, however, to prove that it was by a brooch or bodkin on the breast; and many, curiously wrought of silver, resembling in their general character those of the Scotch Highlanders, have been preserved to us (see Dictionary, p. 60). The value of these ornaments is decided in the Brehon laws. It is singular that the mantles in the illuminated MS. above mentioned are not party-coloured in accordance with the text, nor have they hoods to them. When Prince (afterwards King) John, son of Henry II., landed at Waterford, the Irish chieftains came to pay their respects to him, habited in their national costume, which consisted of a linen vest and a flowing mantle; the truis is not mentioned. They had long hair and bushy beards, which the inconsiderate young nobles in attendance on the Prince not only laughed at, but pulled on their advancing to give the kiss of peace, and finally thrust them with violence from their presence.[1] The weapons used by the Irish in the sanguinary combats to which this unprovoked insult and aggression gave birth are described by Giraldus as of three sorts— short lances, darts, and broad axes excellently well steeled—the use of which they borrowed "from Norwegians and Ostmen." (See Dictionary, article AXE, p. 25.) To these "three sorts of arms" he himself adds another, the sling, telling us "they are also very dexterous and ready beyond all other nations in slinging stones in battle, when other weapons fail them;" and in a description of a battle in the Annals of Innisfallen it is related that the stones came in such rapid showers that they met and blunted the arrows. Giraldus also informs us that "the Irish carry red shields, in imitation of the Danes."

Of the ladies' dresses we know nothing further than it may be inferred from a passage in the Annals aforesaid that they wore a variety of ornaments, as when the wife of King O'Roorke was taken prisoner in 1152 her jewels became the spoil of the enemy. The only female figures in the copy of Giraldus are attired in long tunics, after the Anglo-Norman fashion; but there can be little doubt they wore the mantle fastened on the breast by a brooch or bodkin; and in an Irish romance quoted by Mr. Walker we hear of the fair Findalve's spacious veil hanging down from her lovely head, being fastened to her hair by a golden bodkin (vol. ii. p. 23). The wearing of bodkins in the hair is so common to this day in Spain that we can scarcely question the fashion having been derived by the Irish from that country. The custom has, however, been general in all countries and all ages, and exists in most to the present day. (See BODKIN.)

At this period we get the earliest glimpse of the Welsh from an eye-witness. The same Giraldus whose account of the Irish I have just quoted, tells us that the Welsh use light arms, such as may not "impede their activity; small coats of mail ('loricis minoribus '), arrows, long lances, helmets and shields, and more rarely iron greaves (' ocreisque ferreis rarius '). Those who fight on foot go either barefooted or wear high shoes of untanned leather, constructed in a barbarous fashion " (' Itinerary,' chap. viii.).

In another place he says, " It seems worthy of remark that the people of what is called Venta (Gwentland, *i.e.* Monmouth- and Gloucester-shires) are more warlike and valiant, and more expert in archery, than any other part of Wales;" and, after relating some extravagant stories of their skill and prowess, he adds, "yet the bows used by this people are not made of horn, ivory, or yew, but of wild

---

patchwork, unless by "consutis" we may in this instance understand "woven," indicating a chequered or plaided stuff; but no chequered or striped mantle or truis is to be seen in the illuminations.

[1] John (when afterwards king) addressed an order to the Archbishop of Dublin commanding scarlet cloaks to be made for the Irish chieftains. (Rymer's 'Fœdera.')

elm: unpolished, rude, and uncouth, but stout; not calculated to shoot an arrow to a great distance, but to inflict very severe wounds in close fight" (chap. iv.).

Of their civil attire his account is brief and meagre. "The men and women cut their hair close round to the ears and eyes. The women, after the manner of the Parthians, cover their heads with a large white veil, folded together in the form of a crown" (a turban?). "The men shave all their beard except the moustaches" (*gernobodae*); and both sexes, he informs us, "exceed any other nation in their attention to their teeth, which they render like ivory by constantly rubbing them with green hazel, and wiping them with a woollen cloth" (chap. xi.).

We must now turn our attention again to the vestments of the clergy, which had gradually increased in sumptuousness and number after the ninth century. Rabanus Maurus (A.D. 819), Almarius of Metz

Pope Gregory the Great.
From portal of Cathedral at Chartres.

Archbishop Wulfstan. From Cotton. MS. Claudius, A iv.

(824), and "the reputed Alcuin,"[1] probably in the tenth century, all speak of eight vestments as worn by bishops, beside the pallium proper to archbishops. Walafrid Strabo enumerates only seven, omitting the amice. St. Ivo, writing at the close of the eleventh century, adds but one to them, being the first to include the *caligae byssinae* (leggings or stockings made of linen) as amongst the sacred vestments; but within a period of about fifty years at the most from the time of St. Ivo's writing, the number is exactly doubled. Honorius of Autun reckons seven vestments for priests, seven more (fourteen in all) as belonging to bishops, and two additional appropriated to archbishops; Pope Innocent III., by including two others which he regards as proper to the Bishop of Rome, swelling the list to eighteen within the first few years of the thirteenth century. It must be understood, however, that the term "vestment" is used by these writers in a much wider sense than it would be at present, including not

---

[1] Albinus Flaccus Alcuinus, a writer of the eleventh century, whose treatise was attributed by earlier editors to Alcuin, the pupil of Bede, who died A.D. 804.

only clothing, but ornaments and insignia, with which the wearers were *invested*, such as the episcopal ring, the pastoral staff, the pectoral cross, &c. Mr. Marriott remarks upon these facts, that this rapid development of the vestments in the Roman Church "was effected partly by actual additions to the less elaborate dress of earlier centuries, partly by the promotion, so to speak, to sacred rank of articles of dress or of ornament which had been long in use, but without being consecrated to symbolical significance, or to any specially sacerdotal usage."[1] The magnificence displayed by Thomas à Becket, during his progress to Paris, caused the French peasantry to exclaim, "What a wonderful personage the King of England must be, if his Chancellor can travel in such state!" But this applies more to the splendour and number of his retinue than to his ecclesiastical garments. A set of them, nearly complete, are preserved in the Cathedral at Sens. We have given engravings of his chasuble, stole, and mitre, under their respective headings. It is in the shape

Archbishop, 11th century. From a French MS.   Bishop, 11th century. From a Latin MS.

of the latter that the only alteration takes place, which, during the twelfth century, gradually approached that with which we are familiar. At page 153 of the Dictionary will be found the copy of a drawing representing the general dress of the clergy in the reign of Henry I., and the chromo-lithograph accompanying Part XIII. exhibits an interesting example of a French bishop of the middle of the twelfth century. In both of these undoubtedly contemporaneous authorities the mitre appears as a bonnet depressed in the centre; and Honorius Augustodunensis, who wrote on the sacred vestments and insignia of the Christian Church, *circa* 1125, is the first author who includes a mitre amongst them.[2] The Rev. Mr. Marriott, to whom we are indebted for this information, in his commentaries on St. Ivo's (Bishop of Chartres) earlier work, 'De Ecclesiasticis Sacramentis et Officiis Sermones,' says: "It will be observed that while he (Ivo) mentions the *mitra* or linen cap

---

[1] 'Vestiarium Christianum,' by the Rev. Wharton B. Marriott, M.A., F.R.S., 8vo. 1868. Introduction, p. lxxxi.

[2] "Mitra quoque Pontificis est sumpta ex usu Legis. *Hæc ex typo* conficitur. . . . . Mitra *ex bysso facta* multo above ad candorem perducta caput pontificis exornat"—still, therefore, a cap, made of linen only.

of the Levitical priest, he is silent as to any similar ornament among the Christian vestments. The truth seems to be that in the eleventh century the mitra had been already introduced as a distinctive vestment at Rome (Hefele, pp. 230, 231), and through Rome to particular churches in Germany and elsewhere. But it was not in St. Ivo's time (he died in 1115) regarded as one of the acknowledged vestments of Christian ministry." [1]

Amongst the statues which ornament the grand portal of the Cathedral of Chartres, executed about the middle of the twelfth century, is the figure of Pope Gregory the Great (see p. 60), mistaken by the late Mr. Shaw for an archbishop. The Pontiff is represented as wearing a conical bonnet, terminating in a small knob, and surrounded by a fillet with a vandyke pattern, but no crown. M. Viollet-le-Duc, who has given an engraving of the bonnet, adds to it two pendent ends, which do not appear in this view of the statue.

Bishops and archbishops are frequently represented in the twelfth century with caps more or less ornamental on their heads. A drawing in the Cottonian MS. Claudius, A iii., executed about the end of the eleventh century, purporting to be a portrait of Wulfstan, Archbishop of York, affords us an early example; and from two other MSS. in the Bibliothèque Nationale, Paris, I select the figures of an archbishop and a bishop with richly-embroidered caps (see preceding page).

M. Quicherat, who has given copies of them, has added an engraving of a cap traditionally reported to have been one actually worn by "the Prince of the Apostles," and preserved in the ancient College of Saint-Pierre de Namur. It is at all events an interesting relic, and a valuable illustration of early ecclesiastical costume.

Archbishop Wulfstan is depicted simply in a long tunic and a mantle fastened in a knot on the right shoulder. His cap, which is quite plain, is surmounted by a tuft or button. The cap of the archbishop from the French MS. has the *vittæ* or *infulæ* attached to it; and as he is attired in full canonicals—alb, dalmatic, and chasuble—wearing also the archiepiscopal pall, we must consider the cap to be no less than a mitre, which, by the way, in documents of that date, is itself called *infula*, without any reference to the appendages which have received that appellation. [2] It may be useful here to observe that *infula* is by some early writers employed to designate the chasuble. [3] The confusion created by the application of the same name to several entirely different articles of costume, which I have so frequently noticed and lamented in the Dictionary, seems to have existed as long as costume itself.

The cap of the bishop from the Latin MS. has no infulæ attached to it; but his vestments are most noteworthy, as they include one of which I have not yet spoken—the *superhumeral*. It is here represented as a broad collar of rich brocade, ornamented with jewels, and, according to some ancient writers, was assumed by the Christian priesthood in imitation of the ephod of the Jews, which is Latinized "superhumerale" by St. Jerome, the Venerable Bede, and others, in their descriptions of the Levitical garments. Some, on the contrary, consider it was a name for the amice. Without bewildering ourselves in this controversy, we have in the figure above-named a representation of the superhumeral as worn by bishops in the twelfth century, during which it seems to have disappeared, as it is not mentioned amongst "the nine vestments worn by bishops only," recorded by Pope Innocent III., 1198-1216. [4] The treatise of Germanus, Patriarch of Constantinople, furnishes us with

Cap traditionally ascribed to St. Peter. Preserved in the College of Saint-Pierre de Namur.

[1] 'Vestiarium Christianum,' p. 139.
[2] "Mitra . . . . ex bysso conficitur, et tiara, ydaros (cydaris?), *infula*, pileum dicitur." (Honorius August.)
[3] Hugo à Sancto Victore obiit 1140. "Casula quæ alio nomine planeta vel infula dicitur."
[4] 'De Sacro Altaris Mysterio,' lib. i. cap. 10. "Novem autem sunt ornamenta Pontificum specialia: videlicet, caligæ, sandalia, succinctorium, tunica, dalmatica, mitra et chirotheca, annulus et baculus."

the names and descriptions of the clerical vestments and ornaments used in the Greek Church. I have already mentioned them at p. 42; but there exists a doubt respecting the authorship of that work, which, it is contended by some critics, was written by another Germanus in the thirteenth century. However that may be, the names do not appear to have undergone any alteration, and the epitrachelion and epimanikia (the stole and the cuffs) worn by Bishop Nikita, A.D. 1167, are here engraved from the splendid work 'Les Antiquités de l'Empire Russe.'

In the course of the twelfth century two orders of monks were added to that of St. Benedict (the rule of which, indeed, does not seem to have been very strictly observed by the English till after the Conquest), namely, in 1128 the Cistercians or Bernardines, instituted at Cisteaux, in Latin Cistertium, a town in Burgundy, in 1098, and subsequently greatly patronised by the celebrated St. Bernard; and in 1175, the Carthusians, founded at Chartreux, in France, by St. Bruno, in 1080, but not introduced to England before 1175, where their establishments were corruptly named after them Charterhouses. These, the strictest of all the monastic orders, never became numerous in England. The Cistercians were distinguished from the Benedictines by white garments, and were therefore called "white monks," as the Benedictines were called "black monks." The nuns of that order in Spain appear to have worn dark dresses.

Cuffs of Bishop Nikita.

Stole of Bishop Nikita.

All the following figures present us with the early form of the *cucullus*, the pointed cowl or capuchon of the monastic orders. The monk is attired in the *rock*, a short loose body-garment, worn when assisting in the services, and which subsequently gave

St. Benedict. From an ancient mosaic.

Benedictine Monk. From Montfaucon.

Benedictine Abbot. From Montfaucon.

its name to the *rocket* (Mabillon, 'Annales Ordinis Sancti Benedicti'). It is not very clear how long after the death of its founder, in the seventh century, the above habit of the order was assumed, or at which date it took the form which is more familiar to us: but we borrow from other works the garb of a Benedictine monk, when the rule of the order had acquired stability in England; also the figures of a Bernardine or Cistercian, and of a Carthusian monk.

Benedictine.   Cistercian.   Carthusian.

The two great military and religious orders of the Knights Hospitallers and the Knights Templars remain to be noticed in this chapter of our history. The first of these celebrated fraternities received its name from an hospital built at Jerusalem for the use of pilgrims to the Holy Land, and dedicated to St. John the Baptist, whence their other designation of Knights of St. John of Jerusalem. The principal business of these knights was to provide for the pilgrims at that hospital, and protect them from injuries and insults on the road. The order was founded about 1092, and was much favoured by Godfrey of Boulogne, and his successor Baldwin, kings of Jerusalem. They followed chiefly the rule of St. Austin (St. Augustine), and wore a black mantle with a white cross on it. A house was built for them in London, and they came to England in 1100. They were not originally a military order, but eventually became so in imitation, and in consequence of the success, of the Knights Templars. From a poor and humble beginning they attained to such wealth, honours, and exemptions, that their superior in this country was the first lay Baron and had a seat in Parliament. In a curious satire on the monks, entitled 'The Order of Fairease,' written in the reign of Edward I., and published in Wright's 'Political Songs,' the Hospitallers are ironically described as "very courteous knights, and have very becoming robes, so long that they drag at their feet."

The Knights Templars were instituted A.D. 1118, and were so called from having their first residence in some rooms adjoining the Temple at Jerusalem. Their business also was to guard the roads for the security of pilgrims in the Holy Land, and their rule that of canons regular of St. Austin. Their mantle was white, with a red cross on the left shoulder. "Their coming into England," says Tanner, "was probably pretty early in the reign of Stephen, and their first seat at Holborne. They increased very fast, and in a short time obtained very large possessions. But in less than two hundred years their wealth and power were thought too great. They were accused of horrid crimes, and thereupon everywhere imprisoned. Their estates were seized, their order suppressed by Pope Clement V., A.D. 1309, and totally abolished by the Council of Vienna, A.D. 1312."

The engravings by Hollar, of a Knight Templar and a Knight Hospitaller, in Dugdale's

'Monasticon,' are unauthenticated, and cannot be relied upon. The only undoubted effigy of a Knight Templar is, or was, in the church of St. Ived de Braine, near Soissons, and was engraved for Père Montfaucon's 'Antiquités de la Couronne de France,' published in 1730. The effigy is that of Jean de Dreux, Knight of the Order of the Temple, second son of Jean, 1st Comte de Dreux and de Braine, by his wife, Marie de Bourbon. He was living in 1275, but the year of his death is unrecorded. (See woodcut.) Mr. Fairholt, who has also engraved it, observes that "he is entirely unarmed, but wears the mantle of his order, over the left side of which is the cross of the Greek form, the horizontal arms being rather shorter than the perpendicular ones ; and it is not at all of the *patté* form, which strengthens the conjecture that Hollar's figures (the only ones we possess) have been copied from later representations." I believe them to be altogether fanciful, and therefore have not inserted them here.

Effigy of Jean de Dreux, in the church of St. Ived de Braine.

A propos of crosses, Roger de Hoveden informs us that Philip Augustus, king of France, Richard I., king of England, and Ferrand, count of Flanders, on proceeding to the Holy wars, assumed different coloured crosses—the French *red*, the English *white*, and the Flemings *green*.

A few words before I close this chapter respecting mourning habiliments. We have seen that the Romans wore black or dark-coloured togæ under such circumstances (p. 5), and on the other hand that the Danes never mourned for the deaths of their nearest and dearest relations (p. 43). I have noticed also, at the same time, the remarkable absence of black in the dresses of persons attending funerals, in Anglo-Saxon paintings or needlework. A French writer of the twelfth century, named Baudry, who was Abbot of Bourgueil, mentions the wearing of black by the Spaniards in his time, and describes it as a strange custom. It would appear, therefore, that Spain was the only country in Europe in which, during the twelfth century, black was worn on such occasions ; and it is a curious question whence the Spaniards derived the custom, which does not seem to have been generally adopted in this quarter of the world until nearly two hundred years afterwards. The probability is, that it was copied from the Romans as early as the time of the Emperor Honorius, whose sister Placida became the wife of Atolf or Autolphus, king of the Visigoths, and cemented a strict alliance between the successor of Alaric and the son of Theodosius the Great. Yet in that case it is singular the usage is not found amongst the Franks, who were such ardent imitators of the dress and habits of the Romans.

CHAPTER IV.

THIRTEENTH CENTURY.

NTERING the thirteenth century, we find our sources of information respecting the special subject of these volumes become more numerous and more reliable. The progress of the arts of sculpture and painting, which had fallen into so degraded a state in Europe during the early period of the Christian era, was by no means inconsiderable. The sepulchral effigies of "the illustrious dead" represent all the details of civil, military, or ecclesiastical costume with a minuteness that guarantees their fidelity, which is corroborated by the miniatures in numberless illuminated MSS, drawn with more care and coloured with more brilliancy than in preceding times. The historians and poets also of this epoch indulge in descriptions of armour and dress, appropriating, fortunately for us, the costume of their own time to all ages indiscriminately.

Hector of Troy and Alexander of Macedon are clad in hauberks and chausses of mail, such as were worn by John, king of England, or Philip Augustus of France. And Cleopatra or the Queen of Sheba would be alike depicted in the same attire as Eleanor of Provence or Blanche of Castile. Nor in some respects would the anachronism be so preposterous, for the magnificent fabrics of the East, the purple pall of Alexandria, the woven gold of Baldeck (the ancient Babylon), and the costly stuffs which found their way from China and India to Greece and Italy and were thence disseminated through the Continent, were such as had been worn by "Solomon in all his glory," Sardanapalus, and Semiramis. As a case in point, we have the French poet, Guillaume de Lorris, in his portion of the 'Roman de la Rose,' describing Pygmalion employed in trying on his love-created Galatea all the fashions of Paris in the reign of St. Louis.

Velvet, damask, and a rich silk manufactured in the Cyclades, and thence called "ciclaton," were added to the materials already in use for the confection of habits for the nobility; and amongst furs we now find mention of ermine, marten, squirrel, vair, and minevair or miniver. Two mantles lined with ermine are ordered by Henry III. for his queen and himself. A garment called a *cyclas*, said by some to be so named from the material above mentioned, and by others from a cloak of the same name worn by the ancient Greeks, is mentioned as early as 1083 in Germany, when Judith, daughter of the King of Bohemia, is said to have worn one embroidered or interwoven with gold (see CYCLAS), but appears to have been first known in England at the coronation of Henry III., at which period ciclatons were imported amongst other costly presents from Spain. The name has also been applied to a surcoat shortened in front, worn by knights over their armour; but on no satisfactory authority. At all events it was a garment worn by both sexes, and only known as a *riglatow* in France, which at this period is described by contemporary writers as revelling in riches and luxury. Guillaume le Breton, speaking of the rejoicings of the French after the victory of Philip Augustus over the Emperor Otho at Bouvines, says, "Knights, citizens, villains (country folks) flaunted about in purple. Nothing was to be seen but satin, scarlet cloth, and fine linen. The peasant, intoxicated at beholding himself dressed like an emperor, fancied himself on an equality with sovereigns. It was sufficient for him to have obtained a dress far above that which suited his condition, to make him imagine he was transformed into a superior being;" and M. Nicholas de Bray, describing Paris at the time of the coronation of Louis VIII., exclaims, "It was a pleasure to see the gold embroideries and the dresses of scarlet silk shine in the places, streets, and crossways. Persons of all ages bent equally beneath the weight of the purple. Servants of both sexes exulted in being laden with glittering ornaments, and forgot their position while contemplating the splendid stuffs they were arrayed in. They who could not purchase dresses worthy of display on such an occasion hired them." The nobility, however, found a way to distinguish themselves from the common people. Heraldry had become a science, and armorial ensigns hereditary. No longer limited to the shield of the knight, they were embroidered on his apparel. The effect was as gorgeous as the identification was complete. The Sire de Joinville records the expense of this decoration,

and tells us that he said to Philip le Hardi that in his travels in foreign parts he had never seen such coats worn by St. Louis or any other persons of condition. The king upon that told him that he had dresses embroidered with his arms which cost him 800 livres of Paris,—upwards of 50,000 francs, 2,500*l.* sterling, at the present value of money. The fashion had extended to England. An order is extant for the making of robes of various colours, fringed with gold, for King Henry III.; and one, called a *cointise*, is especially commanded to be made of the best purple-coloured samite, embroidered with three little leopards in front and three behind (see COINTISE). The effigy of Henry in the chapel of Edward the Confessor, Westminster Abbey, represents him in his royal robes, which consist simply of a long tunic and a mantle fastened by a fibula on the right shoulder, no dalmatic being visible. Both garments are at present devoid of ornament or border. It is probable, however, that they were originally painted and gilt similarly to those of his father, King John, and of his ancestors at Fonte-

Base of Effigy.

Effigy of Henry III.,
Westminster Abbey.

vraud. His boots are, however, elaborately embroidered with lattice-work, illustrating the expression *fretatus de auro*, each square of the fret containing a lion passant.

The male costume of England underwent no remarkable alteration during the greater part of the thirteenth century. A large cloak or mantle, with ample sleeves and a capuchon attached to it, called a supertotus or overall, or sometimes balandran, its name in France, was worn by travellers in foul weather. Caps of various shapes were worn—some exceedingly fantastic; but towards the middle of the century a white linen coif, tied under the chin like a child's night-cap, makes its appearance, and is seen upon the heads of men of every class in the kingdom. The judge on the bench, the serjeant at the bar, the nobleman in his mantle, the knight in his hauberk, the huntsman and the messenger, are all depicted in this most unpicturesque, and to our modern notions ridiculous, head-gear, not only in England, but in France and Germany.' To which country we are indebted for its introduction has not transpired; and as it reflects no credit on the inventor, it will be charity to leave its origin in obscurity. (See woodcuts in the next page, and also COIF in Dict., p. 130.)

The dress of the ladies during the first half of the century appears to have undergone no particular change. The inconveniently long and ridiculously-shaped sleeves of the reign of Henry I. and Stephen had gone out of fashion before the accession of John, and the only additions to the female toilet we hear of in his reign are a furred garment for winter called a *pélisson* or *pelice*, a term

K 2

familiar to us at the present day, and a chin or neck cloth of a very unbecoming description, named a wimple. Of the form of the pélisson we have no recognised example. Even M. Viollet-le-Duc

Le Sire de Joinville. From a MS. circa 1300.

German Falconer, circa 1440. From a MS. in the Vatican.

admits that, previous to the thirteenth century, "il nous est impossible d'avoir à cet égard une opinion basée sur des documents certains;" but after that period he gives a host of examples of costumes of every description that we meet with under other designations throughout the fourteenth and fifteenth centuries,—tunics, supertunics, surcoats, gowns, houppelandes, mantles, robes, furred and not furred, all of which he designates *peliçons*, as worn by both sexes in France during three hundred years. Unfortunately, there is no identifying one of them from any description either in verse or prose.

King John orders a grey pélisson with nine bars of fur to be made for the queen, but we are left in the dark as regards the shape or size of the garment, whether it had sleeves or no sleeves, and even the position of the nine bars of fur. Were they to be used for lining the inside, or trimming the outside? What can we learn from such quotations as the following?—

"Un peliçon aveit vestu
Ki del grant freit l'ont defendu
Iver esteit, Noel veneit."
Roman de Rou, v. 15,319.

"Mult i avoit chiers garniment,
Chiers ators et chier vestement,
Rices bliax, rices mantiax,
Rices nosques, rices amax,
Mainte pelice vaire, grise,
Et garnemens de mainte guise."
Li Roman de Brut, v. 10,687.

> " Je te donrai mon pelisson hermin
> A de mon col le mantel sebelin."
> *Li Romans de Garin.*

Absolutely nothing beyond the fact that a garment called a "pelice," lined or trimmed with vair, ermine, grey or other fur (*pellis,* whence its name), was worn by both sexes in winter, and which is indeed important to my argument that the second writer quoted markedly distinguishes the "pelice" from the bliaus, the mantle, and other vestments and "garnimens," as also does the third from the mantle. M. Quicherat, after showing us that a pélisson was a long tunic lined with fur, two of which were allowed to the monks of the order of St. Benedict,[1] speaking of the pélisson worn by women of the twelfth century, says that it was a tunic composed of fur between two stuffs, the fur only appearing at the edges; that it was sometimes worn between the chemise and the bliaud, and at others in lieu of the bliaud itself, also that the same remark applies to the costume of the men, who likewise wore the pélisson. This is a little more definite, but still too vague to enable us to form an idea of its appearance and to identify it in any representation, and M. Quicherat does not offer us a pictorial illustration.

The wimple, introduced about this time, partially superseded the couvrechef of the last century, which wound about the neck as well as enveloped the head. They were sometimes worn together (see WIMPLE, p. 521, Dict.). Examples abound in monuments and MSS. of the thirteenth century throughout England and the Continent. The effigy of Avelina, Countess of Lancaster, in Westminster Abbey, may probably offer an example of it; but later in the century a covering for the chin and neck was invented, which, when worn with a veil, can scarcely be distinguished from it. This was the gorget, called in French "la touaille," a name by which also the Oriental turban was known at this period. The old wimple was abandoned to nuns and widows, but lingered in the wardrobe of women of the humbler classes as late as the fifteenth century. (For these and other female head-dresses of the thirteenth century, see HEAD-DRESS in Dictionary, p. 269.)

A double marriage in the year 1298 contributed also not a little to the introduction of French fashions into England, Edward I. marrying the sister, and his son, the Prince of Wales, the daughter, of Philip IV. of France, surnamed "le Bel."

I have mentioned at p. 67 of the Dictionary that the sleeves worn tight to the wrist, with a row of buttons closely set, reaching up to the elbow. Another contemporary fashion was the sewing them up instead of buttoning them. The lover in the 'Roman de la Rose' is described, needle in hand, so occupied, having just risen in the morning:

> " De mon lit tantost me levay,
> Me vesty & mes mains lavay;
> Lors prins une aisguille d'argent,
> D'ung aisguiller mignot & gent,
> Et cuydant l'aisguille enfiler
> Hors de ville aux talent d'aler.
>   * * *
> En ladite saison nouvelle,
> *Cousant mes manches à vindelle.*"[2]—v. 93.

Effigy of Avelina, Countess of Lancaster, Westminster Abbey.

---

[1] 'Hist. Cost. en France,' p. 190.

[2] In the splendid copy of the 'Roman de la Rose,' in the Harleian Library, British Museum, the lover is depicted in this situation, but as the MS. is of quite the end of the fifteenth century we get no representation of the "manches à vindelle;" and Strutt, who has engraved the figure, takes no notice of the anachronism, nor indeed does he quote the full line, but omits the words "à vindelle." The only explanation I can find of them occurs in the 'Supplément au Glossaire du Roman de la Rose' (Dijon, 1737), which is as follows:—" VINDELLE, BINDELLE. Vient de *binde,* bande, d'où est tiré *bindellus,* bandeau; ainsi *bindelle* étoit ce que nous appellons une *bandelette:* il y a donc apparence qu'une 'manche à bindelle' étoit une manche decoupée à bandelettes."

The same trouble had to be taken by the ladies, as we learn from the same poem—

> "D'une aiguille bien affilée,
> D'argent, de fil d'or enfilée,
> Luy à pour mieulx estre vestue
> Chascune manche estoit cousue."—v. 21,917.

The effigy of a lady in the church of Joigny (date *circa* 1245), engraved in vol. xiii. of the 'Bulletin Monumental' of M. Caumont, affords us an excellent example of this fashion, which, notwithstanding the tediousness of the process, appears to have been in favour for upwards of one hundred years; for Chaucer translates the above passage in the fourteenth century without notice, omitting only the words "à vindelle"—

> "A sylver nedyl forth I droxe
> Out of an aguyler queynt ynowe,
> And gan this nedyl threde anone,
> For out of towne me lyste to gone ;
> And with a threde bastynge my sleeves,
> Alone I went."

And in Hefner I find an example which, from the *coudières*, I should be inclined to attribute to the

commencement of that century, although inexplicably ascribed by him to the tenth. I have met with no example in male attire of any country. The Joigny statue also presents us with the form of cap that was much worn by ladies in the reigns of our Henry III. and Edward I., over a coif or kerchief covering the ears and fastened under the chin. At page 78 of the Dictionary two examples will be found, which give a better notion of it than can be obtained from any verbal description. Of what material it was composed does not transpire, but in all paintings it is represented white, without any ornament whatever. In some instances it is a simple flat-topped cap, much like the paper caps worn by workmen in England at the present day; in others, as in the effigy annexed, it appears to fit the crown of the head and to be turned up all round or encircled by a broad band fluted or plaited into the form almost of a diadem. Caps of the latter description were worn by both sexes in

Effigy in the church of Joigny. 1245.

The daughter of Herodias. From a carving in wood. Hefner.

Germany. (*Vide* the woodcuts next page from the MS. of the Minnesingers, commonly called the Manese MS., No. 7266 in the National Library at Paris.) For the reticulated head-dresses in fashion during this century, see CRISPINE and HEAD-DRESS. The varieties are numberless.

The surquane, sorquanie, or sosquenie is a female garment much spoken of in France and England in the latter part of the thirteenth century, but, as I have stated in the article devoted to it in the Dictionary, it has not, in my opinion, been satisfactorily identified with any pictorial representation. M. Quicherat informs us that the name and the dress were of Languedocian origin; that it was a "façon de cotte déceinte," but shaped so as to develop exactly the form of the bust. A few lines further, he says that the women of Languedoc dispensed with surcoats and cut their sorquanies down the front, displaying, in the intervals left by laces very wide apart, the transparent tissue of a

German Costume, 13th century. From Masson MS., Bib. Nat., Paris.

chemise elaborately pleated and embroidered with silk and gold. He does not, however, illustrate this description by any engraving, and I have been unable to discover a dress of the thirteenth century in any part of Europe which corresponds to it. Two hundred years later we shall find many examples of such a fashion, but the constant allusions to lacing at the period now under consideration refer only to the compression of the waists of the ladies, whose unfortunate ambition it was then, as now, to appear more like wasps than women, to the serious injury of their health and the disfigurement of their persons. In 1298, the Council of Narbonne certainly passed an ordinance forbidding the wearing of "cottes lacées" and "chemises brodées;" but we are still left in the dark as to the particular sort of lacing prohibited. Embroidered shifts were by this edict allowed to be worn by brides on their wedding-day and for twelve months afterwards, but not a day beyond. A powerful preacher, named Jacques de Vitry, who was subsequently made a cardinal, threatened with eternal damnation the fabricators and vendors of such vanities, as worse offenders than those who wore them. I can only give specimens of the costume of this period in the principal countries of Europe from contemporary authorities, and will not attempt to identify certain portions or varieties with the names we find in writings of the time unaccompanied by pictorial illustration. I have already spoken of English, French, and German, and will now turn to Italian and Spanish costume.

Ricardino Malespini, describing the dresses of the Florentines previously to the year 1260, tells us that in those days they did not disdain coarse stuffs for their own garments or for those of their wives. Many even were content to clothe themselves in skins, wearing caps on their heads, and nearly all short boots. A close-fitting dress of a material made of goat's hair, dyed scarlet, a leathern girdle with an old buckle, a mantle lined with *petit gris*, having a hood to cover the head, was the ordinary costume of the women. I have not met with any example of this primitive attire, the change from which appears, from the historian Giovanni Villani, to have been effected during the government of Gauthier, duke of Athens, and by the constant passage of French troops through Florence *en route* to the kingdom of Naples. For Italian costume of the thirteenth century we must turn also to the pages of Vecellio and Bonnard, disregarding unauthenticated dates, and relying on our own judgment for the selection of examples which afford internal evidence that the period of their execution was not later than the days of Cimabue, who died at the commencement of the fourteenth century.

Italian Costume, end of 15th century. From Vecellio.

Of the civil costume of the higher classes in Spain at this period we have some fine and interesting examples in the sepulchral effigies in that country. The effigy of Don Diego Martinez de Villa Mayor, who died *circa* 1214, represents him in a long supertunic, or surcoat, and mantle of State. The former has moderately loose hanging sleeves, terminating at the lowest extremity by a small pendant of metal, apparently but possibly a jewel, and showing the sleeve tight to the wrist of the under-tunic. The waist is loosely encircled by a broad belt, in front of which is a long sword, steadied by his left hand, which rests on the pommel, holding at the same time by its legs or jesses a falcon, the mark of nobility. On the shoulders of the mantle are two circular ornaments (*tassenus*, see Dict., p. 503), to which the cords of the mantle were attached, but no cords are visible in the effigy. The chausses have pointed toes, and the spur that is shown is spear-shaped. The hair, parted on the forehead, passes behind the ears and flows down upon each shoulder, reminding one of the effigy of Edward III. in Westminster Abbey, to which indeed the whole costume bears a certain resemblance, inclining me to believe the tomb to be of later execution than the date assigned to the death of the nobleman deposited in it.

Don Diego Martinez de Villa Mayor.   Beatrix of Suabia, queen of Ferdinand   Maria de Molina, queen of Sancho IV.,   Constance de Aragon.
                                  III., king of Castile. 1234.   king of Castile and Leon. 1295.

The effigy of Beatrix of Suabia, queen of Ferdinand III., king of Castile, A.D. 1234, is remarkable for its peculiar head-dress, which we learn from Señor Carderera was of Oriental origin, and called *Ptolemo*. By Oriental, I presume, is meant Moorish. We have no description of the material it was composed of. It has the appearance of plaited straw, and recalls that of the bonnet of Pope Gregory's statue at Chartres, which M. Viollet-le-Duc likens to basket-work. Several examples appear in the bas-relief on the tomb of Don Diego Lopez de Haro, 1214 (see page 80), which show that the cap or bonnet was secured to the head by a band of the same material passing over the crown and under the chin. The hair, confined by it at the side of the head, flows naturally down behind. The remainder of the costume perfectly accords with that of France and England at the same period, — the tunic with long sleeves tight to the wrist, the mantle sustained on the shoulders by a lace or band, and pointed-toed shoes. There is some indication of a super-tunic, or surcoat, without sleeves, such as we find throughout Europe a century later ; but it is not sufficiently defined to justify my hazarding an opinion respecting it, more especially in the absence of other examples.

The third figure, for which we are indebted to Señor Carderera's beautiful work, is that of Maria de Molina, queen of Sancho IV., king of Castile and Leon, A.D. 1295, and which resembles in its general features the effigies of many noble ladies in England and on the Continent in the thirteenth century. She wears the veil and the wimple, the super-tunic with loose sleeves, showing those of the under-tunic at the wrists ; the waist very short, encircled by a richly-ornamented girdle and pendant ; a mantle of ample dimensions, a rosary in one hand and a missal or *livre d'heures* in the other. If they are her feet that peep from under her tunic, her shoes appear to be round-toed. Another representation of this Queen Maria, in more stately attire and with her hair singularly dressed, is seen in a bas-relief on her monument, where she is represented handing to the Cistercian nuns of Valladolid the charter of formation of their convent (see p. 78). The fourth figure is from the effigy of Doña Constanza de Aragon, wife of Don G. Ramon de Moncada (see p. 77). The date of her death is uncertain, but her will is dated in 1250.

The dress of the commonalty in England remained much the same as it was at the time of the Conquest, with the addition of the bliaus (the blouse and smock of the present day), made for the working classes of canvas or fustian, and worn by both sexes. Coarse woollen cloths, russet, birrus or burreau, cordetum, and sarcillis were principally used for the garments of the people. Cowls, with points or tails to them, were worn more than caps. Jews in England in the time of Edward I. were obliged to have two woollen tablets of different colours, each two fingers broad and four long, sewn on the breast of their exterior garments. Evasions of all sumptuary laws were always found practicable by those who had money sufficient to pay for the prohibited materials or ornaments.

Robert de Suzanne. 1260.

The statutes made at Marseilles in 1276 for the regulation of the dresses of the inhabitants of that city, show that the cloaks and mantles (*huques* and *chapes*) worn by the wives of the well-to-do burgesses were frequently made of cendal and silken stuffs, richly trimmed and decorated. The huque at this time appears to have been a cloak with a hood to it—its primitive Oriental form, and, if not originally introduced to the south of France by the Moors from Spain in the eighth century, may have been first adopted by the Marseillaise from their opposite neighbours on the north coast of Africa.

The armour of the thirteenth century presents us with many novel and remarkable features. To the flat-topped cylindrical helm was added the chapel de fer, with or without a nasal ; and the helm, increased in size, took the form of a barrel bulging at the sides, covering the head completely, and resting on the shoulders (see HELM and Plate XI. figs. 3 and 4, Dict., p. 280). Later in the century the top of the helm assumed the form of the crown of the head, and gradually became more conical. The military surcoats as well as the shield displayed the armorial ensigns of the wearer, and towards the end of the century the curious little shoulder-plates, called by the French *ailettes*, made their appearance in European armour, being also occasionally ornamented with the family arms of the knight, or simply with a St. George's cross. (See AILETTES and Plate II., Dictionary, p. 4.)

We have an early French example in the effigy of Robert de Suzanne, Roi d'Armes *temp.* Louis VIII., who died in 1260, from the incised slab on his tomb in the chapel of the Abbey of Mont St. Quentin.

The ailettes are very large, peculiarly shaped, and placed fully in front, so that they protect the arm-pits as thoroughly as the later palettes or roundels. I would direct the reader's attention also to the coif de mailles, evidently independent of the mail-hood, which covers the whole head beneath it. The surcoat and ailettes are apparently plain, but they may have been originally painted with the armorial ensigns of the family.

The German armour of this period is remarkable for the extravagance of its crests. Annexed is the figure of Wolfran von Eschilbach or Eschenbach (1210), whose helm is rendered almost ridiculous by the superimposition of his crest, which, like the generality of crests at that time, is a repetition of the coat; the charge on which, as displayed on his shield and banner, I will not take upon myself to blazon, as they are unlike any I am acquainted with. Another helm and crest, those of Walter von der Vogelweide (*i.e.*, "Bird meadow"), 1240, is as unpicturesque, though more comprehensible, as it partially symbolizes his name, being "a bird in a cage."

An equestrian statue in bronze of the end of the thirteenth century, in the collection of M. Six, at Amsterdam, affords an example of a Dutch or North-German knight of that time, with a helm on which are two of those horns we meet with so often in German crests at a later period. M. Demmin gives us a front and back view of the figure, showing that the horns spring from each side of the helm. The engraving is unfortunately so rude that the

From a bronze of the 13th century.

Wolfram von Eschenbach. 1210.

details of the armour cannot be depended upon. It would seem, however, to be mail, over which he wears a long surcoat, opened up before and behind for the convenience of riding. Several helms of the thirteenth century will be found at page 281 of the Dictionary.

Of armour presumably Bohemian, M. Demmin presents us with some interesting groups from the MS. of Voleslav of Bohemia[1] in the thirteenth century, preserved in the library of Prince Lobkowitz at Raudnitz, in Bohemia. If of the thirteenth century, it must have been written, or at least illuminated, at very nearly the close of it, for some of the figures are represented in the large bascinet generally supposed to belong to the fourteenth century. M. Demmin observes that the most remarkable feature in this elaborate illumination is the broad-brimmed iron hat with pointed crown, like that of the bascinet, as there is no existing specimen of one with a crown so pointed in

Bohemian Armour, from a MS. of the 13th century.

any collection, nor, he might have added, a similar example as yet noticed in any miniature.

[1] *I* Uladislas, duke of Bohemia, 1218.

Of Italian armour an interesting example is presented to us in a marble bas-relief, in the great cloister adjoining the church of the Annunziata Convent at Florence. It has been engraved for the work of M. Bonnard, and also for Mr. Hewitt, who copied it from a drawing in the valuable collection of Mr. Kerrich in the British Museum, Add. MS. No. 6928. The monument is that of one Gulielmus, who was "Balius"[1] (*i.e.* Lieutenant) to Aimeric de Narbonne, Commander of the Guelphs at the battle of Campaldino, and was killed with his General at the moment of victory. The grateful citizens erected this memorial of him in 1289.

The figure is principally remarkable for the greaves, which it is presumed, from their elaborate ornamentation, were of cuir-bouilli, as engraved or embossed and gilt armour is not known in the Middle Ages, although antique examples have been found at Pompeii and elsewhere of metal, highly ornamented with chasing and embossed work ; and Mr. Hewitt suggests that the Germans may have copied them from classical specimens with which they had become familiar during their wars in Italy. The Italians themselves would most likely be the earliest to adopt them, and the fashion would speedily travel northward. That this style of armour was worn in Italy as late as 1335 is proved by the marble effigy of a knight so dated in the church of St. Dominico at Naples. These greaves are called "Beinbergen" and "Beinschienen" by the Germans, "tumilières" or "grèves" by the French, and "gambala" or "gambiere" by the Italians.

Guillaume Berrard. 1289.

Of Spanish armour of this date one curious relic exists in the Armeria Real at Madrid—a helm with the crest of a demi-dragon, wings expanded, all of polished steel, and attributed to Don James I., king of Aragon, 1213, surnamed "the Conqueror," "el Conquistador." Whether such attribution has the support of any authority more trustworthy than tradition, I am unable to say, and not having seen the original will not undertake to dispute the accuracy of the assertion. The practice of ascribing to celebrated persons any remarkable suit or piece of armour is unfortunately so prevalent that great caution is necessary in adopting the descriptions in catalogues or unverified popular traditions. The helmet tested by English specimens has certainly the character of a later date, but there is nothing in the engravings of it that would justify my rejecting the received opinion.

Helm of Don James I., king of Aragon. 1213.

To Señor Carderera of Solona we are indebted, however, for a sumptuous work containing a series of admirable lithographic representations of the principal

[1] Through the kindness of my friend D. Colnaghi, Esq., her Majesty's Consul at Florence, and that of Count Passerini, rector of the National Library in that city, I am enabled to correct the curious misinterpretations of the monumental inscription which occur in both the works above mentioned. The original runs thus : — "Ahi dhi MCCLXXXIX. hic jacet dñs Gulielmus Balius olim dñi Amerighi de Nerbona." The term *Balius* has been taken for a proper name, and converted into *Balius*, and Bonnard has mixed the names of the General and his officer together, describing the monument as that of " Aimery *de* Guillaume Berrard, Bailli de Narbonne " ! The name of Berrard does not appear in the inscription ; but he is called " Berardi " by Villani, and such was apparently his surname, but he was a distinct personage from Aimery de Narbonne, who was appointed Commander of the Guelphs by Charles II. of Anjou, king of Naples. (*Vide* Villani, lib. vii. cap. 130-131 ; Rammont, 'Tavola Cronologica della Storia Fiorentince,' sub anno 1289.)

Don Guglielmo Ramon de Moncada. 1250.

sepulchral monuments in Spain, from the twelfth to the sixteenth century. I have already availed myself of it for the illustration of the civil costume of Spain, and I now present my readers with copies of the effigies of Don Guglielmo Ramon de Moncada, Seneschal of Catalonia, who died *circa* 1250, from his tomb at Lerida, and of Don Felipe, Infant of Castile, in the Church of the Templars de Santa Maria, at Villasuga, who died in 1273. (The latter, I think, is not in armour; though his mantle so completely envelopes him that it is open to doubt. He has a falcon on his left wrist, the head of which has been broken off, and in other respects the effigy resembles that of Don Diego at page 73 *ante.*)

In ecclesiastical costume, as regards the Church of Rome, the only altera- tion appears to have been in the form of the mitre, which, before the close of the century, had assumed very nearly that which it presents at this day. (See MITRE in Dictionary for its gradual changes.)

In the thirteenth century arose the new religious orders of the Mendicant Friars—the Dominicans or Black Friars,

Don Felipe, Infant of Castile. 1273.

A Dominican or Black Friar.

A Franciscan or Grey Friar.

A Grey Friar or Cordelier without his Mantle.

called also Friars Preachers, instituted by St. Dominic de Guzman, and the Franciscans or Grey Friars, called also Cordeliers, from the rope they wore round their waists, founded by St. Francis of Assisi, which orders were formally established by the authority of Pope Honorius III., the first in 1216 and the second in 1223. Of many others which soon sprung up in imitation of them all were eventually suppressed except two,—the Carmelites or White Friars, introduced from the Holy Land by Louis IX.; and the Augustines, called Grey Friars as well as the Franciscans, from the colour of their cloaks.

The Carmelites, on their first introduction to Europe, became popular from the peculiarity of their dress, which was striped white and brown like the bournouse of the Bedouins of the present day, a garment unchanged from the earliest period. It was, I have little doubt, the bournouse itself, and obtained for them in Paris the name of "Frères barrés." Pope Honorius IV. prohibited, in 1286, this costume, as it occasionally gave rise to unseemly jests, and ordered them to wear grey gowns and white mantles, whence they derived in England their later name of White Friars. They complied with an ill grace, contending that their forefathers had received their striped mantles

The Cistercian Nuns at Valladolid receiving their charter from Queen Maria de Molina.

from the Prophet Eli, an assertion which had probably more truth in it than they were given credit for, as the prophet no doubt wore the ordinary dress of the country.

The habits of the monastic orders and of the other friars appear to have been settled before the end of the century, and have continued unchanged. The same remark will apply to the dress of the nuns, who wore the veil and the wimple, and in many communities adopted the scapulary, which had never been previously worn by women. The peculiar form of the head-dress of the Cistercian nuns at Valladolid must be called attention to; it resembles the aumuse worn by canons (see Dictionary, p. 7). The privilege of bearing a pastoral staff was accorded about this period to Abbesses (vide effigy of a Cistercian Abbess in Dictionary, p. 154). Pope Boniface VIII. (1295-1303) is generally supposed to have added a second crown to the pontifical tiara, but M. Viollet-le-Duc cautiously inquires, Had it already a first? I can only say that if the Cottonian MS. Nero D i. was written, as believed by experts, circa 1250, there is a drawing in it representing Pope Adrian I. receiving a letter from Offa II., king of Mercia, and his Holiness has undoubtedly a crown surrounding his tiara, which would indicate its existence during the pontificate of Innocent IV.

M. Viollet-le-Duc has however copied a curious painting at Pernes (Comtait Venaissin) in which Pope Clement IV. is depicted giving to Charles I., Count of Anjou and Provence, the papal bull which conferred on him the kingdom of the Two Sicilies. This event occurred on the 26th of February, 1265. The Pope is therein represented wearing the conical bonnet, with the knob on its apex, as in the example at Chartres, and the pendent infulæ or vittæ, but no crown.

As the subject leaves no doubt that the painting is as late as 1265, we must take its evidence in preference to that of the Cottonian MS., the date of which is not precisely ascertained, at the same time observing that the latter is only described as *circa* 1250, and may possibly be not older than the painting at Pernes. Innocent IV. was elected Pope in 1243, and died in 1254. We know from Nicholas de Curbion, his confessor, that it was Innocent who conferred on the Cardinals their red hats (*capellos rubros*), accompanying the gift with the observation that the colour should remind them to be always

Pope Clement IV.

Pope, from Cotton. MS., Brit. Mus.

ready to shed their lives for the faith, and that the hats were first worn at the Council of Lyons, A.D. 1245. It is improbable that his biographer, who records this circumstance, would have omitted mentioning one so important as the assumption of a crown by Innocent had such been the case, and certainly previous to his pontificate no sign of such an ornament has been discovered. The learned compilers of 'L'Art de vérifier les Dates,' in allusion to the common opinion that Boniface VIII. added the second crown to the tiara, observe that it is contradicted by the fact that six statues were erected of that Pope during his lifetime, or very shortly after his death, some of which have one crown surrounding the tiara, and the others none at all. It is true, they add, that at Bologna there is a seventh statue of Boniface VIII., on which the tiara is ornamented with a *triple* crown; but it is obvious that the monument is of a much later date. This plain but valuable evidence, which appears to have been overlooked by M. Viollet-le-Duc, answers his question respecting the single crown, and also proves that it must have been added during the forty years between the death of Innocent in 1254 and that of Boniface in 1303. The same authority further observes that the tiara of Benedict XI., the successor of Boniface, in the monuments that exist of him, has only one crown, another proof that his predecessor did not add a second. The fact is, therefore, I think, fully established that the tiara was encircled by one crown during the latter half of the thirteenth century, the exact date of its assumption being still a desideratum. It is traditionally reported that Boniface bestowed the red mantles on the Cardinals, but the evidence is not so satisfactory as that recording the gift of their red hats.

By an edict of the Council of the Lateran in 1215, confirmed by another at Narbonne in 1227, the Jews were commanded to wear a piece of red stuff in the form of a wheel on the breast of their habit, in order to distinguish them from Christians. I believe this is the earliest of these unchristian enactments; the edict of Edward I. in England being, of course, later than 1271.

Rainiero Zeno, Doge of Venice, 1252–1268, is reported to have first surrounded the ducal biretta, or corno, with a circle of gold,—" un circolo d'oro in forma di diadema ;" but the shape was still conical, and continued so throughout the century, as appears by the mosaics which still exist in St. Mark's, the dates of which are exceedingly doubtful, but range from the twelfth to the fourteenth century. I subjoin tracings of three heads of Doges from separate mosaics, which have been most kindly made expressly for me by an English artist resident at Venice.

Three Heads of Venetian Doges. From Mosaics in St. Mark's Cathedral.

A word here in continuation of what I have said at page 65 respecting mourning.

A bas-relief on the tomb of Don Diego Lopez de Haro el Bueno, fifteenth Señor of Biscay, who died in 1214, presents us with a Spanish funeral procession of that date. Being in marble, no

Bas-relief on Tomb of Don Diego Lopez de Haro. 1214.

colours are indicated ; but if we may rely upon the assertion of the Abbé Baudry, it would appear that the black garments worn on such occasions were not distinguished by their form from those in ordinary use. The three male personages following the monks are clad in tunics reaching to the mid-leg ; two of them are confined round the waist by girdles, probably of silk, one being a plain strip tied in a bow knot, the other twisted cord-fashion. The sleeves are long and tight at the wrists, with some sort of trimming at the shoulder. The third figure has a mantle hanging over his right shoulder. All three are bareheaded. The three females are in long tunics and mantles, with the remarkable head-dress we have noticed of Queen Beatrice (page 73), the whole costume being similar to that of the effigy. There is an absence of all personal ornaments. The feet of the male figures have apparently been broken ; but the one perfect leg shows us that the chausses had moderately long-pointed toes.

The bas-reliefs on the tomb of Blanche de Navarre, queen of Sancho III., king of Castile, in the Chapel of Santa Maria de Najara, to which I have alluded at page 55 of this volume, is here appended ; but as the Queen is represented dying in the arms of her attendants, their habiliments cannot, I think, be considered mourning ; and therefore, although highly interesting as examples of female costume of the latter half of the twelfth century, they do not throw any additional light on the question.

Bas-relief from the tomb of Blanche de Navarre, queen of Sancho III., king of Castile.

CHAPTER V.

THE FOURTEENTH CENTURY.

VER as we advance, our materials naturally accumulate, not only from the progress of the arts, but from the increase of authentic documents specially connected with the subject of Costume, such as sumptuary laws, wardrobe accounts, wills, &c. In 1307, Edward II. succeeded his chivalrous father, Edward I., and during the twenty troublesome years of his reign we learn from all sources that luxury increased in proportion to the decline of honour and virtue. Excited by the example of the profligate and presumptuous Gaveston, "the esquire endeavoured to outshine the knight, the knight the baron, the baron the earl, and the earl the king himself, in the richness of his apparel ;"[1] but, after all, what is there new in this complaint ? Have we not heard similar lamentations from the earliest times ? Do we not find them repeated in each successive reign ? and would the remark be utterly out of place at the present day ? The ink is scarcely dry with which we traced the words of Guillaume le Breton and Nicholas de Bray, describing a parallel condition of affairs in France in the reigns of Philip Augustus and Louis VIII.; and, despite the edict of Philip le Bel in 1294, limiting the number and fixing the price of the dresses to be worn by the *bourgeoisie* of Paris, we find them astonishing the spectators by the splendour and costliness of their attire on the occasion of his conferring knighthood on his eldest son Louis in 1313.

Philip V., surnamed "le Long" (1316-1322), contemporary with our Edward II., and who was not remarkable for extravagance, is recorded to have used during the latter half of the first year of his reign no less a quantity than 6364 "ventres de petit gris" for the lining and trimming of his garments.[2] In France, at this date, we first hear of garments called *fond de cuve, garde de corps, garnache,* and *gonnelle,* names which do not occur in the descriptions of English costume, but are applied by M. Viollet-le-Duc to dresses similar to those we are familiar with in this country, at the same period, under other appellations. The *fond de cuve,* for example, presents no special feature that would distinguish it from the houppelande, or at least the gown with long and ample sleeves to which that name has been applied ; the garde de corps is simply a tunic; and the garnache is at one time confounded with the cote-hardie, and at another with the sleeveless surcoat. The pencil can alone enable us to form an idea of these garments, which I, at least, have not been enabled to identify with those named by writers of the time, who rarely do more than mention them. I therefore subjoin engravings of the civil costume of France, from the authorities furnished us by contemporary sculptors and illuminators. Here, for instance, are three representations of what M. Viollet-

[1] William of Malmesbury.   [2] Quicherat, p. 181.

le-Duc informs us is a fond de cuve, mentioned as early as the reign of Philip le Long, and frequently to the end of the century.[1]

Gaston Phœbus, Comte de Foix.

French lady and gentlemen. From MS. in Nat. Lib., Paris; circa 1395.

All three figures are of the latter period ; the first being that of Gaston Phœbus, Comte de Foix, from the MS. of his ' Livre de Chasse,' in the National Library at Paris, and undistinguishable from the loose ample gown with a cowl and very wide sleeves which we find worn in England by persons of rank throughout the fourteenth century (see GOWN and HOUPPELANDE). The other male personage is attired in quite a different sort of garment, made high up in the neck, with a collar fitting the throat closely, as in dresses of the reigns of Richard II. and Henry IV. in England ; no cowl or capuchon, but with wide sleeves, the edges of which are dagged, according to the fashion of those times, and descending very little below the knees. It has buttons up the front from the waist to the throat, and corresponds in general appearance with the short gowns worn by gentlemen in England at the close of the fourteenth century. The MS. from which it is copied is a 'Tite Live,' in the National Library at Paris, written presumably *circa* 1395. The lady is from the same MS. ; and if the upper garment she wears is a fond de cuve, we have a third variety equally destitute of any particular feature by which a fond de cuve can be distinguished from other articles of apparel, known as tunics, supertunics, surcoats, cotes-hardies, gowns, robes, &c.

In the account of expenses for the marriage of Blanche de Bourbon, in 1353, occur these entries : " D'un demi marbré lonc de Bruxelles achaté . . . pour faire une cotte-hardie fourrée de menu-vair et l'autre double . . . Pour huit aunes d'un pers azuré de Broisselles à doubler ledit fons de cuve et faire chauces pour la dicte dame." M. Viollet-le-Duc, who quotes these entries, remarks : " Il semble bien ici que le fond de cuve n'est autre chose que la jupe de la cotte-hardie." In which case,

---

[1] " Item, pour sa robe de la viel de Noel d'un marbré mallé. Pour fons de cuve 380 venures (de menuvair)." (Compte de Geoffroy de Fleury, 1316.)

M 2

if we are to take the figure of this lady as an illustration, the *fond de cuve* is an under and not an upper vestment, or *pardessus*, as he previously calls it.[1] No light is thrown upon the subject by etymology. "Le fond de cuve" is the bottom of a tub. "Une fossée à fond de cuve" is a flat-bottomed ditch.[2] There is nothing in a loose gown, whether long or short, nor in a jacket or a surcoat, to suggest such an appellation, which I find in Quicherat only applied in the seventeenth century to the round tub-like breeches worn in the reign of Louis XII.

We have yet, I think, to identify the fond de cuve of the reigns of Philip "le long" and of Charles VI.

The *garnache, ganache,* or *canache,* is an upper vestment mentioned in wardrobe accounts in France, A.D. 1352, and there is a garment constantly represented in illuminations of that time, which is distinguished by a remarkable feature, called *pattes* by M. Viollet-le-Duc, whereby it may be identified, but the peculiarity appears to have escaped the notice of M. Quicherat, in whose valuable work, to my surprise, I cannot find a single example. The portrait of Charles V. of France in the 'Livre de l'Information des Princes,' written *circa* 1370, affords us an excellent specimen of this dress, whatever may be its name. It is a long gown or surcoat with wide but short sleeves; in this instance, blue powdered with golden fleurs-de-lys, and having attached to it a chaperon lined with ermine, the collar of which surrounds his neck. The remarkable feature I have referred to consists of the two pieces of fur not inappropriately termed "paws" (*pattes*) by M. Viollet-le-Duc, but which the English reader will better recognize by the name of "lapels," turned back on each side of the breast from the opening through which the head was passed, the dress being put on like a shirt. A figure in a bas-relief at Paris still more clearly exhibits the character of these lapels, which, if necessary, could be folded over each other either to close completely the opening at the neck, or to keep the chest warm when travelling. In dresses of state, however, they were only ornaments, and much larger than those in ordinary costumes.

Charles V. of France. 1370.

Bas-relief, Notre Dame, Paris. 1370.

[1] "Fond de cuve. S. M. Sorte de pardessus que portaient les hommes et les femmes." (Tome iii. p. 370.)
[2] "Fond de cuve" is, however, a technical expression in France for any square, hollow, or excavation of which the angles are rounded (Napoléon Landais). How far this may bear on the question I leave to the reader.

It is a singular fashion, having, as far as I can see, nothing to recommend it, and it appears to have been limited to France, as I have not been able to discover an instance of it in the contemporary costume of England or of any other country. M. Viollet-le-Duc says the ganache, which he considers a beautiful and simple garment, disappeared at the end of the fourteenth century. M. Quicherat makes brief mention of it as a surcoat without sleeves or girdle, and neither of those eminent antiquaries throws any light on the derivation of the term *ganache* or *garnache*. Its signification in French is simply "a jaw-bone;" but *garnacha* is still in Spain and Portugal the name for a judge's or counsellor's gown, and the garnache was probably introduced from one of those countries into France in the fourteenth century. The origin of the name is, however, still to seek.

Before leaving this subject, it may be as well to observe that in the middle of this century the term "robe" in the singular signified a complete suit of apparel, consisting of a certain number of articles (*garnemens*), of which at that period one was the ganache. In the account of Etienne de la Fontaine, before quoted, we read: "Pour fourer une robe de 6 garnemens qu'il ot le jour de la feste de Granz Pasques; pour les 2 seurcos et la ganache 3 fourrures de menu vair, tenant chacune 386 ventres; pour manches et poingnez, 60; pour le corps de la houce, 440 ventres; pour elle 96 ventres; pour languetes 6 ventres; pour le chaperon 110; et pour le mantel a parer, 442 ventres." The chaperon or hood is here included amongst the *garnemens* of the robe.

Two remarkable fashions are characteristic of the fourteenth century throughout Europe: one the introduction of party-coloured dresses, and the other that of streamers from the elbows, called *coudières* by M. Quicherat. I find no name for them in English unless it be tippet, which is generally applied to the long tail of the chaperon.

Many foreign fashions were imported into England in the nineteenth year of the reign of Edward III. (1346) by the foreign knights assembled at the round table at Windsor. "The Englishmen haunted so much unto the folly of strangers," says Dowglas, the Monk of Glastonbury, "that every year they changed them in divers shapes and disguisings of clothing, now long, now large, now wide, now strait, and every day clothinges new and destitute and devest from all honesty of old arraye or good usage; and another time to short clothes and so strait waisted, with full sleeves and tapetes (tippets?), of surcoats and hodes over long and large, all so nagged (jagged) and knit on every side, and all so shattered, and also buttoned, that I with truth shall say they seem more like to tormentors or devils in their clothing and also in their shoying (shoeing), and other array, than they seemed to be like men."

Quicherat informs us that costume in France underwent a complete change in the year 1340, when the fashions of the time of Philip Augustus, which had resisted the most important alterations in the constitution of the kingdom, the dynasty, and manners, succumbed without any apparent reason in the middle of the reign of Philip of Valois. The long tunics, supertunics, surcoats, and cyclasses were superseded by the short and tight dresses complained of by the Monk of Glastonbury, for the new fashion was adopted almost simultaneously in France, England, and Italy, and according to an annalist of the latter country had a Spanish origin, travelling from Catalonia through the towns on the coast of the Mediterranean to Marseilles, where it had existed some years previous to its general assumption throughout Europe. This interesting statement of M. Quicherat is supported by an examination of the sculptures and paintings of the period in the countries alluded to. The cotehardie, the doublet, the pourpoint, the court-pie, the paltock (the latter undoubtedly of Spanish origin; see Dictionary), the hanseline or jacket, all appear in the reign of our Edward III., the contemporary of Philip of Valois, and are stigmatized as indecent novelties by the writers of that day. Of these the cote-hardie and the hanseline are claimed for Germany, but may nevertheless have found their way through Italy to the German Empire and have become naturalized there, as the doublet and pourpoint, if of Spanish origin, must, from their names, have evidently been in France. The hair was cropped and long moustaches worn, "comme la portaient les Espagnols," so thoroughly Spanish was the taste which had revolutionized the costume of Europe. The shortness of the pourpoint displayed the chausses or tight hose which had been concealed by the long tunics, and they were therefore made of richer materials and generally party-coloured, one leg differing from the other, rendering the

common term of a pair perfectly inadmissible. Amongst other extravagances the tails of the chaperons were elongated to an absurd degree, reaching almost to the heels. It must be observed, however,
that the regal and judicial costume underwent no alteration, and that the aged and sedate reprobated
and rejected these foreign fopperies. Philip of Valois himself would neither adopt the new fashions
nor suffer his courtiers to wear them. Admonished by Pope John XXII. as to the unseemliness of a
great sovereign's appearing in such scanty and fantastic attire, he continued to wear such garments
as had been in favour with his father and brothers. It would seem that the terms afterwards so
familiar, and still occasionally used in England, viz. "Gentlemen of the long robe" and "of the short
robe," had their origin from the above circumstances ; judges, serjeants-at-law, and other legal dignitaries retaining the gowns and cloaks of the previous century, while the inferior officers wore the short
tunic or surcoat of the day. The author of 'Le Grand Chronique de St. Denis' gravely attributes
the crushing defeat of his countrymen at Crecy to the sins of the people in adopting such indelicate
dresses. "We are bound to believe," says the indignant writer, "that God has permitted this on
account of our sins, for pride was excessive in France, above all amongst the nobility. Great also
was the shamelessness of attire throughout the realm, for some wore robes so short that they
scarcely reached to their hips, and when they stooped to serve a lord they displayed their drawers to
the persons behind them. Their clothes were also so tight that they required assistance to dress and
undress themselves, and when pulling them off it seemed like skinning them. Others had robes plaited
in the waist, like those of the women, and also wore one hose of one cloth and the other of another.
Their cornettes and their sleeves nearly touched the ground, and they looked more like jongleurs
(minstrels or mountebanks) than any other sort of persons ;[1] and for this reason it is no wonder that
God should have punished the excesses of the French by the hand of his scourge, the King of
England." The brevity of the upper garment continued to be a scandal throughout the fourteenth
century. Chaucer, writing in the reign of Richard II., makes his Parson complain of "the horrible
disordinate scantiness of clothing as be these cut slops or hanselines, that through their shortness," he
says, "and the wrapping of their hose—which are departed of two colours, white and red, white and
blue, white and black, or black and red—make the wearer seem as though the fire of St. Anthony, or
some other mischance, had cankered and consumed one-half their bodies."

These party-coloured dresses were the result of the increasing popularity of heraldry, the colours
being taken from those of the arms and worn as the livery of
the family bearing them—a custom which we first hear of in
the reign of Edward I. (see LIVERY), and which became general
during the fourteenth century. In an illumination representing
John of Gaunt sitting to decide the claims on the coronation of
Richard II., Cotton. MS. Nero, D vi., the Duke's long robe is
divided exactly in half, one side being blue and the other white,
the colours of the House of Lancaster.

The reign of the weak and luxurious Richard II. was pro-
ductive of still greater extravagance of attire, and the fashions
of Bohemia, the country of his queen, were added to if they
did not supersede those of Spain, which England had received
not only through France, but from direct intercourse with the
former nation by means of the knights in the service of John
of Gaunt and Edward the Black Prince, whose connection with
it was so near and so frequent. Richard himself was one of the
greatest fops of the day. He had a coat estimated at thirty

John of Gaunt. From Cotton. MS.

thousand marks, the value of which must have arisen chiefly from the quantity of precious stones
with which it was embroidered ; this fashion obtaining greatly in the fourteenth century, as did that
also of working letters and mottoes in the dress, and cutting the edges of the mantles, sleeves, &c.,

[1] See Dictionary, under COAT-HARDY, for an anecdote illustrative of this opinion.

into the shape of leaves and other devices, the latter custom existing as early as the reign of Henry I., and called in France "*barbes d'écrevisses.*"

Knighton, a chronicler of the fourteenth century, tells us the vanity of the common people in their dress was so great that it was impossible to distinguish the rich from the poor, the high from the low, the clergy from the laity, by their appearance—the complaint of all times, and which cannot therefore in fairness be urged as proof of the extravagance of one age or people in particular.

The author of an anonymous work, called the 'Eulogium,' cited by Camden in his 'Remaines concerning Britain,' and apparently of the reign of Richard II., says, "The commons were besotted in excess of apparel, some in wide surcoats reaching to their loins, some in a garment reaching to their heels, close before and strutting out at the sides, so that at the back they make men seem like women, and this they call by a ridiculous name, *gowne.*" This observation is curious, as it marks the first application of the old Saxon word *gunna* to the tunic since the diffusion of the Norman language in England, and also informs us that, with the usual caprice of fashion, the old Spanish dresses were being supplanted by garments as extravagantly long as the others were ridiculously short. From the name of one, the houppelande, it would seem that Spain still contributed to influence the taste of France and England, affected herself by the neighbourhood of the Moors; at all events the words *hopa* and *hopalanda* still exist in the Spanish language. (See HOUPPELANDE.) "Their hoods," continues the censor, "are little, tied under the chin and buttoned like the women's, but set with gold, silver, and precious stones. Their liripipes, or tippets, pass round the neck, and, hanging down before, reach to the heel, all jagged. They have another weed of silk, which they call a *paltock.* (See PALTOCK.) Their hose are of two colours, or pied with more, which they tie to their paltocks with white latchets, called herlots, without any breeches" (*i.e.* drawers) ; "their girdles are of gold and silver, and some of them worth twenty marks. Their shoes and pattens are snouted and picked more than a finger long, crooking upwards, which they call crackowes, resembling the Devil's claws, and fastened to the knees with chains of gold and silver." These crackowes were evidently named after the city of Cracow, and were no doubt amongst the fashions imported from Poland, which had been incorporated with the kingdom of Bohemia by John, the grandfather of Richard's Queen Anne; not that the long, turned-up-toed shoe was a novelty in England, as I have already noticed it as early as the reign of Rufus, but the fastening it to the knee may have been the peculiar fashion of Cracow. In France, these turned-up toes received the name of *poulaines*, for the same reason ; Poulain being an old mode of writing Pologne. This coincidence leaves no doubt of the derivation of the fashion, which might otherwise have been attributed to the Moors of Cordova, a city already famous for its preparations of leather known as Cordovan, and giving the title of Cordwainers to the members of the "gentle craft." Strangely enough, no pictorial representation of these chained-up shoes appears in any of the numerous illuminations of this period, English or foreign ; but the late Major Hamilton Smith, in his 'Ancient Costume of England,' mentions a portrait of James I. of Scotland existing at Keilberg, near Tubigen in Suabia, a seat of the family of Von Lystrums, wherein the peaks of the king's shoes are fastened by chains of gold to his girdle, and in armour there is a most interesting example of the fifteenth century in the Londesborough Collection.

The chaperon or hood was sometimes surmounted by a hat or cap. "The Book of Worcester," says Camden, "reporteth that in the year of our Lord 1369 they began to use caps of divers colours, especially red, with costly linings ; and in 1372 they first began to wanton it in *a new curtal weed they called a cloak,* and in Latin *armiausa,* as only covering the shoulders." It would appear from M. Quicherat, that the French at this date had a mantle which they called *cloche,* "dont l'ouverture était par devant," and which was specially "à l'usage des cavaliers." This must surely have been identical with our cloak, which we first hear of at the same time, and it may be therefore a question whether the word was derived from the Saxon *lach,* as Skinner imagined.[1] (See CLOAK.) At all

---

[1] *Cloca, clochia, clocka,* in Mediæval Latin, signify "a bell" as well as "a mantle" (Ducange, *in voce*). *Clocka* has the same signification in French, and *Klocke* in German. May not the bell-like form of the short shoulder-cloak, the "court manteau" of Anjou, the round "curtal weed" of the Book of Worcester, the "cloca rotunda" of the clergy, have suggested the denomination ?

events, the word first occurs in the English language in the fourteenth century. Extravagance in dress manifested itself in opposite extremes in the reign of Richard II. (1377–99); the scandalously short-skirted and tight-fitting attire retaining a share of public favour, at the same time that long trained gowns with sleeves so wide that they touched the ground were also in fashion,—an enormity reprobated both in prose and verse by the authors of the period, and vainly prohibited by Act of Parliament. Sleeves also called *pokys* and *bag-pipe*, from their shapes, were worn by all classes in England (see SLEEVE).

The same fashions prevailed in France during the reign of Charles VI., who adopted those of Bohemia and Germany, which were at that time the most fantastic, though not the most graceful, in Europe; and to those countries it is, no doubt, we as well as France were indebted for some of the more extraordinary features of the costume of that day, including the " crackowes " before mentioned. The poet Gower, in his ' Confessio Amantis,' alludes to " the new guise of Beme (Bohemia)," and Froissart informs us that Henry, duke of Lancaster (afterwards Henry IV.), on his return to England, entered London wearing a " courte jacques " of cloth of gold, " à la fachon d'Almayne." Camden also expressly asserts that Queen Anne of Bohemia brought in high head attire piked with horns and long-trained gowns for women, but he does not quote his authority, and it could not have been contemporary, as long-trained gowns had been worn as early as the twelfth century, and had never gone wholly out of fashion, and no " *high* head attire piked with horns " appears in England before the reign of Henry V., as we have shown in the Dictionary under HEAD-DRESS, which see. That Queen Anne did introduce some of her country fashions is clear from the words of Gower; and we will now turn to the ladies, who have been too long neglected.

Little alteration is apparent in the female costume of the time of Edward II., 1307–1327. The ugly gorget was still worn occasionally, but the head was more uncovered than in the previous reign. The supertunics or surcoats were of two sorts—one as before, trailing on the ground; the other

Matrons or Nurses, *circa* 1300. Willemin, ' Mon. inédits.'

Lady of rank in surcoat.
Royal MS. Brit. Mus., 2 G ×.

shorter than the under-tunic or kirtle, without sleeves, open at the sides, and worn without a girdle (see woodcuts annexed): I will not attempt to appropriate any special name to it, but it is just

possible that it may be the mysterious sorquanie. (See page 70.) No new term occurs in the catalogue of a lady's wardrobe until we meet, in the reign of Edward III., with the cote-hardie, which
was worn by both sexes. It was buttoned down the front like those of the men, sometimes with
coudières or tippets at the elbows, and in some examples there is the appearance of pockets. In
the 'Vision of Piers Ploughman,' written *circa* 1350, the poet speaks of a woman richly clothed, her
garments purfled (faced or trimmed with fine furs), her robe of a scarlet colour ingrain, and splendidly
adorned with ribands of red gold, interspersed with precious stones of great value. Her head-tire, he
says, he has not time to describe, but she wore a crown; the king had no better. Her fingers were
all embellished with rings of gold set with diamonds, rubies, sapphires, and also with Oriental stones
or amulets to prevent any venomous infection. At the tournaments and public shows the ladies rode
in party-coloured tunics, one half being of one colour and the other half of another, with short hoods
and liripipes (the long tail or tippet of the hood) wrapped about their heads like cords. (See under
HOOD, Dictionary, p. 292, for an illustration of this particular fashion.) The most remarkable article
of female costume of the fourteenth century, however, is a tunic, robe, surcoat, gown, or whatever else
it may be classed with, of which no special designation has yet been discovered, though its peculiarity
must indubitably have demanded one, and which, *faute de mieux*, I ventured forty years ago to give
the name of the "sideless garment." It remains to this day unidentified. Neither M. Viollet-le-Duc
nor M. Quicherat, to my great disappointment, has thrown any additional light upon it. The former
has illustrated its make and shape by many spirited and graceful drawings, but is contented to call it
a surcoat, and considers it of English origin. M. Quicherat says, it is "un habillement à la fois
élégant et majestueuse," but has also no other name for it than a surcoat. Grant that it was a
surcoat, so singular an attire must surely have been distinguished from other surcoats which have no
peculiar character. Were it not seen on the effigy of Blanche de la Tour, daughter of Edward III.,

Gillette de la Fontaine.
From Montfaucon, fol. 134.

Effigy of Blanche de la Tour, Westminster Abbey.

in Westminster Abbey, who died in 1340, I should be greatly inclined to believe it "the new guise of Beme," introduced by Queen Anne aforesaid; but as her arrival was in 1382, that is out of the question. There are many varieties of the dress, however; and as it was worn by royal and noble personages in France and England, and was retained as a state dress in those countries for a hundred and fifty years, it is one of the most important and interesting in the history of Costume, wheresoever it originated or whatever may have been its particular appellation. The engravings on the preceding page from French and English examples will give the reader a clearer notion of it than any verbal description. I find no instance of its being worn in Italy.

Chaucer has furnished us with some graphic descriptions of the dress of the various classes in England in his time. The young Squire in the 'Canterbury Tales' is described as wearing a short gown, with "sleeves long and wide;" his dress was also embroidered

"as it were a mede,
Alle full of freshe flowers, white and rede."

His locks

"Were crull as they were laid in presse."

His yeoman was clad in "a cote and hoode of grene," his horn slung in a green baldrick, a silver figure of St. Christopher was on his breast, and a handsome bracer (a guard to prevent the galling of the arm by the bow-string) on his arm. A sword and buckler hung on one side of him, and he bore a mighty bow in his hand. In the Friar's Tale another yeoman is described wearing a *courtpye* of green, and a hat with black fringes.

The Franklin or country gentleman is merely stated to have worn a gipicierre, or purse of silk, hanging at his girdle, "white as milk," and an anelace or knife.

The Merchant is represented in motley (*i.e.*, party-coloured), with a forked beard and a "Flaunderish beaver hat;" his boots clasped "fayre and fetously."

The Reeve or Steward wore a long surcoat. He had a rusty sword by his side. His beard was closely shaven, and his hair rounded at the ears and docked on the crown like a priest's.

The Miller was clothed in a white coat and a blue hood, and was armed with a sword and buckler. His hose on holidays are said to be of red cloth, and he then twisted the tippet of his hood about his head—a fashion amongst the gallants of that day, as already noticed.

The poor Ploughman wore a tabard, a garment first mentioned in this century, a hat, scrip, and staff.

The Shipman was dressed in a gown of *falding* to the knee, with a dagger slung under one arm by a lace round his neck.

The Haberdasher, Carpenter, Weaver, Dyer, and Tapestry-worker, all wealthy burghers of London,

"were yclothed in a livery
Of a solempne and grete fraternitie."

Their clothes were new, and the chapes of their knives, pouches, and girdles ornamented with silver.

The Wife of Bath wore kerchiefs "full fine of ground" upon her head; her hose were of "fine scarlet redde, full strette yteyed," and her shoes "full moist and new." She was

"Ywimpled well, and on her heade an hat
As broad as a buckler or a targe;
A fote mantle about her hippes large,
And on hire feet a paire of spurres sharpe."

The Carpenter's Wife's outer garment is not described; but her girdle was barred with silk, the collar of her shift and the tapes of her white *volupers* (cap or head-kerchief; see Dictionary, p. 516) were embroidered with black silk, and her "barm-cloth (apron) was as white as morning milk." She had a broad silken fillet round her head, a leather purse attached to her girdle, "tasselled with silk and pearled with latoun." On her low collar she wore a brooch as big as the boss of a buckler, and her shoes were laced high up on her legs.

The same delightful writer also tells us that "a gyte (ghita) of red" was worn by the wife of the Miller of Trompynton on holydays, and the Wife of Bath boasted of the gay scarlet gytes she wore on similar occasions. The gyte (or ghita) being, as I consider, a cloak (see Dictionary, p. 206), it would appear that the familiar red cloak of our country dames and lasses dates at least from as early a period as the reign of Richard II.

Moreover, we obtain from the same unimpeachable authority some interesting glimpses of professional costume, which begins to be distinguishable from the ordinary attire of civilians in the fourteenth century. Legal personages are depicted in illuminations of that date in dresses which we cannot doubt are indicative of their position; and Piers Ploughman speaks of the furred cloak of a serjeant pleading at the bar. Chaucer describes the serjeant-at-law as clad in a medley coat with a girdle of silk, ornamented with small bars and stripes of various colours; and a Harleian MS. informs us that the serjeant-at-law's robe was formerly party-coloured, *in order to command respect as well to his person as to his profession.* One cannot help smiling at the thought of the respect one of her Majesty's serjeants would command in Westminster Hall, or in Lincoln's Inn, at the present day, dressed in a long gown of which one side was scarlet and the other blue striped with red, as he is represented in a contemporary copy of Chaucer in the library of the Earl of Ellesmere; yet it is only custom that renders the wig he now wears less ridiculous in the eyes of her Majesty's lieges. I must refer the reader to the article ROBE in the Dictionary for such information as I have been able to collect on the subject of legal costume, simply noticing in this place the period apparently of its first appearance.[1]

The doctor of physic had assumed, or been ordered to assume, about the same period a distinctive costume. Chaucer tells us, "in sanguine and in perse (purple and light blue) he was clad alle," his gown being lined with taffeta and cendal; but in his 'Testament of Cresseyde,' he describes a physician as wearing a scarlet gown, "furred well as such a one ought to be;" such being still the academic gown of a doctor of medicine.

The clergy, as Knighton has already told us, were not to be known from the laity; and the Ploughman in the 'Canterbury Tales' rails at them for riding, glittering with gold, upon high horses, gayer than any common knight might go, wearing golden girdles and gowns of scarlet and green, ornamented with cut work, and the long piked shoes; nay, being armed even like men of war with broad bucklers and long swords, and baldricks with keen basilards or daggers. Many priests, he says, have mitres embellished with pearls, like the head of a queen, and a staff of gold set with jewels.

In addition to this, Chaucer has also introduced a monk amongst his pilgrims dressed in open defiance of the regulations of the Church. The sleeves of his tunic are edged with fur-de-gris, "the finest in the land." His hood is fastened beneath his chin with a golden pin, curiously wrought, the great end being fashioned like a true lover's knot, or having one engraved on it. His supple boots and the bells on his horse's bridle are mentioned as instances of his foppery and love of display. Even the parish clerk described by the Miller is said to be foppish and most unclerical in his dress. His hose were red and his kirtle sky-blue, set about with many points, and over it he wore a surplice white as a blossom, his shoes having "Paule's windows carven" on them; that is to say, they were cut or embroidered lattice-wise, or in patterns such as we see in painted windows.

The Canon was more decorously dressed in black with a white surplice. He had a hat hanging by a lace upon his back; and the poet says he supposed him to be a canon because his cloak was sown to his hood. The dress of the Parson is not described; but in the valuable MS. before-mentioned he is represented in a gown and hood of scarlet, such being, as Mr. Todd in his edition has observed, the habit of a ministering priest in England until the time of Elizabeth, but how long previous to that of Chaucer he does not state, nor have I as yet ascertained.

---

[1] See also Appendix for correction of date of close roll and other errors in Dugdale's 'Originales.'

N

A prioress is one of the pilgrims; and she is described as most precisely dressed: her wimple neatly plaited, her cloak very handsome (it is black in the Egerton MS. and the under-dress white), her rosary of coral beads, and a buckle or brooch of polished gold—

> "On which there was first written a crowned A,
> And after that 'Amor vincit omnia,'"—

prioresses, we presume, included.

In the thirty-seventh year of the reign of King Edward III. (1363), the Commons exhibited a complaint in Parliament against the general usage of expensive apparel not suited either to the degree or income of the people, and an Act was then passed by which the following regulations, of which we give the substance, were insisted on :—

1. The servants of noblemen, as well as those belonging to tradesmen and artificers, shall not wear any cloth in their vesture or chausses exceeding the price of two marks for the whole piece; neither shall they wear anything of gold or silver upon their garments or attached thereto. Their wives and their children shall wear the same sort of cloth that is appointed for them, and use no veils purchased at a higher price than twelve pence each veil.

2. Tradesmen, artificers, and men in office called yeomen, shall wear no cloth in their apparel exceeding the price of 40 shillings the whole cloth, neither shall they embellish their garments with precious stones, cloth of silk or of silver, nor shall they wear any gold or silver on their girdles, knives, rings, garters, nouches, ribands, chains, *bindz(?)*, or seals, nor any manner of apparel embroidered with silk or in any other way. Their wives and their children shall wear the same cloth as they do, and use no veils but such as are made with thread and manufactured in this kingdom; nor any kind of furs, excepting those of lambs, of rabbits, of cats, and of foxes.

3. All esquires and every gentleman under the rank of knighthood, and not possessed of lands or tenements to the yearly amount of 200 marks, shall use in their dress such cloth as does not exceed the value of 4½ marks the whole cloth. They shall not wear any cloth of gold, of silk, or of silver, nor any sort of embroidered garment; nor any ring, buckle, nouche, riband or girdle, nor any other part of their apparel, gilt or of silver; nor any ornaments of precious stones or furs of any kind. Their wives and children shall be subject to the same regulations; and they shall not wear any purfling or facings upon their garments, neither shall they use esclaires, crinales, or treofles, nor embellish their apparel with any kind of ornaments of gold, of silver, or of jewellery. But all esquires possessed of 200 marks or upwards, in lands or tenements, may wear cloth at the price of 5 marks the whole piece, and cloth of silk and of silver, with ribands, girdles, and other apparel reasonably embellished with silver. Their wives and their children may also wear furs and facings of miniver, but not of ermine or lettice, neither may they use any ornaments of precious stones, excepting on their head-dresses.

4. Merchants, citizens, burgesses, artificers, and tradesmen, as well in the City of London as elsewhere, who are in possession of the full value of 500 marks in goods and chattels, may, with their wives and children, use the same clothing as the esquires and gentlemen who have a yearly income of 100 marks; and such of them as are in possession of goods and chattels to the amount of 1000 marks, may, with their wives and children, wear the same apparel as the esquires and gentlemen who have 200 marks yearly.

It is, however, to be observed that no groom, yeoman, or servant, appertaining to the persons above mentioned, shall exceed the apparel ordained for the grooms and servants of the lords and others specified before.

5. Knights possessed of lands or tenements to the annual value of 200 marks, may wear in their apparel cloth not exceeding 6 marks' value the whole piece, but no cloth of gold; neither may they use any cloak, mantle, or gown, furred with pure miniver, nor sleeves furred with ermine, nor have any parts of their garments embroidered with jewellery or otherwise; and their wives and their children shall be subject to the same restriction, and use no linings of ermine or lettice, esclaires, or any kind of precious stones, unless it be on their heads. But all knights and ladies possessed

of lands or tenements exceeding the value of 400 marks yearly, and extending to 1000 pounds, may use their own pleasure, excepting only that they may not wear the furs of ermine or lettice, nor any embellishment of pearls except upon their heads.

6. Ecclesiastics holding rank in cathedrals, colleges, or schools, and of the King's household, who require the indulgence, may wear such furs as are best suited to their constitutions ; others of the clergy who have yearly incomes exceeding 200 marks are entitled to the same privileges as the knights of the same estate, and those of inferior degree shall rank with the esquire possessed of 100 marks yearly income. It is also ordained that the knights as well as the clergy, who are permitted by this statute to wear fur in the winter, may also wear lining to their garments in the summer.

7. All labourers and lower classes of people not possessed of goods and chattels to the amount of 40 shillings, shall wear no cloth but blankets and russets, and those not exceeding 12 pence the yard, nor use any other girdles than such as are made of linen.

That there might be no excuse for evading the specifications of this Act, it was commanded that the clothiers should make sufficient quantities of cloth at the established prices, to satisfy the demands of the people at large. The penalty annexed to the infringement of these ordinances was the forfeiture of the apparel so made and worn.[1] That they were not only infringed, but utterly set at nought, is obvious from the continuance of the censure and satire of the contemporary writers of this and the following reign. Witness the old chronicler Harding, who says :—

> " There was great pride among the officers,
> *And of all man surpassing their compeers,*
> Of rich array and more contious
> Than was before or sith, and more pretious.
>   *   *   *   *   *
> Yemen and groomes in cloth of silk arrayed,
>   Satin and damask in doublettes and in gownes,
> In cloth of greene and scarlet for unpayd (unpaid for) ;
>   Cut worke was great both in court and towne,
>   Both in men's hoodes and also in their gownes : "

and the poet declares all this he heard Robert Irecliffe say, who was Clerk of the Green Cloth to Richard II.

A peculiar feature presents itself in the costume of the latter years of the reign of Edward III. A single ostrich feather is seen worn right in front of the high bonnet much worn at that period. Taken in conjunction with the celebrated badge of the English royal family, so long popularly supposed to have been derived from the crest of John, king of Bohemia, slain, as the story went, by Edward the Black Prince, in the battle of Crecy, the wearing of a single feather in that position might be fairly considered a fashion introduced in compliment to that mirror of chivalry. We find, however, that the French at that period had a passion for ostrich feathers. The price they paid for them was enormous, in consequence of their rarity. Froissart informs us that the captains of the free companies that were so numerous in France at the commencement of the reign of Charles V. (1364), granted safe conduct to merchants for all descriptions of goods except ostrich feathers, which they seized and appropriated to themselves on every occasion.

M. Quicherat, who quotes this fact in proof of the great value set by the French on these novel ornaments, gives us an engraving of a "damoiseau d'environ 1370," copied from Willemin, "Recueil de Monuments inédits," wearing the single feather ; in this instance, on the left side of a round cap, which, together with the close-fitting hood beneath it and the doublet, is made of "drap de raye," striped cloth, the stripes being perpendicular and not athwart as had been the mode formerly.[2] (See woodcut on the next page.)

---

[1] Rot. Parl. MS. Harl. Brit. Mus., No. 7059.   (Strutt, ' Dress and Habits,' Part v., chap. ii.)

[2]   " Now in every town
              The ray is turned overthwart that should stand adown."
                                          Wright's *Political Songs.*

In the reign of Richard II., the single feather was worn in front of the chaperon (see Dictionary, p. 303; article HOUPPELANDE).

Of the costume of Scotland we are still left in ignorance. The rudely-sculptured stones of uncertain dates that time has spared to us, convey no distinct ideas of the dress of the few human beings that can be distinguished upon them; and her national historians are on that subject as brief as they are vague. Fordun, who wrote in 1350, contents himself with describing the Highlanders as "of goodly person, but misshapen attire;" and even Froissart —the minute, pictorial Froissart— in his account of Edward III.'s expedition in 1326, merely tells us that ten thousand pairs of old, worn-out shoes, made of undressed leather with the hair on, were left behind by the Scotch on that midnight retreat which baffled the English and terminated the inglorious campaign. The Scottish kings and nobility are represented on their seals in robes and armour precisely similar to those worn in England.

Chamberlain, reign 1370. Willemin, 'Mon. inédits.'

Of the Irish we know a little more. Amongst the spoils left by the sons of Brian Rae when they fled from Mortogh, A.D. 1313, were shining scarlet cloaks; and the barbaric splendour or quaintness of the Irish chiefs seems to have caught the fancy of the English settlers in the reign of Edward III., as we find the use of the Irish dress prohibited to them in the celebrated Statute of Kilkenny, passed during the administration of Edward's son, the Duke of Clarence. One clause in this Act ordains that the English in Ireland shall conform in garb and in the cut of their hair to the fashion of their countrymen in England: whosoever affected that of the Irish should be treated as an Irishman, which obviously meant *ill*-treated. Irish frieze, however, was at the time a manufacture highly esteemed in England, for a statute passed in the twenty-eighth year of the reign of Edward III. exempts it from duty, under the description of "Draps appellez frizeware queux sont faitz en Ireland."

In the reign of Richard II. we have a description by Froissart of the four Irish kings who swore allegiance to that monarch, by which it would appear that the truis had been abandoned, or at this time was not a part of the Irish regal habit; for Henry Christall, who gave Froissart the information, complains that they wore no breeches (*brayes*), and that consequently he ordered some of linen cloth to be made for them, taking from them at the same time many ill-made things, "tous d'habits comme d'autres choses," and dressing them in houppelandes of silk furred with miniver and gris, for, he adds, "formerly these kings were well dressed if wrapped up in an Irish mantle." By *brayes*, however, he may have meant *drawers*, always so called at that time, and to go without which was esteemed, both in England and France at that period, a penance and a shame. Christall's ordering them to be made of *linen* cloth is in favour of this supposition, as to supply the place of truis he would have ordered garments of *woollen*, and by the name of hose or chausses. We have no pictorial representation of them at that period except in armour in the 'Metrical History of Richard II.,' as will be seen later in this chapter, and there certainly the king is barefooted. The length of his coat of mail, extending to his ankles, prevents our ascertaining whether he is also bare-legged.

Our authorities for continental costume at this period become overwhelming, and we must limit ourselves to the most interesting and instructive. On the next page are Italian examples, three of which were copied by M. Bonnard from a splendid and profusely illuminated MS. of Titus Livius in the Ambrosian Library, at Milan, of which the date is not precisely ascertained, but may be fairly ascribed to the latter half of the fourteenth century.

With the exception of the round-toed shoes and peculiar head-dress of Can de la Scala, who died in 1329, there is scarcely any difference observable in the male costume from that of France and

England at that period ; and the military belt over the hips, the chaperon with its long cornette, the abacot with a single feather, the supertotus or balandran, and the shoes "À la Poulaine," are all well-known features of European attire subsequent to 1350.

Can de la Scala.   1329.

Can Signorio.   1375.

Italian Costumes.   Latter half of 14th century.

The female costume is more remarkable. The effigy of a lady of the Savelli family, from her tomb in the church of St. Sabina at Rome, dated 1315, offers a peculiar example of a head-dress. The next two, from the Ambrosian MS. above mentioned, are interesting in several particulars. One figure presents us with an early instance of a hood, of which several varieties appear in the following century amongst the head-dresses of the bourgeoisie of Paris. The same figure has a dress the body of which is party-coloured, being divided diagonally, the left side white, and the right as

Lady of the Savelli Family. Church of
St. Sabina, Rome. 1315.

Young Italian woman, circa 1390.

well as the skirt blue. The waist is unconfined by a girdle. The sleeves are of the form known in our own times as *gigot*. The dress of the other figure is so perfectly modern that it might be mistaken for that of a girl about twenty years ago, when the gigot sleeves were in fashion. The hair neatly rolled and braided at the back of the head increases the similitude; but this mode of arranging the hair is classical in its origin, and has repeatedly come into fashion in later times. It was much worn in the fourteenth, and again in the fifteenth century, as well as very recently.

Subjoined are Italian costumes of a date corresponding with that of the reign of our Richard II., and displaying similar features: a signor of Rimini, from a copy of Petrarch's Poems in the Barberini Library at Rome, *circa* 1386; a lady and gentleman of Florence, from an early copy of Boccaccio, in the National Library at Paris, about the same period; young Florentine gentlemen and ladies, from paintings by Ambrogio Lorenzetti and Taddeo Gaddi.

The costume of the lady, copied by Bonnard from a painting by Lorenzetti, who died in 1340, is remarkable for the fashion of the sleeve, which, open from the elbow to the wrist, is confined by buttons at intervals, so as to show the under one of some fine white material, giving it the appearance of the slashed and puffed sleeves of the fifteenth and sixteenth centuries. The male figure, also from Bonnard, was copied by him from the effigy, it is supposed, of one Alexander Vitelleschi, who lived in the time of the Lower Empire, but which was certainly not sculptured previous to the fourteenth century. The character of the sleeve is decisive of the date, and its attribution to Vitelleschi may be erroneous.

The Dream of Life
(Italian Costume of the 14th Century)

From a view ... in the Cloister of the Campo Santo at Pisa

Italian Lady. From a painting by Ambrogio Lorenzetti, circa 1340.

From a painting by Gaddi. 1360.

From an effigy at Carmine, circa 1370.

A Gentleman of Florence. From a MS. copy of Boccaccio, circa 1360.

Florentine Lady. 1360. From the same.

A Signor of Rimini.
From a MS. copy of Petrarch, circa 1380.

Young Florentines.   From a painting by Dello, circa 1500.

Venetian costume, late 15th century.   From Vecellio.

Venetian costume, late 16th century.   From Vecellio.

The costume of Venice is always exceptional. We have been so familiarized with its peculiar features in the sixteenth century, that it is difficult to dissociate our minds from the ideas impressed upon them by the glorious portraits bequeathed to us by Titian, and the spirited engravings of Weigel. There is no disputing, however, that the dresses of the Doge and senators of earlier times differed materially from those we have accustomed ourselves to consider the special costume of that once powerful republic from its earliest foundation. The mosaics still existing in St. Mark's, and the collection of Vecellio, sufficiently prove that fact (see pages 54 and 79), but the latter contains representations of the male and female attire of Venice in the fourteenth century corresponding in some points to that of other European cities at the same period (see woodcuts, pp. 98 and 99).

The large open sleeves ("maniche aperte") of the upper garment, corresponding with those so satirized by English writers in the latter half of the fourteenth century, were not allowed in Venice to trail on the ground and sweep away the filth out of the street, but were discreetly turned back to the shoulders ("voltate sopra le spalle"), to which they must have been fastened by some means not apparent. (See figs. 4 and 5 on last page.) Vecellio informs us that this fashion was called "alla Dogalina"[1] (in the Latin text, "Ducalis vestis cum latis manicis"), and that it was worn by both sexes. The other sort of sleeves, resembling the pokys or bag-pipe sleeves condemned by the Monk of Evesham, are called by Vecellio "a corneo" and "a gomito" (in Latin, "cubitalis" and "cuneatis"). (See figs. p. 98.)

The most important variation is in the biretta or corno of the Doge, which, from the conical cap seen in the earliest mosaics, gradually acquires the well-known form it displays in the sixteenth century, and retained to the last days of the Republic. The subjoined engravings are from the coins of the Doges, from Francesco Dandolo, 1328–1339, to Giovanni Delfino, 1356–1361 :—

Jean Musso, or Mussis, the historian of Placenza, says: "At this present time, that is to say the year of Christ MCCCLXXXVIII, the men and women of Placenza give themselves up to the greatest expenses for their dress and their food, and for everything beyond that which is befitting; for the women wear ample and long simarres of silk-velvet, brocade, and tissues of gold and silk, scarlet and violet woollen stuffs of the most precious description. . . . These simarres have very large sleeves, so long that they cover half the hand, and often touch the ground. They are very wide at the shoulders, and terminate in points something like the Catalonian bucklers, which are broad at top and sharp and narrow at the bottom.[2] Often they enrich their simarres with three, and even five, ounces of pearls; or they ornament them with a broad border of gold about the neck, as well as the ends of their sleeves and the lower edge of their under-garment. They wear little hoods, or chapeaux, ornamented with gold embroidery and pearls, and gird their waists with fine belts of mingled gold and pearls." (Muratori, Rer. Ital. Script., t. xvi., p. 590.) Matrons, he adds, wear a large mantle, long enough to touch the ground, round at the bottom, and entirely open in front. This mantle was fastened by gold buttons or clasps enriched with pearls. Every lady had usually three of these mantles, each of a different stuff, lined with silk or perse, and ornamented with gold embroidery. When they did not wear the capuchon, they covered their heads with a light transparent veil of silk or cotton. Widows wore precisely the same dress, but black, without pearls or gold embroidery. To this they added a black hood, or a thin veil of cotton or linen.

The ample and long *simarra*, as the Italians call the gown, made of precious materials, with exceedingly wide and long sleeves, is well illustrated in the next woodcut, representing an Italian lady, from a picture of this date, copied by M. Bonnard.[3] The hair is neatly rolled and banded

---

[1] Such sleeves were called "à la Duchesse" in France in the sixteenth century.

[2] A curious incidental piece of information respecting Spanish military equipment in 1388.

[3] M. Bonnard attributes the picture from which this and other figures have been taken to an earlier date than I am inclined to do. The Vanni whose name appears upon it must surely be Andreas Vanni of Sienna, who painted between the years 1369 and 1413. The costume is certainly late fourteenth century.

Italian Lady (Bonnard).

German Lady (Hefner).

with gold, and, in lieu of a hood, she wears a turban-shaped "chapeau, ornamented with gold embroidery" of a network pattern. The particular locality is not stated, but the costume has the general character of that described by Musso.

These turban-shaped hats or caps—for they cannot be strictly classed under either denomination—appear to have consisted of a crown fitting the head, surrounded by a stuffed roll of such dimensions as the taste of the wearer suggested, the whole covered with some rich material, and occasionally ornamented with jewellery. Dr. Hefner has selected one from a German example, which is remarkable for its fantastic magnificence. The long sleeves, with their curious borders of cut-work or dagging, which no legal prohibition had the power to suppress, enable us to corroborate the date ascribed to it, viz. the termination of the fourteenth century, and corresponding with the extravagant fashions of the contemporary period in England.

Such "chapeaux" seem to have led to the adoption of the better-known coiffures which immediately succeeded them, and of which numberless varieties are seen during the greater part of the following century. These consisted in the removing of the stuffed roll ("bourrelet," as the French call it) from the border of the crown, and disposing of it in various forms above it. (See Dictionary, under HEAD-DRESS.)

Towards the close of the century, the dresses of both sexes in France and England were made high in the

Charles VI., when young. From a MS. in the Nat. Lib., Paris.

neck. The portrait of Charles VI. of France, shortly after his accession to the throne in 1380, agrees in every respect with the costume we find depicted in the Metrical History of the Deposition of Richard II., from which valuable MS. I have already borrowed some characteristic examples. (See Dictionary, p. 163.) As this fashion was continued during the reign of Henry IV. and his contemporaries, its further illustration is reserved for the next chapter.

In 1306, Rudolph of Nuremberg discovered the art of wire-drawing, by which riveted mail, or suits "à points d'orge," as they are called by French writers, were brought within the reach of almost every man-at-arms. Jointed plate-armour, of which all the defensive improvements and probably the very invention were fairly due to the armourers beyond the Rhine, thenceforth became more generally adopted by knights and nobles, and gradually attained a high degree of perfection. (Demmin, ' Weapons of War.')

A great and total change took place during the fourteenth century in the military equipment. Towards the close of the reign of Edward I., the elbows and the knees had been additionally protected by pieces of plate, known as poleyns and genouillères; in the following reign protections for the legs and arms, jambeaux and brassarts, were added; and before the end of the century the whole body was cased in plate. The principal cause of this alteration was, according to Sir Samuel Meyrick, the excessive weight of the chain mail, with its accompanying garments; so great, indeed, that the knights sometimes sank under it, suffocated with the heat as well as the burden. This great improvement, he tells us, was of Italian origin. The Florentine Annals give the year 1315 as the date of a new regulation by which every horseman who went into battle was to have his helmet, breast-plate, gauntlets, cuisses, and jambs all of iron—a precaution taken on account of the disadvantage which their cavalry had suffered from their *light* armour at the battle of Catina. "So," Sir Samuel remarks, "that what was adopted by them to supply a deficiency, was assumed by the soldiers of Northern Europe as a relief from the superabundance of their defensive armour." He does not tell us, however, what the "light armour" previously worn was composed of, probably cuir-bouilli; but this order could surely apply to certain troops only, as there appears no reason to doubt that the same armour was worn in Italy as in other parts of Europe. Also, if 1315 was the date of the alteration, the "improvement" must have been unusually long in extending to France and England, where complete plate is not found till nearly one hundred years later.

Nor as far as weight goes could there have been much difference during the fourteenth century, for the breast and back plates were actually additions in the first instance to the rest of the armour. What French armour consisted of in 1316, we possess the most precise information in an inventory taken in that year of the armour of Louis X. (le Hutin), king of France and Navarre. I extract from it the following items :—Thirty-three high gorgets, lined with chambli;[1] a panzer[2] and an arm of steel jazerant; a panzer and an arm of ring-mail of superior riveting; a panzer and an arm of steel much stronger, of ring mail of superior riveting; a panzer with an arm of steel, with a camail of the same; three Pizan collars of steel jazerant; a barbière[3] of superior riveting of chambli; a jazerant of steel; a steel haubergeon with hand-coverings; an entire hauberk from Lombardy; two other haubergeons from Lombardy; three pair of chausses of iron; eight pairs of chauçons and one chauçon beside;[4] a new plate covered with vermilion samit; three pairs of greaves, and three pairs

---

[1] " Hautes gorgitres double de chambli." " High double gorgets of Chambli." (Meyrick.) *Doubler* is "to line;" "double gorgets" seems to me inadmissible. Chambli must surely be the name of a material so called after the place of its manufacture. The word occurs a few lines lower—" Une barbière de haute clouure de chamble." I suspect we should read "doublé de chambli," as in the former instance; the "haute clouure" applying only to the *barbire*. I cannot find Chambli elsewhere. Might it mean camlet, much used for lining in the Middle Ages?

[2] " Un *pane*." " Breast-piece." (Meyrick.) The panzer, panchena, is constantly mentioned by later writers. "Haubers et pansibres." (Olivier de la Marche.) The *panser* of the tenth century was a tunic of quilted linen. The *panzer* of the fifteenth century was of steel, and protected the abdomen only. The "pans" here mentioned may be either. It was a time of transition.

[3] " Une barbière de haute clouure." " A head-piece—whence a person wearing armour was said to be barbed." (Meyrick.) A head-piece similar to the bascinet was called *barbuta* in Italy; but *quarre*, should we not read *bauiere*? Meyrick renders *haute clouure* "superior riveting." In the same inventory I find "une couverture de mailles ronde *doury clodes*." " Haute clouure" would consequently indicate stronger workmanship; but the glossarists do not assist us.

[4] " Un chauçons par dessus." Surely this is conclusive as to the meaning of *chausons*. (See Dictionary, p. 95.)

of steel pouloines;[1] six other pairs of steel greaves and two pairs of pouloines; two steel heaumes; five other heaumes, of which one is gilt, and five chaperons, of which two are gilt; two corses of steel;[2] two round bascinets; four swords ornamented with silver, of which two are garnished with samit and two with leather; a parrying sword ornamented with silver, the pommel and hilt enamelled; eight swords of Toulouz,[3] and two misericordes; seventeen swords of Bray; a sword of John d'Orgeret,[4] and two swords and one misericorde of Vezi;[5] fifteen ordinary swords; seven glaive blades of Toulouze; two ordinary ones, and the excellent blade of the king's glaive; a silver fleur-de-lys gilt, not of standard value, to place on the king's heaume; a gauntlet covered with vermilion velvet; a gamboised coat of white cendal; two housses[6] and two tunicles of the arms of France, and the chapeau of the same; two tunicles and a gambeson, each with a border of the arms of France; two tunicles beaten with the arms of France; two embroidered sleeves; three pairs of bracers[7] of leather, of the arms of France; four pairs of spurs garnished with silk, and two pairs garnished with leather; an estuivans[8] of plates garnished with samite; two chapels de fer covered; three wooden shields with the arms of the king, and one of steel; five coats beaten with the king's arms and furred, and one with the fur off; three coats without fur beaten of the king's arms; a collar of the king's arms; a quantity of aiguillettes and laces for arming; six bascinets; a gamboised thigh-piece, and an *esquivalens*[9] of leather; a tunic and housse of cloth, with the arms of France and Navarre of Cypress gold; a housse and tunic of plain cloth with the arms of France and Navarre; an old jupel[10] of the arms of France, with embroidered flowers; a thigh-piece without poulaines of the arms of France; a gamboised coat embroidered with gold trees and goldfinches;[11] one shield and two targets of France and Navarre, and one Indian (or blue) shield with gold letters on it, and a chapeau of cloth of France and Navarre.

The student of costume will find much to interest and not a little to puzzle him in this curious contemporary document (but casually noticed by Mr. Hewitt, and unnoticed by M. Quicherat), out of which I have selected only those items which refer to armour and dress. I confess it has puzzled *me*, and that it is with considerable diffidence I have ventured to differ from Sir Samuel Meyrick in my interpretation of several terms and passages in it, as will be seen by the notes I have appended. Having to consider the general reader, I must refer the more critical inquirer to the original in old French, which is printed *in extenso* in the first volume of Meyrick's 'Ancient Armour,' page 135, second edition, with his translation and commentaries.

As example is said to be better than precept, so is delineation better than description. I will therefore illustrate the armour of the fourteenth century by engravings of the most authentic monuments, paintings, or records of the Transition period throughout Europe.

Our English examples are from the effigies of Sir John de Creke, 1325; Prince John of Eltham, 1334; William de Aldeburg, 1360 (see also Edward the Black Prince, 1376, Dict., p. 317), which exhibit the alterations in the forms of the bascinet and the surcoat and the introduction of the jupon. For other varieties see article ARMOUR in Dictionary, pp. 16 and 17.

As regards Scotland, we learn from the Statutes of Robert I., 1318, that every layman possessed of land, who had ten pounds worth of moveable property, was commanded to provide himself with an acton (or haqueton) and basnet (bascinet), together with gloves of plate, a sword and a spear; those

[1] It is not clear whether these "*pouloines*" were *poleyns* (*i.e.* elbow-pieces) or *poulaines*, pointed-toed solleretts. If the latter, it is an early occurrence of the term. Their association with greaves in the following item would favour such an opinion, added to the fact of their being described as "pairs."
[2] "2 cors d'acier." Meyrick has "bodies."   [3] Toulouse in France, or Tolosa in Spain?
[4] "Jean d'Orgeret." The name of the owner or the maker? If the latter, a fact to make a note of.   [5] Vezi.
[6] "2 housces." Meyrick renders this "two pairs of hose;" an evident mistake. (See Dictionary.)
[7] "Deux paires de braciers en cuer." Either bracers for archers, or brassarts (*brachières*). The context is rather in favour of the first interpretation.   [8] "Estuivans." A boot or leg-guard; from *Stiefel*, Germ.
[9] Meyrick considers "esquivalens" to be synonymous with "estivans." It may be a clerical error for *estivalens*.
[10] "Jupel," for jupon, an early occurrence of the term.
[11] "Une cote gamboisée a arbroussiaux d'or, broudiee a chardonereus." Meyrick translates this "a gamboised coat with a rough surface (like a thicket) of gold embroidered on the nap of the cloth." I cannot possibly follow him. Trees and birds form one of the most favourite patterns in mediæval embroidery. "Chardonereus" must surely mean goldfinches.

who were not so provided were to have an iron jack, or back- and breast-plate of iron, an iron head-piece or knapiskay, with gloves of plate: and every man possessing the value of a cow was commanded to arm himself with a bow and sheaf of twenty-four arrows, or a spear. By the "iron jack" is meant the *jacques de mailles*, which was worn as late as the sixteenth century, when it is described by a French author, and the person who gave Holinshed his account of Scotland.

Sir John de Croke, 1315. Prince John of Eltham, 1334. William de Aldeburg, 1360.

In 1385, an order was issued for every French and Scottish soldier to wear a white St. Andrew's cross on his breast and back, which, if his surcoat was white, was to be embroidered on a division of black cloth.

In 1390, we are told both by Winton and Fordun, that the clan Kay and the clan Quhale were armed in the fashion of the country with bows and arrows, swords and targets, short knives and battle-axes. The short knife was the bidag.

In the Metrical History of the Deposition of King Richard II., Harleian MS. No. 1319, is a

McMorrough, King of Leinster. From Harleian MS. No. 1319.

curious drawing of McMorrough, king of Leinster, wearing a bascinet without a camail and a long hauberk, over which is the mantle with a tailed capuchon, the Irish caputium. His followers wear the capuchon and no bascinet. The king is bare-footed, and apparently bare-legged. Froissart, on the authority of Christall, says, "The Irish have pointed knives with broad blades, sharp on both sides"—the *skein*.

France furnishes us with contemporary monuments in the statues of Philip de Valois, erected by his order in the Cathedral at Paris, in fulfilment of a vow to the Virgin Mary at the battle of Cassel in 1328; Charles, Count of Alençon, killed at the Battle of Creçy, 1346, from Montfaucon; and one of the statues from the Castle of Pierre-fonds, sculptured in 1386, engraved from the copy by

M. Viollet-le-Duc, and affording an excellent example of the fantastic fashion of dagging, as it was called, the edges of every species of attire, civil or military, towards the end of the fourteenth century.

Philip de Valois. 1316.   Charles, Comte d'Alençon. 1346.   Statue at Pierrefonds. 1386.

From a host of Italian examples, I have selected the following:—Statue of a knight, in marble, in the church of St. Domenico, Naples, dated 1335, in armour resembling that of Guillaume Berardi at Florence, given at page 76; effigy of a knight from a sepulchral monument at Pisa, *circa* 1340; Mastino II., from his equestrian statue at Verona, 1352; and Bernabo Visconti, at Milan, 1385. (See next page.)

Venice appears to demand a separate notice on all occasions, having preserved through all ages some peculiar characteristics in her costume. We have here copied, from a painting by Aretino Spinello, a Doge of Venice, in armour, in the attitude of receiving a sword from a Pope. The Pope in the picture is meant for Alexander III., and the Doge consequently for the valiant old Sebastiano Zani, who defended his Holiness against the Emperor Frederick Barbarossa, and, according to tradition, received as a reward the celebrated ring with which he wedded the Adriatic. The painting, however, is late fourteenth century;[1] but I cannot lament with M. Bonnard that the venerable artist depicted these famous personages in the habit of his own time, as we can rely on their accuracy, which I fear we should have hesitated to do had he attempted to represent them in the costume of the twelfth century. The Doge has over his armour of mixed plate and mail a jupon with the arms of Venice within a circle on the back, and probably also on the breast. We give in addition one of the officers in attendance on him. To these interesting figures I add the portrait of the great Venetian general Victor Pisani, who died in 1380, from his statue in the Arsenal at Venice.

Dr. Hefner, in his valuable work 'Des Christlichen Mittelalters,' has given engravings of two knights from a picture in the Gallery at Frankfort, which he attributes to a Flemish painter of the

---

[1] Aretino Spinello is said to have been born at Arezzo, in 1308, and to have painted these frescoes with the assistance of his son, Gaspari Spinello, in 1407! Others place his death in 1400. The biographers of nearly all the early painters are lamentably untrustworthy.

Knight at Naples. 1533.

Knight at Pisa, circa 1300.

Mastino II. 1351.

Bernabo Visconti. 1385.

Doge of Venice, in armour, late 14th century.

Venetian soldier.

Victor Pisani. 1380.

PLATE XXI.

EFFIGY OF AN ALSATIAN KNIGHT, 1350-1370.
(From Schoepflin's *Alsatia Illustrata*, 1751, &c.)

fifteenth century,[1] the subject being the Martyrdom of St. George. The costume induces me to consider the painting must be of earlier date. The absence of all plate in the armour, and the peculiar shape of the surcoats, point to the first part of the fourteenth century; and admitting that

Christian and Pagan Knights. From Hefner.

such fashions may have lasted longer in the Netherlands, and also that the warrior with the sword is presumed to be intended to represent a Pagan, I still doubt the painting being later than 1400. The figures, however, are too curious too omit, and I therefore introduce them in this chapter, by no means insisting on an opinion which has not been formed upon an examination of the original.

Dr. Hefner has liberally provided us with authorities for the illustration of German armour. We have here Gunter von Schwarzburg, king of the Romans, 1349, from his tomb in the Cathedral of Frankfort-on-the-Maine (to the camail is attached a nasal of plate to be made fast to the front of the bascinet, so that the eyes only would be left unguarded; similar nasals are frequently at this period seen attached to the camails of knights); effigy of Hartman von Kroneberg, 1372, from his tomb at Kroneberg; wood-carving in Bamberg Cathedral, *circa* 1370; Conrad von Bickenbach, 1393, from his monument at Roellfeld, near Aschaffenburg.

Plate XXI. affords us an elaborate representation of an Alsatian knight of the first half of the fourteenth century, from a sepulchral effigy engraved by Schœpflin in his 'Alsatia illustrata,' tome ii.

For Spanish armour of the fourteenth century we recur to Señor Carderera's interesting and finely-executed work, and select from it the effigy of Don Ramon Folch, Visconde de Cardona, in the monastery of Poblet, who died in 1320; and also of Don Alfonso, Señor de Ajufria, in the monastery of S. Domingo de Selos, Toledo, who died in 1382. We are also indebted to M. Demmin, who has copied a mural painting in the Cathedral of Mondoneda representing the Massacre of the

---

[1] "Master Wilhelms." I can find no painter of that name living in the fifteenth century. Marcus Willems was born at Mechlin in 1526, and died in 1561. The picture cannot possibly be a work of the sixteenth century.

Günter von Schwarzburg. 1349.

Hartman von Kronenberg. 1372.

Conrad von Bickenbach. 1393.

Wood-carving in Bamberg Cathedral. 1370.

Don Ramon Folch, Visconde de Cardona. 1320.

Don Alfonso, Señor de Aguilar. 1380.

PLATE XXII.

EQUESTRIAL FIGURE AT PRAGUE BOHEMIA

Innocents, a favourite subject with mediæval artists, from which we derive the additional advantage of authorities for the female costume of the period. The figures are so rudely drawn that something must be left to our imagination, but they are well worth studying. "The soldiers," M. Demmin points out, "carry swords with the 'pas d'âne' guard:" that is the name given to the ring-shaped sword-guard below the cross-piece on each side of the blade, and which is not generally met with until the second half of the sixteenth century. Their body armour appears to consist of trellised coats or regulated hauberks, with short sleeves, and jackets or jupons over them. One has a jupon of jazerant work, and all wear conical bascinets and gorgets of plate, that of the figure in the jazerant resembling the one in the effigy of Ramon Folch. Three of the bascinets have oreillets. The legs and forearms have no armour, and the feet are without sollerets or armed shoes. M. Demmin observes that "all the armour of these warriors is on the whole very defective, considering the time (second half or end of the fourteenth century), and inferior to English, French, and German equipments of the same period." The Armeria Real contains no armour of the fourteenth century, and I found nothing of an early period in the collection at Lisbon except a few battle-axes of the fifteenth century.

From a mural painting in the Cathedral of Mondonedo.

At page 476 of the Dictionary I have alluded to the mention of armour of splints in the time of Edward III. of England. I have now the pleasure of illustrating that subject by a plate representing an equestrian figure at Prague, a cast of which is in the Crystal Palace, and affords us a most interesting example of "a suit of splints" of the fourteenth century. The plates are much narrower than those used two hundred years later, but nothing can exceed the exquisite workmanship displayed in their construction. The more the figure is studied, the greater must be our admiration of the delicacy and beauty of the articulations, which must have rendered the hauberk as pliant as if it had been made of silk instead of steel. (See Plate XXII.)

In ecclesiastical costume the principal points to notice are the general increase in the splendour of the sacerdotal vestments, and the appearance of the double and triple crowned tiara of the Roman Pontiff. I have shown, I think incontestably, that previous to the end of the thirteenth century the tiara had only one crown. When and by whom two others were added, is still an open question. It must have been, however, before 1342, as the statue of Pope Benedict XII., who died in that year, is to be seen in the Vatican with a tiara surrounded by two crowns, giving support to the opinion of Marengoni that the second was added by either Clement V. or John XXII. A fragment of an effigy in the Museum at Avignon, said to be a portion of one of Pope Clement VII.,

1378, but which M. Viollet-le-Duc, who has engraved it, considers to be the head of a recumbent statue of John XXII. (1316–1334) which was in the church of Notre Dame des Doms in that city, and was destroyed in 1792, has two crowns round the bonnet, which has assumed a sugar-loaf shape ;

Head of statue of Pope John XXII. (?)

Head of effigy of Pope Urban V.

but the upper part is so dilapidated that it would be hazardous to affirm that there had or had not been a third in its original state. There is also in the same museum a sepulchral effigy of Urban V., elected in 1362, and who died December 10, 1370. The tiara is *triple*-crowned, and from that period remained so. As an example of the sumptuousness of the clerical vestments in the fourteenth century, I have selected that of a canon from Lenoir's 'Statistique Monumental de Paris,' the embroidery of whose chasuble is most elaborate. Part of its ornamentation so closely resembles the pallium of an archbishop, that it might be easily mistaken for it.

In continuation of my notices of the Greek Church, I subjoin the figure of St. James the Apostle, from a fresco on the wall of the Church of St. Sophia at Trebizond, erected *temp.* Alexis, *circa* 1350, and recently discovered by the fall of the plaster with which it had been overlaid by the Turks. The apostle is represented in white robes, wearing the omophorium.

We have now arrived at a period when costume acquires a novel and most interesting feature in the habits of orders of chivalry, the earliest and most famous of all being our own Order of the Garter, instituted by King Edward III. in the twenty-second year of his reign, A.D. 1348. I am not called upon here to discuss the vexed question of the origin of the Order. It has not yet been discovered, and probably never will be. The recorded one is simply the uniting not only of the native knights with one another, but of foreigners with them, in the bonds of fellowship and peace ; and

Canon. From Lenoir's 'Stat. Mon. de Paris.'

Figure of St. James at Trebizond.

my only business here is with the vestments by which the companions of the Order were distinguished. These were originally a mantle, tunic, and capuchon of the fashion of the time, all of blue woollen cloth, those of the knights companions differing only from the sovereign's by the tunic being lined with miniver instead of ermine. The tunic and capuchon were powdered, *i.e.* thickly embroidered with garters of blue and gold, bearing the motto "Honi soit qui mal y pense;" the mantle, lined with scarlet cloth, having one larger than all the rest on the left shoulder, enclosing a shield *argent* charged with the cross of St. George, *gules.* Edward III. had 168 garters embroidered on his tunic and capuchon.

In the thirty-fourth year of his reign the colour of the tunic was changed to black, as a sign of humiliation, in consequence, Ashmole conjectures, of the pestilence then raging; and in the thirty-seventh year it was made of *sanguine ingrain,* which is generally understood to be *purple.* The capuchon always varied with the colour of the tunic.

The garter was of blue cloth or silk embroidered with gold, with buckle and chape of silver-gilt, and worn round the left knee, as appears from the effigy of Sir Richard Pembridge (fiftieth knight) : but it is a curious fact that it is not visible on the effigy of Edward the Black Prince or of any other original Knight of the Garter, nor in any illumination of the period ; neither does any mention of a garter to be worn round the knee occur in any wardrobe account of the period.

No representation of a Knight of the Garter in his habit that I am at present acquainted with is as early as the fourteenth century, in the course of which the tunic (or surcoat) and chaperon underwent several changes of colour. In the seventh year of the reign of Richard II. they were of "violet ingrain;" in the eleventh year, white; and in the twelfth and nineteenth, of long blue cloth, as originally.

The institution of this celebrated Order seems to have excited nearly every sovereign prince in Europe to follow the example of the chivalrous King of England.

Louis of Anjou, king of Sicily and Jerusalem, instituted in 1352 the Order of the Knot, also called "L'Ordre du St. Esprit au droit désir." The history of this Order is so curious that, as it can be very briefly related, I shall not hesitate to give it nearly in the words of M. le Laboureur, to whom we are indebted for it. King Louis having no issue by Queen Jane, his wife and cousin, the Order became extinct at his death, and was so utterly lost sight of, amidst the disorders and revolutions in the kingdom of Naples, that it would have never been remembered had not the original statutes come into the possession of the State of Venice, and been presented by the Senate to Henry III. of France when passing through that city on his return from Poland. He was the more interested in them from the circumstance that he was born on the eve of Pentecost, and had been crowned on the same day king of Poland, and afterwards of France, as Louis had likewise been crowned on the same day king of Jerusalem and Sicily. He resolved therefore to appropriate them, and pass them off as his own composition, and, after having copied and commented on the statutes, commanded the *Sieur de Chiverny* to burn them. But that gentleman felt it against his conscience to destroy so rare a document, which, beside the interest of its subject and its antiquity, was rendered more valuable by the miniatures on vellum, illustrating the contents of each canon or statute. Thus, fortunately, they escaped the flames, and were carefully copied by M. de Gagnières, and subsequently engraved for Père Montfaucon's 'Antiquités de la Couronne de France.' Thanks to the latter, therefore, we are enabled to place before our readers several faithful representations of the habit of this short-lived Order, which are the more interesting and of consequence to this work as they illustrate the remarkable fashion prevailing in England at the same period, and which may probably have been borrowed from Naples.

Fig. 1. This knight is all in white, and bears the St. Esprit on his left breast. His costume is the ordinary one of a nobleman of the period, the sleeves of the surcoat terminating above the elbow, and having attached to them the long strips (coudières) described in Dictionary, p. 464 ; the edges of which, as well as those of the chaperon and of the surcoat, are cut into the shape of leaves—the fantastic fashion alluded to which, during the latter half of the fourteenth century, was carried to the most absurd extent in England and all over the Continent, despite of sumptuary laws, sermons, and satires (see DAGGES, Dictionary, p. 164).

Fig. 2. A knight in the habit of his Order, consisting of a mantle of blue (cloth?), lined with fur, open only on the right side, where it is fastened on the shoulder by a quantity of closely-set buttons,

Fig. 2.   Fig. 3.   Fig. 3.   Fig. 4.

Fig. 5.

and having the badge of the knot embroidered upon it in the centre of the upper portion. The mantle has a capuchon attached to it, and is worn over the ordinary dress. A sword with a peculiarly-shaped hilt hangs on his right side.

Fig. 3 is remarkable for the garment he wears over the surcoat, examples of which I have given and commented upon under HEUK (Dictionary, p. 267). It is frequently represented in these miniatures, the king, in some instances, as well as the knights being attired in it, and has a capuchon attached to it, if indeed it be not the cape of the capuchon itself, rendered unrecognizable by its fantastic cut. In this instance it is black, as are also the hose and shoes; and we learn from the statutes that the knights were ordered to appear so attired on Fridays in commemoration of the Passion of our Lord.

Fig. 4. The surcoat and capuchon of this personage are dark-blue, the borders of the former indented, or, as we should now say, vandyked, a favourite variety of dagging. The coudières are of ermine, and the capuchon has the absurdly long tail or liripipe of the time of Edward III. of England, the contemporary of the founder of this Order. The hose are red.

Fig. 5 is that of Louis of Anjou, distinguished only from his lieges by his crown, and having the badge of the St. Esprit embroidered on the right side of his surcoat, which may be only an ingenious mode of the painter's introduction of it, no other part of the garment being visible. In other instances the king has the badge of the knot on the front of the collar of the capuchon. The knights are enjoined by the statutes to wear the knot at all times on a conspicuous part of their dress, as it was the general badge of the Order ; but the honour of wearing that of the St. Esprit with and immediately over the knot was only conferred on a knight who had distinguished himself by some brilliant achievement in battle. The armed knights are represented with the knot on their surcoats and the St. Esprit on their banners.

For other minute details I must refer the reader to the plates of Montfaucon and the text describing them. They are worthy the study of the antiquary, and have been singularly ignored, or but slightly alluded to, by nearly every writer on costume, English or foreign, with whose works I am acquainted. M. Bonnard, who is one of the exceptions, and who relates the story of the preservation of the statutes, &c., does not give a single figure from the illuminations ; but quotes Montfaucon in order to illustrate the engraving of a knight copied from an effigy in the Church of St. Catherine at Pisa, whom he says, by the knots round his helmet and his shield, is easily recognized as a "chevalier du nœud." Louis d'Anjou died 25th May, 1362. The armour of this knight is of later date, but of course he might have outlived his sovereign and the extinction of the Order. I give it, however, under reservation, as a fine example of Italian military costume of the end of the fourteenth century. No badge of the knot is visible, but there is an ornament round the crest in the form of a knotted cord, and the border of his shield is similarly decorated.

Knight of the Knot (?). From Bonnard.

In 1362, Amadeus VI., Count of Savoy, called the Green Count, from his having appeared at a tournament in a green surcoat and the caparison of his horse being the same colour, founded "The Order of the Collar." Guichenon, in his 'Histoire Généalogique

Coin of the reign of Amadeus VI.

de la Maison Royale de Savoie,' has an engraving of a coin struck during the reign of this Count, on which he is represented seated in his robes of state, with his sword in his right hand and his left supporting his shield charged with the arms of Savoy. Round his neck is the collar of the Order, too minute to be defined ; but on the reverse of the coin it is clearly to be seen composed of lacs d'amour (true lover's knots), of the same shape as those of the Order of the Knot, intermingled with the word "FERT," the meaning of which has never been discovered.[1] This I take to be the earliest collar of knighthood of the existence of which we have

---

[1] It is necessary here, I think, to add a note on this subject. The persistence with which it is still repeated that this device originated in the relief of Rhodes by Amadeus V., called "the Great," Count of Savoy, in 1315, is one of the many proofs of the vitality of error. As long ago as 1660 Samuel Guichenon exploded that theory, by pointing out that it appears on the monument and coins of Thomas Count of Savoy, who died in 1233 ; on a silver pence of his son, Peter of Savoy, before his accession in 1263 ; and also on the coinage of Louis of Savoy, Baron de Vaud, who died in 1301. These facts completely dispose of the assertion that the letters F.E.R.T. are the initials of "Fortitudo ejus Rhodium tenuit," divided by points, as they are seen without such punctuation upwards of eighty years before the event they were supposed to allude to took place. They are also fatal to the grosser interpretation of Favine, and to a third suggestion attributing the invention of the device to Amadeus VI., who founded the Order. Its origin remains in the same obscurity which envelopes that of the "Honi soit qui mal y pense" of the Garter, the "Ich dien" of the Prince of Wales's feathers, the SS. of the Collar of the House of Lancaster, and many other celebrated devices. The tradition that the change of the

satisfactory evidence; but as the Order fell into disuse, and was reinstituted with a new collar under the name of "The Order of the Annunciation" by Amadeus VIII., first duke of Savoy, in 1434.

it must be classed with decorations similarly superseded, and yield priority of rank to such as have remained unchanged to the present day.

In 1370, Louis II., duke of Bourbon, founded the Order of the "Écu d'or," and of this we have also contemporary pictorial evidence in an illumination in the 'Livre des Hommages du Comte de Clermont en Beauvoisis,' which has been copied and engraved in Montfaucon. The Duke is represented admitting a knight into the Order. The only mark of distinction is the gold shield which is embroidered on the breast of Louis and all the knights in attendance on him, however attired. There is no appearance of a collar, though modern writers have assigned to it an elaborate one. The robe of the Duke is noticeable, as the bars of fur upon the shoulder, frequently seen in the succeeding century, put in here a very early appearance. They were evidently the origin of those which subsequently distinguished the degrees of our English peers, and do so to this day.

An order of knighthood called "de la Banda" (the Band) is said to have been founded by Alfonso XI., king of Castile and Leon, in 1332. This date, could it be identified, would give it a priority to the Order of the Garter. The band undoubtedly appears on effigies of Spanish knights of the latter half of the century, like the grand cordon of an order as now worn over one shoulder (see effigy of Alfonso, Señor de Ajufria, page 108 *ante*).

Louis II. and Knight of the "Écu d'or."

The change in colour of the national crosses, French and English, is presumed to have occurred during the reign of Philip VI., surnamed de Valois, 1328–1350; the English assuming the red cross and the French adopting the white, distinctions which have remained unaltered since that period. I have seen no satisfactory reason assigned for this remarkable exchange of the national insignia at this particular date, and confine myself therefore to recording the fact, which is sufficiently established by contemporary pictorial authority.

In this century we first meet with positive evidence of the wearing of black clothes for mourning in France and England, after the fashion, we may presume, of Spain, where I have noticed the usage in the twelfth century. The first instance recorded of it in this country was in 1364, when Edward III. and his court wore black mourning habits for the death of John II., king of France. From this period we find frequent mention of them, and during this century they first appear in monuments and illuminations. Froissart informs us that the King of Cyprus, like Edward III. of England, clothed himself "in black mourning" for the French King John; that the Earl of Foix, on hearing of the death of his son Gaston, sent for his barber and was close shaved, and clothed himself and all his household in black; and at the funeral of the Count of Flanders all the nobles and attendants wore black gowns. Chaucer, in 'The Knight's Tale,' speaks of Palamon's appearing at Arcite's funeral "in clothes black, dropped all with tears." In his 'Troylus and Cressyde' he says, "Creyseyde was in widowe habit blacke;" and again he describes her "in widowe's habit of large samite *broun*;"

arms of Savoy from OR an eagle VERT to GULES a cross ARGENT, was made in commemoration of the assistance rendered to the Knights Hospitallers by Amadeus (the Great) on the above occasion, is equally erroneous, the cross appearing on his seals to charters executed in 1296 and 1310.

by which it would appear that brown was occasionally worn for mourning, and that Froissart's expression "in black mourning" implied that other colours were sometimes worn as mourning and marked the distinction. Strutt has engraved figures in mourning-dress from a MS. of the fourteenth century preserved at Westminster, and the statuettes round the tomb of Sir Roger de Kerdeston, who died in 1337, represent the relations of the deceased knight wearing their own coloured clothes under black cloaks.

Mourning habits. From a MS. of the 14th century, erroneously entitled by Strutt ' Liber Regalis.'

Statuettes from the tomb of Sir Roger de Kerdeston. 1335.

CHAPTER VI.

THE FIFTEENTH CENTURY.

UR sixth chapter comprises the remainder of that period which has received the appellation of "the Middle Ages." In England it includes the reigns of Henry IV., Henry V., Henry VI., Edward IV., Richard III., and all but the last nine years of that of Henry VII.—stirring and troublous times, of which the most deplorable portion was the struggle between the rival houses of York and Lancaster.

But little difference appears in the civil attire of the various classes during the first two reigns from that introduced into England towards the end of the reign of Richard II. The long and short gowns, with sweeping sleeves fancifully indented at the edges, or with *poky* or bagpipe sleeves, mentioned by the Monk of Evesham, formed the general upper garments of high and low, according to their own good-will and pleasure, and in contempt of indignant censors and

From MS. in University Library, Wurzburg.   German Lady, 15th cent.

parliamentary enactments. (See Dictionary, p. 466, for examples of the dress of the commonalty.) I introduce here a German specimen of regal female costume of the first half of the fifteenth century, from the MS. in the University Library at Wurzburg which afforded me an illustration of the fashion of dagging at that period (Dictionary, p. 165). The extreme ugliness and inconvenience of these *pokys* had not been equalled since the days of Rufus and Henry I. in England. A more picturesque costume of a German lady of the same period is copied from a MS. in the Library at Darmstadt. There are few better sources of information respecting costume than the sumptuary laws to which I have just alluded, defining so strictly what should and what should not be worn by men and women of all degrees and conditions. Here is the substance of a statute which Henry IV. considered it necessary to have passed in the fourth year of his reign, A.D. 1403.

No man not being a banneret, or person of higher estate, shall wear any cloth of gold, of crimson, of velvet or motley velvet, nor large hanging sleeves open or closed (*overt ne close*), nor his *gown* so long as to touch the ground, nor use the furs of ermine, lettice, or martins, excepting only men of arms when in armour—"*gens d'armes quant ils seunt armez,*"[1]—who may dress themselves according to their pleasure. No clergyman below the dignity of a resident canon of a cathedral or collegiate church shall wear a large hood, furred or lined, extending beyond the points of his shoulders. Exceptions are made in favour of the Lord Chancellor, the Barons of the Exchequer, and other great officers belonging to the King's Court; Masters of Divinity, Doctors of Law, and the regents of the Universities.[2] Four years afterwards, the privilege was extended to serjeants belonging to the Court, who might wear such hoods as they pleased, for the honour of the king and dignity of their stations. No clergyman below the degrees above mentioned shall wear any furs of pure miniver, of grey, or of biche, nor any kind of gilt harness ("harnays endorrez").[3]

No clergyman beneath the estate of an archbishop or bishop shall use any facings of ermine or miniver upon his garments. To this clause it was afterwards added (8th Henry IV.), that in future no chaplain shall wear a girdle, baselard, or any other implement decorated with silver, and that no esquire, apprentice to the law ("nul esquier, apprentice le loy"), nor clerk of the Chancery or of the Exchequer, or in any other place at the Court, in the household of the king, or residing with any of the lords of the realm, shall use any garments furred with grey, christe-grey, miniver, or biche; nor shall they wear any ornaments of pearls or other jewellery, ouches or beads, nor any other accoutrements of gold: but in this instance the Mayor for the time being of the City of London, the mayors of Warwick, *Brisbie* (perhaps for *Bristol*), and other free towns, accustomed heretofore to wear such furs, had permission to follow the common usage.

No yeoman ("vadlet appellé yeoman") shall wear any other furs than those of foxes, of conies, and of otters.

No person shall use baselards, girdles, daggers, or horns decorated with silver, nor any other harness of silver, unless he be possessed of the yearly income, in lands and tenements, to the amount of twenty pounds, or of goods and chattels to the value of two hundred pounds, except such as are heirs to estates of the yearly value of fifty marks, or to the possession in goods and chattels to the amount of five hundred pounds.

That no yeoman may wear ouches or beads of gold.

That the wife of an esquire, if she be not ennobled, shall not use any furs of ermine, lettice, pure miniver, or grey, excepting the wives of the mayors of London, Warwick, and other free towns, the gentlewomen belonging to the Queen, and the chief maiden attendants of a princess, duchess, or countess.

Four years afterwards another statute was added to the foregoing, by which it was ordained that no man, let his condition be what it might, should be permitted to wear a gown or garment cut or slashed into pieces in the form of letters, rose leaves, and posies of various kinds, or any such like

---

[1] This reads strangely, but cloaks and sleeves of various materials, lined with fur, or with their edges cut into the shape of leaves or flowers, were worn with armour at that period.

[2] The great extravagance of clothing complained of by Occleve, Chaucer, and others, was in nothing more remarkable than in the enormous length of the tippets, cornets, or liripipes, as the tails of the hoods were indifferently called. This clause must therefore be looked at more as a proper restriction on the inferior orders, than as "a curious privilege" accorded to the higher, in which light it is regarded by Mr. Strutt.

[3] Harness at this period signified armour, accoutrements, and ornaments of various descriptions, as well as horse-furniture. In this case it may be taken in all senses as one. Chaucer's Ploughman describes a priest—

"That hie on horse willeth to ride
In glittering gold of great araye."

Fig. 1.   Fig. 2.   Fig. 3.

devices, under the penalty of forfeiting the same.   It was also commanded that no tailor should presume to make such a gown or garment under the pain of imprisonment and fine, according to the

Fig. 4.   Fig. 5.

Figs. 1 and 2. From MS. early 15th cent. Viollet-le-Duc.   Figs. 3 and 5. From MS. in the Louvre. 1410.
Fig. 6. From Montfaucon.   Fig. 7. From Bonnard.   Fig. 4. Willemin, 'Monuments inédits.'

king's pleasure. I have several times noticed, both in the Dictionary and in the preceding pages of this volume, the popularity of the remarkable fashion here alluded to, and which, in despite of all

Fig. 6. Joan de Montagu, killed at Agincourt.

Fig. 7. Fresco in Borromeo's Palace, Milan. 15th cent.

efforts at repression, continued in favour more or less from the reign of Henry II. to that of Henry VII. in England, but no examples I have met with in this country can approach the extravagance to

Italian Costume, 15th century. From Vecellio.

which it was carried abroad. In addition to the examples I have already given of it in the dresses of the Knights of the Knot at Naples, p. 112, I have selected the preceding from a host of authorities for the costume of Europe in the fifteenth century, commencing with two of the designs from French originals in the beautiful work of M. Viollet-le-Duc (figs. 1 and 2, p. 118).

M. Quicherat supplies us with two other examples, taken from a MS. in the Louvre, date about 1410—a nobleman in houppelande and chaperon, the borders of which are cut into lappets, and the sleeves of his under-dress escalloped (fig. 3), and a lady with sleeves similarly incised (fig. 5) ; also Jean de Montagu, killed in the battle of Agincourt (fig. 6), and an Italian lady playing at ball (fig. 7).

On the previous page are also two other Italian costumes, from the work of Cesare Vecellio. He does not give his authority, and attributes the lady's dress to the tenth century ! The chaperon and sleeves, and the high collar of the gown, sufficiently, however, indicate the period of this " habito antico di Roma, la donna il quale era portato per tutta Italia."

Germany furnishes us with a military costume presenting similar features in the figure of a knight of this date, which I have already given at p. 165 of the Dictionary ; and the celebrated engraver on metal, called "the Master of 1466," has represented, in a playing-card, a knight in his civil attire, which

Knight from German playing-card. 1466.

Sancho de Roxas. 1437. From " Iconografia Española."

may be a little exaggerated, but nevertheless illustrates the fashion and indicates the extent to which dagging had been carried in his day.

The effigy of Sancho de Roxas, who died in 1437, affords an example of the practice of dagging in Spain. The border of his mantle, as well as the edges of the sleeves of his under-dress, are escalloped with great precision ; and in Dutch and Flemish costume of the fifteenth century the fashion will be found carried to the greatest extravagance, not only in the civil but in the military costume (see pages 123, 130).

We have seen that, beside the dagging of the borders of dresses, *posies* were prohibited to be worn upon them by persons under certain degrees. These were mottoes. Chaucer tells us of a lady who had the words " Bien et loyaultment" embroidered on the borders and facings of her dress ; but what shall we say to the houppelande of Charles, duke of Orleans, the sleeves of which had embroidered upon them, in gold and pearls, the words *and music* of a song commencing " Madame, je suis tout joyeulx " ? The lines of the music were worked in gold thread, and each note was formed with four pearls; the whole number amounting to 960, at the cost of 276 livres. And this was by no means a singular instance of extravagance. A chronicler of the time, quoted by Quicherat, describes a dress of a gentleman of Normandy, the ornamentation of which consisted of 300 gold pieces disposed in the form of trefoils; and a pair of sleeves made for the Duke of Burgundy in 1411 had sewn upon them 7,500 little silver rings, alternately with 2000 leaves or flowers. After this we need not look with suspicion on Holinshed's account of the dress of Henry, Prince of Wales (afterwards Henry V.), who, when he went to make his peace with his father, was apparelled, he tells us, "in a gowne of blewe satten, full of smal oylet holes, at every hole the needle hanging by a silken threde by which it was worked; about his arme he wore a hounde's collar set full of SS. of golde, and the tyrrettes likewise being of the same metal." Writing in the time of Elizabeth, he is, of course, no authority; but he is not likely to have imagined such a dress, and most probably copied the account from some contemporary MS. then extant. It may certainly be classed with those just described, as far as extravagance of fancy goes, if not of expenditure.

For the general civil costume of this century in England, particularly the coiffures of the ladies, I must refer the reader to the Dictionary, articles GOWN, HEAD-DRESS, &c., illustrating it in this place according to the plan I have laid down, by the dresses of continental nations at the same period.

I must first, however, say a few words respecting foreigners, as they were then held to be, nearer home—the Scotch, the Welsh, and the Irish; and few, unfortunately, they will be, as we have less information about them, as respects their attire in this century, than in any other. Lindsay of Pitscottie, whose Chronicle of Scotland from 1437 to 1542 is in the vulgar tongue, says, "The other pairts northerne are full of mountaines, and very rude and homelie kynd of people doth inhabite, which is called the Reid Shankys, or wyld Scotes. They be clothed with ane schirt, fashioned after the Irisch manner, going bare-legged to the knee." No mention, observe, of any chequered garment. In a wardrobe account of James III. of Scotland, 1471, occurs an entry of "an elne and ane halve of blue tartane to lyne his gowne of cloth of gold;" and of "halve an elne of doble tartane to lyne collars to her Lady the Queen." In 1485, Henry Earl of Richmond displayed in Bosworth field a "banner of yellow tarterne," on which was painted a dun cow; but tartan in those days signified the stuff, not the pattern or the colour (see Dictionary, p. 503, article TARTAN).

Of the national dress of the Irish I find no direct account to add to the little we knew before, but an Act passed in the reign of Henry VI. corroborates the statement in the statute of Kilkenny quoted in the last chapter, respecting the assimilation of attire between the native Irish and the English residents; for it asserts that "now there is no diversity in array betwixt the English marchours and the Irish enemies, and so by colour of the English marchours the Irish enemies do come from day to day together into the English counties as English marchours, and do rob and pill by the high-ways, and destroy the common people by lodging upon them in the nights, and do also kill the husbands in the nights, and do take their goods to the Irishmen: whereof it is ordained and agreed that no manner of man that will be taken for an Englishman shall have no beard above his mouth; that is to say, that he have no hairs on his upper lip, so that the said lip be once at least shaven every fortnight or of equal growth with the nether lip; and if any man be found amongst the English contrary hereunto, that then it shall be lawful to every man to take them and their goods as Irish enemies." Whether this similarity of dress was assumed by "the Irish enemies" for the purpose of facilitating their inroads and depredations, or the consequence of long neighbourhood and intercommunication, does not appear. The long moustaches ("beard above his mouth") prohibited in the above statute must have been retained by the English in imitation of the Irish, as beards were not worn in England during the reign of Henry VI., except by aged and official personages. The faces of even military men are seen closely shaved.

Matters were changed in the following reign, for by an Act of Edward IV. it was no longer the English who were forbidden to dress or wear beards like the Irish, but the Irish dwelling in certain counties were commanded to "go apparelled like Englishmen, and wear beards after the English manner." What that manner was, I am at a loss to say, for in the reign of Edward IV. Englishmen in general shaved as closely as they did in the previous reign, as the reader may satisfy himself by a glance at the chromolithograph issued with Part III., or any of our incidental illustrations of that period ; but as there are exceptions to the rule, the words of the Act must have applied to the peculiar mode of wearing the beard by the native Irish, which was not to be indulged in by those who dwelt within the English pale. Some light will be thrown on this point in the next chapter.

In the reign of Henry VII. (for I may as well finish what little remains to be said of Irish fashions in the fifteenth century), Sir Edward Poynings, in order that the Parliaments of Ireland might want no decent or honourable form that was used in England, caused a particular Act to pass that the Lords of Ireland should appear in the like parliament robes as the Lords are wont to wear in the Parliaments of England. This Act is intituled 'A Statute for the Lords of Parliament to wear Robes,' and the penalty of offending against it was a hundred shillings, to be levied off the offender's lands and goods.

In the sixth year of the same monarch's reign (A.D. 1491), a warm dispute appears to have existed between the glovers and shoemakers about "the right of making girdles and all manner of girdles." Fine cloth, silk, taffeta, and cloth of gold are mentioned as worn by the nobility in Ireland at this time, and worsted and canvas linen for *phaillings* and mantles by the poorer classes. Felt caps are also recorded.

To return to the first half of the century, and the general dress of Europe contemporaneously

Jacqueline de la Grange,
wife of Jean de Montague.   1419.

Hainan Reguier, Trésorier des
Guerres to Charles VI.

From a MS. at Rome.

with the reigns of our fourth, fifth, and sixth Henrys, we find, as usual, the same character pervading the attire of the principal nations of the West and centre, modified slightly in some by local peculiarities or ancient custom, but always bearing unmistakable marks of the date of their make and usage. Take the French in the first place. We perceive the continued existence of two opposite extremes of fashion, the short and the long, both of which excited the wrath and ridicule of the writers of the past century. Little if any change is observable during the remainder of the reign of Charles VI. of France, which comprised those of our Henry IV. and Henry V. The peculiar horned head-dress of the ladies, of which we see so many examples in England of the reign of Henry V., appears to have been limited,

Charles de Savoye. 1408.

Jean de Montaigu, beheaded 1409.

Louis II., Duc de Bourbon. 1410.

Costumes, 1400-1450. From Vosmer's 'Counts of Holland and Zealand.'

according to M. Viollet-le-Duc, to the Isle de France, and never to have assumed the exaggerated proportions it did on this side the Channel. All the other fashions seem to have been common to both countries. There are the same long and short dresses, hats, chaperons, shoes, &c., that we have in English examples.

The statues round the monument of Louis le Male, Count of Flanders, erected by Philip the Good, Duke of Burgundy, exhibit a great variety of male and female costume of the middle of the fifteenth century. A work printed at Antwerp in 1578 contains also some spirited engravings of the Counts and Countesses of Holland, evidently from paintings of the fifteenth century, though many are absurdly appropriated to personages who lived five or six hundred years previously.[1] (See preceding page.)

Italian costume of this period is profusely represented in the paintings of Domenicano Bartoli (1426–1470), from one of which I select the annexed figure, on account of the hat, which is of a form we find in contemporary pictures in France, Flanders, and England.

M. Quicherat corrects an error of Brantôme, who states that Isabella of Bavaria had brought with her into France the most extravagant fashions, and taught the ladies to attire themselves in the most gorgeous manner: on the contrary, it would appear that the Court of Bavaria, in which the young princess was brought up, was by no means distinguished for its magnificence; and when she was conducted to Paris to become the wife of Charles VI., she was so simply dressed that as soon as she alighted her aunt, the Countess of Hainault, felt obliged for the honour of the family to procure for her better clothes. The truth is, she had first to be instructed by this aunt, and afterwards by the ladies of her court, in all the mysteries of the toilet; but she was an apt scholar, and learned her lessons so well that she was very soon capable of instructing her teachers. She possessed more jewels than any queen of her time; and it became a passion with her to invent all kinds of attire which would enable her to display her diamonds, sapphires, rubies, and pearls to the greatest advantage. Her inordinate love of splendour, which neither the misfortunes of her own house nor the distresses of the kingdom could abate, was chiefly the cause of the execrations she was ultimately laden with by the people.

From a painting by Domenicano Bartoli   1426–1470.

France, torn to pieces by faction and handed over by her own sovereign to the English, was reduced to the greatest distress. "The year 1420," says one of her historians, "was the hardest of all times, and clothing was dearer than everything else;" and two years later Charles VII. had the mortification of seeing a cordwainer take away with him a pair of boots he had made for the king because his majesty had no money to pay for them. Philip the Good, Duke of Burgundy and Count of Flanders, maintained meanwhile the most splendid state in his cities of Ghent and Bruges, and for a time Fashion issued her decrees from them to the world instead of from impoverished Paris.

So many fantastic head-dresses had succeeded each other during the early portion of the fifteenth century, as the pages of our Dictionary will testify, that it becomes difficult to affix a precise date to the introduction of any one in particular, or to define from verbal description which are specially entitled to certain names we meet with in contemporary chronicles or satires. One of the best known by name to us is the *hennin*, a term of which the derivation or etymology has not been even suggested by the latest French writers on Costume. We first hear of it in the sermon of the monk, or more properly the Friar preacher, Thomas Connecte, which has been mentioned at p. 274, Dictionary, as quoted by Addison from Paradin in his 'History of Lyons,' who was himself indebted to Monstrelet

[1] ' 'Principes Hollandiæ et Zelandiæ Domini Frisiæ.' Auctore Michaele Vosmero. Antwerpiæ excudebat Christophorus Platinus Philippo Gallæo, MDLXXVIII.

for the story. According to the latter, it was in the year 1428 that the zealous Carmelite commenced his crusade in Flanders against "les bobans et autours de tête" of various shapes, which were at that date the fashion amongst the ladies in the cities of Artois, Cambrai, Amiens, and the Flemish Marches, and excited the children to follow the wearers in the streets and shout at them "*Au hennin! au hennin!*" But no description is given us either by the preacher or the chronicler of the particular form of head-dress that provoked the wrath and ridicule of the reverend censor. M. Quicherat has, however, informed us that the fashions at that time were imported to France from Flanders. (See woodcut annexed of Flemish fashions, from an illumination executed in Flanders about the middle of the fifteenth century.) It is in Flanders we first hear of the *hennin*, and it is to the language of that country we must look for its meaning. Now *hennen* is Flemish for "a cock," and some fancied resemblance to the crest or

Flemish costume, circa 1440-1470.

comb of that bird might have suggested a comparison : but *hennen* is also rendered "*jau coccou,*" and in the case of married ladies, for such alone wore elaborate coiffures, would have implied conduct so dis-

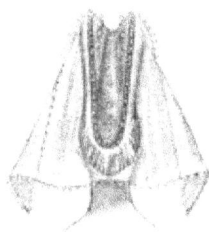

Back view of Hennin. From Viollet-le-Duc.

Flemish lady. 1400

Triple horned head-dress. From Viollet-le-Duc.

graceful to them that their husbands, from self-respect, would deem it expedient to add their influence to that of the Church for the suppression of the obnoxious head-tire. (See woodcut above of Flemish lady in a hennin, from a miniature *circa* 1470.) That the hennin, whatever its shape in the early part of the fifteenth century, was introduced from Flanders, I think there can be little doubt. That it was not specially the designation of the steeple head-dress of a later period is also, I think, sufficiently clear; and that high and magnificent head-dresses were not brought from Bavaria to France by Isabella, queen of Charles VI., in 1385, has been disproved by M. Quicherat, who quotes Monstrelet to show that their first appearance in Paris was in 1429. I am inclined to go further still, and contend that the *hennin* denounced by Friar Thomas was not that exaggeration of the heart-shaped head-dress in which Isabella has been represented in Montfaucon,[1] and which I doubt she could ever have seen;[2] and that the "hault atours" mentioned by Monstrelet were the "escoffions à cornes" (horned coiffes) so peculiarly characteristic of the reign of our Henry V., of which a variety of shapes are seen in French and English monuments and miniatures of the first three decades of the fifteenth century. (See Dictionary, p. 272 and also p. 132, for an extraordinary example in the head-dress of Beatrix, Countess of Arundel, but which certainly can be matched, as far as eccentricity is concerned, by an escoffion aux cornes represented in a Latin missal in the Bibliothèque National in Paris, of the first half of the fifteenth century. See triple-horned head-dress, last page.)

In 'Le Dit des Mariages des Filles au Diable,' a French poem written at the commencement of the fifteenth century, quoted by M. Viollet-le-Duc, the author says—

> "Or venons es dames *cornues*,
> Chies de Paris *testes tendues*,
> Qui se vont pour offrant à vente
> *Com cerfs ramu* vont par rues
> En bourriaus, enfurs en tambues
> Usent et metent lor jouvente."

Here is an example of a hennin or escoffion cornue from M. Viollet-le-Duc, which he tells us was worn in l'Ile de France in 1415, and also of one of the varieties in fashion much about the same period.

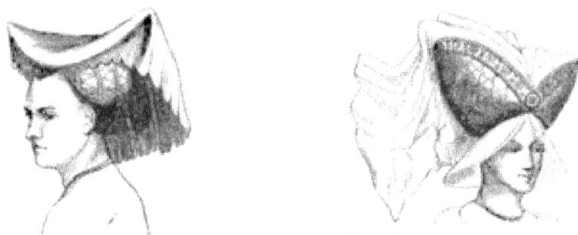

Escoffions aux cornues. From Viollet-le-Duc.

The description of the latter I will give in the learned antiquary's own felicitous language : "Ils se composaient d'une coiffe de mousseline empesée, formant couvre-nuque et venant joindre ses pans saillants et roides au sommet du front. Sur cette sorte d'auvent, qui donnait des reflets très-doux et clairs à la peau, se posaient les cornes assez semblables à deux valves d'une coquillage s'ouvrant. Ces cornes étaient plus ou moins richement ornées de broderies, de passementeries, de pierres et de perles.

---

[1] The print was engraved from a drawing in M. Gagnière's celebrated portfolio, but there is no proof of the assertion that the original painting from which the drawing was made was "fait du temps même de la Reine Isabeau," and the dresses of her attendants are of a later period.

[2] In our chromolithograph from Christine de Pisan's MS. in the British Museum, which is really contemporaneous with Isabella, the queen is represented in the usual head-dress of that day, which was as extravagantly *wide* as the later fashion was *high*.

De l'intervalle qu'elles laissaient entre elles s'échappaient, en gros bouillons, un voile de gaze ou d'étoffe très-légère et transparente."

I have dwelt upon this particular subject longer perhaps than some of my readers may think necessary; but I find so much confusion and contradiction in the very best writers respecting it that I deemed it a duty to the public as much as it was interesting to myself to endeavour to obtain and impart some clearer notion of the hennin than has hitherto been entertained by antiquaries in general. I will not venture to say that I have succeeded.

In the reigns of Henry VI. of England and of Charles VII. of France, *circa* 1440, we find in both countries well-authenticated examples of the towering head-dress attributed to Isabella of Bavaria, who had then been in her grave some five years, and the costume of her train-bearers points distinctly to at least as late a period. (See annexed engraving from some tapestry in the Library of Berne in Switzerland, published by M. Jubinal in the second volume of his 'Anciennes Tapisseries historiques' of that date, and another of the effigy of Joan Keriell, who died *circa* 1453-4, from her brass in the church of Ash-next-Sandwich.) Louis Guyon has an anecdote related in a MS. written in 1450, of a lady of Sens, who, coming to Paris on some law business, found the height of her " bonnet " so inconvenient when she went to solicit the judges that she adopted a head-dress completely flat, with a bag behind to enclose her hair. This fancy is supposed to have caused the revival of the chaperon; but whether or no, a hood of some description was worn occasionally throughout the fifteenth century, and in the latter days of Charles VII. one of his fair favourites was called "Madame des Chaperons," from her mode of wearing them.

Under the date of 1467, Monstrelet, or rather one of his continuators—for Monstrelet himself died in July 1453, and the portion actually written by him of the 'Chroniques' bearing his name terminates in 1444—tells us that the ladies wore on their heads round caps gradually diminishing to the height of half or three quarters of an ell, with a loose handkerchief atop, sometimes hanging as low as the ground. This was that form of the hennin which has been designated the steeple head-dress, and of which we have given an excellent example in the figure of Marie, Duchess of Burgundy, at p. 274 of the Dictionary; but although this fashion lasted far into the latter half of the century, and lingers still in Normandy and the Pays de Caux, it appeared as early as 1450, simultaneously with another variety of the hennin which is seen on the head of one of the train-bearers of Queen Isabella in M. de Gagnière's drawing before mentioned, and also occurs in conjunction with it in the Tourney book of King René of Anjou, illuminated by himself about the above date, one of the miniatures in which forms the subject of the chromolithograph issued with Part IX. of this work. A more elaborate representation on a larger scale from the same manuscript will give a better notion of its form and mode of construction. The bonnet or cap, the proper name for which was *cornet*,[1] is seen through the veil of gauze,

Brass in Ash Church.

From Tapestry at Berne.

---

[1] The words *cornet, cornette*, had in French a variety of significations. It was applied to caps of different descriptions, to the tippet of the chaperon, and at a later period to the pointed standard carried by the cavalry, the bearer of which is called a cornet, as the officer of infantry who carries the colours of the regiment is entitled an ensign. Anything with a peak or point was so designated. The *capan cyrnicyll* of the Welsh, and the *corno* of the Doge of Venice, were not *horned*, but simply conical. Inattention to this fact has misled many English writers on this subject.

which is sustained, curiously folded, high above its apex by wires so fine as to be invisible, instead of being loosely thrown over it, or attached only to the top and allowed to stream down behind almost

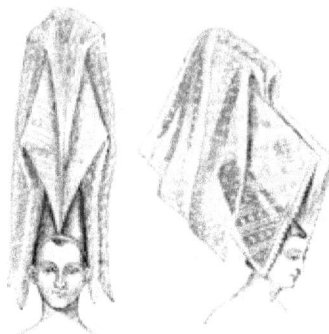

to the ground. In the latter instance a smaller veil was worn over the head beneath the cornet, shading the face and neck. (See woodcuts annexed, and also p. 275 of the Dictionary.)

The hennins, or whatever name may be given to these preposterously high head-dresses, do not appear to have been worn in other European countries so much as in France and England. A few examples may be found in Germany and Holland, but the classical taste of Italy appears to have prevented their crossing the Alps; and I am not aware of their having ever been adopted in Spain or Portugal. Although Flanders has the reputation of their introduction, I much suspect their origin to have been Oriental and of great antiquity.

The important changes that took place in European armour at the close of the fourteenth century, appear to have been completed by the time of the accession of Henry V., A.D. 1413. The

Front and side views of Hennins. From the "Traité de Tournois" of René d'Anjou.

brass of Sir John Fitzwaryn in Wantage Church, Berkshire, 1414, is one of the earliest, affording an example in England of a knight in complete steel from head to foot. The camail has given place to the plate-gorget, and circular gussets of plate, to which English antiquarians have given the names of palettes and roundels, protect the arm-pits. There is no authority for the use of either name; and as these plates are frequently oval, oblong, crescent, and otherwise shaped, the latter denomination could not correctly be applied to them. (See PALETTE.) The skirts of tassets overlapping each other, encircled by the military belt, and the rings dependent from the edge of the apron of mail beneath them, are indicative of this period. As we have given in the Dictionary at p. 18, under the article ARMOUR, the effigy of Sir Robert Suckling, 1415, from his brass in Barsham Church, Suffolk, which is so nearly identical with that of Fitzwaryn, I have selected that of Sir Thomas de Quentin, circa 1420, for illustration in this place of the armour of the reign of Henry V., on account of the curious ornamental wreath upon his bascinet, composed of leaves or feathers, which may have been real or of metal. A similar head-dress was worn with the civil dress at this period. (See Dictionary, p. 75.) The left gusset in this instance has the shape of a shield used at the same time. For the various changes in the form of the breast-plate and the bascinet during the first half of the century, I must refer the reader to the Dictionary.

Feathers were first worn in bascinets at this period (see that of Robert Chamberlayne, Esquire to Henry V., Dictionary, p. 515); and cloaks with or without sleeves and tabards of arms were worn by military men over their armour, the jupon still appearing occasionally. The beaume of Henry V. in Westminster Abbey is figured in Plate XI. of this work, and is undoubtedly an authentic relic which he may have worn; but it is not "the very casque that did affright the air" at Agincourt, as stated in the Catalogue of the Antiquities and Works of Art exhibited in the Ironmongers' Hall, London, in 1861, if we are to believe St. Remy, who was an eye-witness, and who tells us that "after masses had been said they brought him the armour for his head, which was a very handsome

Effigy of Sir Thomas de Quentin.

bascinet à barierre" (bascinet with a barred vizor, or a beaver—*bascinet à bavierre*), "upon which he had a very rich crown of gold, arched like an imperial crown," part of which, we afterwards learn from Monstrelet, was struck off by the battle-axe of the Duke of Alençon.[1] St. Remy, who says he saw what he relates, describes the French as "so loaded with armour that they could not advance. First, they were armed in long coats of steel reaching below their knees and very heavy, below which was armour for their legs, and above, white harness and bascinets with camails;[2] and so heavily were

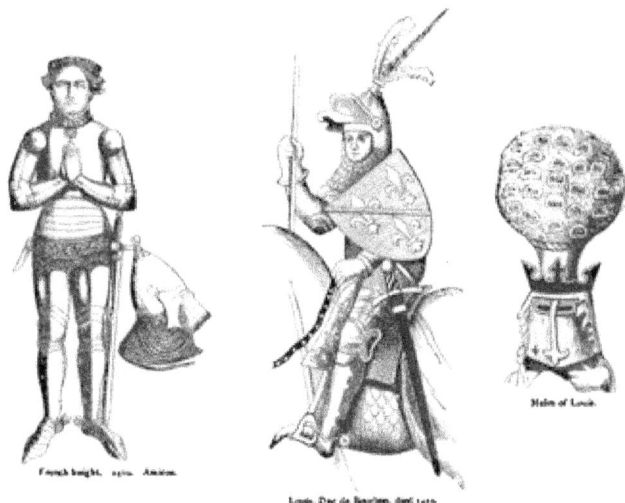

French knight. 1410. Amiens.

Louis, Duc de Bourbon, died 1410.

Helm of Louis.

they armed that, together with the softness of the ground, it was with great difficulty they could lift their weapons." White harness signifies plain polished steel, but what the long coats of steel reaching

[1] As a controversy respecting the heaume in Westminster Abbey has arisen since the publication of Part VIII. of this work, in which it was mentioned and figured, I find it necessary to say a few words on the subject. It is quite true, as Mr. Hewitt states, that a helmet appears to have been made by a certain John Daunt for the funeral of the king, and it is consequently probable that the said helmet was borne in the funeral procession, but *non constat* that it was the one now in the Abbey. There are many reasons for discrediting such an assertion, which the nature of this work will not permit me to enter into discussion of ; but the strongest argument in favour of the authenticity of the heaume is deducible from the well-known custom of the period. The armour, standard, or horse of a deceased knight was during the Middle Ages *solemnly* presented to the church in which his body was deposited, and it would have been a profanity, as well as an insult to the authorities, to have offered them anything but a personal relic of the departed warrior. What are called "undertakers' helmets" were unknown previous to the Reformation ; and even as late as the reigns of Elizabeth and James I. the veritable helmet, gauntlets, &c., were suspended above the tomb of their former owner, although the devotional motive no longer existed. No doubt has ever been entertained respecting the heaume of Edward the Black Prince at Canterbury. That of Sir Richard Pembridge, transferred from Hereford Cathedral to the Collection of Sir S. Meyrick, has been discovered by Sir Noel Paton, its present possessor, to be plated with silver. The heaumes of Sir John Foggs, from Ashford Church, Kent, and of Sir John Crosby, from Great St. Helen's, London, both now in the Londesborough Collection, are *bonâ fide* relics of these worthies. The standard of the Dun Cow, reverently deposited in St. Paul's Cathedral by Henry VII., was not "made to order," but had been actually borne at the battle of Bosworth.

[2] "Premièrement, estoient armés de cottes d'acier, longues passants les genoux, et moult pesantes, et par dessous harnois de jambes et pardessus blanc harnois, et de plus bachinets de camail."

to their knees could have been I am at a loss to say. If the skirt of tassets, as Meyrick suggests, the English at that period wore the same, and therefore would not have attracted the special observation of St. Remy, as they must have been equally incommoded; but yet I see nothing else in French armour to which it could apply. Above is an engraving from the tomb of a French knight preserved in the Museum at Amiens, date *circa* 1410. His armour corresponds as nearly as possible with that of English suits at the same period, and there is his vizored bascinet, with its camail, which St. Remy distinctly states was worn by the French knights in the battle. Another authority for French armour of this date is the figure of Louis, Duc de Bourbon, from the 'Livre des Hommages du Comté de Clermont,' engraved by Montfaucon. He also wears the vizored bascinet (very ill drawn), with its camail and penache; but the body-armour is not visible. No further light is thrown on the subject by representations of the military costume of Flanders and Holland, as preserved to us in the prints to Michael Vosmer's work, already mentioned (p. 124), engraved

William of Bavaria, 27th Count of Holland.   1417.   From Vosmer's "Counts of Holland."

from a series of drawings of the time of our Henry V. I select one of William of Bavaria, twenty-seventh Count of Holland, who died 31st May, 1417, and may therefore have some claim to authenticity. To his globular breast-plate is appended a skirt of mail, worn over a tunic, the lower portion of which, as well as the edges of the ample sleeves, display a specimen of the *dagging* so much indulged in, and so reprobated for centuries. (See also the two following figs. from the same work.)

Of German armour of this date we have already given a specimen at p. 165 of the Dictionary, illustrating the same fashion; but steel coats "reaching to the knees," save in the shape of tassets, find I none.

The effigy of a knight of the family of Haberkorn in the church of St. John of Jerusalem at Wurzburg, dated 1421, is figured by Hefner in his 'Trachten,' and presents us with a skirt of *scale* mail, attached to the globular breast-plate—a curious variety. The under-garment with its wide sleeeves marks the time. Leather appears to supply the place of cuishes. The bascinet is of the old pointed form, with no pipe for a penache. (See opposite page.)

It remains to speak of the general soldiery—the archers and the bill-men. The brigandine was the principal defence of the former, and the jazerant of the latter. The jack was also much used. The English archers at the Battle of Agincourt were, for the greater part, "without armour to their pourpoints, their hosen loosened, having hatchets and axes or long swords hanging from their girdles, and some with *their feet naked*; some wore humettes or caps of boiled leather or wicker-work, crossed over with iron." (St. Remy.) Those with their feet naked were probably Irish, as Monstrelet in his 'Chronicles,' chap. xxiv., says, "that at the siege of Rouen, in 1417, there were several bodies of Irish in Henry's army, of whom the greater part had one leg and foot quite naked. The arms of these were targets, short javelins, and a strange kind of knives." The strange kind of knife was, of course, the *skene.* Speed, in his 'Chronicle,' p. 638, giving an account of the forces raised by Henry V. for his invasion of France, says, "With the English sixteen hundred Irish Kernes were enrolled from the Prior of Kilmainham; able men, but almost naked. Their arms were targets, darts, and swords."

The equipment of the Breton archers and pavisers in 1425 is described in an ordinance of John, fifth Duke of Bretagne, of that date, respecting the arming of the nobles and others, as a precaution against the enterprises and descents of the English. "Nobles possessing property and revenues from one hundred and forty to two hundred livres, are to be personally in the state and apparel of a man-at-arms, mounted on a good horse, and attended by a coustilleur and a page mounted on competent horses. Nobles of less estate are to furnish themselves with the habiliments of archers in brigandines, if they know how to use

Knight of the Haberkorn Family, Wurtzburg.

the bow, otherwise they are to be furnished with good guis-armes and good salades and leg-harness, and have each a coustilleur and two good horses. Nobles of still less revenue are to wear brigandines and good salades, or at least good *paletocks*, armed *in the new fashion* without sleeves, with overlapping plates of iron or mail on their arms, with good guisarmes or bows, if they know how to use them."

Charles VII. of France instituted in 1448 a body of men called Francs-archers or Francs Taupin. He ordained that in each parish in the kingdom there should be an archer, who should keep himself ready with a sufficient and suitable equipment, with huque of brigandine or jack, salade, sword, dagger, bow and quiver, or arbalast furnished ("arbalestre garnie"). They were to be free of all taxes—whence their name of Francs or Free Archers.

Montfaucon has engraved the effigy of Guillaume le May, a captain of Francs-archers, who died in 1480. He wears a jazerant jacket, with an indented skirt of mail and a gorget, or, as it was called, a standard of mail. On the breast of the jacket is a Latin cross. He has plate-armour on his arms and legs; the former having pauldrons attached by points.

Effigy of Guillaume le May. 1480.

The choice of armour and weapons allowed within a limited degree to the persons specified in the above and similar ordinances rendered uniformity next to impossible. In all representations, therefore, of battle-pieces of the Middle Ages, whether English or foreign, while a general similarity is observable in the equipment of the men-at-arms, the archers, whether long or cross bowmen, the billmen, guisarmiers, and other common soldiery, appear in every variety of apparel, the only "sign of company" occasionally discernible being a badge, either national or of the family of the leader under whose standard they served. Of these distinctions, which multiplied in England amazingly during this century, I shall speak further presently.

In the third year of Edward IV. a new Act was passed, in order to promote a reform in dress, and heavy penalties were annexed to the infringement of it, the substance being as follows :—

1. No knight under the estate of a lord, or his wife, shall wear any sort of cloth of gold, nor any kind of corses worked with gold, nor any furs of sables, under the penalty of twenty marks, to be paid to the king ; lords' children excepted.

2. No bachelor-knight, or his wife, shall wear any cloth of velvet upon velvet, under the forfeiture of twenty marks to the king ; the knights of the Garter and their wives excepted.

3. No person under the degree of a lord shall wear any cloth of silk of a purple colour, under the penalty of ten pounds.

4. No esquire or gentleman under the rank of a knight, or their wives, shall wear any velvet or figured satin, nor any counterfeit resembling velvet or figured satin, nor any counterfeit cloth of silk, nor any wrought corses, under the penalty of ten marks. The sons of lords, with their wives and daughters, and esquires of the king's body, with their wives, excepted.

5. No esquire or gentleman, or any other man or woman under the rank aforesaid, shall wear any damask or satin, under the penalty of one hundred pence. There is a long exception to this clause, including *esquires moinauls* (household esquires ?), serjeants, officers of the king's household, yeomen of the crown, yeomen of the king's chamber, esquires, and gentlemen possessing the yearly value of one hundred pounds.

6. Remembering always that the seneschal, chamberlain, treasurer, comptroller of the king's household, his carvers and knights of his body, and their wives, may wear furs of sables and ermines, and the mayors of London and their wives may wear the same array as the bachelor-knights and their wives : the aldermen and recorder of London, and all mayors and viscounts of the cities, towns, and boroughs of the said realm ; the mayors and bailiffs of the Cinque Ports, and the barons of the same ; and the mayors and bailiffs of the shire-towns, with their wives, may use the same apparel as esquires and gentlemen having possessions to the annual amount of forty pounds.

7. No man not having the yearly value of forty pounds shall wear any fur of martins, or pure grey, or of pure miniver ; nor shall the wife, the son, the daughter, or the servant of such a man, the son and daughter being under his government ; nor shall any widow of less possession wear a girdle ornamented with gold, or with silver gilt in any part of it, nor any corse of silk made out of the realm, nor any coverchief exceeding the price of three shillings and four pence the *plite* (fold or square ?), under the penalty of five marks. The same exceptions are made as in the sixth clause, and the persons excepted and their wives were permitted to wear the furs of martins, foynes, and lettice, and also gilt girdles, and coverchiefs at the price of five shillings the plite.

8. No man, unless he be possessed of the yearly value of forty shillings, shall wear fustian, bustian, or fustian of Naples, or scarlet, or cloth ingrain, or any furs but of black or white lamb's skin, under the forfeiture of forty shillings. The former exceptions are also added to this clause.

9. No yeoman, or any other person under the degree of a yeoman, shall wear in the apparel for his body any *bolsters*, or stuffing of wool, cotton, or caddis, in his pourpoint or doublet, but a lining only according to the same, under the penalty of six shillings and eight pence.

10. This clause is directed against the wearing, by any person under the rank of a lord, of the indecently short gowns, jackets, and cloaks, at that time so notoriously general ; and any tailor making such garments or doublets, stuffed or otherwise, contrary to the Act, was to forfeit the same garments.

11. No knight under the estate of a lord, no esquire or gentleman, or any other person, shall

wear any shoes or boots having pikes or points exceeding the length of two inches, under the forfeiture of forty pence. This penalty was increased the next year, and it was then ordained that no cordwainer or cobbler in London, or within three miles of the same, should make, or cause to be made, any shoes, galaches, or buskins, with pikes or poleyns exceeding the length of two inches, under the forfeiture of the sum of twenty shillings; and the year following it was proclaimed throughout England that the *beaks* or pikes of shoes or boots should not exceed two inches, upon pain of *cursing by the clergy*, and forfeiting of twenty shillings—one noble to the king, another to the Cordwainers of London, and the third to the Chamber of London. The extent to which this ridiculous fashion was carried at this period is well illustrated in the annexed figure, from a MS. of the reign of Edward IV., in the Royal Library, British Museum, marked 14 E iv. (See also CLOG and SHOE.)

12. No servant of husbandry, or common labourer, or servant of an artificer, inhabitant of any city or borough, shall wear in their garments any cloth exceeding the price of two shillings the broad yard. Their wives shall be restricted to the same, and they shall not wear any coverchief of more value than twelve pence the plite. It is also ordained that the servants and labourers aforesaid shall not wear any hosen, *close* or *open*, beyond the price of fourteen pence the pair, neither shall their wives use any girdles garnished with silver under the penalty of forty pence.

13. No person in any part of these realms shall sell *lawn nifels,*[1] wimples, or any other sort of coverchiefs, whereof the price of such plite shall exceed the sum of ten shillings, under the forfeiture of thirteen shillings and fourpence to the king for every plite so sold.

In the twenty-second year of the same king's reign, all the former statutes against excess of apparel were repealed, and the following substituted for them :—

From Royal MS., 14 E iv.

1. That no person, of whatsoever degree or condition he might be, shall wear any cloth of gold or silk of purple colour, excepting the king, the queen, the king's mother, his children, his brothers and his sisters, upon pain of forfeiting for every default the sum of twenty pounds.

2. No person under the estate of a duke shall wear any cloth of gold of tissue, under the forfeiture of twenty marks.

3. No person under the estate of a lord shall wear any plain cloth of gold, under the penalty of ten marks.

4. No person under the degree of a knight shall wear any velvet in their doublets or in their gowns, nor any damask or satin in the same, excepting only the esquires of the king's body, under the forfeiture of forty shillings.

5. No yeoman of the Crown, or any other person under the degree of an esquire or gentleman, shall wear damask or satin in their doublets or gowns of camlet, under the penalty of forty shillings.

6. No person under the estate of a lord shall wear any manner of woollen cloth manufactured out of the king's dominions (at that time consisting of England, Ireland, Wales, and Calais), nor any furs of sables, under the forfeiture of ten pounds.

7. This clause relates to the servants, and is the same as the twelfth clause of the preceding Act, excepting only that their wives are hereby permitted to wear a *reyle*, called a kerchief or coverchief, of any value not exceeding twenty pence, and the men such hose as were not of higher price than eighteen pence, the penalty being the same as previously.

8. This clause is precisely the same as the tenth in the former Act, against indecently short jackets, &c., saving only that the prohibition to the tailors is not included.

These statutes were renewed from time to time during the succeeding reigns, but with so few

[1] Strutt says, "probably a sort of veil." The literal meaning is "*trifles*" (*vide* Halliwell *in voce*). "Trash, rags, *nifels*, trifles" (Cotgrave).

alterations that it is unnecessary to recite them. It is notorious that all such enactments were generally evaded or disregarded ; but it would be interesting to ascertain what amount was received for penalties, and who were the principal offenders amerced.

The short reign of Richard III. is distinguished chiefly by the latest form of the hennin, the bonnet of which is cylindrical instead of conical, and of moderate dimensions ; no longer emulating a steeple, but rather suggestive of a drum, and projecting from the back of the head almost horizontally. The veil, stiffened out by wires, expands in two angular wings, entitling it to the appellation of "the butterfly head-dress," bestowed by Paradin less appropriately on the one preceding it. (See Dictionary, p. 274.) The piked poulaines, "two feet long," we are told by the same writer (who must, however, speak at second hand, as he was not born till 1513), were succeeded by shoes denominated "ducks' bills," from the shape of the toes, and still four or five fingers' breadth in length ; and in the following reign of Henry VII. they became round and wide, gradually increasing to the end of the century.

The shamefully short garments prohibited in the tenth clause of the foregoing statute (22nd Edward IV.), were equally fashionable and equally condemned on the other side of the Channel.

Jacques Duclercq, under the date 1467, complains that in that year the men wore such short dresses that their chausses were of little use to them, and they might as well have gone naked. At the same time he says that, if they did not attire themselves in that fashion, they went to the other extreme, and wore robes so long that they trailed on the ground, appearing one day in short dresses, and the next in long. There was scarcely a little shop-boy that had not a long robe of cloth reaching to his heels. They wore long hair and high cloth caps, and the nobility and rich persons had great chains about their necks. Their pourpoints were of velvet or cloth of silk ; their shoes had long poulaines—as long as their caps were high ; and they had great mahoîtres on their shoulders and much stuffing in their pourpoints, in order to give themselves the appearance of being powerfully made. This description perfectly corresponds with similar lamentations in England, and is faithfully illustrated by the paintings of the time. He mentions also the commencement of a practice which in the subsequent century was carried to an enormous extent all over Europe : "Ils faisoient fendre les manches de leurs robes et de leurs pourpoints de telle sorte qu'on voyoit leurs bras à travers une déliée chemise qu'ils portoient, laquelle chemise avoit la manche large." The fashion at this time was confined to the sleeves, but very soon was extended to every portion of the dress, even to the caps and the shoes. The earliest examples are anything but picturesque, giving the gentlemen only the appearance of being "out at elbows." (See Dictionary, p. 171.) Coquillart, a satirical poet of this period, alludes to this fancy of showing the shirt, and of the trick of those who could not afford expensive linen, placing fine handkerchiefs at the openings of their sleeves to do duty for it, the shirt itself being as coarse as sackcloth :

> "Mais la chemise elle est souvent
> Grosse comme un sac de moulin."

Sumptuary laws had been found as ineffective in France as in England, and since 1292 none had been enacted. The reign of Charles VII. had been distinguished for the costliness and fantastic character of the dress of the people generally, and the old complaint of extravagance and immorality, of the confusion of classes, the ruin of families, and the perdition of souls, was made officially to the king, as appears by a memorandum in the archives of the city of Paris, quoted by M. Quicherat, in which it is stated that it was represented to the king that "of all the nations on the habitable earth there was not one so changeable, so outrageous, so extravagant, or capricious, as the French nation." He was therefore prayed to prohibit the sale of cloth of gold, silver, or silk, velvet, satin, or cramoisie, to anyone save princes and persons of the blood royal, and to the clergy, to make vestments, under the penalty of the confiscation of the said clothes and sixty livres parisis. Nothing was however done, but during the reign of the hypocritical and sanctimonious Louis XI. the example of the king, who affected great simplicity in his attire, had a discouraging effect on splendour and display in everything. On the accession of his son in 1483, a reaction took place, and two years afterwards an ordinance

PLATE XXII.

Aeneas Silvius Cardinal Bishop of Siena, afterwards Pope Pius II
introducing Eleanora of Portugal to the Emperor Frederick in 19th February, 1452.
From a Fresco Painting by Pinturicchio at Siena, circa 1506

was issued, founded amongst other considerations upon the belief that an excess of expenditure on dress was an offence against the Creator. The wearing of cloth of gold was absolutely forbidden. Silk was permitted only to nobles with sufficient incomes to live according to their rank, and no esquire or gentleman might wear velvet under penalty of fine and confiscation of the garment.

The king, the royal family and household, were as usual unrestricted; and when Charles VIII. set out for Italy, his dress, and that of his retinue, was of the most gorgeous description; the hose even of the halberdiers of his guard were of cloth of gold. The costume of France, Italy, Holland, and Flanders has been already sufficiently illustrated at pp. 118, 119, 122, 124. I have now to speak of that of Germany, Spain, and Portugal, during the second half of the fifteenth century to within a few years of its close.

The following figures of a noble lady and gentleman of Spain were copied by M. Bonnard from a beautiful copy of the Office of the Virgin, which belonged to the Court, and was written towards the

Spanish lady.

Spanish nobleman.

end of the fifteenth century; but, as he observes, the costume of these personages possesses the character of a much earlier period. Had Señor de Carderera's valuable work preceded in date of publication that of M. Bonnard, the latter antiquary might have pointed to the effigy of Doña Constanza de Aragon (see p. 73 *ante*), who died in the latter half of the thirteenth century, and of which the head-dress bears great similarity to that of the noble lady engraved above. In Spain, however, a fashion may have lasted much longer than in France or England.

Germany and Portugal are mutually illustrated at this period by the fresco-painting in the fifth compartment of the library of the Cathedral of Siena, executed by Pinturicchio and Raphael by order of Cardinal Francesco Piccolomini, afterwards Pius III., and representing Bishop Æneas Silvius introducing Eleanora of Portugal to the Emperor Frederick III. at Siena, 19th February, 1452 (see Plate XXII.*). The costumes are of course of the time of the painting, and not of the event.

For the defensive armour of this period we have a mass of authorities, sculptural, pictorial, and documentary. Its general features in England have been described in the Dictionary, art. ARMOUR, pp. 17, 18, and the separate pieces and weapons under their respective headings. I shall therefore, in pursuance of my plan, deal principally with foreign specimens, the characteristics of which will be found, as in the case of civil costume, extremely similar throughout Western Europe to those in English examples; a fact less to be wondered at, as the greater proportion of what the dealers call "Gothic armour,"—that is, armour of the fifteenth century,—is of German or Italian manufacture,[1] differing in nowise from such as we find in the national collections at Dresden, Vienna, Turin, Paris, Madrid, and London.

The salade and haussecol were introduced about the middle of the fifteenth century, superseding the vizored bascinet and the heaume, no longer worn except in the lists. The statue of Guillaume de Bibra, who was ambassador from the Emperor Frederick III. to Pope Innocent VIII. (1484–1492), in the church of St. Anastasius, is a fine example of Italian armour, just previous to the next great change which took place in the reign of the Emperor Maximilian. It affords a late instance of the

| Statue of Guillaume de Bibra. 1489. | Italian suit, circa 1480, in the Musée d'Artillerie. | Richard III. From Warwick Roll. |

wearing of palettes or roundels to protect the arm-pits, which are said to be rarely met with after 1435. Another occurs in a fine Italian suit of about the same period, in the Musée d'Artillerie, Paris, the roundels being furnished with spikes.

The sollerets retained their long-pointed toes to within some twenty years of the end of the century. At p. 473 of the Dictionary I have given an engraving of one belonging to the recently discovered suit at Tewkesbury, supposed, with great probability, to have belonged to Edward, Prince of Wales, son of King Henry VI.; and in the Londesborough Collection are a pair of jambs with long-toed sollerets, which present the interesting feature of rings by which the peaks or poulaines could be chained up to the knees. The toes subsequently became round and then square, in conformity with the fashion of the shoes in civil attire; but it is incumbent on me to notice that the effigy of the great Talbot, Earl of Shrewsbury, slain at Chastillon in 1453, has round-toed sollerets, which, unless it were executed long after his death, as was frequently the case, is a unique example at that period.

[1] In Italy this manufacture was conducted on so large a scale that the armourers of the single town of Milan were able after the battle of Macalo, in 1427, to supply in a few days arms and armour for 4000 cavalry and 200 infantry soldiers. (Demmin.)

The long-toed solerets are also visible in the chromolithograph issued with Part X., copied from a picture in our National Gallery, stated in the Catalogue to be the Battle of St. Egidio, by Paulo Uccello. This is not the place for a long argument respecting the *subject* of the picture. My business with it in this work is confined to the armour represented in it, which is Italian, and of quite the close of the fifteenth century. At p. 284 of the Dictionary I have given my reasons for doubting the date ascribed to it—at least by implication—in the Catalogue aforesaid; and will only here repeat my opinion that if that picture be the work of Uccello, who, it is assumed, died in 1479 at the advanced age of eighty-three, he must, like Titian, have painted to the last days of his existence. In that case, also, the armour worn in France in 1507 must have been in use in Italy thirty years previously.

Tabards of arms were much worn by knights in France and England during the latter half of the century. The tabard of Henry VI. hung over his tomb at Windsor in the reign of Henry VIII. (see Dictionary, p. 499); and Richard III. is represented in one in the Warwick Roll, written in his reign (see previous page).

A second change took place in English costume, both civil and military, during the last fifteen years of the century. In the civil costume the hood was discarded completely for hats, caps, or bonnets, except in official, legal, civic, or collegiate dresses, the habit of the Knights of the Garter, &c., and feathers were worn in profusion. Every article of dress, with the exception of the cloak, was slashed and puffed to the greatest extent; not only the pourpoint, but the hose, the shoes, and even the boots and the bonnets. The latter were worn much on one side of the head, displaying a close cap beneath them. The large felt hats laden with feathers were occasionally worn slung behind the back (see p. 172, Dictionary), a small bonnet covering the head. The toes of the shoes and boots, which had previously been absurdly pointed, were made so broad that an edict was issued to limit their width in lieu of their length. Paradin asserts that this change took place in Flanders in the year 1474. The slashing of dresses is said to have arisen from the conduct of the victorious Swiss after the defeat of Charles the Bold in the battle of Granson, in 1476. Amongst the plunder was found a mass of magnificent stuffs, silk, velvet, and cloth of gold and silver. These, it is reported, were cut or torn up by the soldiery and fastened on their dresses, the variety of colours producing the effect which was subsequently attained systematically by the tailors, and may still be seen in the uniform of the Swiss Guard of the Pope.

The invention of hand fire-arms about the middle of the fourteenth century, probably in Flanders, as the Flemings appear to have used them some time before other nations, had a marked effect on defensive armour, and towards the close of the fifteenth century the arquebus had become a formidable rival to the bow.

In 1485 Henry VII. instituted a body-guard in imitation of that of the kings of France, and which may be considered the first formation of a standing army in England. Rapin, who calls them Archers, says they were instituted on the day of his coronation (30th of October), and that they consisted of fifty men, whose office it was to attend him and his successors for ever. By the first regulations, every yeoman of this corps was to be of the best quality under gentry, well made, and fully six feet high; one-half carried bows and arrows, the other half arquebuses, and all had large swords by their side.

Louis XII., king of France, was the first who took into his service the troops called stradiots or estradiots. They were Greek mercenaries, who under their leader offered their services alike to Turks or Christians, calling themselves Στρατιώται, a word abbreviated to stradiots. They were first known to the French during the wars in Italy, and are thus described by Philip de Commines: "The estradiots are troops like the Janizaries, equipped as horse and foot like the Turks, with the exception of their heads not wearing that fabric twisted round them called a turban. . . . . The Venetians make great use of them, and place in them great confidence." Their armour, according to M. de Montgomeri Courbousson, seems to have consisted of a cuirass with sleeves and gloves of mail, over which they wore a jacket without sleeves, and on their heads an open salade. Their weapons were a large sabre; a mace, which they carried at their saddle-bow; and the zagaye or arzegaye, which was a lance twelve feet long, pointed with iron at both ends. With this latter arm, according to a book attributed to M. Langey, they would sometimes dismount and act as pikemen against cavalry, using it with both hands, sometimes presenting one point and sometimes another. They were generally called in France "Albanian cavalry."

I have mentioned a few pages back the badges by which the soldiery of different nations, or retainers of particular leaders, were distinguished at this period. The English had now finally adopted the red cross and the French the white. The exact period at which this change was effected has not been ascertained; but a French antiquary has suggested that it originated in the pretension of Edward III. to the crown of France during the reign of Philip de Valois, the probability being that Edward assumed the French badge at the same time that he quartered the French arms. The red cross of St. George may also have influenced him in the matter; but I have not met with any example that would support a theory. All we know for certain is that the change had taken place in the days of Charles VII. and of our Henry VI., the former having also made a white standard the principal national flag, and which thenceforth was styled "la cornette blanche," the red oriflamme being no longer displayed in battle;[1] also that the English troops are always depicted in the illuminated MSS. of the fifteenth century with red crosses on their backs, and the French with white. The troops of the Dukes of Burgundy bore either a saltire raguly gules, or, after the institution of the Order of the Golden Fleece, the briquet or steel that formed part of its insignia. (See Burgundian archers at p. 11, Dictionary.) At the battle of Barnet in 1471, a strange misfortune happened to the Earl of Oxford and his men; "for they having a star with streams on their liveries, as King Edward's men had the sun, the Earl of Warwick's men, by reason of the mist not well distinguishing the badges so like, shot at the Earl of Oxford's men that were on their parts." (Baker's Chron., p. 211.)

Of the twenty-four years of the reign of Henry VII., fifteen were comprised within this century; and as a great change appears to have taken place in European costume before the expiration of it, we must cast a parting glance over the principal countries, including our own, and note the more important alterations.

"At the close of the fifteenth century," Strutt observes, "the dress of the English was exceedingly fanciful and absurd, insomuch that it was even difficult to distinguish one sex from the other." Our readers will remember that this complaint, nearly in the same words, has been made by contemporary writers from the reign of Rufus.

The application at this later period of certain terms to articles of male apparel which we have been accustomed to associate with female attire, may certainly justify the remark of Strutt as to the petticoat mentioned in the reign of Henry V., was now added the stomacher (see Dictionary, p. 487). This sort of habit, however, was worn only by the upper classes. The elegant fashion of slashing, as already noticed, makes its appearance about this time; and the opening of the sleeve at the elbow, first observable in the costume of the reign of Edward IV., led to another curious fancy —the complete division of the sleeve into two or more pieces, and their attachment to each other by means of points or laces, through which the shirt or chemise protruded, for the fashion was not confined to the male sex. The upper part of the men's hose was also occasionally slashed and puffed, or embroidered and coloured differently to the lower portion,—an indication of their approaching separation. Whatever truth there may be in the tradition I have mentioned, that this remarkable character of the costume of Europe towards the end of the fifteenth century originated with the victorious Swiss troops, after the defeat of Charles the Bold, duke of Burgundy, at Granson, it is certain that some of the most extravagant examples of the fashion are to be found in the military costume of Switzerland, shortly after this date, and that the Swiss Guard of the Pope continue to wear a similar habit to this day. Germany perhaps, next to Switzerland, affords the greatest variety of this remarkable style of habiliment; but the vogue appears to have pervaded all civilized Europe, and to have outlived the following century. As it is more characteristic of the latter portion of the reign of Henry VII., we shall reserve our illustrations of it for the next chapter, and confine ourselves here to the costume prevailing in England and on the Continent during the last

---

[1] 'Traité des Marques Nationals,' par M. Beneton de Morange de Peyrins. Paris, 1739.

decade of the fifteenth century. Under the article GOWN in the Dictionary, we have already given several examples of both male and female attire at that period, including the figures of Henry and his queen from their portraits by Holbein. To these we now add the highly interesting portrait of the King from the original drawing in the Sutherland 'Clarendon,' which I had the pleasure of first making public, by permission of Mrs. Sutherland, in my 'History of British Costume.' Under CLOAK and HEAD-DRESS will also be found a variety of costumes of the same date, and of which the most remarkable feature is the profusion of feathers worn by the young gallants in the broad-brimmed hats which they wore over skull caps, or slung behind them. That the latter fashion prevailed in France is testified by the annexed figures of courtiers from the frontispiece of a 'Traité de Tournois' by Louis de Bruges, in which the author is depicted presenting his book to King Charles VIII. That it also was followed in Germany is equally proved by the group accompanying them from the celebrated 'Triumph of Maximilian' by Hans Burgmair. I have found, however, no instance of it either in Italy or Spain. In the former country, small caps, short-waisted jackets, and tight-fitting, party-coloured hose more especially characterise the costume of the youth of this epoch, only differing from that immediately preceding it in the fashion of the sleeves, which are slashed and puffed, or composed of several pieces fastened together by points, as already described. (See page 141.) The elder and graver persons retained the gown, and wore a more ancient form of bonnet.

Henry VII.

French Nobles, temp. Charles VIII. From the 'Traité de Tournois.'

German Nobles. From the 'Triumph of Maximilian.'

The shoes became as absurdly broad at the toes as they had been previously peaked. The new

T 2

Italian costume, end of 15th cent. From Cesare Vecellio, and a painting by Bartholomé Montagna, 1498.

Italian female costume, late 15th cent. From Cesare Vecellio.

fashion is said to have commenced in Flanders, about 1470. Paradin says the two-feet long poulaines were succeeded by duck-bills, the toes being so shaped, but still four or five fingers' breadth in length, and that subsequently slippers were worn so very broad in front as to exceed the measure of a good foot. This latter fashion does not appear to have found favour in Italy, where the poulaines, however, had been worn as generally as in Northern Europe. The female costume south of the Alps presents us with features similar to those of France and England at the same period, with the exception of the head-dress, which seems never to have been carried to such extravagant dimensions as in France and England. I have never met with an example of the steeple head-dress, or of the horned head-dress, of either the time of Henry V. or of Henry VI., nor do I find any allusion to the *hennin* in any of the Italian writers of that period. The hood worn by Anne de Bretagne, wife of Charles VIII. of France, and much in fashion in England, is also absent from the Italian portraits and statues of the same epoch. I subjoin a Milanese lady from Vecellio, illustrating the remarkable fashion of sleeve alluded to at page 139.

Milanese Lady, circa 1490. From Vecellio.   Young Venetian Noble.   Companion of the Calza.

Of Venetian costume we have several examples in Vecellio and Bonnard. The most remarkable are those of a fraternity or association of young men entitled 'La Compagna della Calza,' or the Stocking. With the sanction of the Government they gave, at their own expense, public entertainments, masquerades, concerts on the water, gondola races, and festive displays of every description.[1] They wore for distinction long, tight hose, of which the right leg was of a different colour to the left,[2] and embroidered with gold or silver, and sometimes with pearls.

The short jacket, the divided sleeves, the small cap, the long hair, are all features of the costume of England at the commencement of the reign of Henry VII.

We have not yet done with Venice. The habits of the Doge, the senators, and nobility of that famous city had assumed, during this century, the form familiarized to us by the pencils of Titian

[1] Morelli, 'Diss. sulle Pompe Veneziani,' vol. i. p. 159.

[2] One account says the hose on the left leg was green, but the assertion is not corroborated by paintings. The company survived to the year 1589.

Michael Steno, Doge of Venice.   1413.

Venetian Senator, circa 1400.

and his contemporaries. The monumental statue of the Doge Michael Steno, in the church of
St. John and St. Paul, Venice, 1413, is one of the earliest authorities for the state dress of the chief

Venetian Senators. 1450.

Fig. 1. Magistrate of Florence.

Fig. 2. A Lord of Padua.

of the republic. It presents us with the mantle of cloth of gold, with its deep cape or collar (*mozetta*) of ermine, and the *corno* of crimson velvet, encircled by a band of gold and jewels, and

Fig. 3. A Paduan.

Fig. 4. Pietro Lione, Governor of Rome.

worn over a white coif. To this figure we add that of a senator of the early part of the fifteenth century, as indicated by the hood of that period ; also those of two other senators, at the close of it, from a painting by Gentile Bellini, 1496. (See p. 142.)

Before leaving Italy in this chapter, I must direct attention to such state and official costume of other Italian Governments as have been handed down to us by painters of the fifteenth century, with the observation that, being official dresses, we cannot undertake to affix a date to their first assumption, which may have been much earlier than the time of their representation. Fig. 1 represents a magistrate of Florence, from a splendid copy of Dante in the library of the Vatican. The costume has all the character of the fourteenth century ; but it must have been still worn in the fifteenth, during which the manuscript was illuminated. Fig. 2 is from a portrait of one of the, family of Carrara, Lords of Padua,[1] and it may be questioned whether the dress he wears is official or simply the ordinary one of a nobleman of that city, and of "altri personaggi d'Italia." The sceptre in his hand, however, inclines one to the former supposition, and the form of the sleeve marks the period to be not earlier than the termination of the fourteenth century. No inference can be drawn from the absence of a mantle, for gowns are as frequently seen unaccompanied by them in portraits of Italian princes or magistrates of this period in robes of state : witness fig. 3, a podestà or mayor of an Italian city, from a picture by Pinturicchio, at Sienna, painted circa 1500, and for which some of the designs were made by Raffaelle, at that time barely of age. Fig. 4 is that of "the senator" or governor of Rome, copied by Bonnard from the sepulchral effigy of Pietro Lante in the church of Araceli at Rome, who exercised that important office in 1380 and 1381.

The works of Albrecht Dürer and Hans Burgmair are replete with examples of German costume of the latest years of this century. (See below ; also woodcut on p. 139.)

German Noble, in hunting costume. From a painting by Albert Dürer.

German costume, 15th cent. From Holbein.

German Lady, 15th cent. From Holbein.

Of Danish costume we have an example in the portrait of John, king of Denmark, 1481-1513, corresponding in its general features with that of our Henry VII, his contemporary, at page 139.

[1] The last lord of Padua of that family was murdered in 1456.

John, king of Denmark. 1481-1513.

Count of Holland, in costume 15th cent.

and Vosmer's 'Counts of Holland' supplies us with similar costumes worn by the nobility in the Low Countries at the same period.

During this century three celebrated orders of knighthood were added to those I have already noticed:—1. The Golden Fleece, in Burgundy; 2. St. Michael, in France; and 3. The Elephant, in Denmark. The Order of the Golden Fleece is, next to that of the Garter, the most coveted of such distinctions in Europe, and its collar is the earliest decoration known in the history of chivalry. It was founded by Philip the Good, duke of Burgundy, Brabant, and Earl of Flanders, on the occasion of his marriage with his third wife, the Infanta Isabella of Portugal, in compliment to whom the motto of the Order was devised, which originally ran thus: "Aultre n'auray Dame Isabeau tant que vivray;" but, like many other such mottoes, has been shorn of its fair proportions, and only the first two words, "Aultre n'auray," retained. The consequence has been an erroneous interpretation of it by several modern writers, from their ignorance of its original construction and obvious meaning. Three other matters are also connected with it : the collar, of which we have given an engraving in Dictionary, Plate V., composed of briquets or steels joined two and two together as if they were double B's (the monogram of Burgundy), and flint stones emitting sparks and flames, absurdly described as the ancient arms of the sovereigns of Burgundy of the first race, with their motto, "Ante ferit quam flamma micet;" the badge, consisting of a golden lamb or fleece, with a flint stone of gold enamelled blue, on which is engraved a motto from Claudian,

Philip the Good, duke of Burgundy. From Harleian MS. 6199.

"Pretium non vile laborum ;" in addition to which, on the border of the mantle, is embroidered the third motto, " Je l'ay empris," several times repeated.

Our business here is limited to the illustration of the costume of the knights at the period of the foundation of the Order, and an admirable one exists in the portrait of the founder himself. This portrait is taken from a MS. in the Harleian Collection, Brit. Mus., No. 6199, containing the minutes of all the feasts and chapters of the Order from its formation to 1481, and the miniature of Philip is considered to have been painted about 1460, some six or seven years before his decease. The whole dress, including the chaperon, is of crimson velvet, embroidered with gold.

The Order of St. Michael was founded on the 1st of August, 1469, by Louis XI., king of France, at the Castle of St. Amboise, in honour of St. Michael, the protector of the kingdom. The cause of its establishment is unknown. Mathieu, in his Life of Louis, states that the king hoped by its means to appease the great nobles, who were at that time excited against him, and to put an end to the division amongst them, as well as to attach them to himself. The collar was composed of

Louis XI. in the robes of the Order of St. Michael.
From a MS. of the Statutes.

Effigy of Don Gomes de Manriquez.

escallop shells, and the badge was a representation of St. Michael killing the dragon. The motto, " Imenso tremor oceani," is supposed to have reference to the tradition that whenever the foes of France approached by water the rock of St. Michael, the archangel appeared and scattered the enemy. Montfaucon has engraved a painting representing the first chapter holden of this Order, from a book of the statutes written for the use of Louis himself. I have given an engraving of the collar in Plate V. (see Dictionary, p. 124). We have in the above woodcut the king in the robes originally worn, with the tall sugar-loaf cap of the period.

The third Order, that of the Elephant, founded by King Christian of Denmark, 1470, has also been already noticed at p. 124 of the Dictionary, and the collar engraved in all its varieties.

In 1434 (as I have stated at p. 114 ante) Amadeus VIII., first duke of Savoy, reformed the Order of " the Collar" instituted by Amadeus VI. in 1362, and changed the name to that of " the Annunciation." It is still the principal Order in Piedmont. The pendant of the collar, which had previously been engraved with the figure of St. Maurice, the patron of Savoy, on horseback, now represents the

Annunciation of the Virgin Mary, surrounded by *lacs d'amour* in open work. The first knights of the new formation were a class of hermits.

To these well-known orders of knighthood must be added that of La Jarra, or the Lily, in Aragon, founded by Ferdinand I., king of Aragon, brother to Henry III., king of Castile, in 1410, on the occasion of his victory over the Moors. In M. Carderera's 'Iconografia Española' is the copy of a painting on wood of King Ferdinand and his queen, and both wearing the collar of the Order, which consisted of pots of lilies and griffins, with a medal or badge dependent, on which was the image of the Virgin enamelled in the proper colours. (See Chromolithograph issued with Part XVI.) Beside the king are the Emperor Sigismund and, it is believed, Pope Martin. The other figures, no doubt, are also portraits, but they have not been identified. The original picture was in the College at Majorca, founded by the celebrated Raimond Lulle. It is now the property of M. José Genesca, of Barcelona. To this illustration I add that of the effigy of Don Gomez de Manriquez (also from Carderera's 'Iconografia Española'), who is represented wearing the collar with the griffin appended to it, in lieu of the medallion of the Virgin (see preceding page).

Portraits of Francesco Aringhieri at Sienna.

The Knights Hospitallers, of whom I have spoken at page 64, driven finally out of the Holy Land by Sultan Khalil, 1291, first took refuge in the island of Cyprus, and in 1307 obtained a footing in the island of Rhodes, of which they completed the conquest in 1310. From that period they were known for two centuries as Knights of Rhodes. The pencil of Pinturicchio has preserved for us, in a chapel of the Cathedral of Sienna, two portraits of Francesco Aringhieri, Knight of the Order, *circa* 1485—one in his military costume, which is a fine example of the armour of that period, and the other in the robes of the Order, exemplifying the fact that the surcoat of the knight when armed for the field displayed the *arms* of the Order, viz. gules, a cross argent ; while the mantle of the professed knight in his religious capacity was distinguished by a cross of eight points, to which their subsequent removal to Malta in 1530 gave the name of the Maltese cross, by which it is now familiarly known.

The Order of the Knights Templars was abolished, as I have already stated, by the Council of Vienna, in 1312 ; but in Portugal the various establishments of that Order were upheld and their property protected by King Denis, in open defiance of Church and Pontiff. The contention was ended in 1319 by a compromise. Pope John XXII. agreed to the proposition of the king to re-establish them under the name of Knights of Christ, on condition that it should be a Roman as well as a Portuguese Order, and that he and his successors should have equal power with the kings of Portugal to make knights thereof—an arrangement continued to the present day. (See below.)

"The Order of the Dragon overthrown" was instituted by the Emperor Sigismund in 1418, to "*commemorate*" the burning of those great Reformers, John Huss and Jerome of Prague; the Order of St. Hubert, in the Duchy of Juliers,—traditionally, by Gerrard V., third duke of Juliers, in memory of a victory obtained by him over Arnold of Egmont on St. Hubert's Day, A.D. 1447; and no less than four orders of St. George were founded—one by a private gentleman of Burgundy named Philibert de Miolans, on account of his having brought from the East some relics of the saint; a second in Austria; a third at Genoa, in 1472, of which the Doge of Venice was to be perpetual grand master; and a fourth in Rome, founded by Pope Alexander VI., in 1492. The brief existence of these orders renders any description of their decorations unnecessary.

Several other orders of knighthood, the institution of which has been ascribed by their respective historians to the twelfth and thirteenth centuries, claim our attention in the fifteenth, as whatever may be the value of the authority on which such early dates have been assigned to them, it is only with reference to the special subject of this work that I am bound to speak of them, and I know of no trustworthy examples or descriptions of the habits of such orders previous to the year of grace 1400.

Of the Spanish orders of Calatrava and of Alcantara, for instance, the origins are most misty, not to say mythical. The former is said to have been founded by Sancho III., king of Castile, in 1158, and confirmed by Pope Alexander III. in 1164. That of Alcantara, otherwise called "St. Julian or the Pear-tree," is dated as early as 1156. According to some writers, it was at one time incorporated with the Order of Calatrava, but subsequently separated: a portion of the knights became a distinct fraternity, under the government of Denis, king of Portugal, in 1319, the remainder establishing themselves in Spain; and at the end of the fifteenth century Ferdinand, king of Aragon, constituted himself Grand Master of the Order, as he had already done of Calatrava, with the sanction of Pope Innocent VIII., annexing the offices to the crown of Spain for ever.

It is probable that the habit, so far as regards mantles and badges, which we see depicted some hundred years later, may have been in use at this period; but we know enough of heraldry at present to feel satisfied from their form that the crosses, fleurs-de-lys, and escallop shells distinguishing these orders of knighthood are designs of the Middle Ages, and the earliest representations of them hitherto met with cannot be assigned to an earlier date than the fifteenth or sixteenth century, whatever may have been that of their first assumption. The same observations apply to the Order of "St. James of Compostella," or "St. James of the Sword" (S. Iago della Spada), traditionally founded by Don Ramirez, king of Castile, in commemoration of his victory over the Moors at Clavos, in 846 (?), and in consequence of the asseverations of several of his officers that they distinctly saw St. James fighting on their side, bearing a banner on which was a red sword in form of a cross. Suffice it to say that in 1493 Ferdinand of Aragon, king of Castile, was constituted Grand Master of the Order by Pope Alexander VI., being already Grand Master of the Order of Calatrava, and subsequently of the Order of Alcantara.

In Portugal we find three orders of knighthood existing in the fifteenth century, viz.:—1. "The Order of Christ," which, as I have explained above, was simply a re-institution of the old Order of Knights of the Temple under a new name; 2. "The Order of the Sword," founded by Alphonso V. on his return from a successful expedition in Africa, July 2nd, 1459, and which I take to be an offshoot from that of "St. James of the Sword" just mentioned, the form of the cross being precisely the same; and, 3. "The Order of Avis," of which it is acknowledged nothing certain is known either of its institution or the origin of its name (some say from a castle so called, and others from *avis*, a bird), but which the mere blazon of the allusive badge assigned to it—viz. "*or*, a cross flory vert, accompanied in point by two birds *affronté* sable "—sufficiently disproves its existence previous to that of heraldry as a science. In Chapter VIII. figures will be found of knights of all the above orders in their proper habits of ceremony; but how long they had been in use at that date (1695), in the absence of documentary evidence I will not undertake to determine.

Of the habit of one Order instituted in the fifteenth century, we possess, happily, undoubted evidence. It is that of "the Crescent," founded by René, count of Anjou and king of Sicily, in 1446 (?). Montfaucon has given us, in plate clxvi of his 'Trésor des Antiquités de la Couronne de France,' an engraving from a painting in the portfolio of M. de Gagnières, representing a meeting of a chapter of the Order, and at the foot of it the portrait of Jean Cossa, Comte de Troie and Seigneur de Grimault, one of the knights in 1451, in the habit of the Order. It is very peculiar, the badge of the crescent being embroidered on a red robe under the right arm, with the motto "Los en croissant." The knights seated in chapter wear flat-crowned, broad-brimmed hats of a very modern character, but the figures are ill-drawn and poorly engraved, and the portrait of Cossa is the most interesting and reliable illustration. (See annexed woodcut.)

Several alterations in the colour of the surcoat and chaperon of the Knights of the Garter took place during the fifteenth century. In the first year of the reign of Henry V. it was changed again to white, the whole of the dress being still of cloth.

Jean Cossa, Comte de Troie, Knight of the Crescent, 1451.

In the thirteenth of Henry VI. the surcoat and chaperon were of scarlet, and subsequently again of white. The Earl of Shrewsbury, in our chromolithograph from the splendid Shrewsbury book, is in a scarlet surcoat, the chaperon being of a rather lighter red. The number of garters to be embroidered on them was limited in this reign to one hundred and twenty for a duke, one hundred and ten for a marquis, one hundred for an earl, and so less by ten down to a knight bachelor, who wore sixty. The king was unlimited, and on Henry's surcoat and chaperon there were one hundred and seventy-three. The mantle about this period was first made of velvet, and lined with white damask or satin.

Of Family collars I have given some notice under that heading in the Dictionary: that of the House of York consisting of suns and roses, with its various pendants; the white lion of March, for Edward IV.; the black bull of Ulster, for the Duke of Clarence; and the white boar for the Duke of Gloucester,—all first appearing in the latter half of the century.

Legal and official personages continue to be distinguished in England by party-coloured dresses, long gowns girdled round the waist, and chaperons with tippets, by which they are occasionally slung over the shoulder. (See chromolithograph of the Court of King's Bench issued with Part XIV. of this work for the official costume of the judges, counsel, and officers of the court in the reign of Henry VI.)

When that king returned to England after being crowned in France, A.D. 1432, "the Lord Mayor of London rode to meet him at Eltham, being arrayed in crimson velvet, a great velvet hat furred, a girdle of gold about his middle, and a baldrick of gold about his neck trailing down behind him; his three henchmen in suits of red spangled with silver; the aldermen in gowns of scarlet, with purple hoods; and all the commonalty of the city in white gowns and scarlet hoods."

In France we learn that the colours of the official dresses were continually changing, and it would appear they were generally those of the sovereign or the seigneur of the day, or adopted according to circumstances. In 1418, the gowns of the members of the Hôtel de Ville in Paris were entirely blue; during the English rule there they were wholly red; and on the entry of Charles VII. after the retirement of the English, they were party-coloured, scarlet and blue. The counsellors of the Cour de Bourgogne wore robes of black velvet in 1468, which was one of the family colours of Charles the Bold. The Parliament of Paris was an exception to this custom of change. Its members were always robed in red. The procureurs and avocats of the king in Parliament also wore red gowns and large furred hoods.

The Presidents of Parliament wore, in addition to their scarlet gowns, a mantle of the same colour, open only on the right side below the shoulder. The mantle of the First President was distinguished by three strips of gold lace and three of white fur upon each shoulder. The Presidents also wore round hats of black velvet over their chaperons, the hat of the First President being ornamented with a gold lace round the top. This hat or bonnet, called "*barette*," from the Italian *biretta*, was the general mark of literary eminence. Students in the Universities received it on their being made Masters of Arts. In form it originally resembled the Turkish fez; but in the year 1460, and for a short time afterwards, it was affected by the fashion of the time, and became tall and pointed. Such is the information we receive from M. Quicherat; but, unfortunately, he does not give us any pictorial illustration of it in this altered form. It is probably, however, represented in the annexed figures of legal personages in a MS. in the Harleian Library, No. 4374, a copy of Valerius Maximus, late fifteenth

Legal personages, 15th cent. From a MS. in Harleian Library, British Museum.

century. The two smaller figures offer us also an interesting illustration of the hyke worn by serjeants-at-law (see Dictionary, p. 287. Compare also the figures at pp. 288 and 289 with these, and I think there can be no doubt of the identity of the garments).

Jean Chartier, in his account of the entry of Charles VII. into Rouen in 1449, describes the Chancellor of France as "drest in a royal habit, that is to say a mantle, robe, and chaperon of scarlet furred with miniver, and having on each of his shoulders three gold ribands and three purfles of lettice." These three bands of gold lace and white fur appear to have been the origin, as I have already remarked, of the bars on the mantles of our peers (see Dictionary, under ROBE, p. 424); and they are seen on the mantles in France not only of judges or chancellors, but on those of kings, sovereign princes, and nobles. (See figures of Louis II., duke of Bourbon, pp. 115 and 123.)

I have met with no explanation of their particular significance, or record of their first assumption.

M. Bonnard has given us examples of magistrates and legal functionaries in various Italian states in the fifteenth century; but no such distinction is visible on any part of their vestments, which differ in no particular degree from those of the generality of the upper classes of their separate periods. The first woodcut represents two magistrates or judges, and the second two artisans consult-

THE TRIUMPH OF ST. THOMAS AQUINAS

From the painting in the Louvre by Benozzo Gozzoli, 15th cent.

ing a notary. Both subjects were copied by M. Bonnard from a MS. copy of the statutes of the Republic of Sienna, written *circa* 1400.

Italian Magistrates, 15th cent.

Artisans and Notary.

The ecclesiastical costume of the fifteenth century is generally represented in our accompanying plate (XXIV.) from Benozzo Gozzoli's picture of 'The Triumph of St. Thomas Aquinas,' an event which took place in the thirteenth century (A.D. 1256), but depicted by Gozzoli (who was born in 1400 and died in 1478) in the habits of his own time. The Pope, the cardinals, a bishop, and the heads of various religious houses and orders are here seen in council, attired as they would have been about 1450.

At the close of the fifteenth century the superfluous usage of cloth, and the vast expenses incurred at the funerals of the nobility and gentry in England, occasioned the promulgation of an edict, by which the habits and liveries, as they were called, were limited to certain quantities. Dukes and marquises were allowed sixteen yards for their *slopps* (mourning cassocks so called[1]) and mantles; an earl, fourteen; a viscount, twelve; a baron or banneret, being a Knight of the Garter, eight yards for his gown and hood; a knight or esquire of the body, six; and all inferior personages five yards for their gowns: and the number of liveries for their servants decreased proportionately, from eighteen for a duke down to two. An archbishop was allowed the same as a duke; and to this edict was added a prohibition to wear hoods to all persons under the degree of an esquire of the king's household, except in time of need, that is to say bad weather,—only tippets of a quarter of a yard in breadth. Hoods "with a roll *sleved* over the head, or otherwise being of that fashion," were forbidden to all persons below the rank of a baron, or the son and heir of an earl; all of lower degree were to wear their hoods without rolls. Margaret, Countess of Richmond, the mother of King Henry VII., issued in the eighth year of his reign an ordinance for "the reformation of apparell for great estates of women in the tyme of mourninge," wherein it is ordained that "the greatest estates shall have their surcotes with a trayne before and another behynde, and their mantles with traynes, the greatest estates to wear them longest, with mantles and tippets, and that *bekes* be no more used in any manner of wyse, because of the deformitye of the same."

[1] See under SLOP, in the Dictionary, for the curious usage of this word.

The Queen is to wear a surcoat with "the traynes" as aforesaid, "a playne hoode without clockes, and a tippet at the hood lying a good length upon the trayne of the mantell, being in breadth a nayle and an inche;" and after the first quarter of a year the hood may be lined with black satin or furred with ermine, and all ladies, down to the degree of baroness, are to wear similar mourning, with the tippets and trains shorter, and to be barbed above the chin. Baronesses were to wear surcoats without trains, and mantles "accordinge;" and lords' daughters and knights' wives surcoats with "meatlye traynes," but no mantles, hoods without clockes, and tippets only a yard and a half long "to be pynned on the arme." These estates are to wear the barbe under their chins. The inferior gentry were to wear "sloppes and coat hardies," hoods with clockes, and tippets a yard long and an inch broad pinned upon the side of the hood; all chamberers and other persons, hoods with clockes, and no manner of tippets to be found about them. The barbe also was to be worn by them below "the throat goyll," or gullet; that is, the lowest part of the throat.

Amongst other regulations it is provided that "great estates when they ryde, wearing mantells, may have short clokes and hoodes, with narrow tippettes to be bounde about their hoodes, and as soon as they come to the courte to laye awaye their hoodes;" also, "and after the first month none shall wear hoodes in presence of their betters, excepting when they are at labour or on horseback."

A duchess may have sixteen yards of cloth for her "mantell, surcote, slop, hood, and kyrtell;" and in a more modern manuscript she is allowed one barbe, one frontlet, and four kerchiefs, and livery for twelve servants. A countess is allowed twelve yards, one barbe, one frontlet, and two kerchiefs, and liveries for eight servants; a baroness the same, with liveries for four servants.

In a MS. in the Harleian Library, British Museum, No. 6064, and also in one in the College of Arms, are figures illustrating some of these ordinances. (*Vide* next page and Dictionary, page 34.)

The surcoat with the train before and behind, the former being tucked up and passed through and falling over the girdle, the hood with the long tippet, all as worn by the highest nobility, are visible enough in the figures given therewith; but what "bekes" may have been I cannot discover by an examination of the mourning habiliments at any period. Throughout the MSS. of the fifteenth century, mourners are represented in long black cloaks and cowls, the latter greatly resembling some "cowls" we see upon chimneys at the present day, which must have been modelled from and named after them; but nothing like a beak or peak is discernible.

Some curious information respecting continental customs is conveyed to us by a treatise on etiquette written by a lady of the Court of Philip the Good, duke of Burgundy, quoted by M. Quicherat. "The fashion of robes and mantles," she tells us, "differs in France from that in Flanders, for in France they wear long cloths, here they do not." "I have heard," she continues, "that the Queen of France must remain for a whole year in the room wherein she received the tidings of the king, her husband's, death; and every one should know that the queen's chamber should be hung entirely with black, and the halls with black cloth also."

Madame de Charolois, daughter of the Duke of Bourbon, as soon as she heard of her father's death in 1456, remained from that moment in her chamber for six weeks, and always reclined on a bed covered with white cloth, her head supported by pillows. She wore her "barbette," her mantle, and her chaperon, which were furred with miniver. The chamber was all hung with black cloth, and under foot was a great black cloth in lieu of a velvet carpet. We are given to understand, however, that this was only the state in which the Princess received visitors; for "Quand Madame estoit en son particulier, elle n'estoit pas *toujours couchée ou en une chambre*," which is a great relief to our feelings, and reconciles us to an account we might otherwise have regarded with some suspicion.

Furthermore, the lady informs us that "all other princesses should do the same, but that the wives of knights bannerets need keep their beds only nine days on the deaths of their fathers or mothers, and the rest of the six weeks they might sit in front of their beds on a great black cloth. For their husbands, however, they must mourn recumbent for the whole six weeks."

For a husband also the hood and mantle were to be worn for six months, the barbette and kerchief over it three months, the robes to be always furred with miniver, the "gris" being taken out, and the white alone seen. While the barbe was worn no girdle or ribbon of silk was allowed ; and in deep mourning ("grand deuil") for husband or father, rings and gloves were equally prohibited.

The queens of France were expected to observe similar regulations rigidly ; but they had the privilege to wear white during their "long deuil." This custom, M. Quicherat informs us, was the origin of the term " Reine blanche," popularly applied to all queen dowagers ; also of many traditions that have been incorrectly linked with the name of Queen *Blanche* of Castile, the mother of Louis IX. (St. Louis). The notorious Isabella of Bavaria was the model of " Reines blanches," who never moved out of Paris, nor even left her chamber, but remained shut up in the Hôtel de St. Paul the whole time of mourning, "comme veuve doit faire."[1]

Mourning habit, *temp.* Henry VII. From Harleian MS. 4425.

On the death of a king of France, it was the custom at this period for the heir to the throne, wherever he might be at the time, to assume black clothes immediately, and wear them till the termination of the first service for the repose of the soul of the deceased, after which he changed them for red (*vermeil*), the equivalent for purple, which was considered royal mourning. That consummate and eccentric hypocrite, Louis XI., obeyed this custom after his own fashion, by attiring himself at the end of the ceremony in a hunting suit, parti-coloured red and white, *hat included.*

[1] French Chronicle, quoted by Quicherat, p. 290.

Michelle de Vitry, widow of Jean Juvenal des Ursins. 1456. From the Museum at Versailles.

CHAPTER VII.

THE SIXTEENTH CENTURY.

UR difficulties are actually increased by our advantages. The trouble of hunting up scraps of information in ancient records, of identifying sepulchral effigies and testing popularly-received authorities, is trifling compared with that of selecting from the mass of authentic material available for our present purpose, pressed upon us from all countries in civilized Europe, those examples which may be most interesting and instructive, as it would be manifestly impossible to include in this work a tithe of them. Russia, an empire which in the sixteenth century began to take a prominent position amongst the continental Powers, would alone demand a volume for its illustration. Engraving, an art in its infancy in the previous century, now boasted the master hands of a Burgmair, an Albert Dürer, and a Crispin de Passe. Holbein, Sir Antonio More, Titian, and Zucchero painted, and the first works on Costume were published in the reign of Elizabeth. It is a positive *embarras de richesses*, out of which we are at a loss to know what to choose, what to neglect. Take, for instance, the magnificent *Ehrenforte*,—the 'Triumphal Arch of the Emperor Maximilian,' as it is otherwise called, displaying in its infinite variety the civil and military costume of Germany, contemporary with the reign of Henry VII. in England. Which out of that volume of sumptuous engravings is to be preferred to another? Yet it is obvious that our examples must be limited to two or three at the outside. Of this, however, anon. Our first business is with England under the Tudors. We have had a glimpse of it in the last chapter, and must now take up the tale at the sixteenth year of the reign of Henry VII., which was the last of the century.

There is little to add in the way of description to what I have already said respecting the costume of this reign. The fashion of slashing all portions of attire increased in popularity, and fluted skirts to the doublets are specially characteristic of this period. The doublets were cut exceedingly low in the neck, a fashion stigmatized by Barclay in his 'Ship of Fooles of the Worlde,' printed by Pynson in 1508, in which the gallants of that day are described as

> "——charged with collars and chaines;
> In golden withes, their fingers full of rings;
> *Their necks naked almost unto the raines;*
> Their sleeves blazing like unto a crane's wings."

Others are called on to "come neare" with their shirts, "bordered and displayed in forme of surplois." Shirts bordered with lace and curiously adorned with needlework continued for a long time in use amongst the nobility and gentry. A shirt that belonged to Arthur, Prince of Wales, the eldest born son of Henry VII., made of long lawn with very full sleeves, and beautifully embroidered with blue silk round the collar and wristbands, was in the possession of the late John Gage Rokewood, Esq.,

King Henry VIII

director of the Society of Antiquaries. The baring so much of the throat and neck induced the wearing of the hair much longer on each side of the head, and the general substitution of hats, caps, and bonnets of various fantastic forms for the now rapidly disappearing hood (see Vol. I. p. 76). The face was still closely shaved, soldiers and old men alone wearing moustaches or beards. One cap peculiar to this period is still visible on the heads of the knaves in our playing cards, the whole costume, indeed, not only of the knaves but of the kings and queens, being rude representations of the dress of that day; and a pack of cards engraved by Martin Schongauer, a celebrated painter-engraver and goldsmith, who died 2nd February, 1499–1500, presents several designs illustrative of the costume of his own time, slightly exaggerated in the details (see woodcut forming the initial of the first word of this chapter, representing "the Knave of Pinks"). The costume in England at the accession of Henry VIII. appears to have been considerably influenced by that of Germany, although France was still the *arbiter elegantiarum* in the world of Fashion. As M. Paul Lacroix has happily observed, "France was then, as it is now, fickle and capricious, fantastical and wavering, not from indifference, but because she was always ready to borrow from every quarter anything which pleased her. She, however, never failed to put her own stamp on whatever she adopted, thus making any fashion essentially French, even though she had only just borrowed it from Spain, England, Germany, or Italy."[1] It is exactly that "stamp" of hers which makes French fashions current through Europe. In the Dictionary we have pretty well exhausted the variety of costumes of Henry, his queens and subjects, gentle and simple, and shall therefore, in accordance with the plan already pursued, continue the illustration of it by foreign examples, beginning as previously with France.

Francis I. was fond of dress, and encouraged the love of it in his lieges, especially in the ladies of his court, to whom he liberally presented most splendid dresses. "I have seen," says Brantôme, "coffres and wardrobes belonging to old ladies of that time, so full of gowns the king had given them, and of so magnificent a description, that it was a very great fortune."

Rabelais has given a minute account of the costume of his time, both for men and women, in his description of the imaginary Abbey of Theleme, founded by Gargantua, in which the votaries, in lieu of being restricted to the dress of the monastical orders, attired themselves in that most fashionable at the period, viz. 1533.[2] How much are we indebted to the satirists of all ages for the greater portion of such information as we possess respecting the habits of their contemporaries. "The men," he says, "wore stockings (*chausses pour les bas*) of stamine or milled serge of scarlet, *migraine*,[3] white or black, and upper stocks (*pour les hauts*) of velvet of the same colours or nearly so, embroidered or slashed according to their fancy; the pourpoint of cloth of gold or silver, or of velvet, satin, damask, or taffeta, of similar colours, slashed, embroidered, and garnished gracefully; the points (*aiguilettes*) of silk of the same colours, with tags of gold well enamelled; the cloaks and gowns (*saies et chamarres*) of cloth of gold or silver, or velvet trimmed or guarded (*pourfilé*) at pleasure; robes as rich as those of ladies; girdles of silk of the colour of the pourpoint, and each man with a handsome sword by his side, the hilt gilt, the sheath velvet of the colour of the chausses, the chape of goldsmiths' work; a dagger to match; the bonnet of black velvet, garnished with many rings and buttons of gold; the feather white, delicately interspersed with gold spangles, from which hung fine rubies, emeralds, &c." Elsewhere he speaks of the various hats that were worn, "les ungs sont ras, les aultres a poil, les aultres veloutez, les aultres taffetassez, les aultres satinisez."

In the wardrobe accounts of the reign of Henry VIII., and the elaborate descriptions of his banquets and entertainments in the pages of Hall, Stowe, and Howe, all these articles of attire are continually mentioned as made of the same costly materials and ornamented as richly with gold-smiths' work and jewellery. Under their separate heads will be found ample quotations from the above authorities, and it is needless to repeat them here.

[1] 'Manners, Customs, and Dress during the Middle Ages,' p. 549.
[2] "Comment estoyent vestus les religieux et religieuses de Theleme."—Livre I., chap. lvi. "Theleme, mot grec qui signifie *volonté*."—Glossaire, ed. 1820.
[3] Another shade of scarlet, the colour of the pips of the pomegranate.

The bas-relief of the Hôtel du Bourthéroulde at Rouen, representing the celebrated meeting of Henry and Francis on the Field of the Cloth of Gold, so named from the profusion of that magnificent material displayed on that occasion, enables us at a glance to recognize the similarity in apparel and equipment of the rival sovereigns and their respective suites.

Meeting of Henry VIII. and Francis I. From a bas-relief at Rouen.

Nevertheless, a great alteration took place in the costume of the two countries during the first half of the sixteenth century. The hats, which we have seen so large and crowned with a forest of feathers—a fashion that lasted with little intermission from about 1488 to 1520, the date of the royal interview aforesaid—gradually decreased in size till they scarcely covered the head, and in 1540 had moulted their plumage so completely that nothing was left of it but a single *marabout.* The *haut de chausses,* about the same date, became trunk hose, and the *bas de chausses,* called "stocking of hose" in English, foreshadowed its approaching independence of the more important article of apparel, and finally monopolized the names of stocking, hose, and *bas.*

Rabelais still more minutely describes the dress of the ladies. Their *chausses* (stockings), he tells us, were of scarlet colour or migraine. Their shoes and slippers were of crimson, red, or violet velvet, slashed "à la barbe d'écrevisse." They wore "la belle vasquine" (the *basquina* of the Spanish doñas), made of silk camlet, and the "vertugale" (farthingale) of white, red, tawny, or grey taffeta, over which was placed the "cotte," made of silver taffeta embroidered with fine gold needlework, or, as it seemed best to them according to the weather, of satin, damask, or velvet of various colours—orange, tawny, green, ash, blue, yellow, crimson, or white—or of cloth of gold or silver, or of stuffs embroidered with gold and silver; their gowns ("robes"), according to the season, of similar rich materials,—in winter of taffeta trimmed with fur of lynx or leuzerns ("loup cervier"), black genets, martins of Calabria, sables, and other valuable furs. In summer, in lieu of gowns, they sometimes wore *marlottes* (mantles) of the above-named materials, or *bernes à la Moresque,*—the *bournouse,* a Moorish cloak with a hood to it, and introduced from Spain, where it was called *beruia,*— of violet velvet embroidered with gold and silver, or of gold net with small pearls at the angles, and

Nobleman of the reign of Louis XII.   Claude de Guise. 1516.   French Gentleman. 1520.

always a fine plume of feathers *of the colour of their cuffs*, plentifully ornamented with gold spangles. Their head-dresses also varied with the seasons. In winter it was "à la mode française ;" in spring,

Flemish costume, circa 1505.

French Lady, *temp.* Louis XII.

"À l'espagnole ;" in summer, "à la tusque" (Tuscan): except on Sundays and fête-days, when the French head-dress was always worn, "parcequ'il est plus honnête et sent plus pudicité matronale." This "accoutrement français," as he terms it, was the peculiar hood we see worn by Anne de Bretagne, queen first of Charles VIII. and afterwards of Louis XII., and, I presume, known in England as "the French hood," of which we have given numerous examples so far as we can venture to judge from the vague and puzzling accounts of it. That it underwent many changes and varied according to the taste of the nation adopting it, the varieties engraved in illustration of it will sufficiently prove (see Dictionary, pp. 277, 296, 298); in addition to which we have the assertion of Holinshed, that Anne of Cleves, the day after her arrival in England, wore a French hood *after the English fashion*. M. Quicherat distinctly describes it in accordance with my view of it : "L'accoutrement de tête à la mode française était *le chaperon de velours avec templette et quelque pendante*" (p. 360). M. Viollet-le-Duc simply calls this particular head-dress "une coiffe" (art. "Coiffure," 'Mobilier Français,' tome iii, p. 248), and altogether ignores it in the article "Chaperon" (ibid., pp. 131, 142).

Claude de France, first wife of Francis I.　　　　　　　　Eleanor of Castile, second wife of Francis I.

There are many other points in the above descriptions of Rabelais which are commented upon by M. Quicherat, and some that call for notice from me, as they tend to illustrate certain unexplained terms met with in inventories of costume in England at this period. In chronicles and inventories of the reign of Henry VIII., we meet with the words shamew and chammer (see Dictionary, p. 450), which is said by Hall to be "in effect a gowne cut in the middle." Now, though Rabelais does not add to our information as to its shape, we learn from him that shamew and chammer are corruptions of the French *chamarre;* and furthermore, from M. Quicherat, that it was a long loose garment ("veste" he calls it) composed of bands of silk or velvet, united by lace of gold or silver, from which the verb *chamarrer*, applied to the richly-laced liveries of the valets of the nobility in after-days, was originally derived.

The ornamentation of feathers with jewels was a fashion in the previous century : the *paillettes* and *papillettes* they hung from, which I have translated "spangles," were most likely the "aglets" with which the Milan bonnets were so profusely decorated in the time of Henry VIII.

The vasquine is described in the Glossary to Rabelais (ed. 1820) as a sort of corset worn next to the chemise, and this description is adopted by M. Quicherat.[1] The *basquine* of Spain is undoubtedly a petticoat ; and if the above description be correct, it is only another proof of the perplexity occasioned by transferring the name of one article of attire to another entirely dissimilar. The *vertugal*, again, is here undoubtedly an under-petticoat, more resembling the modern crinoline than the vardingale or farthingale to which it bequeathed its name some fifty years later. In the reigns of Francis I. and Henry VIII. it was shaped like an inverted funnel (" en entonnoir "), and distended the lower portion of the dress, giving it the form of the capital letter A, an infinitely more graceful one than that of a wheel or a drum, which was the effect of its successor. The Spanish and Tuscan or Florentine head-dresses, which these gay Thelemites wore in spring and summer, will be considered in their proper places. *Calabrer*, a fur so frequently mentioned in the thirteenth and fourteenth centuries, and which is only defined by the glossarists as derived from Calabria, we are told by Rabelais, is the fur of the Calabrian martin, "martres de Calabre," a much more satisfactory definition.

But we have not yet done with the devotees of Theleme. The personal ornaments of the fair recluses were paternosters (rosaries), rings, *jaserans*, and carcanets of fine jewels, carbuncles, balas rubies, diamonds, sapphires, emeralds, turquoises, garnets, agates, beryls, pearls, and the rarest sort of pearls called unions.[2] The word *jaserans* requires explanation. M. Quicherat informs us they were gold chains disposed in festoons (*guirlands*) on the corsage of the gown, recalling, I presume, though he does not allude to it, the effect of the gold-studded armour so named, scarcely then disused, and at all events familiar to the sight of the existing generation.

Other accessories to the toilet make their appearance at this period. The fan composed of feathers is mentioned by Rabelais as an *éventoir de plumes*. It was suspended by a gold chain to the girdle with other pretty trifles, called *contenances*, such as scent bottles, pomanders, keys, seals, &c., and deriving that appellation from the circumstance that toying with them during a delicate or embarrassing conversation gave confidence to the fair owner. To these were added, by Eleanora of Castile, a small hand mirror, either alone in a frame and with a handle of carved ivory or gold-smiths' work, or inserted at the back of the feathered fan.

The wearing of swords in civil attire also dates from this epoch. The dagger had long been considered a necessary appendage to the full dress of a gentleman. To it was now added the sword, the hilts and guards of both being often *chefs-d'œuvre* of workmanship. Rabelais ridicules this fashion by giving to his pacific Gargantua a sword of gilt wood and a poniard of cuir-bouilli, and attributes its origin to the "Indalgos bourrachous," as in corrupt Castilian he designates the drunken, brawling, hectoring Spanish adventurers that swarmed on the Continent during the wars of the sixteenth century.

I hope I have not over-estimated the value of these extracts from the pages of the immortal Doctor of Medicine of Montpellier, and that I need not apologize to my readers for the length to which they have extended.

As late as 1521 the hair was worn long behind and at the sides of the head, and short in front, as it had been from the commencement of the reign of Henry VII., but an accident which occurred to Francis I. occasioned a change of fashion. Having received a wound in the head from a torch flung at him by Captain de Lorges, Sieur de Montgomery, during a frolic at court in that year, it became necessary to cut his hair close, in order to apply the requisite remedies. In compliment to their sovereign, his courtiers hastened to be similarly cropped, and, as usual, their example was followed by the public generally.[3] Beards and moustaches were still worn by the laity.

---

[1] " Vasquine ou basquine, sorte de corset que les femmes mettaient par-dessus la chemise. Nous avons un livre intitulé ' Blason des Basquines et Vertugales.' "—Benoist Rigaud, Lyons, 1563.

[2]   " And in the cup a *union* will I throw,
      Richer than that which twelve successive kings
      In Denmark's crown have worn."
              Hamlet, Act V. sc. last.

[3] Pasquier, ' Recherches,' liv. vii.

Two other celebrated sovereigns, contemporaries of Henry and Francis, the Emperors Maximilian I. and his successor Charles V., must, by the interchange of magnificent courtesies, have influenced considerably the taste in dress of the courts they visited, and through them, as usual, that of the people. In 1494 the marriage of the former with Blanche Marie, widow of Philibert duke of Savoy, at Milan, was celebrated with the greatest pomp and splendour ; and the great work of Hans Burgmair, known as the 'Triumph of the Emperor Maximilian,' is as illustrative of the costume of England as it is of that of France at the same period. The reception of Charles V. by his generous rival, Francis I., at Paris, 1st of January, 1540, on the Emperor's passing through France to his Flemish dominions, in point of splendour might almost be ranked with the celebrated interview of Henry and Francis at Ardres.

We have already heard complaints of the adoption of French fashions by the Florentines, and we find Milan bonnets the rage in England in the reign of Henry VIII. The pencil will demonstrate these facts much more readily than the pen, and the reader is therefore referred to the engravings of Milan bonnets at page 76 of the Dictionary.

The marriage of the Emperor Frederick III. with Leonora, Infanta of Portugal, has furnished subjects for the pencils of Pinturicchio, Raphael, and Burgmair. The representations of this ceremony, which took place at Sienna in 1452, are all of a date full half a century later than the event, but they are valuable illustrations of the costume of Germany, Italy, and Portugal at the period of their execution, when, as I have just observed, a sort of fusion took place in the fashions of the principal countries of Europe. In the fresco of Pinturicchio—from the designs, as it is asserted, of Raphael in 1502—representing the introduction of Leonora to Frederick by Æneas Sylvius, then Bishop of Sienna, we have a most interesting variety of costume, male and female, civil and ecclesiastic. M. Bonnard has selected several of the principal figures and given them singly in his 'Costumes,' but Mr. G. Scharf has copied a photograph of the fresco in Her Majesty's collection at Windsor, which was engraved to accompany a communication of his to the Society of Antiquaries (published by it in the forty-third volume of the 'Archæologia' in 1870), and thereby greatly added to our information (see Plate XXII.).

Marriage of the Emperor Frederick and Leonora.

The dress of the Emperor, who is not in his robes of state, that of the officer in attendance on him, and the curiously arranged hair of the lady-in-waiting on the Infanta, are well deserving the reader's attention.

The woodcut by Hans Burgmair, in the well-known volume entitled 'Der Weis Kunig,' represents the *marriage* of Frederick and Leonora by Pope Nicholas V. at Naples. In this the Emperor is crowned, but not with the Imperial crown, nor is he in the Imperial robes, but attired in a rich gown of cloth of gold, with broad collar of miniver, the usual dress of princes and nobles at the end of the fifteenth and commencement of the sixteenth centuries. (See portraits of Henry VII., Dictionary, p. 219, and the present volume, p. 139.) "The Infanta," Mr. Scharf remarks, "is here made to look thoroughly German, and wears the costume of the sixteenth century peculiar to that country." Only, let me add, in character, the form being that of the period generally. The bulging sleeves, with the cuff projecting over the back of the hand, the cut of the body, and the caul or crespinette confining the hair, are all features of female attire in England and on the Continent from 1480 to 1509.

Turning next to Spain and Portugal—for these two countries were so closely connected with Germany at the period now under consideration, that the costume of one is reflected by the other as perfectly almost as in a glass—I will first call the reader's attention to the portraits of the three

Charles.   Leonora.   Isabella.
The three children of Philip of Castile.

children of Philip of Castile, called " Le Beau," son of the Emperor Maximilian I. by his wife Jeanne la Folle, daughter of Ferdinand king of Aragon and Isabella queen of Castile ; a marriage which conveyed the crown of Spain to the house of Austria, in the person of Charles V., one of the children here represented—at the age, it is presumed, of five or six ; his sisters Leonora and Isabella, the former two years older and the latter a year younger, being the other two depicted. The portraits are only half-lengths, but fortunately they present us with the most important portion of the costume.

Charles, at this time known only as the Duke of Luxembourg, and his younger sister Isabella, both wear caps of the pattern seen on the head of Henry VII. in his portrait at p. 139 *ante.* Leonora's head-dress is the well-known hood with its pendent drapery, so conspicuous in all the portraits of Anne de Bretagne and the ladies of France and England *circa* 1500. The doll in the arms of Isabella has a similar coiffure, and, what is particularly noteworthy, the hair is plaited in a long tail behind, and recalls the head-dress of the Portuguese lady attending the Infanta Leonora in Pinturicchio's fresco (Plate XXII.*). The laced body of the gown and the sleeves expanding from the elbow will be recognized as the characteristic features of the fashion immediately preceding (see Dictionary).

A splendid manuscript in the British Museum, containing a richly-illuminated genealogy of the royal house of Portugal by Flemish artists during the first half of the sixteenth century, furnishes us with several fine examples of male and female costume of Spain and Portugal during part of the reigns of Charles V. and John III., though some of the portraits, as they may be called, are of persons of a much earlier period : for instance, Constantia, natural daughter

Constantia, duchess of Lancaster.

of Peter the Cruel, king of Castile, and second wife of John of Gaunt, duke of Lancaster, and Philippa,

Philippa, queen of Portugal.

the duke's daughter by his first wife and queen of John I., king of Portugal. Although some doubt may be thrown on the horned head-dress of the duchess having been worn in Spain at the date at which this figure was painted, it is probable that it may have been copied from an earlier picture. The mode of wearing the hair, the square-cut body, the open robe displaying the petticoat, the girdle with its long jewelled pendant, are distinct characteristics of the dress of the six-teenth century; while the head-dress is certainly not of the time in which the duchess lived (she died in 1394), nor indeed resembling that of any time sufficiently to enable us to speak confidently about it. I would not, therefore, undertake to say that such a coiffure was not worn in Spain or Flanders *circa* 1520, through one of those evanescent caprices of Fashion which induces her to repeat herself at intervals with slight alterations, generally betraying the date of the revival. One thing is certainly clear, that it is the only part of the dress which leaves a doubt of its authenticity. Queen Philippa is represented in her state dress, wearing crown and mantle, and there is nothing in the remainder of her attire that is visible at variance with the costume contemporaneous with the age of the manuscript.

A-propos of the horned head-dress in Spain, it is certain that in one form or another it was worn in the Basque pro-vinces in 1530. Subjoined is the figure of a woman of Biscay, from Vecellio, and another of a woman of Bayonne, from Duplessis' 'Costumes historiques,' t. i.

Woman of Biscay. 1592.

Woman of St. Jean de Luz.

Woman of Bayonne, 16th cent.

M. Quicherat, who gives a similar figure to the former as a Basquaise de St. Jean de Luz, from a collection of costumes *à la gouache* of the time of Francis I., describes both these dresses, and quotes

Queen Eleanor of Aragon.

John, King of Castile.

an account of the young married women of Bayonne complaining of their coiffure to the envoys of Francis I. in 1530, and adds from the same authority, that at Dax the women wore hoods with

Francis I. (?)

Charles V.

Y 2

horns in front and small tails behind. One of them being asked what was the use of such things,
replied, "To catch fools."

Of the male costume, the portrait of John, king of Castile
and Leon, though barely a half-length, presents all the features
of the time of Francis I.—the slashed and puffed sleeves,
the cloak with lining and broad collar of fur spread over the
shoulders, and the broad-brimmed hat seen in so many
portraits of this time, and notably in those attributed to
the Emperor Charles V. and Henry VIII., in the picture
formerly at Strawberry Hill, and engraved in Harding's work
(see woodcuts in the preceding page).[1]

Queen Eleanor of Aragon is also represented in the
same work, in one of those turban head-dresses so frequently
seen in European costumes of the early part of the fifteenth
century ; and Queen Johanna of Castile, with her hair in a
resille, and the slashes in her sleeves connected by jewels.

Italy further exemplifies the fusion of national costumes
at this period. At the commencement of the century we
find the turban-like head-dresses worn by both sexes ; the
fluted bases (*falde*) to the doublets of the men, "like
the Germans ;"[2] the gowns of the women less formal perhaps in shape, but all with the sleeves bulging, puffed,
slashed, and some decorated with ribbons flying in all
directions, as are those of the "knave of pinks" at the head of this chapter. The varieties are

Queen Johanna of Castile.

Italian Lady, early 16th cent. From Vecellio.

Italian Nobleman, early 16th cent. From Vecellio.

[1] Doubts have been expressed by connoisseurs respecting the personages represented. The portrait assigned to
Henry VIII. is conjectured to be that of Francis I., whom it certainly more resembles. As illustrations of the costume
of the time, however, they are not affected by the question.   [2] " Simili à quei de Tedeschi." (Vecellio, p. 71, ed. 1598.)

all to be found in the dresses of the other nations of Europe of the same date ; and even in Venice, except in official costumes, there is no special difference to be discerned, the descriptions in Vecellio being usually headed " Habito usato in Venetia & *per l'Italia*," or " d'altri luoghi d'Italia."

Beatrix D'Este. From Bonnard.

Countess de Cellant. From Bonnard.

The following extract from a curious old writer affords us a piece of contemporary information specially concerning Genoa, which is interesting as it illustrates a fashion in Spain in the following

Merchant of Venice. From Vecellio.

Merchant of Venice. From Bonnard.

century which was probably derived from it. The women of Genoa, we are told, "though their uppermost garment be but of plain cloth *by reason of a law*, yet underneath they wear the finest silks that may be had, and so finely hosed and shoed as I never saw the like." They are also described as "open-faced and for the most part bareheaded, with the hair so finely trussed and curled that it passeth rehearsal." (Wm. Thomas, 'Historie of Italie,' 4to. London, 1549.)

Some fifty years later, it would appear, from the engravings and descriptions of Vecellio, that the law Mr. Thomas speaks of had been repealed or no longer regarded, as the "Donna nobile moderna" (1598) is represented by Vecellio in a *guippone* of the most elaborate gold embroidery.

Examples, however, of the dresses of the merchants and citizens of Venice of the first half of the century may be useful as well as interesting. I have given, therefore, on the previous page, two from early examples, as some fifty years later we shall find a complete change in their attire. Till that period I defer any further notice of the attire of the Doge, senators, and great officers of the Republic, as in the fifteenth century they appear to have assumed the character they continued

Children in Christian II., king of Denmark.

to bear to well-nigh the end of the seventeenth, with the exception that the chaperon may not have entirely disappeared before 1500. Vecellio, in 1594, gives the figure of a Venetian senator in a costume which, he says, was worn two hundred years previously (see p. 145).

In the Royal Collection is a painting of three children, half-lengths, formerly said to be the portraits of Princes Arthur and Henry, sons of Henry VII., and of their sister Mary; and as such they were engraved by Vertue for the Society of Antiquaries. Mr. George Scharf, Keeper of the National Portrait Gallery, to whom we are all so deeply indebted for the correction of many erroneous descriptions of ancient pictures, has identified these portraits as the children of Christian II., king of Denmark;[1] and they are valuable to us as corroborating the opinion that the upper classes, at all events, were during the Middle Ages pretty nearly attired in the same fashion throughout Europe. I give a copy of them, as I have not said anything of Denmark for some time, nor indeed of Sweden and Norway. I shall endeavour to atone for this apparent neglect before the end of this chapter.

It is time to turn to the armour of Europe during the first fifty years of the sixteenth century. It may be said to have reached in 1500 the culminating point of its manufacture, if not of ornamentation. "It was more particularly at the period of the Renaissance," remarks M. Demmin, "that Italian armour attained its highest perfection. During the Middle Ages it could not bear comparison with German, Hispano-Moorish, French, and English workmanship." Yet, in the reign of Richard II., we hear of armour being sent for from Milan, and the armour of the period we are now speaking of obtained the name of "Maximilian." The form of the breast and back plate was not so graceful as in the latter half of the fifteenth century, but the lamboys had an imposing effect; and the close helmet, with its vizor, beaver, and splendid plume, decidedly surpassed in appearance the salade and hausecol it had superseded. The art of engraving had also arrived at such excellence that its application to the ornamentation of armour and weapons added greatly to their beauty. Nevertheless, a tendency to exaggeration of form is specially observable in German examples, and the decline of taste in both civil and military costume is singularly traceable from the revival of the arts! The

[1] John, born 1518, died 1532; Dorothea, who married Frederick II., Elector Palatine; and Christine, wife first of Francis duke of Milan, and secondly of Francis duke of Lorraine.

invention and rapid improvement in hand fire-arms also contributed in a great measure to the production of this result. It became necessary to make armour bullet-proof, and strength therefore was more studied than outline. For the same reason the globose form of the breast-plate—a fashion we have remarked of the reign of Henry V., and which scarcely survived his time—was re-introduced in the reign of Henry VII., with considerably increased prominence, some varieties verging on the ridiculous, the convexity being calculated to cause the ball to glance off, and which, if even struck point-blank, broke the force of the blow on the wearer, there being so much space between the plate and the body. During the reign of Henry VIII. and his contemporaries, the ingenuity of armourers appears to have been incessantly exercised in the invention of means to resist or evade the effects of these new and formidable weapons, while, on the other hand, the gunsmiths were equally active in increasing their power and improving their construction. The battle between guns and armour, which at the present day is exciting so much attention, has never ceased from the time of the Tudors, and its issue is still undecided.

It is unnecessary for me to repeat here the details into which I have entered upon this subject in the Dictionary. The reader will find at pp. 54 and 55 the various forms of the breast-plate at this period, when the salient angle was adopted in succession to the curved line, and gradually descended from the centre to the waist before disappearing altogether. At pp. 19, 35, and 134, will be found examples of complete suits of armour of the same time; and at pp. 65, 85, and 285, engravings and descriptions of the different head-pieces—burgonets, casques, and helmets—of the sixteenth century. Other portions of the military equipment of that date are described and engraved under their separate headings. I shall here therefore confine myself to the illustration of one or two varieties of knightly armour, and the costume of the body-guards of the sovereign and general soldiery.

In the first place, here is the representation of a German suit in our national collection in

German Suit. Tower of London.   Suit of Henry VIII. Tower of London.   German armour, after Albert Dürer.

the Tower of London, with the preposterously prominent breast-plate of which I have spoken; also a suit made for King Henry VIII., in the same collection, with a skirt of taces working on

Almaine rivets, so that they could be moved up or down as easily as a Venetian blind.   This interesting suit has the collar of the Order of the Garter engraved on the gorget.   To which I add a figure from the work entitled 'Vita Imperatoris Maximiliani,' engraved by Burgmair from the designs of Albert Dürer.

Of the yeomen of the guard established by Henry VII. in 1485, I have not been able to find a representation ; but in the picture at Hampton Court of the procession of Henry VIII. to the Field of the Cloth of Gold, they are conspicuously depicted.   It is noticeable that though their coats are all alike of scarlet cloth guarded with black velvet, and having the Tudor rose and crown embroidered on the breast and back, their underclothing, as much as is seen of it, the sleeves of their doublets, their puffed and starched hose, and their stockings vary in colour and form in nearly every instance.

The doublet of one yeoman is black, with black sleeves, quite plain ; his hose are yellow puffed

Yeomen of the Guard, *temp.* Henry VIII.

John Borel, Sergeant-at-arms to
Henry VIII. 1531.

with white, and his stockings white.   Another yeoman wears a black doublet, with green sleeves puffed with white ; his hose are white slashed with black, and white stockings.   A third figure has an under-dress and stockings all black, the hose slashed with red.   I think we may learn from this that in the sixteenth century the liveries given by the sovereign and great noblemen to their retainers were limited to coats and badges, sometimes including caps, and that the rest of their garments were their own, and of whatever colour or fashion they fancied.   They all have swords, and carry halbards.   The sergeants-at-arms carried maces surmounted with crowns in the Middle Ages (see under MACE).   At Broxbourne, in Hertfordshire, there was formerly the brass of John Borel, Sergeant-at-arms to Henry VIII., 1531.   He was represented in full armour, with a mace in his hand.   (See woodcut above, from an engraving in the Rev. Herbert Haines' 'Manual of Monumental Brasses,' 8vo, 1861, Part I., p. 226.)

The Swiss guards in the time of Francis I. were attired similarly to our yeomen guard : they had red bonnets (*toques*), and their coats were of three colours—white, black, and tawny.   The Scotch guards had coats of three colours, which were those of the king—blue, scarlet, and tawny ; over which they wore what M. Quicherat calls "le haqueton traditionnel."

Garden du Corps of Francis I.

The example, however, which he gives from the collection of M. Gagnières, is not, I think, one

French Soldiery. From a bas-relief on the tomb of Francis I.

of the Scotch guard, as his dress does not correspond with the description; and Montfaucon, who has given an engraving of the same figure with a companion, simply entitles them "Gardes du Corps du Roy François premier." There were several companies of "Gardes du Corps" at this period. They are minutely described by Père Daniel in his 'Histoire de la Milice Françoise,' t. ii., livr. ix.; and neither of the figures above mentioned appears to be either Scotch or Swiss guards, but probably represent gentlemen of the two companies of "Gardes du Corps," which corresponded with our "gentlemen pensioners," now called "Gentlemen-at-arms." They were named "Gentils-hommes du bec de Corbin,"[1] from the weapon they carried, which I presume is represented borne by the second figure, and resembles the axes, as they are called, carried by our gentlemen-at-arms, only with a longer *bec* or pick (see also Dictionary, p. 364). The other figure bears a halbard, as did and do our yeomen of the guard, and on his back is embroidered the salamander, which was the badge of Francis I., surmounted by a crown.

For the general character of the French troops at this period we give the preceding group from the bas-relief on the tomb of Francis I., armed with pike, partisan, sword, dagger, and harquebus.

German, Swiss, and Italian soldiers of all arms in the first half of the sixteenth century are depicted in the 'Weiss Kunig' and the 'Ehrenpforte' or 'Triumph of Maximilian,' Holbein's 'Costumes Suisses,' the Entry of Charles V. into Bologna, and the 'Déploration de Gennes,' already quoted. From some of these we have given examples, and here add others in illustration of the military costume of Germany from the works of several of the greatest artists of that period, directing also the attention of our readers to Plate XXIII., from a piece of tapestry representing the chiefs of the Swiss army receiving the hostages delivered to them at the siege of Dijon in 1513.

The five woodcuts immediately following are copied from engravings in the 'Triumph of Maximilian,' and exhibit many of the varieties of military costume of the above period. The close helmet with its forest of feathers, the long fluted *bases*, the puffed and slashed sleeves and chausses, the Milan bonnet with its peculiar border, all the characteristics of the age, have been faithfully delineated by the pencil of Dürer and the burins of Burgmair and other engravers.

From the 'Triumph of Maximilian.'

---

[1] "Appelez 'Gentils-hommes du bec de Corbin.'" (Du Hallian, 'État des Affaires de France,' fol. 306.) In 1557 the weapon was called *bec de faucon*, "becum falconis." (Lupanus, 'De Magistratibus et Præfecturis Francorum,' p. 29.)

PLATE XXIII.

THE SIEGE OF DIJON IN 1513.

Chiefs of the Swiss Army receiving the hostages under the terms of capitulation.

(From Achille Jubinel's "Anciennes Tapisseries.")

From the 'Triumph of Maximilian.'

From the 'Triumph of Maximilian.'

From the 'Triumph of Maximilian.'

A design for the sheath of a dagger of the same date, the subject being the 'Dance of Death,' incidentally illustrates the general costume of the early portion of the sixteenth century, as it presents us with the figures of a king, a queen, a standard-bearer, a woman of the middle classes, and a monk or friar. The sheath of a dagger of the reign of Elizabeth, engraved at p. 451 of the Dictionary, is equally instructive of the costume of the latter half of the century; and the dress, civil,

Z 2

military, and ecclesiastic, of Europe from 1600, might be adequately illustrated by the embossed and engraved armour of the time alone.

Design for sheath of Dagger, early 16th century.

It is stated by some writers, amongst them M. Demmin, that these magnificent arms were not intended for warfare, but "only to be worn on gala days, when the nobles rivalled one another in the magnificence and artistic richness of their equipments."[1] But that they were occasionally worn in conflict is proved by the splendid embossed silver cuirass in the possession of Mr. Magniac, which has been pierced by a bullet.

The superbly wrought shields in the Ambras and other collections, called pageant shields, may very probably have been only borne on such occasions.

Picturesque costume gradually disappeared during the remainder of the sixteenth century, to be for a brief period revived in the seventeenth. No beauty of material, no splendour of decoration, could give grace to the outline, disguise the ugliness, and reconcile to the eye of taste the ridiculous peascod-bellied doublet and its accompanying bombasted breeches, the hideous ruffs, the interminable stomachers, and preposterous farthingales, in which Fashion, one might imagine with *malice prepense*, in order to fool her votaries to the top of their bent, disfigured "the human form divine," both male and female, in the times of Elizabeth and her contemporaries. We have so fully illustrated the dress of this period under the various heads of its component parts in the Dictionary (see particularly the articles CLOAK and GOWN) that I have little to add in the way of drawings or descriptions. Ben Jonson has, however, given us so minute a description of a gallant of the latter days of Queen Elizabeth, in his play 'Every Man out of his Humour,' first performed in 1599, that I must not neglect quoting it. Fastidioso Brisk, giving an account of his duel with Signor Luculento, says: "I had a gold cable hat-band, then new come up, which I wore about a murrey French hat I had. Cuts my hat-band, and yet it was massy goldsmiths' work;—cuts my brims, which by good fortune being thick embroidered with gold twist and spangles, disappointed the force of the blow, nevertheless it grazed

'Weapons of War,' p. 307.

on my shoulder ;—takes me away six purls of an Italian cut-work band I wore,—cost me three pounds in the Exchange but three days before . . . making a reverse blow falls upon my embossed girdle ; I had thrown off the hangers a little before ;—strikes off a skirt of a thick laced satin doublet I had lined with four taffetas ; cuts off two panes embroidered with pearl ; rends through the drawing out of tissue and skips the flesh. . . . Not having leisure to put off my silver spurs, one of the rowels catch'd hold of the ruffle of my boot, and being Spanish leather and subject to tear, overthrew me ; rends me two pairs of silk stockings that I put on, being somewhat a raw morning, a peach colour and another" (Act iv. scene 4). We may truly say with Macilente, "By this we may guess what apparel the gentleman wore."

By the kindness of a gentleman whose acquaintance I have recently had the advantage of making, I am enabled to supplement the information contained in my 'History of British Costume,' respecting the national dress of the Irish at this period, with some valuable material.

To begin, however, with the sumptuary regulations of Henry VIII. in the years 1535 and 1539. The first is an order, dated April 28, 1535, for the government of the town of Galway, in which the inhabitants are directed "not to suffer the hair of their heads to grow till it covers their ears," and "that every of them wear English caps." "That no man nor man-child do wear no mantles in the streets but cloaks or gowns, coats, doublets, and hose shapen after the English fashion, but made of the country cloth or any other cloth it shall please them to buy ;" and by the latter Act it was ordained "that no person or persons, the king's subjects within this land (Ireland), being or hereafter to be from and after the first day of May, which shall be in the year of our Lord God 1539, shall be shorn or shaven above the ears,[1] or use the wearing of hair upon their heads like unto long locks, called *glibbes*, or have or use any hair growing on their upper lips called or named a *crommeal*,[2] or use or wear any shirt, smock, kercher, bendel, neckerchour, mocket, or linen cap coloured or dyed with saffron ; nor yet use or wear in any of their shirts or smocks above seven yards of cloth, to be measured according to the King's standard ; and that also no woman use or wear any kyrtle or coat tucked up or embroidered or garnished silk, or couched, nor laid with *usker* after the Irish fashion ;" and any person so offending was liable not only to forfeit the garment worn against the statute, but certain sums of money limited and appointed by the Act.

In these documents we find mention made of the custom of dyeing the shirts and tunics with saffron, said by many writers to have existed in Ireland from the earliest period, but without quoting any ancient authority in support of their statement. Subsequently the allusions to it are frequent, but it is certainly not mentioned by Giraldus, unless by "some colour" and "various colours" we are at liberty to conclude that saffron or yellow was amongst them. Had it been the prevailing colour, so minute a chronicler as Giraldus would assuredly have particularized it ; and yet, on the other hand, the shirt and truis in the illuminated copy in Sir Thomas Phillipps' library are both frequently painted light yellow or tawny.

In the reign of Elizabeth we find Spenser strongly recommending the abolition of the "antient dress," which, it is clear, continued to be worn in defiance of the above enactments. "The mantle," he remarks, "is a fit house for an outlaw, a meet bed for a rebel, and an apt cloke for a thief." He speaks of the hood as "a house against all weathers," and observes that while the mantle allows him to go "privilie armed," the being close-hooded over the head conceals his person from the recognition of any on whom he has dangerous designs. He also alludes to the custom of wrapping the mantle hastily about the left arm when attacked, "which serves them instead of a target"—a common practice in Spain to this day, and probably derived from thence.

His objections to the use of mantles by females are as strongly and more grossly urged ; and of

---

[1] There must be some mistake here, for the wearing their hair "till it covered their ears" was especially forbidden to them ; and the English, from the king downwards, were "shorn and shaven above the ears."

[2] Amongst the unpublished MSS. in the State Paper Office is another earlier order of Henry VIII., dated April 28, 1536, for the government of the town of Galway, in which these moustaches are termed *crompoualis*. *Crom* in Celtic signifies anything crooked, also the nose ; *peau* is the beard of a goat, and *lis* wicked or mischievous. *Crompoualis* appears therefore to be one of those curious compounds continually met with in that ancient language, and resembling Greek in condensed force of expression.

the long plaited and matted locks called *glibbes* he speaks in terms of equal reprobation. "They are as fit maske as a mantle is for a thief; for wheresoever he hath run himself into that peril of the law that he will not be known, he either cutteth off his glibb, by which he becometh nothing like himself, or pulleth it so low down over his eyes that it is very hard to discern his thievish countenance." He concludes, however, by admitting that there is much to be said in favour of the fitness of the ancient dress to the state of the country, "as, namely, the mantle in travelling, because there be no inns where meet bedding may be had; the leather-quilted jack in journeying and in camping, for that it be fittest to be under his shirt of mail and for any occasion of sudden service, as there happen many *to cover his trouse* on horseback." Thus we learn that the Irish chieftain still wore a shirt of mail as he did in the reign of Richard II., and that he wore it over a leathern-quilted jack, which was long enough to cover his truis, descending, perhaps, as low as his ankles; but in that case inconvenient on horseback, and necessarily divided before and behind. It was probably a jacket with long flaps, which hung over the thighs. He speaks also of "the great linen roll which the women wear to keep their heads warm after cutting their hair, which they use in any sickness; besides their thick folded linen shirts, their long-sleeved smocks, their half-sleeved coats, their silken fillets, and all the rest they will devise some colour [excuse] for, either of necessity, of antiquity, or of comeliness."

Stanihurst, who wrote in this reign, and whose account of Ireland is published in Holinshed's 'Chronicles,' speaking of Waterford, says, "As they distill the best *aqua vitæ*, so they spin the choicest rug in Ireland. A friend of mine being of late demeurant in London, and the weather by reason of a hoare frost being somewhat nipping, repaired to Paris Garden clad in one of these Waterford rugs. The mastiffs had no sooner espied him but, deeming he had beene a beare, would fain have baited him: and were it not that the dogs were partly muzzled and partly chained, he doubted not that he should have been well tug'd in this Irish rug, whereupon he solemnlie vowed never to see beare-baiting in any such weed."

Camden, in his 'History of Queen Elizabeth,' relates that in 1562 O'Neal, Prince of Ulster, appeared at the English Court with his guards of Galloglachs bareheaded, armed with hatchets, their hair flowing in locks on the shoulders, attired in shirts dyed with saffron ("vel humana urina infectis"), their sleeves large, their tunics short, and their cloaks shagged ("tuniculis brevioribus et lacernis villosis").

To the above descriptions must be added that of Derricke, who gives a poetical and picturesque account of the Kerns or common soldiers in the sixteenth century :—

" With skulls upon their powles
 Instead of civil cappes;
With speare in hand and sword by sides
 To beare off afterclappes;
With jackettes long and large,
 Which shroud simplicitie,
Though spiteful dartes which they do bore
 Importe iniquitie:
Their shirtes be very strange,
 Not reaching past the thigh,
With pleates on pleates they pleated are,
 As thick as pleates may lie,

Whose sleeves hang trailing down
 Almost unto the shoe;
And with a mantle commonlie
 The Irish Kerne doe goe.
And some amongst the rest
 Do use another wede—
A coate, I wees, of strange device,
 Which fancie first did breed.
His skirts be very shorte,
 With pleates set thick about,
And Irish trouse more to put
 Their strange projectours out."

In my 'History of British Costume' is a woodcut from a copy made by me of a rare print in the collection of Mr. Francis Douce, who kindly lent it to me for that purpose. That collection is now in the Bodleian Library at Oxford, to which it was bequeathed by its eminent possessor, and I have now the pleasure of inserting in this work, by the courtesy of the gentleman alluded to at page 173, the fac-simile of a photograph of the print, taken of the full size of the original. (See annexed Plate.)

Now, on referring to this indubitable authority, which is superinscribed "Drawn after the qvicke," that is, "from the life," we find the full-pleated shirts with long trailing sleeves; the short coat or jacket with half-sleeves, very short-waisted, embroidered, and short-skirted, "with pleates set thick

DRAVN AFTER THE QVICKE

Irish Chieftains.

From a wood cut in the Bodleian Library, Oxford.

about " the middle ; the iron gauntlet on the left hand mentioned by Stanihurst, the skull cap, the mantle with its shaggy edges, the hair flowing on the shoulders, the lock of the *glib* hanging over the forehead lower than the eyes, the *skein* or long dagger and peculiarly-shaped sword, with a remarkable hilt and as strange a sheath, corresponding exactly with those upon the tombs of the Irish kings engraved in Walker's ' History '—the absence of the leather-quilted jack mentioned by Spenser, which may perchance be the jacket " long and large " spoken of by Derricke, of the truis and shoes (all the figures being bare-legged and bare-footed), being the only varieties of the ancient Irish male costume not depicted.   The truth of the print is curiously corroborated by a drawing in a *Flemish* MS. in the British Museum, containing a description of England and Ireland, executed about 1574, the last date in a diary contained in it being in that year.   (See annexed woodcut.)   Here we have

Irish Costume, A.D. 1574. From a drawing in the British Museum.

two male figures precisely resembling those in the plate before us—one in the short jacket, with tabs or pleated skirts and half-sleeves hanging open from the shoulder, the shirt reaching only to the knee, the bare legs and feet, and the remarkable sword and sheath ; the other also bare-legged, wrapped in the mantle, and with the *glib* hanging over his forehead.   These figures have written above them " Wilde Irische," and, what is still more interesting, they are accompanied by two females, one superinscribed " Edel vroue " (noble or gentlewoman), and the other " Burges vroue " (townswoman), so that we have here the dress of the civilized portion of the female community in the Irish cities, who appear to have adopted some of the fashions prevailing at that period in Europe.   The long sleeve to the shirt or tunic of the men, "trailing down almost unto the shoe," while the body of the garment was so short and fully pleated, was a European fashion in the fourteenth century, and if not adopted from the English in the reign of Richard II., when we find the Irish chieftains condescending to receive additions to their scanty wardrobe, probably reached Ireland from Spain.

A yet more valuable illustration of ancient Irish costume has been contributed to this work by Mr. Harold Arthur Dillon, the gentleman already alluded to, and to whom I am indebted for the photograph of the Doucean print. It is a photograph of a portrait at Ditchley (the seat of his uncle, Lord Dillon), of a Captain Thomas Lee, in the national dress of Ireland at this period.

Captain Thomas Lee. From a portrait at Ditchley.

He is represented in an embroidered shirt with full sleeves, open at the neck nearly to the waist, and terminating but little lower than the hips in a singular skirt, composed of horizontal pleats or bands like the steel taces of a knight of the fifteenth century. Over this shirt is a short loose black jacket without sleeves, but with tabs at the shoulders and waist, apparently trimmed with gold and lined with scarlet. A scarlet cord with a running barrel and tassels is round his neck, but whether connected with the jacket or the round buckler slung behind his back is not distinguishable. He carries a morion on his left arm, a long dag hangs at his girdle, a sword in a black scabbard at his side; he has a long spear in his right hand, and with all this equipment is entirely bare-legged and bare-footed! It is certainly most remarkable that, notwithstanding we have not only written and pictorial evidence that the truis formed a portion of the national dress of Ireland from the earliest period of which we possess authentic information, but also actual specimens in the museum of the Royal Irish Academy, which were dug out of bogs in Ireland within the present century,[1] we have here before us these indubitable proofs of their being dispensed with, or, if not utterly, temporarily abandoned in the reign of Queen Elizabeth. I confess myself at a loss to account for the discrepancy, particularly as Thomas Lee, in selecting to be painted in the national dress, would surely, one would think, have worn them if they had been specially characteristic of his country.

Some analogy may be found, however, in the equally mysterious habits and customs of the Scotch Highlanders. Lindsay of Pitscottie, whose Chronicle of Scotland extends from 1437 to 1542, says: "The other pairts northerne are full of mountaines, and very rude and homelie kynd of people doth inhabite, which is called the Reid Shankis (red shanks) or Wild Scotes. They be clothed with ane mantle, with ane schirt faschioned after the Irish manner, going *barelegged to the knee.*"

John Major, who wrote the history of his native country in Latin, also remarks their being without stockings or coverings for the legs, and wearing a cloak for an upper garment. Here we find a similar ignoring of any nether clothing, and yet we know that the truis was a portion of the national costume of Scotland at this very period.

Lesley, Buchanan, and Beague, all writers of the sixteenth century, bear unequivocal testimony to the existence and prevalence of party-coloured attire in Scotland; and to the above three

[1] "In 1824 a male body, completely clad in woollen garments of antique fashion, was found in a bog sixteen feet deep beneath the surface, in the parish of Killery, county Sligo. No weapon was found near the body, but a long staff lay under it, and, attached to the hand by a leather thong, was said to have been a small bag of untanned leather, containing a ball of worsted thread, and also a small silver coin. On the above body were the truis or breeks now in the Museum. The truis with the rest of the clothing found on the body were presented to the Academy by his Grace the Duke of Northumberland, who purchased them with the collection of the late R. C. Walker, Q.C." (Catalogue of the Museum.) What the colour of them may have been originally it would be hazardous to say: they now appear as dingy brown, with a black check, and have straps to fasten under the feet, as was the fashion in England some years ago with trousers.

authors may be added the writer of a chronicle of the same date, preserved in Lord Somers's Tracts, who tells us the inhabitants of the Western Isles delighted to wear "marled cloths, especially that have long stripes of sundry colours. Their predecessors used short mantles or plaids of various colours, sundry ways divided, and amongst some the custom is observed to this day; but for the most part now they are brown, most near to the colour of the hadder (heather), to the effect that when they lie among the hadder the bright colours of their plaids should not betray them." Heron also, in his 'History of Scotland,' says that in Argyll and the Hebrides, before the middle of the fifteenth century, tartan was manufactured of one or two colours for the poor, and more varied for the rich; yet the earliest contemporary mention of this singular habit, which is identified throughout modern Europe with the name of Scotland, occurs, as I have already stated, in the time of the Tudors. (See TARTAN.) The authentic portraits of royal and noble personages of Scotland engraved in Mr. Lodge's beautiful work, comprising those of Henry Lord Darnley, second husband of Mary Queen of Scots; David Leslie, first Lord of Newark; James Hamilton, Earl of Arran; James Grahame, Marquis of Montrose; Archibald Campbell, Marquis of Argyll; William Kerr, Earl of Lothian; John Leslie, Duke of Rothes, and others, exhibit no trace of a national costume: and the painting of the Surrender of Mary Queen of Scots at Carberry Hill, representing the royal English and confederate Scotch forces in battle array, exhibits no distinctions of dress, though the banners of the respective leaders are scrupulously emblazoned, and the artist, one would suppose, could not have been ignorant of the existence of a national habit at that time in Scotland.

There appears but one way of accounting for such strange discrepancies, as I pointed out long ago in my 'History of British Costume.' The striped and chequered "garb of old Gaul," as well as the truis, must have fallen into disuse throughout the southern and most civilized portion of Scotland at a very early period; and the manufacture of the one and the wear of the other have been confined to the Western Isles and the most remote retreats of the ancient Keltic population, from whence they may have been gradually re-adopted during the seventeenth century, and their popularity increased by their assumption by "the young Chevalier" and the subsequent prohibitory statutes which the rebellion gave rise to.

Respecting the female attire, Lesley, in 1578, says it consisted of a long tunic reaching to the ankles and generally embroidered, a mantle *woven of different colours* (here we have evidence of the tartan, but no name for it), bracelets, and necklaces. White twilled cloth, made from fine wool and called *cuirtan*, was used for under-garments, and hose by those who indulged in such superfluities. The latter, denominated *ossan*, evidently from *hosen*, were of different dimensions, and the larger sort were called *ossan preasach*.

The hair before marriage was uncovered, the head bound by a simple fillet or *snood*. Sometimes a lock of hair of considerable length was allowed to hang down on each side of the face, and was ornamented with a knot of ribbons—a Teutonic fashion. When privileged to cover it, the *curch curaichd* or *breid* of linen was put on the head and fastened under the chin, falling in a tapering form on the shoulders. The female costume, especially of the higher orders, varied in the Lowlands according to the fashionable barometers of London or Paris. Amongst the hundred and one portraits, authentic or imaginary, of Mary Queen of Scots, not one represents her in what could be called a Scotch dress (see our example, Dictionary, p. 226), and the verbal descriptions of her attire are equally contradictory of any such assumption.

An Englishman who visited Edinburgh in 1598 (31st of James VI.) says that "the citizens' wives and women of the country did weare cloaks made of a coarse cloth of two or three colours in chequer-work, vulgarly called *ploddan*;" and *plaiding* is still the term for the chequered tartans in the Lowlands; and his silence respecting the dress of the upper classes is strong negative evidence that it differed in no remarkable particular from that of ladies of similar rank in England.

I have continued my notices of the costume of Ireland and Scotland to the end of the century; but I must now retrace my steps and give the reader the best information I can concerning the dress and arms of the peoples of Europe generally, and England in particular, during the latter half of the period allotted to this chapter, which includes the reigns of the three children of Henry VIII.

—Edward VI., Mary, and Elizabeth, and of their contemporary sovereigns; amongst whom the most notorious—for such is the mildest epithet we can apply to them—are Philip II. king of Spain, husband of Mary, Charles IX., and Henry III. of France.

The brief reign of the young King Edward is principally remarkable for the introduction of the small flat round bonnet worn on one side of the head, and worn till recently by the boys of Christ's Hospital, whose whole dress is indeed the costume of the citizens of London at the time of its foundation by that amiable sovereign. Blue coats were, the common habit of apprentices and serving men, and yellow stockings were very generally worn at that period. The jackets of our firemen previously to the formation of the fire-brigade, and of the watermen attached to the City companies, are also of this date; the badge, now made of metal and placed on the sleeve, being in the sixteenth century embroidered on the back and breast of the jacket or coat, as are those of the yeomen of the guard.

Minstrels, players, and all retainers of the nobility were similarly attired. The well-known print engraved by Vertue from the painting by Holbein, in Bridewell Hospital, representing Edward VI. confirming his father's charter of foundation of that charity, and our chromo-lithograph of a very inferior picture, erroneously attributed to Holbein, of the same sovereign presenting to the Lord Mayor the charter of foundation of Christ's Hospital, may be consulted for the regal, official, ecclesiastical, and civic costume of that period; the only reason for including the latter in our illustrations being the fact that it had never been engraved, and presented some interesting features not to be found in Holbein's picture.

The last sermon preached by Latimer before King Edward contains a passage illustrative of the dresses in 1550 and of the rage for foreign fashions. Speaking of the ladies, he says: "They must wear French hoods, and I cannot tell you what to call it. And when they make them ready and come to the covering of the heade, they will call and say, Give me my French hood, my bonnet, and my cap, and so forth. But here is a vengeance devil. We must have our *power*" (the name he gives to the bonnet) "from Turkey, of velvet. 'Far fette dear bought,' and when it cometh it is a false signe. I would rather have a true English signe than a signe from Turkey. It is a false signe when it covereth not their heads, as it should do. For if they would keep it under the *power*, as they ought to do, there should not be any such *tussocks* nor *tufts* be seen as there be, nor such laying out of the hair, nor braiding to have it open."

Mary's still briefer reign of five years is equally barren of important changes of fashion. An engraving of her from a portrait by Antonio More will be found at p. 225 of the Dictionary, and may fairly serve as an example of the costume of ladies of rank *circa* 1558. Only one sumptuary law appears to have been passed in her reign, in the second year of which it was ordained by Parliament that no person under the degree of the son and heir of a knight shall wear silk upon his hat, bonnet, nightcap,[1] girdle, scabbard, hose, shoes, or spur leathers, excepting mayors and aldermen, under pain of imprisonment for three months and the forfeiture of 10l. for each day's offence. It further states that if any person, knowing any servant of his to offend by the breach of this Act, shall not put him from his service within the space of fourteen days, he shall forfeit one hundred pounds. What could have been the cause of such a prohibition? Three months' incarceration and a forfeit of ten pounds for wearing a groat's worth of silk for a shoe-tie! Strutt, who quotes this passage from the Act, makes no observation upon it, and I have met with nothing in the history of commerce that can be suggested as accounting for it. In the third and fourth years of the joint sovereignty of Philip and Mary an order was agreed upon by the four Inns of Court, in which, amongst other things, it was required that none of the companions or members of those Inns should wear their study gowns in the City any further than Fleet Bridge or Holborn Bridge, or as far as the Savoy, on pain of forfeiting 3s. 4d., and, for the second offence, that of expulsion; also that none of the said companions, when in commons, might wear Spanish cloaks, sword and buckler or rapier, or gowns and hats, or gowns girded *with a dagger on the back*, upon the like pain.[2]

---

[1] Nightcaps, it must be remembered, were much worn in the day-time at this period, with rich laced borders.

[2] Reeves' 'History of the English Law,' vol. iv. p. 573.

Bulwer, in his 'Pedigree of the English Gallant,' p. 548, tells us that, in the reign of Queen Mary, the people in general caused their shoes to be made square at the toes, with so much addition to their breadth that a proclamation was made limiting the width to six inches. He does not, however, give the date of the proclamation; and I suspect that he, not being a contemporary, has confused two different epochs, as the long piked shoes he speaks of had ceased to be worn for sixty or seventy years before the accession of Mary, and the equally preposterous broad or square toes had arrived at their widest extravagance in the reign of Henry VIII., and disappeared before the close of it. The shoes and boots of the second half of the century, whether round or pointed, had never exceeded the limits to which thenceforth they have been restricted. (See BOOT and SHOE.)

The costume of the reign of Elizabeth has been so fully illustrated under the heads of the separate articles of which it was composed that I should be simply repeating pages of text already in the possession of our subscribers if I entered into a detailed account of it. I shall therefore speak in this place of it generally, and leave its further illustration to incidental notices of contemporary foreign fashions. Vain to a contemptible degree, the anything but "*Good* Queen Bess" possessed costumes of all countries, and is said to have left three thousand habits in her wardrobe at her miserable death.

In 1579 the Queen gave her "commandment" to the Lord Chancellor and Privy Council to prevent certain excesses in apparel, and it was ordered by them that after the 21st of February in that year "no person shall use or weare such excessive long clokes, being in common sight monstrous, as now of late are beginning to be used in this realme. Neither, also, shoulde any person use or weare such great and excessive ruffles, in or about the uppermost part of their neckes, as had not been used before two years past; but that all persons shoulde, in modest and semely sort, leave off such fonde, disguised, and monstrous manner of attyring themselves, as both was insupportable for charges and undecent to be worne."

Mr. Fairholt remarks upon "the womanish spleen of the latter part of this manifesto, where the Queen's jealousy of any rivalry in extravagance of costume peeps forth very plainly," her own ruffs being always of larger dimensions than those of her ladies. Paul Hentzer, who visited England in 1602, gives the following description of her dress on one occasion:—"The Queen had in her ears two pearls with very rich drops; she wore false hair, and that red; upon her head she had a small crown; her neck was uncovered, and she had a necklace of exceedingly fine

Queen Elizabeth. From a print in her Prayer Book.

jewels. Her gown was white silk, bordered with pearls the size of beans, and over it a mantle of bluish silk, shot with silver threads; her train was very long. Instead of a chain she had an oblong collar of gold and jewels."

2 A 2

Strange to say, there is no mention of a ruff, yet she surely must have worn one ; at least, no portrait of her, after her accession to the throne, is painted without one. Four have been engraved for the Dictionary, and will be found at pp. 79, 187, 225, 246. We here give a fifth, from a woodcut in a book known as 'Queen Elizabeth's Prayer Book,' printed in 1569 (see preceding page) ; also a plate from the picture erroneously described as her Procession to Hunsdon House, but shown by Mr. Scharf to represent her progress to Blackfriars, to celebrate the marriage of Anne Russell with Lord Herbert, son of the Earl of Worcester, in June 1560. This print affords also examples of the costume of the nobles and ladies of her court, and renders it unnecessary for me to say more on that subject, referring the reader to the above pages of the Dictionary for further illustration.

Of the female costume of the end of her reign the annexed figure of Mary Rust, from a brass

Mary Rust. 1596.

Robert Rampston, Yeoman of the Guard. 1585.

Yeoman of the Guard. From Grose.

at Necton, 1596, engraved by Cotman, is a fair example, and presents us with an illustration of the hooded cape, the precursor of the calèche and capuchin of the eighteenth century.

Of the yeomen of the guard in 1585 we have an excellent representation in the monumental brass of Robert Rampston, lately at Chingford, Essex. Grose has also given an engraving of one of the corps on horseback, which supplies the hat wanting in the Chingford brass. He carries a harquebus, those on foot bearing halbards.[1] The brass of Thomas Noke, Yeoman of the Crown or Crown Keeper, 1567, at Shottesbrooke, county Berks, represents him in a furred gown with long sleeves, with two openings in each, so that the arms might be passed through either at pleasure, and on the shoulder of the left sleeve the Tudor rose and crown in embroidery. An earlier example without the rose is seen on a brass, A.D. 1480, in the possession of the Society of Antiquaries (see opposite page).

Henry II. of France ascended the throne in the same year that Edward VI. became King of England, 1547, and in 1549 his Chancellor Olivier renewed the sumptuary law of the late King

[1] In the College of Arms is a curious pen-and-ink drawing of the procession of Queen Elizabeth to Parliament, in which some of the Yeomen of the Guard are represented wearing high-crowned hats, a circumstance which gives support to the opinion I have expressed at p. 167.

The Visit of Queen Elizabeth to Blackfriars, 16th June 1600
From a Painting at Gorhambury Castle

Francis I., respecting the wearing of gold and silver ornaments, with other regulations affecting apparel generally.

Gold and silver were limited to buttons and the tags of laces (points), and silk alone was allowed to be used for the guarding, *i.e.* trimming, or embroidering of garments. No persons under the rank of royalty were permitted to dress in crimson. Gentlemen and their wives were only allowed to wear an under-garment of that colour. Ladies in waiting on the queen or princesses of the blood royal might wear velvets of any colour except crimson, but the attendants on other princesses were limited to black or tawny.

Crown Keeper's badge. From a brass. 1480.

Women of the middle classes were forbidden to wear velvet except in their sleeves or *cottes*, and their husbands prohibited from the wearing of silk upon silk; and if their upper garments were of velvet, the lower portion of their dress was ordered to be of cloth, or, if they preferred it, *vice versâ.*

Tradesmen, artisans, and workmen in town or country were interdicted the use of silk or velvet in any way whatever, but the servants of the nobility might trim their dresses with either, the dress itself being of cloth.

This edict causing great dissatisfaction, and, as usual, being either boldly disobeyed or ingeniously evaded, some concessions were made to public opinion, especially to the fair sex, who were the most harshly treated. Gold bands for the head, chains for the neck, and girdles for the waist were

Thomas Noke, Keeper of the Crown. 1567.

conceded to the upper and wealthier classes; and the lower orders were allowed to use silk for the trimmings and linings of their dresses or hanging sleeves (*fausses manches*). But velvet was strictly forbidden to the men except in bands on their "haut de chausses," or bindings of the slashes in their dresses. At the same time the wording of the regulations was rendered more precise, and the magistracy was armed with greater power to enforce them. The poet Ronsard compliments the king on his limiting the use of velvet to the nobility, in some verses commencing—

> "Le velours, trop commun en France,
> Sous toy reprend son viel honneur."

The nobility, however, appear to have paid little attention to the Chancellor's directions, and to have dressed themselves according to their own fancy.

M. Quicherat, in his interesting notice of this period, quotes the description of a dress by Blaise de Montluc, in 1555, wherein he observes nearly every article worn is in direct contradiction to the ordinances. It consisted of a pourpoint of crimson velvet (specially restricted to princes), chausses of the same with gold lace, a shirt embroidered with crimson silk and gold thread, a *casaquin* (a loose jacket) of grey velvet laced with silver, at the distance of two little fingers' breadth between each lace, and lined with cloth of silver, and a hat of grey silk made in the German fashion with "un grand cordon" (*i.e.* a cable hat-band) of silver, and a plume of feathers "en aigrette" spangled with silver ("bien argentée").

Fascinating as is the subject, I must limit verbal description, and resort to pictorial illustration, which is more readily and clearly comprehended. Subjoined therefore are examples of French costume during the period corresponding with the reigns of Edward VI., Mary, and Elizabeth, and which will be found in its general character similar to that of England.

Here are four kings of France and three queens, viz.: Henry II., after his portrait by Clouet, in the Museum at the Louvre, his dress being composed of two colours only, black and white striped

Henry II.

Catherine de Medicis.

(*traced*) with gold, which Brantôme says he adopted as his livery out of compliment to "La belle veuve qu'il servoit," *i.e.* Diane de Poitiers ;—Catherine de Medicis, his queen, of detestable memory,

Francis II.

Charles IX.

Henry III.

and their three sons, who consecutively succeeded to the crown—Francis II., first husband of Mary
Queen of Scots; Charles IX., the bigoted murderer of the Huguenots; and the contemptible Henry III.,
with the wives of the two latter, Elizabeth of Austria and Louise de Lorraine.   As the Court is the
fountain of fashion, I need scarcely say that in selecting the portraits of royal personages for my
examples, I am not only securing the most accurate representations of the costume of the nobility
and upper classes, but also of the prevailing dress of all whose means would enable them to imitate it.

Elizabeth of Austria.   Louise de Lorraine.

It was in the latter half of the sixteenth century that pockets seem to have been first made in
the trunk-hose of the gentlemen, superseding the pouch (*escarcelle* in French), which in one form or
another had been suspended from the girdle during some six hundred years.   At least we first hear of
pockets in France in the reign of Henry II.   They were suspected, however, in that of his successor,
Charles IX., as being receptacles of pistols and poniards ; and by an ordinance issued in 1565 tailors
were expressly forbidden to make pockets in haut de chausses.   By the same ordinance the haut de
chausses were ordered not to be stuffed with horse-hair or cotton, a fashion which, under the name of
bombasting, we have seen prevalent at that time in England ; but these, like all other such laws, were
evaded or defied, and soon ceased to be enforced.   The convenience of pockets speedily occasioned
their restoration to these nether garments, from which they have never since then been estranged,
though the garments themselves have taken every variety of form imaginable.

Their appellations also, during the remainder of the sixteenth century, were correspondingly
numerous.   M. Quicherat records the following chausses :—*à l'italienne, à la napolitaine, à la flamande,
à la martingale, à la marine, à la matelotte, à l'espagnole*, and *à prêtre*.   What the "chausses *à prêtre*"
can have been like, I am at a loss to imagine, and M. Quicherat does not enlighten us.   The shape of
the others may be ascertained by reference to the contemporary costumes of the countries and classes
they are named after, which will be found in these volumes.

In the reign of Henry III. were added chausses *à la polonaise, à la provençale, à la savoyarde,
à la niçarde, à la gargeuse* or *grequesque* (i.e. *à la grecque*, and which was abbreviated to *greques*),

and *à la gigotte ;* and in 1580 the young gallants took to wearing tight and short breeches, which received the name of *culotte* in derision from Desperriers, and have bequeathed it in a slightly altered form to their successors.

I must not omit to notice a singular fashion of this period. Whilst the gallants of the Court in Paris generally affected a great variety of colours in their dress, the Duke of Alençon took a fancy to attire himself from top to toe entirely in green, and the mode was followed by many for a short time.[1]

The bas de chausses, or stockings, which completed the clothing of the legs, were of two sorts, long and short. The long were fastened by aiguillettes (points) to the chausses ; the short, a pair of which was frequently worn over the others, terminated at the knees, beneath which they were secured by garters. Ben Jonson, in 'Every Man out of his Humour,' speaks of "the Switzer knot on his French garters."

The cloaks were equally numerous in shape and name :—The cape *à l'espagnole,* without a collar, and wrapped round the body, one end being thrown over the shoulder, as worn by Spaniards at present ; the cape *à collet droit,* i.e. with a high-standing collar, and *à collet rabattu,* with a falling or turnover collar ; the cape *à capuchon,* with a hood to it ; and the *manteau à la reitre* (*Ritter,* Germ.), or horseman's cloak, of very ample dimensions ; one sort of which, with a capuchon attached to it and made of thick woollen cloth, such as was worn by the peasants in Gascony, was adopted by gentlemen in rainy weather, and called from the locality whence it came "cape de Béarn."

The cassock, or jacket with hanging sleeves, called "mandille," which will be found described and illustrated at page 353 of the Dictionary, article MANDILION, appears in France about this time. These hanging sleeves were called "manches pendues."

D'Aubigné, describing the dress of Henri III., says :—

> "Il montroit des manchons goufré de satin blanc,
> D'autres manches encore qui s'étendoit fendues,
> Et puis jusques aux pieds d'autres *manches pendues.*"

In a proclamation respecting the performance of 'The Mystery of the Apostles' is the following passage :—"Deux hommes vestuz de sayes de velours noir portant manches pendues de trois couleurs :" Paris, 1540.

Of the two co-existent fashions in female attire, the "robe montante," made high in the neck, was not allowed to be worn at court *fêtes* or ceremonials. The low dress, the corsage of which was cut very square, had a collerette (the partlet in England) of the finest cambric, terminating just below the chin in a moderately-sized ruff. The sleeves, of a lighter material than the gown, were tight to the wrist, and slashed or puffed throughout their length. The length of the trains was in proportion to the rank of the wearer. They were worn even on horseback. At the entry of Elizabeth of Austria into Paris, 1571, the princesses in her suite rode upon hackneys ; their trains, seven French ells long, being borne by their squires. The young Queen's train measured twenty ells—upwards of seventy feet English—"the longest train," as M. Quicherat justly observes, "of which history makes mention." These trains were worn even with ball dresses, but they were then occasionally looped up by metal hooks or ivory buttons. But not always ; for when Elizabeth de Valois (afterwards Queen of Spain) danced in the Salle de St. Louis, at the marriage of Mary Stuart with the Dauphin of France, she is said to have delighted the spectators with her grace and dexterity in the management of her train, which, being six yards long, was borne after her by a gentleman throughout the mazes of the lively *couranto.*[2] Should not some share in the dexterity be accorded to the gentleman ?

The petticoat is now for the first time called the *cotillon.* The *vertugal* (vardingale) had been adopted in France for some time, as in 1563 their width was restricted to an ell in circumference.

Notwithstanding I have dwelt so long upon French costume, I cannot resist adding the two

[1] Quicherat, p. 415.   [2] Godfrey, 'Grandes Cérémonies de France,' tome ii.

following groups : the first from a painting in the Louvre, representing the festivities at the marriage of the Duc de Joyeuse, the favourite *mignon* of Henry III., celebrated with such prodigal magni-

French Costume. 1581.

ficence in 1581 ; and the second from another picture in the same collection, of ladies and gentlemen dancing at Court before the King in 1585.

French Costume. 1585.

And now we must pass on to Spain, which for a few years was so closely connected with England by the marriage of Philip II. with Mary Tudor.

Of Philip himself there are many portraits, but for this portion of our work we select that painted by Sir Antonio More, in the same picture from which we engraved the portrait of Mary (see Dictionary, p. 225), and another crowned and in mantle of state from an engraving in 1590. The

Philip II. of Spain: ordinary attire.

Philip II. as King. 1590.

reign of Philip was nearly conterminous with that of Elizabeth, his death occurring in 1598; and we have now a mass of authorities not only for the costume of the Court of Madrid and of the nobility of the kingdom, but also for that of the various provinces which continued to preserve the fashions of earlier periods, as is the case to this day in many parts of the Continent, though gradually, I regret to say, disappearing in some districts, which, within my recollection, retained a national costume of the most picturesque description.

At p. 108 of the Dictionary will be found the figure of a Spanish gentleman of the close of the reign of Philip II., from the work of Cesare Vecellio, printed in that king's reign. From the same work, which now becomes a most valuable contemporary authority, we give on the next page three figures of Spanish ladies of that date, 1590–1598. From the text we learn that the ordinary dress of a lady of quality was a robe or gown of silk or velvet, with a long train, over a petticoat of silk and gold or silver embroidery, according to fancy; that black was the colour generally prevailing, but that on festive occasions others were worn at pleasure; and when abroad the head was covered with a long veil of black silk (the *mantilla* of the present day, but much longer); the whole dress resembling, we are told, that of the ladies of Rome and other Italian cities. The third figure, it will be perceived, wears wooden clogs of considerable thickness (" pianelle," a term used also for the Venetian *chioppine* and the ordinary *pantoufle* or slipper), resembling the *patins de bois* worn by French peasants as early as the eleventh century.

The costume of a woman of Toledo, which follows, recalls the dress of the previous century by the turban-like head-dress, the square cut of the corsage, and the form of the sleeves. The elaborately ornamented apron we shall find at the same period in Italy. In the text it is described as of bombasin or silk, and in this example fills up the space between the two sides of the upper garment, showing a small portion of the petticoat below it. On her feet are boots or buskins.

Spanish Ladies. 1590-1596.

Spanish Lady.

Woman of Toledo.

The costume of a woman of Granada in Vecellio's time is said to have been " simile all' habito delle more di Barbaria." At any rate it differs considerably from any European dress of that period. She is represented in a cloak which has apparently no sleeves or lateral openings for the arms, which therefore could be only used by lifting up the cloak on each side, as the clergy in the early days of the Church did the original chasuble, to which it bears some resemblance, the head being passed through a circular aperture in the centre. What form of dress was worn beneath it he leaves us ignorant of. The cap with a brooch or medallion on it, the long hair, and the slashed boots are, however, relics of the early part of the century in Europe, and his collection contains no Moorish dress that bears any resemblance to his engraving. I give it, nevertheless, not having any reason to doubt its fidelity.

A man of Granada excites no suspicion. His dress is conformable to that of persons of the

Woman of Granada.   Man of Granada.

middle class at the commencement of the century, the hat being a lineal descendant of the abacot of the Middle Ages, differing but little from the one worn by the Spanish nobleman at p. 135 ante.

Two of the following woodcuts from the same work represent a lady of Bilboa and a country-woman of Biscay. Both retain traces of older fashions, a few of which linger out an existence at the present day, especially the varieties of the horned head-dress in the Basque Provinces, earlier examples of which we have given at p. 162 ante. The next two exhibit the male and female costume of Navarre.

Bertelli affords us but one example from Spain—the wife of a merchant of Valencia—which in general character very closely resembles an engraving of a woman of Portugal in Vecellio (see p. 190) ; but this lady is mounted on wooden clogs, which appear to be highly ornamented. Her dress is guarded with broad bands of velvet.

We have still to glance through another hundred years before the modern traveller in Spain will recognize features familiar to him in some of its national costumes.

Lady of Bilboa.

Countrywoman of Biscay.

Man of Navarre.

Woman of Navarre.

Wife of a Merchant of Valencia.

Our four subjoined figures represent the male and female costume of Portugal and the province of Gallicia, both kingdom and province being, at the period of the publication of Vecellio's work, incor-

Portuguese Gentleman.

Portuguese Lady.

Gallician Gentleman.

Gallician Lady.

Marriage of Francis, Grand Duke of Tuscany, with Joanna of Austria, daughter of the Emperor Ferdinand I., 1565. By Callot.

porated with Spain under the sceptre of Philip II. There is nothing specially remarkable in the dress with the exception of the loose trousers of the Gallician gentleman, which first appear in this century, and perhaps the form of the hat of the Portuguese, which differs from that of the hats worn in other European countries, and nearly approaches its successor, the sombrero. The costume of the woman of Portugal is almost identical with that of a woman of Valencia given by Bertelli.

For the costume of Italy in the latter half of the sixteenth century, the various works which issued from the press during that time amply supply us with authorities not only for the habiliments of princes and nobles, but for those peculiar to the inhabitants of each particular city or district. In addition to the 'Habiti Antiche e Moderni' of Vecellio, still our most prolific purveyor, and the 'Diversarum Nationum Habitus' of Pietro Bertelli, to which we have been already indebted, we have now the 'Sacri Romani Imperi ornatus' of Caspar Rutz, and the 'Habitus Variarum Orbis Gentium' of Jan Jacques Boissard, the engravings in which are not only larger, and the details consequently more distinct, but infinitely superior as works of art. From these and other less important publications it becomes a difficult task, not to search for authorities, but to select from the abundance of them; as, where all are so interesting, the indispensable necessity of rejecting many increases the responsibility. As the sources from whence they are derived will be recorded, the reader may, with very little trouble, obtain any further illustration he may desire.

Beginning with Rome, the reader will find at page 109 of the Dictionary the figure of a Roman gentleman, circa 1590, from Vecellio, to which we add below a nobleman of the same date

Roman Baron. From Vecellio. 1590.   Roman Ladies. From Boissard. 1581.

from the same work, and two ladies from Boissard, 1581, which perfectly correspond with engravings of similar personages in the work of the former, but are better executed.

The male costume, Vecellio observes, was not confined to the Romans, but was the habit of the gentry and the mercantile community in Florence, Naples, and Milan (see figure of Roman merchant, next page). The long cloak of the Italian gentleman in the Dictionary probably represents the one adopted in England some time previous to 1579, in which year the wearing of them was prohibited. Caspar Rutz furnishes us with a senator of Rome of this date in a grave and magisterial costume, but, as there are no letter-press descriptions, we are ignorant of the colours. The accompanying

Roman Merchant.   Roman Senator.

Plate, copied from Bertelli, representing the procession of the Pope in full state, affords an excellent example of the ecclesiastical, official, and, I may add, the military costume of the Court of Rome, as the Swiss Guards of his Holiness are depicted in it.

Vecellio most liberally supplies us with the costumes of ladies of all the principal cities in Italy, independently of Venice; but as there is a great similarity between many of them, and he specially observes in several instances that the fashion was not limited to one locality, but was worn in "altre citta circonvicine di Lombardia," or "en altre luoghi di Toscana," and even by "altre signore *de tutta Italia*," I feel justified in selecting from the host such marked varieties as will not only give the reader a choice of Italian costume, but also tend to the illustration of that of Europe generally at this period.

First, we have the garb of "a duchess of Parma and of other noble ladies throughout Italy." It consists of a richly-embroidered body and skirt, with moderately tight sleeves reaching to the wrists, over which is a "zimarra ò sopra-veste" of stamped velvet ("vellute stampate"), ornamented with gold lace and having large sleeves open from the shoulders. Round the neck is a ruff of moderate dimensions. From her head-dress of jewels a veil of transparent silk, striped with gold, falls behind her, one corner of it being brought up under the left arm and fastened on the breast to a gold ornament or jewel in the form of a lion's head.

A lady of Belluno is attired in a *settana* of velvet, over which is a gown with wide sleeves, open in front, and showing those of the under-dress; the body made high in the neck and buttoned up the centre; a small ruff close round the throat, and the indispensable veil; the gown open from the waist, displaying the petticoat with a row of buttons down the front; a girdle and pendant of gold and jewels, and a chain of gold round her neck.

The sleeves of the upper dress of a Florentine lady are open at the elbow-joint for the inner sleeve to pass through, and hang behind to a great length—a fashion of which many examples will be found in both male and female European costume in the sixteenth century.

The upper dress of a lady of Milan "& altri luoghi di Lombardia" presents us with a

Audientiā periā. Vescone Cardenali il Santi Pontifice. Camerieri Secreti

Secreti Mastere di Camera Clistieri di Camera Camerieri Croceanari. Lagardia Squalieri a 200 PALAFRENIE

Procession of the Pope

Duchess of Parma.

Lady of Bellano.

variety in form, being shorter than the under one, unconfined at the waist, and the lower portions connected by gold cords and buttons. The veil of black sarcenet or taffeta (*ormesino*) is wrapped

Lady of Pisa.

Lady of Sienna.

Lady of Florence.

Lady of Brescia and Verona.   Lady of Milan.   Lady of Mantua.

round the throat. The sleeves of the under-dress are ample and fastened by points. The veil of a lady of Padua is brought round and attached by the corners to the girdle.

Lady of Ferrara.

Lady of Naples.

Genoese Lady.

A lady of Verona and Brescia wears a mantle of black silk over her shoulders, the lower corners being fastened in front.

The ladies of Belluno, Milan, Florence, Mantua, Pisa, Naples, Genoa, Ferrara, and Sienna, I must leave to speak (to the eye) for themselves. The list might be largely augmented; but unless distinguished by some national peculiarity, which we are assured by Vecellio they are not, I should not be justified in occupying space and incurring expense by increasing the number of engravings without a corresponding addition of interesting information. I have only to call the attention of the student to the fact that, in all the examples given of female Italian costume, there is not one instance of that monstrosity so characteristic of English and French dress of the same date, the ridiculous and unbecoming wheel farthingale.

Before recrossing the Alps I must say a few words upon the costume of Venice, which from the earliest period has been distinguished from the rest of Italy by some features more or less peculiar. No great difference, perhaps, may be found between the dress of a Venetian lady and that of her Italian contemporaries; but yet there is a character about it that associates it with the Piazza

Venetian Ladies. 1590.

di San Marco, the Liddo, and the Canale Grande. The hair is dressed in two horns,[1] similar to those we have seen on the head of the Spanish Queen Maria de Molina, two hundred years at least previously. The corsage is more *décolleté* than in other localities, and the height of the lady can only be accounted for by her being stilted on the preposterous chioppines that provoked the ridicule and reprobation of English travellers and writers of the sixteenth and seventeenth centuries, and occasioned one to say that "the Venetian ladies were made of three things—one part of them was of wood (meaning their chopines), another part their apparel, and the third part was a woman."[2] The fan in the hand of the above figure appears to have been specially Venetian, though fans of ostrich feathers are also seen in some pictures. Other varieties are occasionally met with.

[1] "Che fanno la forma d'una mezza luna, con le punte o corna (che questo nome ancora hanno sortito) rivolte all' insu." (C. Vecellio, p. 100.)

[2] James Howel, 'Survey of the Signory of Venice.' London, 1651.

2 C 2

Venetian Lady in winter dress.

Venetian Woman on chioppines.

Venetian Lady at her toilet.

Vecellio has given us an engraving of a lady at her toilet, combing her hair, which is drawn through an aperture in the top of a broad-brimmed straw hat protecting her head from the sun. Evelyn, writing in the next century, describes this practice in the following words :—" They" (the women) " weare very long crisped haire of severall strakes and colours, which they make so by a wash, dischevelling it on the brims of a broad hat that has no head, but an hole to put out their heads by ; they drie them in the sunn, as one may see them at their windows." Vecellio's engraving not only represents the lady so employed, but affords us an interesting example of her *déshabille*, her chioppines, her looking-glass, the instrument with which she *streaks* her hair, and other articles of her toilet, and we therefore give it in its entirety.

With this I shall conclude my notice of the female costume of Venice in this century, premising that much more information concerning it will be found in the next chapter, which, though derived from later writers, throws considerable light upon the habits, manners, and customs of the times immediately preceding them.

The male costume of Venice, ducal and official, had arrived in the fifteenth century at the forms which are most associated with the ideas popularly conceived of them. Of the Doge we have given an engraving in our last chapter, and here annex one of a Dogaress in 1590, from the work of Vecellio, which, but for the peaked stomacher and partlet, which mark the date, might pass for a lady of that rank in her cap and mantle of state in the previous century. The following woodcuts require scarcely any description beyond the designation of their class or office ; and, as I have just observed respecting the female costume, they will be further illustrated in the next chapter. They consist of the ordinary attire of the Venetian gallant indoors in 1590 ; the costume of a " most potent, grave, and reverend signor," chief of the Council of Three ; of the general of the Venetian forces ; the *Capitano grande* ; a minister of justice ; a cavalier and an esquire of the Doge ; and of a merchant or superior shopkeeper. To these we must add examples of what may be called the free forces of the signory : the scappoli and galeotti, who served in time of war on board the galleys ; the stradiots, soldiery in the service of the State—a class of troops of which I have

A Dogaress of Venice.

Venetian Gentleman at home.

Chief of the Council of Three.

General of the Venetian Forces.

The Capitano Grande.

Minister of Justice.

Venetian Knight.

Squire of the Doge.

Cavalier of the Doge.

Merchant.

Procession of the Doge of Venice

previously spoken; and the gondolieri,—all but the latter being Greeks or Sclavonians, and the stradiots alone preserving some sort of uniformity in their clothing.

Bertelli, who furnished us with the procession of the Pope, has also engraved a procession of the Doge, which is equally illustrative of the general state costume of "the Queen of the Adriatic," and it forms the subject of the accompanying Plate.

Switzerland calls next for our attention; the works published towards the close of the sixteenth century supplying us for the first time with authorities for the costume of that celebrated little republic, and it is interesting to compare the dresses of its inhabitants at that period with those familiar to the modern traveller through its various cantons. The upper classes appear in 1581 to have been attired as nearly as possible after the prevailing German fashion, which, considering that from the time of Rodolph of Hapsburg (1251) the republic had been subject to the influence or domination of the Emperors of the house of Austria, is not surprising. Whether the cantons were distinguished by such marked peculiarities of dress as they have been for at least the last two centuries, I will not presume to say; but in none of the works I have been able to consult do I find an intimation of it. The figures are simply described as "Swiss," "Dame Suisse," "Femme Suisse," "Frau in Schweitzerland," "Schweizerin," "Donzella " or "Matrona-Suizzera," which, I think, may be taken as negative evidence that local distinctions of dress were at least unknown to the contemporary draughtsmen and authors who have transmitted to us their information, and moreover, being Germans and Italians, could scarcely be ignorant of the habits of their nearest neighbours. Vecellio, describing the dress of a Swiss nobleman, makes the curious remark, "Vestone colori diversi, vaghi & belli & portano habiti *differenti de tutte le altre nationi.*" Now, when we possess such abundant proof of the general similarity of the costume of Germany to that of Switzerland which is furnished to us by the writers and artists above mentioned, Vecellio himself included, the unqualified assertion that the dress worn by the people of the latter country differed from that of all other nations is rather perplexing. Vecellio, an inhabitant of Venice, in that day the mart of the world—"the place where merchants most *did* congregate "—must have constantly seen foreigners of all countries in juxtaposition, and, as the author of so comprehensive a work on costume as the 'Habiti Antiche e Moderni *de tutto il Mondo*,' must have had some reason for so deliberate an assertion. I can only attempt to account for it by suggesting that the difference was not in form, but in colour.

I have mentioned in the last chapter (page 137) the tradition that the extravagant fashion of the haut de chausses worn in Germany originated with the Swiss, who, after their victory at Granson in 1476, cut or tore in shreds the magnificent materials of every description found in the tent of Charles the Bold and arrayed themselves fantastically in the pieces. The difference Vecellio alludes to, but does not specify, appears to be the "colori diversi" which were particularly noticeable in the "calce" (hose), described as "assai larghe con tagli grande" (with great slashes), composed of silk or taffeta and fine cloth, "diversato de piu colori;" such, in fact, as the Swiss guards of the Pope are depicted wearing in the procession copied from Bertelli in our plate, and which, with slight modification, they wear to the present day. I have been unable to meet with any representation of Swiss costume earlier than the sixteenth century, and therefore can only imagine that no particularity of attire distinguished the citizens, soldiers, hunters, or herdsmen of those romantic regions from men of the same classes in Germany previously to the battle of Granson, when the strips of gold and silver cloths, damasks and velvets of different colours, with which they ornamented their ordinary habiliments, gave rise to a fashion which became national amongst the military portion of the population, and distinguished those who were in the pay of foreign princes from the troops of any other country. I trust my readers will not consider I have been too prolix in my endeavour to reconcile this apparently conflicting testimony. It is in such cases, and the history of costume is full of them, that critical investigation is imperatively demanded.

Here is the figure of a Swiss nobleman, as given by Vecellio, who admits that the shoes are of

Swiss Nobleman.   Women of Switzerland.

an ancient form and of German fashion ("alla Tedesca"). They are square-toed, with a strap over the instep, such as were worn in France and England *temp.* Francis I. and Henry VIII. Every other article of his attire can be found in delineations of German costume of the time of our Queen Elizabeth, when in variety and extravagance it seems to have equalled, if not surpassed, that of

England and France, so censured and satirized by their respective historians. The four female figures are those of Swiss women, but, with the exception of one with her hair in two long plaited

Women of Switzerland.

tails behind, a fashion as old as the time of Rufus in England, there is no vestige of their costume which resembles anything seen in Switzerland in our days.

Moving eastward, we find in Lorraine some relics of an earlier age. The women of Verdun

Noble Lady of Lorraine.   Lady of Verdun.   Noble Lady of Alsace.

retained in 1581 a head-dress of a fashion at least a hundred years old, the rest of the dress being of their own time, and in accordance with that of France or Germany.

In Metz the French hood appears to have been adopted, while in Alsace a female costume is presented to us of a perfectly different character from anything we have yet met with in the west of Europe.

The dress of an Alsatian soldier (as Vecellio says he is more to be considered of that class

Woman of Alsace.   Alsatian Soldier.

than of any other) reminds one of the Gallician at page 190 *ante.* Persons of condition in Alsace dressed, however, like those of the same rank in other countries, leaning a little, it would seem, to the taste and style of Germany.

West of the Rhine we have still to notice the Low Countries, at that period under the sceptre of the King of Spain, and therefore we may conclude that the intercourse between the two nations affected in some degree the costume of the people; but whether or no, we find in that of the Netherlands some peculiar features which impart to it a national character worthy of observation.

The gentleman from Boissard has undoubtedly a Spanish air; and so, indeed, has the lady. The *chambrière* has no distinctive character of dress: but the lady of Antwerp, or of Brabant generally, as Vecellio describes her, is fortified against the weather by a cloak forming a hood of the most capacious dimensions, the point in front being fastened to the hair over the centre of the forehead, and the sides stiffened out by a copper wire, "filo de rame,"—the origin, I imagine, of the "hood à calèche," of which so many examples are seen in English effigies of the seventeenth century. Caspar Rutz[1] also engraves a lady "cum palla Belgica." Minsheu calls it a *huycke*— "Peplum muliebre Brabanticum, Flandres *huycke*—a mantle such as women use in Spaine, Germanie, and the Low Countries, when they goe abroad" (see Dictionary, p. 287, under HEUK).

"A woman of Antwerp" depicted in Vecellio's work presents us with a straw hat or bonnet in the shape of an inverted bason ("un capello de paglia fina tutto a giusa di catino"). The cross

[1] 'Sacri Imperi Romani Ornatis.' 1585.

Gentleman of Brabant.

Lady of Brabant.

Flemish Waiting-maid.

visible on the left side of it is not alluded to in the text, and I will not pretend to account for it. Straw hats of all sorts of shapes—baskets, trays, dishes, &c.—were common at this period on the northern coast of Europe.

Belgian Lady. From Cæsar Rota.

Lady of Antwerp in her dayrie.

Woman of Antwerp.

2 D 2

In the adjacent country of Holland, the dress of the higher orders differed in no particular respect from that of the nobility and gentry of their neighbours, and it would be almost unnecessary to give examples in addition to the many costumes of the latter portion of the sixteenth century to be found in various parts of these volumes, were it not that they illustrate the fluctuating fashions of England and help us to identify certain articles of attire mentioned by our historians and dramatists.

The women when out of doors wore the same kind of cloak or heuk, but there is also seen a variety in the form of the upper portion being made with a projecting peak, and fitting the head like a cap. The figure of a Dutch gentleman, from Vecellio, has been given in the Dictionary, p. 108, article CLOAK; and from Caspar Rutz we give some examples of the naval and military costume of Holland and Zealand.

Dutch Woman.   Zealand Sailor.   Dutch Soldier.

Germany offers us a most tempting multitude of singular and picturesque costumes at this period, but our limits will not allow more examples than are fairly sufficient to illustrate the principal localities. The pen must also give place to the pencil, for the eye will comprehend at a glance what would take pages to explain even imperfectly.

Cologne will interest many of our readers, who no doubt remember, as I do, its market-place crowded with women in quaint head-dresses, nearly all of which, alas! have recently disappeared. When I last passed through the city, not one was visible. On the opposite page are representations of how they dressed in 1585.

The figures which follow, in the works previously quoted, are simply described as German, and are given as examples of some of the prevailing varieties of male costume worn in the Empire in the time of Rodolph II. Bertelli has engraved between thirty and forty figures holding shields with the armorial bearings of all the principal duchies, cities, &c., in Germany, and no two of the whole number are dressed precisely alike, though the majority undoubtedly are faithful representations of dresses of the day; and if I could be satisfied that the costume of the supporters of these shields was actually that of the particular locality indicated by the arms and sub-inscriptions—i.e. Bamberg,

A Magistrate of Cologne.

Gentlewoman of Cologne.

Ratisbon, Ulm, Salzburg, &c.—I would strain a point for their admission: but the work, like those of Caspar Rutz, Boissard, and Weigel, has no descriptive text appended to it, and, as some of the figures are in ancient Roman armour, I cannot rely upon the others being authorities for anything beyond the general costume of the period, presenting a most interesting series of ingeniously

Young Lady of Cologne.

Lady of Cologne in wedding-dress.

designed varieties, and affording the artist a valuable opportunity of selection for his especial purpose. To the work itself, therefore, I must refer the student who is desirous of fuller pictorial illustration than is here afforded him. (See also Dictionary, p. 108, article CLOAK.)

Of female costume we have examples in Boissard from Bavaria, Suabia, and the city of

Ladies of Bavaria.

Lady of Suabia.

Lady of Augsburg.

Ladies of Nuremberg.

Augsburg, which may be depended upon ; while Weigel and Vecellio supply us with those of Nuremberg, the Palatinate, Saxony, and Austria. With Bohemia we reach the utmost limits of Central
Europe, which comprised in the sixteenth century all the nations that, to use a familiar phrase,

Lady of the Palatinate.

Noble Lady of Austria.

followed the fashions of the West, whether set by the Court of Paris or of Madrid. Even within its boundaries some indications are noticeable of Oriental influence or connection. Subjoined are figures from Vecellio of a Bohemian gentleman and lady, and a man and woman of the middle classes.

Noblewoman of Bohemia.

Bohemian Gentleman.

Man of Bohemia.

Bohemian Woman.

The national characteristics are, as usual, more marked in the dress of the latter. The gentleman wrapped in his fur-lined cloak with wide sleeves, of a fashion general throughout Western Europe in the beginning of the century, would probably have under it a doublet and hose of a corresponding date, as his broad-toed shoes with a strap over the instep are additional warrants for supposing. The lady is much more advanced in her knowledge or her taste, and is attired conformably to her German contemporaries. On the other hand, the commonalty of both sexes present us with a style of costume not yet met with west of the Oder. The cloak with hanging sleeves, it is true, was not a novelty in France or England at this period; but as we proceed eastward we shall probably satisfy ourselves whence it was imported. The high fur cap and the leathern boots, the blue or red tunic, also lined with fur, and the fur collar or cape ("bavarro"), betoken the wilder and colder regions we are approaching.

In Saxony, at the period under consideration a fief of the Empire, the fashions of Germany were naturally followed by the higher classes. Subjoined are examples of the costume of ladies of condition, preserved to us by Vecellio.

Female Costume of Saxony.

Prussia was in the sixteenth century, like Saxony, only a fief of the Empire, and styled the Margraviate of Brandenburg. Its Margraves were also Electors of Brandenburg, but, long under the domination of Poland, the costume of the people appears to have been more characteristic of the east than of the west of Europe; and Vecellio makes little if any distinction between them in his descriptions. He gives, in fact, only the figure of a Prussian merchant, whose dress, he tells us, was common to persons of that calling in Poland, Russia, and Tartary. I shall not hesitate therefore to treat under one head the countries lying between the rivers Oder and Vistula and north of the Carpathian mountains, including Pomerania, Lithuania, Livonia, and Silesia, all at the close of the sixteenth century more or less connected by common descent or political necessity.

Crossing the Carpathians, we find ourselves amongst people who retained with Oriental tenacity the costume of their ancestors, unaffected by the caprices of fashion, which were constantly working

2 F

Lady of Dantzig in bridal-dress.

Servant Girl of Pomerania.

changes in the West. The tide of immigration flowing steadily from the " teeming north " of Asia had
been arrested in the ninth century by the consolidation of the empire of the Franks under the

Noblewoman of Livonia.

Lithuanian Officer.

Gentlewoman of Lithuania.

Woman of Grodno.

sceptre of Charlemagne. A barrier was raised from the Baltic to the Adriatic against which the advancing waves of population beat in vain, and the last comers had no alternative but to settle

Silesian Bride in winter dress.

Silesian Citizen's Wife.

Silesian Woman and Child of the Middle Classes.

2 E 2

down as best they could in the countries they had succeeded in reaching.   Here then we find
the descendants of two great families—the Sclavonians or Slaves, and the Magyars or Turks—who
established themselves in Pannonia in 889, in succession to the Huns and the Avars, two Scythic
tribes, from the former of which it derived its modern name of Hungary.[1]

Writing at a moment when all Europe is watching with anxiety the progress of affairs in the
Principalities and provinces comprised at present in what was anciently called Sclavonia, it would
be interesting to examine the costume of its inhabitants three hundred years ago ; but, unfortunately,
Vecellio limits his illustration to the portions now possessed by Austria on the borders of Servia and
the Herzegovina, viz. Croatia and Dalmatia, whilst Weigel and Bertelli contain no information on
the subject whatever.   Of the costume of Hungary, however, all three have examples, and Vecellio
intimates that there was a general similarity in his time to be observed in the dress of all these
neighbouring nations.

Croatian.   Noble Croatian or Hungarian.   Prussian.

In this and the four following pages will be found all the figures from the above works that can
assist us in our inquiries into this portion of our subject.

Greece, overrun by the Goths and the Sclavonians, divided by the French and the Venetians,
parcelled out into Norman and Italian duchies, ruled by a Flemish Emperor, and finally conquered
by the Turks in 1453, must have passed through as many changes of apparel as of masters, retaining
probably in all some traces of that ancient Oriental character visible in the costume of the Lower
Empire in the sixth century ; but between that and the sixteenth we have no reliable evidence concerning it, if we except the engraving from a Greek MS. of the tenth century, given at page 33 of
the present volume.   It is therefore interesting to contemplate the costume of the inhabitants of
such fragments of the old kingdom of Greece as had fallen to the share of Austria in the time
of Rodolph II., as well as some of the provinces possessed by the Turks under Amurath III., when

---

[1] " Magiar " is the national and Oriental denomination of the Hungarians ; but among the tribes of Scythia they
are distinguished by the Greeks under the proper and peculiar name of *Turks*, as the descendants of that mighty people
who had conquered and reigned from China to the Volga.

Bosnian.

Pole.

Noble Hungarian.

the authors we have been already so indebted to published their collections. The reader will not recognize in the Epirot or Albanian depicted by Boissard "the wild Albanian kirtled to the knee" of

Hungarians.

Prussian and Polish.　　　　　　Livonian.　　　　　　Wallachian.

Lord Byron, nor do I find a representation reminding me of his "dark Suliote" with "his snowy camise and his shaggy capote." The picturesque attire considered the national costume of modern Greece is not to be found in any work I have met with, and must have been adopted by the subjects

Greek Merchant.　　　　　　　　Greek Noble.

of the Sultan at a later period. If Vecellio and Boissard are to be relied on, there were certainly no
"well-greaved Greeks" in the sixteenth century. The hat of a Greek gentleman is like a caricature
of the chimney-pot hat of the present time; but the head-dress of the lady of Macedon recalls to

Noble Lady of Macedon.

Woman of Macedon.

Lady of Thessaly.

Dalmatians and Sclavonians.

us the *escoffion* or *hennin* of France in the middle of the fifteenth century, and suggests the probability of those preposterous coiffures having been derived from the East, as it appears to have been worn in the Island of Mytilene, the ancient Lesbos, which was unlikely to have received it from the Continent. Vecellio describes it as made of thin, light wood, in the shape of a box, covered with cloth of gold, terminating in a species of horn, and having a veil of variegated silk pendent at the back. The ladies of Thessalonica are represented wearing a head-dress still more resembling those of the fifteenth century in France and England, but the foundation made of other materials (brass or copper wire, or of felt [1]), also covered with cloth of gold, and richly ornamented with jewels.

Ragusa being in that portion of Dalmatia at that period under the dominion of the Doges, the ladies are attired after the Venetian fashion. Bertelli gives us the costume of what he calls a letter-

Ragusa.

carrier (*Tabellarius*, but *quære* Tabularius, a scrivener) of Ragusa, which appears to be a mixture of Asiatic and European habiliments. The hat is indescribable.

I approach, not without trepidation, to the European provinces of the now enormous empire of Russia, but which was in the sixteenth century only known as the Grand Duchy of Muscovy. Ivan Vassilliewitch in 1545 caused himself to be solemnly crowned by the Metropolitan, a ceremony previously unknown in Russia, and assumed the title of Tsar or Czar, which his father, Vassili Ivanowitch, had occasionally used towards the end of his life, but was never accorded by the Muscovites generally to any of their princes before Ivan IV., his son and successor, who is distinguished in Russian history as the first Tsar of Muscovy. Under his reign Russia beheld, for the first time, a regular and disciplined army, ready at his command to march against an enemy; and the bow was abandoned for the matchlock. By the death of his son Feodor, in 1598, the dynasty of Rurik, which had furnished fifty-two sovereign princes to Russia in seven hundred and thirty-six years, became extinct.

One of the earliest descriptions of Russian costume that I have met with is that of the chronicler Hall, who has left us an account of a Masque at Westminster in 1509. "In the first year of the

[1] " Fatto de rame, con certi fili de rame."

reign of Henry VIII," he tells us, "at a banquet made for the foreign ambassadors in the Parliament Chamber at Westminster, came the Lord Henry, Earl of Wiltshire, and the Lord Fitzwalter, in two long gowns of yellow satin, traversed with white satin, and in every bend (*i.e.* diagonal broad stripe) of white was a bend of crimson satin, after the fashion of Russia or Russland, with furred hats of

Grand Duke of Muscovy.

Muscovite Ambassador.

Lady of Muscovy.

Muscovite Soldier.

grey on their heads, either of them having an hatchet in their hands, and boots with pikes turned up."
In Vecellio we have engravings of "Il Gran Duca di Moscovia," a "Nobile Moscovita Ambasciatore,"
and a "Donna di Moscovia." What were the authorities for these costumes he does not tell us; but
at the time of publication of his first edition Feodor was on the throne of Russia. But it was during
the reign of his great-grandfather, Ivan III., who died 7th October, 1505, that Moscow first saw
within its walls ambassadors from the republic of Venice, and from that period may be dated the
entrance of Russia into the comity of European nations. We may therefore fairly suppose that
Christopher Chraegar, a German by birth, who engraved the woodcuts for Vecellio, was furnished by
him with accurate drawings of Russian personages in their national costume, taken from the life
about the middle of the sixteenth century. The reader will observe that the Muscovite *Ambassador*
(a significant description) is attired, with the exception of the turned-up pikes of the boots and the
pattern of the long satin gown, in perfect accordance with the account given by Hall of the dresses of
the Masque at Westminster in 1509 (see previous page).

The magnificent work published by the Russian Government, copies of which were liberally
presented to the British Museum, the Royal Academy, and other public institutions in this country,
by his Imperial Majesty, Alexander II., has already furnished us with illustrations of the vestments
of the Greek Church, and from this date will supply us with most authentic materials for the
costume, civil, military, and ecclesiastic, of Russia in Europe during the sixteenth, seventeenth, and
eighteenth centuries; the earliest examples I can avail myself of in it being the portrait of Ivan IV.
(the first crowned Czar of Muscovy aforesaid) and of his son Feodor I., also above mentioned; the
former in ordinary costume, and the latter in his Imperial robes.

Ivan IV.   Feodor I.

In the account of Sir Hugh Willoughby's Voyage in 1553, we find the following description of
his reception at Moscow by the former sovereign, whom he styles "the great Duke of Muscovy and
chief Emperor of Russia, John Basilewich."

"Being entered within the gates of the King's Court, there sat a very honourable company of

1. *Tiara of Gold Brocade called the Siberian, A.D. 1684.*
2. *Turra of the First Order, or Crown of the Czar Peter the Great, 1687.*
3. *Tiara of the Grand Dukes and Czars of Russia used in Crowning the Heir to the Throne.*
4. *Ancient Episcopal Tiara preserved in the Cathedral of St. Sophia, Novogorod.*
5. *Crown of the Empress Anne, 1730.*

courtiers, to the number of one hundred, all apparelled in cloth of gold down to their ankles ; and then, having been conducted into the chamber of presence, our men began to wonder at the majesty of the Emperor. His seat was aloft, on a very royal throne, having on his head a diadem or crown of gold, apparelled with a robe all of goldsmith's work, and in his hand he held a sceptre garnished with precious stones." Afterwards he assumed "a robe of satin and another diadem," and was attended by "one hundred and forty servitors arrayed in cloth of gold."

Cap of the Metropolitan Job.

It was in 1586, during the reign of his son the Czar Feodor, that a patriarch of Constantinople, named Jeremiah, arrived at Moscow to collect alms to enable him to re-purchase his seat from the Grand Vizier, who had deprived him of it. He was requested to create a patriarchate in Russia, and the Metropolitan Job was invested with that dignity. His cap or mitre is here engraved from the same valuable volume.

The sixteenth century witnessed the commencement of "the decline and fall" of armour. I have given sufficient examples of it in the completest state to which it had attained in the reigns of our Edward VI. and of the European sovereigns his contemporaries. After the accession of Elizabeth cap-à-pied suits were used only for jousting, and not always even for that purpose, knights often appearing in the lists without armour for the legs or thighs. The breastplates were made much thicker in order to be bullet-proof, and the point of the tapul reappeared at its lower extremity and projected downwards, in conformity with the shape of the peascod-bellied doublet of the civil dress of that period. (See example under BREASTPLATE, Dictionary, p. 55.) The taces or tassets appended to them were sometimes made in two parts, to accommodate the bombasted breeches of Queen Elizabeth's time. The morion was more generally worn than the helmet, in 1578 with a large comb (see Dictionary, p. 372). Carabines and petronels are frequently mentioned amongst the fire-arms of this period, and the rest for the long, heavy matchlock musquet was introduced into France in the reign of Henry III.

It must not be forgotten that in this century we have authentic information of the existence of something like uniformity of clothing in the English army. A MS. in the College of Arms, marked W. S., contains the following orders of the Duke of Norfolk to the conductor of the wayward of an army raised in the 36th of Henry VIII., in 1544-5, respecting the dress of the troops :—" First, every man sowdyer (soldier) to have a cote of blew clothe, after such fashion as all footmen's cotes be made here at London, to serve his majestie in this jorney, and that the same be garded with redde clothe after such sort as others be made here, and the best sene [i. e. the best-looking men] to be trymmed after such sort as shall please the captayn to devise." Every man is to be provided with "a payer of hose ; . . . the right hose to be all red and the left to be blew, with one stripe of three fingers brode of red upon the outside of his legg, from the stocke downward." Badges of any sort are strictly prohibited, with the exception of a red cross to be sewn upon the uppermost garment. No soldier, or victualler or other, to presume to come within the precincts of the camp without such cross, "upon payne of fifteen dayes imprisonment, and to be further ordered at my Lorde Lieutenante's pleasure." From another MS. in the same Library, marked D, folio 109, it would appear by a letter written by Thomas Lord Wharton to the Earl of Shrewsbury, that with the above exception the colour of the clothing of the English infantry in this reign was usually white.

In the reign of Elizabeth, anno 1584, the soldiers raised in Lancashire for service in Ireland are directed to be furnished with "convenient doublets and hose, and also a cassocke of some motley or other sad (dark) grene coller or russet." Also every soldier to have five shillings to provide a mantle in Ireland, beside his livery coat, when he shall be there arrived. From the same source we learn that the uniform cloaks of the cavalry were red.

Sir John Harington, in his 'Nugæ Antiquæ,' gives a particular account of the articles of clothing provided for the officers and men serving in Ireland in 1599, and the prices paid for them : cassocks of broad Kentish cloth, and *Venetians* (*i.e.* loose breeches reaching to the mid-leg) of the same material, with buttons and loops, canvas doublets, shirts and bands of "Osnabridge Holland," kersey stockings, neat leather shoes, and "hats and caps coloured," but no colours specified.

An order was issued in the reign of Elizabeth that all commanders in the navy should wear scarlet. Cesare Vecellio, at the end of his fourth book, gives us a representation of an English sailor, *circa* 1598, which I think may be fairly relied on as to form. He mentions no colours (See cut annexed.)

The portraits of François, duc d'Alençon, afterwards Duc d'Anjou, one of the pretenders to the hand of Queen Elizabeth, of François de Montmorency, Maréchal de France, 1578, and the figure of a *manœuvre* or man-at-arms of the French royal army in 1593, from a print in a work of that date, will suffice as examples of the armour worn in France in the latter half of the century by commanders and by the cavalry. (See cuts below.)

By the infantry, armour was discarded nearly altogether, except for the head. The figures in the next page are from prints of the time, reproduced by Montfaucon and Quicherat, viz. a harquebusier and a halbardier, *temp.* Charles IX., 1565 ; a halbardier of the Royal Guard, *temp.* Henry III., 1586—the three crowns embroidered on his breast, I presume, indicate the three kingdoms of France, Navarre, and Poland—and a Swiss of the Royal Guard of the same reign, the last two from a painting of that date.

English Sailor. 1598.

Duc d'Alençon.

François de Montmorency. 1578.

French Man-at-arms. 1593.

Harquebusier. 1585.

Halbardier. 1589.

Halbardier and Swiss of the Royal Guard. 1586.

The Spaniards seem to have retained the use of armour to a later period than the English. Sir Richard Hawkins, in his 'Voiage into the South Sea, anno Domini 1593,' says, "I had great preparation of armours, as well of proofe as of light corsletts, yet not a man would use them ; but esteemed a pott of wine a better defence than an armour of proofe, which truely was great madnesse,

Philip II., king of Spain.

Don Juan of Austria.

for if the Spaniard surpasseth us in anything, it is in his temperance and suffering ; and where he hath had the better hand of us, it hath beene for the most part through our own folly, for that we will fight unarmed with him being armed : besides that, the sleightest armour secureth the parts of a man's body from pike, sword, and all hand weapons ; it likewise giveth boldnesse and courage. Therefore, in time of warre, such as follow the profession of armes, by sea or by land, ought to covet nothing more than to be well armed. Wherein the Spanish nation deserveth commendation above others, every one, from the highest to the lowest, putting their greatest care in providing faire and good armes. He which cannot come to the price of a corslet will have a coat of mayle, a jackett, at least a buffe-jerkin or a privie coate, and hardly will they be found without it, albeit they live and serve for the most part in extreame hott countries."

Spanish Sergeant. From Caspar Rutz.

Above is the portrait of Philip II., king of Spain, from an engraving in Le Petit's 'Grande Chronique de Hollande,' &c., a contemporary publication ; also a half-length of the celebrated Don Juan of Austria, from a painting attributed to Alonzo Sanchez Coello, a Portuguese painter, engraved for Señor Carderera's great work ; and annexed a sergeant of Spanish infantry, from Caspar Rutz. The sleeves of chain-mail in the portraits of Philip and Don Juan are peculiarly characteristic of Spanish armour at this period. (See also Dictionary, under MORION.)

In form the armour of Spanish manufacture differed in no

particular from that made in Germany or Italy; or which was worn in the north, south, or east of Europe, on this side the Oder. The distinction, where any existed, was in the ornamentation, which, in the latter half of the sixteenth century, was of the most superb description. Private as well as public collections of any celebrity contain suits or portions of suits of engraved or embossed armour, the workmanship of which is unsurpassably beautiful. In this country the late most unhappily dispersed Meyrick Collection contained, amongst other priceless treasures, a suit of Italian armour chased and engraved in the highest style of art; it was covered with arabesques, interspersed with human forms, trophies of arms, and instruments of music; the whole chiselled out and then engraved, the relief gilt, and the ground russet; date *circa* 1560 ;—a suit which belonged to Alfonso II., duke of Ferrara, 1558, to whom Tasso dedicated his 'Gerusalemme liberata,' which Sir Samuel did not hesitate to assert was "one of the most splendid suits in Europe, if it be not, indeed, entitled to pre-eminence ;"—also a third suit, nearly as fine, which had belonged to an officer of the guard of Cosmo de Medici, Grand Duke of Tuscany. In the yet fortunately intact collection of Lord Londesborough, are some exquisite specimens of Italian repoussé work, and a superb cap-à-pie suit of engraved and gilt armour, purchased at the sale of Mr. Bernal's collection, and which, from the double-queued lion upon it, is conjectured to have been made for a Count of Luxembourg. The suit of armour of Sir Philip Sidney, formerly at Strawberry Hill, which the apathy of the Tower authorities allowed to be lost to this country, had figures in high relief on it of solid gold ; but it is needless to swell the catalogue of these magnificent relics, to which no engraving can do justice. I will only mention the suit known as the "Armure aux Lions," in the Louvre at Paris, as amongst the most celebrated of those preserved in national collections on the Continent.

William Thomas, the old traveller I have already quoted, gives us a little insight of the armour in Venice in the first half of this century: "And now methinketh it convenient to speak in this place of the armory that is in an hall of the Duke's palace called La Sala del Consiglio d'idieci, which surely is a very notable thing. There be (as they reckon) a thousand cotes of plate, part covered with cloth of gold and velvet, with gilt nails, so fair that princes might wear them, besides divers other fair harnesses, made of late, which are bestowed in so fair an order, with their divers kinds of weapons furnished of the best sort, that a great while looking on would not satisfy me." (History of Italie, 1549.) The "cotes of plate, part covered with cloth of gold and velvet, with gilt nails," were evidently jazerants, such as are described in the Dictionary, p. 314.

Italian Nobleman. By Moroni.

The portrait of an Italian nobleman by Moroni, lately added to the collection in our National Gallery, reveals to us the mode of attaching sleeves of mail to a body of buff leather, thereby relieving the wearer of the weight of a considerable portion of chain under the breastplate. (See woodcut annexed.)

In the east of Europe the Oriental type still predominates. Poland, Russia, and Hungary present us with examples of long coats of mail which might have been worn by the satraps of Persia, and yet distinguish the Circassian cavalry. The casques have nasals or nose-guards, the raising or lowering of which is regulated by a screw; a fashion we find adopted in England in the following century, and obviously derived from Turkish, Persian, or Mongol examples, of which several are to be found in the national collections at St. Petersburg and Paris.

In the Imperial Arsenal of Vienna there is an Hungarian suit of the end of the sixteenth

century, composed of chain and plate. "The whole equipment," observes M. Demmin, "has an
Oriental character about it, especially the cuishes and knee-pieces, composed of plates joined by rings

Hungarian Armour, 16th cent.

such as are used in Persia. The casque is made with a low
crown and covered with a mail-hood, the front part of which
protects the forehead and cheeks" (see annexed figure); the
round shield is ornamented with a painting representing a
crossbow. The Russian casques are of three descriptions—
the Chlem, the Chichack, and the Missiourki, but their distinguishing peculiarities are not sufficiently obvious to me,
and the names appear to have been applied to head-pieces
indifferently. The adjoined cuts of Russian casques are from
examples in the Musée d'Artillerie, Paris, and the Tsarskoe
Selo Museum at St. Petersburg. The Hungarian casque is
described by M. Demmin as having belonged to the hero
Nicalao Zringi, 1566.

Respecting orders of Knighthood, it is to be observed
that the earliest mention of a collar of the Order of the
Garter occurs in the reign of Henry VII. The mantle,
kirtle, hood, and collar are stated as composing the whole
habit of the Order sent to Philip, king of Castile, in 1504
(22nd of Henry VII.). The dress was then entirely of purple
velvet, lined with white silk, sarcenet or taffeta, and no longer
embroidered with garters. The collar and the great and
lesser George, as at present worn, were given to the Knights
of the Garter by King Henry VIII., who reformed the
statutes of the Order and altered the dress. The surcoat
was made of crimson velvet, and a flat black velvet hat of

Russian.

Russian.

Hungarian.

the fashion of the time superseded the hood, which was still, however, worn for ornament only,
hung over the shoulder, and thence called the *humerale*. It was of crimson velvet, the same as
the surcoat. The lesser George was not worn before
the thirteenth year of this king's reign, when it hung in a
gold chain or ribbon upon the breast; and from a memorandum of the thirty-eighth year of the same reign, we
learn that the colour of the ribbon at that date was black.
In the reign of Elizabeth the flat hat was exchanged for
one with a higher crown, of the fashion of the time, but
no other alteration took place in the dress. I annex an
engraving of the Queen in the habit of the Order, from
the print in Ashmole's History of it.

The principal order of knighthood instituted in the
sixteenth century is that of the St. Esprit, by Henry III.
of France, December 31st, 1578. As I have stated in the
Dictionary, p. 133, there is an engraving in Montfaucon's
'Monarchie Française,' from a painting of the period, of
the Count de Nevers being invested with the collar of
the Order, in the first chapter of it, held January 1st, 1579.

Queen Elizabeth in the habit of the Order of the Garter.

An engraving of the collar will be found in Plate V., fig. 5, but our accompanying plate is copied
from the print in Montfaucon above mentioned, showing the knights in the robes of the Order at
the time of its foundation. Several Orders of minor importance are stated to have been founded
in the course of the century, namely :—

The Order of St. Peter and St. Paul, in Rome, by Pope Leo X., in 1520, and re-established in

HENRY III OF FRANCE HOLDING THE FIRST CHAPTER OF THE ORDER OF THE SAINT-ESPRIT IN 1578

THE COURT OF WARDS AND LIVERIES

Temp Q Eliz

1540 by Pope Paul III. The last-named pontiff is supposed to have instituted the Order of St. George of Ravenna, in 1534. It was, however, abolished by Pope Gregory in 1572, and became extinct.

The Order of the Golden Spur, in Rome, is said to have been founded by Pius IV. in 1559, and to have fallen into disuse on his death, in 1565.

The Order of St. Stephen, in Tuscany, founded by Cosmo de Medicis, 1561, and that of Our Saviour in the same year by Eric, thirteenth king of Sweden, which had a very brief existence.

The Order of the Lamb of God, also in Sweden, by John the Great, at Upsal, on the day of his coronation, 1564.

The Order of St. Maurice and St. Lazarus, an amalgamation by Philibert, duke of Saxony, with the permission of Pope Gregory XIII., of two earlier institutions.

The Order of Loretto, by Pope Sixtus V. in 1587, abolished by Pope Gregory XIV.

There is nothing in these fraternities that calls for illustration in our pages. The reader who desires further information respecting them is referred to Edmondson or the earlier work of Favine, 'Théâtre d'Honneur et de Chevalerie,' who industriously collected the few facts and many fictions concerning them.

Of the legal costume of England in the reign of Elizabeth, we have an interesting illustration in painting on panel of the Court of Wards and Liveries, executed presumably about 1585, and, if that date be correct, presenting us with portraits of the Master and several officers of the Court, more or less distinguished, in their robes of office. It was engraved by Vertue for the Society of Antiquaries of London, and published in the 'Vetustamenta.' The personages represented are supposed to be Lord Burleigh, Master of the Court, in the chair, with the mace in his right hand, and supported on each side by a Chief Justice as Assessors. The person in a high-crowned hat, seated on his right, is said to be Thomas Seotford, the Surveyor, and immediately behind him stands a Queen's Serjeant. Next to the Surveyor is seated the Receiver-General, at that time G. Goring, and standing beside him with a staff, Marmaduke Servant, the Usher. On the left of the Master, and next to the Chief Justice, is the Attorney, Thomas Kingsmill, and behind him stands a counsel pleading. Seated next to Kingsmill is William Tooke, the Auditor, and next to him, with the royal arms on his gown, Leonard Taylor, the Messenger of the Court. In front, outside the Bar, stand two Serjeants with white coifs, one in a party-coloured gown, indicating his recent appointment, and consequently conjectured to be Thomas Grnt, made Serjeant in 1585. (*Vide* accompanying plate.)

I approach with diffidence the alterations in ecclesiastical costume consequent on the momentous event of the Reformation, and, in order to avoid offending any of my readers, will confine myself to the quotations of the Rubric without comment.

The vestments ordered in the Prayer-book of 1549 are at the Holy Communion, "for the priest that shall execute the ministry, the vesture appointed for that ministration; that is to say, a white alb, plain, with a vestment or cope, and, where there are priests or deacons ready to help, these are to wear albs with *tunicles*." By the alb, when distinguished, as it here is, from the surplice, is meant a white tunic of much scantier dimensions than the surplice, and, as such, suited for wearing under the vestment or cope. By plain (*pura*) is meant without "apparels," which in mediæval times had been adopted as ornaments to the alb. (See Dictionary, pp. 5 and 9.)

Mr. Marriott remarks upon the above direction, that "in strictness of grammar one wearing 'a vestment *or* cope' would be understood to mean but one vestment, of which cope was an alternative name. But it appears clear that in the fifteenth and sixteenth centuries the word 'vestimentum' was often used with a limited meaning of that which was then regarded as the special vestment of Christian ministry; viz. the chasuble." And further, that though an option is given in the rubric already quoted between "vestment or cope" for the priest at Holy Communion, yet in the rubric providing for services on Wednesdays and Fridays, when there is no Communion, a cope is prescribed without any alternative.

In the second Prayer-book, A.D. 1551, a further change was made, the question of the vestments having in the interval been brought prominently into discussion in consequence of Bishop Hooper refusing to be consecrated unless the use of the pontifical vestments were dispensed with. The second rubric before Morning Prayer ran therefore as follows :—" The minister at the time of the Communion, and at all other times in his ministration, shall use neither alb, vestment, nor cope ; but being archbishop or bishop, he shall have and wear a rochette ; and, being a priest or deacon, he shall have and wear a surplice only."

In the injunctions issued in the first year of Queen Elizabeth, A.D. 1559, no mention is made of vestments ; but in the interpretations appended to them by the archbishop and bishops, there occurs the following direction :—" That there be used only but one apparel : as the cope in the ministration of the Lord's Supper, and the surplice in all other ministrations " (Cardwell, ' Doc. Ann.,' p. 203, *et seq.*).

The Prayer-book of 1559, the use of which was enjoined by the Parliament of 1558–59, has the following rubric on vestments :—" And here it is to be noted, that the minister at the time of the Communion, and at all other times of his ministration, shall use such ornaments in the church as were in use by authority of Parliament in the second year of the reign of King Edward VI., according to the Act of Parliament set in the beginning of this book."[1]

In the 'Advertisements' of 1564, put forth at the Queen's injunction by the Archbishop of Canterbury, Metropolitan, the Bishops of London, Ely, Rochester, Winton, and Lincoln, " Commissioners in causes ecclesiastical with others," occurs the following :—

Protestant Bishop. 16th cent.

" Item, in the ministration of the Holy Communion in cathedrall and collegiate churches the principall minister shall use a cope, with gospeller and epistoler agreeably ; and at all other prayers to be sayde at the Communion table to use no copes, but surplesses.

" Item, that the dean and prebendaries weare a surplesse with a silk hood in the quyer, and, when they preach in the cathedrall or collegiate churches, to weare their hood.

" Item, that every minister saying any publique prayers or ministring the sacraments or other rites of the churche, shall wear a comely surplea with sleeves."

The Reformation, as Mr. Fairholt observes, " by the change produced in the officiating costume of the clergy, appears to have deprived it of its symbolical meaning and consequent form, discarding all that was peculiarly the feature of the Church of Rome." These changes, however, were not sweeping or immediate, but took place gradually with the rejection of the many observances and ceremonies held by that Church. The woodcut title-page to Cranmer's Bible, printed in 1539 (see Dictionary, p. 220), which is said to have been designed by Holbein, is an excellent authority for the clerical costume of that time. In one of its divisions Henry VIII. is depicted on his throne, giving the Bibles to Cranmer and Cromwell for distribution to the people. The Archbishop and his attendant chaplain are habited in long white gowns falling to the feet, over which are worn plain white surplices reaching to the calf of the leg, and having full sleeves. A black scarf (apparently adapted from the stole) gathered in folds round the neck, hanging down at each side in front over the shoulders, to a little below the waist. The portraits of Bishop Latimer,

---

[1] Mr. Marriott has appended to this passage the following note :—" The Parliament which authorised the first Prayer-book of Edward VI. met Oct. 15th, 1548, and was prorogued till Nov. 24th by reason of the plague. The Bill for conforming the Order of Divine Worship, which had been drawn out 'by the Archbishop of Canterbury, with other learned and discreet bishops and divines,' was brought on December 10th to the Lords, and was agreed to January 15th, 1549. The Parliament was not prorogued till March 14th ; and as Edward's accession dates from January 28th, 1547, the session is technically described as 2 & 3 Edward VI., and yet the authority of Parliament is said to be given to this book 'in the second year of King Edward VI.'" (p. 231). It must have escaped Mr. Marriott's notice that the second year of Edward's reign did not expire till January 27th, 1549, and the consent of the Lords had been given to the Bill twelve days previously.

who was burned 16th October, 1555, and of other prelates of that period, present similar features. But the various articles of a Protestant bishop's dress will be best understood from the woodcut in the preceding page, copied, with the necessary elucidations, from Palmer's 'Origines Liturgicæ.' Fig. 1 is the scarf or stole; 2, the chimere; 3, the rochette; and 4, the cassock, or under garment of the chimere. Dr. Hody says that in the time of Edward VI. it was worn of a scarlet colour by our bishops, like the doctor's dress at Oxford, and placed over the rochette, and in the time of Elizabeth was changed for the black satin chimere worn at present.[1] The cap is of the form of that generally worn by clerical, legal, and learned personages in the sixteenth century, and which was superseded shortly after the Reformation by the square cap still worn in our Universities.

The Rev. J. Jebb, in his work on the 'Choral Service of the Church,' p. 219, says: "From a comparison of the various dresses of the primitive Church with those of Rome, it appears that the tendency of the Western Church has been to curtail the flowing vestments of the East, and make up for what they want in majesty by the frippery and effeminate addition of lace, &c. The long English surplice, reaching to the ground, with flowing sleeves, is acknowledged by one of their own ritualists (Dr. Rock) to be more primitive than the short sleeveless garment of Rome."

The quotations from the early Prayer-books show that the cope was still authorized to be worn on certain specified occasions. Archbishop Cranmer, at the consecration of a bishop in 1550, wore not only a cope but a mitre, and the assistant bishops had copes and pastoral staves ('Life of Cranmer,' book ii. chap. xxiv.). In 1564 copes were worn by the officials and assistant priests at Canterbury on Communion days, and by the gentlemen of the Queen's Chapel in the reign of Elizabeth (see Dictionary, p. 131); and we shall find them in use in the Protestant Church till the Great Rebellion.

The alb being directed to be always worn plain, or without apparels, and thereby one of its principal distinctions from the surplice removed, and the use of the two vestments permitted indifferently, the alb appears to have been soon discarded, but the chasuble was occasionally worn as late as the seventeenth century. Accordingly we find on the brasses of priests in the early part of Queen Elizabeth's reign the surplice or plain alb, and sometimes a hood, but afterwards the usual dress is not the surplice, but the Genevan or ordinary civilian's gown. A skull-cap is also found on the head of a doctor in divinity.

The Church of Rome, unused to fluctuation, richly endowed and firmly established, admitted of no change in a costume which it had adopted with a mystic reference to its tenets, and to which it added nothing but splendour of decoration as it increased in wealth and power.

In our next chapter I shall have something more to say respecting the costume of the clergy of the Greek Church, reliable authorities for which abound from the commencement of the seventeenth century.

Louis de Lorraine, Cardinal de Guise.

The portrait of Louis de Lorraine, Cardinal de Guise, illustrates what were called "the forked caps of Popish priests," to which I have alluded (with an engraving) at p. 80 of the Dictionary. In the more depressed form which it presents in this example, it may have suggested the square or trencher cap of the following century.

M. Camille Bonnard has given us the figure of a pope in his ordinary costume, copied, he informs us, from a painting preserved in the Vatican, and described as the portrait of Sixtus IV. by Piero della Francesca. If Vasari is correct, however, in stating that Della Francesca, born in 1398, became blind in 1458, it is impossible he could have painted Sixtus IV. as pope, as he was not elected till 9th of August, 1471, and died 13th of August, 1484. It is, however, an interesting picture of a

---

[1] In consequence, it is said, of the objections of Bishop Hooper at his consecration, previously mentioned.

pope in his daily dress at the commencement, I should say, of the sixteenth century, our earlier illustrations representing him only in full pontificals.

Pope in ordinary dress.   Emmanuel Welser, Canon of Basle.   1576.

I adjoin also the portrait of Emmanuel Welser, Canon of Basle, who died 1576. His aumuse, or tippet, is of ermine, illustrating the observation of the late Mr. Pugin in his 'Glossary of Ecclesiastical Costume,' which I have quoted in Dictionary, p. 7 (article AMESS). The Bishop of Basle being a temporal prince, the chapter of his cathedral were consequently entitled to this peculiar distinction.

George Villiers, Duke of Buckingham and Family

CHAPTER VIII.

THE SEVENTEENTH CENTURY.

HIS period of our history embraces the reigns of the sovereigns of the House of Stuart, including the twelve years of the Commonwealth.

The costume of England in the reign of James I., who succeeded to the throne 24th March, 1603, was little more than a continuation of the dress in the latter portion of the reign of Elizabeth. The long-waisted, peascod-bellied doublet remained in vogue, and the conical-crowned hat and large Gallic or Venetian hose, slashed, quilted, stuffed and guarded (laced), were worn as before, but increased in size, from the quantity of stuffing used in them, which owes its adoption, according to a contemporary writer, to the pusillanimity of the new monarch, who "had his cloathing made large, and even the doublets quilted, for fear of stellets (stilettoes). His breeches in great plaits, and full stuffed." (Dalzell, ' Fragments of Scottish History :' see figure of James, Dictionary, p. 57.) Towards the close of his reign some alterations are observable. Short jackets or doublets, with tabs and false sleeves hanging behind, succeed to the long-waisted doublets ; and the hose, instead of being slashed or laced, were covered with loose, broad straps, richly embroidered or adorned with buttons, the silk or velvet trunk being visible at the intervals.

Jewellery was in great favour during this reign with such of each sex as could indulge in so costly a fashion. In a MS. in the Harleian Library is the following description of the dress of the famous George Villiers, duke of Buckingham, the favourite of James I. :—" It was common with him at any ordinary dancing to have his clothes trimmed with great diamond buttons, and to have diamond hatbands, cockades, and ear-rings ; to be yoked with great and manifold knots of pearl ; in short, to be manacled, fettered, and imprisoned in jewels ; insomuch that at his going over to Paris in 1625, he had twenty-seven suits of clothes made, the richest that embroidery, lace, silk, velvet, gold, and gems could contribute ; one of which was a white uncut velvet, set all over, both suit and cloak, with diamonds valued at fourteen thousand pounds, besides a great feather stuck all over with diamonds, as were also his sword girdle, hatband, and spurs." The fashion of wearing jewels in the hat has been noticed in the Dictionary, p. 265, where the reader will find extracts from the letters of James to this same Duke of Buckingham and Charles Prince of Wales respecting it. Silk, worsted, and thread stockings were in this reign almost universally worn, and cloth or woollen stockings considered unfashionable (see Dictionary, p. 485).

The ladies' dress was still disfigured by the vardingale : see portrait of Anne of Denmark, queen of James I., in Dictionary, p. 187, and to that portion of our work I may also refer the reader for information respecting all the separate articles of attire necessary to complete the costume, male and female, of this period in England. A portentous list of the latter is contained in an old play, called 'Lingua ; or, the Combat of the Tongue and the Five Senses for Superiority,' published in 1607. " Five hours ago," says one of the characters, " I set a dozen maids to attire a boy like a nice gentlewoman, but there is such doing with their looking-glasses ; pinning, unpinning, sitting, unsitting, formings and conformings ; paintings of blue veins and cheeks ; such a stir with sticks, combs, cascanets, dressings, purls, fall-squares, busks, bodices, scarfs, necklaces, carcanets, rabattoes, borders, tires, fans, palisadoes, puffs, ruffs, cuffs, muffs, pusles, fusels, partlets, fringlets, bandlets, fillets, corsletts, pendulets, amulets, annulets, bracelets, and so many lets (stops or hindrances), that she is scarce dressed to the girdle, and now there is such calling for fardingales, kirtles, busk-points, shoe-ties, and the like, that seven pedlars' shops, nay, all Stourbridge fair, will scarcely furnish her. A ship is sooner rigged by far than a gentlewoman made ready."

Henry Fitzgoffery, in his satirical 'Notes from Black Fryers,' 1617, furnishes us with a description in rhyme of a fashionable gallant of that date, which is nearly as instructive respecting the wardrobe of the male sex :—

> " Know'st thou yon world of fashion now comes in,
> In Turkie colours carved to the skin,
> Mounted Polonianly till he reeles,
> That scorns so much plain dealing at his heels ;
> His boots speak Spanish to his Scottish spurs ;
> His sute cut Frenchly rounde, bestuck with burres ;
> Pure Holland is his shirt, which proudly faire
> Seems to outface his doublet everywhere ;
> His haire like to your Moores or Irish lockes,
> His chiefest dyet Indian mixed with dockes ;
> What country May-game might wee this suppose ?
> Sure one would think a Roman by his nose ;
> No ! in his habit better understand
> He is of England, by his yellow band."

And Dekker, in his 'Gull's Horn Book,' published in 1609, contrasting the fashions of his day

with the simplicity of the old times (though where he found simplicity in any later than the Deluge I am not aware), says : "There was then neither the Spanish slop nor the skipper's galligaskins ; the Danish sleeving, sagging down like a Welsh wallet ; the Italian's close strosser, nor the French standing collar ; your treble, quadruple, Dædalion ruffs ; nor your stiff-necked rabatos, that have more arches for pride to row under than can stand under five London bridges, durst not then set themselves out in print, for the patent for starch could by no means be signed. Fashion then was counted a disease, and horses died of it." The disease is a very old one, and Dekker would have been puzzled, I fancy, to point out an age in which it was not deplored as epidemic.

The annexed portraits of the Earl of Somerset and his infamous wife illustrate the ordinary dress of the nobility of this kingdom in the reign of James I. ; and those of Prince Henry, the promising son of that sovereign, and a young nobleman in

The Earl and Countess of Somerset.

attendance on him [1] (see next page), furnish us with the hunting costume of the same period.

[1] Supposed to be Lord Harrington, from a shield of arms suspended from a branch of the tree above him in the original picture ; but in a replica of it the shield is charged with the arms of another family.

To the above quotations may be added another from Samuel Rowland's tract, 'A Pair of Spy-Knaves,' in which, speaking of the "roaring boys" of his time, he says:—

> "What our neat fantastics newest hatch
> That at the second-hand he's sure to catch :
> If it be feather-time, he wears a feather,
> A golden hat-band or a silver either ;
> Waisted like to some dwarfe or coated ape,
> As if of monster's misbegotten shape
> He were engendered, and, rejecting nature,
> Were new cut out and sticht the taylor's creature ;
> An elbowe cloake, because wide hose and garters
> May be apparent in the lower quarters ;
> His cabbage-ruff of the outrageous size,
> Starched in colour to beholder's eyes."

I have mentioned at p. 179 of the Dictionary a singular fashion of this period, viz. the wearing of one or more black strings in the ear by gentlemen in lieu of ear-rings, and illustrated it by two

Prince Henry and attendant Lord.

examples from portraits in Hampton Court Palace. The following anecdote respecting it is preserved in Peck's 'Desiderata curiosa,' p. 575 :—

"In 1612 (10th James I.), Mr. Edward Hawley of Gray's Inn, coming to Court one day, Maxwell (a Scotsman) led him out of the room by a black string which he wore in his ear, a fashion then much in use : but this had like to have caused warm blood. Not only Gray's Inn Society, but all the gentry in London thought themselves concerned in the affront, and Hawley threatened to kill

Maxwell wherever he met him if he refused to fight, which so frightened the king that he sent for the benchers and made up the quarrel."

I have the pleasure of further illustrating this eccentric fashion by the annexed engraving, from a drawing by Mr. Dillon, of a portion of the portrait of Henry Prince of Wales, now in the possession

From portrait of Henry Prince of Wales.   From portrait of Richard Lee.

of his uncle, Viscount Dillon, at Ditchley. Mr. Dillon has also obliged me by copying for me part of the face of the portrait of Richard, brother of Sir Henry Lee, in the same collection, which illustrates the contemporaneous fashion of wearing a rose in the ear, alluded to by Shakespeare in 'King John,' act i. sc. 1 :

> "That in mine ear I durst not stick a rose,
> Lest men should say, Look, where three-farthings goes!"

and referring to a thin silver coin of the reign of Elizabeth, called the "three-farthing rose." This contribution of Mr. Dillon's is the more valuable, as the example is the only one, I believe, known to exist of the practice. (See also Dictionary, p. 433.)

We do not learn from this the origin or birthplace of the fashion; but I am inclined to think it travelled hither from Denmark with Anne, the queen of James I., as it is first seen after her arrival, and one of the portraits at Hampton Court to which I have alluded is said to be that of Christian, king of Denmark.

The reign of Charles I. (1625–1648) introduces us to the most elegant and picturesque costume ever worn in England ; and from the circumstance of its having been the habit of the time in which Vandyke painted, it has become associated with his name, being frequently called "the Vandyke dress." At the commencement of his reign, however, the fashions of the latter years of his father were retained, and there was scarcely a nation in Europe that had not contributed its share to them. In Ben Jonson's comedy, 'The New Inn,' first acted in 1629, Sir Glorious Tipto says :

> "I would put on
> The Savoy chain about my neck, the ruff,
> The cuffs of Flanders ; then the Naples' hat
> With the Rome hatband and the Florentine agate,
> The Milan sword, the cloak of Genoa set
> With Brabant buttons : all my given pieces,
> Except my gloves, the natives of Madrid,
> To entertain him in."—Act ii., scene 2.

It is rather remarkable that France, the head-quarters of Fashion, is not mentioned amongst the countries to which the knight confesses his obligation.

The "Spanish quellio ruffs" are mentioned by Massinger in his 'City Madam,' act iv. sc. 2, which play was produced in 1632. Gifford, in a note on this passage, has : "Quellio, a corruption of *cuello*," and offers us a derivation of the word which appears perfectly satisfactory. *Cuello* in Spanish certainly signifies "the collar of a shirt, a large plaited neck-cloth formerly worn;" but *quellio*, as used by Massinger, implies a particular kind of ruff, and I have lighted on another word of which I think *quellio* is an abbreviation. Lachuquwilla is Spanish not only for "a frill, formerly worn round the neck," but for "a small lettuce;" and in Fletcher's play, 'A Wife for a Month,' licensed in 1624, I find (act ii. sc. 4) the expression "*lettice* ruff," which, if not a translation of "*quellio* ruff," is, at all events, I think, worth "making a note of."

Peck, the antiquary, states that he had seen a portrait of Charles I. in which the king was represented in a falling band, a short green doublet, the arm part towards the shoulder wide and slashed zigzag, turned-up ruffles, very long green breeches, tied far below the knee with long yellow ribbons, red stockings, great shoe-roses, and a short red cloak lined with blue, with a star on the shoulder. Anything more hideous than such a mixture of red, green, blue, and yellow, can scarcely be imagined, and, I should think, was never seen in any dress but that of a jester. The portraits of Charles best known and authenticated may be appealed to in refutation of the stigma on the good taste of the sovereign implied by the villanous daub described by Peck. The full-length portrait of Charles by Vandyke, in white satin, is here annexed as an illustration of the dress of the day. At the commencement of the Civil War, when the Royalist party began to be denominated Cavaliers, and the republican Roundheads, the costume of England was as divided as its opinions; but the dress of the Cavalier was gallant and picturesque in the extreme. It consisted of a doublet of silk, satin, or velvet, with large loose sleeves slashed up the front; the collar covered by a falling band of the richest point lace, with that peculiar edging now called Vandyke. A short cloak was worn carelessly on the shoulder. The long breeches, fringed or pointed, as we have already mentioned, met the tops of the wide boots, which were also ruffled with lace or lawn. A broad-leafed Flemish beaver hat, with a rich hatband and plume of feathers, was set on one side the head, and a Spanish rapier hung from a magnificent baldrick or sword-belt, worn sash-wise over the right shoulder. The beard was worn very peaked, with small, upturned moustaches; the hair long in the neck, and sometimes, it would seem, powdered.

Charles I. From a painting by Vandyke, in the Louvre.

Bulwer, in his 'Pedigree of the English Gallant,' says, "Our gallants' witty noddles are put into such a pure witty trim, the dislocations of every hair so exactly set, the whole bush so curiously candied, and (what is most prodigious) the natural jet of some of them so exalted into a perfect azure, that their familiar friends have much ado to own their faces; for by their powdered heads you would take them to be mealmen." John Owen, Dean of Christchurch and Vice-Chancellor of Oxford, appears in 1652 "in querpo, like a young scholar, with powdered hair, snake-bone band-strings, a lawn band, a large set of ribands pointed (*i.e.* tagged) at the knees, Spanish leather boots, with large lawn tops, and his hat most curiously cocked,—a dress," as Strutt remarks, "improper enough for a clergyman," but which, fortunately, affords us a description of the dress of "a young scholar" affecting a gallant of that day. (See also article POWDER (HAIR), in Dictionary, p. 484.)

The ladies of this period wore their hair low on the forehead and parted in ringlets, or else curled like a peruke, or braided in a knot on the top of the head. "Why do they adorn themselves," inquires Burton, "with so many colours of herbs, fictitious flowers, curious needleworks, quaint devices, sweet-smelling odours, with those inestimable riches of precious stones, pearls, rubies, diamonds, emeralds, &c.? Why do they crown themselves with gold and silver, use coronets and tires of several fashions, deck themselves with pendants, bracelets, ear-rings, chains, girdles, rings, pins, spangles, embroideries, shadows, rebatoes, versicolor ribands? Why do they make such glorious shows with their scarfs, feathers, fans, masks, laces, tiffanies, ruffs, falls, calls, cuffs, damasks, velvets, tinsels, cloths of gold, and silver tissue? It is hard," he observes, "to derive the abominable pedigree of cobweb lawn, yellow starched ruffs which so much disfigure our nation, and render them ridiculous and fantastical."

The following "catalogue" of the apparel and ornaments of a fantastical lady of fashion appears in the dramatic pastoral 'Rhodon and Iris,' first acted in 1631, and from which several extracts will be found under separate heads in the Dictionary. It is here given *in extenso*, as conveying the best general picture of the female costume of that time. The speaker allows it to be " as tedious as a tailor's bill," but a tailor's bill of the seventeenth century is anything but tedious to the student of costume in the nineteenth, and this catalogue is too interesting, from its containing the names of "all the devices" he is "commanded to provide," to require any such apology for its insertion.

> "Chains, coronets, pendant, bracelets, and ear-rings,
> Pins, girdles, spangles, embroyderies, and rings ;
> Shadowes, rebatoes, ribbands, ruffs, cuffs, falls,
> Scarfes, feathers, fans, maskes, muffs, laces, cauls,
> Thin tiffanies, cobweb lawn, and fardingals,
> Sweet fals, vayles, wimples, glasses, crisping-pins,
> Pots of ointment, combs, with poking-sticks and bodkins ;
> Coyfes, gorgets, fringes, rowles, fillets, and hair-laces ;
> Silkes, damasks, velvets, tinsels, cloth of gold,
> Of tissues with colours of a hundred fold.
> But in her tyres so new-fangled is she,
> That which doth with her humour now agree
> To-morrow she dislikes : now doth she sweare
> That a loose body is the neatest weare ;
> But ere an hour be gone she will protest
> A straight gowne graces her proportion best.
> Now calls she for a boisterous fardingal,
> Then to her hips she'll have her garments fall ;
> Now doth she praise a sleeve that's long and wide,
> Yet by and by that fashion doth deride.
> Sometimes she applauds a pavement-sweeping traine,
> And presently dispraiseth it againe.
> Now she commends a shallow bande so small
> That it may seem scarce any bande at all ;
> But soon to a new fancy doth she reele,
> And calls for one as big as a coach wheele.
> She'll weare a flowing coronet to-day,
> The symboll of her beauty's sad decay ;
> To-morrow she a waving plume will try,
> The emblem of all female levitie.
> Now in her hat, then in her hair is drest ;
> Now of all fashions she thinks change the best.
> Nor in her weeds alone is she so nice,
> But rich perfumes she buys at any price :
> Storax and spikenard she borns in her chamber,
> And daubs herself with civet, musk, and amber.
> *   *   *   *   *   *   *
> Waters she hath to make her face to shine,
> Confections eke to clarify her skin ;
> Lip-salves and clothes of a rich scarlet dye
> She hath, which to her cheeks she doth apply ;
> Ointment wherewith she pargets o'er her face,
> And lustrifies her beauty's dying grace."

I give here an elegant example of a standing collar of lace from the portrait of the celebrated Mary, Countess of Pembroke—"Sidney's sister, Pembroke's mother"—A.D. 1621, from the engraving in Walpole's 'Royal and Noble Authors.'

Wenceslaus Hollar, in his 'Ornatus Muliebris Anglicanus,' 1640, has admirably depicted the dresses of all the various classes of the women of England, and copies of the most important we have already given in the Dictionary (see pp. 186, 227, and 228), to which we must refer the reader. See also the figures of Anne Stotevill and Dorothy Strutt, from their effigies, inserted below.

The practice of patching the face commenced during this reign. Glapthorne mentions it in his 'Lady's Privilege,' published in 1640; and Bulwer in his 'Artificial Changeling,' printed in 1650, speaks of it as "a vaine custom" which had been "*lately* entertained" by the ladies. It was carried to a preposterous extent, and continued in vogue with both sexes to the end of the century. (See Dictionary, p. 388, where the fashion is fully illustrated.) The wearing of love-locks by men was another absurd and effeminate custom which arose at the same period, and was bitterly denounced by the Puritans. (See Dictionary, p. 246, article HAIR.)

Mary, Countess of Pembroke. 1621.

"During that distracted period of our history when Cromwell obtained the ascendency,

Effigy of Anne Stotevill in Westminster Abbey. 1631.

Effigy of Dorothy Strutt in Whalley Church, Essex. 1641.

Mr. Fairholt observes, "the dresses of the various classes of the community presented a considerable mixture, for each followed the bent of his own inclination."

While extravagance and splendour characterised the Royalists or Cavaliers, everything worn by the Republicans, whether Puritans or Roundheads, became meanly and ridiculously plain, and the short-cut hair and little plain Geneva bands were marks by which they were particularly known. (See Dictionary, p. 247.) The contrast is amusingly described in a poem entitled 'The Way to Woo a zealous Lady,' published in 'The Rump Songs' at that period, and relating the reception of a fashionable gallant by a Puritan lady who had won his affections :—

"She told me that I was much too profane,
    And not devout, neither in speech nor gesture ;
And I could not one word in answer gain,
    Nor had not so much grace to call her sister ;
For ever something did offend her there,
Either my broad beard, hat, or my long hair.

"My band was broad, my 'parel was not plain,
    My points and girdle made the greatest show ;
My sword was odious and my belt was vain,
    My Spanish shoes were cut too broad at toe ;
My stockings light, my garters ty'd too long,
My gloves perfumed, and had a scent too strong.

"I left my pure mistress for a space,
    And to a snip-snap barber straight went I ;
I cut my hair, and did my corps uncase
    Of 'parel's pride that did offend the eye :
My high-crown'd hat, my little band also,
My peaked beard, my shoes were sharp at toe.

"Gone was my sword, my belt was laid aside ;
    And I, transformed both in looks and speech,
My 'parel plain, my cloak devoid of pride,
    My little skirts, my metamorphos'd breech,
My stockings black, my garters were ty'd shorter,
My gloves no scent—thus march'd I to her porter."

Mr. Fairholt, to whom we are indebted for the above extracts, remarks, "This display of plainness, however, was anything but a type of innate modesty, as those persons were no whit less vain of their want of adornment than the gallants were of their finery." Of the arch-rebel Cromwell himself, Sir Philip Warwick has left us a minute and graphic description. "The first time," he says, "that I ever took notice of him was in the beginning of the Parliament held in November 1640, when I vainly thought myself a courtly young gentleman : for we courtiers valued ourselves much upon our good clothes. I came one morning into the house well clad, and perceived a gentleman speaking whom I knew not, ordinarily apparelled, for it was a plain cloth suit, which seemed to have been made by an ill country tailor ; his linen was plain, and not very clean ; and I remember *a speck or two of blood* upon his little band, which was not much larger than his collar : his hat was without a hatband, his stature was of a good size, and his sword stuck close to his side." Once in power, however, he became more particular in his dress, wearing a suit of black velvet or cloth trimmed with velvet, trunk-hose, a scarf round his waist, long boots, and a grey hat with a silver clasp. His body after death was more gorgeously attired than that of any deceased sovereign, with purple velvet, ermine, and the richest Flanders lace ; and his effigy, carved by one Symonds, was clad in a fine shirt of Holland, richly laced with bands and cuffs of the same, and the clothes covered with gold lace. Nor did the mother of Cromwell sacrifice her taste to the puritanical affectation of her day. She wore a handkerchief of which the broad point lace alone could be seen, and a green velvet cardinal trimmed with broad gold lace.

The Puritan ladies, indeed, as well as the men of birth, had no fancy for exchanging the rich dress of the Court of the Stuarts for that of the Roundheads. Sir Thomas Fairfax, father of the great Parliamentary general, is described as wearing a buff coat richly ornamented with silver lace, open sleeves slashed with white satin, his breast-plate partly concealed by a falling collar of broad and costly Flanders lace ; trunk-hose trimmed with the same materials, russet leather boots, and a sash of silk and gold. It was not till the arrival of the first Spanish envoy accredited to "the Protector" that Harrison begged Colonel Hutchinson and Lord Warwick not to appear in gold or silver lace. The former complied, and presented himself next day in a plain black suit ; but Harrison, to the astonishment of everyone, arrived in a scarlet coat so laden with lace that the material of which it was made was scarcely visible. "The more we read," says Mrs. Bury Palliser, alluding to this anecdote, "the more we feel convinced that the dislike manifested by the Puritan leaders to lace and other luxuries was but a political necessity to follow the spirit of the age ;" which, she might have added, was one of disgusting hypocrisy.

The dress of a Puritan in 1649 will be seen at p. 109 of the Dictionary, and that of a notorious

Roundhead in the portrait of Colonel John Lilburne at page 248 of the same volume. Long hair was not, however, generally discarded. Cromwell himself wore hair of a moderate length behind, and the effigies of Hyacinth and Elizabeth Sachevarel, 1657, in Morley Church, Derbyshire, are fair examples of the costume of an English merchant and his wife just previous to the Restoration. The canions round the knees of the trunk-hose of the male figure are a late example of them in their original form.

An English writer of this latter date, bitterly commenting on the follies and fashions of his countrymen, says, "If thou beest for bravery, I cannot follow thee by the track nor find out thy various motions. The gallant is counted a wild creature—no wild colt, wild ostrich, wild cat of the mountain comparable to him. He is indeed the buffoon and baboon of the times; his mind is wholly set on cuts and slashes, knots and roses, patchings and pinkings, jaggings, taggings, borderings, trimmings, half shirts, half arms, yawning breasts, gaping knees, arithmetical middles, geometrical sides, mathematical wastes (waists), musical heels, and logical toes. I wonder he is not for the Indian's branded skin and ringed snout. . . . . Know ye not the multitude of students, artists, graduates, that are subliming their notions to please this one light head? Then hear them by their names—perfumers, complexioners, leather-

Hyacinth and Elizabeth Sachevarel. 1657.

makers, stitchers, snippers, drawers; yea, what not! yet among them doth the knighted spark spend out his time. This is the gallant's day." ('Plea for Nineveh,' 1657.) Again, he says, "The man now is become as feminine as the woman. Men must have their half-shirts and half-arms, a dozen casements above and two wide luke-homes below. Some walk, as it were, in their waistcoats, and others, a man would think, in their petticoats; they must have narrow waists and narrow bands, large cuffs upon their wrists, and larger upon their shin-bones; their boots must be crimped and their knees guarded. A man would conceive them to be apes by their coats, soap-men by their faces, meal-men by their shoulders, bears or dogs by their frizzled hair—and this is my trim man!"

On the fair sex he is equally severe. "The kings of Egypt were wont to give unto their queens the tribute of the city of Antilla to buy them girdles; and how much girdles, gorgets, wimples, cauls, crisping pins, veils, rails, frontlets, bonnets, bracelets, necklaces, slops, slippers, round-tires, sweet-balls, rings, ear-rings, mufflers, glasses, hoods, lawn, musks, civets, rose-powders, gossamy-butter, complexion-waters, do cost in our days, many a sighing husband doth know by the year's accounts.

"What ado is there to spruce up many a woman either for streets or market, bankets (banquets) or temples! She is not fit to be seen unless she doth appear half naked, unless she hath her distinguishing patches upon her; she goeth not abroad till she be feathered like a popinjay, and doth shine like alabaster; it is a hard thing to draw her out of bed, and an harder thing to draw her from the looking-glass. It is the great work of the family to dress her; much chaffing and fuming there is before she can be thoroughly tired (attired); her spungings and perfumings, lacings and lickings, clippings and strippings, dentrificings and daubings, the setting of hair methodically, and the placing every beauty spot topically, are so tedious, that it is a wonder that the mistress can sit, or the waiting-maid stand, till all the scenes of this fantastic comedy be acted through. Oh, these birds of Paradise are bought at a dear rate! the keeping of these lannerets is very chargeable!" N.B.—This was in 1657, three years before the Restoration. Our lady readers may triumphantly refer their satirists of the present day to this picture of their ancestresses in the time even of the Commonwealth!

"With the restoration of the House of Stuart, Fashion also regained the throne from which she had been driven by the stern and puritanical Republicans, and, like the Merry Monarch with whom she returned, many were the mad pranks she played in the delirium of her joy; many the excesses she committed. Taste and elegance were abandoned for extravagance and folly; and the male costume, which in the time of Charles I. had reached the highest point of picturesque splendour, degenerated and declined from this moment, and expired in the square coat, cocked hat, full-bottomed wig, and jack-boots of the following century." ('Hist. of Brit. Cost.,' p. 323.)

The birth of these odious articles may be traced from the close, indeed, of the reign of Charles II., at the commencement of which a few fantastical additions to the Vandyke costume injured but did not totally destroy it. The doublet was made exceedingly short, open in front, without any under waistcoat, and displaying the fine holland shirt which bulged out from it over the waistband of the loose breeches, which, as well as the full sleeves, were laden with points and ribbons. Beneath the knee hung long, drooping lace ruffles, to which was now transferred the name of canions or cannons, which previously was applied to the rolls of cloth or ribbon which terminated the trunk-hose. The falling collar of lace, and high-crowned hat with drooping feathers, still preserved some of the old gallant Cavalier character.

The following contemporary account of Charles II.'s entry into London contains many particulars of costume deserving notice:—

"All the streets being richly hanged with tapestry, and a lane made by the militia forces to London Bridge; from London Bridge to Temple Bar by the train bands on one side, and the several companies in their liveries on the other side by the rails; from Temple Bar to Westminster by the militia forces, regiments of the army, and several gentlemen officers of the King's army, led by Sir John Stawell. First marched a troop of gentlemen, led by Major-General Brown, brandishing their swords, in cloth-of-silver doublets; in all about 300, besides their servants. Then another troop, led by Alderman Robinson, with buff coats, silver sleeves, and green scarfs. After this a troop with blue liveries and silver lace, colors red,[1] fringed with silver, about 130. After that a troop, 6 trumpets, 7 footmen in sea-green and silver, their colors pinck, fringed with silver. Then a troop with their liveries gray and blew, with silk and silver laces, 30 footmen, 4 trumpets, consisting of about 220, their colors sky, fringed with silver. Another of gray liveries, 6 trumpets, colors sky and silver, of about 105 gentlemen. Another troop of 70 gentlemen, 5 trumpets, colors sky and silver. Another troop, led by the Lord Cleveland, of about 200 noblemen and gentlemen, colours blew, fringed with gold. Another troop, of about 100, black colors, fringed with gold. Another troop of about 300," colours not described.

"After these came 2 trumpets, with His Majestie's arms; the Sheriffs' men in red cloaks and silver lace, with half pikes, 79 in number. Then followed the several companies of London,[2] with their several streamers, all in black velvet coats, with gold chains, every company having their footmen of their several liveries, some red and white, some pinck and white, some blew and yellow, &c. Three trumpets, in liveries richly laced, and cloth of silver sleeves, went before the Company of the Mercers. After all these came a kettledrum, 5 trumpets, and 3 streamers, and very rich red liveries with silver lace. The number of the citizens were about 600. After these 12 ministers, another kettledrum, 4 trumpets. Then His Majestie's Life-Guard, led by the Lord Gerrard; another party led by Sir Gilbert Gerrard and Major Rosecarron, and the third division by Colonel Pragues. Then 3 trumpeters in rich coats and satin doublets; the City Marshal, with 8 footmen in French green, trimmed with crimson and white; the City Waits, the City officers in order, Dr. Warmstry, the two Sheriffs, and all the Aldermen in their scarlet gowns and rich trappings, with footmen in liveries, red coats laced with silver and cloth of gold; the heralds and maces (mace-bearers), in their rich coats; the Lord Mayor, bare (headed), carrying the sword; his Excellency the Duke of Buckingham, bare; and then the glory of all, His sacred Majesty, rode between the Dukes of York and Glocester. Afterwards followed a troop, bare, with white colours; then the general Life-Guard; after which

---

[1] It is not quite clear to me what we are to understand by this and several subsequent mention of "colors." It certainly cannot mean flags, and I can only suppose that, being named in addition to "liveries," these "colors" must have been scarves or knots of ribbon assumed for this particular occasion.

[2] The writer has previously informed us that they were ranged from London Bridge to Temple Bar, "by the rails," facing the trained bands. We must therefore suppose they fell into the procession as it passed.

Banquet given to Charles II at the Hague, May 30th 1660, by the Estates of Holland
From an engraving of the period

another company of gentry, sky, fringed with gold; after which five regiments of the army horse led by Colonel Knight, viz. His Excellencie's (General Monk's) regiment, Colonel Knight's, Colonel Cloberrie's, Lord Faucosberg's, Lord Howard's. After whom came two troops of nobility and gentlemen, red colors, fringed with gold." ('Mercurius Politicus,' May 1660.)

Lady Fanshawe, in her 'Memoirs,' gives us the following description of the costume of a gentleman at this period:—

"Then came my husband in a very rich suit of clothes, of a dark phillamot brocade, laced with silver and gold lace, every one as broad as my hand, and a little silver and gold lace between them, both of very curious workmanship. His suit was trimmed with scarlet taffeta ribbands. His stockings of white silk, upon long scarlet silk ones. His shoes black, with scarlet shoe-strings and garters. His linen very fine, laced with rich Flanders lace. A black beaver, buttoned on the left side with a jewel of 1200£ value. A rich upright, curious gold chain, made at the Indies, at which hung the King his master's picture, richly set with diamonds, and cost 300£, which His Majesty, in his great grace and favour, had been pleased to give him on his coming from Portugal. On his fingers he wore two rich rings. His gloves were trimmed with the same ribbands as his clothes, and his whole family were richly clothed according to their several qualities."

The diaries of Pepys and Evelyn teem with descriptions of the costume of this period. I have already, in the Dictionary, quoted freely from both in illustration of various portions of attire under their separate heads, and shall therefore limit my extracts here to a few general notices. In April 1662, Pepys says: "I saw the King in the Park, now out of mourning, in a suit laced with gold and silver, which, it is said, was out of fashion."

In October 1663, he tells us that he has spent "55£, or thereabouts," in clothes for himself, amongst which he enumerates a velvet cloak, two new cloth skirts, black, plain both; a new shag gown, trimmed with gold buttons and twist, a new hat, and silk tops for his legs.

Under the date of November 30, the same year, he records: "Put on my best black suit, trimmed with scarlet ribands, very neat, with my cloak lined with velvet, and a new beaver, which altogether is very noble."

A-propos of his "new beaver" he tells us, under the date 22nd September, 1664, that he caught cold by "flinging off his hat at dinner." And in a note to this passage in Lord Clarendon's 'Essay on Decay of Respect due to Age,' he says that in his younger days he never kept his hat on before those older than himself, *except at dinner*. We shall find the custom of wearing hats at dinner continued in the following century. The circumstance of there appearing no person covered in the print of the banquet given to Charles II. at the Hague, in 1660, may be accounted for, perhaps, by the presence of the King and the royal family.

The engravings by Hollar, of the procession of Charles II. through London the day before his coronation, published in Ogilby's History of that ceremony, affords ample illustration of the State and official costumes at the commencement of his reign; and our accompanying plate, representing Charles at the banquet given to him at the Hague by the Estates of Holland, in May 1660, just referred to, from a work of that date,[1] is extremely interesting, as it contains portraits of his aunt, the Queen of Bohemia; his sister, the Princess of Orange, and her young son, afterwards William III.; and his two brothers, James, duke of York, who succeeded him as James II., and the Duke of Gloucester, who died 13th September, 1660.

In the year 1658 one William Ravenscroft is recorded, by Randal Holmes, as having arrived at Chester from France, and introduced the petticoat breeches known by the name of Rhingraves,[2] which owed their origin to a Count de Salm, bearing the title of Rhingrave, who resided several years in Paris as the political agent of the United Provinces, and assiduously frequented the Palace of the Luxembourg. The fashion rapidly spread from the Court through the country, and in due

[1] 'A Relation, in form of a Journal, of the Voyage and Residence which the most excellent and most mighty Prince, Charles II., King of Great Britain, &c., hath made in Holland; rendered into English out of the original French by Sir William Lower, Knight. Hague: printed by Adrian Vlack, anno M.DC.LX.'

[2] They seem to be alluded to in 1657 by Reeve in his 'Plea for Nineveh' (*vide* p. 236).

course to England, where it was generally adopted at the time of the Restoration, and was shortly followed by that absurd monstrosity, the periwig. Two stories are current respecting the origin of the periwig: one that Louis XIV., when a little boy, had remarkably beautiful hair, which hung in long waving curls on his shoulders, and the courtiers, out of compliment to their young sovereign, had heads of false hair made to imitate his natural locks, which obtained the name of perukes—when the King grew up, he returned the compliment by adopting the article himself; the other, that they were first worn by a Duke of Anjou to conceal a personal deformity, and were adopted by the Court in compliment to him. I find no positive authority for either story, and M. Quicherat does not even allude to them. On the contrary, he distinctly says that Louis, who possessed a head of hair which would have assured to him the title of "Grand Roi" in the time of the Merovingians, would not conform to the fashion until he was thirty-five years old (1673), and then had openings made in the caul of the wig, through which his own luxuriant locks could be drawn, as he refused to sacrifice them; while we know, from the minute Mr. Pepys, that the Duke of York first put on a periwig February 15th, 1663-4, and that he saw the King (Charles II.) in one for the first time in the April following.

The fashion seems, however, to have arisen in France, about 1660; but not only false hair, but the terms peruke and periwig had been known in England a hundred years previously (see PERIWIG, in Dictionary, p. 392).

In 1666 Charles II. declared in Council his design of adopting a certain habit which he was resolved never to alter. It consisted of a long close vest of black cloth or velvet, pinked with white satin, a loose coat over it of the Polish fashion, and, instead of shoes and stockings, buskins or brodequins (see VEST, Dictionary, p. 513). The fashion was, however, very short-lived, and "Monsieur's vanities" (as Evelyn calls the dresses of the Court of France) resumed their ascendency. By the way, there is an anecdote respecting this particular habit which may claim a word or two of explanation. Pepys says, under date of 22nd November of the same year, that Mr. Batelier brought him "the news how the King of France hath, in defiance of the King (Charles), caused all his footmen to be put into vests, and that the noblemen of France will do the like, which if true, he declares, is the greatest indignity ever done by one prince to another." Now, I find no mention of any such circumstance in M. Quicherat's elaborate 'Histoire du Costume en France,' or in any other French work on that subject; but, in contradiction of it, that in 1670 the vest was generally substituted for the short doublet, and became, with the coat, a costume specially affected by the military. Was Mr. Batelier hoaxing the inquisitive Secretary, or was it the idle gossip of the day, as untrustworthy as such gossip is in general?

In 1679 we find, in an inventory of apparel provided for Charles II., a complete suit of one material, under the familiar designation of coat, waistcoat, and breeches. Pantaloons are also mentioned in that document, with holland drawers, and flannel and cotton trousers.

The band was succeeded by the cravat of Brussels or Flanders, and the enormous periwig required a different covering to the high-crowned hat, or the broad-leafed Spanish sombrero. So the crown was flattened, and the brim, reduced in width, was garnished with feathers, and turned up, or cocked, as it was termed, in various ways, according to the prevailing mode or the fancy of the wearer.

One would suppose the periwigs of that day would have kept the head sufficiently warm without a hat, and yet we have seen that Pepys records he caught cold by taking his off at dinner.

No remarkable change has to be noticed during the brief reign of James II. (1685-88). A little more formality in the cut of the coat indicates the advent of that square-skirted, stiff garment which speedily succeeded it. Gentlemen appeared in little low hats, with a bow at the side. The long, straight coats and waistcoats had close-set rows of buttons down the front, a fashion of which we see examples as early as 1670, in the dresses of the persons attending the funeral of General Monk; and I can therefore scarcely understand the complaint of the author of a rare little book, published in 1683, that in wearing Dutch hats with French feathers, French doublets with collars after the custom of Spain, Turkish coats, Spanish hose, Italian cloaks, Venetian rapiers, with such like, we had likewise stolen the vices and excesses of these countries'—unless he is speaking of the past, as far as the costume is concerned, for it is that of the time of James and Charles I., and was never seen after the Restoration.

Malcolm, in his 'Manners and Customs,' has collected many curious notices of dress in the latter days of Charles II., some of which I have quoted under particular headings in the Dictionary.

An advertisement in 1680, respecting the loss of a watch, informs us that it has been found by a gentleman that "goes in a sad-coloured cloth suit,[2] with a green shoulder-knot figured with silver, and the facings of his coat of green velvet. He wears a light-coloured periwig, with a grey hat, and a green taffety ribband round it, and a sword-knot of the same."

Green appears to have been a favourite colour in 1680. Thomas Taylor, a youth who had wandered from his home, was described by his friends as wearing a grey cloth suit, lined with green, with plate buttons, a green vest, a grey cloth monteer (montero?) cap, lined and edged with green, a pair of green stockings, and a lace neck-cloth.

In 1681 we read of a young gentleman in "a suit of sad-coloured cloth, lined with flowered silk, the ground buff colour, with peach and green-coloured flowers, and a waistcoat of the same silk ; a pair of silk stockings of the same colour of the cloth ; and a sad-coloured cloth cap, turned up with sable, and laced down the seams with gold breed" (braid). Blue plush caps, we are told, were much worn in this year, and, from the occurrence of the word " monteer " in the above advertisement, and the description of the cloth one turned up with sable and laced with gold braid down the seams, which follows, I surmise that the cap known in Spain as the *montero* had been introduced here about this period ; or the Spanish name given to a peculiar cap which we find worn by Bamfylde Moore Carew, the famous King of the Beggars, and, with some unimportant variation of form, by the lower orders to the time of George II.

In the same year (1681) "a light-coloured cloth coat, lined with blue serge, the cape and sleeves faced with blue shag, gold and silver buttons, and silk, gold, and silver loops, and the cape bound round with broad gold galloon, above three inches broad, was left in a coach," and the finder was directed to return it to the Master of the Rolls, in Chancery Lane.

Cloth coats lined with red, and satin ribbons of different colours round the hat (the latter reminding us of the hats still worn by the Yeomen of the Guard, whose dress remains much the same as it was at the beginning of the last century), were the fashion at the above period ; also "campaign coats" of cloth and mixed silk, and silver buttons, and three frost (frosted silver) loops at each pocket flap ; waistcoats made of shalloon, faced and bordered with flowered silk, the buttons small and of silver.

In 1682 Lord Windsor was robbed by a man who had on a sad-coloured cloth suit, lined with a striped crape, with silver buttons and loops, a white hat with gold-twisted hatband, and an (over) coat of dark-coloured hair camblet, lined with blue, the sleeves turned up with blue plush, with silver buttons and loops—one of "the swell mob," it would seem, of that date. A thief of a lower order wore "a frize coat ; a waistcoat and breeches *speckled with red, green, and orange colour ;* a brown periwig, and silver or gold rings in his ears."

The Princess Anne, the Countess of Pembroke, and several other ladies, are described in the 'Loyal Protestant Intelligence' of March 13, 1682-3, as having taken the air on horseback, "attired very rich in close-bodied coats, hats, and feathers, *with short perukes.*"

A female servant of that day was clad in "a red petticoat, a grey cloth waistcoat, a linsey-woolsey apron, a red handkerchief, a black hood, and a white hat."

In 1688 we hear of a young man attired in a coat of the still favourite sad colour, with black buttons and white sleeves, breeches of purple shag, black fringed gloves, a black *caster*, with a silver-twisted hatband.

In 1697 Spanish drugget coats and waistcoats, lined with Persian silk, are recorded as fashionable, the waistcoat being trimmed with silver orris lace, and the buttons and button-holes silver frosted.

---

[1] 'England's Vanity, or the Voice of God against the monstrous Sin of Pride in Dress and Apparel.'
[2] Sad-coloured cloth : " Brun obscur qui tire sur le noir " is the French definition of it.

The 'Protestant Mercury' of February 11, 1698, announces that "some gentlemen lately come from France report that the fashion there for men is as follows; a hat about two inches broad, a peruque very thin of hair, a coat fully plaited all round, with short cuffs, and the quarters of their shoes not over an inch broad; a small neck-cloth tucked within their coat, with a very full cravat-string tied upon the same." "Shoulder-knots," it is added, "were introduced by some ridiculous persons, but without success." For the *form* of these habits we must refer the reader to the engravings illustrating the various articles under their separate headings in the Dictionary, where, also, as I have stated, some portions of the above passages will be found.

The costume of the ladies in England, during the latter half of the seventeenth century, has had for its illustration the pencils of Lely and Kneller, and been made familiar to the public by the paintings at Hampton Court, and the numerous engravings of them; but they must not be depended upon as strictly accurate representations of female attire in the reign of Charles II. The "beauties" sat for their portraits, and there is obviously some fancy, either of the courtly painter or his fair subject, in the character of the costume of the majority. I must refer the reader to the engraving of the Duchess of Newcastle, from her portrait at Wentworth, in the Dictionary, p. 229, for a more reliable example, and to Evelyn's description of the Queen's (Catherine of Braganza) arrival in England, 25th May, 1662, which I have printed at page 188 of the Dictionary (article FARTHINGALE).

Evelyn's 'Mundus Muliebris, or Voyage to Maryland,' contains a rhyming catalogue of a lady's toilette, some lines of which I have quoted under certain heads in the Dictionary, but which I here give *in extenso*, as it deserves.

"One black gown of rich silk, which odd is
Without one coloured embroidered boddice;
Three manteaus, nor can Madam less
Provision have for due undress;
Nor demy-sultane, spagnolet,
Nor fringe to sweep the ground forget;
Of under-boddice, three neat pair
Embroidered, and of shoes as fair;
Short under-petticoats, pure fine,
Some of Japan stuff, some of Chine,
With knee-high galoon bottomed,
Another quilted, white and red,
With a broad Flanders lace below;
Four pair of *bas de soy*, shot through
With silver, diamond buckles too
For garters, and as rich for shoe;
Twice twelve day-smocks of holland fine,
With cambric sleeves rich point to joyn
(For she despises Colbertine);
Twelve more for night, all Flanders lac'd,
Or else she'll think herself disgrac'd;
The same her night-gown must adorn,
With two point waistcoats for the morn;
Of pocket *mouchoirs*, nose to drain,
A dozen laced, a dozen plain;
Three night-gowns of rich Indian stuff,
Four cushion-cloths are scarce enough;
Of point and Flanders not forget,
Slippers embroider'd on velvet;
A manteau girdle, ruby buckle,
And brilliant diamond rings for knuckle.
Fans, painted and perfumed, three;
Three muffs of sable, ermine, grey;
Nor reckon it among the baubles,
A palatine also of sables,
A sapphire bodkin for the hair,
Of sparkling facet diamonds there;
Three turquoise, ruby, emerald rings

For fingers, and such pretty things
As diamond pendants for the ears
Must needs be had, or two large pears;
Pearl necklace, large and Oriental,
And diamond and of amber pale.

*   *   *   *

In pen-up ruffles now she flaunts;
About her sleeves are *engageants*,
Of ribbon various *eschelles*,
Gloves trimmed and lac'd as fine as Nell's;
Twelve dozen *Martial*, whole and half;
Of jonquil, tube-rose (don't laugh),
Frangipan, orange, violett,
Narcistus, jessamin, ambrett,
And some of chicken skin for night,
To keep her hands plump, soft, and white;
Mouches for pushes, to be sure,
From Paris the *très fine* procure;
Calembac combs in pulvil case,
To set and trim the hair and face,
And that the cheeks may both agree,
Plumpers to fill the cavity.
The *settee*, *cupée*, place aright,
Frelange, *fontange*, *favorite*,
Montil la haute and *palisade*,
Sorti, *flandan* (great helps to trade),
Bourgoigne, *jardine*, *cornett*,
Frelal next upper *panier* set,
Round which it doth our ladies please
To spread the hood called *rayonnées*.
Behind the noddle every baggage
Wears bundle *shows*—in English, cabbage;
Not *cruches* she nor *confidants*,
Nor *passagers* nor *bergers* wants;
And when this grace Nature denies,
An artificial *tour* supplies;
All which with *mauritiers* unite,
And *crève-cœurs*, silly fops to smite."

The terms in italics will nearly all be found explained under their separate heads in the Dictionary, from a book entitled 'The Lady's Dictionary,' published in 1694, and therefore, as well as Evelyn's work, of the early time of William III.; but the fashions were of the reign of James II., and continued in favour for some years, a few being introduced from Holland by Queen Mary, amongst them that monstrosity the commode, of which a full account will be found in the Dictionary, p. 130. This period, indeed the whole of the seventeenth century, will receive so much illustration in my notice of the costume of France, that I shall abstain from any further observations here on that of England, which as usual, with very few exceptions, drew its inspiration from the Court of Versailles. I shall only draw the reader's attention to our chromo-lithograph issued with Part XVIII. of this work, from a picture at Hampton Court, which has some peculiar features of interest, not only as an example of costume, but as an instance of the uncertainty attaching to the descriptions of ancient paintings, derived apparently from the best contemporary authority. The one in question is said to be the portrait of "the famous Mr. Lacy" (as he is called by Wilkes in his 'View of the Stage,' 1759), "an excellent low comedian, and so pleasing to King Charles." He was also the author of several comedies, which have been recently collected and published in one volume, with prefatory memoir and notes by the editors of the series, entitled 'Dramatists of the Restoration.'

Langbaine records that Lacy "was so well approved by Charles II., that he caused his picture to be drawn in three several figures in the same table, viz. Teague in *the Committee*, Scruple in *the Cheats*, and Galliard in *Variety*, which piece is still in being in Windsor Castle." Aubrey's account slightly differs as far as regards the characters represented : "His Matie (Charles II.) has severall pictures of this famous comedian at Windsor and Hampton Court, in the postures of severall parts that he acted, *e.g.* Teag, Lord Vaux, the Puritan." We need not concern ourselves here respecting the identity of the last two. The Puritan is most probably Scruple, in 'The Cheats,' and whether the centre figure is meant for Galliard or Lord Vaux is of no importance to us, as our business is simply with the costume, which so faithfully represents the dress of a Puritan and of a gallant of the period. The important question is, whether we are to believe Aubrey and Langbaine are correct in ascribing the third figure to Teague, in 'The Committee.' I think they are not.

Evelyn in his Diary, under the date of October 3, 1662, expressly says : "Visited Mr. Wright, a *Scotsman*, who had lived long at Rome and was esteemed a good painter," and states that in his opinion his best portrait is that of "Lacy, the famous Roscius, or comedian, whom he (Wright) had painted in three dresses, as a gallant, a Presbyterian minister, and *a Scotch Highlander in his plaid*." Surely this is conclusive, as Evelyn must have been so informed by the painter, who was a Scotchman himself.[1]

Lacy was the author of a play called 'Sauny the Scot, or the Taming of the Shrew' (an alteration of Shakespeare's well-known comedy of the same name), and acted the part of Sauny himself.[2] Surely the figure in this picture is that of a Scotchman, and not of an Irishman. Moreover, Teague could never have worn such a dress at any time, as he first appears wrapped in a blanket and afterwards as a running footman in the livery of Colonel Careless. In the latter dress Mr. Moody is painted as Teague in a fine picture in the Garrick Club, in the act of exchanging his velvet cap, such as is still worn by the Royal footmen, with the Puritan hat of Abel, who is in a maudlin state of drunkenness, the latter being a portrait of the popular low comedian Parsons. (See following chapter.)

The descriptions of Aubrey and Langbaine are evidence that in the seventeenth century the Irish national dress was either similar to that of the Scotch, or was ignorantly supposed to be so. That the truis of a chequered pattern was worn in Ireland to a late date is unquestionable ; but the Irish

[1] Mr. Michael Wright painted the twelve judges in Guildhall after the Great Fire. There is a long account of him in Walpole's 'Anecdotes of Painting.' It is a remarkable instance of the obstinacy of error that Bray, the editor of Evelyn's Memoirs in 1827, while recording the above fact, should in a foot-note repeat without comment the statement of Aubrey and Langbaine that the third figure is that of "Teague in the Committee." Wright is not mentioned in the latest edition of Bryan's 'Dictionary of Painters and Engravers.'

[2] "To the King's house, and there saw the 'Taming of the Shrew,' which hath some very good pieces in it, but generally is but a mean play, and the best part, Sauny, done by Lacy."—*Pepys' Diary*, 9th April, 1667.

2 I 2

cloak or mantle bore no resemblance whatever to the "belted plaid" of the Gaelic Highlander, nor was the skein of a "Kerne" to be mistaken for the dirk of a "Dougal creature."

Some glimpses of Scotch costume are to be gleaned from the Kirk Session books at Glasgow.

Under the date of 1604 we read that "the Session, considering that great disorder hath been in the Kirk by women sitting with their heads covered in time of sermon *sleeping*, therefore ordains intimation to be made that afterward none sit with their head covered with plaids during sermon time." In 1637, we have a more detailed description of the female attire :—"Forasmeikell as, notwithstanding of divers and sundrie laudibill actes and statutes maid be the provist, baillies, and counsell of the burg in former tymes, discharging that barbarous and uncivil habitte of women's wearing of plaids, yit such hes bein the impudencie of many of thame that they have continewit the foresaid barbarous habitte, and hes added thairto the wearing of their gownes and petticottes about their heads and faces, so that the same is now become the ordinar habitte of all women within the cittie, to the general imputation of their sex, matrones not being abitt to be decerned from strumpettes and town-living women, to their owne dishonour and scandal of the cittie, which the proviest, baillies, and counsall have taken into their serious consideration ; thairfore have statutt and ordaynst, and by presentis statutis and ordaynes, that none of whatsome ever degree or qualitie presume after this day under payne of escheat of the said plaids, not only be such as shall be appoyntit for that effect, but be all persones who sall chalenge the same ; and that nae woman weir their gownes or petticottes about their heads and faces under the payne of ten pundis, to be payit by women of qualitie for the first falt, and twenty pundis for the second, and under such farder paynes as shall pleas the counsall to inflict upon them for the third falt." Smaller penalties were to be paid by servants and others of lower degree, who for the third fault were to be banished from the city. (Maitland's ' History of Edinburgh.')

For the Irish dress in the seventeenth century we have considerable authority, both verbal and pictorial. Mr. Walker has engraved what he terms "a rude but faithful delineation of O'More, a turbulent Irish chieftain, and Archer, a Jesuit retained by him," both copied from a map of the taking of the Earl of Ormond in 1600. O'More, he tells us, is dressed in the barrad or Irish conical cap, and a scarlet mantle. Archer's mantle is black, and he wears the high-crowned hat of the time. Both appear in the tight truis, but there is no indication of chequers.

Irish Chieftain and Archer, a Jesuit.

Morryson, a writer of the reign of James I., has left us a graphic account of the dress of the Irish in his time. The higher orders and better-educated classes had, in the seventeenth century, pretty generally conformed in their costume to that of England ; but "touching the meare or wild Irish," observes Morryson, "it may be truly said of them which was of old spoken of the Germans ; namely, that they wander slovenly and naked, and lodge in the same house (if it may be called a house) with their beasts. Amongst them the gentlemen, or Lords of counties, wear close breeches and stockings of the same piece of cloth, of red or such light colour, and a loose coat and a cloak, or three-cornered mantle, commonly of coarse light stuffe made at home, and their linen is coarse and slovenly, because they seldom put off a shirt till it be worn, and those shirts in our memory, before the last rebellion, were made of some twenty or thirty elles, folded in wrinkles and coloured with saffron. . . . Their wives living among the English are attired in a sluttish gown, to be fastened at the breast with a lace, and in a more sluttish mantle and more sluttish linen, and their heads be covered, after the Turkish manner, with many elles of linen, only the Turkish heads or turbans are round at the top ; but the attire of the Irish women's heads is more flat in the top and broader in the sides, not much unlike a cheese mot if it had a hole to put in the head. For the rest, in the most remote parts, where the English lawes and manners are unknown, the very chiefs of the Irish, as well men as women, goe naked in winter time." Speed, who wrote in the same reign, confirms the account of Spenser and Morryson respecting the large, wide-sleeved linen shirts, stained with saffron, their mantles, skeins, &c., and adds that "the women wore their hair plaited in a curious manner, hanging down their backs and shoulders from under the folden wreaths of fine linen rolled about their heads"—a custom in England as ancient as the eleventh century, and, though not mentioned by Giraldus, a fashion no doubt of equal antiquity in Ireland, and still existing in Germany, Switzerland, and other countries. Speed, in his Map of Ireland, has given representations of an Irish gentleman and woman, a civil Irish man and woman, and a wild Irish man and woman, but whether drawn from "the quick," as the curious group in our photograph, p. 174 *ante*, is declared to have been done, or from his own descriptions, I cannot pretend to say. There is an air of truth about them that inclines me to think they have some pretensions to accuracy. The long-sleeved shirts are certainly not visible, but the turban-like head-dress of the woman with a child in her arms, and the rough mantles of Irish frieze (?), are characteristic, and the latter point to the Spanish descent of the southern inhabitants of the island.

Irish Gentleman and Lady.

Wild and Civil Irish Men and Women.

It was in the reign of James I. that the Irish dress began to feel the influence of fashion, and to assume a new form. The circuits of the judges being now no longer confined within the narrow limits of "the pale," but embracing the whole kingdom, the civil assemblies at the assizes and sessions reclaimed the natives from their wildness, caused them to cut off their glibbs and long hair, to convert their mantles into cloaks as then worn in England, and to conform themselves to the manner of England in all their behaviour and outward forms. The order from the Lord Deputy Chichester, in his instructions to the Lord President and Council of Munster, to punish by fine and imprisonment all such as should appear before them in mantles and robes, and also to "expel" and cut off all glibbs, is dated May 20th, 1615.

For some years this statute was rigorously enforced, but Charles I., in the tenth year of his reign, caused an Act to be passed at Dublin for "repeale of divers statutes heretofore enacted in this Kingdom of Ireland," and the beard was once more allowed to flourish on the upper lip, and the people generally left at liberty to wear either their own national apparel, or the English dress of the day, as best suited their fancy or convenience.

The periwig is supposed to have found its way into Ireland in Cromwell's time, the first person who wore it being a Mr. Edmund O'Dwyer, who lost his estates by his loyal opposition to the Parliamentary forces, and consequently obtained the appellation of "Edmund of the Wig." It must have been late, however, in the days of the Interregnum, I fancy, that the gallant Irishman assumed that article, as its invention in France does not appear to have taken place much before 1660.

An order issued by the Deputy-Governor of Galloway during the Commonwealth, grounded on the old statute of Henry VIII., prohibiting the wearing of the mantle to all people whatsoever, and which was executed with great rigour, is the last we hear of these vexatious and invidious enactments.

Sir Henry Piers, in his description of the county of Westmeath about this period, says, "There is now no more appearance of the Irish cap, mantle, and trouzes, at least in these countries." That they were worn, however, to a much later period in some provinces has since been sufficiently proved; and it will be obvious that, from the earliest notice of Ireland to a late period, the national dress was handed down from generation to generation amongst the peasantry, and that many gentlemen wore it within the last two hundred years. Persecution, as usual, but attached them more strongly to the prohibited garb; and it is probable that the free exercise of their fancy granted to them by Charles I. conduced more to the ultimate neglect of the long-cherished costume of their ancestors than the peremptory order to abandon it issued by the officer of Cromwell, or even the exhortations of the Romish clergy to that effect, which are acknowledged to have been of little avail. Certain it is that the Lord Deputy's Court at Dublin was in Charles's reign distinguished for its magnificence; the peers of the realm, the clergy, and the nobility and gentry attending it being arrayed of their own free will in robes of scarlet and purple velvet, and other rich habiliments, after the English fashion.

We will now turn to the country the tastes or follies of which have been found throughout this history most directly influencing those of our own. The Huguenot movement in France had much the same effect on the national costume as that of the Puritans had in England; but there was not the contrast afforded to it which was produced on this side the Channel by the gaiety and splendour of the Cavaliers. The Catholic party affected a greater sobriety of apparel. Paris, reduced by the Ligue to the greatest misery, had, even before the death of Henry III., abjured magnificence in attire. Cloth took the place of silk, and silk that of tissues of gold and silver. To such an extent was this feeling carried, that a contemporary writer informs us that if a girl appeared in a ruff or band of the plainest description, if it exceeded a certain size, however little, other girls would set upon her and tear it from her neck. On the restoration of tranquillity throughout the kingdom, and the return of the Court to the capital, some reaction took place; but Henri Quatre, though a "vert gallant," cared little about dress, and though Fashion regained her sovereignty, the costume of both sexes, however costly, was destitute of grace and dignity. The stiffened-out trunk-hose, the ruffs and rebatoes of the end of the last century, hats not differing much in shape from those worn at present, and cloaks with collars to them, are the general features of the male costume of the reign of "the Béarnais," as Henry of Navarre was familiarly called. It is related of him that, in 1598, he said to the deputies of the clergy, "My predecessors gave you words, but I, with my grey jacket, will give you deeds. I am all grey outside, but all gold within." He often referred to the state of his wardrobe. A few weeks before he entered Paris, his stock of linen was limited to five pocket-handkerchiefs and a dozen shirts, many of which were in holes. His best clothes consisted of a pourpoint of white satin, with a black cloak, and hat with black feathers. Whenever, after his re-establishment, he put on rich clothes, it was from a sense of duty, and not from taste. The principal novelties were gloves, with tops reaching almost to the elbow, some of which were of green satin, others of carnation-coloured velvet, with a deep fringe round the edges, and long boots of Russia leather (cuir de roussy), the latter being worn even for dancing. Their introduction, according to D'Aubigné, was by the King, in compliment to one of his equerries. M. Quicherat is inclined to attribute the fashion rather to the exigencies of trade. Henry had sent a tanner named Roze to study the process of dressing leather practised in the Danubian provinces, and he brought from Hungary the secret, which gave rise in France to the fraternity of the Hongroyeurs, who dressed the leather from which these boots were made. It is probable that the material obtained its appellation of cuir de roussy from Roze, the name of the tanner, and not from that of Russia, a country with which it does not appear to have been associated.

The dress of the ladies became daily more ugly in form, however costly in material. M. Quicherat justly observes, "Lorsque les vêtements deviennent de l'architecture, ils cessent d'être des vêtements et alors la mode est absurde, et elle a beau coûter cher, elle n'arrive qu'à produire des effets sans grâce et de l'étalage sans goût." The stiffness and formality of these architectural dresses—

these structures of velvet and whalebone—the unnaturally long and pinched-in waists, and the ridiculous farthingale, we have already seen in England. There was a continual struggle for mastery between the ruff and the standing collar (*collet montant*). So monstrous were some of the former, that spoons were made with long handles to enable women to carry soup to their mouths over these obstructions. There was a fashion which sprung up at the end of the last century, of affixing to the back of the dress two shell-shaped constructions of some fine tissue, the larger below and the smaller above the waist, which were called mantles, but which M. Quicherat says seem made rather to fly with than for the purpose of clothing. The hair was at one time combed up from the head, over a foundation of some description, in the form of a large melon (see next page). False hair was also much worn, and perfumed hair-powder of various colours used. Colour, indeed, was all the rage with the ladies, and invention seems to have been racked to produce a sufficient variety. D'Aubigné has bequeathed us a list of upwards of seventy names of the colours in fashion in his day, some of which

Henri IV., *circa* 1600.   Henri IV., 1606-10.   Gentleman *circa* 1600.

are ridiculous to incredibility : "Triste amie," "par tel," "face grattée," "de Judas," "singe mourrant," "de veuve rejouie," "de temps perdue," "singe envenimé," "ris de Quenon," "trepasse revenue," "Espagnol malade," "Espagnol mourrant," "couleur de baise-moi, ma mignonne," "couleur de peché mortel," "les désirs amoureux," and "détalleur de cheminée." Of the latter alone would it be possible to form an idea, and one would almost be inclined to look upon the list as a joke, were it not that it contains the names of "Isabelle," "feuille morte," "sang de bœuf," and other well-known colours, and that one of the most fashionable a few years ago in Paris was "Bismark malade."

Three petticoats were worn beneath the gown, each different in colour, and a mode of walking was assumed enabling the wearer to show a portion of each in turn. Brocades were also in great favour. A petticoat belonging to the celebrated Gabrielle d'Estrées is described as being "de drap d'or de Turquie, figuré à fleurs incarnat bleu et vert."

After all, the pencil is the best illustrator of costume, and I have, therefore, given engravings of Henri IV., his queen, Marie de Medicis, and ladies and gentlemen of his reign, from authentic portraits (see above and next page).

Catherine Duchess du Bar, sister of Henry IV. Died 1604.

Gentleman. 1617.

Lady of Quality. 1600.

Lady of Quality. 1605.

Marie de Medicis in widow's dress. 1615.

Lady of Quality. 1610.

The reign of Louis XIII. introduces us to fashions of which we see the reflection in England in the reign of Charles I., previous to the costume which has obtained the name of Vandyke. The plates to the well-known work of Pluvinel, riding-master to the young French monarch, engraved by Crispin de Passe, present us with every variety of the male costume of France in 1620 (see next page). The doublet or pourpoint, with hanging sleeves, is characteristic of this period ; but the principal feature is the long boot introduced, as I have already mentioned, by Henri Quatre. D'Aubigné, in his satirical work, 'Le Baron de Fœneste,' gives a minute description of these boots, and observes that they save the wearer all sorts of silk stockings. "If you are seen walking in the streets, it is supposed that your horse is close at hand." So general was this usage, that it is related that a Spaniard answered an inquiry respecting the state of Paris by saying that he had seen a great number of people, but he thought there must be no one left in it at that moment, as they were all booted and apparently on the point of departure. The few who did not wear boots could not present themselves in society in any but silk stockings. Woollen stockings were only worn by the inferior clergy, pedants, and the lowest classes : "un honneste homme," *i.e.* a person of condition, would scarcely venture to wear them under his silk ones in winter, and therefore in very cold weather wore generally three pairs of silk stockings at least, one over the other. Malherbe, the poet, is said to have worn so many that, in order to avoid having more on one leg than the other, he threw a counter into a saucer for each as he drew them on. The Marquis de Racan advised him to have his stockings marked with letters, and to put them on in alphabetical order. He did so, and wrote to Racan the next morning, "J'en ai dans l'L." He had therefore eleven pairs on his legs at that time !

Red was the favourite colour for stockings and also for the trimmings of dresses, but not for the dress itself, unless it was to hunt in. The popular "pink" of our modern sportsmen appears, therefore, to have been first worn in France in the early part of the seventeenth century.

What was known in England as a love-lock seems also to have had its origin in France at this period, where it was called *cadenette*, from Marshal Cadenet, who was celebrated for his fine hair, a lock of which he wore hanging on one side of his face, tied at the end with a bow of coloured ribbons. Ribbon was indeed worn in as much profusion by both sexes in France at this time as in England. Knots, bows, and roses of ribbon are continually alluded to : "Deux paires de roses à souliers garnies de dentelles d'or." (Invent. de Madame Sœur du Roi (Henrietta Maria) : 'Arch. de l'Empire.')

> "De large taffas la jartiere parée,
> Aux bouts de demy-pied de dentelle dorée."
>
> *Satyrique de la Cour.*

To the question "Vous avez des roses en hiver ?" Fœneste replies, "Oui, sur les deux pieds traînantes à terre, aux deux jarrets, pendantes à mi-jambe, au busc du pourpoint, une au pendant de l'espée, une sur l'estomac, au droit des brassards et aux coudes." Cut-work (*point coupé*) and lace ("point de Venise," "point de Flandres," and "point d'Espagnes") were introduced, and at the commencement of the reign of Louis XIII. so prodigal had the nobility become in these articles of attire that the Queen Regent, Marie de Medicis, was compelled to issue an ordinance prohibiting all lace and embroidery.[1] This edict gave rise to a satire entitled 'Consolations des Dames sur la Réformation des Passemens,' 1620, in which it is said—

> "Ces poincts couppez, passemens et dentelles,
> Las ! qui venaient de L'Isle et de Bruxelles,
> Sont maintenant descriez, avilis,
> Et sans faveur gisent ensevelis."

This edict was followed by several others, at short intervals, to nearly the end of the reign.[2] One

[1] 1620, Feb. 8th : "Declaration portant deffenses de porter des cliquants, passemens broderie," &c.—*Archives de l'Empire.*

[2] 1625, March 20th : "Declaration qui deffend l'usages des étoffes d'or." 1625, Sept. 30th : Declaration prohibiting the wearing of "collets, fraises, manchettes et autres linges des passemeots, point coupez et dentelles, comme aussi des broderies et decoupures sur quenon ou autre toil." 1634, May 30th : "Lettres patentes pour la reformation du luxe des habits." 1636, April 3rd : "Declaration contre le luxe," prohibiting both foreign and home-made *points coupés*. 1639, November 14th : "Points de Gênes" specially prohibited. Not to wear on the collar, cuffs, or boots, "autre chose que de la toile simple sans aucune façon."

known as the Code Michaud, entering into the most minute regulations for the toilet, especially excited the risibility of the people, and was never carried out.

The vardingale was still worn by the ladies, but much reduced in size. The head-dress known in England as "Mary Queen of Scots'" also lingered on, with some slight alteration, amongst the bourgeoises and in the provinces; but it was only worn in the fashionable world by widows (see page 248). In a satirical poem, 'La Mode qui court au temps présent,' printed in 1612, we hear of

> "Coiffures de cinq cents façon,
> Quand on les veut voir en brassière,
> En nymphe ou à la cavalière.
> *   *   *   *   *
> Et la coeffe à la Jacobine,
> Qui donne encor très bonne mine."

Also of

> "Grandes pyramides de gaze,
> Pour celles qui ont tête rase,
> Et perruques pour qui le front
> De près ne paroist que trop rond ;
> Moulles avant, moulles arrière,
> Hausse-col en arc et bas terre,
> Tresses, nœuds, cordons et laets,
> Assez pour charger dix mullets."

Dr. Heylin, who visited France in 1625, speaking of the Dames de Paris, says, "Their habit, in which they differ from the rest of France, is in the attire of their heads, which hangeth down their

French Costume, temp. Louis XIII., from Plorioal (1600) ; and Lady of Quality (1640), from Hollar.   Lady in demi-toilette, from De Boose (1640)

backs in fashion of a veil" ('France painted to the Life'). But it is time to bring the pencil once more to the aid of the pen. Above therefore are examples of French costume during the reign of Louis XIII., 1610-43, which includes the period known as the "époque de Richelieu," and introduces that most picturesque of male costumes, which I have already spoken of as appearing in

England in the reign of Charles I. (See following pages for illustrations from the works of Abraham Bosse, a French engraver, born at Tours in 1610, and who imitated the style of Callot.) The dress had its origin no doubt in Flanders about the same time the marriage of Anne of Austria to Louis revolutionized the female costume, and superseded the "mode Italienne" by the "mode Espagnole."

Menage attributes to that princess the mode of dressing the hair as it appears in the portraits of ladies contemporary with our Charles I. The hair combed out was separated into three parts. Two of these, called *buffons*, were massed "en petites frisures" on each side of the temples and above the ears: the third was thrown back over the head, to be rolled in plaits behind; but a portion of it, cut short, formed a fringe on the forehead of small curls, which were called *garcettes*, a Spanish word signifying "little aigrettes." Subsequently the *buffons* were done away with, and the hair, instead of being massed at the side, was allowed to fall in ringlets (*tire-bouchons*, corkscrews), or in tresses, tied with bows of ribbon, like the *cadenettes* of the men, and were called *moustaches des dames*.

The ruff and the *collet-montant* could not be worn with this style of head-dress, and were replaced by a kerchief just covering the shoulders, of a diaphanous material called *quintin*, with a turnover broad collar, either of plain linen or costly lace, to which the name of *rabat* (rebato) was transferred from its predecessor, and many varieties of it distinguished by special appellations, viz. *rabats dentellés, rayonnés, cannuts, houppeilés; rabats à la Reine, à la Guise, à la Guimbarde, à la neige, à la fanfreluche*, &c. &c.

The odious vardingale was now completely banished in France, the waist was shortened, and the gown (*robe*) fell in graceful folds to the feet, with a small train. And here I think it is desirable that I should notice the change that took place at this period in the sense of the word *jupe*, which had previously signified a sort of cassock or coat with long skirts, the upper part of which was called the *corps de jupe*, and the lower the *bas de jupe*. By degrees these terms were abbreviated to *corps* and *jupe*, the latter being applied to the skirt alone; and on this alteration in female costume, whereby the gown open from the waist displayed the *cotillon* (in English called, by a similar deduction, a petticoat), the word *jupe* was arbitrarily transferred to it, and retained by it to the present day, in conjunction with the older appellation. *Jupon*, another form of the word, and which had undergone equal transmigrations, was still left to designate the cassock, jacket, or justau-corps aforesaid, a variety of which was called a *hongreline*, being of Hungarian derivation, worn by men as well as women. A *hongreline* of fine cloth or velvet, with a man's hat and feathers, constituted the riding-habit of a lady of fashion. Women of lower rank, peasants, and servants, who could not wear-gowns, also wore *hongrelines* of coarser materials, with jupes and aprons, as did the Sœurs de Charité, whose institution dates from this period. It appears to have been identical with the jackets worn by persons of the same class in England as late as the seventeenth century (*vide* "Maid-servant, *temp.* George II.," Dictionary, p. 311); and, in point of fact, the short doublet with skirts or bases, so constantly seen in the costumes of both sexes in the reign of Charles I.

The length of the gowns and petticoats (I use the English terms) in the reign of Louis XIII. rarely allowed the stockings, or even the shoes, to be seen. The former were, nevertheless, of the brightest-coloured silks—scarlet, apple-green, or sky-blue; and the latter (of a fashion called *à la Choisy*), of red or blue satin, with high heels or slippers (*muletins*) of violet, yellow, or white morocco. Women of rank rarely went on foot out of doors, but on such occasions they wore velvet clogs (*patins*) with thick cork soles.

Of gloves, the names were legion, principally derived from the perfumes with which they were scented. There were "gants à l'occasion" and "à la nécessité," "à la Phyllis" and "à la Cadenet;" the latter so named because their perfume was the favourite one of Marshal Cadenet, who had set the fashion of *cadenettes* (see p. 249). Then there were "gants à la Frangipani," after the Marquis de Frangipani, a Roman nobleman, and "gants de Neroli," their perfume having been invented by the Duchess of Bracciano, Princess of Nerola, and therefore, as M. Quicherat observes, they should have been called "de Nerola;" but "la mode, qui n'est pas forcée de respecter la géographie, consacra Neroli."

The same writer informs us that the most expensive article of female costume at that day was

2 K 2

the *demi-ceint d'argent*, a girdle or sash of silk decorated with plates of silver, either chased or enamelled. Even chambermaids did not hesitate to spend thirty or forty crowns on their *demi-ceint*, independently of the chain, also of silver, which was attached to one side of it, and whereby hung their keys, scissors, knives, purses, &c.

I have entered into this detail respecting the dress of the French ladies in the reign of Louis XIII., because it throws so much light on that of our countrywomen at the same period, and feel assured that, although I may have wearied some of my male readers, my fairer students will not think their time has been wasted in perusing this summary of facts, selected and condensed from a mass of evidence produced by the able author of 'Histoire du Costume en France,' to whom I am already so much indebted.

There is yet a word or two to be said about the gentlemen, as a marked alteration took place in their attire, as well as in that of the ladies, during this reign. Boots were universally worn by men

French Men of Fashion. 1616.

French Gentleman. 1630.

of fashion throughout it; but about 1625 they were reduced in length, and the tops increased in width, turning over about the middle of the leg, and displaying an extra stocking—*bas de bottes*, or boot-hose, as they were called in England. The haut de chausses, or breeches, took the form of short trousers, hanging straight down lower than the knees, almost meeting the boots, which had formerly aspired to meet them. These breeches were called

"Le haut de chausse à *fond de cuve*"

by Le Sieur Auvray, who wrote a poem called 'Le Banquet des Muses,' printed at Rouen in 1628, in which he graphically describes a gallant of the day. The shoulder-cloak, with a large cape or fall-over collar to it, was, according to the same writer,

"Le manteau à la Balagnie,'

from a son of the Mareschal de Balagny, who must have been more popular than his father, who lost Cambrai in the reign of Henri Quatre, in 1595. He speaks also of

"Le bas de Milan, le *cotter*
Orné d'un riche cordon d'or,"

silk stockings of Milanese manufacture being then in favour, and beaver hats dividing the suffrages with felt hats, both being of the flat, broad-leafed, Spanish sombrero form, with long drooping feathers ("l'ondoyant et venteux pennache").

The beard, at that date pointed, was shortly afterwards reduced to a small tuft on the chin, such as is now called an "imperial," in consequence of an eccentric act of the King, who took it into his head to shave the principal gentleman in attendance on him, a circumstance commemorated in the following couplets :—

> "Hélas ? ma pauvre barbe,
> Qu'est-ce qui t'a faite ainsi ?
> C'est le grand Roi Louis,
> Treizième de ce nom,
> Qui trait à rebarbé sa maison."

Ridiculous as it may appear, everybody followed the fashion, and wore what was called "la barbe royale," with the exception of Cardinal Richelieu, who continued to wear the "barbe en pointe."

We will now proceed to the reign of Louis XIV., which, commencing in 1643, extended into the following century. A child in the sixth year of his age when he ascended the throne, the early part of his reign may be called the epoch of Cardinal Mazarin, as that of his father had been entitled the epoch of Richelieu. The fashions at this date were set, not by the Court, but by two men—a financier named Montauron, who had accumulated an enormous fortune, and Gaston de Nogaret, Duc de Candale. The former—a vain upstart, whose sole

Louis XIII. knighting a Gentleman. 1651.

ambition was to make himself the talk of the town—paid large sums to everybody who would give his name to a new invention, and for three years every novelty in Paris was entitled "à la Montauron." Shortly after 1646 Montauron, having run through all his fortune, sank into obscurity, and was heard of no more. His successor, the Duc de Candale, was not only a man of rank, but of most refined manners. His ambition, however, was limited to the desire of being "the glass of fashion," as he was really "the mould of form." He was distinguished for nothing but the taste of his ribbons and the fineness of his linen. Some style of breeches invented by him received the name of "chausses à la Candale." He died 28th January, 1658, at the early age of thirty, of double mortification of being defeated by the Spaniards and of losing the affections of a woman he adored. The Cardinal de Retz is reported to have said there was nothing great about him but his *canons*, i.e. the rolls of ribbon at the termination of the breeches, and which appellation was subsequently transferred to ruffles of lace at the knees, and also, as it would seem, from a passage in 'Les Lois de la Galanterie,' to those which filled up the wide tops of the shortened boots at this date, such tops being called *genouillères*, because they had formerly covered the knees. I have already, at p. 73 of the Dictionary, under the head of CANONS, pointed out the perplexity attending this article of attire, and must beg the reader's patience for a brief re-examination of the subject by the light of French authorities now before me. In 'Les Lois de la Galanterie,' above mentioned, it is said : "Quant aux canons de linge que l'on establie au-dessus des bottes, nous les approuvons bien dans leur simplicité quand ils sont fort larges et de toile de batiste bien empesée, quoique l'on a dit que cela ressembloit à des lanternes de papier et qu'une lingère du Palais s'en servit ainsi un soir, mettant sa chandelle au milieu pour la garder du vent. Afin de les orner davantage nous voulons aussi que d'ordinaire il y ait double et triple rang de toile, soit de batiste, soit de Hollande, et d'ailleurs cela sera toujours mieux s'il y peut avoir deux ou trois rangs de point de Gênes, ce qui accompagnera le jabot, qui sera de mesme parure." There is no question here of ribbon. The canons are expressly described as of linen, either of well-starched batiste or Holland cloth, to which it is recommended two or three rows of Genoa point lace should be added, of the same quality as formed the *jabot*, i.e. front of the shirt.

Upon this passage M. Quicherat observes that these canons were the "genouillères de linge," which had their origin in the reign of Charles IX., but that the difference in them consisted in their increasing in width at the bottom, so far as to cover the opening of the boot, "qu'elles s'élargissaient *par le bas* de façon à recouvrir l'épanouissement de la botte." This, taken in conjunction with the words of the contemporary writer, "au-dessus des bottes," might be supposed to indicate the position of the canons above the boots and not within them, and therefore more descriptive of the lace ruffles that dangled from below the knees of the gallants of the Court of our own Charles II.: and that such is apparently the idea of M. Quicherat, one would infer by his adding, "elles prirent ainsi l'apparence des *manchettes ;*" but at the same time he tells us that the edict of 1644 having prohibited the use of lace in collars, cuffs, or boot-hose, the old term of *canons* was exhumed and applied to the latter, thanks to which change of name it was pretended " que cette pièce " (the said hose) might legally be "garnie de dentelles." Here, then, he distinctly alludes to the lace tops of the "bas à bottes," which fill up the genouillères of the boots, and are well illustrated in the accompanying engraving from a print of the period annexed by him to his description, wherein the double row of tagged ribbons terminating the breeches, which I should be inclined to call canons, are represented as well as the lace tops to the "bas à bottes." When, in addition to all this, I find that the breeches themselves were sometimes called canons,[1] I frankly confess myself unable in the present state of my information to explain satisfactorily the conflicting evidence of the pen and pencil.

Man of Fashion. 1650.

Like the word *slop*, on which we have sufficiently discussed, that of canon appears to have been applied to all sorts of articles of attire at different periods of the seventeenth century.

The edict of 1644, issued by Cardinal Mazarin, which has been just alluded to, prohibited not only point lace, but all sorts of gold, silver, and copper lace (*clinquant*), and thereby brought ribbons more into request for the trimming and decoration of male as well as female apparel ; and the excess to which this fashion was carried induced the Cardinal in 1656 to issue another edict, denouncing the *galants*, as the bows of ribbon were called, and from which the word *galon* is presumed to be derived. Another term for those used by ladies was *faveurs*, which still exists in England. After the troubles of the Fronde, coifs were introduced. I say "introduced," because they differed altogether from the coifs of the previous centuries. They were simply pieces of crape or taffeta thrown over the head and tied under the chin. This was the hood of the same period in England, which was as distinctly different from those which had preceded it. Black was the principal colour, and they were therefore called " *thérèses*."

Released from the tutelage of Mazarin and the Queen-mother, Louis XIV. himself set the example of sumptuousness of apparel, restricting, however, for some years the wearing of gold and silver stuffs and lace to the royal family, and such of his Court as he was pleased to honour with the especial permission. In 1664, he ordered the making of some body-garments of blue faced with red, and magnificently embroidered with gold mixed with a little silver. These were called "justaucorps à brevet," and were bestowed by him on a limited number of his nobility, with his majesty's letters

[1] " Le haut de chausses fut corrigé d'un manière conforme à ce svelte habit ; on en réduisit l'étoffe de plus de moitié et les jambes (on disait alors les *canons*) tout en restant flottantes," &c. (Quicherat, p. 480.)

patent according the privilege to wear them, whence their name, "à brevet." On the death of one, another was elected to fill his place, and as much Court interest and personal solicitation was required as was necessary to obtain an office or a pension. I have not been able to identify this particular dress. The costume of the middle of this reign is well illustrated by the following engravings and the lines of Sganarelle in the 'École des Maris' of Molière, 1661.

Royal Pages in 1664. Duke of Orleans, 1685. From a print of that date.

> "Ne voudries-vous pas, dis-je, sur ces matières
> De nos jeunes muguets m'inspirer les manières?
> M'obliger à porter de ces *petits chapeaux*,
> Qui laissent éventer leurs débiles cerveaux,
> Et de ces blondes cheveux de qui la vaste enflure
> Des visages humains offusque la figure?
> De *ces petits pourpoints* sous les bras se perdant,
> Et de ces *grands collets* jusqu'au nombril pendant?
> De ces *manches* qu'à table on voit tâter les sauces,
> Et de ces *cotillons* appelés haut-de-chausses?
> De ces *souliers mignons de rubans revêtus*,
> Qui vous font ressembler à des pigeons pattus?
> Et de ces *grand canons* ou comme en des entraves
> On met tous les matins *ses deux jambes esclaves*,
> Et par qui nous voyons ces messieurs les galants
> Marcher écarquillés ainsi que des volants."—Act iv., sc. 1.

Some commentary upon them is nevertheless indispensable.

" Les petits chapeaux " are observable in the figures of the pages engraved above, and succeeded in Paris the broad-brimmed castors of the reign of Louis XIII., but I have not seen an example in English costume of any reduction in the size of the hat earlier than 1670, ten years later than the change of fashion in France; it does not follow, however, that small hats may not have been introduced previously to that period, though I have not met with an allusion to or representation of them. "Les petits pourpoints," graphically described as "sous les bras se perdant," are articles of attire familiar to us in the dress of the time of Charles II., and generally throughout Western

Europe, but I am at a loss to recognize the "grands collets jusqu'au nombril pendant," allowing even a large margin for the exaggeration of satire, which is, I think, discernible in the description of the sleeves.

Of the "cotillons" and the shoes there are specimens enough; but the most important feature in the picture drawn by Sganarelle of the "muguets" (scented fops) of the time is their "grands canons," which in this instance are spoken of without any relation to boots, and surely indicate the frills or ruffs of lace, or linen edged with lace, of which I have upheld the claim to be entitled to that appellation. They are here compared to fetters on the legs of the wearers, which compel them to straddle in walking, keeping their limbs apart from each other as widely as the sails of a windmill; the natural consequence of the stiffness imparted to the canons by the starching to which they were subjected. It may be fairly retorted that the expansion of the tops of the boots would necessitate a similar mode of progression; but shoes, and not boots, are in this instance associated with the canons,—a point I submit in favour of my view of the passage, though still leaving the

Persons of Quality. 1684-1688.

question unsettled. M. Quicherat evidently shares my opinion as to the appropriation of the name of canons to these genouillères in the time of Louis XIV.; for in his account of the *rhingrave* he says it was an ample *culotte*, which hung straight down like a petticoat, but the lining of it was tied round the knees by a running cord. The band through which the cord ran served also for the attaching of the canons, which were still in fashion, though boots had ceased to be worn in full dress.

In 1670 the little pourpoints with their short sleeves gave way to the *justaucorps* and the *veste*; Anglicè, coat and waistcoat. Each, descending to the knee and buttoning all the way down, covered the rhingrave, which, notwithstanding, existed later than 1680, and, though reduced in dimensions, retained its garnish of ribbons; outliving the canons, which the introduction of the *culotte* (veritable breeches) and of stockings rolled over above the knees definitively abolished about two years previously.

In 1677 'Le Mercure Galant' announced that rich materials were no longer used for the making of the exterior garment. Cloth, poplin, camlet, and other less costly stuffs, superseded velvet, satin, and gold or silver brocades, which were confined to the waistcoat. A large bunch of ribbon on the right shoulder was the only decoration of the coat. Even the button-holes were only worked with yellow or white silk, in imitation of gold and silver. The rabat, or falling-collar, could not be worn with the coat, and was discarded for the cravat of lace or muslin, tied at the neck with a bow of ribbon. Swords—which had been laid aside by civilians since the Fronde—were again worn, despite the edict of Parliament and the vigilance of the police, who took them from every one unprivileged to go armed in public. They were carried by such as were properly qualified in broad baldricks fringed with silk. (See engravings subjoined of French men of fashion, 1678–1693.)

Men of Fashion in France. From prints of the period.

Scarfs, or rather sashes, were worn over the baldrick round the waist in 1668;[1] and in winter a muff, suspended by a ribbon round the neck, was the constant companion of a man of fashion —the first appearance of it as an accessory to the costume of a gentleman. (*Vide* engravings in the preceding page.)

The influence of Madame de Maintenon over her Royal admirer induced him to discountenance anything approaching to magnificence of attire during the latter years of the seventeenth century. Dangeau describes his dress at this period as consisting of a coat of some whole-coloured dark velvet, very slightly embroidered, with simple gold buttons; a waistcoat of satin or cloth, red, blue, or green, considerably embroidered. He never wore rings or any jewels, with the exception of those in the buckles of his shoes or garters. His hat was bordered with "point d'Espagne," and had a white feather. He was the only member of the order of the St. Esprit who wore the insignia under the coat, but on grand occasions he wore it outside; the collar and badge being set with jewels to the amount of eight or nine millions of francs. In 1697, however, on the marriage of the Duke of Burgundy, the King expressed his desire that the Court should appear as sumptuous as possible, and he set the example by ordering clothes as superb as he had latterly worn them plain. The last three years of the century, therefore, saw the commencement of a new rage for dress of the most costly description, which, as the fashion continued to nearly the end of his reign, will be noticed in our next chapter.

We must now retrace our steps and speak of the ladies, whom we have too long neglected.

Of the magnificence of the female costume in France in 1676, the often-quoted account given by Madame de Sévigné in her letter to her daughter, of the dress presented by Langlée to Madame de Montespan, is a fair example: "Une robe d'or sur or rebrodé d'or rebordé d'or, et pardessus un or frisé rebrodé d'un or mêlé avec un certain or qui fait la plus divine étoffe qui ait jamais été imaginée." She speaks also in the same letter of *transparens*, which she describes as "des habits entiers des plus beaux brocards d'or et azur qu'on puisse voir, et pardessus des robes noires transparentes ou de bel dentelle d'Angleterre ou des chenilles veloutées sur un tissu, comme ces dentelles d'hyver que vous avez vues : cela compose un transparent qui est un habit noir et un habit tout d'or ou d'argent ou de couleur, comme on veut—et voilà la mode."

Between 1660 and 1680 there was not much alteration of form in the female dress. Although an infinite number of trifling varieties were introduced from time to time, none attained celebrity, and few had a prolonged existence. The long waists, "tailles en pointe," the short sleeves, and the full petticoats, or rather skirts tucked up, displaying the close petticoat beneath, continued the general fashion. These tucked-up skirts were called *manteaus* in the language of that day, and we must therefore be careful not to confound them with mantles properly so called. Those worn at Court had trains, the length of which was regulated by the rank of the wearers. The Queen's train measured nine ells; the King's daughters' ("filles de France"), seven; other princesses of the blood, five; and duchesses, three. On creating a new rank for the King's grand-daughters, they were allowed seven ells for their trains, which occasioned the extension of their mothers' trains to nine ells, and that of the Queen to twelve.

A loose dress, called a "robe battante," is said to have been invented by Madame de Montespan, which seems to have been simply a dressing-gown, or "robe de chambre;" and as it imparted a youthful air to the wearer, it obtained the second name of *innocente*.

> "Une robe de chambre, étalée amplement,
> Qui n'a point de ceinture et va nonchalemment,
> Pour certain air d'enfant qu'elle donne au visage,
> Est nommée *innocente*, et c'est du bel usage."
>
> BOURSAULT, *Mots à la Mode.*

M. Quicherat informs us that the *négligé* or undress of a lady in 1672 was a black gown, with a short white apron, called by Boursault "laisse tout faire."

---

[1] M. Quicherat says, "Cette écharpe n'était que *pour l'été.*" It appears in a print published in 1678 at Paris, "avec privil. du Roy." (See figure in preceding page.)

The large collars of lace or point coupé went out of fashion after the death of Queen Anne of Austria, and disappeared entirely in 1672. At Court or in full dress the shoulders were uncovered, and out of doors a kerchief of lace, called a palatine, was worn in summer, and in winter a fur tippet, to which was given the same name, derived, I imagine, from the Princess Palatine, who wrote her Memoirs at that period.

Jet ornaments were in great favour with women who could not afford diamonds, imitation jewellery having fallen into contempt amongst all classes. Real gems were, however, worn in the greatest profusion by the wealthy. 'Le Mercure Galant,' describing the marriage of Mdlle. de Blois with the Prince de Conti at Versailles in 1680, says, her dress was "white, bordered with diamonds and pearls; and as it is the custom for brides to wear at the back of their heads a sort of small crown of flowers, which is called *le chapeau*, this princess had one made of five rows of pearls instead of flowers."

The lower orders—from the small tradeswomen, shopkeepers, work-women, &c., downwards— who were unable to purchase expensive stuffs, contented themselves with Dutch *camlet*, a mixture of

Matron of Paris.   Wife of a Mechanic of Paris.   French Countrywoman.

silk and wool, or *ferrandine*, composed of silk and cotton; serge, and other inferior manufactures, especially one called *grisette*, from its colour, whence the name of *grisette*, which subsequently became the appellation of girls of all occupations. Hollar's admirable etchings of female costume, executed in 1642–44, afford us the best authorities for the dress of French women of all classes at that period. (See above engravings, and page 250 *ante*.)

Masks, patches (*mouches*), and muffs continued in favour. In the latter it was considered the height of fashion to carry a little dog. Muffs made expressly for that purpose are advertised in the 'Livre des Adresses' for 1692 as *chiens mouchons*, and they were to be bought at the Demoiselle Guérin's, Rue du Bac, Paris.

Previous to 1645 the hair of ladies had always been dressed by their own women. About that period, however, a man named Champagne contrived to establish a reputation as a ladies' hairdresser. Tallemant de Reaux says, "Ce faquin, par son adresse à coeffer et à se faire valoir, se faisoit rechercher et caresser de toutes les femmes." His skill appears to have been surpassed by his insolence. He would sometimes arrange one side of a lady's head and refuse to dress the other unless she kissed him. He declined taking money for his services, preferring presents, which were of more value. While attending to one lady, it was his custom to tell her what he had received from

2 L 2

others, and give her to understand that anyone whose donations had not been satisfactory would thenceforth send for him in vain—a threat which rarely failed to produce double what had been originally intended.

In 1671, a woman named Martin, who had succeeded Champagne, brought into fashion a style of dressing the hair called *hurlupée*, or *hurluberlu*, in which the long ringlets were exchanged for

Merchant's Wife of Paris. 1642.

French Lady of Quality. 1690.

several rows of close curls, and which received the name of "À la Maintenon," from its adoption by that lady at the time the king first noticed her. Verbal descriptions of such fashions are more likely to mislead than to instruct; the reader is therefore referred to our engravings.

The latest head-dress of this century was the fontange, which gave rise to the commode, of which it formed part. It will be found fully described in the Dictionary, p. 191.

I have dwelt longer than I calculated upon the costume of France in the seventeenth century, but it is so illustrative of that of England at the same period, so remarkable as presenting us with the last dresses in Western Europe which can fairly lay claim to be entitled costume in the picturesque sense of the word, and the numerous memoirs and correspondence of the time so teem with information on the subject, that it has been a task of no ordinary difficulty to compress my digest of them into these limits.

I must now turn to Spain and Portugal, those countries being especially associated in our minds with England from many circumstances; *inter alia*, the journey of Charles I., when Prince of Wales, to Madrid in 1623, and the marriage of Charles II. with Catharine of Braganza.

The costume of Spain during the first half of the seventeenth century is abundantly illustrated by the paintings of that admirable artist and most amiable of men, Velasquez. His picture in our National Gallery, "The Boar Hunt at the Pardo," affords us several examples of the dress of the caballeros of the reign of Philip IV., who is himself depicted on horseback, but it is not sufficiently distinct in details to render it of service in this work; and the celebrated one, "Las Mucinas" (the Maids of Honour), his last great work, painted in 1656, which would be most instructive, is unfortunately inaccessible to us at the present moment.

Dekker, in his 'Seven Deadly Sins of London,' 1606, and also in his 'Gull's Hornbook,' 1609, alludes to "the Spanish slop" (large loose breeches). In the former he says,

"His huge slops speak Spanish;"

and in the latter, as I have already observed (page 230), he contrasts them as a novelty in fashion with "the Italian's close strosser," and other nether garments of an earlier period :

"There was then neither the Spanish slop,
Nor the skipper's galligaskins."

It would seem, therefore, that the ample but unstuffed breeches which we observe in the time of Charles I. had been adopted by English gallants from Spain as early as the third year of the reign of his father, who nevertheless stuck to his "great round abominable" upperstocks to the last. The word "slop" has, however, been so capriciously applied to all sorts of articles of attire by our forefathers (see Dictionary, p. 469), that, unaided by the pencil or more detailed description, I would not undertake to identify the form of slop worn in Spain during the first decade of the seventeenth century.[1] The Low Countries also had been so long under the domination of Spain that I suspect many fashions may have been originally Spanish which have passed for Flemish, and *vice versâ.*

In 1623 an ordinance was issued against the wearing of lace, and enforcing plain rebatos without any trimming of *point coupé* or *passement* for the men, and ruffs and cuffs for the ladies, but all without starch. This regulation was, however, suspended during the visit of Charles, Prince of Wales, in February that year. In 1649 Evelyn informs us that "y⁰ Spanish habit was in Paris the greatest bugbear imaginable."

Howell, in a letter from Madrid, dated 12th August, 1623, tells his brother that the Infanta was "preparing divers suits of rich cloathes for his Highness" (Prince Charles, at that time her intended husband) "of perfumed amber leather, some embroidered with pearl, some with gold, some with silver;" but unfortunately he does not describe their form, nor does he give us any information respecting the costume of the Court of Philip IV., or of the people of Madrid. Of the women, he only tells us, that "when they are married they have a privilege to wear high shoes and to paint, which is generally practised here, and the Queen useth it herself. . . . . All the women going here veiled, and their habit so generally alike, one can hardly distinguish a countess from a cobbler's wife." (Letter to Lord Colchester, 1st February, 1623.)

The celebrated Countess d'Aulnoy, who visited Madrid in 1679, is, as might be expected, much more communicative on the subject.[2] "The King" (Charles II. of Spain, son of Philip IV. and Marie-Anne of Austria) "was there," she tells us, "in a black lutestring taffety suit, a shoulder-belt of blue silk, edged with white. His sleeves were of white taffety, embroidered with silk and bugles; they were very long, and open before."

The following is her description of the son of the Alcalde of Aranda :—"His hair was parted in the middle and tied behind with a blue riband four fingers broad and two ells long, which hung down its full length. He had black velvet breeches, buttoned by five or six buttons above the knee, without which it would have been impossible to take them off without tearing them to pieces, so tight are they worn in this country ; a vest so short that it did not cover the pockets, and a pourpoint with long skirts of black cut velvet and hanging sleeves four fingers broad. The sleeves of his pourpoint were of white satin with jet borders, and his shirt sleeves were of black taffeta instead of linen, extremely wide and with ruffles of the same. His cloak was of black cloth, and, as he was a *guapo* (*i.e.* a fashionable swaggerer), he had twisted it round his arm, because that was considered more

---

[1] In a masque or play *temp.* James I., the reference to which I have unfortunately lost, a character is described wearing "a slop on one leg and a trunk on the other."

[2] 'Voyage en Espagne.' A translation of which, entitled 'Ingenious and diverting Letters of a Lady's Travels into Spain,' was published in England, and reached its eighth edition in 1717. It was reprinted in two volumes, with corrections (much needed), in 1808. A new edition of the original, with notes by Madame B. Carey, was published in Paris in 1874.

gallant, having a *broquel* (a light sort of buckler with a steel point in the centre) in one hand, and in the other a sword as long as a half-pike. He had also a poniard with a narrow blade, which was attached to his girdle at his back. His *golilla* (collar) of pasteboard, covered with a thin quintin (a fine cloth), kept his neck so stiff that he could neither bend nor turn his head. Nothing can be more ridiculous than this high collar, for it is neither a ruff nor a band nor a cravat. His hat was of a prodigious size, low-crowned, and lined with black taffeta, and with a great piece of crape round it, such as a husband would wear who was in mourning for his wife." This, she tells us, was the height of fashion. Those who prided themselves on their dress wore no trimmings on their hats, or feathers, or knots of gold or silver ribands, but a thick and large crape, which was irresistible in the eyes of the fair sex. "His shoes were of morocco leather, as thin as glove leather, and full of slashes, notwithstanding the cold weather, fitting the foot as if glued to it, and without heels."

Much information is contained in this minute description of a Spanish *exquisite* of the seventeenth century ; for perhaps this modern epithet may be the nearest rendering of the "*guapo*" of Madame d'Aulnoy in the sense in which it is used by her, as amongst the many significations of *guapo* one is a person who takes an exceeding pride in dress. The "golille de carton couverte d'un petit quintin," of which she speaks, demands especial notice. *Golilla*, from *gola*, "gullet," or "upper portion of the throat," is Spanish for a kind of collar forming part of the dress of magistrates of some superior courts in Spain. A footnote of the editor informs us that it was first adopted by Philip IV., who was so delighted with it that he instituted a fête in its honour, and with his court went annually in procession to the chapel of the Bridge of the Guardian Angel, to return thanks to Heaven for the blessing of its invention ! In 'A History of Costume' the omission to record this singular tribute to the popularity of a particular article of apparel would have been so serious a defect that I feel assured no apology is needed for this digression. *Quintin*, the material with which the pasteboard was covered, is a fine sort of cloth, called *Kentin* in English. The height and rigidity of this collar, which prevented the wearer from bending or turning his head, is exemplified by the fact that one form of the word in Spanish signifies "to strangle." From its retention to the present day by the magistracy in their official costume, its name is in familiar language used to designate the judge himself : "Ajustae a uno la golilla." There is also a saying in Spanish which has a curious affinity to an English one : "Levantar la golilla" is "to become passionate," which, literally translated, is "to raise the collar." Query : Is the popular expression "to raise one's *choler*" in any way indebted to the Spanish ? Madame d'Aulnoy's account of her visitor having curtseyed to her like a woman may not be altogether ascribed to the stiffness of his pasteboard collar preventing his making a bow, for her editor states that "Les grands d'Espagne, lorsqu'ils saluèrent le roi, faisaient *encore de notre temps* une révérence semblable à celle d'une femme ;" but, at the same time, we may ask, can this peculiar mode of salutation be traced to an earlier period than that of the invention of the golilla ? If not, might it not be a courtly custom originated by it in the reign of Philip IV. ?

"Till of late, women wore fardingales of a prodigious bigness. This fashion was very troublesome to themselves as well as to others. There were hardly any doors wide enough for them to go through, but they have left them off now, and only wear them when they go to appear in the queen's or the king's presence. Commonly, in the city, they wear a certain sort of vestment which, to speak properly, is a *young* or little fardingale (called a *sacriston*). They are made of thick copper wire in a round form. About the girdle there are ribands fastened to them, with which they tie another round of the same form, which falls down a little lower and is wider, and of these rounds they have five or six, which reach to the ground and bear out their petticoats and other garments." In point of fact, the primitive hoop which succeeded the farthingale.

Of petticoats she tells us they wear a vast number, and that "one would hardly believe that such little creatures as the Spanish women are could bear such a load. The upper one is always of a coarse black taffety, or a plain grey stuff made of goat's hair. . . . Under this plain and upper garment they have a dozen more, one finer than another, of rich stuffs, and trimmed with galloons and lace of gold or silver to the girdle. When I have told you a dozen, pray don't think that I exceed the truth : during the excessive heats of summer they only wear seven or eight, of which some are of velvet and others of thick satin. They wear at all times a white garment under all the rest, which is called *sabenina*. It is made either of fine English lace or muslin embroidered with gold, and so wide that they are four ells in compass. I have seen some of these worth five or six thousand crowns."

The petticoats, she tells us, were worn so long in front that they could not walk in them without treading upon them, and were therefore obliged to hold them up "à fleur de terre." This fashion, we are informed in a note, was called the *tontillo*, and had the honour of being the subject of a correspondence between the courts of France and Spain in the reign of Louis XIV. Louise de Savoie, queen of Philip V., objected to the length of the dresses of the dames du Palais, whilst the husbands of those ladies vehemently opposed any curtailment.[1] The object of their length was the concealment of their feet, for, celebrated as the Spanish dames have ever been for the smallness and beauty of their feet, the sight of them was at that time accounted one of the greatest favours a lady could grant to a gentleman, and was the first privilege accorded to an accepted lover.

"The bodies are worn pretty high in front, but behind you may see them to the middle of their backs. They put red on their shoulders, which are bare, as well as on their cheeks. Nor do they want for white, which is very good, but there are few who know how to use it. . . . Their large sleeves, which they fasten to their wrists, are made of taffety of all colours, like those of the Egyptians (gipsies), with broad lace ruffles. Their stays are commonly of gold or silver stuffs mixed with lively colours. . . . About their necks they wear bone lace, embroidered with red or green silk, or gold or silver.[2] They wear girdles ornamented with medals and relics, also the cord of some order, either of St. Francis, of the Carmelites, or some other. It is a small cord, made either of black or white or brown wool, and is worn outside their stays and hangs down before to the edge of their petticoats. They are full of knots, and on every knot there is usually fastened a diamond. At the top of the stays ladies wear a broad knot of diamonds, from which depends a chain of pearls or ten or twelve knots of diamonds, which they fasten at the other end to their sides. They never wear any necklace, but only bracelets, rings, and ear-rings, which last are longer than my hand, and so heavy that I have wondered how they could carry them without tearing out the holes of their ears ; to which also they add whatever they think pretty. I have seen some have good large watches hanging there, others padlocks of precious stones, and even your fine-wrought English keys and little bells. Their heads are stuck full of bodkins, some with heads made of diamonds in shape of a fly, others like butterflies, the colours of their wings imitated by various precious stones. They dress their heads after various fashions, but never wear any sort of coif, either by day or by night. They part the hair on one side and lay it across the forehead. It shines so that one might truly say one may see oneself in it. I have seen some who had their heads dressed up with feathers like little children. These feathers are very curious, and spotted with different colours, which made them much more beautiful. I cannot imagine why they do not make such in France."

In another place she says, "The Marquesa de Palacios wore a little hat trimmed with feathers, according to the fashion of the Spanish ladies when they go into the country."

Respecting their *chaussure*, for which Spanish ladies have been immemorially celebrated, she writes, "I have already told you their feet are so small that their shoes look like those of our babies. They are made of black Spanish leather, cut up on coloured taffety, without heels, and fit as closely as a glove." Out of doors they wore *pattins*, which the Countess describes as "a sort of little sandal, made of brocade or velvet, set upon plates of gold, which raise them half a foot," apparently the counterpart of the Venetian *chioppine*. She adds that "they walk very ill" in them, "and are apt to fall down."

I confess there are portions of this elaborate description of the costume of a Spanish doña that puzzle me, and my fair readers will, I think, be unable to comprehend the object of the

---

[1] Mémoires du Maréchal de Noailles.

[2] The 'Mercure Galant,' 1679, describes the Spanish ambassadress as "vetue de drap noir avec de la dentelle de soye ; elle n'avait ni dentelle ni linge autour de sa gorge."

astounding number of splendid petticoats worn one over the other, and the effect of watches and keys suspended from ear-rings. It would be very interesting to discover a portrait that would illustrate the latter curious caprice. It is also remarkable that Madame d'Aulnoy makes no mention of the veil that Howell states was universally worn by Spanish women at the time of his visit, and which, we know, has been characteristic of their national costume for the last three centuries.

One singular custom Madame d'Aulnoy describes I must not omit to notice. "At my first coming in," she says, "to visit the Princess of Monteleon, I was surprised to see so many young ladies with great spectacles on their noses and fastened to their ears; but that which seemed yet more strange to me was that they made no use of them where it was necessary, but only discoursed whilst they had them on." The Marquesa de la Roza, to whom she referred for an explanation, "fell a laughing" at her question, and told her that they wore them only for gravity's sake and to command respect. "'Do you see that lady?' said she to me, meaning one that was near us. 'I do not believe that since she was ten years old she ever left them off but when she went to bed. . . . I must needs tell you,' continued she, 'that some time ago the Jacobite Friars had a lawsuit of great importance, to secure the success of which they neglected no means in their power. One of the young Fathers in the convent had some very influential kinsmen of high rank, who, on his account, promised to use their interest in behalf of the fraternity. The Prior assured the young man that, if the suit was gained through his credit, he could ask nothing that should not be granted to him. The suit was gained, and the young friar, transported with joy, ran to the convent with the news and to claim his reward by the grant of a special favour which he had long desired to obtain; but the Prior,

immediately on hearing the good tidings, embraced him, and in the most solemn tone said, "Hermano, pongo los ojulos;" that is, "Brother, put on spectacles." The honour of this permission was so highly appreciated by the young friar that he felt the recompense exceeded his desert, and that he could ask for nothing more.'" The Countess relates some other anecdotes illustrative of this extraordinary custom, and states that she heard there were spectacles of various sizes allotted to men and women according to their several degrees of rank or property. "Proportionably," she says, "as a man's fortune increases, he enlarges the glasses of his spectacles and wears them higher on his nose. The grandees of Spain wear them as broad as one's hands, and for distinction call them *ocales*. They fasten them behind their ears, and leave them off as seldom as they do their collars." She concludes by saying, "I have since observed several persons of quality in their coaches, sometimes alone and sometimes in company, with those great spectacles hung upon their noses, which in my mind is a strange sight."

Spanish Nobleman, circa 1690.

In justice to one of the most intellectual women of her age—in grateful recollection of the delight her immortal 'Contes des Fées' has afforded us in child-hood, and, I may specially add, of the advantage I have personally derived from them as a dramatist —I cannot bring myself to believe that the above account was deliberately written by her for the purpose of deception, or that she could possibly have been credulous enough to have taken *au sérieux* the gossip of the Marchioness de la Roza, whom she describes as a person of "a neat wit and a Neapolitan." At the same time it is difficult to understand how such an eccentric custom should have escaped the notice, not only of other foreign travellers, but of the contemporary national authors, the Spanish novelists and dramatists of the seventeenth century. If it be true, according to one of the stories, that the Marquis de Astorgas, Viceroy of Naples, insisted upon his spectacles being represented in his marble bust, how is it that we do not find them forming a pro-minent object in the portraits of the nobility and gentry of Spain, which have been handed down to us by the painters or engravers of that period? How long had the custom existed previously to the visit of Madame d'Aulnoy, and at what date was it discontinued? One thing at least is certain: the fashion was never adopted in any other country, if, indeed, it was ever heard of. I have simply discharged a duty in laying this account before my readers, few of whom, I suspect, are acquainted with the original work or its translations; but I decline the responsibility of vouching for its accuracy.[1] Some other of the writer's notices of costume may be received without suspicion. "Those which they call the life-guards have partizans, and march near the (king's) coach, and next the foot go a great many of the king's pages, clothed in black, and without swords, which is the only mark to distinguish them from other pages." Are we to understand by this that black was as universally worn by pages in Madrid as blue by serving-men in London in the days of Elizabeth?

"The captains of the guard and other officers . . . . are clothed in yellow velvet or satin, which is the livery of the king, trimmed with tufted or crimson galloon, mixed with gold and silver. The yeomen of the guard, which I call the life-guard, wear only short cloaks of the same livery over black clothes.

"Footmen of nobles and ambassadors wear long swords, with shoulder-belts and cloaks. They are all clothed either in blue or green, and their green cloaks are frequently lined with blue velvet cut in flowers. You would think," she observes, "that these would be handsome liveries; but yet I assure you nothing is uglier. They wear bands, but without any collars, which is ridiculous."

The portraits by Velasquez already alluded to may be depended upon as authorities for the dress of the nobility and upper classes in the capital during the seventeenth century; and I am of opinion that the various costumes of the different provinces with which the paintings of our modern artists and the representations of the modern stage have made us familiar, date from the latter portion of it, as I shall endeavour to show in the next chapter.

Christian IV., king of Denmark; died 1648.

Danish Women. From Moller, 1642.

Of the costume of the North of Europe—Norway, Sweden, and Denmark—at this period, we have some very imperfect descriptions scattered through the pages of the various voyages and travels into those regions, collected by Pinkerton, Moore, and others. What, for instance,

[1] In corroboration, however, of Madame d'Aulnoy, let me add that her latest editor in the Paris edition, 1874, appends the following note to this description: "Le Conseiller Bertault fait également mention de cette étrange mode" (p. 285).

can we understand by the French poet Regnard's account of the women of Denmark? "The women carry all kinds of baskets made of very fine twigs on their heads." Is he speaking of head-

Peasants of the Parish of Mora, in Dalecarlia.
From Picart.

dresses? I presume so, as there are numerous examples of hats or head-coverings, whatever they may be called in the adjacent countries of Holland, the Hanse Towns, and the North of Germany, which may fairly be called baskets, but they differ in shape as much as baskets do, and we therefore gain little information of use to us. The portraits of royal and noble personages shed no light on national costume: their dress resembles that of persons of the same rank in England, France, or Germany. In the preceding page is an engraving of the full-length portrait of Christian IV., king of Denmark, at Hampton Court, which might equally well represent an English nobleman at the court of James I., even to the strings in his ear, which may be the only national feature of his costume, as it is presumable that it was introduced into England from Denmark during that reign. I know of no portrait of Anne of Denmark before her marriage with James, but believe little if any difference existed in it to that in which she is represented at p. 187 of the Dictionary.

Of Sweden I have found a curious illustration in an engraving by Bernard Picart (born in 1673) of the costume of the peasantry of the parish of Mora, province of Dalecarlia. Two females, an old and a young one, are soliciting money from an old countryman, who holds a well-filled purse or money-bag in his left hand. The women have their heads bound in handkerchiefs in a peculiar fashion, and wear the jacket, bedgown, or nightrail, so general amongst the peasantry and lower classes throughout Europe at this moment. The man has a similar jacket, loose breeches, with tremendously long canions, as they were called, to the knees.

Of Norway, Lapland, and Iceland, the travellers alluded to are more instructive, and the magnificence of the dress of a Lapland lady is remarkable; but of all these Scandinavian nations I shall speak more fully in the next chapter, as the numerous collections of costume published during the last hundred years exhibit all the characteristics of the seventeenth century, at which period the peasantry and labouring classes appear to have desisted from further progress in their dress, although some peculiar features distinguish one district from another, as in Western and Southern Europe. Our illustrations will then be contemporaneous with the accounts of later travellers, and yet depict faithfully many of the earlier fashions of which we have not found dependable representations by artists of their time.[1]

Flanders, the Netherlands, or Low Countries, as that portion of Europe, which has resumed its classical appellation of Belgium, was usually called in the days of the Stuarts, was, as I have already

[1] For this reason I have refrained from introducing copies of the engravings in Vecellio and Bertelli of these people, as I doubt the drawings having been made from nature.

observed, so long under the dominion of the kings of Spain of the house of Austria, that an assimilation of the costumes of the two countries amongst the higher orders must be naturally expected,
influenced also as both would be by the decrees of Fashion in France, issued then as now from the
head-quarters of the capricious divinity, Paris, to her votaries throughout Western Europe. Vandyke
and Rubens have grandly and faithfully illustrated the dresses of the Flemish nobility, and the burin
of Hollar has transmitted to us those of the townswomen and domestic servants of his own time. In
the former little difference is to be seen from the dresses of the English of the same date. In the
latter there is more national character; and the *huycke*, described by Minsheu as " a mantle such as
women use in *Spain*, Germany, and the *Low Countries* when they goe abroad " (see Dictionary, p. 288).

Gentlewoman of Brabant.

Noblewoman of Antwerp.

Woman of Antwerp.

From Hollar. 1643.

Woman of Cologne.

2 N 2

is particularly remarkable, with a little saucer-shaped piece of black velvet with a tuft of black silk
projected from it, by which it was secured on the forehead, and which Rubens has depicted in the

Citizen's Daughter, Cologne.   Servant-maid of Cologne.   Lady of Brabant. Winter dress.
                                 From Hollar.

well-known portrait of his second wife.   It is also seen in representations of Spanish duennas.
Ducange specially calls it "peplum muliebre *Brabanticum*," and one of Hollar's etchings of a lady

Game of Tric-Trac. By Teniers.

so attired is described in English and Latin, "a gentlewoman of Brabant," "mulier generosa
Brabantica."   (See engravings in the preceding page.)
    The portrait of Jean Baptiste van Deynum, a popular Flemish painter, taken by himself, as

captain of a company of the burgher guard of Antwerp, his native city, in 1651, is given on p. 266, from a rare engraving of the period by Waumans. Although only a half-length, it affords us

Teniers and his Daughters. From a picture in the National Gallery.

Dutch Woman. From Hollar.

Dutch Women. From Hollar. 1640.

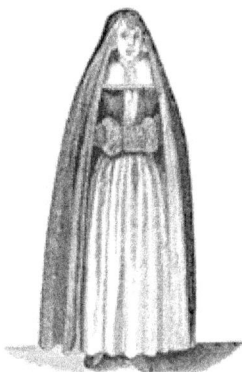

some useful details of costume. The ornamentation of the sleeves, the mode of feathering the hat, the gloves, ruffles, and cane, are all well defined and characteristic.

The painters and engravers of the seventeenth century furnish us with ample authorities for the costume of all classes, in Holland, Germany, and Italy. Teniers and Terburg alone would supply us with hundreds of examples of dress in "the United Provinces," from the prince to the boor, from the stadtholder's lady to the ale-wife and the market-girl. In addition to these, we have the etchings of Hollar and Romayn de Hooghe, not to mention many others. The prints in Sir William Lower's work, described at p. 239 *ante*, are also of assistance to us in this portion of our history. The engravings from paintings by Teniers (see previous pages) illustrate the general costume of the Dutch in his day, in addition to which we give a chromolithograph from Terburg's celebrated picture of 'The Music Lesson,' and four woodcuts from the etchings of Hollar. All these engravings speak so clearly to the eye that verbal description is little needed.

As in England, the costume of the termination of the sixteenth century continued in fashion for the first few years of the following, the shortening of the waist being the earliest remarkable alteration. Dekker alludes to it in 1606 as though it had originated in Holland. Appropriating each article of an English gallant's attire to some particular foreign nationality, he says, "The short waste hangs over a Dutch botcher's stall in Utrich" (Utrecht).

Maria of Austria, Queen of Bohemia. 1649.

Elector of Germany, in his State Dress.
From Vecellio.

Hunting Dress. 1639.

Coifs are generally worn by women of the middle classes, and enormous ruffs remain in favour with the wives of the merchants and shopkeepers. The short linen or cotton garment which I remember being called a bedgown, and seems to have been the night-rail, so often mentioned in England at the period in question (see Dictionary, p. 379), makes its appearance in Dutch female dresses *circa* 1640, and probably was first worn in Holland, where it is seen to this day, and now generally of a flowered pattern. Of the various kingdoms, duchies, &c., comprised in the Germanic empire during the time the crown of Charlemagne was worn by Matthias, Ferdinand II., Ferdinand III., and Leopold I., all previously kings of Hungary and Bohemia, I can only say that the sovereigns and their courts literally followed *suit* whatever France might lead. The above woodcut, from a portrait by Vandyke, of Maria of Austria, wife of Ferdinand III. king of Bohemia, 1649, displays all the characteristic features of that date. In the portraits of the Electors of Hanover, Brunswick, Saxony, Wurtemburg, Bavaria, the Palatinate, and their respective wives and families, no marked difference is to be observed between their dress and that of their contemporaries

of the same rank in Paris and London. The chromolithograph issued with Part XII. represents
a group of distinguished personages and their attendants, who, if not German, as reported, display

Woman of Nuremberg. 1640.

Women of Nuremberg. From Münzer, 1581.

Roman Catholic Widow of Augsburg,
in Mourning Dress. From Münzer, 1587.

Woman of Strasburg, in Mourning Dress.

at least in their attire all the fashions peculiar to the costume of the higher classes in Central
Europe at the end of the seventeenth century, as will be evident on comparison with the portraits

and prints of that period and reference to the descriptions of contemporary travellers and biographers. We give the state robes of an Elector of Germany from Vecellio, and the hunting dress of the time from a figure carved on the stock of the wheel-lock rifle of the Archduke Leopold, afterwards Emperor of Austria, dated 1653, formerly in the Meyrick Collection.

Woman of the Lower Palatinate. 1640.

Woman of Upper Austria.

Woman of Franconia.

Woman of Mayence.

Merchant's Wife at Frankfort.

Native of Frankfort.

Misson, who travelled in 1687–88,[1] gives us descriptions and representations of the bourgeoisie of Nuremberg, Augsburg, and Strasburg at a later period, which are of the most eccentric description. A bride of the first-named city was attired at her wedding in "a black *casaquin*, with long

[1] 'Voyage d'Italie,' par Maximilian Misson. 4 vols. 12mo. La Haye, 1702.

basques, something like the hongrelines worn not long ago in France; the basques loaded (*chargées*) with little bows of black ribbon (*nœuds pressés de ruban satine noir*), and the sleeves long and tight, reaching to the wrist; over this a collar of fine old lace, made in front like a man's, but ending in a point behind, falling to the middle of the back; a short petticoat trimmed with gold and black lace, and gold chains round her neck and her waist." Of Augsburg he tells us that the variety and *bigarrure* of the dresses are greater than those of Nuremberg. "They are under the regulation of the police, and one knows the religion of the majority of the inhabitants by the distinctions in the clothes they wear." Unfortunately he does not particularize those distinctions, and I have therefore been unable to select examples from the number of hideous and ridiculous figures he presents us with. "I will only describe to you," he says, "the mourning habit worn by a Roman Catholic tradeswoman for her deceased husband." "This," he informs us, "consists of a white muslin couvrechef, well starched, with the usual wings and horns; a black petticoat and a black cloak made like a man's, reaching to the knee; an ample white veil attached to the back of the couvrechef, and widening as it descends to the heels." But the singular and absurd mark of widowhood is an oblong piece of starched muslin, four feet long and about two in width, extremely starched, stretched on a frame of copper wire and suspended immediately beneath the lips, so that it hangs in front of them, covering the whole figure from the chin downwards. Of this eccentric and unmeaning costume he gives an engraving, which I have had copied as a curiosity, and also the mourning habit of a lady of Strasburg (see page 271). The other monstrosities I considered it unnecessary to reproduce, as they are neither picturesque nor instructive. Should they be required for any special purpose, they will be found in the first and third volumes of the edition published at the Hague in 1702.

In the provinces, however, and principal towns generally throughout the Continent, great variety existed. Nearly every city and district was distinguished by some characteristic costume of an earlier date, which had become localised and remained unaffected by the caprices of Fashion, some of which have lingered to the present day, but are gradually, I regret to observe, disappearing, even in the Tyrol and some parts of Switzerland.

The same remarks will apply to Italy with the exception always of Venice, where the Doge and the Signori continued to preserve their stately habits, and in some degree of Naples, which, under the dominion of Spain, was naturally influenced by the fashions of Madrid. Dekker, who in his 'Gull's Hornbook,' 1609, speaks of "the Italian's close strosser," and in his 'Seven Deadly Sins of London,' 1606, mentions "the wing and narrow sleeve of Italy," in neither instance names the precise locality.

Richard Lassells,[1] describing the people of Genoa, says, "They wear broad hats without hatbands, broad leather girdles with steel buckles, narrow breeches, with long-waisted doublets and hanging sleeves. The great ladies go in *guard infantas*; that is, in horrible overgrown *vertigoles* of whalebone, which, being put about the waist of the lady, and full as broad on both sides as she can reach with her hands, bear out her coats in such a manner that she appears to be as broad as she is long. The men look like tumblers that leap through hoops, and the women like those that anciently danced the hobby-horse in country mummings" (p. 96).

Our engraving from the portraits of Ferdinand II. (de Medici), Grand Duke of Tuscany, and his duchess, Victoria, attributed to Velasquez, formerly in our National Gallery, admirably illustrates the costume of the nobility of Italy in the middle of the seventeenth century, 1631–1660 (see next page).

Misson describes the dress of the citizens of Ancona in 1687. "The principal men," he says, "usually wear a black cloak lined with green; blue or reddish-brown (*feuille-morte*) stockings; their shoes whitened with chalk, tied with coloured ribands; their pourpoints unbuttoned, with trimmings of coloured brocades, the long sleeves of their shirts (ruffles?) reaching to their fingers' ends. The women had a sort of cloth upon their heads with long fringes, which protects the face from the flies like a hood (*en guise de capuchon*). The body of their gown is either red or yellow, laced together on all four sides and ornamented with livery lace; short waists and petticoats, and the whole dress of fifty colours."

[1] 'A Complete Journey through Italy.' Sm. 8vo. 1686.

The great ladies are "ajustées et en fontanges tant qu'elles peuvent à la Française."

Annexed is an engraving from an original portrait of a young Italian gentleman, one of

Ferdinand II., Grand Duke of Tuscany, and his Duchess.   By Velasquez (?).

Young Italian Gentleman.   1690.

the Madeloni family, painted about 1690, the costume corresponding with that of the reign of William III. in England.

Of Venice in the seventeenth century we possess a mass of contemporary information, transmitted to us by English travellers, some of whom I have already had occasion to quote in the Dictionary (article CHIOPINE). Avoiding repetition as far as possible, I extract the following passages from the works of Coryat, Evelyn, and Howell, in chronological order.

Coryat, who travelled in 1608, tells us there were no less than three thousand gentlemen of Venice who were called "Clarissimoes." "All of which," he continues, "when they goe abroad out of their houses, both they that beare office and they that are private, doe weare gownes wherein they imitate the Romans . . . . Most of their gownes are made of black cloth, and over their left shoulder they have a flappe made of the same cloth and edged with blacke taffata, also most of their gownes are faced before with blacke taffata. There are others, also, that weare other gownes according to their distinct offices and degrees, as they that are of the Council of Tenne (which are, as it were, the maine body of the whole estate) doe most commonly weare blacke chamlet gownes, with marvellous long sleeves that reach almost down to the ground. Again, they that weare red chamlet gownes with long sleeves are those that are called Savi, whereof some have authority only by land, as being the principal overseers of the podestates and prætors in their land, cities, and some by sea," &c.

The chiefs of the Council of Ten—who were three in number, elected by lot, changed every month and possessed tremendous authority—wore "red gowns with long sleeves, either of cloth, chamlet, or damask, according to the weather, with a flappe of the same stuff and colour over the left shoulder, red stockings and slippers."

"Upon every great festivale day," says Coryat, "the senators and greatest gentlemen that accompany the Duke to church or to any other place, doe weare crimson gownes, with flappes of crimson velvet cast over their left shoulders. All these grand men doe weare marvaillous little blacke caps of felt, without any brims at all, and very diminutive falling bandes, no ruffs at all, which (the bands) are so shallow that I have seen many of them not above a little inch deepe. . . . . The fifth day of

August being Fryday," he tells us, "I saw the Duke in some of his richest ornaments. . . . . He himself then wore two very rich robes, or long garments, whereof the uppermost was white cloth of silver, with great massy buttons of gold ; the other cloth of silver also, but adorned with many curious workes made in colours with needlework." Speaking of the ordinary male attire, he remarks that " the colour they most affect and use for their other apparel—I mean, doublet, hose, and jerkin—is blacke, a colour of gravity and decency," and that "all of them use but one and the same form of habite, even the slender doublet made close to the body, without much quilting or bombast, and long hose, plain, without those new-fangled curiosities and ridiculous superfluities of panes, plaites and other light toyes used by us Englishmen, yet they make it of costly stuffes, well beseeming gentlemen and eminent persons of their place, as of the best taffataes and sattins that Christendom doth yield, which are fairly garnished also with lace of the best sort." [1]

Respecting the female sex, he says, " Most of their women, when they walk abroad, especially to church, are veiled with long vailes, whereof some do reach almost to the ground behinde. These vailes are eyther blacke or white or yellowish. The blacke eyther wives or widowes do wear ; the white, maydes, and so the yellowish also, but they wear more white than yellowish. It is the custom of these maydes, when they walke the streets, to cover their faces with their vailes, the stuffe being so thin and slight that they may easily look through it, for it is made of a pretty slender silke and very finely curled," qualifying this account as follows : " Now whereas I said that only maydes doe weare white vailes and none else, I mean these white silke curled vayles, which (as they told me) none doe weare but maydes. But other white vayles wives doe much weare, such as are made of holland, whereof the greatest part is handsomely edged with great and very fair bone lace."

Evelyn, writing some forty years later, says of the Venetians, " The truth is, their garb is very odd, as seeming allwayes in masquerade ; their other habits are also totally different from all nations. They weare very long crisped haire of several streakes and colours, which they make so by a wash, disch-evelling it on the brims of a broade hat that has no crown, but an hole to put out their heads by ; they drie them in the sunn, as one may see them at their windows (vide page 196). In their tire they set silk flowers and sparkling stones, their petticoates coming from their very armpits, so that they are neere three quarters and an half apron. Their sleeves are made exceedingly wide, under which their shift sleeves as wide and commonly tucked up to the shoulder, shewing their naked armes thro' false sleeves of tiffany, girt with a bracelet or two, with knots of points richly tagged about their shoulders and other places of their body, which they usually cover with a kind of yellow vaile of lawn, very transparent. Thus attired, they set their hands on the heads of two matron-like servants or old women to support them, who are mumbling their beades. 'Tis ridiculous to see how these ladys crawle in and out of their gondolas by reason of their choppines, and what dwarfs they appeare when taken down from their wooden scaffolds. Of these I saw nearly thirty together, stalking halfe as high again as the rest of the world ; for courtezans or the citizens may not wear choppines,[2] but cover their bodies and faces with a vaile of a certaine glittering taffeta or lustrée, out of which they now and then dart a glance of their eye, the whole face being otherwise entirely hid with it. Nor may the com'on misses take this habit, but go abroad barefac'd. To the corners of these virgin-vailes hang broad but flat tossells of curious point de Venize. The married women go in black vailes. The nobility weare the same colour, but of fine cloth lin'd wᵗʰ taffeta in summer, with fur of the bellies of squirrells in ye winter, which all put on at a certain day, girt with a girdle emboss'd with silver ; the vest not much different from what our Batchelors of Arts weare in Oxford ; and a hood of cloth made like a sack, cast over their left shoulder, and a round cloth black cap fring'd with wool, which is not so comely : they also weare their collar open to shew the diamond button

---

[1] His assertion that their attire "is the same that hath been used these *thousand yeares* amongst them," must be understood to apply only to the "*gownes*," and then most be taken *cum grano*. The reader will find at p. 54 of this volume the form of gowns worn in Venice five hundred years before Coryat wrote. The "long sleeves that reach almost to the ground" were not *three* hundred years old at the time he travelled.

[2] This regulation must have been a comparatively recent one in 1645, for in 1591 an engraving testifies to the contrary.

of the stock of their shirt . . . . The Doge's vest is of crimson velvet; the Procurator's, &c., of damask, very stately."

It is to be noticed that Evelyn uses the word "vest," in the above description, in the general sense of a vesture or garment, and is in this instance speaking of the gown worn by the whole "Signory" of Venice. This must also be taken into consideration when he and Pepys, some twenty years later, mention the introduction of vests, "after y* Persian mode," by Charles II.

The hood of cloth cast over the left shoulder is the "flappe" mentioned by Coryat. Its being "made like a sack" can only indicate that it was double, as it is always represented lying quite flat on the shoulder like a band or stole, and not like the hoods worn by Doctors and Masters of Arts in our Universities. There was an order of knighthood in Venice called "the Golden Stole," and it is difficult to distinguish in engravings that which is a decoration from the ordinary "flappe" or tippet of the hood observed by Evelyn and Coryat, who say nothing about the order.

Howell in his 'Survey of the Signorie of Venice' (London, 1651), after telling us that the Doge always goes clad in silk and purple, observes that "sometimes he shewes himself to the public in a

Venetian Nobleman. 1687.

robe of cloth of gold and a white mantle; he hath his head covered with a thin coif, and on his forehead he wears a crimson kind of mitre with a gold border, and behind it turns up in form of a horn; on his shoulders he carries ermine skins to the middle, which is still a badge of the Consull's habit; on his feet he wears embroidered sandals,[1] tied with gold buttons, and about his middle a most rich belt embroidered with costly jewels, so much so that the habit of the Duke, when at festivales he shews himself in the highest state, is valued at above 100,000 crownes." The dress of the Doge was regulated by particular days and ceremonies. On all days sacred to the memory of the Virgin his robes were white, and the colour of the corno was always that of his robes.

Misson, a still later traveller, tells us that in 1687 the Venetian ladies of rank were allowed the privilege of giving such striped or parti-coloured jackets to their gondoliers as pleased them during the first two years of their marriage ("bigarrer comme bon leur semble les hoquetons de leurs gondoliers"), a privilege at other times restricted to the Doge; also to wear jewels on all occasions during the same period. He gives us also an engraving of a noble young Venetian of that date, which is interesting from the novel introduction of the periwig (see figure annexed).

The magnificent work on Russian Antiquities published by the Imperial Government supplies us with ample authorities for the costume of all ranks and classes in that part of the empire which concerns us in this chapter. Portraits of the Tzar Alexis Michaelowitz (1645-1676), of his wife Maria, and of the Patriarch Nikon will be found in the chromolithograph issued with Part XIX., faithfully copied from it; and the plate issued with Part XX. presents us with accurate representations from the same source of the crowns and caps of the sovereigns of Russia in the seventeenth century, and may probably illustrate those of anterior times of which no relics have been handed down to us.[2] Baron Mayerberg, who was sent by the Emperor Leopold as Ambassador to the Tzar Alexis, has left a minute description of the Hall of Audience at Moscow; but simply

---

[1] Cesare Vecellio, in 1594, says, "*slippers*,"—"Porta in piedi le *pianmells* par del medesimo usani anche da cavallieri nobile di Venetia."

[2] N.B. By an unfortunate oversight the third, fourth, and fifth figures have been incorrectly numbered. No. 4 should be No. 3; No. 5, No. 4; and No. 3, "Crown of Empress Anne." No. 5, as in the marginal reference.

Eudocia, wife of Tzar Mikhail Romanoff. 1645.

Natalia, 2nd wife of Tzar Alexis Michaelowitz. 1671.

tells us that "the Czar had on his head a cap of a sugar-loaf form (*bonnet en pain de sucre*), with a border of sable and surmounted by a crown of gold enriched with jewels" (Le Clerc). Of Feodor II. (his son), we learn that he was the first Tzar who suffered his hair to grow, all his pre-

Grand Falconer, temp. Alexis Michaelowitz.

Russian Boyard. 17th cent.

Summer Costume of a Woman of Torjock. 17th cent.

decessors having had their heads shaven and worn a *calotte.* He also assumed the Polish dress, probably in compliment to his first wife, who is said to have been a Polish lady, and the Court followed the example of their sovereign. We find Peter the Great subsequently in a Polish costume. From the same work we borrow the above engravings of the Czarina Eudocia, wife of Mikhail Romanoff, founder of the present dynasty ; of Natalia, second wife of Alexis Michaelowitz, and mother of Peter the Great ; the costume of the Grand Falconer, *temp.* Alexis ;[1] of a Boyard, and the summer dress of a woman of Torjock.

Of the Poles and Hungarians there is nothing new to be said in this chapter. We shall find them even in the one following little changed from what they were in the last.

From the commencement of the seventeenth century, defensive armour of plate gradually fell into disuse throughout Europe. In England James I. had satirically described it as an excellent invention, for it not only protected the wearer but prevented his hurting anyone else. The increasing improvement in fire-arms combined with other causes to bring it into disrepute, and before the close of James's reign the armour of the heaviest cavalry terminated at the knees. Cap-à-pie suits are rarely met with at this period. Boots had begun to supersede jambs in the time of Elizabeth. Cuisses were next dispensed with. Brassarts were rendered unnecessary by the sleeves of the stout buff-coat, which eventually cast off its superincumbent cuirass, leaving nothing but the helmet and gorget of all the pieces which had composed the complete panoply of a knight of the Middle Ages.

Amongst the latest of the complete suits of this period is the beautiful one made for Henry, Prince of Wales, eldest son of James I., in 1610, and now in the royal collection at Windsor. We have already given (Plate IX.) an engraving of an additional right-hand gauntlet belonging to the suit which had found its way into the possession of Sir Samuel Meyrick, and the reader will be enabled to judge of the effect of the elaborate engraving with which it is covered. The same Prince armed only to the waist will also be found engraved at p. 20 in the Dictionary (article ARMOUR). In the Tower is a fine suit which was presented to King Charles I. by the City of London. The surface is entirely covered with scroll-work, and gilt throughout. The tassets are articulated from the waist to the knee. In the same collection is also a beautifully-chased and gilt suit made for him when a boy.

The infantry in the reigns of James and Charles consisted of pikemen and musketeers. Examples of the equipment of these troops will be found in the Dictionary, at pp. 20, 376, and 398 ; and during the former reign the intercourse with Spain changed the name of Lancer into Cavalier—an appellation which, during the Civil Wars, was bestowed generally on the loyal and gallant gentlemen who devoted their lives and fortunes to the defence of their king.

To the rest for the musquet or matchlock was added a long rapier blade called the Sweyn's feather, the precursor of the bayonet (see Dictionary, p. 496).

In 1604, King James confirmed the order of Elizabeth respecting the scarlet dress of commanders in the Royal Navy, and the material was directed to be furnished at a specific price.

In the reign of Charles I., armour with the exception of helmets, backs and breasts, with tassets, which were worn by the pikemen and musqueteers, was confined to the pistoliers and heavy cavalry. Many officers contented themselves with a cuirass over a buff-coat, and some entire regiments were armed in this fashion, and were thence called Cuirassiers.

Dragoons, first raised in France in the year 1600 by the Marshal de Brissac, were now introduced into our army, and wore "a buff-coat with deep skirts and an open head-piece with cheeks."

In 1632, we learn from a work published in that year at Cambridge, entitled 'Military Instructions for the Cavalrie,' that that force consisted of four classes—"the lancier, the cuirassier, the harquebuse and carbine, and the dragone."

"The dragone," we are told, "is of two kinds, pike and musket : the pike is to have a thong of leather about the middle of it, for convenience of carrying. The musketeer is to have a strap fastened to the stock of his piece, almost from the one end to the other, by which, being on horseback, he hangeth it at his back, keeping his burning match and the bridle in the left hand."

---

[1] On the breast of this officer is the double-headed eagle, and we are informed by M. le Clerc that armorial bearings were first adopted in Russia during the reign of Alexis.

The harquebusier, "by the late orders rendered in by the Council of War," is to wear, besides a good buff-coat, a back and breast, like the cuirassier, more than pistol-proof, a head-piece, &c. ; a harquebus two feet and a half long, hung on a belt by a swivel; a flask, touch-box, and pistols. While the carbineer, armed in the same fashion, his carbine or petronel hanging in like manner as the harquebus, carried a flask and touch-box, but in lieu of pistols had a sword with girdle and hangers.

The lancier was to wear a close casque or head-piece, a gorget, breast and back, pistol and caliver proof, pauldrons, vambraces, two gauntlets, tassets, culassets (culets or garde de reins), a good sword, "stiff, cutting, and sharp-pointed," with a girdle and hanger so fastened that he might easily draw the sword ; a buff-coat with long skirts to wear under his armour; his lance either of the usual or pike shape, only thicker at the butt-end, eighteen feet long, with a thong of leather to fasten it round the right arm ; one if not two pistols, of sufficient bore and length ; a flask, touch-box, and "all appurtenances fitting."

The cuirassier, armed as already described, is directed to wear a scarf, the only sign of company at this time, when the buff-coat and cuirass presented no distinguishing colours. Scarlet, however, had long been the prevailing colour of the clothing of the Royal troops in England, and was retained by Cromwell ; but his personal guard of halberdiers was clad "in grey coats welted with black velvet" (Whitelock's 'Perfect Politician').

In 1645, the harquebusiers were accounted the second sort of cavalry, and wore triple-barred helmets, cuirasses with garde de reins, pauldrons, and vambraces, at the same time the dragoons changed their muskets for the shorter piece, called a dragon, from which it is said they had derived their name abroad (see Dictionary, p. 175). In 1649, they carried the caliver.

The modern fire or flint lock was in use in England in the reign of Charles I. Previously to its

Musqueteer. 1668.   Pikeman. 1668.

introduction the wheel-lock was frequently called fire-lock, but that term was afterwards used for the improved piece alone. Much uncertainty exists as to the origin and date of the invention (see Dictionary under FIRELOCK and SNAPHAUNCE), but the arm was not common in this country before the second half of the seventeenth century. Musket rests and Sweyn's feathers were abandoned during the Civil Wars.

Vambraces were discarded by the harquebusiers in the first year of the Restoration ; and the helmet and corslet, or cuirass, or the gorget alone worn over a buff-coat, formed, as I have already stated, the total defence of steel borne by officers.

The arms offensive and defensive of the cavalry are directed by the statute of the thirteenth and fourteenth of Charles II. to be as follows : " A back, breast, and pot, the breast and pot to be pistol-proof ; a sword and a case of pistols, the barrels whereof are not to be under fourteen inches in length."

The infantry, consisting of musketeers and pikemen, were ordered, the former to be armed with a musket, the barrel not to be under three feet in length, a collar of bandeliers and a sword ; the pikemen, with a pike made of ash, not under sixteen feet in length, with a back, breast, head-piece, and sword.

To the engravings of pikemen and musketeers *temp.* James I. and Charles I., in the Dictionary, pages 20, 375, 376, already referred to, I have added above the figures of a pikeman and a musqueteer from Colonel Elton's 'Complete Body of the Art Military,' 1668.

The present familiar names of the regiments comprising the British Army commence from this reign. The Life Guards were raised in 1661, composed and treated, however, like the Gardes du Corps of the King of France, being formed principally of gentlemen of family and distinction, who themselves or their fathers had fought in the Civil Wars. In the same year a troop was raised in Edinburgh, one hundred and twenty in number, commanded by the Earl of Newburgh, and called the King's Life Guard, or his Majesty's troop of Guards. On the 2nd of April, 1661, "after their taking their oath to be loyal to his Majesty, they made a parade through the town of Edinburgh, with carbines at their saddles, and their swords drawn." (Wodrow Cannon's 'Historical Records of the British Army,' &c.) The accompanying cut is copied from the engraving by Hollar of the procession of Charles II. from the Tower to Westminster, for his coronation, 22nd April, 1661.

At the same period the "Horse Guards Blue" were embodied and called the Oxford Blues, from their first commander, Aubrey de Vere, Earl of Oxford.

Life Guardsman. 1661.

The Coldstream Foot Guards date their formation from 1660, when two regiments were added to one raised about ten years previously by Captain Monk at Coldstream, on the borders of Scotland.

Also the First Royal Scots, brought from France at the Restoration ; the Second or "Queen's," raised in 1661 ; the Third, or "Old Buffs," so called from their accoutrements being made of buffalo leather, embodied in 1665 ; the Twenty-first, called Fusiliers from their carrying the fusil, a lighter firelock than the musket, raised in 1678 ; and the Fourth, or "King's own," raised in 1680.

James II. added to the British Cavalry the First or King's Regiment of Dragoon Guards, 6th June, 1685, and the Second or Queen's Dragoon Guards in the same year. They were trained to act either on foot or on horseback, the men being armed with firelocks and bayonets in addition to their swords and pistols.

A-propos of bayonets, at p. 38 of the Dictionary I have described the varieties of this weapon, which eventually superseded the pike, and given the hitherto received derivation of its name from Bayonne, in Spain, where it is said to have been first invented. M. Quicherat, however, demurs to this opinion, and says it is only the corruption of a Spanish word, *vayneto*, which signifies a little sheath—"une petite gaine"—and in this particular case "une pièce qui s'engaine," which *sheathes itself !* I am too familiar with the eccentricities of etymology to deny the possibility of such a derivation, in face of the old classical example of "lucus a non lucendo." I have also too much respect for M. Quicherat to doubt that he has sufficient authority for his assertion, although he has not considered it necessary to impart it to us. In the absence of such information, and my consequent inability to test the value of the evidence, I must reserve my own opinion, simply observing that M. Demmin, while he rejects, with his usual lofty disdain of "authors of encyclopædias and dictionaries," the hitherto accepted derivation of the name of the weapon from the town of Bayonne, does not condescend to favour us with any other, and that I am not aware of any writer having attributed the *invention* and *manufacture* of the weapon to M. de Puysegur, as he asserts. That the bayonet succeeded the Sweyn's feather, and was in use in England in its plug form in the reign of James II., does not admit of dispute. The other questions remain for the present open ones.

To the infantry were added in 1685 the 5th and 7th Regiments, the latter called the Royal Fusiliers; and in 1688 the 23rd Regiment, or Welsh Fusiliers.

I need scarcely observe that the regular uniforms of the British army were gradually adopted as armour and buff-coats were discarded by the old regiments, or as the new were embodied; so that by the termination of the seventeenth century, in the eleventh year of the reign of William and Mary, nearly the whole of our land forces had their distinctive clothing of either scarlet or blue, varying only in the facings. Red, as I have elsewhere remarked, had been for centuries the national colour of England, in conformity with the heraldic rule which prescribes its assumption from that of the field of the armorial bearings; and blue, which we have also recognized in the family colours of our sovereigns, may have originated with the quartering of the arms of France by Edward III. and his successors down to the middle of the present century.

Pepys mentions the Militia of the Red Regiment being on duty at the Old Exchange, 28th February, 1659.

Evelyn, describing the procession to the coronation of Charles II., 22nd April, 1661, mentions "the King's own troop of Life Guards, the Duke of Albemarle's troop of Life Guards, a troop of volunteer horse, and lastly, a company of volunteer foot," but only informs us that "this magnificent traine on horseback" were "as rich as embroidery, velvet, cloth of gold and silver, and jewells could make them," not specifying any particular colours.[1]

In 1678 we learn from Evelyn that Grenadiers were first brought into our service, "so called," he says, "because they were dexterous at flinging hand-grenades, every one having a pouch full. They had furred caps with coped crowns, like Janizaries, which made them look very fierce; and some had long hoods hanging down behind, as we picture fools, their clothing being likewise pyeball, yellow and red." He does not seem to recognize that yellow and red were the livery colours of the House of Stuart. I have not been fortunate enough to meet with a pictorial illustration of this peculiar costume.

In the same year State clothing for the kettledrummers and trumpeters of the troops of Life Guards was issued from his Majesty's Great Wardrobe, consisting of velvet coats trimmed with silver and silk lace, and silver and silk buttons and loops, embroidered with his Majesty's cypher and crown on the back and breast, with cloth cloaks trimmed with silver and silk lace buttons and loops; boots, stockings, hats, gloves, swords, bands, cuffs, and shirts. The colour of the velvet coats is not mentioned.[2]

In 1679 we glean a little more information from Chamberlayne's 'Anglica Notitia.' The Life Guards, he tells us, "are divided into three troops—the King's troop, distinguished by their blue ribbons and carbine-belts, their red hooses and houlster-caps embroydered with his Majestic's cypher and crown; the Queen's troop, by green ribbons, carbine-belts covered with green velvet and gold lace, also green hooses and houlster-caps embroydered with the same cypher and crown; and the Duke's troop, by yellow ribbons and carbine-belts, and yellow hooses embroydered as the others." Still there is no mention of the colour or material of the clothing.

A contemporaneous account of a grand review on Putney Heath, 1st October, 1684,[3] gives us,

[1] Our woodcut on the previous page, from Hollar's engraving of this procession, illustrates the form of the dress, which was of the ordinary fashion of the period.

[2] 'Historical Records of the British Army.'

[3] 'A General and Complete List Military of his Majesty's Land Forces at the Time of the Review upon Putney Heath, 1st October, 1684.'

however, a further insight as to the colour of the uniform. The King's troop are described as "coated and cloaked in scarlet lined with blue," and the Grenadiers of this troop had "blue loops tufted with yellow upon red coats lined with blue, with grenadier caps lined with the same, and a blue round mark on the outside"—the grenade, as described subsequently. The Grenadiers of the Queen's troop had green loops, with yellow tufts, and those of the Duke's troop yellow loops, in accordance with the colours of the carbine-belts, &c., by which the three troops were distinguished, as already stated.

In the first year of the reign of James II. we at length obtain a full and particular account of "the splendid appearance of the first troop of Guards" at the coronation of the king and queen, 23rd April, 1685. "The officers of the first troop are richly habited, *either* in coats of *crimson velvet* embroidered with gold and silver, *or of fine scarlet cloth* embroidered or laced with gold and silver, both intermixed. They wear scarfes about their waistes, *either* of gold and silver network, *or* of crimson taffata richly fringed with gold and silver on the edges, and with a deep fringe of the same at the ends. Their cloaks are also of fine scarlet cloth embroidered on the cape and down before with gold and silver, both intermixed. In their hats they wear tours[1] of white feathers. The housses and holster-caps being of crimson velvet, are richly embroidered and embossed with gold and silver; and the manes, cruppers, and tails of their horses are garnished with large knots of broad blue taffata ribband. The gentlemen of this troop are cloathed in coats and cloaks of scarlet cloth lined with blue shalloon. The facings of their sleeves, of the same stuff, are laced about with a figured galloon of silver edged with gold, two inches broad. Their buttons are of silver plate. They are accustomed to have each of them a good buff-coat and a large pair of gantlet gloves of the same; and in their hats (which are black and turned up on one side and edged with a broad silver lace) they wear large blue knots of broad taffata ribband (blue being the distinguishing colour of their troop), and the heads of their horses are adorned with knots of the same ribband. They have their housses and holster-caps of scarlet cloth, embroidered with the king's cypher and crown, with a border of foliage." The writer prefaces this description with a notice of his intention of omitting those of the other troops—"they being in manner the same, except as to the distinguishing colour of each troop; that of the first troop being blue, that of the second green, and that of the third yellow." [2]

Some additional particulars are to be gleaned from Sandford's 'Account of the Coronation of James II.' (folio, London, 1685). The first troop of Horse Grenadiers had coats of fine red cloth, lined and faced with blue shalloon and buttoned with white metal; on breast, arms, and facings of sleeves, loops of fine blue worsted, edged and tufted with black and white. "The crowns of their caps were raised high to a point, falling back at the top in form of a *capuoch* (capuchon ?), which were turned up before and behind triangular, and faced with blue plush; and on the back of the crowns a roundell or granado ball of the same"—*i.e.*, of blue plush, as it is alluded to in the former account.

The officers appear to have worn "black hats laced about with silver and adorned with knots of blue ribbands." The second and third troops were similarly clothed, distinguished only by the colours of their ribbons, as aforesaid.

Of the Foot Guards, we learn from the same source that the officers of the 1st Regiment were attired, "some in coats of cloth of gold, others in crimson velvet embroidered with gold or silver, but most of them in fine scarlet cloth, buttoned down the breast, and on the facings of the sleeves with silver plate, scarfs, &c." The captains wore corslets or gorgets of silver, double gilt; the lieutenants, corslets of steel, polished and sanguished (*i.e.*, tinted red, *sanguined*), and studded with nails of gold; ensigns, corslets of silver plate. "The private soldiers all wore coats of red broadcloth, lined and faced with blue; blue breeches and stockings; hats laced with silver and decorated with blue ribbands."

Pikemen wore sashes or scarfs of white worsted fringed with blue. The caps of the Grenadiers were of red cloth lined with blue shalloon and laced with silver; on the frontlets, very high, the king's cypher and crown.

The 2nd Regiment like the 1st, only *gold* embroidery, lace, and fringe, instead of *silver*; and the breeches and stockings of the private soldiers blue instead of red.

---

[1] Feathers lying flat around (*autour*) the brim.   [2] ' Historical Records of Life Guards,' p. 73.

In 1693 we learn from an original contract made in that year between Lord Castleton and Mr. Francis Molineaux, a clothier, that the coats and breeches of the soldiers and sergeants in an infantry regiment were at that time made of grey cloth, the coats of the drummers being purple and their breeches grey. The latter also wore badges. (MS. Harleian Coll., Brit. Mus., No. 6844. Grose, 'Mil. Antiq.' vol. i. p. 329.)

In 1699 King William III. made great alterations in the uniforms of his three English troops of Life Guards: the lace on the coats, which had for several years past been silver edged with gold, was now ordered to be gold lace only. The feathers worn in the hats of the private gentlemen had been discontinued more than twenty years; but the king commanded the whole to resume wearing feathers in their hats—the first troop to have scarlet feathers, the second white, and the third green; and 'The Post Boy' of 11th November in the above year, describing a review by the king in Hyde Park, so describes them.

It will be observed that no mention is made of cuirasses, the private gentlemen being only ordered to wear buff-coats, while the officers are allowed to dress in crimson velvet or scarlet cloth at their pleasure. Other cavalry regiments are recorded to have worn cuirasses as late as 1688. In that year the 3rd Horse or 2nd Dragoon Guards being ordered to Salisbury, on the news of the landing of the Prince of Orange at Torr Bay, deposited their defensive armour in the Tower before leaving London, the king giving the officers permission to continue to wear their cuirasses if they chose to do so.[1] The same option may have been accorded to the officers of the Life Guards.

It must be obvious that the limits of this volume will not allow of similar extended notices of all the regiments in our service. The above has been given as an illustration of the progress of uniform, and a sample of the information attainable by the reader who will consult the works above quoted.

The precise time when that valuable force, the Marines, was first incorporated, has not, I believe, been ascertained, but the oldest corps of the kind discovered by Grose is entered in the list of the army for the year 1684. It there appears as "the Lord High Admiral of England, his Royal Highness the Duke of York and Albany's maritime regiment of foot, commanded by the Honourable Sir Charles Littleton, called also the Admiral Regiment." It then consisted of twelve companies without grenadiers. The men were clothed in *yellow* coats lined with red; their colours were a red cross with rays of the sun issuing from each of its angles. Upon this I may remark that yellow was the Duke of York's livery colour, and was selected no doubt to distinguish his own regiment of infantry, as it did his own troop of Life Guards (see page 282). In the reign of James I. the order of Queen Elizabeth that commanders in the Navy should wear scarlet was confirmed, but does not appear to have been much attended to. In 1677, we find from Wycherley's comedy of 'The Plain Dealer,' that red breeches were the mark of a sailor.

Of the Yeomen Guard I give examples from the coronation processions of Charles II., in 1661, and of James II., in 1685.

Of the Gentlemen-pensioners, now Gentlemen-at-arms, and the Yeomen of the Guard in the time of Charles II. and James II., the engravings of their respective coronations, in the works of Ogilby and Sandford, present us with trustworthy delineations. Those of the yeomen are especially valuable to us, as the popular idea is that the guard of to-day are attired in the fashion of the sixteenth century, and are facsimile representations of their predecessors in the reigns of Henry VIII. and Queen Elizabeth.

Our illustrations at pp. 168 and 180 may have partially dissipated this illusion. Our readers will perceive, by comparing the subjoined figures with the preceding, that as late as the end of the seventeenth century their uniform partook of the fashion of the time, and that the long coats worn by them at present were not known even in the reign of James II.

I must now proceed to notice the military equipment of other European nations in the seventeenth century.

To begin with France. The disuse of armour, which commenced in the reign of Henri Quatre, the contemporary of our Elizabeth and James, continued at the same gradual pace on each side of the

[1] War Office.

Channel. The French army was remodelled. The companies of halbardiers were disbanded, and the infantry consisted of pikemen, musketeers, and harquebusiers. The pikemen retained for some time

Yeoman of the Guard. 1661.

Yeoman of the Guard. 1685.

Gentleman Pensioner. 1661.

Gentleman Pensioner. 1685.

Fifer in Coronation Procession of James II.

their usual armour. The others were clothed in the ordinary dress of the day, the musketeers wearing hats, and the harquebusiers morions (see Dictionary, pp. 20, 375, 376).

The cavalry consisted of cuirassiers (*gens d'armes*), having a company of lancers at the head of each squadron, the weapons of the main body being pistols and swords, the latter now assuming the shape of the modern cavalry sabre, carabineers, and mounted harquebusiers. Piece by piece, as in England, armour of plate disappeared, and the gorget alone was worn by officers over a buff-coat.

Buffalo leather was, however, an expensive article at the beginning of the seventeenth century, and for some twenty years it could only be obtained from Germany.

About 1630 a citizen of Nérac acquired a reputation for making buff-coats which were pike- and sword-proof, and shortly afterwards coats were made at Niort and Poitiers of calf and sheep skin, at of course much less price, but not greatly inferior.

Towards the end of the reign of Louis XIII. a sort of cassock or loose coat, called a *hongreline*, of Hungarian origin, was introduced into the army. A jacket of the same name had for some time past been worn by women as well as men of the middle class. The vestment now so called was buttoned down the front, and cut round about the hips. The hongreline and buff-coat enabled the officers to dispense with the cuirass. The king, who had long objected to its disuse, at length gave way, and the gorget alone was worn by officers of the infantry; but he rigidly insisted on the cavalry, which in 1655 was first formed into regiments, being armed with all pieces—casque, hausse-col, cuirass, brassarts, and tassets to the knees—under pain of degradation.

The famous corps of King's Musketeers, who served on foot and on horseback and formed the body-guard of the sovereign on all

French Infantry, temp. Louis XIII.

occasions, was first formed in 1622. They had been previously carbineers, but now had their carbines exchanged for muskets, and apparently were privileged at the same time to lay aside the casque and the cuirass, and substitute for them the plumed hat and peculiar cassock by which they were specially distinguished. This cassock, as it was called, is represented in engravings of the time as a tabard. (See engraving in the next page.) It was made of blue velvet with a silver cross having gold flames issuing from each angle, embroidered on the front, back, and sleeves.

To Père Daniel we are indebted for minute information respecting the alterations in the uniform of this celebrated corps, divided in 1665 into two companies, distinguished by the colour of their horses as "Mousquetaires *gris*" and "Mousquetaires *noir*."

For some time after the re-establishment of the first company, in 1657, the cassock was the only distinctive portion of their equipment (*habit d'ordonnance*). The rest of their attire was left to their own fancy, or rather to that of the king, who, when he desired to make a grand display at some review or particular State ceremony, issued instructions on the subject. On one occasion they were ordered to wear buff-coats, and the richest amongst them had their sleeves lavishly embroidered with diamonds. Another time he commanded them to appear in black velvet. On the formation of the second company, in 1665, each troop had its particular uniform, whatever that might be; but after the siege of Maestricht, in 1673, the king ordered that both companies should wear the same, with the exception of the lace, which for the first company was to be all gold, and for the second gold and silver mixed. In 1677 their coats were scarlet, and so continued. Their cassocks were very short and barely descended to the croup of the saddle, in 1660, when some magnificent ones were made

for the entry of the king into Paris after his marriage. Subsequently, on being sent to the wars, the cassocks were lengthened so as to reach to the knees. They were embroidered with four crosses—one in front and one behind, and one on each sleeve; the one in front being divided by the opening of the cassock.

Mousquetaires du Roi and Swiss Halberdier. 1657

In 1688 the cassocks were exchanged for surcoats (*soubrevestes*), which are described as being like "*juste-au-corps sans manches.*" They were blue and laced, like the cassocks, and had one cross in front and another behind of white velvet edged with silver lace, the fleurs-de-lys in the angles of the crosses[1] being of the same, the front and back of the surcoat being attached to each other at the sides by hooks or clasps.

The only difference between the surcoats of the first and second companies was in the embroidery of the cross, the flames issuing from the angles being red and three in number for the first company, and for the second *feuille-morte* and five in number. The hats of the first company were laced with gold, and those of the second with silver. Originally the mousquetaires wore the stiff heavy boots of the ordinary cavalry, but in 1683 calf-skin turnover boots with fixed spurs were substituted for them; and these, being considered ungraceful, were subsequently exchanged for a lighter sort of an improved shape, and easier to march in.

M. Quicherat has engraved for illustration of his description of the mousquetaires a cut from a print which he dates 1637 (I presume a typographical error), representing the mousquetaires in their tabard-like cassocks, as described by Père Daniel in 1657. The latter writer has left us the figure of a mousquetaire in the surcoat which superseded the cassock. The latest alteration of the uniform will be found in the next chapter.

The equally celebrated body-guard, Les Cents Suisses, dates from 1616, according to Bassompière, who states in his journal that it was formed at Tours by Louis XIII, on his return from his journey to Guienne, and that it first mounted guard at the king's lodgings there on Thursday, 12th of March in that year (see woodcut above of a Cent Suisse in the costume worn by that corps in 1657).

Dragoons and Hussars were added during this reign to the French forces: the former wore long

[1] This is inaccurately expressed. The fleurs-de-lys were not "aux *angles* de la croix," heraldically speaking. The cross itself was "fleur de lisée" (see woodcut).

Officer of Infantry. 1680.   Garde du Corps. 1687.   Mousquetaire du Roi. 1688.

leather gaiters and a conical cap, the point of which hung down almost to the shoulder, with a bourrelet round the forehead in form of a turban or turned up with fur. The predominant colours were yellow, green, and red. The hussars, of Hungarian origin, were at first attired in a sort of Turkish costume. Their heads were shaved, leaving only a single tuft of hair on the crown of the

Hussar.   Dragoon.

Troop. Louis XIV.

skull. They wore a fur cap with a cock's feather in it, a tight jacket and large loose trousers and boots, with a tiger-skin on their shoulders, which they shifted from one side to the other according to the way of the wind. Above are engravings from drawings and prints of the period.

Both in Spain and Italy armour was retained longer than in France and England.

A portrait, said to be that of Philip V., by a pupil of Velasquez, formerly in the possession of John Auldjo, Esq., Noel House, Kensington, presents us with a highly characteristic costume of a young Spanish officer of distinction. He wears a corslet, short tassets, and pauldrons, all gilt and engraved; brown leather boots, with lace ruffled boot-hose; a hat laden with feathers, the brim turned up all round and fastened by a jewelled ornament; a scarf over the left shoulder, and the Order of the Golden Fleece appended to a simple gold chain.

Nearly half a century later we find the Portuguese general, Matthias de Albuquerque, represented

Philip V., from an original portrait.   Matthias de Albuquerque. 1646.   Count Pappenheim. 1630.

in armour which we might attribute to the middle of the sixteenth century. Mr. Hewitt has given an engraving of him from his portrait in the 'Livro do Estado da India Oriental,' dated 1646, of which I annex a copy.

Hollar's engraving of the portrait of Count Pappenheim, the celebrated Imperial general, slain at Lützen in 1632, furnishes us with an example of the military equipment of an officer in Germany at that period, where, as in France and England, the gorget was the only piece of defensive plate armour retained by the generality of commanders.

Turner, in his 'Pallas Armata,' 1670, says, "In former times a captain marched at the head of his company with a head-piece, a corslet, and a gorge, all high proof, and so did the lieutenant in the rear. But now you may travel over many places of Christendom before you see many of those captains or lieutenants. The difference of the armour was none but that the captain's helmet was decorated with a plume of feathers, the lieutenant's not. The feathers you may peradventure yet find, but the head-piece for the most part is laid aside."

No particular alteration is observable in the military equipment of the Hungarians, Poles, or Russians during the seventeenth century. In the Museum at Dresden there is preserved a casque of imbricated scales in polished steel, with a movable nose-guard, cheek-pieces, and a circular plate at the back to protect the neck, curiously similar to those attached to the helmets of the early part of the sixteenth century, on which I have commented in the Dictionary, p. 85. The socket for the feather and several other parts are in copper gilt, and it is said to have been worn by John Sobieski, king of Poland, before Vienna in 1683 (fig. 1). In the same collection is one of the casques worn

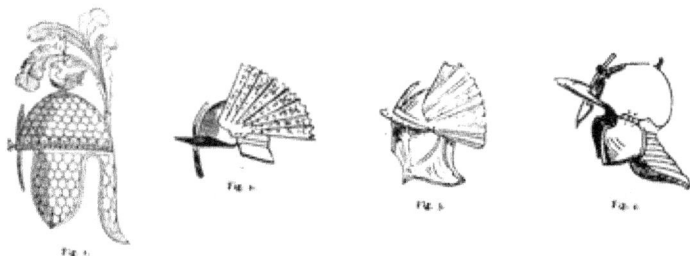

Fig. 1.   Fig. 2.   Fig. 3.   Fig. 4.

by the *Jazala Skrzydlata*, or "Winged cavalry" of the Polish army of Sobieski, so called from the wings or fans on the sides of their head-pieces (fig. 2). Another is in the Tsarskoe-Selo Museum at St. Petersburg (fig. 3); and fig. 4 is an Hungarian lobster-tailed helmet called *Dschycksc*, from the Royal Arsenal at Turin, of the same date.

Concerning orders of knighthood, I have first to mention the changes that took place in the robes and decorations of that of the Garter during the seventeenth century. The hat worn by the knights retained the higher crown it had assumed in the reign of Elizabeth; but in the tenth year of the reign of James I. ostrich feathers, which had been for some time neglected (perhaps in favour of the jewelled hat-band, which is frequently seen at that time unaccompanied by a plume), were re-introduced.

By the kindness of Mr. Harold Dillon I am enabled to present my readers with an engraving of a portrait of Prince Charles, second son of

Charles, Prince of Wales. 1611.

Jewel and band of Hat.

James I. (and ultimately king), as a Knight of the Garter (to which order he was elected in 1611), from the original picture in Lord Dillon's possession at Ditchley. The hat is a most interesting object, as in front of the feathers (which are worn on the right side of the hat, and not in front as subsequently) is an elaborate ornament, consisting of two sprays supporting a ship, all in (apparently) garnets. The hat-band is formed of large pear-shaped pearls, set upright.

In addition to the figure I give a cut from a tracing of the hat-band and jewel.

The ribbon also to which the lesser George was appended round the neck was changed from black to blue. One of sky colour is ordered in the twentieth year of the reign of James I. (Ashmole's Hist. of the Order).

Some variation appears to have been made in the colour of the mantle of foreign princes elected Knights of the Garter. The mantle sent to Frederick, duke of Würtemburg, by James I. in 1607, was "of a mixed colour; to wit, purple and violet." Charles I., in the twelfth year of his reign, determined to restore the mantle of the order to its original colour, and it was accordingly worn on the installation of the Prince of Wales of a rich *celestial* blue; the surcoat and humerale remained crimson; the hat was of black velvet, with the plume of white ostrich feathers as before. As early as the second year of his reign he had directed that the badge of the order (the cross of St. George surrounded by the garter) should be worn by the knights on their daily dresses, and in 1629 it was formed into a star by the addition of rays at first of a wavy or flamboyant character, and subsequently straight, as at present.

In the reign of Charles II. the costume of the order became, with the exception of the lighter colour of the blue, exactly what it is at this day; for in the chapter held 1st April, 1661, "The

Henry, Prince of Wales, as Knight of the Bath.

sovereign and knights, thinking it fit there should be some under habit as well as outer habit of the order, appointed for the under habit a cloth of silver doublet or vest and trunk hose, from that time to be constantly used" (Existing Statutes, p. 35): the black velvet hat, with its mass of tall white ostrich feathers, in the midst of which was inserted a heron's plume, and the ribbon worn over the left shoulder and brought under the right arm, where the jewel or lesser George hangs, being introduced in their present form shortly before the publication of Ashmole's History of the Order in 1685. Mrs. Jamieson records the following anecdote respecting the lesser George. Shortly after the young Duke of Richmond, son of Charles II. by the Duchess of Portsmouth, was installed Knight of the Garter, he was introduced to the king with the ribbon so arranged, and his Majesty was so pleased with the alteration that he commanded it to be adopted in future. It is probable that the duchess had seen the portrait of Charles I. by Vandyke, and had taken a hint from it. The first knight formally so invested with the ribbon was Henry, duke of Norfolk, by James II., 6th May, 1685.[1]

James I. is stated to have revived or newly instituted the Order of the Bath at or immediately after his coronation; and Sir George Buck, in his 'Eclog treating of Crownes and Garlandes, and to whom of right they appertaine,' printed in 1605, undoubtedly testified in a marginal note to the existence of a device or badge of King James of three crowns, with the motto "Tria juncta in uno." Manerius also, whose work was published in 1613, says that the Knights of the Bath wore as their badge three golden crowns within a golden circle, and this inscription round it, "Tria in unum" ("tres aureas coronas in orbicello aurea expressas addita hac circumscriptione, Tria in unum"). Favine likewise, in 1619, says that the Knights of the Bath were also called Knights of the Crowns, because, to distinguish them from esquires, "they wear upon their left shoulders an escutcheon of *black* silk, with three crowns of *gold* embroidered thereon."

[1] 'London Gazette,' No. 2032.

The badges or jewels of that date which have descended to us flatly contradict these assertions, as will be shown in the following chapter. In the meanwhile I am enabled to illustrate this portion of my work by an engraving of a portrait of Henry, Prince of Wales, as a Knight of the Bath, from the original at Ditchley. (See preceding page.)

In 1611, Christian IV., king of Denmark, added to the Order of the Elephant the Order of the Arm in Armour (" Le bras armé "), in commemoration of the defeat of the Swedes at Colmar, 3rd December. Annexed is the portrait of one of the first knights, and also an engraving of the decoration, from the work of Bercherode, published in 1704, and quoted under COLLAR in Dictionary, p. 124.

In 1671, Christian V., king of Denmark, founded the Order of the Danebrog, of which an account will be found, with an engraving of the collar, at p. 125 in the Dictionary. The same king added a star to the Order of the Elephant, and annexed is the portrait of him in the robes of the order from the print in Bercherode's work aforesaid. The star resembles that of the Garter, and the under-dress of white silk and satin seems to have been copied from that of the Knights of the Garter at that period. The mantle is of crimson velvet lined with white satin, the

Knight of the Order of the Arm in Armour. 1611.

Decoration of the Arm in Armour.

Christian V., king of Denmark.

Knight of the Order of the Danebrog. 1697.

2 P 2

train two yards long, cords and tassels of silver and red silk; hat, black velvet, with two rows of ostrich feathers. A black heron plume is the only distinction of the sovereign, but it is not distinguishable in the engraving.

In a work published at Amsterdam in 1697, containing a history of all the orders of knighthood and engravings of the knights in the habits of their orders,[1] there is a representation of a Knight of the Danebrog, which may be fairly considered a contemporary authority. (See engraving in preceding page.) In Schoonebeck's engraving it will be observed that on the mantle is embroidered a wreath of laurel, within which some words are indicated. These appear from the text to be "Pietate et Justitia."

The Order of St. Louis was instituted in France by Louis XIV. in 1693. The decoration consisted of a gold cross of eight points, intersected by fleurs-de-lys, having the full-length figure of St. Louis in the centre, and worn by the Knights Grand Cross appended to a broad red ribbon over the right shoulder, and passing under the left arm, a similar cross being embroidered on the coat and cloak or mantle. Knights Commanders wore the cross and ribbon *en kharpe* only, and Knights Companions the cross attached to a small piece of ribbon, *couleur de feu*, on the breast. There were no robes, strictly speaking, of the order; but, on occasions of ceremony, the Grand Crosses, Commanders, and great officers wore black velvet or silk coats, with gold buttons and button-

Knight of the Order of St. Louis. 1697.

holes, lined with some material, *couleur de feu*, and cloaks of black velvet or silk with similar linings.[2] In the Dutch work, however, before mentioned, there is an engraving of a Knight of St. Louis in a mantle embroidered with fleurs-de-lys. If meant for the king himself, as Grand Master of the order, it may be only the royal mantle, which was of violet velvet, the fleurs-de-lys gold. The hat and under-dress, periwig, and cravat, are characteristic of the costume of the period. (See engraving above.)

The Order of St. Andrew in Russia, founded by the Tzar Peter Alexiowitz ("Peter the Great") in 1698, has been already noticed, and the collar engraved

Jewel and Collar of the Order of the Amaranth.

in the Dictionary, page 126. The badge or jewel of the order is appended to a sky-blue riband worn over the right shoulder. The habit consists of a sky-blue surcoat and a scarlet mantle, richly embroidered with gold.[3]

In addition to these may be named the Order of the Amaranth in Sweden, founded by Queen Christina in 1645, and

Knight of the Order of the Amaranth. 1697.

[1] 'Historie van alle Ridderlyke in Kryge Orders.' Adriaan Schoonebeck. Amsterdam, 1697.
[2] Hermant, 'Histoire des Ordres militaires et des Ordres de Chevalier.' 2 tomes. Rouen, 1726.
[3] Hanson. See next chapter.

noticeable more on account of the eccentricity of the foundress, who assumed the name of Amarantha at one of her Court entertainments, than for any celebrity connected with it. The collar was composed of interlinked letters A and small escutcheons, to which was appended a wreath of laurel, entwined by a band inscribed with the motto "Dolce nella speranza," and encircling two letters A, of gold set with diamonds, interlinked as in the collar. By a small chain attached to the collar on the right side appears suspended the figure of a horse, but I find no mention of such an addition in any history of the order.

From the work published at Amsterdam in 1697, I give an engraving of the decoration, and also of a knight in the habit of the order, as it affords a good example of the costume in Sweden in the latter half of the seventeenth century.

It will be sufficient to name the Order of "Concord," founded by Christian Ernest, Margrave of Brandenburg, in 1660; the Order of "Ladies slaves to Virtue," at Vienna, for ladies of noble birth, founded by the Empress Eleanora in 1662; of "the Starry Cross," by the same Empress, in 1668; and of "Generosity" by Frederick III., Elector of Brandenburg, afterwards King of Prussia, in 1685.

Venice, though a republic, had its orders of knighthood, which were existing in the seventeenth century, at whatever date they might have been instituted.

1. The Order of St. Mark, of which the Doge for the time being was Grand Master, and was strictly limited to men who had rendered signal services to the State. The decoration consisted only of a gold cross charged with the arms of Venice, the winged lion of St. Mark holding an open copy of the Gospels, with the motto, "Pax tibi Marce Evangelista meus," and which was worn attached to the vest in front.

2. The Order of the Golden Stole, conferred only upon noblemen who had been ambassadors to an emperor or a king. Envoys to sovereign dukes or princes were not eligible. These "Cavalieri

Knight of the Golden Stole in Venice. 1697.

Knight of St. James in Portugal. 1697.

della Stola d'Oro" were distinguished by wearing a stole of black velvet with a gold border over their left shoulder on ordinary occasions, but of cloth of gold in grand ceremonies or on grand fête days. They were also permitted to wear a red under-dress by an *ordonnance* promulgated in 1636. Above is an engraving of one of these knights from Schoonebeck's work before mentioned. Vecellio gives the "stola di brocato d'oro" and the red under-dress to all the "senatori & cavallieri della città de Venetia" without exception. It is not specially mentioned by Coryat, Evelyn, or Howell; but seems by an engraving in Hermant's work to be distinguished by having tassels at the four corners.

Knight of Calatrava. 1697.

Knight of Alcantara. 1697.

Schoonebeck's work, as I have already stated, affords us representations of the knights of several of the orders I have recorded in the habits of their orders as they appeared at the time of its

Neapolitan Knight of Malta.

Lutheran Minister.

Russian Imperial and Ecclesiastical Costume

publication, and which are extremely valuable as contemporaneous examples of the costume of the different countries to which they appertain. To those already given I therefore add copies of the knights of Calatrava and Alcantara in Spain, and of St. James in Portugal.

In 1687 James II. of England and VII. of Scotland "revived and restored," as he phrased it, an imaginary Order of St. Andrew or of the Thistle, but the letters patent never passed the Great Seal; and though eight knights were made and invested, the Revolution and the abdication of the king, a few months afterwards, stifled the order in its birth, and its institution is generally ascribed to Queen Anne in 1703. (See following chapter.)

No alteration of consequence is noticeable in the costume of the Roman or Reformed clergy of the Church of England during the seventeenth century—that is to say, in their officiating vestments; but Archbishop Tillotson is the first prelate represented in a wig. It is, however, of moderate dimensions, and not much unlike a natural head of hair.

The figure of a Nonconformist (Calvinist) minister of the time of Charles II., from a print by Pierre Tempest, is given in the preceding page. The dress of a Puritan minister is given in our chromo-lithograph of Lacy, the actor, in three characters.

The habit of a Lutheran minister of Frankfort, "saluant du chapeau et de la calotte," is copied from a drawing "fait après nature," by B. Picart.

A flood of authentic information respecting the vestments of the Greek Church at this period has been recently made accessible to us by the publication of the superb work already so frequently referred to in these pages, 'Antiquités de l'Empire de Russie.'

Amongst the many magnificent illustrations contained in it may be enumerated the mitre of Job, the first Patriarch of Russia (engraved at p. 219 of this volume); the mitres given by the Tzar

Cowl of the Patriarch Nikon.

Back View.

Alexis to the Patriarch Nikon in 1652 and 1653; the cowls or capuchons of the Patriarchs Nikon and Philarete; the rich collar of the latter and the habitual dress of the former dignitary; the capuchon of Basile, Bishop of Novgorod; the bonnet of Bishop Nicetas, and those of the Archbishops of Novgorod.

Subjoined are the figures of St. Sampson, St. Methodius, and St. Germanus. The first wears the phænolion over the sticharion or white tunic; the ends of the peritrachelion or stole are visible beneath it. St. Methodius is represented in the polystaurion, differing from the plain phænolion by

St. Sampson.   St. Methodius.   St. Germanus.

being embroidered all over with crosses. Over it he wears the omophorium (the pallium of the Roman Church), and on the right side hangs the genuale, a lozenge-shaped satchel or pocket, of which the use is not clearly described, but it is the distinctive ornament of Patriarchs or Metropolitans.

A Greek deacon.   Patriarch Bekkos, in his walking-dress.

The sticharion or alb of St. Germanus is distinguished by the stripes proper to a bishop. He wears the sakkos in place of the ordinary phænolion, marking his dignity as a metropolitan.

Goar, in his 'Enchologion,' has given a representation of the Patriarch Bekkos in his walking dress. Mr. Marriott, who has copied it on his LIX. Plate, says, "He wears on his head the outer and the inner καμηλαύχιον, and in his left hand carries a broad-leafed hat (the καπάσιον, also known as καπέλλος), the strings of which are seen pendent below it. The long-sleeved coat, worn as a body dress, corresponds to the cassock of an English clergyman. The outer garment is the mandyas, with its three stripes (ποταμοί). In his right hand he holds the δικανίκιον, or ῥάββος, the pastoral staff, which has a head the reverse of the *tau*, or crutch-head of the staff, seen in the hands of the earliest Christian bishops. His hat has also a cruciform decoration of the type in heraldry termed *Moline*." (See Dictionary, page 154, for figure of Patriarch of Constantinople, 1590, from the work of Bertelli, whose authority in this case I am inclined to doubt.)

Judicial and official costume in England during the latter half of the seventeenth century is amply illustrated by the prints of the processions of Charles II., James II., and William and Mary, to their several coronations. Some examples have already been given from them in the Dictionary,

Sir John Scarborough.

under the article ROBE, at page 429. Annexed is an engraving of the portrait of Sir John Scarborough, physician to King Charles II., and in his gown as Doctor of Medicine. He is represented wearing a bonnet of a form fashionable in the reign of Elizabeth, and not the square cap appropriated to men of his degree in their academical costume.

CHAPTER IX.

THE EIGHTEENTH CENTURY.

E now enter the last section of our history ; the period comprising the latter years of the reign of William III., the reigns of Queen Anne and of the first two Georges, in England, and of their contemporaries, more or less illustrious or notorious. Peter the Great of Russia and Charles XII. of Sweden, the Empresses Catherine and Elizabeth of Russia, and the brave and beloved Maria Theresa of Austria, " King" of the Hungarians, are all personages of importance in the annals of Europe, and their names are " familiar in our mouths as household words," however opinions may vary in the estimation of their characters. Picturesque costume had, however, died out in the last century as far as the courts and cities of Europe were concerned. In the provinces it was cherished and transmitted from generation to generation for upwards of a hundred years, and even within my recollection much of what is popularly termed National costume distinguished the peasantry of one canton, district, or department from the other. During the last fifty years, however, it has been rapidly disappearing. The influence of fashion has actually begun to be felt in the hitherto unchangeable habits of the East. The blue frock-coat is ousting the caftan from Constantinople and Cairo, and it has been confidently reported in Paris that a recently-accredited Ambassador from the Sublime Porte to the French Republic has been seen in that most odious invention, a chimney-pot hat.

The last two years of the reign of William III. are remarkable for nothing in the history of costume but increase in the size of the wigs and the amplitude of the sleeves of the men, and the disappearance of the *commode* or *tower* from the heads of the ladies. With the accession of Queen Anne, in 1702, vanished every relic of our chivalric costume except the sword, which still accompanies the full dress of the Court of St. James's. Square-cut coats and long-flapped waistcoats, the latter meeting the stockings still drawn up over the knee, so high as to entirely conceal the breeches, but gartered below it ; large hanging cuffs and lace ruffles ; the skirts of the coats stiffened out with wire or buckram, from between which peeped the hilt of the sword, deprived of the broad and splendid belt in which it swung in preceding reigns ; blue or scarlet silk stockings with gold or silver clocks ; lace neckcloths ; square-toed, short-quartered shoes, and high red heels and small buckles ; very long and formally curled perukes, black riding-wigs, bag-wigs, and nightcap-wigs ; small three-cornered hats, laced with gold or silver galloon, and sometimes trimmed with feathers,—composed the habit of the noblemen and gentlemen during the reigns of Queen Anne and George I.[1]

Minuter fashions were of course continually arising and disappearing, adopted and named after some leader of the *ton* or in commemoration of some public event, such as the famous battle of Ramilies, which gave a name to a wig and a tail ; but for all the items in the inventory of a gentleman's wardrobe of the first half of the last century, I must refer the reader to the notices of the articles themselves under their separate heads in the Dictionary, and to the accompanying plates and woodcuts for a general view of the subject.

[1] ' History of British Costume.' 12mo. 3rd edit., 1874.

The same advice must be given respecting the dress of the ladies during the same period. Under the headings of CAP, GOWN, HAIR, HEAD-DRESS, HOOP, PETTICOAT, SHOE, &c., information will be found which it is needless to repeat in this portion of the work, and to which I can make no important addition. The costume of France, which I shall have next to notice, will however, as usual, assist in the illustration not only of our own, but of all the principal countries of Europe, and our old friend Malcolm has gathered some particulars respecting the costume in the time of George II. The following descriptions of the dresses worn by the Royal Family and the nobility on the occasion of the marriage of H.R.H. Frederick, Prince of Wales, father of his Majesty King George III., in 1736, are extracted from Read's 'Weekly Journal,' of May 1 of that year.

"When her Royal Highness the Princess" (Augusta, youngest daughter of Frederick II., Duke of Saxe-Gotha), "came to St. James's, she was dressed in a suit of rich silk, deep ground, trimmed with gold and embroidered with green, scarlet, and purple flowers. . . . . Between six and seven o'clock her Highness, dressed in her wedding-clothes, which were of silver-tissue and silk over white, with her hair curled and stuck with jewels, after the German fashion, was presented to her Majesty, who presented her to the Prince, whose clothes were of silver-tissue, with white stockings and shoes."

"His Majesty (George II.) was dressed in a gold brocade, turned up with silk, embroidered with large flowers in silver and colours, as was the waistcoat; the buttons and star were diamonds. Her Majesty (Queen Caroline) was in a plain yellow silk, robed and laced with pearls, diamonds, and other jewels of immense value."

"The Dukes of Grafton, Newcastle, and St. Albans, the Earl of Albemarle, Lord Hervey, Colonel Pelham, and many other noblemen, were in gold brocades of £300 to £500 the suit. The Duke of Marlborough was in a white velvet and gold brocade, upon which was an exceeding rich *point d'Espagne*. The Earl of Euston and many others were in cloths flowered or sprigged with gold; the Duke of Montague in a gold-brocaded tissue. The waistcoats were universally brocades with large flowers."

The writer adds, and it would be unpatriotic to omit the information: "It is assured that most of the rich cloths were the manufacture of England, and it must be acknowledged in honour of our own artists, that the few which were French did not come up to these in richness, goodness, or fancy, as may be seen by those of the Royal Family, which are all of the British manufacture."

"The ladies were principally in brocades of gold and silver, with large flowers, and wore their sleeves much lower than had been done for some time."

"On the Wednesday following, at noon, there was the greatest appearance of the nobility, quality, and gentry at Court that has been known in the memory of man, to congratulate their Royal Highnesses on their nuptials."

"The ladies were variously dressed, though with all the richness and grandeur imaginable; many of them had their heads dressed English, of fine Brussels' lace of exceeding rich patterns, made up on narrow wires and small round rolls, and the hair pinned to large puff-caps, and but a few without powder; some few had their hair curled down on the sides; pink and silver, white and gold, were the general knots worn. There was a vast number in Dutch heads, their hair curled down in short curls on the sides and behind, and some had their hair in large ringlets behind, all very much powdered, with ribbands frilled on their heads, variously disposed; and some had diamonds set on ribbands on their heads; laced tippets were pretty general, and some had ribbands between the frills; treble-laced ruffles were universally worn, though abundance had them not tacked up. Their gowns were either gold stuffs or rich silks, with gold or silver flowers, or pink or white silks, with either gold or silver nets or trimmings; the sleeves to the gowns were middling (not so short as formerly), and wide, and their facings and robings broad; several had flounced sleeves and petticoats, and gold or silver fringe set on the flounces; some had stomachers of the same sort as the gown, others had large bunches of made flowers at their breasts; the gowns were variously pinned, but in general flat, the hoops French, and the petticoats of a moderate length, and a little sloped behind. The ladies were exceedingly brilliant likewise in jewels; some had them in their necklaces and ear-rings, others with diamond solitaires to pearl necklaces of three or four rows; some had necklaces of diamonds and pearls intermixed, but made up very broad; several had their gown-sleeves buttoned with diamonds, others had diamond sprigs in their hair, &c. The ladies' shoes were exceeding rich, being either pink, white, or green silk, with gold or silver lace braid all over, with low heels and low hind-quarters and low flaps, and abundance had large diamond shoe-buckles."

" The gentlemen's clothes were generally gold stuffs, flowered velvets, embroidered or trimmed with gold, or of cloth trimmed, the colours various. Their waistcoats were also exceeding rich silks, flowered with gold, of a large pattern, all open sleeves and longer than formerly, and the cuff broader; the clothes were longer-waisted than of late, and the plaits of the coat were made to stick out very much (in imitation of the ladies' hoops), and long.

" The wigs were of various sorts; the tyes higher foretops than formerly, and tied behind with a large flat tye; the bag-wigs, &c., as usual. White stockings were universally worn by the gentlemen as well as the ladies."

" The officers of the Horse and Foot Guards that mounted on Tuesday at St. James's, wore Ramilie periwigs by his Majesty's order."

From similar contemporary authorities I select the following notices of English costume during the first half of the last century, in chronological order, premising that isolated passages from some have already appeared under separate heads in the Dictionary.

Of female fashions, we find the following recorded as prevailing in the year 1700:—

Coloured gowns lined with striped silk, the bodice or stays sometimes made of silk, with black straps to fasten with buckles, and set with jewels or paste. Girdles fastened by buckles were also common. Holland petticoats, embroidered with coloured silks and gold, and with broad border of orrice at the bottom. Flanders laced hoods, double ruffles and tuckers, aprons of point or other lace, and black scarfs embroidered with gold.

1701-2. On the 1st of January in this year, an order was issued by the Earl Marshal, that in consequence of many mischiefs and dangerous accidents having happened and been occasioned by footmen wearing of swords, no footman for the future should wear any sword, hanger or *bayonet*, or other such like offensive weapon, during such time as they resided or were within the cities of London and Westminster, and the liberties and precincts of the same. ('Gazette' of that date.)

1703. A youth in the middle rank of life is advertised as being dressed in "a dark brown frieze coat, double-breasted on each side, with black buttons and button-holes, a light drugget waistcoat, red shag breeches with black stripes, and black stockings." Such a "get up" would be invaluable to a low comedian in a play of that period. Black silk facings to coats were worn by gentlemen, and the old fashion of patches was carried to great extravagance, and assumed for political party designation.

1709. The following articles of female attire were advertised as stolen, in 'The Postboy' of 15th November:—

" A black silk petticoat with a red and white calico border, cherry-coloured stays trimmed with blue and silver, a red and dove-coloured damask gown, flowered with large trees, a yellow satin apron trimmed with white Persian, and muslin head-cloths with crow's-foot edging; double ruffles with fine edging, a black silk furbelowed scarf, and a spotted hood."

Though an umbrella cannot strictly be called an article of costume, it has become as constant an out-of-door companion as a walking-stick; and as a notice of that familiar object is to be found in the Dictionary, an anecdote implying that in 1709 umbrellas were considered too effeminate to be carried by men, will not be thought out of place in the History.

'The Female Tatler' for 12th December in that year satirically says: " The young gentleman belonging to the Custom House, that for fear of rain borrowed the umbrella at Wills' Coffee House in Cornhill, of the *Mistress*, is hereby advertised that to be dry from head to foot on the like occasion, he shall be welcome to *the maid's pattens*."

1710. The extravagantly long wigs worn in this year were very expensive, costing from five to forty guineas. In 'The Tatler,' a satirical advertisement announces a stage-coach as departing from Nando's Coffee House for Mr. Tiptoe's Dancing School every evening, and adds :—" N.B. Dancing shoes *not exceeding four inches' height in the heel*, and periwigs *not exceeding three feet in length*, are carried in the coach-box *gratis*."

Ladies are censured for the extremely *décollété* character of their dress ; and fringed gloves, feathers in the hat, and pearl-coloured stockings are spoken of in connection with the fashionable gentleman of the period.

A lady's riding dress was advertised for sale in 1711, which is described as consisting of " a coat, waistcoat, petticoat, hat and feather," all " well laced with silver."

Another advertisement in 1712 mentions " an Isabelle-coloured *Kincob* gown, flowered with green and gold." Now, Isabella was a dun colour, as I have explained in the Dictionary, *sub voce ;* but *Kincob* is the name of the most magnificent cloth of gold, interwoven with coloured silk, that is known in India, and the principal place of its production is Benares. It is not quite clear whether this lost gown was actually made of that most costly Oriental material, or whether the name had been applied in England to an *inferior* manufacture resembling it. In the same advertisement occur the descriptions of Atlas and Allejah gowns and petticoats, which I have noticed under those names in the Dictionary, with the admission that I was unable to suggest the derivation of those terms. I am still in the dark respecting the "purple and gold" and "blue and gold" Atlas gowns and petticoats, and can only conjecture that the material was manufactured in the empire of Morocco, which is divided by the celebrated mountain chain of the Atlas, the goats in the neighbourhood of which are celebrated for the quality of their wool and also of their skin, from which is prepared the valuable leather known as Morocco.

Allejah alludes, I suspect, as much to the pattern as to the place from which the stuff was obtained. A similar word in the Turkish language signifies *striped*, and the particular garment in question is described as " an Allejah petticoat, *striped* with green, gold, and white." The recent disaster to the Turkish forces under Mukhtar Pasha in Armenia occurred on the Alledja-dagh, or " *Striped Mountain*."

The man of fashion in 1720 wore the full curled flowing wig, which fell in ringlets half-way down his arms and back ; a neckcloth tied tight round his neck ; a coat reaching to his ankles, laced, straight, formal, with buttons to the very bottom and several on the pockets and sleeves ; his shoes were square at the toes, had diminutive buckles, a monstrous flap on the instep, and high heels ; a belt secured the coat and supported the sword.

The ladies wore hooped petticoats, scarlet cloaks, and masks, when walking. The hoops were fair game for the wits, and they spared them not.

> " An elderly lady, whose bulky squat figure
> By hoop and white damask was rendered much bigger,
> Without hood and bare-neck'd to the Park did repair
> To show her new clothes and to take the fresh air.
> Her shape, her attire, raised a shout and loud laughter :
> Away waddles Madam, the mob hurries after.
> Quoth a wag, then observing the noisy crowd follow,
> ' As she came with a hoop, she is gone with a hollow.' "

The ' Flying Post ' of June 14, 1722, states that " the Bishop of Durham appeared on horseback at a review, in the King's train, in a lay habit of purple, with jack-boots, and his hat cocked, and a black wig tied behind him, like a military officer." This account is interesting, as it proves that the clergy, even down to this date, continued to defy public opinion as well as legal authority by their assumption of military and unseemly attire when not in the actual exercise of their sacred duties ; a practice which had provoked the censure and satire of the chroniclers and poets of the fourteenth century (*vide* page 91 *ante*). As early as 1343 a Constitution of Bishop Stratford recites that the clergy had apparelled themselves " like soldiers rather than clerks," and ordains that offenders should incur suspension or be disabled from obtaining a benefice for a certain period. In the Canons of 1603. it is ordained that, in private houses and in their studies, persons ecclesiastical may use any comely and scholar-like apparel provided it be not cut or *pincks* (slashed), and that in public "they go not in their doublet and hose without coats and cassocks, and that they wear not very light stockings."

In 1652, we have read of a Dean of Christchurch and Vice-Chancellor of Oxford disporting himself "*in querpo*, like a young scholar," with powdered hair, Spanish leather boots with lawn tops, and his hat most curiously cocked; and here, a century later, we find a bishop insulting his sovereign—as it would seem with impunity—by riding in his company in the dress of a trooper!

In 1727, the following description of a beau was published in a paper entitled 'Mist's Journal:'—

> "Take one of the brights from St. James's or Wright's,—
> 'Twill best be if nigh six feet he proves high;
> Then take of fine linen enough to wrap him in;
> Right Mecklin must twirl round his bosom and wrist;
> Red heels to his shoes, gold clocks to his hose,
> With calves *quantum suff.*—for a muff.
> In black velvet breeches let him put all his riches;
> Then cover his waist with a suit that's well laced.
> 'Tis best if he wears not more than ten hairs,
> To keep his brains cool on each side of his skull.[1]
> Let a queue be prepared twice as long as a yard,—
> Short measure, I mean; there is great odds between.
> This done, your beau place before a large glass.
> The recipe to fulfil, mix with powder pulvil,
> And then let it moulder away on his shoulder;
> Let a sword then be tied up to his left side,
> And under his arm place his hat for a charm;
> Then let him learn dancing, and to ride horses prancing,
> Italian and French, to drink and to wench:
> Oh, then with what wonder will he fill the *beau monde* here!"

The following description of the dress of a running footman in 1730 will be found perfectly illustrated by subsequent engravings in this and the next chapter:—"They wear fine holland drawers and waistcoats, thread stockings, a blue silk sash fringed with silver, a velvet cap with a great tassel, and carry a porter's staff with a large silver handle."

1731. An advertisement in the month of March this year furnishes us with information respecting several articles of female attire then in fashion, amongst which were a black velvet petticoat, a rose-coloured paduasoy mantua, lined with Mantua silk of the same colour; a suit of black paduasoy; a long velvet scarf lined with a shot-silk of pink and blue; a long velvet hood; a long silk hood, laced; two white short silk aprons, one embroidered with silk at the edges; one green silk apron, embroidered with silk and silver; three new muslin India half-handkerchiefs, spotted with plated silver; two gauze half-handkerchiefs, one brown embroidered with gold, silver and silk; a short crimson satin cloak, lined with white silk; a gold and silver girdle, with buckles set with Bristol stones.

1735. On his Majesty's birthday in this year, "The Queen was in a beautiful suit, made of silk of the produce of Georgia, and the same was universally acknowledged to excel that of any other country. The noblemen and gentlemen wore chiefly at Court brown flowered velvets, or dark cloth coats laced with gold or silver, or plain velvets of various colours, and breeches of the same; their waistcoats were either gold stuffs or rich flowered silks of a large pattern with a white ground; the make much the same as has been worn some time, only many had open sleeves to their coats.[2] Their tie-wigs were with large curls, setting forward and rising from the forehead, though not very high; the ties were thick and longer than of late, and both behind.[3] Some few had bag-wigs."

---

[1] I am at a loss to account for this allusion, unless it refers to the natural hair under the wig, as long perukes were worn by beaux much later than 1727, and queues with them.

[2] I am not aware of any coat sleeves at this period that could be called "open;" but the term is constantly applied to them without explanation.

[3] Some wigs had two locks tied at the ends, one of which was worn in front. In these instances they were "both behind."

"The ladies wore flowered silks of various sorts, of a large pattern, but mostly with a white ground, with wide short sleeves and short petticoats; their gowns were pinned up variously behind, though mostly narrow. Some few had gold or silver nets on their petticoats and to their facings and robings; and some had gold and silver nets on their gown-sleeves, like flounces; they wore chiefly fine escalloped laced heads, and dressed mostly English. Some few had their hair curled down on the sides; but most of them had it pinned up quite straight, and almost all of them with powder both before and behind. Some few had their heads made up Dutch, some with cockades of ribands on the side, and others with artificial flowers. They wore treble escalloped lace ruffles—one full, tacked up before, and two down, but all three down behind; though some few had two fulls tacked up and one down before. Laced tippets were much worn: some had diamond *solitaires* to hook them together; others had their jewels made up bows and ends. Those without tippets had mostly very broad laced tuckers, with diamond necklaces and ear-rings. Diamond buckles were much worn in the shoes both of the gentlemen and ladies."

The writer goes on to inform us that "Lord Castlemain made a very splendid appearance in

The Mall, St. James's Park, in 1738.

a rich gold stuff coat; as Lady Harcourt did among the ladies in a white ground rich silk, embossed with gold and silver and fine coloured flowers of a large pattern."

1738. The editor of the 'London Evening Post' for December in that year thus describes, under the *nom de plume* of Miss Townley, the fashions then prevailing in London: "I went the other night to the play with an aunt of mine, a well-bred woman of the last age, though a little formal. When we sat down in the front boxes, we found ourselves surrounded by a parcel of the strangest fellows that ever I saw in my life: some of them had those loose kind of great coats on which I have heard called *wrap rascals*, with gold-laced hats, slouched in humble imitation of stage coachmen; others aspired at being grooms and had dirty boots and spurs, with black caps on, and long whips in their hands; a third sort wore scanty frocks, little shabby hats put on one side, and clubs in their hands." A print published in this year of the Mall, viz. St. James's Park, enables us fully to illustrate the above observations. (See woodcut above.)

The fashion of carrying these "clubs" is noticed in 'The Universal Spectator' about that date. "The wearing of swords at the Court end of the town," says the writer, "is by many polite young gentlemen laid aside, and instead thereof they carry large oak sticks with great heads and ugly faces carved thereon."

In an account of Bartholomew Fair in 1740 is a description of the renowned Tiddy Doll, who was dressed in a *very fashionable suit* of white cloth trimmed with gold lace, a lace ruffled shirt, and a large cocked hat formed of gingerbread, fringed and garnished with Dutch gold ; and in the same account, Frederick, Prince of Wales, is described as wearing a ruby-coloured frock coat, very richly guarded with gold lace, and having his long flowing hair curiously curled over his forehead and at the sides, and finished with a very large bag and courtly queue behind.   He wore the blue ribbon, star and garter, and a small three-cornered silk court hat (the *chapeau bras*).

Claret-coloured cloths were much used for suits, and light blue suits with silver button-holes and silver garters to the knees were very fashionable between 1740 and 1751.

A print published in 1745 illustrates the form of dress worn by persons of the *beau monde* at

The Mall in 1745.

that date, and another of the drawing of the lottery in 1751 supplies us with much information as to that of the general public.   (See accompanying Plate.)   "Soon after the year 1745," we are told, "the French curls made their first appearance in Paris. . . . They look like eggs strung in order on a wire and tied round the head.   At the same time appeared the French crape (*crêpe*) toupee, and also the strait, smooth, or English dress.   All these the English made in false hair, from a notion of cleanliness, which they improved by being first averse to powder, but soon after they had all their hair dressed in all the different fashions.   Some time after came up the scallop-shell or Italian curls, done back from the face in their several shapes.   The German were a mixture of scallop-shell and French in the front, curled all over behind, or *tête de mouton*."   (Plocacosmos, 1781.)

To proceed to France.   The last years of the reign of Louis XIV. have received the appellation of "Les années sombres."   "The courtier," observes La Bruyère, "formerly had his own hair, was dressed in chausses and pourpoint, wore great *canons*, and was a libertine.   This is no longer befitting.   He wears a perruque, a tight coat, long stockings, and is religious."   "The change could not be better expressed," remarks M. Quicherat, who quotes the above passage, "which took place not only at Court, but throughout the higher classes of society, after the king resigned himself to the spiritual direction of Madame de Maintenon."

Stuffs of all descriptions were whole coloured.   Embroidery was employed so sparingly that it was scarcely to be seen at a distance.   Lace was restricted to the cravat and the ruffles.   Buttons superseded points and ribbons, which became limited to shoulder-knots and cockades, and were subsequently discarded altogether.   Tight and short breeches took the place of the *rhingraves*, which had become ridiculous.   Everything was reduced in size except the wigs and the coat sleeves.

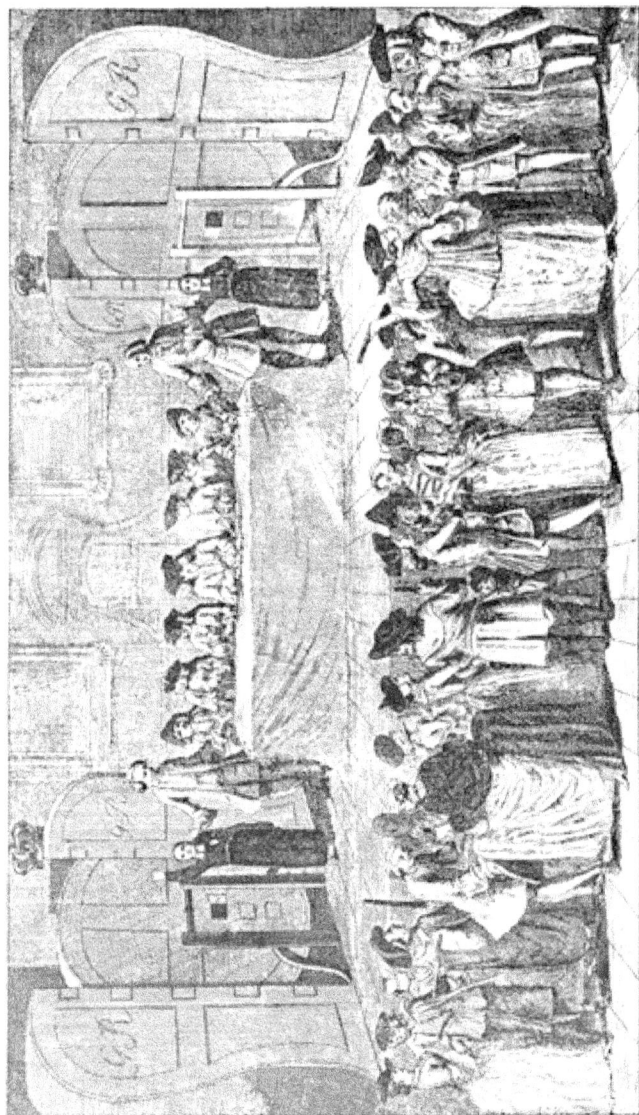

DRAWING OF THE STATE LOTTERY AT GUILDHALL 1751

An edict issued in 1700 authorized the use of gold and silver by noblemen and great officers of State; but it was strictly forbidden to citizens, shopkeepers, and the working classes. The last sumptuary law of which there is any record or recollection was passed in 1708, and prohibited the use of gold to all persons whatever. It was disregarded, as such laws had generally been, and it is worthy of notice that gold and silver were never less used in the decoration of civil costume than after statutes had ceased to denounce the employment of them. Hats were worn with large brims turned up on three sides, and retained their feathers till 1710. The wigs were immensely increased in length

and descended almost to the waist. According to the peculiar fashion of their curls or mode of wearing them, they were called Spanish, cavalier, or square (*carré*). In 1705, the wigs were powdered white, and not only the wig but the shoulders of the wearer, which caused a satirist to exclaim—

> " Poudrer un juste-au-corps ! Quelle étrange parure !
> Tel est le dos d'une âne au sortir d'un moulin !"

It is necessary to mention here, that at the commencement of this century a conventional dress existed in the Court of France perfectly distinct from the full dress or ordinary attire of a man of rank or fashion. It was a habit of ceremony worn by the great officers of State and certain gentlemen in the king's household on special occasions, and composed of portions of the costume of former periods combined with some of those in vogue at that day. The trunk hose of the reign of Henry III., the open doublet of Louis XIII., were incongruously associated with the lace cravat and ponderous periwig of the latter days of "Le Grand Monarque." (See engraving on next page of the Duc de Gesvres, first gentleman of the chamber, in State dress, from a portrait by Vanloo the younger, 1735.) The same fashion will be found existing in Germany in 1703, but which nation has the questionable credit of its invention I have not been able to discover. It does not appear to have been adopted in England or other European countries, except as an under-dress for Knights of the Garter and of other fraternities in the full habit of the order (see p. 290).

In female costume, it is to be observed that the term *manteau* was at the beginning of the eighteenth century applied to the exterior petticoat, or rather the skirt of the robe or gown which was trussed up behind, much as we have seen it lately. Bustles as they might now be termed, made

Duc du Genevre le Staat dress. 1712.

of gummed cloth, were placed under the manteaux to give them greater amplitude ; and as their stiffness caused them to crackle at the least motion, they were called *criardes*. The ornaments of the petticoat were called *falbalas* and *pretantailles*. The former, anglicised *furbelows*, were rows or flounces of pleated silk or lace, the invention of the celebrated Langlée, as it would appear from an expression of Voltaire, who says, " J'ai mis les poemes à la mode comme Langlée y avait mis les falbalas." Between these rows were occasionally inserted broad bands of gold lace or fringe. The *pretantailles* were stripes of various colours sewn on to the borders of the petticoats, a fashion which led to the revival of brocaded stuffs of gold and silk, the patterns of which were so large that they were more fit for window curtains (see description of the petticoat lost by Mrs. Beale in 1712, Dictionary, p. 396).

Respecting the hoop, which appeared in France in the following reign, M. Quicherat observes, " L'origine des *paniers* est obscure comme toutes les origines." Some say it was introduced from England, others from Germany, and a third opinion is that it was derived from the theatre. His own suggestion is, that the farthingale having been retained in some little obscure and old-fashioned German Court had found its way back to England in the time of Queen Anne, and that, being worn by some English ladies who visited Paris after the Peace of Utrecht, it was adopted in the first instance by the actresses, as the heroines of tragedy, ever since the time of Corneille, had always endeavoured to give their stage dresses an artificial amplitude. This theory combines the three opinions. At the same time he relates an amusing anecdote which gives us a fourth derivation.

Two extremely corpulent ladies, who were much incommoded by their *embonpoint*, had caused to be made for them under-petticoats mounted on hoops, which they only wore in the privacy of their own apartments. One summer evening, however, they were tempted to take a stroll in the Tuileries so accoutred. In order to avoid the remarks of the mob of footmen at the gates they entered by the orangery, but lords and ladies are not less curious than their lacqueys. As soon as the pair appeared they were surrounded. The numbers rapidly increased; they had barely time to retreat behind a bench, and but for the protection of a musketeer they would have been smothered or crushed to death by the pressure of the crowd. The poor women reached home more dead than alive, believing they had caused a great scandal. Far from that, they had set the fashion to the Court as well as the city.[1] As M. Quicherat gives the date 1718 for the occurrence of this incident, I presume it is recorded in some contemporary publication; but as we have indubitable evidence of the existence of the hoop-petticoat in England in July 1711,[2] the story, if true, must have reference to some variety in the form of the hoop and not to its first introduction. As in England, the earliest hoops gave a triangular form to the petticoat, "la forme fait d'abord celle d'un entonnoir et produisit les paniers à guéridon."[3] The next shape was termed in French les paniers à coudes, because, the arches springing from the waist, the wearer could rest her elbows upon them. This fashion lasted longest in favour and attained the most extravagant dimensions. It is reported that in 1728 they were the cause of considerable anxiety to Cardinal Fleury. He was informed that when the Queen was at the theatre she was scarcely to be seen in consequence of the hoops worn by the princesses, who sat one on each side of her, which were so large that they covered her Majesty almost entirely. What was to be done? Etiquette demanded that the two princesses should accompany her; at the same time decorum protested against her being, as it were, eclipsed before her subjects. After much reflection the Minister decided that in future a fauteuil should be placed on each side of the Queen, which was to remain unoccupied. The princesses submitted to this arrangement on condition that a similar distance separated them from the duchesses. The dukes objected to this, and circulated an anonymous libel against the princesses, which was ordered to be publicly burnt by the hands of the common hangman.

The hoops en coupole continued to expand till they reached three or four French ells in circumference, and were from their expense restricted at first to the higher or wealthier classes; but a workwoman of Amboise, known as Mademoiselle Margot, coming to Paris and establishing herself there, contrived to make and sell hoop-petticoats of the largest size at very low prices, and consequently they were soon worn by every one, down to the vendors of herrings or lemonade. Some ladies took to wearing short under-petticoats lined with hair-cloth (the modern crinoline) and quilted, reaching only to the knees. These were called paniers jansénistes, indicating a concession to the Jansenist clergy, who denounced the abomination of hoops; but they protested indignantly against the application of the name of their sect to a fashion which they objected to in any form whatever. Nevertheless, in one shape or another hoops remained in favour long beyond the period at which this history is announced to terminate.

The commode disappeared early in the eighteenth century, and the fontange had for some time previously become what it was in the first instance—a simple bow of ribbon. 'Le Dictionnaire de Furetière,' re-edited in 1701, describes it as such, and speaks of it as only an ornament of the towering head-dress to which it had given its name. When the latter had reached such an altitude that the fair wearers could not pass through the doors of their rooms without stooping (an exaggeration recalling the old story of Isabella of Bavaria), Louis XIV. began to regret that he had expressed so much admiration of the improvised coiffure of Mademoiselle de Fontange; and after repeatedly but vainly expressing to the princesses of the blood his vexation at being compelled to tolerate in his old age and in his own household such absurd frivolities, he formally commanded them to lay aside commodes, fontanges, and palissades. The order was obeyed for a time, but at the end of a few months the prohibition was forgotten, and the head-gear of the ladies soared as high if not higher than ever, till one day in the year 1714, an English lady presenting herself at Court in an extremely low head-dress, destroyed in the twinkling of an eye all these Babel-like constructions.

[1] Quicherat, p. 551.   [2] 'Spectator,' Nos. 109, 129.   [3] Quicherat, p. 551.

On observing this sudden change of fashion, the king could not refrain from saying: " I own that I am mortified when I think that all my royal authority could not succeed in suppressing those extravagantly high head-dresses. No person, even out of complaisance for me, would reduce hers an

Parisian Ladies. 1715.

French walking and hunting Dress. 1735.

inch. A stranger arrives, 'une guenille d'Angleterre,' with a little low head-dress, and instantly the princesses rush from one extreme to the other."

Horace Walpole has a very different version of this story ; but I believe M. Quicherat to have given us the true one, although he does not quote his authority.

Abbess and Abbot, in out-of-door Dress. 1730. From Dupin's 'Costumes Français.'

During the reign of Louis XV. the low head-dresses continued in fashion. Powder was invariably worn by all ladies, and in such profusion that their heads, whatever might be the colour of their hair, were as white as snow. Aigrettes of jewels, real or false flowers, lappets of blond lace, ribbons striped of two colours termed *boiteux*, were the ornaments usually worn in it. A work published in 1724 mentions coiffures *à la culbutte* and *à la deguine*; and in another, published in 1730, are named coiffures *en doriotte, en papillon, en vergette, en équivoque, en désespoir*, and *en tête de mouton*. The latter, in which the hair was all in curls at the back of the head, was very fashionable in England. White cotton stockings with coloured clocks were much worn by ladies. When the stockings were of silk, the clocks were of gold or silver. White shoes were also in favour about 1730, with enamelled or diamond buckles. Long silk mittens were worn for dress and of dimity in déshabille. Coiffes called *baguelettes*, a variety of those worn in the previous reign, and *mantes*, a sort of capacious cloak or mantle lined with fur and buttoned all down the front (see opposite page), were assumed in cold or windy weather. In summer, a scarf, the *mantille* (borrowed from the Spanish *mantilla*), was thrown over the head and the ends loosely tied in front, or merely round the neck, crossed on the bosom and tied behind.

Before we quit France, it will be necessary for us to notice a few of the dresses peculiar to certain provinces, the relics of former fashions, retained until what were once general became characteristic of one locality only. Brittany is a remarkable instance of this adhesion to old customs. The Bretons still wear a costume which must have been first assumed by their forefathers two hundred years at least ago; and the curious question occurs to me, why, having been influenced by fashion up to that period, they should suddenly cease to follow it altogether? Here is the figure of a Breton farmer of the present day, in the dress generally worn in his district.

It has all the features of European costume in the early part of the seventeenth century, and, what is of more importance, of that time only. No portion of it can be traced to a previous period. The leggings are suggestive of a Spanish origin, as indeed are the loose jacket and broad-brimmed, low-crowned hat, which first appear in English costume of the time of Charles I. Although I confess myself utterly unable to account for the fact, it is incontestable that what is popularly termed national costume, so far as the south-western part of Europe is concerned, dates from the same epoch, and has undergone little change till within the last fifty years, during which, as I have already observed, with great regret, it has been slowly disappearing.

The descriptions, therefore, of comparatively modern travellers may be justifiably resorted to for information on this subject; and respecting Brittany, the following have been extracted from the work of a popular writer (Mrs. Stothard) at the beginning of the present century.

"The common people in some parts of Brittany wear a goat-skin dress, and look not unlike Defoe's description of Robinson Crusoe. The furry part of the dress is worn outside; it is made with long sleeves, and falls nearly below the knees. Their long shaggy hair hangs dishevelled about their shoulders, the head being covered by a broad-flapped straw or beaver hat. Some few of the Bretons go without shoes or stockings; but the generality wear sabots (wooden shoes), and thrust straw into them to prevent the foot being rubbed by the pressure of the wood."

Breton Farmer.

"The better classes of the peasantry wear coats generally of a dark mulberry colour, lined with scarlet; white waistcoats, also lined with scarlet; and broad belts, corresponding in colour with the lining, or else plaided like the Scotch tartan. The most singular feature of their dress is the taste and caprice displayed in the coat, which, instead of being of a uniform colour, has the skirts often of quite a different shade from the upper part. The broad-flapped hat was worn by all classes."

A countrywoman of Bignan is described as being "dressed in a petticoat or skirt of white flannel, bordered with a scarlet band above the hem: this skirt is sewed to the body in large full

Head-dress of a Countrywoman of Bignan.

plaits. The body or jacket was made of scarlet cloth, tight to the shape, and reached nearly up to the throat. The sleeves were of the same colour, sitting close to the arm and turned up at the wrist, with a deep cuff, both the body and sleeves being trimmed with a braiding composed of a black velvet riband embroidered with coloured worsteds. Her apron was of a deep mulberry colour, fastened with an ornamental sash, tied in a bow at the side. Her cap of white linen sat quite tight upon her head, and was covered with another cap that served the purpose of a bonnet. This last was made of a coarse starched cloth like brown holland, the form conical, with two long flaps hanging down her back, or sometimes pinned up, at the pleasure of the wearer. Her necklace was of amber and black beads; she wore also, suspended by a velvet string, a little ebony crucifix. Her brooch, that fastened her shift in front, was made of white bugles and green glass beads, tastefully arranged."

"In the district of the Léonais, the dress is, like its wearers, grave and formal; it is generally made of black cloth or serge, which gives it a most sombre appearance. The coat is cut quite square, but sometimes reaches half-way to the knee; at others it is only like a long jacket. The waistcoat is very long. The breeches of the better farmers are very large and tied in at the knees; the poorer peasants have them not nearly so wide. The stockings are black, and a blue scarf encircles the waist. The hair always hangs at its full length over the back and shoulders; the hat is of immense size, and the shoe buckle enormous. Those peasants who cannot afford to wear cloth clothes have them made of linen, and wear straw hats with a black cotton rosette."

"Unlike the Léonards," says the author of ' A Summer in Brittany,' "the inhabitants of the hills delight in the most gay and contrasted colours. Violet is a very favourite colour for the coat, which is usually adorned with crimson trimmings and buttons. Gaiters, or leggings rather—for they do not cover any part of the foot—are worn of the same hue and similarly ornamented with crimson. The *bragou bas*, or enormous breeches, are almost always of linen or of a coarse brown woollen cloth. The coats and waistcoats of the richer farmers, and the bodices and petticoats of their wives, are usually made of a coarse cloth; those of the poorer classes of a woollen material they call *gainé*, which is full of little knots and resembles the sort of stuff of which greatcoats are sometimes made. The poorer classes are dressed entirely in linen, or else in a sort of coarse brown thick flannel. The hats in Cornouaille are broad-brimmed, but not so immensely large as those of the Léonards; and instead of the simple broad band of black velvet, which is used by the latter, they are ornamented with two or three circles of string, prepared with the gayest and most varied colours for the purpose, in the same manner that the handles of bell-ropes are made. Between these variegated strings, the Kernewote or Cornouaille man puts a circle or two of silver thread, and all the various strings are united into a tassel, which hangs down behind."

For the following information we are indebted to the authoress of ' The Book of Costume,' 8vo, London, 1846.

In the neighbourhood of St. Pol de Léon the peasants wear flannel jackets and violet-coloured breeches; men from near Brest, red coats and breeches, and white waistcoats with crimson buttons. On the western coast, a blue cloak with a falling cape distinguishes the native peasant from those of other districts. The Roscovites have close green jackets, white trousers, and crimson belts; while the men from the remote villages of the northern shore wear small, close, blue caps, dingy woollen jackets, and short linen trousers. They do not even adopt the sabot, but leave the feet and legs bare.

At Quimper, the peasants wear the large broad-brimmed hat, the crown of which is ornamented with two bands of gold lace, a long blue waistcoat, a jacket made so tight that only the lower button can be fastened, thus leaving it very open to show the waistcoat to advantage. On the edges of the jacket and round the throat is a band of gold or gold-coloured lace. The *bragou bas* are of immense size, made of white linen; the stockings brown, large sabots, and a broad brown leather belt round the waist, fastened with a large buckle; their hair hanging in long curls half-way down their backs.

In the department of Morbihan, the men wear short square-cut coats of white cloth or drugget; the edges of the coat, the buttons and button-holes, also the flaps of the large pockets (which latter are vandyked), are all trimmed with crimson cloth, and on the breast of the coat is frequently embroidered the date of the year in which it was made.

Of the women, those of Quimper generally wear a jacket laced up in front, with tight sleeves that reach only to the elbows; below which are white sleeves reaching to the wrist. The petticoat is often white, very full and short to show the gold or gilt buckles in their shoes. Sometimes the jacket and petticoat are blue, trimmed with gold and red lace; half the sleeves being blue, then pink, and lastly, near the hands, white tied with yellow or red ribbons. The chemise reaches to the throat, where it is fastened with a collar of various colours. An orange-coloured apron completes this gaudy dress.

In the Morbihan, some of the women wear close caps or hoods, of a violet or green colour; but the variety in the shape of their head-dresses is remarked as "a great peculiarity of dress in this province." Some of these coiffures look like folds of linen laid one upon another, others are immensely high, and some closely encircle the face, but have long lappets hanging down the back. Their hair, unlike the custom of the men, is never seen, even from infancy, and this may account for their strange want of variety in this ornament of female beauty, for in many parts of Brittany they actually part with their tresses at the fairs to regular hair merchants, who buy for a few sous what they afterwards sell in other towns for large prices when curled and made into perukes.

In the adjacent province of Normandy we find relics of costume of an earlier date than in Brittany, particularly in the head-dresses of the women, several of which bear evidence of their having been adopted about the middle of the fifteenth century, being varieties of the steeple and butterfly caps worn by the ladies in France and England in the reigns of Charles VII. and Henry VI.; a circumstance attributable, no doubt, to the half-English character of Normandy, its final and absolute severance from England not occurring till 1450, after which period no

Countrywoman in the Morbihan.

important change appears to have taken place in the head-dress of the country-women, called *cauchoise* from its popularity in the Pays de Caux, and in some places, according to Mrs. Stothard, *bourgoin*, a name of which I do not know the derivation.

The general costume of the women is described by Mrs. Stothard as consisting ordinarily of "a woollen petticoat striped with a variety of colours, as red, blue, &c., and an apron, also of red or blue. The jacket of the gown is most commonly made of maroon, white, black, or red worsted, the long sleeves being sometimes of maroon as far as the elbow, and the lower half of a scarlet colour. A little shawl (white or coloured) with a fringe round it, pinned in plaits upon the back, covers the shoulders . . . Several *paysannes* on Sundays or holy days appear clothed entirely in white instead of in this costume; but they still retain their *bourgoin*, which on such occasions is always composed of fine muslin or lace." In the next page are given examples of varieties of the *cauchoise* or *bourgoin*, familiar, no doubt, to many of my readers.

The men more frequently wear white or red cotton caps than hats, and when they do wear a hat they have generally a cap beneath it. A blue cotton blouse (the *bliaus* of the Middle Ages) takes the place of the coat or jacket, and loose trousers of the same colour and material are substituted for the *bragou bas* of the Breton. Wooden shoes are worn by both sexes.

Although not so picturesque as the costume of Brittany, the simple dress of a Norman peasant may be traced back to an earlier period, and is at least coeval with the steeple head-dress which has been retained by the women. A modern writer on the subject says, "When travelling in Normandy, I was shown one of these coiffures, belonging to the wife of a rich peasant: it had descended from mother to daughter for several generations, and was looked upon with as much reverence as a box of family diamonds would be among the higher classes."

In the southern parts of France and the department of the Pyrenees, the national dress has

Varieties of the Canchoise or Bourgoin.

been naturally affected by the neighbourhood of Spain. The large dark brown woollen cloak with a hood to it, known in France in the reign of Charles IX. as the *cape de Béarn*, has never been discarded. The author of 'A Summer in the Pyrenees' describes the usual head-dress of the women as "a handkerchief made of a manufacture of the country which never fades or crumples. The middle is usually brown, drab, or fawn colour, with a broad border to suit. It is adjusted so as to give a Grecian contour to the head and face, and I suspect, notwithstanding its appearance of artless simplicity, that there are degrees of coquetry by which it is arranged so as best to suit the appearance of the wearer. Beneath this head-dress we see soft bands of dark hair, carefully parted on the forehead and placed against the cheek, so as to contrast in the best manner with a complexion at once glowing and delicate, healthy and pure. Add to this the neatest little collar round the neck, the universal shawl pinned down in front, over which the hands, in curiously coloured mittens, are closely folded. The peasant women, besides the handkerchief above described, wear a hood called a *capulet*, made of white or scarlet cloth of the finest texture, often bordered with black velvet, and has a striking effect, whether hanging loosely from the head to the shoulders, over which it extends, or folded thick and flat on the head, as we see in Italian pictures. When at church, they wear a cloak of black or blue stuff lined with red.

"The rest of the dress is of the simplest description: usually a thick woollen petticoat of brown or blue, with a stripe of a different colour, a blue cloth jacket tight to the waist, and the shawl pinned over it. This dress being dark and durable, and exactly suited to their occupation, never looks shabby or dirty; nor is there such a thing as a ragged garment to be seen, even upon the poorest or the most inferior.

"With regard to shoes and stockings, they are not particular, and we often see the women stopping to put them on before they enter the towns. The peasants and mountaineers wear universally rudely-shaped shoes of wood, immensely thick, turned up with a pointed toe."

In the Pays des Landes, the costume of the men consists of long trousers, a kind of garment between a jacket and a spencer, and a worsted cap stuck on the back of the head like a Scotchman's bonnet. The dress of the women generally resembles that above given of Béarn. The female peasants at Aubagne, near Marseilles, have broad black hats, adorned with little scraps of silver lace, smart jackets, and gorgeous petticoats; while their male companions, by the display of the gayest stockings and vests, seem determined not to be outdone in finery. ('Book of Costume,' by a Lady of Rank.)

Working round by the south-east, we find the influence of Italian fashions; the women at Drappo, near Nice, wearing their hair bound in a silk filet or net, one of the earliest modes of head-dressing in Europe, fastened at the top with a long pin. The men wear short vests, blue belts and stockings, and their hair tied up behind. (Ibid.)

Ascending northward, we come to Alsace, which in the eighteenth century was a portion of the kingdom of France, but in speech and manners remarkably German, and consequently we find a much later fashion of dress prevailing; the cocked hats and long square-cut coats of the reign of our King William III. having displaced the costume of those earlier periods of which we trace so many remains in the south and west of Europe. Père Laguille, in his 'Histoire de la Provence d'Alsace,' printed in 1727, has given us a most curious representation of an Alsatian female in holiday attire (see annexed woodcut). The body of her gown is made with the immensely long pointed stomacher of the period, trimmed with bows of ribbon, lace, and jewels. Over it is a mantle or tippet, apparently of black silk, with long pointed ends edged with white lace; a handkerchief also of white lace is round her neck, tied in front, the ends depending. The sleeves are short, with broad cuffs terminating above the elbow, with ample lace ruffles. Her petticoat, or it may be apron, is of some white material, the upper half being laid in very fine close plaits, the lower in broader plaits and escalloped all round the bottom. She has a necklace composed of several chains with a cross pendent to them, long gloves, and shoes with very pointed toes, high heels, and large rosettes: but her coiffure is the peculiar and extraordinary feature of her costume, and I am ignorant of anything approaching it in eccentricity, excepting always the monstrous head-gear of the women of Nuremberg and Augsburg delineated by Misson in 1687 (see page 271). It is an enormous triangular construction of black silk or satin, lace and ornaments of some description of which the pencil alone can convey an idea. Her hair, turned back from the forehead, hangs in a very long plaited tail behind

Alsatian Woman in holiday dress. 1727.

her; a fan suspended by a ribbon is slung on her right arm, and the bouquet in her hand completes the festal character of this singular and elaborate toilet.

For Italian and Spanish costume we have numberless examples in the portraits of the celebrities of the day, and in the collections of national costumes published during the present century, so many of the dresses retaining the features which distinguished them a hundred years ago, and some re-calling the fashions of the Middle Ages. I may particularly point to the well-known head-dress of the Roman women, so frequently seen in the streets of London in the present day, in company with some of those itinerant organ-grinders who are the torment of the student and the invalid—that mass of white linen folded square and laid flat upon the head, the ends hanging down upon the shoulders behind, and recalling the French hood of the sixteenth century, and the still earlier coiffure of Anne de Bretagne, which appears to have been its prototype (see pages 277 and 298 of Dictionary, and page 191 of this volume). The rest of the dress of the Roman female pea-santry consists of a petticoat of a dark colour, a bodice laced across the bosom, frequently gaily ornamented, and usually of some bright colour, different from the petticoat. The sleeves are those of the shift and reach to the wrist. A kerchief is pinned across the bosom, and an embroidered apron completes the picturesque costume. Their love of finery is great. Those who can afford such ornaments usually wear gold necklaces, chains, and crosses, and in their shoes immense silver buckles, which are the most modern articles comprised in their attire, being introductions of the last century.

The dress of the Trasteverini, who form a large portion of the population of Rome, distinguishes them from the rest of the Romans. The men wear a silken net on their heads *à l'espagnole*, a jacket of black velvet thrown over the shoulders, a broad crimson sash, and enormous silver shoe-buckles. The women braid their hair in silken nets and ornament it with silver bodkins, and in their gala dress appear in velvet bodices, laced with gold ; silken petticoats, white and coloured ; showy silver buckles and scarlet aprons. (See footnote next page.)

The female peasantry of Terni wear a veil of embroidered linen, projected like a shade over the eyes by a piece of whalebone, and called *cuffa* (a corruption probably of the French *coif*, or its offspring *coiffure*), showy scarlet jackets, and coloured petticoats.

Lady Morgan mentions the great resemblance between the dress of the peasantry in parts of the Pontifical States to that of the common Irish, the men being muffled to their chins in dark and ragged mantles. "It is remarkable," she says, "that some of the women in this district wear a head-kerchief precisely like that worn in the remote parts of Ireland ; and that others had on the Irish mantle, a piece of bias-cut cloth drawn over the head, almost always of a dingy red. The Irish mantle

is, in fact, the Roman cloak so universally worn by all ranks. Another point of resemblance was that almost all the women were bare-legged and frequently bare-footed."

I may add to these observations that nearly all the costumes familiar to the traveller on the northern coast of the Mediterranean have been transmitted from the opposite coast of Africa, and much of it may be traced back to the Phœnicians, the Carthaginians, and their successors the Arabs and the Moors. Those who scoffed at Colonel Valancy's theory of the Milesian origin of some portion of the Irish are now dead and gone, but we have lived to acknowledge the truth of it.

The women in the Apennines Lady Morgan describes as "resembling in their dress the peasantry of Wales, universally wearing little round black beaver hats with high crowns and a stiff plume of black feathers. Their gala dress is principally characterised by a profusion of ribbons floating from their shoulders, their waists, and their sleeves. The beaver hat is then replaced by combs and bodkins, and at all times their necks are encircled with pearl and coral, usually an heirloom of many generations' descent, but occasionally the purchase of years of labour and the most rigid economy."

Of Bologna the same author says, "The costume appears to belong to other ages. The French toilet prevailed in Bologna among the higher classes nearly a century ago, but the females of the lower ranks still wear the becoming *zendado*, a scarf or veil, which falls from the head, and which they drape prettily enough round their shoulders. Their hair is ingeniously plaited and set off with showy combs or bodkins ; and coral, mock or real, is abundantly and universally worn."

In her account of Genoa she remarks that "the women's heads are ornamented by a quantity of silver bodkins, forming a sort of coronet or star at the back, and confining a profusion of plaited tresses. Many of the elder women wear square linen veils, embroidered and trimmed with coarse lace. Dresses are here considered heirlooms. Many a silken vest and quilted bodice, many a chain of gold and coral purchased in the days of Genoa's prosperity, still remain to deceive the eye with the appearance of rural and commercial wealth." These observations justify my statement that the national costume of the greater part of Europe in the past century continued to be worn in the present, and that it might consequently be illustrated by the descriptions of modern travellers. At the same time we occasionally meet with apparent discrepancies which it is difficult to reconcile. For instance in the case of Genoa. In the 'Notes of a Wanderer,' we read, "In Genoa the women were all gracefully dressed without bonnets, wearing merely a *white muslin scarf* fastened to the crown of the head by its centre, and the ends hanging down over the shoulders ;" while Gray, in his 'Germany,' says of the women of Genoa, "The *painted linen veil* which they wear is called *messaro*, though it resembles a flowered gown thrown over the head and hooded."

At Mola di Gaeta the women roll their long tresses mingled with silken bands round their heads with an antique grace, and Swinburne tells us that amongst the Neapolitan peasants "may be seen almost every mode of hair-dressing found on the Roman and Grecian coins. The coiffure of the younger Faustina, with the coil of hair plaited upon the crown of the head, occurs frequently in the old town; that with the coil lower down, which may properly be styled Lucilla's head-dress, is common among the younger part of the sex in the Chiaia; and Plautina's among the women more advanced in years."

"Forty years ago," says the same writer, "the Neapolitan ladies wore nets and ribbons on their heads, as the Spanish women do to this day, and not twenty of them were possessed of a cap, but hair plainly dressed is a mode now confined to the lowest order of inhabitants, and all distinctions of dress between the wife of a nobleman and of a citizen are entirely laid aside."

"Very little," he observes, "suffices to clothe the Lazzaro, except on holidays, and then he is indeed tawdrily decked out with laced jacket and flame-coloured stockings; his buckles are of enormous magnitude, and seem to be the prototype of those with which our present men of *mode* load their insteps."

"The costume of the Tuscan peasantry varies much according to the district they inhabit. In Florence the out-of-doors dress of the middle classes is generally black. The Tuscans on Sundays and fête-days wear their hair becomingly ornamented, with a very small hat elegantly poised over the left ear, while the hair on the opposite side is interwoven with a string of pearls or adorned with a shining comb. They have earrings formed of several drops of pearl set in gold, and necklaces composed of two rows of pearls and coral. Their feet are enclosed in black velvet slippers, and in their hands are to be seen gaudily ornamented fans. They have jackets without sleeves, laced with riband. When at work or market, they confine their hair in a net of crimson, scarlet, or blue silk, tied by two strings and ornamented by tassels, which are often of gold or silver. They are also often seen with the hair drawn into a knot at the top of the head, and a veil hanging down behind." Our readers will recognize in the silk net for the hair one of the earliest of mediæval fashions, and the veil depending from a knot of hair on the top of the head is commonly to be seen in engravings of Italian females in works of the sixteenth century.[1]

For the costume of Venice some interesting authorities are contained in a volume of engravings published at Nuremberg in 1703, the work of the celebrated Christopher Weigel. The plates are unfortunately unaccompanied by text, but the figures are so admirably executed and of such a size that the smallest details are clearly discernible. The Venetian dresses are especially interesting, as they exhibit the ducal and senatorial habiliments in that remarkable republic, at nearly the latest period to which this work is limited. The inevitable periwig, we find, has established itself on the heads of all the signors, with the exception of the Doge, and the Procurator of St. Mark still wears the stole or "flappe" over his left shoulder.

At this period there was a college at Venice, the officers of which were charged with the regulation of dress by the republic, and the introduction of foreign cloth was prohibited. Formerly it was necessary that a nobleman should have eight cloaks: three for the masks, one of which was for the spring fête of the Ascension, when the Doge married the sea; one for the autumn, the *ridotto* and theatre; and one for the Carnival. These three were called *baceta*. In addition to these, they had two for summer of white taffeta, one of blue cloth for winter, one of white cloth for grand State occasions, and one of scarlet cloth for great Church ceremonies. Weigel's work, unfortunately, does not contain any examples of the costume of Venetian ladies of the early part of the eighteenth century, and we have no information, so far as I am aware, of the exact period when the *chioppine*

[1] Since these pages were written, I have visited the greater portion of the localities above mentioned, and, except in Rome during the Carnival, saw nothing that could be called a national costume. In the Trastevere, as well as in the environs of Turin, Florence, Genoa, and Nice, the dress of the peasantry, male and female, resembled generally that of persons of their own class in other parts of Europe.

was discarded. We know from several accounts that it was worn very late in the seventeenth century ; but it had certainly disappeared in Mrs. Piozzi's time, when it would seem that an entire revolution had taken place in Venetian female attire, not a trace of the old characteristic costume of the Queen

Doge of Venice. 1703.   Procurator of St. Mark.

of the Adriatic being found in her description. "Their morning dress," she says, "consists of a black silk petticoat, sloped just to train on the ground, a little flounced with black gauze. On their heads they have a skeleton wire, like what is used for making up hats ; over it they throw a large piece of black mode or persian, so as to shade the face like a curtain ; the front is trimmed with deep black lace or soufiet gauze, very becoming. The thin ends of silk they roll back and fasten in a puff before on the stomacher ; then, once more rolling it back from the shape, tie it gracefully behind and let it hang in two ends.

"The evening coiffure is a silk hat, shaped like a man's, with a white or worked lining, and some-times with one feather, a great black silk cloak, lined with white, and perhaps a narrow border down before, with a very heavy round handkerchief of black lace, which lies over the neck and shoulders, and conceals the shape completely. Here is surely little appearance of art ! No crêping, no frizzing the hair, which is flat at the top, all of one length, and hanging in long curls about the back and sides, as it happens. No brown powder ; no rouge at all."

Lady Millar, who visited Venice much about the same time, corroborates the latter statement. "A custom," she observes, "here prevails of wearing no rouge, and increasing the native paleness of the face by lightly wiping a white powder over it." Her account of a Venetian wedding contains some notices of dress which are interesting, as they show the gradual inroad of French or German fashions into this most exclusive of European governments. "All the ladies, except the bride, were dressed in their black silk gowns, *with large hoops ;* the gowns were straight-bodied, with very long trains, the trains tucked up on one side of the hoop with a prodigious large tassel of diamonds. Their sleeves were covered up to their shoulders with falls of the finest Brussels lace, a drawn tucker of the same round the bosom, adorned with rows of the finest pearls, each the size of a gooseberry, till the rows descended below the top of the stomacher ; then two rows of pearls, which came from the back of the neck, were caught up at the left side of the stomacher, and finished in two fine tassels. Their heads were dressed prodigiously high in a vast number of buckles and two long drop curls in the neck. A great number of diamond pins and strings of pearls adorned their heads, with large *sultanes* or feathers on one side, and magnificent diamond ear-rings. The bride was dressed in cloth of silver, made in the same fashion, and decorated in the same manner, but her brow was quite bare, and she had a fine diamond necklace and an enormous bouquet. Her hair was dressed as high as the others, with this difference, that it had curls behind and before. These curls had a singular appearance, but not near so good an effect as the other ladies', whose hair was plaited in large folds, and appeared much more graceful. Her diamonds were very fine and in great profusion."

Unfortunately, I have not been able as yet to discover any representations of Venetian costume that would illustrate this description, which in general, however, corresponds with what we have seen and heard of the dress of the ladies in the reigns of George II. of England and Louis XV. of France, the principal exception being the coiffures. The skeleton wire, covered with black mode, mentioned by Mrs. Piozzi, almost suggests a revival of the butterfly head-dress of the fifteenth century; but no example of the latter has ever been found in Venice. The "silk hat, *shaped like a man's*," must in her time have been three-cornered; and such, with feathers in them, were worn by ladies in England and elsewhere in the early part of the eighteenth century, but only with the riding habit. Here it is said to have been worn with evening dress.

The paintings of Antonio Canal, better known as Canaletto, who died in 1768, are the best authorities for the costume of his contemporaries, whom he has depicted by hundreds swarming in the Piazza de San Marco and other localities of his native city, but too small to be instructive.

I must now hark back to Spain, in the national costume of which there yet remain much variety

Man and Woman of Aragon.

and interest, and but little, if any, alteration has taken place since it was described in the last century by Townshend, Swinburne, Bourgoin, or by other still more modern travellers.

Much of it, as I observed in the preceding chapter, dates from the days of our Charleses, when Spanish fashions were imported to us either direct from Madrid or by way of the Netherlands, wherein the long domination of Spain had naturalized them. In some provinces the Moors have left their impress behind them, while in others the costume might be traced back to the times of the Romans. As examples of the first description, take the subjoined figures of a man and woman of the mountainous part of Aragon. The cassock with open hanging sleeves of the former, the ruff and slashed sleeves of the latter, must be familiar to the students of these volumes, while the sandalled legs take us back almost to Keltic times, the *lingettes* of the Frank and the Norman.

Observe in addition the costume of a Mauregato, with his tabbed doublet, ample hose, and flat-crowned, broad-leafed hat, and compare his appearance with an Englishman of the first half of the seventeenth century. Dalrymple, who travelled in Spain in 1775, gives the following account of this peculiar race, whom he conjectures are the descendants of those who followed the fortunes of the usurper Mauregato, natural son of Alphonso the Catholic, who, by the aid of the Moors, succeeded in seating himself on the throne of Leon, *circa* A.D. 783, and who, during his brief reign of five years

Costume of the Mauregatos.

and six months, encouraged Moorish settlers. "In the morning," he says, "I observed a number of women in a peculiar kind of dress; on inquiry I found they were called Mauregatas. Their habit is very particular; they wear large ear-rings, and a kind of white hat, which at a little distance, both as to size and shape, resembles what is worn in like manner by the Moorish women. Their hair is divided in front, and falls on each side of the face; they have a number of little pictures of saints set in silver, and other trinkets, pendent to large beads of coral, tied round the neck and spreading all over the bosom; their shift is stitched at the breast and buttoned at the collar; they wear a brown woollen cloth bodice and petticoat, the sleeves of the bodice very large, and open behind.

"The Mauregatos (the men) wear very large drawers, which tie at the knee, and the loose part hangs over the tie as far as the calf of the leg. The rest of their dress is a short kind of coat, with a belt round the waist."

Flores, in his 'España Sagrada,' says the Mauregatos are a people noted for their integrity: "that the women retain a dress so ancient that its origin is not known, being the most uncommon in all Spain." I confess I am at a loss to understand what kind of a white hat was ever worn by a Moorish woman, and I have not seen a representation of a Mauregata; but the dress of a Mauregato is, as I have already pointed out, of the fashion of the reign of our Charles I., and I should imagine that of the women would pretty nearly correspond with it. *Maragato* is Spanish for a particular ornament on a woman's tucker, and the name is probably derived from the dress of a Mauregata; but no great antiquity is associated with a tucker, that article of a lady's wardrobe not occurring before the seventeenth century.

In La Mancha, Dalrymple tells us that the men are dressed "in waistcoats and breeches of dark-coloured cloth made from the undyed wool of black sheep, each family fabricating a sufficient quantity for its own use. The women wore jackets and aprons of the like stuff, with a kind of linsey-woolsey petticoat, red stockings, beads, and many trinkets about their necks, with their black hair tied behind, the smarter girls wearing silver combs."

In the Basque provinces the adherence to ancient fashions will be obvious to our subscribers by the comparison of the costumes of the women of Biscay in the sixteenth and seventeenth centuries (pp. 162 and 189) with those copied from prints in a 'Coleccion de Trages de España,' recently

Man and Woman of Roncala.   Countrywoman of Biscay.

published. The peculiar knot of the kerchief which forms the head-dress will be immediately recognized.

Murcia and Valencia present us with picturesque attire, recalling the Celtiberian and the Moor. The bright silk kerchief folded diagonally and tied in a knot behind or at the side is said to be a bequest of the latter people, as may also be the white linen shirt reaching barely to the knees, like the camise of the Albanians, if, indeed, it be not the tunic of the Romans. The striped cloak (*al bornos*) is undeniably Moorish, and so I believe are the *alpergatas*, or sandals, of Esparto rush, beaten and bound together and fastened to the foot by leathern thongs or strings.

"The most singular thing in the dress of the men," says Swinburne, "is the covering of their legs: they wrap a piece of coarse grey or black woollen cloth round them, and fasten it with many turns of tape; it answers precisely to the idea I have of Malvolio's cross gartering in the 'Twelfth

Valendan Costume.

Night.'" Had Mr. Swinburne survived, he might have corrected that idea ; and, even in his day, I
am surprised that he should consider this custom singular, as it has existed from the earliest periods
in the Abruzzi and some parts of Russia, and, as I have remarked, is of Frankish origin. The

Valencian Costume.

spatterdashes, or *bottines* of calf-skin, worn by the better classes, partially cover shoes (*zapatos*) of the same leather, so that they look like high boots. They are fastened with leather loops on the outside of the leg, but left open at the calf to give the appearance of a full and handsome limb. They are made with the rough side outwards, when new of a beautiful light colour, and are tastefully worked on the front and back with flowers of darker leather, or are sometimes stitched with silk of various colours. The *bottines* of Seville were most in fashion, and a handsome pair cost not less than four or five dollars. "I have seen them," says a modern writer, "though rarely, of black tanned leather studded with brass tacks."

The Valencian costume consisted, according to Swinburne, of a monstrous slouched hat, cropped hair without a net,[1] a short brown jacket, white waistcoat, and *trousers*, stockings gartered below the knee, and packthread sandals; a dress differing not less remarkably than that of the Aragonese from the Catalonian. "The common dress of a Catalonian sailor," he says, "is brown; and the distinc-

Peasant of Murcia.   Peasant of Segovia.   Countrywoman of Segovia.

tive mark by which they are known in Spain is a red woollen cap, falling forwards like that of the ancient Phrygians,"—undoubtedly its lineal descendant, and the head-gear to this day of all the populations on the coasts of the Mediterranean (see next page). "The middling sort of people wear hats and dark clothes, with a half wide coat carelessly tossed over the shoulders. The dress of the woman is a black silk petticoat over a little hoop, shoes without heels, bare shoulders, and a black veil stiffened out with wire so as to arch out on each side of the head, somewhat resembling the hooded serpent."

The costume of Barcelona, we are told by Townshend, "is the usual Spanish dress. The ladies of every condition wear the *basquina* (petticoat), *saya* (body or spencer), and *mantilla* (veil), together with silk stockings, and shoes embroidered either with silk or with gold and silver fringe, spangles, or pearls. The veil is the only covering worn on the head, and by the material of which this is made the higher class are chiefly distinguished. A Spanish lady's full dress is generally black, with the

---

[1] In another place he says, "They strut about all day in *redecillas* or *nets*, monstrous hats, and dark-brown cloaks."

veil either white or black, more commonly the latter; her undress is of any colour. They are fond of adorning their hair, neck, arms, and fingers, with jewels. The fan is a most indispensable article; and to wield this sceptre of the fair with grace, and to make it perform all its telegraphic purposes, is a prime accomplishment." Respecting the male attire, we are only informed that "the gala dress of the noblemen is as superb as gold and silver embroidery can make it." Nothing is said as to form or colour; but, as it has been too truly observed by a modern writer, "The ever-varying modes of France have long crept across the Pyrenees; French clothes, French fashions, and French colours have quite superseded the ancient costume of the country among the higher classes." The innovation had commenced before the time of Townshend and Swinburne; but their descriptions are valuable, inasmuch as they point out what was still remaining of old Spanish costume in the latter half of the last century, the period to which my inquiries at present are limited.

A later French traveller, speaking of the province of Murcia, says, "The Murcian peasant wears,

Sailor, North Coast.   Sailor, South Coast.

instead of a cloak, a piece of coarse striped woollen, half an ell wide and two ells long, thrown over the shoulder, a white jacket, short white trousers, not covering the knee, a red woollen girdle, shoes of hemp or bass, and either a round or slouched hat or a leathern cap called a *montero*. The common people in towns wear a round hat over a black net, a black waistcoat, and a large brown or black mantle. The women dress as in other parts of Spain; but instead of the elegant satin or velvet basquinas and mantillas which are seen elsewhere, the basquina is of yellow, red, green, brown, or black serge, wide-spreading, and short, showing, in place of the handsome shoe and stocking of a Spanish belle, red or yellow woollen hose half-way up to the knee. The mantilla worn here is heavy and dismal, and, instead of the usual Spanish head-dress, the Murcian ladies have their sleek, shining black hair combed backward tight and flat; while the graceful fan is superseded by a huge chaplet of large beads reaching nearly to the ground, which they carry almost always about with them, even when not going to church.

"The military, merchants, and the official persons," he adds, "dress in the French fashion."

Swinburne describes the dress of an inn-keeper's daughter at Lorca in this province. "Her hair," he says, "was tied in a club with a bunch of scarlet ribands, large drops hung from her ears, and on her breast she wore a load of relics and hallowed medals ; the sleeves of her gown were fastened together behind by a long blue riband that hung to the ground."

From the work of an English officer in 1809, I add the following : "The Estramaduran has a brown jacket without a collar, and with sleeves which lace at the shoulder, so that they are removed at pleasure" (a fashion, observe, of the fifteenth century). "The red sash is universally worn, and a cloak is generally carried on the left arm. A jacket and waistcoat profusely ornamented with silk lace and buttons of silver filigree, the hair clubbed and tied with broad black ribbon, and a neat cap of cloth or velvet (the montero), mark the Andalusian. The ass-driver of Cordova is clothed in a complete dress of the tawny brown leather of his native province. The lemonade-seller of Valencia has a linen shirt, open at the neck, a fancy waistcoat without sleeves, a kilt of white cotton, white stockings rising to the calf, and sandals."

In quitting Spain I have to remark that I have only called attention to such examples of national dress as afford evidence of an origin anterior to 1700, and that I have not thought it necessary to give descriptions or engravings of bolero dancers or bull-fighters, with whose conventional costume the modern stage and modern publications have made the general public so familiar. The immortal Barber of Beaumarchais is apparently privileged to wear the costume usually appropriated to him, for the locality of the drama is Seville, and Figaro may be fairly presumed to hail from Ronda, where Mr. Jacob describes the dress in 1809 ; but I hesitate to suggest even the date of its introduction. The women of that district, when walking abroad, wear veils made of pink or pale blue flannel, which, with a petticoat of black stuff, form their principal dress. The men wear the montero cap, made of black velvet (something in the shape of a sugar-loaf), adorned with tassels and fringe.

There is but little to be said about Portugal in the eighteenth century. As in other European kingdoms, the Court and the higher orders of society received their fashions from Versailles, and the costumes we have described in the reigns of Louis XIV. and Louis XV. found as much favour on the banks of the Tagus as on those of the Thames.

Gaudy colours were, however, not much affected by them, both sexes ordinarily wearing black.

The ladies wore large heavy ear-rings, and in their hair quantities of precious stones, generally set in the form of butterflies and other insects.

The women among the peasantry wore their hair as now, in a net of silk called *redecilla*. "Their gowns," says a recent writer, "usually have a bodice and short sleeves reaching to the elbow, of a different material from the jupe : this bodice is made with a long pointed stomacher, and is cut round at the bosom ; beneath it is worn an under-dress with long sleeves, and a body that fastens round the throat. White dresses are much worn, ornamented with coloured ribbons." (Book of Costume.)

"No young woman ever conceals her hair under a lace or muslin head-dress. Elderly ladies wear a cap shaped like a caul, of very fine clear muslin." Speaking of the better orders, "Their gowns," the writer adds, "of which they sometimes wear two or three, one over the other, are richly embroidered. The upper one forms a long train, which sweeps along the ground and is of black stuff. Their hoops are quite enormous, and their sleeves immensely wide. Instead of a girdle they encircle their small waists with a string of diamonds ; the ends hang to the ground and have knots of diamonds in them. Their shoes are of Spanish leather, without any heels ; but when they go out they put on pattens, or silk sandals fastened with gold clasps, by which they are raised several inches from the ground," (a sort of chioppine ?) "They wear paint not only on the cheeks, but on the shoulders also." A fashion I have already noticed.

The dress of the muleteers, the drovers, and the water-carriers, the latter particularly, who are principally Galegos, i.e. natives of the Spanish province of Gallicia, resembles in every respect that of the same classes in Spain—a short round jacket and tight knee-breeches, a red sash, a broad-leafed hat, the edges curled up all round, with a tuft of black silk on one side and a gilt ornament dangling on the other ; leathern gaiters and a striped cloth flung over the shoulder ; the head sometimes bound in a gaily-coloured silk handkerchief, which is worn with or without the hat.

2 T 2

The cloak is universally worn by all ranks and in all seasons. The women retain the black cloth huke which is so common in Belgium, and was most probably derived from the Moors, many of whose manners and customs are still to be traced in the country. Perhaps from them they derive their love of jewels; even the fishwomen wear gold necklaces and bracelets. The women who sell fruit frequently wear boots instead of shoes or sandals, and black conical caps. "The costume of the lower orders of Lisbon," observes a lady tourist,[1] "would not be unbecoming if they had a more thorough notion of personal cleanliness. It invariably consists, when they walk out in summer or in winter, of a long ample cloth cloak, generally of a black, brown, or scarlet colour,[2] with a deep falling cape called a capote, which forms a graceful drapery both to men and women. The latter wear a white muslin handkerchief doubled cornerways, carelessly thrown over their dark braided locks and fastened beneath the chin. When they go to mass on festivals or Sundays, they carry a fan in the hand. . . . All wear pink, green, or yellow silk shoes, or even white satin, and worked stockings (the latter knitted very ingeniously by the peasants), even in the midst of the most disgusting dirt and mud. . . . The class one step higher in the scale of society indulge in tawdry, ill-chosen finery, in sorry imitation of the French and English fashions; but at mass they exchange this gaudy attire for a black silk gown and a deep transparent veil of the same sombre hue, which latter they throw over their heads without any other covering, even in the coldest day in winter." This is of course the mantilla, which, with other relics of national costume throughout Europe, is rapidly disappearing. During two visits I have paid to Lisbon during the last twenty years, I do not recollect seeing, even at a bull-fight, half-a-dozen women in mantillas.

For the costume of Germany, Holland, and the greater portion of Eastern Europe in 1703, we

The Emperor Leopold.   The Empress Leonora.

have the invaluable authority of the work published at Nuremberg in that year, which I have already been indebted to for illustrations of that of Venice. Of the Court of Vienna it presents us with a gallery of portraits. The series commences with the Emperors Leopold I. and Joseph I., their

[1] 'The Book of Costume, or Annals of Fashion.' By a Lady of Rank. 8vo. London, 1846.
[2] Black and brown are common. I never saw one of scarlet.

Prince Eugene of Savoy.　　Rector of the University.　　Lady of the Bedchamber.

empresses, and the principal members of their family, great officers of State and attendants, pages,
guards, &c., from which are selected the following :—The Emperor Leopold and his Empress Leonora ;
Prince Eugene of Savoy; the Rector of the University of Vienna; Lady of the Bedchamber;

Gentleman of the Bedchamber.　　　　　　　　Pages.

Gentleman of the Chamber ; pages, herald, trumpeter, halbardier, trabant guard, and running footman ;
also a gentleman in a hunting dress and lady of Vienna in her ordinary attire.

Herald.

Trumpeter.

Halbardier.

Trabant Guard.

Running Footman.

Hunting Dress.

Lady Wortley Montague, in 1716, represents the dress of the Austrian ladies as very disfiguring ; and the Baron de Pollnitz, who visited Vienna in 1729, remarks that the ladies there dressed with

Lady of Vienna. 1703.

Lady of Ratisbon. 1703.

Ladies of Strasburg. 1703.

more magnificence than taste, but states to their credit that very few painted, either red or white, or wore patches. Reisbeck, on the contrary, says, "French fashions prevail here universally; all the women are painted up to the eyes and ears, as in Paris."

Of the ordinary female costume of Vienna, Ratisbon, and other German cities, in 1703, examples have also been selected from the work above mentioned (see p. 327).

The numerous varieties of costume, especially in head-dresses, which even still distinguish not only particular States, but particular towns and districts in each of them, although gradually disappearing, have already been alluded to in my notices of the costume of Germany in the two previous centuries, and I can only here repeat my observation on the necessity of limiting our illustrations to those which are most remarkable or instructive. In the great cities throughout the entire Fatherland, the fashions of Versailles or St. James's were eagerly and promptly adopted by

Nuremberg Peasant. 1703.   Jews of Frankfort. 1703.

the nobility and gentry, and may in fact be fairly considered the costume of Europe from the Danube to the Atlantic Ocean. A traveller in Prussia during the last century, speaking of the ladies of Berlin, mentions the practice even then existing of the extravagant and absurd mode of patching which was used in England in the days of Charles II. "The damsels," he says, "frequently cut their patches in the shape of flies, beetles, hares, asses, bears, sheep, oxen, and hogs; so that the French have not devised anything, be it ever so silly and absurd, that the Germans have not made still more silly and absurd in the imitation." And this, too, was in a kingdom the sovereign of which prohibited paint, and was a decided enemy to gaudy dresses and new fashions of every description. While yet a boy, Frederick William had vowed vengeance against French wigs and gold brocade dresses. When not in uniform, he wore a brown coat and red waistcoat, with a narrow gold border. He observed with indignation that the large laced hats and bags in which Count Rothenburg and his retinue appeared in public found admirers at Court, and to prevent imitation he ordered at the great review held at Tensplehoff, near Berlin, in 1719, that the regimental provosts, who like the executioners were reputed infamous, should appear in the French costume, only with the brims of the hats and the bags enlarged to an extravagant size. Fashion and the fair sex proved more than a match for Frederick William I. of Prussia.

His son, Frederick the Great, was as simple in his own tastes as his father. The whole of his wardrobe consisted of "two blue coats faced with red, the lining of one a little torn, two yellow waistcoats, three pair of yellow breeches" (such being the uniform of the Potsdam Grenadiers), "and a suit of blue velvet, embroidered with silver, for great occasions." His personal appearance is as familiar to us, from the many portraits and statues existing of him, as that of his contemporary, our own King George III.

The female peasantry throughout Germany were then as now full and short petticoats of cloth, generally woven by themselves, laced bodices of black velvet or other materials, and coloured stockings. Those who wore leathern shoes rejoiced in buckles. Their head-dresses were, however, as various as they were extravagant, recalling some of the most preposterous coiffures of the fifteenth century, and in some instances actual relics of that period, reverently handed down by mother to daughter from generation to generation. At Linz, the capital of Upper Austria, I was asked, in 1827, several guineas for one of the caps of gold brocade worn by the young women of that locality, and thence called *Linzen-hauben*. It was not inelegant in form, and had two bows of black satin ribbon, one on the top and another larger behind, from which a couple of long ends streamed down the shoulders.

The authoress of the 'Book of Costume,' published some thirty years ago, collected a considerable quantity of materials for her account of the "Toilette in Germany;" and from that portion of her pages which treats of the national dress of Europe in her time, and principally from her personal observation, I have already made several extracts.[1]

"In the neighbourhood of Bamberg and Augsburg," she observes, "the female peasants wear a chemise with short sleeves, and which fits close to the throat, with a small collar, not unlike a modern habit shirt. The bodice fits tight to the shape, and is ornamented with buttons or gilt beads. The petticoat reaches just below the knees; it is very wide, and of a different coloured stuff from the bodice. The stockings are white or blue, with scarlet clocks. The shoes have buckles. A riband often encircles the waist, and is tied in front. The hair is arranged flat on the forehead, or rolled back in front, and allowed to hang in a short *chignon* on the neck. Some wear a close neat cap, much like a night-cap; others a coiffure resembling a caul, that fits the head and ties under the chin. A good deal of the back hair is seen, and long ribands hang from it." The "coiffure" last mentioned by the writer was daily seen in the streets of London some fifty years ago on the heads of the Bavarian broomgirls, and may be traced back to the thirteenth century. "The better class of peasants," adds the Lady, "have curiously shaped caps, some of black satin or velvet, others of lace or muslin, plaited and stiffened like wings. The upper part, of coloured silk, resembles a skull-cap, and is ornamented with two large bows." The form of the first one in the engraving

Caps of Bavarian Peasants.

accompanying the latter description resembles that of the Linzen-hauben above mentioned. The other recalls a head-dress of the second half of the fifteenth century.

"The gowns," she continues, "are high up the throat, which is frequently encircled with a broad necklace or band. The women are fond of gaudy colours, and often wear dark-blue or scarlet shoes. The men in this district have black hats, turned up behind, and surrounded with a gold-coloured band, scarlet waistcoats, long blue coats, black breeches, and shoes, with large buckles."

"The Bavarian peasants, near Munich, wear broad felt hats or bonnets, with a knob on the crown the size of a walnut, or a droll little silver turban *with two peaks behind*, which is fastened on the very back of the head.[2] The dark petticoats of the women are very short, and the bodice, which

[1] Pages 310, 312, 324.

[2] Fifty years ago I saw such a head-dress worn generally in the market-place at Cologne, but it had entirely disappeared when I revisited that city in 1857.

resembles a cuirass, is made quite stiff, with silver buttons, chains, and ornaments, which shine brightly upon the scarlet or blue stuff of which the body is made. The sleeves are white and short, the stockings usually of a bright blue, with long stripes and clocks of scarlet and white. The men as well as the women wear broad-brimmed hats of black felt, with scarlet or yellow bands round them, sometimes with bunches of riband suspended from the crown, and not unfrequently a feather. Their nether garments scarcely reach to their knees, which are usually bare, for the blue and white stockings are gartered beneath. Their waistcoats are green or blue, their jackets black and very short, and those who can afford it ornament their vests, like the women's bodices, with every kind of silver trinket."

I annex a woodcut from a coloured print of Bavarian costume, published at Frankfort, which illustrates many points of the above description, particularly that of the men. It represents a man and woman of Langries, and slight differences exist in every district.

Man and Woman of Langries, Bavaria.					Costume of Ulm, Würtemberg.

In the adjoining kingdom of Würtemberg, the women wear generally a black jacket over the bodice; it has long sleeves to the wrist, and is often left open to the waist, so as to show the bright-coloured vest beneath. The petticoats scarcely hang over the knees; they are very full, and have a coloured border round the bottom. The chemise is often tied at the throat with a broad riband; sometimes it has long sleeves and a worked corsage. The bodice is usually scarlet, laced over a blue stomacher with yellow; and the wide petticoat is white, with a broad border of blue and yellow. Stockings are worn of all colours, also girdles and belts. The coiffures are various: sometimes a little black skull-cap is seen, with a bow at the top, or the hair hangs in long plaits behind, and a large gilt comb ornaments the top of the head; frequently, however, an immense cap of black lace is worn, and forms a fan that stretches far beyond the face; the crown is merely two rolls of scarlet silk, with ribands hanging from it. The men wear either broad-brimmed or three-cornered hats, and dark clothes, except on holidays, when they may be seen in white coats lined with blue, scarlet waistcoats, and leather breeches.

Here is a young man of Elbingen in the holiday dress described, and his chosen fair one in her bridal costume. She has the black jacket mentioned above, over a black bodice, with a blue stripe in it, cut very low to display as much as possible of the scarlet or crimson under-vest or stomacher, above which is seen the neatly-pleated chemisette. Her girdle is of silver or gilt metal-work ; her stockings scarlet or crimson, as the vest ; her shoes black. Her hair, parted on the forehead, is plaited in a long tail, to which are attached streamers of coloured ribbon ; and on her head is a small coronet or cap of gold brocade, which is usually a family relic of many generations.

Bride and Bridegroom of Ebingen, Würtemberg.

Peasants in the Rhinegau, near Pfalz.

In the district of Baden the lower class of peasants are gaily attired. The men wear a broad-brimmed black hat; a coat of lilac or blue, lined with scarlet ; a scarlet waistcoat, striped with green ; black breeches, blue stockings, and shoes bound with red. The women comb back all the hair from the forehead, and plait it into one tress, which hangs down the back ; or else cover the head with a straw hat, tied under the chin with a black riband. Their shift has full sleeves to the elbow ; the bodice of crimson, black, or blue, is usually laced across, striped, and adorned with some other bright colour. The petticoat is often green, the apron purple, and the stockings scarlet. Frequently, however, the peasants, instead of stockings, wear linen or cloth leggings, which leave the ankles and feet uncovered.

Near Friburg they have little velvet caps, white petticoats, black jackets, laced with crimson ; white stockings, and black shoes, with crimson rosettes. The men in some of the districts tie their hats on to their heads with a broad riband, and wide riband neckcloths knotted in large bows. Frequently, too, they draw their white stockings above the knees, and fasten them with broad black garters. The engravings in a collection of German Costumes published some fifty years ago furnish us with examples of the dress of the people in and about Friburg, which display some curious varieties.

The costume of a man of Morat, in the canton of Friburg, carries us back to 1600. That of the women is only remarkable for the manner in which the head and throat are closely bound up in a kerchief, over which is placed a broad-leafed straw hat. The laced bodice, jacket with long tight

2 U 2

Peasant of Morat, Canton of Friburg.

Villagers of Baden in Wedding Dress.

Peasantry of Wallach, in Baden.

sleeves, striped petticoat, and apron, have the common features of those with which we are familiar in the dress of German or Swiss peasantry. Some are attired in a *mélange* of fashions of various

Country people of Rahbeim, environs of Frankfort.

Country people near Dresden.

dates, the adoption of which has probably been gradual, the shoes and buckles being the latest introductions.

A collection of Costumes published at Frankfort affords an example of the wedding dresses of a young couple in the Kirchzarter Thal, in the Margraviate (now Grand Duchy) of Baden. The floral coronet of the bride is prettily constructed. The braces of the bridegroom (a peculiar feature in nearly all German costumes) are highly ornamented. (See opposite page.)

Near Frankfort-on-the-Main the women wear the full petticoats so generally seen in the other districts, but usually of a dark colour, the bodice laced with crimson and ornamented with silver buttons; the shift sleeves tied in at the elbow. A coloured kerchief covers the neck, a crimson sash encircles the waist, and a little blue cap conceals all the hair except the chignon behind. The

Men and Woman of Upper Austria.   Costume of Loeben, Styria.

men wear striped night-caps, with a tassel at the end; dark blue jackets, with gilt buttons; pale blue waistcoats, with silver buttons; short leather breeches, and white stockings, pulled up over the knee and fastened beneath with wide black garters. The shoes are made with a broad piece of leather, which lies on the instep, and are clasped with immense buckles.

A curiously-shaped cap is worn by the women in a portion of this district. It bears some slight resemblance to one of the many forms of the French hood, but whether an intentional imitation or not I will not venture to say.

In Saxony we find a variety of singular costumes, some of the head-dresses rivalling in extravagance and eccentricity any of the monstrosities of the fifteenth century, of which I have given so many examples. One of the least grotesque is seen in the neighbourhood of Dresden. It consists of a tight cap or coif of crimson, with a white border round the face, and entirely concealing the hair. An immense frill surrounds the neck, tied in front with a large blue bow, the cap behind being adorned with one equally large of crimson.

The most extraordinary costume remaining in Europe in the eighteenth century may, I think, fairly be said to distinguish the female peasantry of the district of Altenburg, in Saxony. No verbal description of it would be comprehensible by any person who had not visited the locality. Fortu-

Costume of Altenburg, Saxony.

nately it has been depicted by native artists in all its grotesque and hideous varieties, and from a host of examples I have selected the accompanying, humbly confessing my utter inability to suggest their origin or the date of their adoption.

Winter Costume, Altenburg.

The male costume has a general resemblance to that of the majority of German provinces, with some slight indications of the neighbourhood of Poland, the toes of the boots and shoes evincing in several instances an inclination to turn the points upwards.

Summer Costume, Altenburg

The subjoined group of head-dresses is described " Kopfputz der Altesten Zeit," and may therefore be considered as no longer worn; but the high-crowned hat of the male figure (No. 1) cannot be older than the sixteenth century, while figures 4 and 5 appear to be reflections of fashions of the seventeenth. Of the remaining six, Nos. 3, 8, and 9 resemble head-dresses occasionally seen here and elsewhere in Germany, and, like Nos. 2, 6, and 7, may have been relics of a very early period. The singular fish-tailed head-dress of the women, in what we may term modern costume (see woodcut above), must therefore have been a comparatively late assumption, and I cannot suggest even its derivation.

The noble authoress of 'The Book of Costume,' which I have so often quoted, in her notice of Bohemian costume says: "The women often wear little jackets trimmed with fur, scarlet stomachers, black petticoats, scarlet stockings, and have on their heads a tight band of linen with a red crown and long ribands hanging from it. The chemise is never seen; a black handkerchief covers the neck, and a black cloak is often worn, lined with scarlet, and carelessly hanging from the shoulders. The men have long coats and waistcoats of scarlet or blue, adorned profusely with silver lace and buttons; the shirt is seen above, tied with a black riband. The nether garments are large and wide, the stockings blue, and the shoes black edged with scarlet."

This partiality for black relieved by red or blue is particularly noticeable at Eger, in Bohemia, a place celebrated for its chalybeate spring. The

Old National Head-dresses worn in Altenburg.

following figures are from a local print, representing a wedding procession. The whole party, including bride and bridegroom, are clothed in black and red, with the exception of the man-servant, who has a blue sleeveless jacket, and the maid-servant, who wears a blue apron. The heads of the women are bound with black kerchiefs, and the hats of the men adorned with large bunches of

Costume of Eger, in Bohemia.

black watered ribbons. Their loose breeches are of black leather, and meet the tops of the black close-fitting boots in which their legs are encased. The coats and jackets of both sexes are profusely furnished with gilt buttons.

Of the costume of Upper Austria and Styria, examples have been given at p. 333. The Tyrol

Tyrolese Costume.

presents us with a mixture of German and Italian costume. Broad-leafed hats of black or green felt; gay-coloured waistcoats, over which are worn braces, connected by a band across the chest; and jackets with tight sleeves, or square-cut coats with large sleeves, usually compose the upper and most ancient portion of the dress of the men in Upper Austria and Styria, the lower consisting of comparatively modern knee-breeches, coloured stockings, and half-boots. The women also wear broad-brimmed hats over kerchiefs; black or coloured jackets, with stomachers; short, full-pleated petticoats and aprons: a style of dress which, with slight modifications, has probably been worn for the last three hundred years.

The same remark may be made respecting the Tyrol, where the dress of the men differs from their German neighbours' principally in the shape of their hats and the clothing of their legs, the crowns of the former being conical, like the Roman peasant's; and the protection of the latter entrusted to pieces of linen or cotton tied round the ankle, and looped up to the breeches behind the knee, which, as in some Bavarian costumes, is always left bare. The women are distinguished by the number and amplitude of their petticoats, some wearing nine or ten, all very full and very short. The head-dress of a woman of Stoerzing is remarkable. She carries in her hand, beside, a broad-brimmed straw hat, lined with green silk and adorned with ribands, the ends of which have gold or gold-coloured fringes.

The costumes of the various cantons of Switzerland must be familiar to the majority of our readers, and have so many features in common with those above described, that the introduction of several would appear to be

Woman of Stoerzing.

Canton of Schaffhausen.

Costume of Zurich.

Vaudoise.

repetitions. With the exception of the almost universal custom of plaiting the hair in long tresses with ribands—a fashion as old in Europe as the twelfth century—there is nothing in the appearance of a Swiss maiden or matron to carry the student of costume back to the Middle Ages, as is the case

Costume of Lucerne.

Costume of Thurgovie.

Costume of Berne.

in other countries. Bating powder and periwig, hoop and patches, men and women seem to have inherited the clothes of their grandfathers and grandmothers, and only in the cantons of Berne and Appenzell is there even a head-dress that would attract his attention. It may be a question, indeed, if even the well-known fan-shaped cap of black lace worn by the women there is of national origin, for a coiffure extremely similar is worn in Würtemberg, and the mode might have found its way into Switzerland in the eighteenth century, together with the three-cornered cocked hat and the shoes and buckles of the men of that period. There is certainly no representation of it previous to the seventeenth century. The caps of the Swiss women depicted in Vecellio, Boissard, Weigel, &c., are such as are commonly seen on the banks of the Rhine and in various parts of Germany, as well as in some cantons of Switzerland at the present day, and have no remarkable peculiarity. It appears to me a singular fact, and one which I have not found noticed by any writer with whose works I am acquainted, that the Swiss, who for three hundred years at least have been so specially distinguished by their dress when serving abroad, should have retained no particle of their characteristic attire in their own valleys, and that, with the trifling exceptions above mentioned, there is nothing in the costume even of their wives and daughters to mark their nationality, to identify them with the land they are reputed to be so passionately attached to.

Christopher Weigel supplies us with some characteristic costumes of Holland in 1703,—a merchant reading his letters, a boatman, and a fisherman and his wife. By the dress of the merchant

Dutch Merchant. 1703.

Dutch Boatman.

one may understand that the better classes of the Dutch nation followed the French fashions, and rely upon the truth of the following description of the attire of the gentry of Amsterdam in the last century, quoted by the authoress of the 'Book of Costume:'—

"The Dutch burgomaster always dresses in black. His lady appears in a bell-hoop and a lace head-dress worth 100*l.*, but the daughter not unfrequently walks between this antiquated couple tricked out in all the bravery of the last Paris fashions."

An Amsterdam belle of that period is thus described. " To begin with her head; it is covered with a small muslin cap, and a tiny round black silk hat, which is balanced on the back of the head. A

2 X 2

neat white handkerchief is fastened across the bosom with a pin, and carefully pinned underneath the arm; round her neck, upon the handkerchief, hangs a necklace made of rows of gold beads. Her upper garment is a short striped cotton bed-gown; the body is laced before the gown, part reaching just below the hips, which are swelled out to a large size by her hoop. The sleeves of this garment are tight, and do not fall beyond the elbow; the petticoat, which reaches to the ankles, is of a red or

Dutch Fisherman and Wife. 1703.

green stuff, spread out to the size of a barrel, forming a strange contrast to the small head; the feet are encased in black shoes with red heels and enormous buckles." A beau of the same date is said to have "his hair rolled up above the ears, his hat is three-cornered, and in size about three-quarters of a yard from corner to corner, the waistcoat very long, the coat closely buttoned, and the shoes ornamented with Brobdignag buckles." These descriptions read as though they were out of a page of the 'Spectator.'

It was my good fortune, some years ago, to pick up a collection of Dutch Costumes published at Amsterdam by E. Maaskamp in 1804, with descriptions in French and English. The worthy editor informs us, in what he evidently believed to be the latter language, that "very often he found himself obliged to deny the traveller who asked him for such a Custom book of the kingdom, by answering that nothing of this nature as yet existed," and that "the one and the other has made him resolve to put hand to work himself in fulfilling the deficiency of this province." The result of his laudable labours was the publication of a series of very neat copperplate engravings carefully coloured; woodcuts of some of which, although uncoloured, will be better comprehended by our readers than "the ample *explication* in English" by which each is "attended;" though, as a relief to the dryness of archæological disquisitions, I may be tempted to quote *ipsissima verba* M. Maaskamp's interesting though absurdly written work, entitled 'A Representation of the Dresses, Morals, and Customs of the Kingdom of Holland at the beginning of the Nineteenth Century.'

I perfectly agree with him that "it is greatly to be regretted to see the vanishing of the national dresses which were either original or introduced at the removing of the nations . . . At present the fashion has confused everything. Hardly there are in some corners of Europe patterns of the original dress to be seen. *This* in particular is existing in the kingdom of Holland" (meaning that the patterns of the original dress *can* be seen there), "and so our country makes an exception in this respect." Upon which he calls our attention to a print of two women of Friesland, "drest in the very same strange manner as in *the fifth century*, when their predecessors, united with the Saxons, established colonies in Great Britain"! I need hardly take the trouble of correcting this very romantic description. My readers have only to turn to the Dictionary or the first two chapters of this volume to form their own opinion of its veracity. Even the fifteenth century would be quite early enough for the date of any dress in Holland. Nevertheless the dress of the Dutch women in some of the provinces is very quaint and of some antiquity. Take, for instance, these young maidens of Marken,

a small island in the Zuyder Zee, and who are very incorrectly described by M. Maaskamp. One is a bride, or rather a *fiancée*, according to the plate, and "glitters," we are told, "with all the gloss of the variously coloured dress of the *thirteenth* century." The *fifteenth* would be the earliest to which any portion of it could be traced, viz. the sleeves and the bodice. The cap is peculiar, and may probably be of the same date. It is described as being made of fine white linen, bordered at top with a red silk riband, and at the lower edge by two ribands— one red, the other black or blue. The collar of her chemise is embroidered with black silk, and fits tight round her throat. Over the chemise is a stomacher, or what the editor calls a breast-plate of red cloth, and over that a waistcoat of the same colour, with a black border and fastened across the chest with a broad gold clasp. Over this, again, she wears a brownish-yellow jacket, without sleeves, embroidered with roses and stiffened in the sides with whalebone. On her arms are brown half-sleeves, displaying the chemise between the elbow and the shoulder— a fashion of the time of Edward IV. and

Young Women of Marken.

Henry VII. in England. The rest of her costume consists of a full blue woollen petticoat ; a white apron with embroidered borders, the upper portion pleated in very fine horizontal pleats, and the rest in broad longitudinal ones ; blue stockings, and black leather shoes with round silver buckles. The other girl (miscalled an elderly woman), who is congratulating her companion on her approaching nuptials,[1] is in the ordinary dress of her class—a brown jacket with *tabs* at the waist, a blue petticoat, and light brown apron, the upper part of which is of black and white check. Her neckerchief or whisk of white muslin, with a point and tassel behind, is seen in Dutch paintings of the time of Charles II. The pointed cap of white linen, undecorated with riband, is the only article of dress which identifies her with the Island of Marken. The caps of married women are said by M. Maaskamp to be embroidered in black with the initials of their husbands' names. "Whether," he adds, "this is a precaution, or a relic of barbarity in ancient times, when a man marked his wife even as his cattle, we do not know." Neither do I, having never heard of such a custom.

A-propos of husbands, whatever antiquity may be attributed to certain articles of the female toilette in Holland, the costume of the men leaves no room for speculation. When it was not of the date of Queen Anne or the first two Georges—the usual habit of the merchant and citizen class—it was that which we have found prevailing all over Western Europe, and traceable, with few exceptions,

---

[1] "Belle fiancée, toutes sortes de prospérité," is the superscription.

to the reign of our James I. In illustration of these remarks I append two engravings from Maas-kamp's collection : the first representing a well-to-do Frieslander and his wife in their Sunday clothes, returning from church ; and the other, a fisherman and his wife, of Ens or Shockland, an island in the Zuyder Zee.

The dress of the man in the former has the general character of that of the first half of the eighteenth century ; the long straight-cut collar-less coat, with its double rows of buttons, loose breeches tied with bunches of riband at the knees, being relics of the days of William III. The cocked hat, wig, and shoe-buckles are of a later date ; the shortness of the waistcoat alone suggesting the introduction of a fashion of the time of publication. Waistcoats as short and even shorter were, however, worn in much earlier times, and we must not therefore hastily infer that they were novelties in the United Provinces before 1760. The good wife presents us with an admirable specimen of a Dutch woman of the middle classes, by whom the fashions of at least fifty years had been utterly

Costume of Friesland.   Fisherman and Wife of Shockland.

disregarded. She wears the printed calico jacket which was called a bedgown in England within my recollection, and was probably imported from Holland in the days of William and Mary ; a flowered petticoat of damask or Indian chintz over an ample hoop, a neat checked apron, a white muslin neckerchief with a coloured silk one over her shoulders, and black lace mittens, as might any London housewife have done ; but her nationality is distinguished by the large flat straw hat lined with chintz, and the North Holland cap with its gold ornaments, of which more anon.

The second couple afford an example of national costume retained from an earlier period. The coat of the man has fuller sleeves, but in other respects does not differ widely from that of the Frieslander ; but the breeches are those very loose wide ones known as Dutch slops, as early as the sixteenth century. They are fastened at the waist over two waistcoats, the under one scarlet, with silver buttons, and the upper blue with red stripes and similar buttons, but not meeting any-where in front, the under one alone being visible, except at the waist. He wears a cap of close-knitted wool, grey woollen stockings, and white scoured wooden shoes. The woman's costume is specially interesting. She wears a scarlet under-vest, with sleeves reaching a little below the elbows, with yellow or gold lace at the terminations and on all the seams. Over this is a blue waistcoat, without sleeves, also trimmed and laced like the under one, meeting only at the neck and the waist, leaving an oval opening displaying the red under-vest, over which it is laced with yellow or gold cord nearly half-way from the waist upwards; a brown stuff petticoat and blue apron; a purple silk kerchief, knotted, about her neck; and a cap bound on the head by a broad piece of linen, which only allows the crown to be seen, and from under which a row of small curls are permitted to peep upon the forehead, and a corkscrew ringlet to hang on each side the face. The upper part of this costume may hail from the fifteenth century in Europe, whither I suspect it travelled from the East.

Subjoined are two other Friesland women. One of them is a person of some condition; though wearing the costume of her locality, it is all of finer materials. The hat is of a remarkable form—"somewhat alike," M. Maaskamp suggests, "to a large oyster shell." Rather, I should say, to the lid

Costume of Friesland.

Young Woman of Alkmaar (North Holland).

of a large basket. It is made of the finest plaited straw, lined and covered with a gay chintz, and having a broad silk riband streaming down from the back and brought over the shoulder to secure it, in case of necessity; as the poetical editor observes, "against the indiscreet curiosity and rude attacks of the wild children of Æolus"! The long gloves of green kid, the black lace embroidered apron, and the pink slippers are indications of gentility not to be mistaken; she is also ordering the other woman, who has brought her some fresh butter, to take it to her servant.

The straw hat of the latter is of a different form, and under it she wears the cap which is specially considered the head-dress of the women of all ranks in North Holland. There appears to be several varieties of the gold ornaments belonging to it. This coiffure, as worn at Alkmaar, is thus described: "It consists, firstly, of a white under-cap, with embroidered black flowers, which, just fitting the head, encloses and covers all the hair except two very small curls, which hang down, one on each side the face. On this under-cap lies a broad band of thin beaten gold, surrounding the back of the head and extending to the ears. From the square ends of this band, in some examples, small slightly-curved plates of gold, terminating in points, rise up and secure the cap in front, while in others a plate partly encircles the forehead, terminating in a rounded end above the right temple; over this cap is worn another of transparent gauze, the ends of which hang down behind on the shoulders, covering but not hiding the broad gold band aforesaid." Such descriptions are rarely intelligible unassisted by the pencil. The annexed engravings will better acquaint the reader with the form and effect of this remarkable and picturesque head-dress, which is no doubt of considerable antiquity, and

North Holland head-dresses.   Cap worn at Vollendam.

confined, as far as I have been able to ascertain, to this particular locality. Not the least curious consideration is, that it should have remained unnoticed by writers and delineators of costume down to the beginning of the present century. Some of these head-dresses, M. Maaskamp assures us, cost as much as four hundred guilders.

With the representation of one more head-dress, the cap worn by the women of Vollendam, I shall conclude my notice of the costume of Holland. The crown of this cap is made of fine linen. It is slightly conical, and terminates with a plain band above the forehead, having a broad border of lace, called *laugit*, very stiffly starched, and forming a peak in front, while at the back it is turned up in two sharp ears, and in this example, M. Maaskamp informs us, "embroidered in black," with the "*fore*-letters (initials) of her husband's name"—the custom I have already alluded to.

The numerous works of the Dutch and Flemish painters of the last two centuries, familiarised to us by the originals in the public and private collections in this country, and the engravings of those abroad, furnish such ample and accessible authority for the dress of all classes in the Netherlands, that as no material alteration took place in the first half of the eighteenth century, it is happily not imperative upon me to increase the bulk and expense of this volume by the introduction of any examples.

Ancient Scandinavia, represented at the present time by the three kingdoms of Denmark, Sweden, and Norway, has retained many of its primitive customs and habiliments. In the capital cities the nobility, gentry, and principal inhabitants have, as we have already seen, constantly followed more or less rapidly the fashions invented or adopted in France or England; but the peasantry, as in other European countries, have been little influenced by the changes without, and retain most of the costume that has been worn by their fathers for many generations.

In Norway the men wear broad-brimmed hats, or grey, brown, or black woollen caps. The Gulbrandsdalen peasants are distinguished by red caps. Some wear breeches and stockings all in one (the *chausses*, in fact, of their ancestors in the eleventh century), waistcoats or jackets to match, that is of wool of home manufacture, which those who wish to be smart cover the seams with cloth of a different colour. The Hardanger peasants wear black, edged with red; the Vaasserne wear all black; the Strite, white, edged with black; and those in the neighbourhood of Soynefiord, black, with yellow: so that, as that agreeable traveller, Inglis (*alias* "Derwent Conway"), observes, "every division has its distinguishing costume."[1]   Their shoes are without heels, and consist of two pieces of leather; the upper part sits close to the foot, and the other is joined to it in folds.   In winter they have laced half-boots, but when on the ice they put on skates about ten feet long, covered with seal-skins.   They never wear a neckcloth, but leave their throats and necks entirely uncovered.   Sometimes they fasten a leather belt round the body, to hold their knives or other implements.

At church, or on holydays, the Norwegian women wear laced jackets and leathern girdles adorned with silver.   Their kerchiefs and caps are covered with plates of silver, brass, and tin, buttons and rings; and of the latter they wear quantities on their fingers.

In some parts of Norway the men wear coats of stone-coloured cloth, the button-holes being worked with scarlet, and the buttons made of white metal.

Inglis, describing the meeting of the Diet at Christiania, says that the assembly of delegates presents, in consequence of the variety of local costume he has alluded to, "a very motley and almost ludicrous appearance to a stranger.   Several of the deputies wore jackets and girdles: these I recognized as natives of Tellemarken, through which I had recently passed; others, whose coats were as much beyond the length of an ordinary coat as the jackets of the former were shorter, and who might be seen walking to the hall, their heads covered with something of the shape of a Kilmarnock nightcap, I was informed were the deputies of Gulbrandsdalen, the mountainous district bounded on the north by the Dovre Field and its range.[2] . . . On the occasion of opening the Diet a public ball was given, which I attended.   The wives and daughters of a few of the deputies had come to Christiania and were present, their home-spun and home-made dresses singularly contrasting with the more fashionable attire of the belles of the metropolis."

Costume of Hernusad, Sweden.

Of Sweden Mr. Inglis gives us no information whatever on the subject of dress; and the

[1] 'A Personal Narrative of a Journey through Norway, Sweden, and Denmark.' Edinburgh, 1829.
[2] In a Norwegian legendary ballad translated by the author, the wood demon borrows the jacket and red cap of a peasant, in order to pass for "a child of clay," and it is stated in a footnote that such "is the universal dress of the peasantry in Gulbrandsdalen, and the districts bordering on the Dovre Field" (p. 248).

sumptuary law of Gustavus III., enacted for the purpose of repressing the extravagances and luxuries indulged in by his subjects, being passed in 1777, is too late for our notice. The regulation also affected only the higher orders, and especially those who attended the Court. The dress of the peasantry, the really national costume of the country, appears to have had many features in common with that of the North of Europe at the same period, which, as I have already noticed, seems to have been not older in fashion than the commencement of the seventeenth century. A collection of Costumes, published at Stockholm in 1827, enables me to illustrate this portion of my work with some very picturesque examples of the dresses worn in particular localities and on special occasions. To these I shall confine myself, as exhibiting relics of bygone times which I cannot venture to give a date to, as they have an Oriental character about them exceedingly deceptive always as to age, from the tenacity with which types and patterns are adhered to.

Take, for instance, the figures in the previous page of peasants in the district of Herrestad.

The bosses and buttons with which the jackets of the two women and the collar of the cloak of one are laden, may have been centuries old or of modern

Costume of Herrestad.

manufacture. The jackets themselves are probably of Tartar origin. We have seen them wherever

Costume of Wingaker, Sweden.

Bride and Bridegroom, Wingaker.

Winter Dress, Wingaker.

Peasant Girl, Wingaker.

an Asiatic race had settled in the West, and they had found their way to France and England from Spain in the seventeenth century. The jacket of the man is of the form that garment assumed during its journey northward at the latter period, when it encounters its original in Scandinavia,

Costume of Werend.

Costume of Blekinge.

Bridal Costume, Blekinge.

after having made the tour of Europe. The remainder of the man's costume, minus the boots, is scarcely different from that of an English countryman in the time of Charles I., from which date it was to be seen nearly all over the Continent. The more modern jacket of another man of the same district is in strange contrast with a high standing ruff of the sixteenth century (see p. 346). The only variety is the long straight coat and cocked hat which appeared at the end of the century. In Sweden the coat is generally of white woollen cloth, in winter well lined with fur.

On p. 346 also are a young couple of Wingaker in Sodermanland, in their ordinary costume, and another pair in their bridal attire. The bride, in her hooped petticoat and stomacher, with short sleeves ruffled at the elbows, recalls the dress of the days of Queen Anne in England ; she wears the crown which in one shape or another is as indispensable in Sweden as the wreath of orange blossoms with us. The bridegroom, in his long white coat, high topped gloves, broad-leafed hat with band and buckle, and square-toed shoes, only requires a lace cravat or muslin neckcloth to pass for a well-to-do English commoner of William III.'s reign. A woman of the same district,

with her young son, in their winter clothing, the outer garments of each being well lined with fur, are worthy of notice, principally for their head-gear (see preceding page). The woman has a voluminous one of white linen, tied in a knot behind, the ends hanging on the shoulders. The boy has the red cap common to the male population of a portion of Norway ; the little peak it forms in front giving it a thoroughly Phrygian character, as well as recalling the caps of their Scandinavian ancestors, the Norsemen of the ninth and tenth centuries.

Beneath them is a woman of Warend, in the district of Smaland, in her riding-dress, and two female costumes from the district of Blekinge, one of which is peculiarly graceful, recalling to us some of the more picturesque dresses of the time of our Henry VII. ; the

Group of Mourners, Torna.

other is that of a bride with her indispensable coronet, and her hair flowing down her back according to European custom in the Middle Ages.

I conclude my notice of Sweden with a group of mourners in the Harad of Torna. The hat of the man is the bycocket of the fifteenth century, but there was a revival of the form in the seventeenth, and I cannot, therefore, draw any inference of its antiquity in Sweden from this modern example.

Of Lapland and Iceland, in the first half of the eighteenth century, we possess the contemporary accounts of Ehrenhalen (1745). He says the Laplanders "pretend to have preserved the attire of ancient times, yet I do not believe it ; they live and dress as the climate permits." But so they most undoubtedly did " in ancient times," and consequently there may be more truth in their tradition than M. Ehrenhalen is willing to admit. "They use," he tells us, "no linen cloth ; this only accords with warm countries. All their foreign luxury consists in a very coarse woollen cloth. They have caps of it, which they border on all the seams with a lace of a richer or more shining cloth. They make their doublet of it. It is a greatcoat with long sleeves, wide about the neck, and open at the breast ; yet they cover the skin with a stomacher. In the bad weather of summer this piece of cloth is covered with an old furred robe ; in the winter with a warmer fur. In the severe cold of that long season they

Laplander in Winter Dress.   Laplanders, Male and Female, in Summer Dress.

wear caps or cloaks of skin. The Laplanders of the forests wear shoes made of the bark of birches ; those of the mountains in winter have shoes of reindeer skin. The Lapland women," he observes, " differ little in their dress from the men, but wear round their heads a fillet of crimson cloth for want

Portions of Lapland Costume, from Pinkerton's 'Voyages.'

of ribbons of silk, and a light border of wool instead of lace." The London public have recently had an opportunity of seeing at the Royal Aquarium, Westminster, a family of Laplanders in their ordinary dress, which remains to this day precisely the same as it was at least a hundred years ago, and as represented in the preceding page from prints in the volume I have been indebted to for the costume of Sweden, published at Stockholm in 1824. I add from Pinkerton's 'Collection of Voyages' various articles of dress worn in Lapland.

A later traveller than Ehrenhalen (Professor Lessing, 1757) describes the dress of the men of Iceland as consisting of a jacket shaped like a coat, good cloth waistcoat, and breeches of the

Lady of Iceland.

same; the waistcoat trimmed with four or six rows of copper or other metal buttons. The women wear cloaks of different colours, mostly black, and called *hempe*. The richer classes decorate the front of the *hempe* with various ornaments of gold or silver, and wear a collar or neck-band of velvet, three or four inches wide, embroidered with gold or silver; but the most remarkable feature of their costume is the conical head-dress, composed of stiffened coarse cloth, covered by a finer material, and forcibly reminding us of the steeple head-dress of the fifteenth century, and its modern varieties in Normandy and the Basque provinces. From whence could this singular fashion find its way into Iceland? With what people did it originate? May we trace it back to the mountains of Lebanon and other parts of Asia Minor, where, from the time of Zechariah (B.C. 520), and probably long previously to the present day, it has existed and obtained a proverbial immortality? The horn worn by the women of Lebanon is called *tantoura*, and has a veil attached to it, as in the case of the steeple head-dress of the Middle Ages. Mr. Buckingham describes one worn by a female at Tyre: "She wore also upon her head a hollow silver horn, rearing itself upwards obliquely from her forehead, being four or five inches in diameter at the root, and pointed at its extremity. . . . This peculiarity reminded me very forcibly of the expression of the Psalmist (lxxv. 5)." Bruce also found the fashion existing in Abyssinia, where silver horns, four inches long, are worn by the chiefs and military men. It is there called *kern*, the same word as the Hebrew *keren*, and from whence the French *corne* and our own *corner*.

The men wear a tunic called *tork*, of sheepskin, the wool inside, with a stiff high collar of cloth, embroidered with different colours—the tunic is bordered with kersey, and the edge trimmed with otter's fur, the left side ornamented with gold or silver tassels; cloaks of kersey or wadmol, called *Ladde kafte* and *Gogges kafte*, with stiff collars covering the whole neck to the shoulders, also embroidered; other cloaks, made of the skin of the female reindeer, the hairy side outwards and called *Paesk*; gloves called *Rappenbuk*, made of the skin of the feet of the young reindeer or the black fox, and lined with dried grass called *sunnek*; no stockings, but leggings of wadmol, reaching from hip to ankle, called *Gogges Busak*, or of dressed leather, called *Kamark Busak*; shoes, called *galloshek* (can this word have any connection with our galloches?), fastened with thongs about the calf and up above the knee, (the old Scandinavian custom)—some with turned-up toes, called *sopokek*; girdles and pouches of leather, with tin ornaments. The women shave their heads almost to baldness, and usually wear linen caps, seldom woollen—if the latter, they are of kersey, or some such cloth, bound on the head with ribbons or counterfeit gold or silver lace; hoods of green or blue cloth, trimmed with a different colour; sheepskin tunics, like those of the men, only longer and without the stiff collar, and more profusely tasselled with gold or silver on the left side; others of wadmol, kersey, or reindeer skin; long trousers like the men, and gloves and shoes of the skin of the white reindeer; girdles of cloth or leather, covered with tin plates, the wealthier women wearing gold or silver girdles.

A Russian Nobleman. 1703.   Sailor's dress.   Peter the Great, 1689-1714.   Polish dress.

Of Russian costume Weigel in 1703 gives us but one specimen. We have, however, abundant material in the grand work we have been already so much indebted to, illustrative of all ranks and both sexes in the European portion of that empire, and from which we select the figures of the

Empress Natalie.   Prince Potemkin.

A Polish Nobleman.

A Polish Heyduck.

celebrated Tzar Peter the Great in his sailor's dress and a Polish dress, the Empress Natalie his mother, and the celebrated Prince Potempkin.

Respecting the military costume of this period, the warlike character of the nations in the East

Heyduck.

A Polish Peasant.

of Europe, and the influence of their Asiatic origin on their dress as well as on their manners, render it difficult to distinguish the apparel of every-day life from that of the camp and the battle-field, particularly as all classes save the mercantile and the clerical went on all occasions armed to the teeth, and regimental uniform, but recently introduced into France and England, had not in 1703 (the date of the publication of Weigel's work) been adopted by the Governments of Hungary, Poland, or Russia. I shall not therefore, in this instance, attempt to separate the civil from the military costume of those countries, reserving, however, some observations on the latter for that portion of the chapter which is appropriated to the illustration of the regular army.

To begin with Poland, at this period under the sceptre of Frederick Augustus, Elector of Saxony, the successor of the valiant John Sobieski, soon, however, to be driven from his throne by the power of Charles XII. of Sweden, and supplanted by Stanislaus Lecziusky, Palatine of Posnania, elected July 12th, 1704. Here we have, 1, "Ein Polnisch armiter Edelman," the costume but slightly differing from what it appeared in the sixteenth century; 2, a Polish Heyduck, with the ample trousers that indicate an Oriental origin; 3, another Heyduck, of inferior rank, who might be described as "in heavy marching order;" and, 4, a Polish peasant. Unfortunately there is no example of Polish female attire in the collection; but I am enabled, by the kindness of a Polish gentleman, to supply the deficiency from a collection of Costumes published in 1841 by Leon Zienkowicz, from which I have selected such examples of national attire as have reached our own times uninfluenced by the fashions of Western Europe, guided also by the valuable descriptions and notes of the learned editor, whose text, in French, is full of the most valuable information.

The dress of the peasantry in the vicinity of Cracow, on the left bank of the Vistula, consists of a shirt, the collar and wristbands of which are fastened by ribbons. They never wear any sort

Cracovians in Sunday dress.   Man and Woman of Sdialmiers.

of neckerchief or cravat, even in winter. Over this shirt they wear a tunic or coat, called *sukmana* or *karazya*, fastening in front, and a girdle, ornamented with bright copper studs, to which, by a leathern thong, is appended a small knife, called *kozik*. Loose trousers of white or striped red and white cloth, or sometimes of yellow leather, are stuffed into their boots, which come up to the knees, and are made of leather called *juchta*, known to us as "Russia leather," with very thick iron heels. Their caps are square, of red cloth, and bordered with black fur. The overcoat differs in colour in particular districts. That of the peasants nearest to Cracow is blue, with crimson silk or cotton embroidered borders (the *karasya*), and has a falling collar or cape hanging over the shoulders, ornamented with little plates of copper. The inhabitants of Szkalmierz wear brown coats, with white cords; those of Proszow, white, with black cords. In summer time the men generally wear white cloth coats and linen trousers, high boots, a large low-crowned hat, ornamented with ribbons and peacock's feathers. The young women wear their hair long behind, and tied with coloured ribbons. Their shift sleeves are embroidered on the shoulders and at the wrists with crimson. The bodice is of blue or red cloth, silk or satin; the petticoat, of various colours, descends to the ankles, and, by those who can afford it, is bordered with gold or silver lace. Necklaces of coral or coloured beads are universally worn. In summer a light shawl or scarf, of linen or muslin, called *rantuck*, is

Peasant of Proszow.   Polish Peasants of Skavina.

thrown over the shoulders to protect them from the dust. They wear also aprons, which they fling over their heads when at work in the fields. Over this dress they wear sometimes a coat like that of the men, generally of blue cloth, and in winter lined with sheep's wool, and boots with high heels instead of shoes.[1] In fine weather they sometimes wear neither shoes nor stockings. On fête-days the young Cracoviennes wear a *bandeau* of velvet or gold lace round their heads in form of a diadem, surmounted by flowers and long streaming ribbons. Married women wear a white kerchief on their heads, or a hood (*chaperon*), trimmed with gold lace.

The people on the right bank of the Vistula (the Kijacks and the Skavinians) are also called Cracovians. The former, inhabiting the country between the salt mines of Wieliezka and Podgorse, wear blue coats, lined and trimmed with crimson; green vests and girdles, ornamented with gold and silver; green velvet caps, square in form, and bordered with grey or black fur. The Podgorsian women wear blue coats, like the men, red corsets, yellow petticoats, and various-

[1] It is worth noticing that the toes of both boots and shoes are devoid of any such peculiarities as those of the *cracowes* in the Middle Ages, which are presumed to have derived their name from this locality.

coloured aprons. The girls dress their hair with flowers; the matrons wear white kerchiefs. The Skaviniens wear blue bodices; green petticoats, with red borders; a flowered apron; and a scarf or shawl about their shoulders.

A spirited sketch of a Harvest-home Procession in the neighbourhood of Sandomir illustrates a singular local custom. A crown of wheat is placed on the head of some village beauty who is a bride-elect,

Back of cap of Man of Podolia.

and, after it has been blessed by the priest in the church, she is conducted with music and song to the house of the Mayor, who attaches a cock to the top of the crown, which is reconciled to its position by pecking the grain out of the ears. If on the road it expresses its satisfaction by crowing, it is con-

Peasants in the neighbourhood of Warsaw.

sidered a happy omen for the ensuing season; but if it remain sulky and silent, the reverse is to be expected. As there is nothing special in the dress of the persons composing the procession, I have not thought it necessary to have it engraved.

Hunters in the Forest of Bialowicz.

Costume of Mountaineers called Hamly.

2 Z

Galician Male and Female Costume.   Countrywoman of Jaroslaw.

In the woody and mountainous parts of Poland the foresters and hunters of these districts bind their legs, like the peasants in the Abruzzi and some parts of Spain, from the ankle to the knee with a sort of cross-gartering, such as we see in Frankish, Anglo-Saxon, and Norman costumes of the tenth and eleventh centuries; but in lieu of linen and leather the Polish bands are made of the bark of the beech-tree. White linen shirts and trousers, brown cloth jackets, coats or cloaks (*kapota,*

Hungarian Nobleman.   Hungarian Officer in summer dress.   Hussar Officer.

siermienga, sukmana), leathern girdles, and fur caps of various shapes, or low-crowned, broad-brimmed hats, form the ordinary attire of the inhabitants of the Bialowicza and the mountaineers of Kolomya. The women trim their holyday dresses with gold and silver lace, and the girls braid their hair with a profusion of ribbons.

With the above examples of the costume of the people in the environs of Lemberg and Jaroslau, towns in Gallicia or Austrian Poland, I must terminate my selections from the interesting work of M. Zienkowicz, which contains no less than thirty-seven carefully drawn and coloured plates illustrative of national dress and military uniform; the latter, however, being of too recent a date for introduction in this History.

Hungary is more liberally illustrated by Weigel, as may be imagined, considering the Viennese origin of the work. Subjoined are eight engravings of Magyar costume, male and female :—1, a Hungarian nobleman (*ein Hungarischer Herr*); 2, a Hungarian officer in summer dress (*ein*

Hussar.   Colonel of Hussars.

Hungarischer Beamter in Somer-Kleid); 3 and 4, an officer and private soldier in a Hussar regiment; 5, a colonel of Hussars; 6, *ein Hungarischer Banteerstecher*,[1] in a coat, hood, and chausses of mail, and who but for the boots might be mistaken for a soldier of the fourteenth century; 7, a Hungarian lady of quality; 8, a Hungarian lady in summer dress, and 9, a lady in winter clothing; also a Honak and a Honakin or female peasant of the same district. (See woodcuts, pages 358, 359.)

Armour, excepting gorgets and cuirasses, was entirely abandoned at the commencement of the eighteenth century by all European nations west of the Danube, and regular uniform adopted for every arm in the service, Prussia setting the fashion in military costume as well as military tactics.

---

[1] I have been unable to obtain even from Germany a satisfactory interpretation of this word. Heinsius defines it a sort of rapier with hard blade, which served to pierce a coat of mail (Bantzer, Banner, or Panzar). I can only suggest that such troops were named from the weapon peculiar to them, as we find Halbardiers and Harquebusiers; or at present, Lancers, Carbineers, and Fusiliers. This, however, entails the inference that such mail-clad men were employed against troops similarly equipped, as the Circassian cavalry are to this day.

Hungarian Rearersmchet.

Hungarian Lady of Quality.

Hungarian Lady in summer dress.

Hungarian Lady in winter dress.

Scarlet and blue had long been the two principal colours of the cloth ordered for the array of the king's troops, in accordance with the tinctures in the armorial ensigns of the Royal Family

March of the Guards to Finchley. 1745.

From the Engraving by Hogarth

Homak.

Homakie.

of England from the time of Edward III., the guide from the beginning of Heraldry for the liveries
of retainers and domestics having been the colours in the arms of their lord or leader. The uniform
of the Guards was therefore, in the reign of Queen Anne, definitively made red with blue facings ;
those of the regiments of the Line being also red, but dis-
tinguished from each other by different coloured facings. The
red and white feather appears during the same reign. The black
cockade, about the time of George II., was probably assumed in
opposition to the white cockade of the Jacobite party. The
pointed Grenadier cap was introduced from Prussia between
1713 and 1740, *i.e.* during the reign of Frederick William II., first
King of Prussia, and father of Frederick the Great.[1] The pike
ceased to be carried in the English army in the reign of Queen
Anne, and the musquet and bayonet became the general weapons
of the infantry. The cartouch-box supplied the place of the
bandelier ; and the gorget, worn only by officers when on duty,
dwindled into the gilt toy that I remember it in the reign of
George III. The British Hussars were enrolled in 1757.

Grose has printed the regulations for the clothing of his
Majesty's forces in 1729, 1736, and 1746; but as no colours are
mentioned, they add nothing to our information on this subject.
For more minute details I must again refer the reader to the
'Records of the British Army,' published by authority, from
official documents, by Richard Cannon, Esq., London, 1837.

The only Scotch regiments in the English service previous to
the accession of George III. were the Royal Scots and the 42nd Foot. The former, under the

Life Guard. 1742.

command of the Earl of Orkney, was in 1700 still "armed in the old Highland fashion, with bows and arrows, swords and targets, and wore steel bonnets."

The 42nd Foot was composed of independent companies, raised for the protection of the country against robbers, and thence called the Highland Watch. They were regimented October 25, 1739, when John, Earl of Crauford, was appointed Colonel. Grose, writing at the end of the century, says: "The 42nd Regiment of Foot differs from all others in his Majesty's service in their dress and appointments, their uniform being the ancient habit of the Scottish Highlanders, consisting of the bonnet, plaid, red jacket faced with blue, the philibeg, and tartan hose. Their arms, besides those borne by the other regiments of infantry—namely, firelocks and bayonets—are large basket-hilted swords, and daggers about eighteen inches long, called dirks" (vol. i. p. 163). To this account he

Officer and Sergeant of Highland Regiment.

adds a foot-note, as follows : " I doubt whether the dirk is part of their general arms, but I remember in the year 1747 most of the private men had them, and many were also permitted to carry targets. The regiment then was in service in Flanders." Now this statement is of considerable importance to us, as it justifies our introduction of copies of the engravings which accompany Mr. Grose's description, as, recollecting the equipment of the regiment in 1747, had any particular alterations taken place in it previous to 1800, when the drawings must have been made for the work (published in 1801), he would surely have alluded to them. I have, therefore, no hesitation in giving reduced copies of figures from his plates, depicting an officer, soldiers, sergeant, and piper of a Highland regiment at that date, although it is later than the period to which this History is limited. The good old antiquary's remark, that their uniform was "the ancient habit of the Scottish Highlanders," raises a smile in these more critical days ; but the *sporans* worn by them are of a primitive form, and the hose of the officer and soldiers are longer than those worn at present, reaching up to the knee, and gartered close beneath it.

Soldiers, Highland Regiment.   Piper.

In France the progress of uniform was much the same as in England, and similarly influenced by the regulations in Prussia. In the first years of the reign of Louis XV. the square-cut coats and large three-cornered cocked hats were worn by the majority of the forces, leather breeches and high boots distinguishing the cavalry, with the exception of the Dragoons and the Hussars—the former wearing long gaiters, and a cap the point of which hung down nearly to the shoulders ; while the Hussars had exchanged their original Turkish style of dress for the Hungarian. Their cap resembled that of the Dragoons, only not so long in the point. The jacket had tight sleeves and short skirts. The pantaloons were close-fitting, and the boots of soft leather, with turn-over tops. A short mantle of fur hung on their shoulders, and the pouch called *sabretache* was appended to their waist-belt. Père Daniel, in his ' Histoire de la Milice Française,' published in 1721, has given us contemporary representations of a Dragoon and a Hussar, and also an engraving of the standard-bearer of the Cent Suisse at the same period, who must not be confounded with the Swiss Guards. (See next page.)

Regiments were distinguished principally by the colour of their facings, their lace, or their *brandeburgs*. Dark blue and bright red were the colours of the Royal regiments. The former was appropriated to the *Gardes du Corps*, the *Gardes Françaises*, and the *Grenadiers à cheval* ; the red to the Swiss Guards, the *gens d'armes*, and the Musqueteers. In the troops of the Line the *"rouge garance"* (a deep red, approaching claret colour) and sky-blue were assigned to foreign regiments in the French service, whilst every shade of brown and grey, with different coloured facings, distinguished the French regiments from each other. But while uniform had been accepted without protest by the army generally, the officers took great liberties, and dressed according to their fancies. Those of the Gardes Françaises, who were privileged to wear private mourning when on duty, would march at the head of their companies in plain black vests, without any mark of military distinction except the gorget, usually worn at that period.

The bearskin fur cap was introduced from Prussia in 1740. It was first worn in the French

Standard Bearer, Great Britain.

Officer of Mousquetaires du Roi. 1700.

army by some German regiment in the service, and subsequently adopted by the Horse Grenadiers. By degrees the colonels of infantry regiments gave them to their grenadier companies, some, however, preferring the pointed cap without fur.

Hussar. 1555.

In 1745, Marshal Saxe, after his exploits in Bohemia and Bavaria had given him celebrity, obtained permission from Louis XV. to raise at the expense of the State a corps of Hulans or Uhlans—irregular cavalry of Asiatic origin, but naturalized at that period in Poland and Lithuania. Several other corps of foreigners were formed, and amalgamated with the French army shortly after-wards—composed of Croatians, Gallicians, Biscayans, and Corsicans —who were allowed to retain the most characteristic portions of their national costume. To these were added legions of volunteers from Dauphiny, Flanders, and Hainault. Amongst the best-known were the legions of Fischer and of La Morlière.

During the "War of the Succession," as the contention respect-ing the crown of Spain was called, which commenced in 1702 and terminated by the Peace of Utrecht in 1713, the uniforms of all the regiments of infantry, which had previously been clothed in grey or in brown, were changed to white, with various-coloured facings ; on the shoulders were buttoned straps to correspond, and the squares cut skirts of the coats were turned back at the corners.

Besides the grenadier companies attached to the different regiments, there were formed in 1745 and 1749 some regiments com-posed of Grenadiers only. They were called Royal Grenadiers and Grenadiers of France, or French Grenadiers. Their uniform was blue with red facings. They would seem to be the first that possessed pioneers, for we are told that ten men of each company had leathern aprons and carried hatchets and pickaxes. They all wore tall bear-skin caps, the fur being only in front, according to the Austrian fashion. In 1760, the uniform of the Hussars was sky-blue, and

Soldier of the Legion La Morlière.

that of the Dragoons red. The alterations after that date do not call for my notice in these pages. For them and for further minute particulars respecting the French army in the eighteenth century, the reader is referred to the excellent work of M. Quicherat and the many collections of engravings of French military costume which have been published in Paris, and are generally accessible, amongst which may be specially recommended the "Recueil des Uniformes" of Chéreau.

I have said that the equipment of the European armies in the eighteenth century was particularly influenced by the alterations made in those of Prussia. One of the most remarkable, the substitution of the sugar-loaf cap of the Grenadiers, rendered so familiar to us by the pencil of Hogarth, in place of the three-cornered cocked hat (noticed at page 359), is reported to have originated in the following circumstance during the reign of Frederick II., king of Prussia, father of Frederick the Great. The Prussian Grenadiers in 1730 were armed with the lighter fire-locks called *fusils*, which they carried slung behind them while they were flinging their hand-grenades. The large cocked hats were found exceedingly inconvenient under these circumstances ; at every movement of the soldier, he ran the risk of his hat being knocked off by the contact of one of its corners with the muzzle of the gun. The king, to obviate this difficulty, invented a conical cap with a metal plate in front, which presented no impediment to the swing of the musket. Some of these caps were of fur, and others of paste-board, covered with cloth, and became so popular in the army that they were worn long after hand-grenades had been done away with.

The Baron de Polnitz, writing from Berlin, June 5, 1729, testifies to the strictness of the regula-tions of dress at that time established in the Prussian service : "L'uniformité," he says, "régna en toutes choses dans l'armée, jusqu'aux boucles des souliers."

He tells us also, that "Les Prussiens ont une chose qui n'a jamais été pratiquée par aucunes troupes ; c'est d'habiller tous les ans de neuf." It appears, therefore, that they set the example of this important practice to Europe, issuing cloth breeches for winter and linen for summer, shirts, collars, and gaiters. He further informs us, that the uniform of the whole of the infantry was blue ; but that it was left to the colonel of each regiment to settle the colour of the waistcoats and facings according to his own pleasure.

The uniform of the Cavalry and Dragoons was white; that of the Hussars, red. The *gens d'armes* had blue coats with gold brandeburgs. Some regiments which he does not specify had laced waistcoats ; all the heavy horse had buff coats and cuirasses.

A book entitled 'Geschichte aller Königlichen Preussischen Regimenter,' published at Nuremberg in 1760, a copy of which was kindly given me by Sir Samuel Meyrick, enables me to illustrate this latest portion of my work, as regards Prussia, very completely. Annexed are figures of an officer and soldier of each of the principal regiments existing at the above period, with the date of its formation.

1. Infantry—Musqueteers, raised 1715. Uniform blue, with red facings, collar and turnbacks, gold-embroidered button-holes and gilt buttons. Officer, boots, gorget, black and silver sash, straight

Officer and Private of Musqueteers. 1715. Officer and Private of Grenadiers. 1740.

sword. Private, gaiters and curved sword. Some regiments have pink and some white facings, and some yellow or buff waistcoats and breeches ; all cocked hats.

2. The Grenadier battalion, raised in 1740. Uniform blue, with red facings and turnbacks, white waistcoats and breeches. The officer wears a gold-laced cocked hat with bullion tassel, high black boots, a black and silver sash (the colours of Prussia) fastened in front with two large tassels, a black ribbon round his neck tied in a bow behind, and a gorget. The private has the grenadier cap, the back of which is of scarlet cloth, and the point is surmounted by a red and white pompon. He wears long black gaiters, a broad belt buckled in front, from which depends a curved sword or sabre, called in French *sabre briquet* or *coupe-chou*.

3. Infantry—Fusiliers, 1741. Blue, with various facings—yellow, orange, white, red, and pink. Private, pointed grenadier cap, the colour of the back generally but not always corresponding with that of the facings.

4. Cuirassiers, 1718. White coats with various-coloured facings, black cuirasses, high black boots, and cocked hats, lined with gold or silver according to the lace and buttons of the coat ; broad

Officer and Private of Fusiliers. 1742.

Private and Officer of Cuirassiers. 1718.

carbine belts, white with red or blue stripes or chequered borders, long cavalry straight swords and
sabretaches.

5. Dragoons, 1741. Light blue coats with black, yellow, red, pink, and white facings and turnbacks, white breeches, high black boots, black and silver sashes, cocked hats laced with gold or

Private and Officer of Dragoons. 1741.

Officer and Private of Hussars. 1741.

silver according to the lace or embroidery and buttons of the coat, and aiguillettes of gold or silver on the right shoulder.

6. Hussars, 1741. Jackets edged with fur, white, brown, light blue, black, and red ; waistcoat and pantaloons generally of the same colour ; yellow or black morocco leather boots of the form known as Hessian ; high cloth caps with very broad bands and pendent ends—a curious illustration of the original form of the well-known Hussar cap of the present day ; curved sabres and sabretaches.

The troops of all arms wore powder and pigtails *circa* 1760, except the Hussars, who had side-locks, either plaited or tied up with ribbons, and wore moustaches, as did some of the other cavalry regiments. The infantry were all closely shaven.

In addition to these regiments were the corps of *gens d'armes*, formed by King Frederick I. in 1701, the officers of which wore scarlet coats with blue cuffs and collars, richly embroidered with gold, yellow waistcoats and breeches, high black boots, gold-laced cocked hats, and black and silver sashes—the privates being represented in yellow coats, with red collars and cuffs, blue waistcoats edged with red, yellow breeches, and black boots, and wearing long straight broad swords and sabretaches ; the Leib Carabinier regiment, armed similarly to the Cuirassiers ; the mounted Jäger corps (" Jæger corps zu Pferde "), in green and scarlet uniforms, and a foot regiment in the same dress ; the Artillery, Engineers, and " a Pionier Regiment," formed in 1741, which latter, however, displays no special distinction suggested by the name. A Royal Body Guard (Gardes du Corps), formed in the same year, appears to have been dressed as nearly as possible like the *gens d'armes*, save that the embroidery, lace, and aiguillettes were of silver, and that the waistcoats of the privates were red with blue bindings instead of blue with red.

The cut of the clothes and form of the hats of the above regiments differing in no respect from those of which I have already given examples, it is unnecessary to multiply the illustrations, as without colour they would appear to be simply repetitions. Nor do I consider it necessary to pursue the subject of uniform any further. Similar gradual changes took place in the attire and equipment of the armies of Spain, Portugal, Italy, and the Northern kingdoms of Europe, which it would be tedious to record, however briefly ; and while some national character might probably be preserved in the costume of certain foreign auxiliaries, the general features of the uniform adopted in France and England from contemporary Germany were thoroughly represented by the regular forces of all.[1]

Of the navies of Europe, as far as costume is concerned, our information is meagre.

To commence with that of our own country, we find that a regular uniform was not introduced previous to 1748. Naval commanders were ordered to wear scarlet in the reign of Elizabeth, and that order was confirmed by James I., as I have stated in the last chapter ; but during the subsequent reigns that regulation was neglected, and naval officers appear to have been habited according to their own fancy and armed like the military, while their ships' companies were sometimes clothed like the land forces, in the colours of their captain. At page 116 of the Dictionary will be found the figure of an English Admiral in 1703 ; but as it is copied from an engraving, we are ignorant of the colour of his dress.

In the Guard Room of Hampton Court are, or were, the portraits of Admiral Churchill and Vice-Admiral Sir Stafford Fairburn, *temp.* Queen Anne. The first is in red velvet, with gold-laced button-holes ; the second in plain blue velvet.

Mr. Fairholt has engraved an English sailor from a print of the date of 1746, and says, " He wears a small flat cocked hat, an open jacket displaying his shirt, the collar being turned loose over his shoulders, and loose slops similar to the petticoat breeches of the reign of Charles II., and which are still seen on Dutch sailors, as well as upon our own fishermen." He might have referred to Chaucer for proof of the great antiquity of the latter portion of the dress amongst nautical men. The Shipman in the Canterbury Tales is described as dressed in " a gown of *falding* to the knee ;" the *phalinges* mentioned, as early as the reign of Henry II., by Giraldus Cambrensis in his descrip-

---

[1] A traveller who visited Vienna at the end of the eighteenth century describes the Emperor's Trabant Guard (see page 320) as " clothed in black, all in a cloak laced with yellow," the colours of the Empire.

tion of the ancient dress of the Irish. Like the Scottish kilt, it was originally the skirt of a body garment, from which, eventually separated, it became a petticoat, and is still generally worn by sea-faring men on the shores of the Adriatic and the Mediterranean.

In 1748, George II. accidentally met the Duchess of Bedford on horseback in a blue riding habit faced with white, and was so pleased with the effect of it, that a question having been just raised as to the propriety of deciding upon some general dress for the Royal Navy, he immediately commanded the adoption of those colours,—a regulation which appears never to have been gazetted, nor does it exist in the records of the Admiralty, although a subsequent one in 1757 refers to it (vide 'Journal of the British Archæological Association,' No. 5).

The flat three-cornered cocked hat which we have seen on the head of the sailor in 1746 continued to be worn down to the reign of George III., for in 'The London Chronicle' for 1762 we are told that "sailors wear the sides of their hats uniformly tacked down to the crown, and look as if they carried a triangular apple-pasty upon their heads;" and Swinburne, in his Travels in Spain, describing the dress of a class of irregular soldiers called Miquelets, says, they "wear a broad silver-laced hat, squeezed flat, *like those of the English sailors.*" In our Plate representing the drawing of the Lottery in 1751, a sailor is seen with his three-cornered cocked hat and petticoat trousers.

In France, previous to the reign of Louis XIII., there was no dis-
tinction between the land and sea forces. The Naval Armies ("Armées Navales") were composed of merchant vessels taken up by Govern-

English Sailor. 1746.

ment, armed for the occasion and filled with troops from the regiments on shore. Cardinal Richelieu established a new system, and from his time there has always existed a regular marine army, specially formed and reserved for service at sea. Louis XIV. instituted in 1670 a corps of 200 Gardes Marines, and in 1682 added to their number and founded academies for their instruc-
tion in mathematics, fortification, hydrography, *dancing*, fencing, and exercise of the pike and the musquet.

Père Daniel, who furnishes us with ample details of their organization, duties, &c., is silent respecting their clothing; but M. Quicherat states that it was the same as that of the land forces, and we must therefore consider these troops to have been similar to our own marines. The crews or regular sailors seem to have been only employed to work the ships, and wore dragoon caps ("bonnets à la Dragonne"), flat-soled slippers, short jackets with sleeves that buttoned at the wrist, a sort of petticoat (*jupon*) called a *vareuse*, a black silk cravat, and a blue silk scarf. Unfortunately, we have no engraving accompanying this rather vague description; but it would seem that, with the exception of the cap, the dress could have differed little from that of seafaring men in general.

The distinction between the sailors and the maritime forces on board ships of war, in all European nations, seems therefore to have been officially established during the first half of the eighteenth century, and originated probably in England, the nation of which the navy has been so long the most popular service, and, to use an appropriate simile, "the sheet anchor" of her power and prosperity.

Following the order I have hitherto observed in this work, I have next to speak of the clerical costume of Christian Europe, 1700--1760.

In the Roman Church, no addition was made to the vestments and ornaments of the clergy. They continued to be six in number for the general priesthood—viz., 1, the amictus or amice; 2, the alb; 3, the girdle; 4, the stole; 5, the maniple; 6, the chasuble—and nine additional proper to bishops only: viz., 1, the *caligæ*, leggings or stockings, otherwise called *tibialia*, originally of linen, but in later times always made of silk; 2, the shoes (*sandalia, soleæ, campagæ*, or *campodi*); 3, the under girdle (*subungulum, succinctorium*); 4, the episcopal tunic (*tunica pontificalis*); 5, the dalmatic; 6, the

Canon Regular in Bologna.

Canon Regular in Austria.

mitre; 7, the gloves; 8, the episcopal ring; 9, the staff or crozier. All these have been specially noticed under their separate headings in the Dictionary; and engravings of prelates and other church dignitaries in full pontificals and ministerial vestments will be found throughout these pages.

Canon Regular in Poland.

Croston Monk in his Choir Habit.

Some variation, however, appears to have existed in the dress of canons in different European nations. We give therefore, from prints of the last century, figures of—1, a canon regular of the congregation

Pope Clement XI.

Leopold, Cardinal Archbishop of Cologne.

Abbot of Benedictine Monastery.

French Abbé.

of St. Salvator in Bologna ; 2, a canon regular in Austria ; 3, a canon regular in Poland ; and 4, a Croxton monk in his choir habit. (See page 368.)

In the preceding page are given the portrait of Pope Clement XI. from an engraving by Christopher Weigel ; of Leopold, Cardinal Archbishop of Cologne in 1703, of the abbot of a Benedictine monastery, and of a French abbé.

The following woodcuts from engravings of a series of sovereigns and saints prefixed to an heraldic work in the Russian language, in my possession, published in 1714, may also be adduced in

St. Ladislaus.   Russian Archbishop and Patriarch.   Pope or Priest of the Greek Church.

proof of the clergy of the Greek Church having retained their officiating vestments, unaltered in form and number, from the earliest days of its separation from that of Rome, the particular names and descriptions of which have been handed down to us from Germanus of Constantinople in the eighth century and Simeon of Thessalonica in the fifteenth, to the present day. The sacerdotal character of the imperial state habiliments, as exemplified in the figure of St. Ladislaus, is in conformity with those of the Emperors of Germany, who bore the title of Apostolical, the style retained by their descendants, the Emperors of Austria, and who were sovereigns of the Holy Roman Empire ; the orarium, the especial vestment of Christian priesthood, being most prominent in the costume of the autocrats in both countries. I have also noticed its assumption by an English sovereign as early as the thirteenth century (see Dictionary under STOLE, p. 486). The third figure is that of a pope or priest of the Greek Church, in ordinary attire.

In the English Church no alteration took place in the dress of the officiating minister, but the clergy were distinguished from the laity in society by their wigs and gowns which they wore in ordinary. In those days Englishmen appear not to have been ashamed of their honourable professions. The divine, the physician, the "counsel learned in the law," and the military officer, were conspicuous in all places of public resort or social assemblages, and their costume not only commanded the respect due to their position, but had a salutary effect on their behaviour. That wholesome check is now removed ; and with the exception of the clergy, who have recently (the High Church party especially) been more demonstrative in their ordinary attire (though as a matter of

THE HOUSE OF LORDS, *temp. George II.*

taste, I confess, the sporting of soft shapeless "wide-awakes"[1] in the streets of London does not, in my humble opinion, add to the respectability of their appearance), the members of all other professions eagerly shuffle off every article of apparel that would indicate the rank one would imagine they would be naturally proud of, and become lost in the mass from which their learning, their valour, and general abilities have raised them.[2]

The pencil of Hogarth has preserved to us the usual costume of the clergyman and the barrister in more than one of his admirable pictures of society (see 'The Marriage Settlement,' issued with Part XXII.). The numerous portraits of our eminent divines, judges, and other high official personages which are now happily so accessible to the general public in the National Portrait Gallery at South Kensington (to the intelligent curator of which, Mr. George Scharf, it is always a pleasure to me to express my many obligations), render it unnecessary for us to multiply engravings of what may be fairly termed familiar examples. The accompanying woodcuts of the Houses of Lords and Commons in the reign of George II., and the House of Commons in the time of Sir Robert Walpole, will sufficiently illustrate the general senatorial costume of the middle of the eighteenth century. The present University dresses also date from about this period; the trencher caps and apologies, or rather absurd substitutes, for the mediæval hoods, being inventions of an age which was remarkable for its wretchedly bad taste.

Sir Levett Hanson, in what he calls "a critical dissertation" prefixed to his 'Accurate Historical Account of all the Orders of Knighthood at present' (1802) 'existing in Europe,' computes the number at sixty-six, which he divides into seven classes—viz. 1, chapteral; 2, papal; 3, imperial; 4, royal; 5, electoral and archiepiscopal; 6, ducal or princely; and 7, "destined particularly for the fair sex." Of these sixty-six Orders, twenty-two were instituted between 1700 and 1760, the limit of our inquiries; of these some expired with their founders, others became dormant and have never been revived, and the majority were of so little general importance that it is unlikely their insignia would be a matter of interest to our readers, or the representations of them required by the artist or the actor.[3] I shall therefore limit my illustrations to those Orders which have a European reputation and an authentic history, and of the habits and decorations of which accurate descriptions or engravings are accessible. In addition to the work above mentioned, Edmondson's 'Complete Body of Heraldry,' Clark's 'Concise History of Knighthood,' and Nicholas Carlisle's 'Concise Account of the several Foreign Orders of Knighthood,' the latest contribution to our knowledge on this subject, may be consulted by any student desirous of obtaining information on some special point in connection with it. He must be careful, however, of trusting to dates of institution or traditions of origin, as few, if any, concerning the more ancient Orders can be depended upon. Even the world-renowned "Garter" and "Golden Fleece" are to this day enveloped in mystery, as I have already pointed out.

My selection, for the foregoing reasons, amounts to ten foreign and two British Orders, the two latter being those of "St. Andrew" and "the Bath," previously noticed in the Dictionary, p. 123. Of the foreign Orders, the first in date, as well as of consequence, is that of the Black Eagle of Prussia, also previously noticed in the Dictionary at the above page, and of which the collar is engraved on Plate V.

This Order was instituted at Königsberg by Frederick I. of Prussia (inadvertently called Frederick the Great, in the article alluded to), on January 18, 1701, the day preceding his coronation. The badge is appended to a broad watered, orange-coloured riband, worn over the left

---

[1] The broad-brimmed, flat-crowned hat of a clergyman of this date is engraved from a painting by Hogarth at p. 260 of the Dictionary, but is much more respectable.

[2] It is actually at present one of the punishments to which an officer guilty of some dereliction of duty is *condemned.* He is sentenced to wear his sovereign's *uniform* for a certain period as though it were a *degradation*, when it should be his proudest privilege to do so in public on every befitting occasion, and not eagerly merge in *mufti* the honourable position he has the good fortune to occupy.

[3] In the library of the College of Arms are four volumes, folio, illustrating Sir Levett Hanson's work by cuttings from foreign publications and carefully coloured drawings of the decorations, collars, crosses, stars, and ribbons of nearly all the existing orders of knighthood, made from the originals.

shoulder, in honour, it is said, of the mother of the founder, who was a princess of the House of Orange.[1] The habit of the Order consists of a sky-blue velvet vest or tunic, with long sleeves and a carnation-coloured velvet mantle, lined with blue mohair, having the star of the Order embroidered on the left side ; a black velvet hat turned up on one side, with a diamond loop and button, and a plume of white ostrich feathers. All the knights wear the like robes, excepting princes, the trains of whose mantles are considerably longer.

The Order of the White Eagle of Poland, traditionally founded by Vladislaus V., king of Poland, in the fourteenth century, had no substantial existence previous to the reign of Augustus II., who instituted it in 1705. It fell into disuse on the partition of Poland in 1795, and was revived by the Emperor Napoleon I. in 1807. The habit assigned by the first founder consisted of a long surcoat of *ponceau* velvet, lined with white satin ; a sky-blue velvet mantle, also lined with white satin, on which was originally embroidered a white eagle, and a cap "made after the Polish fashion," of the same velvet as the surcoat. That there was, however, an Order of the White Eagle known in Bohemia and Poland previous to the institution of Augustus in 1705 is indisputable, as it is described and figured in a work published at Amsterdam in 1697. The tradition is therein repeated of the origin of the Order, being the discovery of a nest of white eagles, and the habit and insignia are stated to have been a white eagle appended to a gold chain, and a blue mantle with a white eagle embroidered on it.[2]

This description is accompanied by an engraving ; but as no authority is quoted for it, and as Bäckler, Haagen, and all writers on the subject are agreed, that even if instituted in 1325, "having soon fallen into disuse, it lay in oblivion until the year 1705," the figure is more likely to have been designed from fancy than any contemporary representation in sculpture or painting. The form of the shield and the arms upon it are not of the Middle Ages,[3] and at the time of the publication of the book shields had "fallen into disuse" as well as the Order.

The Order of St. Alexander Newsky, instituted by Peter the Great and confirmed by the Empress Catherine in 1725, does not appear to have had any habit assigned to it. The knights are distinguished by a broad *ponceau*-watered ribbon worn over the right shoulder, with appendent badge and a star on the left breast.

The Order of St. Januarius of Naples was instituted by Charles, King of the Two Sicilies (afterwards Charles III. of Spain), 3rd June, 1738. Hanson describes the habit of the Order as a vest and coat of cloth of silver, or white and silver tissue, and a mantle of crimson mohair bestrewed with fleurs-de-lys in gold embroidery, and lined with pearl-coloured taffety, beset with black spots after the manner of ermine ; cords and tassels of gold and silver ; hat, black velvet with a white feather. The ribbon is flame-coloured and watered, and worn over the right shoulder with pendent badge ; the star on the left breast.

The Order of the Sword in Sweden is supposed by some writers to have been founded by Gustavus Vasa in 1522 ; but "owing to many circumstances, such as the mental derangement of Gustavus Erichsen, the embracing of the Catholic religion by one branch of that family, their subsequent retreat into Poland, and the long wars occasioned by a disputed succession to the throne, this Order was in a state of dormancy until the year 1748, when it was established by Frederick I., King of Sweden and Landgrave of Hesse-Cassel. The insignia consist of a star and a badge, the latter being worn appended to a yellow-watered ribbon with a dark-blue border." I find no mention of robes, though Hanson says that Sir Sidney Smith, on the occasion of his investment at Stockholm, "appeared in the robes or habit of the Order."

The Order of the Polar Star was instituted by the same king, Frederick of Sweden, on the 17th April, 1748, and it was renewed with some alterations by Adolphus Frederick, Duke of Holstein-Gottorp, his immediate successor, in 1751. No robes are assigned to it, but in addition to a badge

[1] Louise Henriette, daughter of Frederick Henry, Prince of Orange, and wife of Frederick William, Elector of Brandenburg.

[2] "Een witten trent onder aan een grude keten hangende, en een blaauwe Mantel, dar den witten trent mede ofe, af gebeeld was gaf." ("Historie van alle ridderlyke en Krygs-Orders,' vol. ii. p. 172.)

[3] The arms of the kingdom of Poland, crowned and surmounted by the insignia of the White Eagle.

THE HOUSE OF COMMONS, temp. George II

pendent to a black-watered riband the knights wear on high festivals a collar composed of white-enamelled five-pointed stars, and the letter F in blue enamel and crowned regally. There is no separate star.

The Order of St. Anne of Holstein was instituted by Charles Frederick, Duke of Schleswig-Holstein Gottorp, in the month of January 1735, in honour of the Empress Anne of Russia, and of his own consort, Anne Petrowna, the eldest daughter of Peter the Great; but it was not until Peter, Duke of Schleswig-Holstein Gottorp, Grand Duke of Russia, succeeded to the Imperial throne on the decease of the Empress Elizabeth in 1762, that it became of much consideration, by being declared the fourth Order of the Russian Empire.

Hanson describes the habit of the Order as consisting of a black velvet full-dress coat (suit), with the star richly embroidered on the *right* breast, and a mantle of crimson velvet, embroidered with three devices in gold, silver, and colours—the first being the star of the Order, the second the monogram A. I. P. F.[1] in a cypher, and the third the image of St. Anne kneeling. These three devices are disposed alternately in such wise that the whole mantle is covered therewith. The mantles of princes are lined with ermine, but those of the knights with "ermine velvet" (*i.e.* white with black spots in imitation of ermine), and fastened on the breast with a rich clasp of gold. The hats are of crimson velvet, somewhat broad-brimmed, lined with ermine velvet, and "worn in the Spanish fashion." Sir Levett does not inform us whether this habit was assigned to the knights on the institution of the Order in 1735, or on its being established as an Imperial Order in 1762; but the latter date is so nearly within our limits that I feel justified in including the account in this chapter. The riband, not mentioned by Hanson, is scarlet, watered, with narrow yellow border.

The only Order for ladies which concerns us is "The Order of St. Catherine of Russia, which acknowledges for its founder," according to Hanson, "the Emperor Peter I. of Russia, who, desiring to immortalize the heroic spirit of his august consort, Catherine, shown in the danger he had been in at the Pruth, instituted the Order in 1714." This Order is conferred only on ladies of the highest rank, be they natives or strangers. Previous to her marriage with his Serene Highness the then reigning Duke (afterwards King) of Würtemberg, H.R.H. Charlotte Augusta, Princess Royal of Great Britain, was created a Lady of the Order, and wore the insignia at the ceremony of her nuptials, 18th May, 1797. The badge is worn suspended from a narrow *ponceau*-coloured riband with a silver border, scarf-wise over the right shoulder, and the star on the left breast.

Of the Orders of St. Andrew (1703) and the Bath (1725) the collars have been already engraved on Plate V. and the stars at pages 480-81 of the Dictionary. I should have here, therefore, only to describe the habits of the Knights at their investiture, but that I consider this the proper place to avail myself of the information derived from the labours of that distinguished herald and antiquary, the late Sir Harris Nicolas, who, in his valuable 'History of the Orders of Knighthood of the British Empire,'[2] has collected a mass of most interesting facts relative to this subject, which more recent writers have overlooked or neglected. So interesting are they indeed that I regret that the special character and limitation of this work preclude my quoting the greater portion of them *in extenso*. I must, however, confine myself to notices of dates and dress, referring the more general inquirer to the History from which they have been extracted.

And first, as to dates. Although it is as unquestionable that the present Order of St. Andrew or the Thistle was founded by Queen Anne in 1703, as it is ridiculous to assume with John Lesley, Bishop of Ross,[3] that it was instituted by Achaius, King of Scotland, a century after his death,[4] there is documentary evidence to prove that the honour of placing the Order upon a regular foundation, similar to that of the other knightly fraternities of Europe, was reserved for King James VII. of Scotland and II. of England, who, on the 29th May, 1687, issued a royal warrant for letters

[1] Being the initials of the motto, "Amantibus, Justitiam, Pietatem, Fidem."

[2] 4 vols. 4to. London, 1842.

[3] 'De Origine, Moribus, et rebus Gestis Scotorum;' 4to. Romæ, 1578. Lib. v.

[4] Achaius died (if he ever existed) upwards of a century before the reign of Athelstan, King of the West Saxons, in commemoration of whose defeat Achaius is said to have instituted the Order.

patent to be passed under the Great Seal of Scotland, in which, after reciting the fabulous tradition of the origin of the Order by Achaius and the causes of its desuetude, he declares it to be his pleasure to "revive and restore the same to its full glory."

This patent, however, though prepared, never passed the Great Seal; but certain statutes for the governance of the Order were ordained at the same time, in which were the following regulations for the habits and decorations of the Knights:—

"That the habits of the Sovereign and brethren be a doublet and trunk hose of a cloth of silver; stockings of pearl-coloured silk, with white leather shoes, garters, and shoe-strings of blue and silver; the breeches and sleeves of the doublet decently garnished with silver and blue ribbands, and surcoat of purple velvet lined with white taffeta, girt about the middle with a purple sword-belt edged with gold, and a buckle of gold at which a sword with gilded hilt, whereof the shell is to be in form of the badge of the Order, and the pommel in the form of a thistle, in a scabbard of purple velvet; over which a mantle or robe of green velvet lined with white taffeta, with tassells of gold and green; the whole robe parsemée or powdered over with thistles of gold embroidered; upon the left shoulder of which, in a field of blue, Saint Andrew the Apostle his image, bearing before him the cross of his martyrdom, of silver embroidery. About the shoulders is to be borne the collar of the Order, consisting of thistles and sprigs of rue going betwixt, in the middle of which, before is to hang the Saint Andrew in gold enamelled, with his gown of green, with the surcoat purple, having before him the cross of his martyrdom, enamelled white, or if of diamonds consisting of thirteen just, the cross and feet of St. Andrew resting upon a ground of green; the collar to be tied to the shoulders of the robe with a white ribband. Upon their heads, in days of solemn procession or feasting where the Sovereign himself is present or his commissioner, for that effect they are to wear at these times of permission a cap of black velvet faced up with a border of the same, a little divided before, wide and loose in the crown, having a large plume of white feathers with an egret or heron's top in the middle of it, the border of the cap adorned with jewels; the Sovereign's cap for difference to have two rows of diamonds cross the crown thereof, in form of a royal crown; the Sovereign's robe to be of a length proportionable to his royal dignity, and the badge on the shoulder to be adorned with pearl, besides with other distinctions he shall think fit to appoint."

"And we, having considered that it was the ancient custom for the Sovereign and Knights-brethren on their daily apparel to wear the jewel of the Order, in a chain of gold or precious stones, and that *the use of ribbands has been brought in since the most noble Order of the Thistle was left off, and that chains are not now in use*, we have therefore thought fit to appoint the jewell of the said Order to be worn with a purple-blue ribband watered or tabbied; the jewel to have on the one side the image of St. Andrew, with the cross of his martyrdom before him, enamelled as above said, or enriched with precious stones on the cross and round about, on the back of which shall be enamelled a thistle of gold and green, the flower reddish, with a motto written round it, 'Nemo me impune lacessit:' the ground upon which the thistle is to be done shall be enamelled blue.

"Upon the left breast of the coat and cloak shall be embroidered a badge of proportionable bigness, being St. Andrew's cross, of silver embroidery, on the middle of which a circle of gold, having the motto of the Order in letters of blue, in the middle whereof a thistle of gold upon a field in blue."

Similarly precise regulations follow for the habits of the Secretary, "the Lyon," and the Usher, which it is unnecessary to record, my object being to show that the Order of St. Andrew or the Thistle was not only projected but actually founded by James II. in 1687, who on the 6th of June following the date of the warrant nominated eight Scottish noblemen Knights of the Thistle, four of whom—the Earls of Melfort, Moray, Seaforth, and Dumbarton—were invested by the King at Windsor the same day; the others being in Scotland, were knighted, took the oaths, and received the insignia at Edinburgh shortly afterwards. The Revolution and abdication of James, which occurred a few months after the institution of the Order, caused it to fall into desuetude. Of the eight Knights, the four above mentioned followed their sovereign to France, and lost all their honours by attainder; but the others retained the dignity and wore their decorations until their deaths. Even though no longer *de facto* King of Scotland, James VII. never abandoned his pretensions to the sovereignty of the Order of the Thistle ; and on Christmas day, 1723, he invested his eldest son, Charles James (afterwards better known as " the Chevalier de St. George "), then only three years old, with its ensigns as well as those of the Garter.

At the same time that Sir Harris Nicolas throws all this light on a previously little known circumstance, he renders us a still greater service by critically examining all the traditions and legends concerning the Order, and disposes of the arguments and theories which they have given rise to.

Admitting that a collar of Thistles was worn by James V. of Scotland before 1541, that a similar collar to which the cross or effigy of St. Andrew was attached was placed round his achievements and those of Mary, Queen of Scots, of her son King James VI. of Scotland and I. of England, and of his successors Charles I. and Charles II., he maintains that " as far as has yet been discovered there is no evidence of a conclusive or satisfactory nature that before the reign of James VII. any person either received the collar from his Sovereign, or was styled a Knight of the Order of St. Andrew or of the Thistle. The name even of such an institution has not been found in any record, nor is there a trace of its charter of foundation, or of statutes, chapters, elections, installations, investitures, nominations, or a list of the Knights." [1]

The Order remained in abeyance in these dominions during the whole of the reigns of William III. and Queen Mary, but, in the second year of the reign of Queen Anne, her Majesty was pleased to revive it, and letters patent were passed under the Great Seal of Scotland on the 31st of December, 1703, in which the absurd history of the original institution by Achaius was repeated, its long discontinuance after the decease of James V. attributed to the minority of succeeding sovereigns and to other circumstances, and its restitution by King James VII. was recited.

The regulations respecting the habit and decorations are nearly word for word those of King James above quoted ; the only alteration in the dress being that the garters, shoe-strings, and ribands are ordered to be of *green* and silver instead of *blue* and silver, and in the decorations that the riband to which the jewel or medal was attached should be *green* instead of purple-blue, and the ground on which the thistle was to be done in the badge should be green instead of blue as well as the letters of the motto round it. To the original decorations the Queen added at the same time a medal all of gold, with the image of St. Andrew bearing his cross, and encircled by the motto ; and at the lower part of the circle, at the joining of the words, a thistle : this medal to be worn in a green riband as the jewel when the jewel is not worn. It is remarkable that there is no mention of a *star* of the Order in any of the above statutes ; but in a memorial addressed to George I. by eight of the Knights on the 9th of November, 1714, it is alluded to in terms which seem to imply that it was identical with a *badge*, which was ordered to be worn on the coat or cloak of the Knight in his daily dress. The passage is as follows :—" That the thistle in the middle of the star to be worn on the coat or cloak be green brightened with gold upon a field gold, and that the circle round the thistle and field be green and the motto in letters of gold ; " and that instead of the image of St. Andrew, &c., which was directed to be embroidered on the left shoulder of the mantle, " it is humbly proposed there be on the shoulder of the mantle the star, such as is appointed to be worn on the coat or cloak ;" and on the 17th of February, 1714-15, the prayer of the memorial was fully complied with by his Majesty, who issued an additional statute authorizing the proposed alterations.

Since that date no change has been made either in the habit or the ensigns, and they are here therefore described and illustrated from Sir N. H. Nicolas's costly work aforesaid. The mantle or robe is made of rich green velvet lined with white taffeta. On the left shoulder the star of the Order, and the right shoulder is tied up with white riband streamers ; it is fastened at the neck with a cord and tassels of green silk and gold. The mantle appointed by King James II. was much more splendid, it having been parsemée or powdered all over with thistles of gold embroidery.

The surcoat and hood are made of rich purple or Garter-blue velvet, lined with white taffeta, girded with a sword-belt of purple velvet trimmed with gold lace, and having a buckle and runner of gold. The sword has a gilt hilt, of which the shell is in form of the badge of the Order, and the pommel in that of a thistle. There is no mention of a hood in any of the statutes.

The under-habit, which is the installation dress, consists of a doublet and trunk hose of cloth of silver, the breeches and sleeves garnished or ornamented with silver and green ribands; the stockings are pearl-coloured silk, the shoes of white leather, the garters and shoe-strings green and silver.

The cap is of black velvet, as before described.

The collar of the Order described in the statutes of James II. was adopted by Queen Anne, and has never been altered; but the image of St. Andrew appended to it was commanded by George I. to be made of a larger size than heretofore, and surrounded by rays of gold in the form of a halo or glory.

"All that is known of the jewel," says Sir N. H. Nicolas, "is the account given of it in the statutes, as it has long ceased to be worn;" the exact time of its disuse, however, is not ascertained.

Collar in Portrait, James V.

Collar on Great Seal of Mary, Queen of Scots.

Collar on another Seal of Mary.

Collar on Great Seal of James VI.

It appears to have been altogether superseded by *the medal*, first mentioned in the statutes of Queen Anne, and was at that time directed to be worn in the riband whensoever the jewel was not used.

The riband, which was changed by Queen Anne to green from blue, is not "watered or tabbied," as the blue was. It is four inches wide, and worn over the left shoulder, the medal appended to it under the right arm.

The star was altered by George I., as stated above, and has been engraved at p. 480 of the Dictionary.

The latest British Order of Knighthood instituted within the limits prescribed for this History is the Order of the Bath, created by King George I. in 1725, which has been erroneously represented as a revival only of an institution of the fifteenth century, as the expression "Knights of the Bath" occurs in a Patent Roll of the first of Henry VI.: but bathing was one of the ceremonies observed in the making of Knights generally, from almost the commencement of the institution of chivalry, and the earliest evidence of a special Order of Knights of the Bath distinguished by insignia appears in the reign of James I., A.D. 1614, when the badge or jewel worn by John, Lord Harrington of Exton, who was knighted at the king's coronation and died in 1613, was engraved for the Funeral Sermon of that nobleman, and displays the three crowns, not of gold, however, as now seen in the star and jewel of the Knights of the Bath, but of green leaves and with a different motto, viz. "Honoris singulum (cingulum?) militare." The jewel also that was worn by Sir Edward Walpole (grandfather of Sir Robert Walpole, first Lord Orford), who was made a Knight of the Bath at the coronation of Charles II., was made of gold, the centre white, charged with three garlands, wreaths, or crowns of

Jewel of the Order of the Bath. 1604.   Jewel, temp. Charles II.

foliage, enamelled green. (See cuts above, copied from the engravings from the original in Sir N. H. Nicolas's valuable work.) A third contradictory and contemporaneous piece of evidence is furnished us by the portrait of Lord Herbert of Cherbury, at Powis Castle, who is painted in the robes of the Order, but without any badge, either on the mantle or attached to a chain or riband; while a shield, supposed to represent the arms of the Order, and suspended by a red riband from the ceiling of the apartment, displays gules, three *garlands*, with the motto "Virtus sibi præmium."

In the face of all this conflicting evidence, what have we to rely upon either as to origin, meaning, or even consistent regulation, until we arrive at the reign of George I., when "the military Order of the Bath," now existing, with its statutes, limitation of number of Knights, collar, star, and habit of the Order, undoubtedly was founded by that sovereign on the 18th of May, 1725; and the statutes, dated the 23rd, were issued after the investiture of the first Knights on the 25th of the same month?

As these statutes have never, I believe, been printed *in extenso* in any work but that of Sir N. H. Nicolas, above quoted, I shall not hesitate to extract from them such passages as contain information, not only of the habit and ensigns of the Order, but of the ceremonies preliminary to investiture which were obligatory on the Companions elect of the Order.

The 7th statute commands "that all persons herein nominated to be Companions . . . and all other persons that may hereafter be elected into this Order shall have signification of their election made unto them by the Great Master, and shall also, upon the summons of the Great Master for their creation into the said knighthood as also for their installation, repair to the Prince's Chamber within the Palace of Westminster (which is hereby declared to be the Chapter-room of this Order), at the time or times to be appointed in the said summons, each of them to be attended by two Esquires of Honour, Gentlemen of blood, and bearing coat-arms (to be approved by the Great Master), who shall be worshipfully received at the door of that Chamber by the King of Arms and the Gentleman Usher of this Order; and the person thus elected shall enter into that Chamber with the Esquires, who, being experienced in matters of chivalry, are to instruct him in the nature, dignity, and duties of this military Order, and to take diligent care that all the ceremonies thereof (which have their allegorical significations) shall be powerfully recommended and punctually observed; and such Esquires who from this service have usually been denominated Esquires Governors shall not permit the Elected to be seen abroad during the evening of his first entry, but shall send for the proper barber to make ready a bathing vessel, handsomely lined on the inside and outside with linen, having cross hoops over it covered with tapestry, for defence against the cold air of the night, and a blanket shall be spread on the floor by the side of the bathing vessel : then, the beard of the Elected being shaven and his hair cut, the Esquires shall acquaint the Sovereign or Great Master that, it being the time of evensong, the Elected is prepared for the bath; whereupon some of the most sage and experienced Knights shall be sent to inform the Elected, and to counsel and direct him in the Order and feats of chivalry ; which Knights, being preceded by several Esquires of the Sovereign's household, making all the usual signs of rejoicing and having the minstrels playing on several instruments before them, shall forthwith repair to the door of the Prince's Chamber, while the Esquires Governors, upon hearing the music, shall undress the Elected and put him into the bath, and, the musical instruments then ceasing to play, these grave Knights, entering into the chamber without any noise, shall severally, one after the other, kneeling near the bathing vessel, with a soft voice instruct the Elected in the nature and course of the Bath, and put him in mind that for ever hereafter he ought to keep his body and mind pure and undefiled, and thereupon the Knights shall each of them cast some of the water of the bath upon the shoulders of the Elected and then retire, while the Esquires Governors shall take the Elected out of the bath and conduct him to his pallet bed, which is to be plain and without curtains ; and as soon as his body is dry, they shall clothe him very warm, in consideration that he is to watch that whole night ; and therefore they shall array him in a robe of russet, having long sleeves reaching down to the ground and tied about the middle by a cordon of ash-coloured and russet silk, with a russet hood like to an hermit, having a white napkin hanging to the cordon or girdle ; and the barber having removed the bathing vessel, the experienced Knights shall again enter, and from thence conduct the Elected to the Chapel of King Henry VII. (wherein it is our pleasure that the religious ceremonies relating to this Order shall for the future be constantly performed), and they being there entered, preceded by all the Esquires making rejoicings, and the minstrels playing before them, during which time wine and spices shall be laid ready for these Knights, the Elected, and the Esquires Governors ; and the Elected having returned thanks to these Knights for the great favours of their assistance, the Esquires Governors shall shut the Chapel door, permitting none to stay therein save the Elected, one of the Prebendaries of the Church of Westminster to officiate, the chandler to take care of the lights, and the verger of the Church, where the Elected shall perform his vigils during the whole night in orisons and prayers to Almighty God, having a taper burning before him held by one of his Esquires Governors, who, at the reading of the Gospel, shall deliver it into the hands of the Elected, which being read, he shall re-deliver it to one of his Esquires Governors, who shall hold it before him during the residue of divine service, and when the day breaks and the Elected hath heard Matins or Morning Prayer, the Esquires Governors shall re-conduct him to the Prince's Chamber and lay him in bed and cast over him a coverlet of gold lined with *cards* (f); and when it is a proper time these Esquires shall acquaint the Sovereign or Great Master that the Elected will be ready to rise from his bed, who shall again command the experienced Knights, preceded as before, to repair to the Prince's Chamber ; and the Elected being awakened by the music, and the Esquires Governors having provided everything in readiness, the experienced Knights at their entry shall wish the Elected a good morning, acquainting him that it is a convenient time to rise : whereupon, the Esquires Governors taking him by the arm, the most ancient of these Knights shall present to him his shirt, the next his breeches, the third his doublet, another the surcoat of red tartarin, lined and edged with white sarcenet ; two others shall take him out of his bed ; two others shall put on his boots, in token of the beginning of his warfare ; another shall gird him with his white girdle without any ornament ; another shall comb his head ; another shall deliver him his coif, or bonnet ; and, lastly, another shall put upon him the mantle of this Order, being of the same silk and colour of the surcoat, lined and edged in like manner, which shall be tied and made fast about the neck with a lace of white silk, having a pair of white gloves hanging at the end thereof; and on the left shoulder of the said mantle shall be the ensign of this Order, that is, three Imperial Crowns, or, surrounded with the motto of the Order upon a circle, gules, with a glory of rays issuing from the centre; and on the same shoulder of the said mantle the lace of white silk anciently worn by the said Knights."

It is scarcely possible to read the above farrago of absurdity and believe it was seriously concocted in the reign of George I., and issued by his authority under his sign manual. We may rest assured that not one Knight of the Bath created by his Majesty, or any of his successors, was ever compelled to enact the solemn farce which such ceremonies would have been considered in the year of Grace 1725.

Dispensations were no doubt granted in every case as respected the vigils, the washings, the dressings, the lectures of the experienced Knights, &c.; and the statutes were revised and rendered acceptable to the common sense and conformable to the manners of the eighteenth century.

An alteration took place in the Order of the Garter during the reign of George II., when the colour of the riband was changed from sky-blue to its present dark blue in consequence of "the Pretender's" making some Knights of that Order. Philip Dormer Stanhope, Earl of Chesterfield's portrait in the British Museum, is believed to present us with one of the latest examples of the light blue riband.

The under-dress, first adopted by order of Charles II. in 1661 (see p. 290), has undergone little alteration, and appears in all portraits of Knights in the full habit of the Order shortly after that date. Whether due to the taste of an English sovereign, or to that of an English tailor, is uncertain, a similar conventional attire was worn about the same time by Knights of the Order of St. Louis in France and Knights of the Elephant in Denmark (see figure of Christian V. at p. 291 of this vol.); and it is very probable it originated in Paris, and was consequently adopted by Charles II. after the Restoration.[1] It is of no particular time, not even of that of Charles II., when it was invented; and, though hitherto always sent out to foreign princes with the mantle and other habits and decorations of the Order, is not worn by them even on the day of investiture, and the sooner it is abolished and the dress restored to its original form the better.

Respecting official costume, it appears to me some observations are necessary respecting a class in which I am personally interested, viz. Her Majesty's Officers of Arms. Under the heading of TABARD in the Dictionary, an example has been given of that distinctive garb as worn by a Pursuivant in the fifteenth century, differing principally in the mode of wearing it from the tabard of a Herald or a King of Arms; and under that of COLLAR OF SS, an account will be found of the collar distinguishing the latter functionaries from their subordinates; but no mention has been made of the crown worn by a King of Arms, no reliable authority for the form of such article being met with in representations of early English heraldic costume, nor does the sceptre now carried by Garter appear to have been used in its present shape earlier than the end of the sixteenth century: the first representation I have yet seen of it being in a rare engraving by Francis Delaram of a portrait of Sir William Segar, Garter King of Arms, knighted in 1606. At what period these insignia were first introduced in any form has never, I believe, been hitherto ascertained, nor has any recent writer, as far as I am aware, offered even a suggestion on the subject.

In Parker's 'Glossary of Heraldry,' an engraving is given of the crown of a King of Arms of the present day, worn now only at coronations (see p. 382); on all other occasions Garter bears his sceptre, but wears no crown.

The earliest portrait of a King of Arms that has descended to us is that of "William Bruges, King of Arms of all England, called Garter," the first of that title, who was created by Henry V., and so named in a chapter held by that monarch at Rouen on Wednesday, 5th of January, 1420. It occurs in an illuminated MS. in the Ashmolean Museum at Oxford, which is nearly of that date, as is shown by the arms of England on the tabard, in which the arms of France in the first and fourth quarters display but three fleurs-de-lys, the number to which they were reduced in that reign. The tabard is of the present form, but longer, reaching to about mid-leg. The crown, which

---

[1] I believe the last time it was worn in England was at the coronation of George IV., when H.R.H. Prince Leopold (husband of the Princess Charlotte of Wales, and afterwards King of the Belgians) and the Marquess of Londonderry walked in the procession as Knights of the Garter.

principally interests us, is the usual floral one of the English mediæval sovereigns, only not jewelled, and in his hand he holds not a sceptre but a short slender wand.[1]

The next example is the portrait of Sir John Wriothesly, Knight, Garter King of Arms, from a tournament roll in the College of Arms, London, printed *circa* 1534.

William Bruges, King of Arms.

Sir John Wriothesly, Knight, Garter King of Arms.

As he is represented on horseback, he wears a black cap of that or rather earlier date in lieu of a crown. His tabard is shorter, and in his hand he holds a small white wand. He has no collar of SS, badge or medal, or anything to distinguish him from the other kings, heralds, and pursuivants by whom he is accompanied.

The third is the engraving by Delaram already mentioned, but Sir William Segar is depicted in the ordinary costume of a gentleman in the reign of James I., his official dignity being indicated only by the sceptre in his right hand, and his badge or jewel (an addition to the insignia by Henry VIII.[2]) pendent to a riband about his neck: no collar of SS or crown.

It is in the portrait of Sir William Dugdale, Garter principal King of Arms, A.D. 1677–1685, that

Crown of Sir William Dugdale.

we find the first delineation of a crown corresponding in some degree with the modern one, the circle being surmounted by oak-leaves in lieu of fleurs-de-lys, but I can discern no indication of the inscription which is now in use; and there appears to be a jewel in the front which would have interfered with it. The crown surmounts a shield in a corner of the

---

[1] Initial portraits of later Kings of Arms are to be found in the old grants preserved in the Heralds' College. Six of them have been engraved for Dallaway's 'Inquiry,' viz. Christopher Barker, 1530; Thomas Hawley, Clarenceux, 1530; Gilbert Dethick, Garter, 1550; William Harvey, Clarenceux, 1556; Lawrance Dalton, Norroy, 1556; and Robert Cooke, Clarenceux, 1560. Not two crowns out of the six are precisely alike: some are regal, others ducal coronets, and two such as are termed Indian crowns, and all without inscriptions. Neither Barker nor Dethick carry sceptres, none wear collars, but each has in his right hand a slender wand. Their tabards are of the present form, worn over long gowns of a brown or russet colour, if indeed it be not intended for "orange-tawney," which was a livery colour of the House of York, to which family the College is indebted for its foundation.

[2] In Vincent's MSS., No. 151, the "first guifte of a jewel" is ascribed to the 8th of Henry VIII.

picture, charged with the armorial ensigns of his office, impaled with his family arms. He wears also the badge suspended to a gold chain round his neck, as he is in ordinary costume, the collar of SS being worn only with the tabard.

The exact date at which this portrait was painted cannot be ascertained, but the dress is clearly of the latter part of the seventeenth century, and previous to 1685, when Sir Thomas St. George succeeded him as Garter. In the official record of the ceremony of creation of Sir Thomas, on Wednesday, the 29th of March of that year, mention is made of "a crown" which was carried in the procession by Somerset Herald, and afterwards placed on the new Garter's head by the Earl Marshal, but no description is given of it. A gilt collar of SS was also carried by Blue-mantle Pursuivant, and the crown and collar are again mentioned in the account of the creation on the same day of Sir John Dugdale as Norroy King of Arms.

We really have no authority on which we can depend for the form of a crown of a King of Arms previous to the Revolution. There is a drawing in one of Vincent's MSS. in the Heralds' College which completely differs from every other representation, being an arched or Imperial one. In some small rude-coloured drawings in Vincent's ' Precedents,' the crown also appears to have an arch, and the under-dresses of the Heralds are black.

In the "Proceeding to the Coronation" of Queen Anne, 23rd April, 1702, "Two Provincial Kings of Arms" are said to have walked in their rich coats, collars, and medals, "with their coronets in their hands," and "Garter wearing his collar and jewell, his coronet in hand;" no mention of a sceptre.

That the sceptre was borne, however, long before that period is proved by the portrait of Sir William Segar. In Schoonbeek's work, to which we have been already so much indebted, there is a plate representing the Prelate and Chancellor of the Order, Black Rod, and Garter King of Arms or a Herald, the latter in his tabard and bareheaded, but carrying no sceptre. On the staff of Black Rod is a lion rampant, similar to the one now in use. The description of the plate in Latin is as follows, " Cancellarius, Prelatus, *Stator, Rex Armorum et Heraldus*, Equitum, Perisæclidis ;" but there is certainly only one person in a tabard, and if meant for Garter King of Arms he is neither crowned, collared, nor sceptred (see woodcut annexed). The foreign author may have

Group from Schoonbeek. 1697.

confounded Black Rod (Stator) with Garter. Anstis, in his History of the Order, has collected all the evidence bequeathed to us in official documents on this subject, and we find that in Sir William Bruges' petition to King Henry V. he prayed to be allowed to wear a crown on his head and a collar round his neck, " armoyé de blazon," of the most noble company of the Garter, to have the tunic of Arms on his person, and in his hand a long white rod, having at the end a *small banner or pennoncel*, by which rod it would be shown that the king had given him the sovereignty and government within the office of Arms, and these concessions were confirmed by the ' Constitutions' of Henry VIII. It is remarkable that in the portrait of Bruges, which is nearly contemporary, the rod has no "banner or pennoncel " attached to it, nor is it to be seen in any portrait of a Garter King of Arms as yet discovered. Ashmole in his History gives at page 234 a folding plate representing the Prelate,

Chancellor, Treasurer, Registrar, Black Rod, and Garter in their ancient habits, and also the robes and insignia of his own time. The figures are beautiful engravings by Hollar, but no authority for the ancient habits is cited, and they are suspiciously picturesque.[1] The sceptre of Garter has no "pennoncel" attached to it, but terminates in a square plate of solid metal, with the royal arms displayed on it, surmounted by an Imperial crown, and which is still absurdly described as "a banner."

In the absence, therefore, of any positive authority, it may be fairly presumed that the sceptre in its modern form dates from the accession of King James I., as it first appears in a print engraved *circa* 1616, and it is probable also that the form of the crown or coronet of the Kings of Arms was altered and definitively settled subsequent to that period.

The modern crown of a King of Arms is formed of a circle supporting sixteen oak-leaves, each alternate leaf being higher than the rest, and nine only seen in profile. It will be observed that they are more perpendicular and in closer contact with each other than they appear in the Dugdale portrait. It has now also a cap of crimson satin turned up with ermine and surmounted by a tassel of gold. Garter's crown is of pure gold; the crowns of the Provincial Kings of Arms, Clarenceux and Norroy, are of silver gilt. Around the circlet of each is inscribed "Miserere mei Deus secundum magnam misericordiam tuam" (Psalm li. 1). Whether or not a supplication so befitting us, sinners all, is especially requisite for a King of Arms, is a question too delicate to be speculated upon by a member of the Chapter; but the origin and date of its appropriation is a legitimate object of inquiry, and it is vexatious that a diligent search in the records of the College should have resulted in simply an approximate calculation. The wand or rod borne by the ancient heralds appears to have signified their office as marshals, and the collar of SS their status as members of the sovereign's household. Those of the three Kings of Arms are of silver gilt. The badges appended to them originally displayed only the armorial bearings of their respective offices, but in the seventeenth century permission was granted to impale with them their family arms. Various alterations took place in the collar, which was at first composed of SS only. The portcullis was introduced into those worn by judges, &c., in the time of the Tudors, of whom it was a family badge, but not into those of the Heralds. The pendant of the combined rose, thistle, and shamrock was added subsequently to the union of the three kingdoms.

Modern crown of King of Arms.

---

[1] I have therefore decided not to introduce them here.

CHAPTER X.

THEATRICAL AND SPECTACULAR COSTUME.

HISTORY of Costume in Europe would be very incomplete did it not contain some information respecting the dresses assumed by the actors, maskers, and mummers in public or private spectacular entertainments from the days of Roscius to those of Garrick.

The existence of so many amphitheatres in Gaul and Britain may testify to the introduction by the Romans of their favourite sports and pastimes into the countries they conquered ; and though the extinction of the regular drama in Rome has been ascribed to the banishment of the players by Tiberius, in consequence of the factions created by the partisans of particular actors, dancers and buffoons occupied their place, and such entertainments were not entirely suppressed until the irruption of the Goths under Alaric put a stop to every species of diversion throughout Italy. What the substitute for the theatre was amongst the Britons, may be conceived from the Guary Miracles and rude sports of the Cornish in earthen basins like cock-pits. The latter performances were rural or athletic sports, which claim no notice in a History of Costume. The first attempt at regular dramatic exhibitions after the extinction of the Roman Theatre con-

Masks of Roman Actors.

Roman Comedian.

sisted of the Miracles and Mysteries. For these representations dresses were required, as the first two personages of the Trinity, saints, angels, and devils were the characters introduced. Gregory Nazianzen, Patriarch of Constantinople, in the fourth century composed plays from the Old and New Testaments, by way of substitutes for those of Sophocles and Euripides, whilst they were still in possession of the stage. He preserved the Greek model, but turned the choruses into Christian hymns. One only of his plays is extant.

It is a tragedy called 'Christ's Passion.' The prologue declares it to be an imitation of Euripides, and mentions the first personation of the Virgin Mary on the stage. Menestrier considers these exhibitions were introduced into Western Europe by the pilgrims returning from the Holy Land; and Warton adds that the clergy, finding the buffoons who attended at fairs attracted the notice of the people to a degree not to be suppressed by the prohibition of the Church, encouraged the composition of plays founded on scriptural subjects which could be substituted for the profane mummeries increasing in popularity, undeterred even by the threat of excommunication.[1] As a sop, however, to the people, drolls or buffoons were always introduced into these plays, however serious or sacred the subject; a much greater profanity than any it was professed to correct. There were generally two; the principal being the Devil, and the other called the Vice, who was attired in a fool's habit, a cap with ass's ears, and a sword or dagger made of a thin lath, with which it was his business to beat and torment the Devil. He was also furnished with a long pole, with which he laid about him, tumbling the other actors over one another with great noise and riot. The performers were the monks themselves, and of course, where they had special characters to sustain, they assumed some sort of disguises, the decorations of the theatre being the church ornaments.

The costume of the stage in Christian Europe had its origin therefore in the vestiarium of the Church, masks being made for certain characters; but we have no precise description of the dress of any personage earlier than the sixteenth century. Matthew Paris informs us that a play called St. Catharine was written by Geoffrey, a Norman, afterwards Abbot of St. Albans, who being invited over to England by Richard, the then Abbot, to take upon him the direction of the school belonging to that monastery, and arriving too late for that purpose, went to Dunstable and taught there, where he caused his play to be performed about the year 1110, and borrowed from the Sacrist of St. Albans some of the ecclesiastical vestments for the dresses of the actors. The clergy, however, were not unanimous in their approval of public dramatic performances, and there is a violent attack on them in the 'Manuel de Peché,' an Anglo-French poem, written about the middle of the thirteenth century, which is only interesting to us inasmuch as it relates to dresses and decorations. In Robert de Brunne's English version of it we are told that St. Isidore declares all those that delight to see such things, or who lend horse or harness to assist in their representation, do it at their great peril, and that any priest or clerk who lends a vestment which has been hallowed by sacraments is still more to blame, and is guilty of sacrilege.[2]

As I am not writing a history of the drama, but only of dress, it is unnecessary for me to notice the many allusions to the performance of Miracle Plays and Mysteries during the thirteenth and fourteenth centuries, in England, except where they contain indications of the costumes in which they were represented. In order, therefore, to afford our readers a clearer idea than I can by words of the habiliments designed by the costumiers of the Middle Ages, from the fourteenth to the sixteenth century, I subjoin examples from several manuscripts and other pictorial authorities of the disguisings, maskings, and pageants preceding the introduction of regular dramatic entertainments.

---

[1] The 'Passion Spiel,' enacted once in every ten years at Ober Ammergau, in Bavaria, and which has recently excited so much public attention both here and abroad, is, I believe, the only existing example of the old miracle plays of the Middle Ages, and owes its survival to an exception made in its favour by the King of Bavaria at the beginning of this century, when all other such representations in his dominions were forbidden by a royal decree. Good taste has fortunately interfered in time to prevent the scandal of its performance in London—a metropolis in which, it is lamentable to confess, remunerative audiences can be found to attend any exhibition, however repulsive, indecent, or degrading, which the Lord Chamberlain or the magistracy may not feel imperatively called upon to prohibit.

[2]　　　　　" Seynt ysodre seyth yn hys wrytyng,
　　　　　Alle tho that delyte to se swyche thing,
　　　　　Or hors or harneys lenyth partyl,
　　　　　Yyt have they gylt of here peryl.
　　　　　Zyf prest or clerk lene vestment
　　　　　That hawled ys through sacrament,
　　　　　More than euther they are to blame;
　　　　　Of sacrylege they have the fame."
　　　　　　　　　　　　　　　Robert de Brunne.

The annexed woodcuts illustrate plainly enough the appearance of the actors in the disguisings or mummings 'Ludi domini Regis,' in the time of Edward III., described by Warton in his 'History

From Bodleian MS.

of English Poetry,' vol. ii. p. 72, on the authority of the wardrobe accounts of the twenty-first to the twenty-third year of that king's reign, which contain entries of tunics of buckram of various colours, "visours of various similitudes; that is, fourteen of the faces of women, fourteen of the faces of men with beards, fourteen of the heads of angels made with silver, twenty-eight crests or head-pieces of

From Bodleian MS.

fantastic forms (the Latin description of which Warton professes himself unable to understand),[1] fourteen mantles embroidered with heads of dragons, fourteen white tunics wrought with heads and wings of peacocks, fourteen wrought with heads of swans with wings, fourteen tunics painted with eyes of peacocks, fourteen tunics of English linen painted, and as many tunics embroidered with stars of gold and silver."

We have no means of ascertaining what description of beings the wearers of these masks and tunics were intended to represent, but it is to be observed that the number of each sort is limited to fourteen, two sets making twenty-eight; and I think we may fairly conclude that the number of performers were twenty-eight, who entered in two groups of

From Bodleian MS.

fourteen each, and occasionally retired and changed their dresses for another *entrée*, as we shall find was the custom in the reign of Henry VIII. No heads or masks of animals as shown in our wood-

---

[1] The words are these—" 14 crestes cum tibiis reversatis et calceatis : 14 crestes cum montibus et cuniculis ;" sufficiently incomprehensible to the general reader and puzzling to the antiquary. I will not undertake that my interpretation of them is correct, but I venture to suggest the "crests" were armorial, and, literally translated, the passage would read, " 14 crests with legs reversed and booted : 14 crests with mountains and rabbits." Preposterous as this may appear, the student of heraldry will meet with mediæval examples of crests scarcely less grotesque and extravagant, even amongst regular family insignia (particularly in Germany) ; and those assumed for the temporary purpose of a tournament were often more ludicrously fantastic. Human legs, naked, vested, booted, or in armour, and in every sort of posture, are common crests in England ; and for mounds or mountains, with coneys seated upon or burrowing in them, a parallel might also be found.

cuts are mentioned in the extract quoted by Warton ; but the engravings testify to the skill of the manufacturer of "vizours," and the dresses of two of the maskers are embroidered or painted with armorial bearings.

As a further proof of the proficiency to which the "property-makers" of that time had arrived, as well as of the sort of "disguisings" which were popular from the court to the cottage in the fourteenth century, I add the above engravings from a MS. in the Bodleian Library, Oxford, representing a man "disguised" as a stag, another as a goat, and a third as a dog.

Strutt, who has introduced them in his 'Sports and Pastimes of the People of England,' observes that persons capable of well supporting assumed characters were frequently introduced at public entertainments, and also in the pageants exhibited on occasions of solemnity ; sometimes they were bearers of presents and sometimes the speakers of panegyrical orations. In the year 1416, the Emperor Sigismond visited King Henry V. at Windsor, and was magnificently entertained there. A performance of some description was presented before him ; it is not quite clear if it was a miracle play with dialogue or merely a splendid dumb show. What concerns us is, that according to the description of it in a MS. in the Cottonian Library, marked Caligula B. II., we find that the subject was the history of St. George of Cappadocia, that it was divided into three parts and assisted by scenery and dresses. The first part exhibited "the armyng of Seint George and an Angel doyng on his spores" (spurs) ; the second, "Seint George ridyng and fightyng with the dragon, with his spere in his hand ;" and the third, "a Castel and Seint George, and the Kynge's daughter ledyng the lambe in at the Castel gates." Although the wardrobe accounts of Henry V. do not supply us with any information respecting this performance, there can be no doubt, from the description in the MS. above mentioned, that St. George was personated in complete steel armour, the angel in suitable garments with wings, and the king's daughter in royal attire, and very probably the remarkable horned head-dress of that period. The dragon was constructed probably of pasteboard ; but the lamb was most likely a live one, and, if so, has the honour to be the first that trod the boards. As St. George is described as "ridyng and fightyng," there must have been a horse included in this very realistic spectacle. That fancy was also exercised in the dresses provided for these entertainments, more especially when the Miracle Plays and Mysteries were superseded by the Moralities and Mythological Masques and "Interludes" at the close of the fifteenth century, we have sufficient evidence in the items of accounts furnished by the persons whose office it was to purchase the materials. For instance, Richard Gibson, who was an actor in the reign of Henry VII., and early in the following reign appointed Yeoman Tailor to the king, mentions amongst his charges the following particulars of the dresses of two ladies who personated Venus and Beauty in an interlude written by William Cornyshe, and acted before Henry VIII. at Christmas 1514-15 :—

"Itm, bowght by me, Rychard Gybson, one pece of sypers (cypress) 4ᵗ, spent & imployd for the tyer of the lady callyd Bewte, and the oother half for the lady callyd Venus. So spent of sypers 1 pece. Itm, payd to Rychard Rownanger, paynter, for workyng & betyng of a surkytt & a mantyll of yellow sarssenet, with hartts (hearts) and wyngs of sylver for the lady that playd Venus, 10ˢ."

In an inventory of "Garments for Players" of the following year (1516), 7th Henry VIII., we find entries of—"A long garment of cloth of golde ; and tynsell for the Prophete upon Palme Sonday. Itm, a capp of grene tynsell to the same. . . . . Itm, a littill gowne for a woman (the Virgin), of cloth of silver,"—tending to show that the performances for which they were used were Miracle Plays, or at least pieces in which certain Scripture characters were mixed up with allegorical impersonations. Pages might be filled with extracts from such documents during the reigns of Henry VIII., Edward VI., Mary, and Elizabeth ; but until the last half of that of the latter sovereign, there was no theatre existing in England : and the History of Stage Costume properly begins with the erection of the first stage, which in England was in "the Theater," the play-house so called, built about 1570, not to be confounded with the platforms or scaffolds temporarily erected in the yards of great inns, viz., the Boar's-head, Aldgate, the Bell Savage, Ludgate Hill, the Bull, in Holborn, &c., the galleries around which were occupied by spectators.

Previous to the reign of Henry VII., it is rather difficult to distinguish the accounts of dramatic entertainments from those of pageants, maskings, and disguisings, all of which are included in the general term plays (*Ludi*). In an early folio edition of Terence, printed at Strasburg in 1496, by John Gruninger, are several woodcuts intended to represent the scenes of some of the plays, which are evidently the work of a German engraver. I select from them one at the foot of which is printed "THEATRUM." It is questionable, however, whether it is intended to represent the stage of any theatre existing at that date, or merely a fanciful design of an ancient Roman theatre. Its interest to us, however, is in the fact that the actors are dressed in the costume of their own time, and that there is no attempt to even indicate the Roman. The halberdier in conversation with a lady in the steeple head-dress, which had just gone out of fashion, is deserving of particular attention.

From an edition of 'Terence.' 1496.

Scene from Roigny's 'Terence.' 1539

From another edition (circa 1500).

The next earliest representation of theatrical costume is to be seen in a print in Roigny's 'Terence,' 1539. It represents a stage before the introduction of scenery, and the characters Simo and Chremes before the curtain, Davus entering from behind. It will be observed that the actors are in dresses of nearly their own time, and that no attempt was made to imitate the costume of that of Terence. Strutt, in his 'Horda Angel Cynan,' has engraved another example from a sixteenth-century edition of Terence, but has not enabled us clearly to identify it. The costume, however, is much about the same date. It may be a little earlier, and at all events is a valuable addition to our illustrations of the subject.

The inventories taken on the 10th of March, 1598–9—" perhaps," it is suggested, " in anticipation of the removal of the Lord Admiral's players from the Curtain and Rose to the Fortune Theatre,

3 D 2

the project for building which seems about that date to have been entertained by Henslowe and Edward Allen "—give us some information respecting the dresses worn by the actors in Shakespere's time. In the first, quoted by Malone, amongst "goods gone and lost," are entries of "Longshanks' suit," [1] "Harry the Fifth's doublet," and his "velvet gowne." [2] In the succeeding one we find mention of "clownes sewtes and hermettes sewtes," " 1 senitores gowne, 1 hoode, and 5 senitores capes," " 1 sewtte for Nepton (Neptune)," " iiij genesareys (janissaries') gownes," " 1 green gown for Maryan," " vj grene cottes for Robin Hoode," " liij prestes cottes," " ij whitt shepherd's cottes, and ij Danes sewtes and j payer of Danes hosse," " liij payres gownes and iiij hoodes to them, and j fooles coate, cape, and babell (bauble) . . . . and Merlen (Merlin's) gowne and cape," " j carnowll's (cardinal's) hatte," " Eves bodyce," " j hatte for Robin Hoode."

In another, " j Mores cotte," " Tamberlaynes cotte with copper lace," " Junoes cotte," " Tamberlaynes breches of crymson vellvet," " Perowes (Pierrot ?) sewt, which Wm Sley were," " Fayeton (Phaethon) sewte," " Tasoes (Tasso's) robe," " Dides (Dido's) robe," " Harye the V. satten dublet layd with guold lace," " j freyers gowne of graye."

I have extracted from these inventories only the items which had reference to special characters, scriptural, classical, allegorical, or historical, and which might thereby enlighten us as to the degree of attention paid to propriety of costume by managers or actors at that period; and I think the reader will admit that, considering the extent of knowledge then existing, it was commendable, and will bear favourable comparison with that of the stage two hundred years later. We have unfortunately (at least so far as I am aware) no pictorial evidence to produce in illustration of the subject, and no doubt much of the costume would be conventional; but the mention of senators' *gowns, hoods, and caps*, of janissaries' *gowns*, of a cardinal's *hat*, the *robes* of Dido and Tasso, of the green attire of Robin Hood and Maid Marian, and the dresses for priests and friars, evince a desire to represent such personages in their habit as they lived, and the revival of the arts had furnished them with ample authority for its satisfaction. " Perowes sewt," if signifying the dress of a Pierrot, is specially noteworthy at so early a date.

Strict accuracy was not to be expected in the costume of historical characters. Edward I. and " Harry the Fifth " would neither be clothed nor armed in the fashion of their own times; but they would be royally robed and equipped according to that of the sixteenth century. Scriptural personages, we have seen, were before the Reformation indebted to the monasteries and the cathedrals for their attire, and, after it, there were ecclesiastical vestments easily no doubt to be obtained; at all events, their form was familiar to the public, and they could be and probably were sufficiently well imitated. National costume, the dresses of Turks, Russians, Moors, &c., had been assumed by Henry VIII. and his nobility in Court masques, many years previously, and with the great advantage of studying the "genuine articles " on the backs of the ambassadors from the Grand Seignior, the Tzar of Muscovy, the Emperor of Morocco, and other potentates; while the works of the engravers which have furnished us with such abundant illustration of the habits of the principal countries in Europe, and in fact of the whole world at that time, were being daily rendered more accessible to the public. Mythological and allegorical characters had a traditional costume assigned to them at a very early period, which was occasionally varied by the fancy of individuals or the fashions of the passing hour. The heroes and heroines of ancient Greece or Rome were perhaps the most inappropriately represented of any, judging from the ideas prevailing in the Elizabethan age, and to a much later period, of classical attire and armour.

Mr. Collier dates the commencement of the Moralities, which succeeded the Miracle Plays, about the middle of the reign of Henry VI. " Independent of allegorical personages," he remarks, " there were two prominent characters in Moral Plays regarding which it is necessary to speak, as some

---

[1] Edward I. George Peele's ' Famous Chronicle of King Edward the First ' is one of our most ancient historical plays. It was printed in 1599.

[2] If this related to Shakespere's ' Henry the Fifth,' it would be an answer to Malone's objection, that Shakespere could not have been in Scotland in 1599, because he must have been employed in producing his play. This inventory shows that the dress, at any rate, was in existence before March in that year.

FIGURES FROM THE TAPESTRY OF ST GERMAIN L'AUXERROIS

misunderstanding has existed respecting them. I allude to the Devil and the Vice. The Devil was no doubt imported into Moral Plays from the old Miracle Plays, where he figured so amusingly, that when a new species of theatrical diversion had been introduced, he could not be dispensed with : accordingly, we find him the leader of 'the Seven Deadly Sins,' in one of the most ancient Moral Plays that have been preserved. He was rendered as hideous as possible by the mask and dress he wore ; but we have no particular description of it before the sixteenth century."

Masques and pageants were, as I have already remarked, so indiscriminately mixed up with moralities and other dramatic shows, and the dresses provided for the one class of entertainment are so illustrative of those required for the other, that previous to the establishment of regular theatres, during the latter half of the sixteenth century, our information on this subject is necessarily derived from inventories, wardrobe accounts, contemporary descriptions, and a few rare pictorial representations of costume which have been accidentally preserved, and cannot be strictly appropriated to either of the above classes. For instance, Mr. Shaw has given us in his beautiful work, 'Dresses and Decorations of the Middle Ages,' some figures from a piece of tapestry which, at the time he copied it, was suspended in the church of St. Germain l'Auxerrois at Paris. He considered the subject to be an allegorical representation of the Seasons, which may probably have been the case ; but the figures he has selected evidently represent persons forming part of a procession, such as commonly preceded the principal characters in a masque at their *entrée*, and who were always attended by torch-bearers. (See accompanying plate.)

The torch-bearers are, in that example, dressed in the fashion of their own period, and common

Figures of Cupid, from the 'Roman de la Rose.'

throughout Western Europe in the reign of Henry VIII. The ladies they are conducting are also in costume of the same date, but they each bear an arrow, and therefore were evidently intended to support some particular character in the masque, or whatever may have been the form of the entertainment. We may hazard the conjecture that they were attendants upon Cupid, a favourite character in such compositions, and likely to have accompanied Spring, if the subject were, as Mr. Shaw supposed, the Seasons. It is most unfortunate that he did not copy more of the tapestry

(German he considered it), as it would have been a most valuable addition to our knowledge of these curious customs.

A-propos of Cupid, it may be interesting to our subscribers to know how the God of Love was depicted by the artists of the fifteenth century. In the representations of him in the superb copy of the 'Roman de la Rose' in the Harleian Library, which was illuminated *circa* 1490,

> " Le Dieu d'Amours de sa façon
> Ne resembloit pas un garçon."

With the exception that he is winged, and bears a bow and arrows, there is nothing of the classical Eros about him. (*Vide* woodcuts above.) In the words of the author, one would fancy rather

> ". . . que ce fut ung Ange
> Qui venist droictement du ciel,"

but that he is arrayed in royal robes, and crowned either with a regal diadem or

> ". . . ung chapelet
> De roses bel & nettelet."

Hall gives us a most graphic account of one of the "shows" ordered by King Henry VIII., in the first year of his reign, 1509-10, to take place on Shrove Tuesday in the Parliament Chamber at Westminster, for all "the ambassadors that were here out of divers realms and countries." At night, after the banquet was ended, "there came in a drum and a fife, appareild in white damaske, having grene bonnets and hosen of the same sute ;[1] than certayne gentlemen followed with torches, apparayled in blew damaske, purfeled with ames grey, facioned like an awbe (*alb*), and on their heades hoodes with robbes and long tippettes to the same of blew damaske ; visarde (masked). Than after them came a certayne number of gentlemen, whereof the Kyng was one, apparayled all in one sewte of shorte garmentes, little beneath the payntes of blew velvet and crymosyne, with long sleves all cut and lyned with clothe of golde ; and the utter part of the garmentes were powdered with castels and shefes of arrowes,[2] of fyne dokat (ducat) golde : the upper partes of their hosen of like sewte and facion ; the rather partes were of scarlet, powdered with tymbrelles of fyne golde ; having on their heades bonets of damaske silver, flatte woven in the stole, and thereupon wrought with golde and ryche feathers in them ; all in visers. After them entered six ladyes, whereof two were apparayled in crymosyne satyn and purpull, embrawdered with golde, and by vignettes ran flowre de lices of golde, with marvellous ryche and straunge tiers upon their heades ; other two ladies in crymosyne and purpull, made like long slops, embrowdered and fretted with golde after the antique fascion, and over the slop was a shorte garment of cloth of golde, scant to the knee, fascioned like a tabard, all over with small double rolles all of flatte golde of damaske, fret and fringed golde, and on their heads skeynes (scarfs) and wrappers of damaske golde with flatte pypes, that straunge it was to beholde ; the other two ladyes were in kyrtells of crymosyne and purpul satyn, embroudered with a vignet of pomegranettes of golde ; all the garments cut compass-wyse, having demy sleeves and naked downe from the elbowes, and over their garments were rochettes of pleasances rouled with crymsyne velvet, and set with letters of golde-like charectes (characters ?), their heades rouled in pleasauntes and typpets, like the Egipicians, embroudered with golde ; their faces, neckes, armes, and handes covered in fyne pleasaunce blacke,—some call it Lumberdines ; which is marveylous thinne, so the same ladies seemed to be nygrost or blackmores. Of these six ladyes, the Lady Mary, syster to the Kyng, was one. After the Kynge's grace and the ladyes had daunced a certayne tyme, they departed every one to hys lodgyng."

Minute as is this account, it would be impossible for a draughtsman of the present day to illustrate it by the pencil, as, independently of the uncertainty we are in respecting the material and form of

---

[1] White and green were the livery colours of the Tudors.
[2] Badges of the kingdoms of Castile and Aragon.

several articles of dress therein mentioned, there is a confusion of them apparently in their disposition upon the person, which is perplexing in the extreme, and it is therefore much to be deplored that no contemporary representation of one of these magnificent Court spectacles has been bequeathed to us.

That the above-described "show" had a significance to the spectators—"that within which passeth show"—is, I think, discernible from many circumstances. The castles and sheaves of arrows with which "the utter parts of the garments" of the King and his immediate companions were embroidered, were, as I have noted, the well-known badges of Castile and Aragon, and obviously assumed in compliment to the queen. The borders of pomegranates on the kirtles of two of the ladies had also a distinct reference to the Spanish province and formerly Moorish kingdom of Grenada, as those of fleurs-de-lys on the dresses of two other ladies had to the kingdom of France. That the "timbrells" forming the decoration of another portion of the costume of the royal party conveyed an equally comprehensible meaning to the distinguished spectators can scarcely be doubted ; and as the masque is stated to have been designed expressly for the entertainment of "the ambassadors from divers realms and countries," a trustworthy list of their Excellencies might probably enlighten us as regards the allusive import of the "timbrells." There was some meaning, I presume, beyond mere spectacular effect in the appearance of the Princess Mary (consecutively Queen of France and Duchess of Suffolk) and her five attendant ladies in the guise of "Egyptians" or "Blackamoors," and it is uncertain whether by "Egipicians" may not be meant "Gypsies," who were constantly designated by that name, of which indeed our modern term is simply an abbreviation.

I will not, however, detain the reader longer on this subject, which I have commented on only with the object of supporting my opinion that there was much intelligence as well as ingenuity displayed in such exhibitions, and that they were not the "inexplicable dumb shows" so properly reprobated by Shakespere.

It is, however, shortly after this date that we are startled by a statement of the same quaint chronicler, who tells us that in the year 1512-13, "on the daie of the Epiphanie at night, the King with xi other were disguised after the manner of Italie, *called a maske, a thing not sene afore in England.* Thei were appareled in garments long and brode, wrought all with golde, with visers and cappes of gold, and after the banket doen these maskers came in with the sixe gentlemen disguised in silke, beyryng staffe torches, and desired the ladies to daunce. Some were content, and some that knew the fashion of it refused, because it was not a thing commonly seen ; and after thei daunced and commoned together, *as the fashion of the maskes is,* thei toke their leave and departed, and so did the Quene and all the ladies."

I think we cannot hesitate to conclude that this is a record of the first introduction of masquerades into England from Italy—a social amusement differing entirely from the masques or disguisements which had been popular for so long previously in this country, and with which the chronicler was personally so familiar. He consequently recognized the distinction immediately, and describes it as "a thing not sene afore in England."

For that reason I shall defer my notice of masquerades to a later part of this chapter, and continue my inquiries into the progress of the costume of those entertainments, by whatever name they were called, which were more or less dramatic, being regularly constructed with reference to some particular subject, or for representation of incidents in history, sacred or profane, allegorical or mythological—"ballets of action," as we should now term them, for the composition of which Henry VIII., in addition to his many other accomplishments, may have early established a reputation.[1]

On the 10th of November, 1528, in the nineteenth year of his reign, a Latin "morality," in which Luther and his wife were brought upon the stage, and ridicule thrown upon them and the Reformation, was acted before the King, Cardinal Wolsey, and the French ambassadors, by the children of

[1] He is described by Hall as "exercising hymselfe daily" at Windsor, in the 2nd year of his reign, "in shotyng, singing, dauncyng, wrastelyng, casting of the barre, playing at the recorders, flute, virginals, and in settyng of song makyng of balletres," and goodly masses." By "balletres," however, may simply be meant ballads.

St. Paul's School, under the regulation of their master, John Rightwise, who is supposed by Mr. Collier to have been the author of it.

Cavendish, and Stow who copies him, speak of it as " the most goodliest disguising or interlude ;" the dresses of the players being magnificent, "and of so strange devices" that it passed their "capacity to expound."

Richard Gibson, of whom I have already spoken, has left an account of these dresses, which Mr. Collier has printed from the original in his ' Annals of the Stage' (vol. i. p. 108), as follows :—

"The Kyngs pleasyer was that at the sayd revells by clerks in the latyn tong schoulld be playd in hys hy presens a play, whereof insewethe the naames. First, an Orratur in apparell of golld ; a Poyed (poet) in apparell of cloothe of golld ; Relygyun, Eccleasia, Verritas, lyke iij nowessys (novices), in garments of sylke and vayells of laun and sypus (cypress) ; Errysy (Heresy), Falls-interpeytacyun, Compeyo Scryptorris, lyke ladys of Beem (Bohemia), imperelld (apparelled) in garments of sylke of dyvers kolours ; the errytyke Lewter (heretic Luther) lyke a parly freer (friar), in russet damaske and blake taffata ; Lewter's wyef, like a frow of Spyers in Allmayn, in red sylke ; Peter, Poull, and Jhames in iij abyghts (habits) of whyght sarsenet, and iij red mantells and hers (hairs, *i.e.* wigs and beards), of syllver of damaske and pelyuns (pelerines) of skarlet ; and a Kardynell in his apparell ; ij sergeants in ryche apparell ; the Dolfyn (Dauphin) and his brother in koots of vellevet imbrowdyrd with golld and kaps of saten bound with vellvet ; a Messenger in tynsell saten ; vj men in gowns of gren sarsenet ; vj women in gouns of crymsyn sarsenet ; War in ryche cloth of golld, and fethers, and armed ; iij Almayns in apparell all kut and sclyt of syllke ; Lady Pece (Peace) in lady's apparell, all whyght and ryche ; and Lady Quyetness and Dame Tranquylyte rychely besyen (beseen) in ladye's apparell."

This curious document, therefore, presents us with the complete *dramatis personæ*, and the materials and colours of their costumes, fully bearing out the character of splendour and costliness ascribed to them by the old chroniclers. Even the dress of Luther, which was simply that of a friar, was made of damask and taffeta instead of the coarse cloth worn by the mendicant orders. It is also worth noticing that the three "Allmayns" (Germans) were distinguished by their "apparell" being " kut and sclyt," *i.e.* slashed after the fashion which was carried to such an extent in Germany and Switzerland at that period.

There are but few and unimportant records of such entertainments during the reign of Edward VI. The only one of interest to us is a mask at Christmas 1552-3, entitled ' The Triumph of Mars and Venus,' in which the dress of the actor of the God of War is said to have cost £51 17s. 4d. On New Year's Day he had a different suit, valued at £34 14s. He was attended by councillors, pages, ushers, heralds, an interpreter, an *Irishman*, an *Irishwoman*, jugglers, &c., besides six sons (three of them base born), the eldest of whom was apparelled in " a long fool's coat of yellow cloth of gold, all over figured with velvet, white, red, and green ; a hood, buskins, and girdle." Coats were also provided for seven other fools, and the whole cost of dresses was £262 1s. 4d.

In the reign of Mary a strict censorship was instituted respecting plays, in order to prevent the performance of any touching on points of doctrine ; but on St. Mark's Day, 1557, in honour of the arrival of King Philip from Flanders, and for the amusement of the Russian ambassador, who had reached England a short time previously, the Queen commanded for her "regal disport, recreation, and comfort, a notorious maske of Almaynes, Pilgrymes, and Irishmen, with their insidents and accomplishes accordingly."

The expression *notorious* would seem to imply that it was a well-known composition, and may therefore be the earliest instance of the familiar announcement of "a popular drama" in our modern play-bills. A warrant for furnishing Sir Thomas Cawarden, Master of the Revels, with silks, velvets, cloths of silver, &c., for the dresses in the masque, was addressed to Sir Richard Waldegrave, Master of the Great Wardrobe, 30th of April, 1557 ; but we have no details that would afford us any useful information. Miracle plays and such as were founded on scriptural subjects were revived in this reign. ' The miraculous Life of St. Olave' and "a stage-play " of "the Passion of Christ " are named amongst them, but no description of the dresses has descended to us.

We have now arrived at the reign of Queen Elizabeth, in which the English drama, a drama as yet unrivalled by that of any other nation, may be truly said to have been born, and brought rapidly to perfection by Shakspere, who was not the first merely " of an age, but for all time."

Chalmers in his 'Apology' (p. 353) declares that "the persecutions of preceding governments had left Elizabeth without a theatre, without dramas, and without players." This is not strictly the fact. Mr. Collier has pointed out that if by the word "theatre" be meant a building set apart for dramatic performances, her predecessors had none, nor did any exist in the kingdom until many years after she came to the throne. Almost as much may be said of dramas, for the plays, interludes, masques, and disguisings of the first half of the sixteenth century have no claim to be ranked with the national drama of England, while the grand dramatic works of the Greeks and the Romans were not unknown ; and though unacted in public, for the obvious reason that the public were ignorant of Greek and Latin, there is evidence that the plays of Plautus and Terence were occasionally represented to educated audiences at Court ; and George Gascoigne, the author of 'The Princely Pleasures of Kenilworth,' who died in 1577, had some years previously translated Euripides' tragedy of Jocasta into English blank verse, and produced a prose comedy called 'The Supporsi' from the Italian of Ariosto. Again, as to players, Mary had kept up the theatrical and musical establishment of her father at an expense of between two and three thousand pounds a year in salaries only.

It is, however, with the dresses of the players that we have to do, and the gradual improvement of the stage claims our notice only so far as the recorded production of new dramas increases our knowledge of the characters represented and incidentally of the costumes provided for them.

In March 1573-4, a list of the scenery, dresses, and properties which had been required for the acting of six plays and three masks at "Christmas, New Yeartide, and Eastertide last," contains several curious items.

The plays were 'Pedor and Lucia,' 'Alkmeon,' 'Mamillia,' 'Truth, Faythfulness, and Mercye,' 'Herpetulus, or the Blew Knighte and Perobia,' and 'Quintus Fabius.' Amongst the properties, &c., for these, are mentioned "bays for the prologgs," "counterfeit fishes for the play of Pedor," "a jebbet to hang up Diligence," "a dragon's head," and "a truncheon for the dictator."

The three masks, each having their torch-bearers as usual, were composed as follows :—

"Lance Knights vj., in blew sattyn gaskon cottes & sloppes. Torche bearers vj., in black and yelo taffata.

"Forresters or Hunters vj., in green sattyn gaskon cotes and sloppes. Torche bearers attyred in mope and ivye.

"Sages vj., in long gownes of counterfet cloth of golde. Torche bearers in long gownes of red damask."

That these masks were considered as necessary appendages to, if not part and parcel of, the plays represented, is proved by the notice in the above document that in consequence of the *tediousness* of the play 'Timœlia, or the Siege of Thebes,' performed at Hampton Court on Candlemas night, a mask of ladies representing the Six Virtues could not be performed.

The accounts of Blagrave, deputy to Sir Thomas Benger, Master of the Revels in 1574-5, furnish us with some information respecting the dresses and appointments required for certain masks exhibited during the previous year at the Court of Queen Elizabeth, viz. a mask of Shepherds, a mask of Pedlars, and a mask of Pilgrims, and we find accordingly items of "woolverines for pedlars caps," and "bottles for pilgrims." Also of "three devells cotes and heads," "*dishes for devell's eyes*," "long poles and brushes for chymney sweepers in my L. of Leicester's men's play ;" "a cote, a hatt, and buskins all over covered with fethers of cullers (colours) for Vanytie" (in Sebastian Westcott's play of 'Vanity'), and "a perriwigg of beare for King Xerces syster" (in Farrant's play of 'King Xerxes').

In 1578, we learn from 'The Accounts of the Revels at Court' that "a double masque" of Amazons and Knights was represented with great magnificence at Richmond for the entertainment of the French Ambassador. The Amazons are described as being all in "armore compleate, parcel-gilt, with counterfeit morions silvered over and parcel-gilt, and a crest on the top of every of them, having long hair hanging down behind them. Their kirtles were of crimson cloth of gold, indented at the skirt, and laid with silver lace and fringe, with pendants of gold, tassels of gold with gold knobs and set on with brooches of gold, pleated upon the skirt with pleats of silver lawn, with tassels of gold laid under below instead of petticoat, with white silver rich tinsel, fringed with gold fringe. Buskins of orange-coloured velvet. Antique falchions, javelins, and shields, with a device painted thereon."

The Knights were all likewise in armour complete, parcel-gilt, with like counterfeit morions upon their heads, silvered and parcel-gilt, with plumes of feathers on the tops of them. Bases of rich gold tinsel with gold fringe, garded with rich purple silver tinsel; large baldricks about their necks of black gold tinsel, gilt truncheons and shields, "with a posy written on every one of them."

The torch-bearers of the Amazons wore long gowns of white taffeta with sleeves, over which were long gowns of crimson taffeta without sleeves, indented at the skirts, fringed, laced, and tasselled with silver and gold, and tucked up with the girding almost to the knee, bows in their hands, and quivers at their girdles; head-pieces of gold lawn, and women's hair "wreathed very fair." The torch-bearers of the Knights were attired in green satin jerkins and yellow velvet hose, with hats of crimson silk and silver, *thrumed* and wreathed bands and feathers.

The familiar terms of "tragedy" and "comedy" had now made their first appearance, and to them we find added that of "pastoral" in 1580; but these more regular dramatic productions were still intermingled with masques and moralities. In 1589–90 "a mask for six maskers and six torch-bearers" was by her Majesty's commandment sent into Scotland for the celebration of "the King of Scotts mariage." The name of the masque has not transpired, but the following list of the dresses has been preserved:—

"A maske of six coates of purple gold tinsell, garded with purple and black cloth of silver, striped. Bases of crimson clothe of gold, with pendants of maled purple silver tinsell. Twoe paire of sleves to the same of red cloth of gold, and four paire of sleeves to the same of white clothe of copper silvered. Six partletts of purple clothe of silver, knotted. Six bed peeces, whereof foure of clothe of gold, knotted, and two of purple clothe of gold, braunched; six feathers to the same hed peces. Six mantles, whereof foure of oringe clothe of gold, braunched, and twoe of purple and white clothe of silver, braunched. Six vizardes, and six fawchins (falchions), guilded.

"Six cassocks, for torche bearers, of damaske; three of yellowe and three of red, garded with red and yellowe damaske, counterchanged. Six hatts of crimson clothe of gold, and six fethers to the same. Six vizardes.

"Foure heares (hairs, wigs) of silke, and foure garlandes of flowers, for the attire of those that are to utter certaine speeches at the shewing of the same maske."[1]

As we have no indication of the subject of this masque, we can form no idea of the appropriateness of the costume to the characters represented; nor can I pretend to explain what may be meant by head-pieces of cloth of gold with feathers in them. The term was occasionally used for a helmet; and the mention of gilt falchions, and bases with pendants of *maled* purple silver tinsel, induces me to believe that the dresses were intended to represent some conventional kind of classical armour notwithstanding the occurrence of the word "partletts."

These extracts are only interesting as an illustration of the magnificence displayed in these entertainments, and amongst the Lansdowne MSS.[2] in the British Museum is a remarkable proof of the importance attached even in those days to the appropriate splendour and accuracy of theatrical costume, in a letter from Thomas Nevil, Vice-Chancellor of the University of Cambridge, dated 28th Jan., 1594(5), to the Lord Chamberlain, requesting the loan of the royal robes in the Tower for a theatrical performance, and referring to previous instances of such a favour having been accorded:—

"Our bounden dutie in most humble wise remembered. Whereas we intend, for the exercise of young gentlemen and scholars in our Colledge, to set forth certaine comœdies and one tragœdie,

[1] Lansdowne MSS., Brit. Mus., No. 59.　　　　　　　　[2] Ibid. No. 78.

there being in that tragœdie sondry personages of greatest astate to be represented in ancient princely attire, which is nowhere to be had but within the Office of the Robes at the Tower ; it is our humble request your most honorable Lordship would be pleased to graunt your Lordship's warrant unto the chiefe officers there, that, upon sufficient securetie, we might be furnished from thence with such meete necessaries as are required. Which favor we have found heretofore on your good Lordship's like honorable warrant, that hath the rarer embouldened us at this time."

There is no list of the articles borrowed, nor is the name mentioned of the tragedy in which they were to be worn ; but it is probable it was the Latin tragedy of Richard III, written by the previous Vice-Chancellor, Dr. Thomas Legge, and so highly praised by Sir John Harington in his ' Apology of Poetry.' If so, it is actually probable that some of "the *ancient* princely attire " may have been relics of the extensive and superb wardrobe of Richard himself, and his mimic representative would therefore have enjoyed an advantage which no other actor of an historical character has ever at any time possessed.

Fuller, in his ' Worthies,' p. 193, speaking of this wardrobe in the Tower, expressly informs us, " This was not that for the King's wearing apparel, or liveries of servants (kept elsewhere in an house so called in the parish of St. Andrew's Wardrobe), but for vests or robes of state, with rich carpets, canopies, and hangings to be used on great occasions. There were also kept in this place *the ancient clothes of our English kings*, which they wore on great festivals, so that this wardrobe was in effect a library for antiquaries, therein to read the mode and fashion of garments of all ages. These King James, in the beginning of his reign, gave to the Earl of Dunbar, by whom they were sold, re-sold, and re-resold, at as many hands as Briareus had, *some gaining vast estates thereby.*" One can scarcely read with patience of such disgraceful and deplorable Vandalism.

But we have now arrived at a period when regular play-houses had been constructed, and were occupied by special companies of players. When Shakespere wrote and acted, he was himself part proprietor of a theatre, and each establishment had its wardrobe, or each actor his own dresses. Subsequent to the reign of Elizabeth, we hear of no loans of costume from royal or ecclesiastical collections ; and on the destruction by fire of the Globe Theatre, 29th June, 1613, we learn from ' A Sonnett upon the pitiful Burning of the Globe Play-house, in London,' that

> " The perrywigs & drumme heads frie,
> Like to a butter firkin ;
> A wofull burning did betode
> To many a good buffe jerkin."

Also on the occasion of the riots on Shrove Tuesday, 1616–17, when the London apprentices attacked the Cock-pit Theatre in Drury Lane, we are told in the ballad written in their laudation, that

> ". . . to the *tire-house* broke they in,
> Which some began to plunder."

Tommy Brent, one of their leaders, forbids them to steal ; but urges them to "teare and rend," a command which they obey with such alacrity that

> " King Priam's robes were soon in rags,
> And broke his gilded scepter ;
> Faire Cressid's hood, that was so good
> When loving Troylus kept her ;
> Besse Brydges gowne and Muh's crowne," &c.[1]

Whether the dresses and properties in the "tire-house" were the private property of particular actors or of the general company, does not appear ; but we have evidence here of the existence of a wardrobe in a theatre, and may fairly presume that the stage was no longer indebted to the Crown for its costume.

[1] It is a question whether the characters herein mentioned are those in Shakespere's play of ' Troilus and Cressida,' or one on the same subject, as the former could only have been performed at the Cock-pit surreptitiously. Besse Brydges and Muh (Muli-Beg) are characters in Haywood's play of ' The Fair Maid of the West.'

3 E 2

And we are more clearly informed respecting the valuable character of the costumes in the possession of the company by Sir Henry Wotton, who, in a letter to his nephew written three days after the fire, says : " The King's Players had a new play called ' All is True,' representing some principal pieces of the reign of Henry VIII., which was set forth with many extraordinary circumstances of pomp and majesty, even to the matting of the stage, *the Knights of the Order, with their Georges and Garter, the guards with their embroidered coats,* and the like : sufficient in truth, within a while, to make greatness very familiar, if not ridiculous." In contradiction to the ballad, however, he asserts that " nothing did perish but wood and straw, and *a few forsaken cloaks :* only one man had his breeches set on fire, that would, perhaps, have broiled him if he had not, by benefit of a provident wit, put it out with bottled ale." [1]

The masque continued to be at the same time a favourite amusement in private society, on festive occasions, and especially at weddings.

Strutt, in his ' Horda Angel Cynan,' has an interesting illustration of the custom, being an engraving from a painting on board of a masque at the marriage of Sir Henry Utton, and executed shortly after his death, in which Diana and her Nymphs, Mercury with white and black Cupids for torch-bearers, are curiously depicted. (See accompanying plate.)

The masque also continued to share with the drama the favour of the Court, the Royal Family and the noblest personages in the land frequently taking part in it ; the genius of Ben Jonson and the ingenuity of Inigo Jones combining to elevate its literary character, and increase its spectacular effects. In ' The Vision of the Twelve Goddesses,' a masque provided by Samuel Daniel for the first Christmas after James I. ascended the throne, January 8th, 1603-4, the Queen (Anne of Denmark) and her ladies were the principal maskers ; and between that date and 1609, a space of only five years, the " charges for masks " amounted to no less a sum than 4215*l.*, about 10,000*l.* of our present money, a considerable part of which seems to have been expended upon the ' Masque of Blackness ' and the revels of 1604-5 ; 3000*l.* having been delivered from the Exchequer in one sum for the entertainments at Court during Christmas that year.

The sum of 4215*l.* seems likewise, Mr. Collier observes, to have included some of the charges for getting up and bringing out Ben Jonson's masque entitled ' Hymenæi,' on the marriage of the Earl of Essex, celebrated on Twelfth Night, 1605-6, of which some account is contained in a letter from an eye-witness, John Pory, to Sir Robert Cotton, among the MSS. of the latter in the British Museum. The only part of it, however, that concerns the present inquiry is the description of the dresses of " eight men maskers, representing the four humours and the four affections," and " eight ladies who represented the eight nuptial powers of Juno pronubas." " The men were clad in crimson, the women in white. They had every one a white plume of the rochest heron's fethers, and were so rich in jewels upon their heades as was most glorious." The author's own account of the dresses varies considerably from this of " the eye-witness ;" and his minute and most interesting description of the costumes in two of these magnificent spectacles throws so much light on the subject we are considering, that I should not be justified in omitting the information afforded us in the following extract.

The ' Masque of Blackness,' the poet tells us, received its designation "because it was her Majesty's will to have them " (the twelve principal masquers) "blackmoors at first."

The opening scene disclosed six Tritons, " their upper parts human save that their hairs were blue, as partaking of the sea colour, their desinent parts fish, mounted above their heads, and all varied in disposition. From their backs were borne out certain light pieces of taffata, as if carried by the wind." Behind these, on the backs of sea-horses "as big as the life," were seated Oceanus and Niger : "Oceanus presented in a human form, the colour of his flesh blue, and shadowed with a robe of sea-green ; his head gray and horned, as he is described by the ancients ; his beard of the like mixed colour. He was garlanded with alga or sea-grass, and in his hand a trident." Niger, the god or genius of the river so named, was represented "in form and colour of an Æthiop, his hair

[1] Reliquiæ Wotton. Edit. 1672, p. 425.

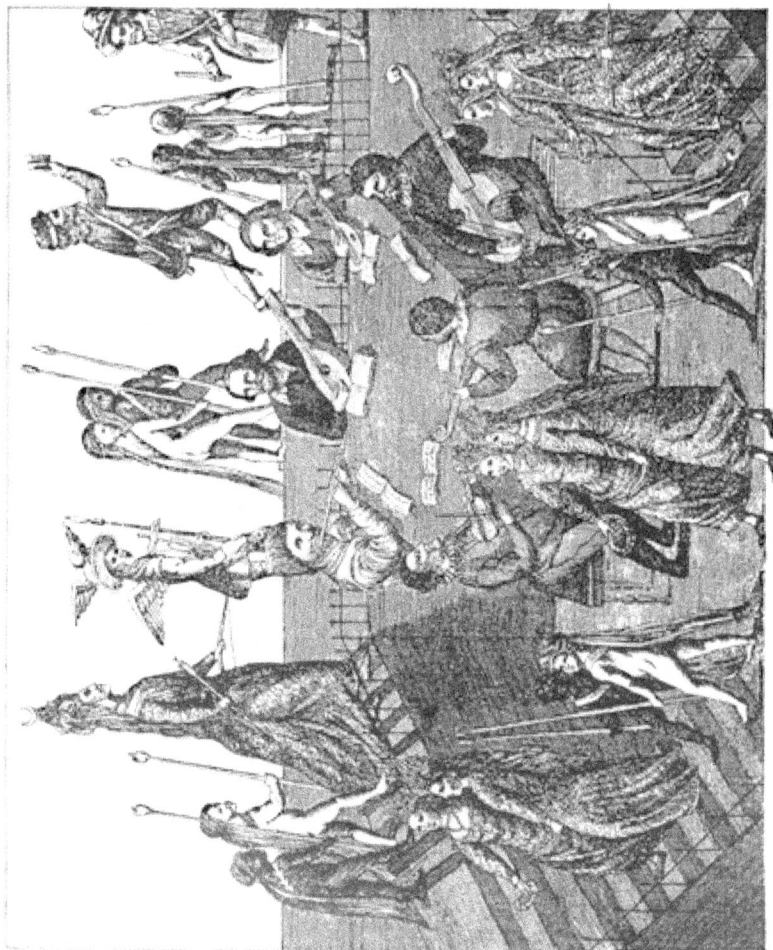

Masque at the Marriage of Sir Henry Unton

From a painting on panel

and rare beard curled, shadowed with a blue and bright mantle, his front, neck, and wrists adorned with pearl, and crowned with an artificial wreath of cane and paper-rush."

The masquers, "which were twelve nymphs, negroes and the daughters of Niger," were attired all alike in "azure and silver, but returned on the top with a scroll and antique dressing of feathers and jewels interlaced with ropes of pearl. And for the front neck and wrists the ornament was of the most choice and orient pearl ; best setting off from the black."

Their light or torch bearers, twelve also in number, were attired "as Oceaniæ or sea-nymphs, the daughters of Oceanus and Tethys. They wore sea-green coloured dresses, waved about the skirts with gold and silver, their hair loose and flowing, garlanded with sea-grass, and that stuck with branches of coral."

It would be difficult, I opine, for the most liberal manager of the present day to reproduce this masque with more taste and splendour.

In the 'Hymenæi or Masque of Hymen,' we find descriptions of dresses designed for allegorical as well as mythological personages, some of which display considerable fancy and ingenuity as well as that familiarity with classical literature which would be expected from "rare Ben Jonson."

Hymen, the god of marriage, was attired in a saffron-coloured robe, his under-vestures white, his socks yellow, a yellow veil of silk on his left arm, his head crowned with roses and marjoram, in his right hand a torch of pine-tree.

The Bridegroom, his hair short, bound with party-coloured ribands and gold twist, his garments purple and white, attended by five pages attired in white (the *Quinque Cerei* of Plutarch) ; and the Bride, her hair flowing, on her head a garland of roses, "like a turret," her garments white, and on her back "a wether's fleece hanging down," her zone or girdle about her waist of white wool, fastened with the Herculean knot.

Reason was represented as a venerable female, with white hair flowing to her waist, "crowned with light" (I presume, a glory), her garments blue, studded with stars ; a white girdle with "arithmetical figures" upon it ; in one hand bearing a lamp, and in the other a bright sword.

Order, "the servant of Reason," a mute personage, wore an under-garment of blue, and an upper one of white, painted full of arithmetical and geometrical figures ; his hair and beard long, a star on his forehead, and in his hand a geometrical staff.

Juno, "sitting on a throne supported by two beautiful peacocks," was richly attired, "like a queen," a white diadem on her head, from whence descended a veil, bound with a *fascia* ("after the manner of an antique bind ") of several coloured silks set with all sorts of jewels, and raised in the top with lilies and roses ; in her right hand a sceptre, and in the other a timbrel. About her sat the spirits of the air in several colours, and on the two sides eight ladies attired richly and alike in the most celestial colours. "The manner of their habits," that is, the *form* of them, is expressly declared to have been copied from "some statues of Juno, no less airy than glorious, the dressings of their heads rare, so likewise of their feet,[1] and all full of splendour, sovereignty, and riches."

Further information is given us by the author in some notes appended to the masque. "The dresses of the lords (eight noblemen representing the humours and affections) were for the fashion taken from the antique Greek statues, mixed with some modern additions, which made it both graceful and strange. On their heads they wore Persic (Persian) crowns, that were with scrolls of gold plate turned outward, and wreathed about with a carnation and silver net-lawn ; the one end of which hung carelessly on the left shoulder ; the other was tucked up before in several degrees of folds between the plaits, and set with rich jewels and great pearl. Their bodies were of carnation cloth of silver richly wrought, and cut to express the naked in manner of the Greek thorax,[2] girt under the breasts with a broad belt of cloth of gold embroidered and fastened before with jewels.

---

[1] Vide *infra*.

[2] The abdominal cuirass which "expressed the naked," *i.e.* the form of the human body. This is evident from the girdle being "beneath the breast," instead of round the waist (*vide* p. 10).

Their labels [1] were of white cloth of silver, laced and wrought curiously between, suitable to the upper half of their sleeves, whose nether parts with their bases were of watchet (blue) cloth of silver, chevronned [2] all over with lace. Their mantles were of several coloured silks, distinguishing their qualities, as they were coupled in pairs,—the first sky colour, the second pearl colour, the third flame colour, the fourth tawny, and these cut in leaves, which were subtilly tacked up and embroidered with O's, [3] and between every rank of leaves a broad silver race (band or stripe). They were fastened on the right shoulder, and fell compass down the back in gracious folds, and were again tied with a round knot to the fastening of their swords. Upon their legs they wore silver greaves, answering in work to their labels.

"The ladies' attire was wholly new, for the invention, and full of glory as having in it the most true expression of a celestial figure; the upper part of white cloth of silver, wrought with Juno's birds and fruits; a loose under-garment full gathered of carnation, striped with silver and parted with a golden zone. Beneath that another flowing garment of watchet cloth of silver laced with gold. . . . The attire of their heads did answer, if not exceed, their hair being carelessly (but yet with more art than if more affected) bound under the circle of a rare and rich coronet, adorned with all variety and choice of jewels, from the top of which flowed a transparent veil down to the ground, whose verge returning up was fastened to either side in most sprightly manner. Their shoes were azure and gold, set with rubies and diamonds; so were all their garments, and every part abounding in ornament." [4]

A volume might be filled with similar descriptions of the dresses in the masques of Ben Jonson, but I think what I have already quoted and commented upon testifies sufficiently to the lavish expenditure, to the extreme magnificence, to the graceful fancy, and, what is more worthy of observation, to the laudable anxiety to represent the deities of ancient Greece and Rome in the costume assigned to them by the poets and sculptors of the classical period. Some of the descriptions are not very clear as regards the form of the garments, and without the aid of the pencil we cannot feel assured of the accuracy of the idea we form of them, but a most valuable illustration is afforded us by the original designs for the dresses in several of these masques by Inigo Jones, preserved in the library at Devonshire House. By the kindness of his Grace the late Duke, a selection of the drawings was published by the Shakespere Society in 1848, with descriptions by Mr. Payne Collier and myself. They are doubly interesting, as they afford us some incidental information respecting the costume of one or two of Shakespere's plays, respecting which no contemporary account has descended to us.

The first plate in the book presents us with the Palmer's or Pilgrim's dress worn by Romeo in the masquerade scene, the figure being simply subscribed "Romeo" in pencil, in the original. It is the usual costume of such personages, consisting of a long loose gown or robe, with large sleeves, and a round cape covering the breast and shoulders; a broad-leafed hat turned up in front and fastened to the crown by a button apparently, if it be not intended for a small cockle-shell, the absence of which customary badge would otherwise be the only remarkable circumstance in the drawing. In the left hand of the figure is the bourdon or staff peculiar to pilgrims. The modern representatives of Romeo have inaccurately carried a cross. In the text of the play Romeo insists upon bearing a torch.

"Give me a torch: I am not for this ambling;
Being but heavy, I will bear the light."

[1] By "labels" I understand those straps of leather known by the name of *lambrequins*, depending from the termination of the cuirass, and the shorter sort attached to the shoulder parts of it.

[2] Chevronned in the heraldic term for a figure derived from a pair of rafters meeting in a point at the top (see shield of Raoul de Beaumont, p. 37). In this instance it was most probably a running zigzag or vandyke pattern, very popular in the Middle Ages.

[3] Probably the initial of 'Opyis, a word which the learned poet in a note on the line, "Are Union's orgies of so slender price?" says, with the Greeks, signifies the same that *ceremonia* does with the Latins; but he does not give any explanation of its appearance on the dresses.

[4] Ben Jonson's Works. By Gifford. 8vo.; Lond.

And again :—

> "A torch for me : let wantons, light of heart,
> Tickle the senseless rushes with their heels ;
> For I am proverbed with a grandsire's phrase :
> I'll be a candle-holder, and look on ;"

and the only indication of his being in a pilgrim's habit is derived from Juliet's addressing him "good pilgrim," &c. The drawing is therefore most interesting authority for the actor. We have given

Roman in Pilgrim's dress.   Torch-bearer.

engravings of torch-bearers of the fifteenth and sixteenth centuries elsewhere. I here annex one of the seventeenth from Inigo Jones's sketches ; but the particular masque for which it was designed is not indicated. Mr. Collier has judiciously observed that we may consider this to be an example of the ordinary costume of such attendants ; but that the apparel of the torch-bearers was often regulated by circumstances, and rendered consistent with the propriety of the whole scene, and that they were occasionally habited with most fantastic variety in Court performances. Another figure in this curious collection is that of a Moresco or morris-dancer, probably designed for the masque of the Four Seasons, in which Spring is described as introducing a morris-dance with which the masque concludes.

As a collateral illustration of this class of performers I subjoin with it two dancers from a French MS. of the latter half of the fifteenth century, the turbaned head-dresses and the bells (*grelots*) attached to their limbs and garments indicating the Moorish character conventionally given to these dances, and from which they derived their name.

A figure under-written "Arlekin, servant to the Mountebank," has a peculiar interest to the student of stage costume, as it illustrates the change which took place in the familiar character of Harlequin during the period of his transference from Italy to England through France in the sixteenth century. We have here the idea entertained of him in the time of Ben Jonson, before that tricksy sprite became so formidable a rival to the dramatist that "the Mountebank," his master, considered him of more importance than Hamlet or Othello. The Harlequin of Inigo Jones is not the particoloured antic of our day, but what used to be called a Zany or Scaramouch (*Scaramuccio*, Ital.), the

Morris Dancers. 19th century.

Pierrot of the French stage and the Clown of our pantomime before the dress was invented (I believe by Grimaldi) which has become identified with that popular personage. I have a dreamy recollection

Morris Dancer. 19th century.

" Arlekin, servant to the Mountebank.

of Laurent, the competitor of Grimaldi at Drury Lane, wearing the white dress, with long sleeves and loose trousers, here depicted ; and occasionally a Clown of this description was introduced, in addition to the more astute and humorous servant of Pantaloon. I shall have much more to say on this subject hereafter. The Harlequin "of the Mountebank" was probably compounded from the French and Italian stages ; and the quack doctor or tooth-drawer at a country fair, within the present century, has been seen with a similar domestic—"a Jack-pudding," as he was called—in attendance upon him.

There are several other characters in the masques of Jonson illustrated by Inigo Jones ; but unfortunately they are so roughly sketched that the details are positively indistinguishable : viz. "an airy Spirit" in the masque of 'The Fortunate Isles and their Union,' designed for the Court on Twelfth Night, 1626, and "the old habit of the three nations, English, Irish, and Scotch," which, if carefully drawn, would have been invaluable to us. I annex the "airy Spirit," premising that the design differs materially from the poet's description of Johphiel, the principal airy spirit in the above masque, which represents him as wearing a chaplet of flowers, pumps, gloves, with a silver fan in his hand.

A volume might be filled with similar notices of the dresses in the Court masques and entertainments of the first half of the seventeenth century, written by Beaumont and Fletcher, Massinger, and their illustrious brethren ; but enough has been said, I think, to demonstrate the progress of stage costume from the earliest period of which we possess authentic records to the time when the regular drama became firmly established throughout Europe ; and Molière in France and Lopez de Vega in Spain had followed in the brilliant path which Shakespere and his successors had opened for the theatre in England.

Airy Spirit.

It is worth observation that, previous to the Restoration of the Monarchy, which may be said to have been also that of the theatre, dramatic entertainments of all sorts having been rigidly suppressed by the Puritan government of Cromwell, considerable attention had been paid to the costume of historical or classical personages, and a laudable desire evinced to render it as accurate as possible ; but it would appear that although Betterton the actor was sent to Paris by royal command expressly to observe the French stage, and transplant from it such improvements in decoration, &c., as might embellish our own, the result was of more advantage to the scenic and mechanical departments than to the wardrobe of the theatre ; and the magnificent but extravagant costume of the reign of Louis XIV. began to render preposterous the tragic heroes and heroines of Greece and Rome and the mythological divinities, for whose appropriate personation so much care and classical knowledge had been displayed by Jonson and his collaborators.

A print appended to Kirkman's Drolls affords us an example of the mode in which many of the principal characters in our national drama were dressed at the Red Bull Theatre, between 1660 and 1663, about which latter date it was entirely abandoned.

The cut represents the stage of the theatre, and the figures upon it are those of Falstaff and Dame Quickly ("the hostess") ; Clause, in 'Beggar's Bush ;' the French dancing master in the Duke of Newcastle's 'Variety ;' the Changeling, from Middleton's tragedy of that name ; the Clown, from Green's 'Tu quoque ;' and the Simpleton, in Coxe's 'Diana and Actæon.'

We here see Sir John Falstaff and Dame Quickly attired in the costume of the reign of Charles I. in lieu of that of the time of Henry IV. or of Henry V., the epoch of the plays into which he was introduced by Shakespere. The rest are more appropriately dressed: the French dancing master wearing the long peruke and the petticoat-breeches (rhingraves) of the courtiers of the Grand Monarque; the Clown, the cap and usual habiliments of the stage; the Jester, Changeling, and Simpleton, such apparel as persons of that class would be clothed in at that date.

Stage of the Red Bull Theatre.

The next illustration of dramatic costume is the portrait of Lacy, the favourite actor of the time of Charles II., in three characters. See chromo-lithographic copy of the original picture by Wright in Hampton Court (issued with the 18th Part of this work), and the description of which given at p. 243 of this volume. I shall, however, have a few more words to say on this subject in the course of the present chapter (see p. 408).

We have now arrived at a period when the English stage began to feel the influence of the French theatre in its literature as well as in its decoration; and in my notice of the progress of the drama in that country, the reader will find much to illustrate the dramatic costume in England during the last decade of the seventeenth century.

The laudable desire to arrive at something like accuracy in the attire of actors representing historical personages, which we have observed prevailing in the Middle Ages, and the graceful fancy exercised in the designs for the dresses of mythological or imaginary beings, appear to have deserted the theatre in the reign of William and Mary, and the two monstrosities that specially characterised the fashions of that day—the peruke and the hoop—extinguished every vestige of the picturesque as well as the appropriate. Who does not remember Pope's lines descriptive of the appearance of the great actor Booth in Addison's tragedy of 'Cato,' which character he originally represented on the production of the play in 1712?

> "Booth enters. Hark, the universal peal!
> But has he spoken?—Not a syllable.
> What shook the stage and made the people stare?
> Cato's long wig, flowered gown, and lacquered hair."

Imagine Cato now appearing in a flowered *robe de chambre* and a profusely powdered full-bottomed wig! Yet the fashion of wearing full-bottomed wigs with the Roman dress (or at least what was intended for such) and other heroic costumes lasted till within the recollection of persons living in my time. My old friend the late Mr. William Dance, of musical celebrity, saw Howard play Tamberlain in such a wig as late as 1765. Aiken, he informed me, was the first who acted the part without one.

Occasionally an attempt was made by theatrical managers at a nearer approach to accuracy, but the ignorance generally prevailing at that period on the subject of ancient costume, and especially armour, had merely the effect of substituting one anachronism for another.

Thus we are reminded by Pope in the poem we have already quoted, that when the play-houses vied with each other in representation of the coronation of Henry VIII., with all due pomp and ceremony, a suit of armour was brought from the Tower for Cibber, who personated the Champion:

> "Back fly the scenes, and enter foot and horse,
> Pageant on pageant, in long order drawn:
> Peers, heralds, bishops, ermine, gold, and lawn;
> The Champion too, and, to complete the jest,
> Old Edward's armour beams on Cibber's breast."

As no armour of "old Edward" has ever been known to exist in the Tower armoury, we may fairly conclude that it was the suit which was at that time, and till very recently, exhibited as that of Edward III, in that much unappreciated national collection, and was of the sixteenth century, with a helmet that did not belong to it, and also that neither peer, herald, nor bishop was apparelled in anything like the costume they would have worn at the coronation of Henry VIII.

That the absurdities of stage dresses and general management at this period in England did not escape the notice and animadversion of persons of taste and education, we have a proof in the remarks of Addison in No. 42 of the 'Spectator,' dated Wednesday, April 18, 1711. "Among all our tragic artifices," he says, "I am most offended at those which are made use of to inspire us with magnificent ideas of the persons that speak. The ordinary method of making a hero is to clap a huge plume of feathers upon his head, which rises so very high that there is often a greater length from his chin to the top of his head than to the sole of his foot. . . . This very much embarrasses the actor, who is forced to hold his neck extremely stiff and steady all the while he speaks ; and notwithstanding any anxieties he pretends for his mistress, his country, or his friends, one may see by his action that his greatest care and concern is to keep the plume of feathers from falling off his head. . . . As these superfluous ornaments upon the head make a great man, a princess gradually receives her grandeur from those additional incumbrances which fall into her tail : I mean the broad sweeping train which follows her in all her motions, and forms constant employment for a boy who stands behind her to open and spread it to advantage. I do not know how others are affected at this sight, but I must confess my eyes are wholly taken up with the page's part, and as for the queen I am not so attentive to anything she speaks as to the right adjusting of her train, lest it should chance to trip up her heels, or incommode her as she walks to and fro on the stage. It is, in my opinion, a very odd spectacle to see a queen venting her passion in a disordered motion, and a little boy all the while taking care they do not ruffle the tail of her gown. The parts that the two persons act on the stage at the same time are very different. The princess is afraid lest she should incur the displeasure of the king her father, or lose the hero her lover, whilst her attendant is only concerned lest she should entangle her feet in her petticoat. . . . In short, I would have our conception raised by the dignity of thought and sublimity of expression, rather than by a train of robes or a plume of feathers."

His comments on another absurdity, the existence of which was protracted to our own times, are so applicable to the state of the stage for upwards of one hundred years after they were written, that I cannot refrain from their quotation :—

"Another mechanical method of making great men and adding dignity to kings and queens is to accompany them with halberts and battle-axes. Two or three shifters of scenes with two candle-snuffers make up a complete body of guards upon the English stage, and by the addition of a few porters dressed in red coats can represent above a dozen legions. . . . The tailor and the painter often contribute to the success of a tragedy more than the poet. Scenes affect ordinary minds as much as speeches, and our actors are very sensible that a well-dressed play has often brought them as full audiences as a well-written one."

Do we not constantly read similar language in our daily papers at present ? And is not the latter paragraph as true in 1879 as it was in 1711 ?

The first reformation in stage costume is said to have been originated in France by the celebrated tragedians M. le Kain and Mdlle. Clairon, and a feeble and very abortive attempt was afterwards made in imitation of it by Garrick. The editor of 'Jeffery's Collection of Dresses,' which was published in 1757, says in his preface : "As to the stage dresses, it is only necessary to remark that they are at once elegant and characteristic, and amongst many other regulations of more importance for which the public is obliged to the genius and judgment of the present manager of our principal theatre (Garrick entered on the management of Drury Lane in 1747) is that of Voltaire's 'Orpheline de Chine,' which was played for the first time in Chinese dresses. The dresses are no longer the heterogeneous and absurd mixtures of foreign and ancient modes which formerly debased our tragedies, by representing a Roman general in a full-bottomed wig, and the sovereign of an Eastern nation in trunk hose."

Now, to say nothing of the fact that the very absurdities specified were then and continued to be for some years afterwards in existence, let us look at the specimens the writer presents us with in his own book of "the elegant and characteristic costumes introduced, or at least tolerated, by the genius and judgment" of Garrick.

Comus.

Zara in 'The Mourning Bride.'

Here is the dress of Comus in Milton's exquisite masque. His coat or "jacket," as he calls it, "is of white curtained sattin; the collar is black velvet set with jewels, and the boots are blue sattin,"

Garrick and Mrs. Yates as Macbeth and Lady Macbeth.

over which is worn what he terms "a robe of pink sattin pufft, with silver gauze fastened over the shoulder, with a black velvet sash adorned with jewels." To his girdle were attached bunches of grapes, and his cap is "stuck over with flowers." Fancy an actor now walking on the stage so attired for Comus!

The next is Mrs. Barry as Zara in 'The Mourning Bride' (a Moorish princess!), from the same collection ; and below, from a little work published by Robert Sayer,[1] and dedicated to Garrick, the "great little Roscius" himself and Mrs. Yates in Macbeth and Lady Macbeth, in the dresses they wore as late as 1769.

This figure of Garrick is stated by Sayer to have been engraved from a portrait in the possession of her Grace the Duchess of Northumberland. There is another in the Garrick Club, representing him as Macbeth in the same gold-laced suit of sky-blue and scarlet in which he played it to the last.

A pamphlet entitled 'The Dramatic Execution of Agis,' published on the production of Mr. Home's tragedy of that name, in 1758, contains a severe attack on Garrick for "disguising himself (*a Grecian chief*) in the dress of a modern Venetian gondolier," and ridicules his having introduced " a popish procession made up of white friars, with some other moveables, like a bishop, his *enfans de chœur*, nuns, &c." into a play the scene of which lies in ancient Sparta. So much for the judgment and taste of Garrick in dramatic costume.

Richard III. he played in a fancy dress, which has been engraved by Sayer, to whom we are also indebted for portraits of him as King Lear and Hamlet.

Garrick as Richard III., King Lear, and Hamlet.

The Prince of Denmark in a full-dress suit of black velvet of Garrick's own time, could at least mislead nobody ; but an ancient British king in knee breeches, silk stockings, shoes with rosettes, a coat with ermine collar and cuffs, lace ruffles, and muslin cravat, was an insult to the most moderately educated audience.

The fancy dress assumed for Richard III. was less preposterous, if not more correct ; but Richmond and the rest of the *dramatis personæ* wore English uniforms of the reign of George III., as if in ridicule of the innovation.[2] A ludicrous anecdote is connected with this particular costume.

[1] 'Dramatic Characters, or different Portraits of the English Stage in the days of Garrick.' Printed for Robert Sayer and Co., Fleet Street, London.

[2] Even in our own times an equally absurd anachronism may be recorded. The late Mr. Charles Mathews, Senior, made his first appearance in public at the Theatre Royal, Richmond, as Richmond in 'Richard III.,' wearing the helmet and jacket of a modern light horseman.

The hat overladen with feathers which he wore with it, being ornamented with mock jewels, was thought a great prize by some bailiffs who were rummaging poor Fleetwood's theatre. Garrick's man and namesake, David, trembling for his master's finery, exclaimed, "Holloa, gentlemen! Take care what you are about. Now look ye, that hat belongs to the king, and when he misses it there'll be the devil to pay." The bailiffs taking for granted, as David meant they should, that the hat was the property of King George instead of King Richard, immediately returned it, with a thousand apologies for the mistake.[1]

Furs or skins were adopted by the French actor Le Kain to distinguish barbaric personages, and the alteration, it can scarcely be called an improvement, was speedily imitated in England. *Teste* Mr. Powell as Cyrus in the tragedy of that name, whose cuffs and boots are edged with fur, and his cap and cloak formed of leopard-skin, while he wears knee-breeches and silk stockings, a vandyke collar of point lace, and his hair is tied with a bunch of riband behind in the fashion of his

Powell as Cyrus.   Mrs. Yates as Mandane.

own day. To complete the farce, Mrs. Yates, as Mandane in the same play, appears in a hoop, court-train, and lace head-dress, which, though not exactly such as might be worn at a drawing room, is as unlike anything Oriental as can well be imagined, and should have induced the manager to remark with King Lear:

"I do not like the fashion of your garments.
You'll say they are Persian; but let them be changed."

It is remarkable that in lieu of an advance in taste and knowledge, as it has been considered, this conventional costume of French origin was in fact a most retrograde movement in theatrical representations, since, as far as Oriental dress was concerned, the Turkish and Persian characters introduced in the pieces played at the fairs of St. Germain and St. Laurent were, as I shall show the reader, attired more accurately as well as more becomingly.

With engravings of some of the dresses worn in the plays of 'Cymbeline,' 'Henry the Fourth,' and 'As you Like it,' in the time of Garrick, I should terminate our pictorial illustration of the stage costume in England, as the period to which this work professes to be limited does not include the reign of George III., but I have to redeem my promise to unravel as far as lies in my power the web of

[1] Cooke's 'Memoirs of Macklin.' 8vo.; London, 1806.

Reddish as Posthumus in 'Cymbeline.'

Mr. Barry as Henry IV.

contradiction that hangs about the portrait of Lacy, the author and actor of 'Sawney the Scot,' in the days of Charles II., and who Langbaine and others have so confidently asserted is represented by

Smith as Iachimo in 'Cymbeline.'

Mrs. Barry as Rosalind in 'As you Like it.'

Wright in his triple portrait of him as Teague in the comedy of 'The Committee.' I have fully argued this question at page 243 of this volume, and shall therefore confine myself only to the production of a copy of the picture in the Garrick Club, of Moody and Parsons in the characters of Teague and Abel in the comedy aforesaid, and to which I have alluded.

Teague is therein depicted in the dress of a running footman, composed of a jacket and petticoat skirt of light blue and silver, such as was worn from the time of Charles II. to the days of Marlborough, and probably much later. He has exchanged the black velvet cap which appertains to his costume for the hat of the hopelessly drunken Puritan, and no reasonable doubt can exist that Moody is attired in the traditional dress worn by the representatives of Teague from the period of the

Moody and Parsons as Teague and Abel. From the
picture in the Garrick Club.

Moody as Teague. From a print 1770.

production of the comedy, and which, if not still seen in England, could not have been so long extinct but that it would be recognized by a majority of the spectators as familiar to them some twenty years or less previously. Moody, who is spoken of in the 'Dramatic Censor' as the best Teague the stage ever knew, and who supported Garrick in the half-price riots of 1763, must have known actors who could remember Lacy in the part, and the dress is too peculiar to have been a subsequent assumption. The portrait at the Garrick Club, therefore, has the additional interest of exhibiting the latest example of the dress of a running footman extant.

I adjoin another engraving of Moody in the same character and dress, from one published by Harrison and Co., April 1770. In this he is represented later in the drunken scene with Abel, whose hat he still wears, and exclaiming over the prostrate form of the drunken man, "Upon my soul, I believe he's dead!"

There is also a portion of stage costume connected with a species of drama peculiar to England, and introduced into it early in the last century, the history of which is so curious and interesting, that I must defer my notice of it to the last, in order to obtain for it the undivided attention of my readers.

I allude to pantomimes, or more correctly harlequinades, which were added to English theatrical entertainments in the days of Queen Anne, and have ever since retained a hold upon the affections of the British public. The principal personage has been the subject of an interminable controversy for more than a century; the origin of his name as well as of his dress having been variously asserted and confidently disputed by every writer, English or foreign, who has undertaken to investigate it. I shall here confine myself to the fact that an actor named Lunn, otherwise Rich, produced the first harlequinade in England, in 1717, and was himself celebrated for his performance of the party-coloured hero, who, except in name and costume, differed widely from his French prototype, and in everything but name from his predecessor in England, "the servant of the Mountebank," in the reign of James I., whose portrait from the pencil of Inigo Jones we have given at page 400 of this volume. The earliest representation of an English Harlequin in the dress now familiar to us, that I have met with, is copied from a painting on an old fan, representing a view of Bartholomew Fair in 1721, an engraving of which was published by Mr. Satchell, printseller in King Street, Covent Garden. A portion of this curious print was copied by Mr. Hone for his 'Every Day Book,' vol. i. pp. 225–6. It contains two figures of Harlequin dressed much as at present,

Bartholomew Fair. 1721.

though still, it would appear from his surroundings, "the servant of the Mountebank," and not the pantomimic performer.

Of his customary companions, Columbine, Pantaloon, and Clown, we have no contemporary representation, and the precise period of the introduction of the latter two has yet to be ascertained. In the following notice of the French and Italian theatre, I shall endeavour to throw a little light on this very obscure subject.

That a thorough reform of theatrical costume did not take place upon the English stage until long after the period to which this history is limited, is now sufficiently acknowledged. The spirit of critical inquiry into these matters has been fairly aroused. The French stage is still in some points in advance of our own; but a few more years will, I hope, produce an entire and complete reformation of our theatrical wardrobes. The persons entrusted with their formation and management will find it necessary to be something more than mere tailors and dressmakers; and though it is too much to expect that every actor will become a thoroughgoing antiquary, it is not too much to presume that before they wear a decoration they will take the trouble to inquire when it was first established, and that the labours of Meyrick, Stothard, and others, having afforded them light enough to dress by, they will not huddle on their clothes in the dark, to be laughed at by a schoolboy in even a transpontine sixpenny gallery.

To turn to France. As early as the fourteenth century, a company of actors of Mysteries and Moralities, such as I have already described, was formed in Paris under the name of "Confrères de la Passion;" and in a theatre which they erected in the Bourg de Saint-Maur des Fossés, they represented the principal incidents from the Passion of Christ. The Prévôt of Paris having by an ordinance issued 3rd June, 1393, prohibited the inhabitants within his jurisdiction from attending the representations without express permission from the King, the "Confrères" complained to Charles VI., who, upon witnessing a performance, was so well satisfied, that by letters-patent of November 4, 1402, he authorized them to perform in the capital and its environs, and to appear in the streets in their theatrical costume.

In noticing the plays founded on sacred subjects in England, I have given ample details of the nature of the dresses assumed on such occasions, and we may fairly conclude that those of the "Confrères" were similar in their form and material.

Froissart, in his account of the entry into Paris of Isabella of Bavaria after her marriage with Charles VI. of France, 1399, gives us several instances of such disguisements. The picture he draws of the pageants presented on that occasion is so graphic and generally illustrative of the manners of the times, that I shall extract from it all the passages bearing upon our subject.

"The citizens of Paris," he tells us, "to the amount of twelve hundred, on horseback, in liveries of green and crimson, lined each side of the road. At the Porte St.-Denis, by which she was to enter the city, was the representation of a starry firmament, and within it were children dressed as angels, also the Virgin holding in her arms a child, *who at times amused himself with a windmill made of a large walnut !* The upper part of the firmament was richly adorned with the arms of France and Bavaria, with a brilliant sun shedding its rays through the heavens ; and this sun was the king's device at the ensuing tournaments. The fountain in the Rue St.-Denis, which ran wine, was decorated with fine blue cloth semée of fleurs-de-lys in gold. The pillars surrounding it were hung with the arms of the chief barons of France, and about them were placed young girls richly attired, having on their heads caps of solid gold, singing sweetly, and presenting cups of gold filled with wine from the fountain to all who chose to drink. Below the Monastery of the Trinity there was a scaffold erected in the street, and on the scaffold a castle, with a representation of the battle with King Saladin, performed by living actors, the Christians on one side and the Saracens on the other. All the lords who had been present were represented with their blazoned war-coats, such as were worn in those times. A little above was seated the King of France (Philip Augustus ?), surrounded by his peers in their proper arms ; and when the queen came opposite the scaffold, King Richard (Cœur de Lion) was seen to leave his companions and advance to the King of France to request permission to fight the Saracens, which having obtained to his knights, and instantly began an attack on Saladin and his forces. The battle lasted for a considerable time, and afforded much pleasure to the spectators. The procession then moved on and came to another gate, which, like the first, had been furnished with a richly-starred firmament, with the Holy Trinity seated in great majesty, and within the heaven little children dressed as angels, singing melodiously.

"As the queen passed under the gate two angels descended from above it, bearing an extraordinarily rich golden crown, set with precious stones, which they gently placed on the head of the queen, sweetly singing the following verses :—

> "' Dame enclose entre fleurs-de-lys,
> Reine êtes-vous de Paris,
> De France, et de tout le pais.
> Nous en n'allons en Paradis.'

"At the gate of the Châtelet was erected a castle of wood, with towers strong enough to last forty years. On the battlements of each was a knight, completely armed from head to foot; and in the castle was a superb bed, as finely decorated with curtains and everything else as if for the chamber of the king, and this bed was called the bed of Justice ('lit de Justice'), in which lay a person representing St. Anne. On the esplanade before the castle (which comprehended a tolerably large space) was a warren and much brushwood, within which were plenty of hares, rabbits, and young birds, that flew out and in again for fear of the populace. From this wood on the side near the queen there issued a large white hart, that made for the bed of Justice, while from another part came forth a lion and eagle, *well represented*, and proudly advanced towards the stag. Then twelve young maidens, richly dressed, with chaplets of gold on their heads, came out of the wood, holding naked swords in their hands, and placed themselves between the hart and the lion and eagle, showing that with their swords they were determined to defend the white hart and the bed of Justice."

The white hart or stag was a special badge of Charles VI., and was afterwards assumed by his son-in-law, Richard II. of England. The lion and eagle most probably typified England and Germany at that period. All three were evidently men or boys in skins, feathers, and masks, made up to counterfeit the beasts and the bird after the fashion of the engravings already given at page 385.

In the same chapter we hear of the presents made to the king, the queen, and the Duchess of Touraine (Valentine de Milan) by the city of Paris. One, a magnificent service of gold plate, was brought to the king in a worked litter, borne by two strong men dressed as savages. Another, consisting of a model of a ship in gold and various flagons, jugs, cups, dishes, &c., of gold and silver, was carried to the queen in a similar litter by two men, one dressed as a bear, the other as a unicorn; and a third litter, laden with a like costly quantity of gold and silver plate, was brought to the chamber of the Duchess of Touraine by two men representing Moors, having their faces blackened and richly dressed with white turbans, "as if they had been Saracens or Tartars."

There is, unfortunately, no contemporary pictorial representation of any of these pageants in the illuminated copies of Froissart, the greater number of which are of the fifteenth century, so we have only the verbal description to guide us. From that, however, we may infer that a laudable endeavour was made to attain something approaching to accuracy in costume.

In the battle between Saladin and Richard, we are told that the most renowned leaders of the Christian forces were represented in their *cottes d'armes*, "such as were worn in those times." I doubt it much, but at all events we may presume that the attempt was made to the extent of their knowledge.

In a play acted before Richard II., A.D. 1389, twenty-one coifs of linen were provided for persons representing lawyers. As the subject of the play is unknown, we cannot of course judge of the appropriateness of the costume; but it was correct if the "lawyers" were to be supposed members of the English Bench or Bar of that date, as the white linen coif was an indispensable article of their professional attire (see Dictionary).

Another remarkable and well-known historical occurrence connected with a masking or disguising is the narrow escape of the same King Charles VI. of France and some of his courtiers from a horrible death, 29th January, 1392–3, in the Hôtel de St.-Pol at Paris. The king and eleven knights and gentlemen dressed themselves in tight-fitting garments of linen covered with fine flax, the colour of hair to imitate savages, and were dancing before the queen, the Duchess de Berri, and other ladies, when the Duke of Orleans, in order to discover who the maskers were, took a torch from an attendant and, imprudently holding it too near one of the party, the flax took fire, and five of them being chained together they were all soon in a blaze. The king was providentially preserved by the presence of mind of the Duchess de Berri, who, without knowing who he was, flung the train of her mantle over him. Four of the six forming the king's party were unfortunately burned to death —two on the spot, and two died a few days afterwards in great agony. A fifth, Jean de Nantouillet, recollecting the buttery was near, broke the chain by which he was attached to his companions and, flying thither, flung himself into a large tub of water which was there for washing the dishes, and so saved his life, but suffered from his burns for some time after. There are representations of this fatal accident in every illuminated copy of Froissart's Chronicles; but none are actually contemporary, the majority being of the middle of the fifteenth century. The appearance of the savages may, however, be not far from the truth, as it was a popular "disguisement" throughout the Middle

From a copy of Froissart, Nat. Lib. Paris.

Ages, and could not have been much diversified. I therefore give an engraving of one of the miniatures from a copy of Froissart in the National Library at Paris, and two of the figures from the copy in the Harleian Collection, Brit. Mus., No. 4380.

From Harleian MS. No. 4380.

These "salvage men," or "wode houses" (i.e. wild men), as they were sometimes called, were prominent features in masques, pageants, &c. They were clothed entirely in skins or imitations of skins, and occasionally with wreaths and girdles of oak-leaves. I shall return to them anon.

During the fifteenth century the rage for dramatic exhibitions rapidly increased in Paris. The clerks of Parliament, called Clercs de la Basoche, formed an opposition company to the Brotherhood of the Passion and acted farces, soties, and moralities on a large marble table in the Palais de Justice. In these pieces they exposed the follies and abuses of society, and the errors and extravagances of the nobility. The clerks of the Châtelet followed their example. Stages were constructed in the market-places and in the colleges as in England, and events of ancient and modern history were publicly performed by the professors and their pupils. To counteract these attractions, the Confrères, who objected to perform in profane dramas—although their plays, founded upon the most sacred subjects, were interlarded with indecencies and licentious allusions of a revolting description—united themselves with a new troupe, called "Les Enfans sans souci," who acted farces enlivened with songs. At the end of each piece, says an old writer, there was always "une chanson fort gaillarde." In 1422, when Paris was in possession of the English, the Confrères performed the Mystery of the Passion of St. George, at the Hôtel de Nisle, before Henry V. of England. The reader will remember I have described a miracle play or masque on this subject, which had been performed in England before the same king six years previously.

In 1548, the increasing indecencies of the farces, and the scandal arising from their association with religious subjects, induced the Parliament to prohibit all plays derived from such sources; and in 1552 we find accordingly a writer, named Jodelle, producing a drama entitled 'Cléopatre,' at the Hôtel de Reims, and a few years afterwards his tragedy of 'Didon.' Still we are ignorant how far the dresses of these classical dramas approached accuracy, or whether the theatrical costumiers of Paris were in advance of those of London.

A great turning point was about to occur in theatrical entertainments, and the movement originated in Italy. Pope Leo X. had encouraged the rise of the drama in Rome during his pontificate, 1513–1522; and the Cardinal de Ferrara, Archbishop of Lyons, built a theatre in the latter city, and expended upwards of ten thousand crowns in the production of a tragi-comedy, for which a company of Italian actors was engaged and imported.

An Italian tragedy, entitled 'Sophonisba,' performed before the Pope, was translated into French, and acted at Blois before Catherine de Medicis, by the princesses and ladies and gentlemen of the Court.

Between 1570 and 1597, several Italian companies came to Paris; but their representations exciting the jealousy of the Confrères de la Passion, whose privileges were always highly respected by the Parliament, their success was of short duration. Henri IV., however, had a private company of Italian actors, who performed both at Paris and Fontainebleau; but in his reign the French theatre had not shaken off the barbarism, puerility, and grossness which in all countries disfigured the earlier productions of the stage, although in England Shakspere had brought out nearly all his immortal dramas.

To this rapid résumé of the history of the French stage to the end of the sixteenth century I have been unable to add any information respecting the costume of the actors, beyond what we may gather from the descriptions of the pageants or performances in the streets on great public occasions, or Court entertainments, such as have been already noticed; but judging from analogy, we may fairly presume that it was similar to that adopted in England, and of which so many curious particulars have been preserved to us by the chroniclers, and in the inventories and official documents of the time. Henceforth, however, we shall find ample authority for the illustration of the especial subject of this chapter.

In 1595, a theatre was opened in the Foire St.-Germain, which, after much opposition and litigation, was permanently established, the company paying two crowns per annum for their licence to the monopolizing fraternity of the Passion. Of the peculiar pieces enacted in this theatre, a

collection was printed and published at Amsterdam at the beginning of the eighteenth century, with
engravings of the principal scenes and characters. This theatre was the cradle of the Vaudeville and
the Opéra Comique.

The higher order of drama received much about the same period considerable impetus and
encouragement from Cardinal Richelieu, who built two theatres in his palace (now the Palais Royal),
one of which was erected for the purpose of acting his own tragedy, called 'Mirame,' the getting-up
of which cost him nearly three hundred thousand crowns. On the boards of this theatre, Corneille's
famous tragedy of 'The Cid' was acted in 1636, and was followed in 1639 by 'Les Horaces' and
'Cinna.' The costume in which the representatives of these Roman celebrities was attired I shall
attempt to illustrate by contemporary designs, but some of a conventional character were invented
at this period by a few comic actors—originally, it is reported, bakers, who hired a tennis-court near
the Estrapade, which they converted into a theatre, with some coarse decorations, and where they
acted low and most ridiculous farces with such extraordinary success, that their names have
descended to posterity, and, what is of more consequence to us at present, their full-length portraits
were engraved by the first artists of the day, and had an extensive sale throughout Europe.

The names of these actors were as follows :—

1. Henri le Grand, surnamed Turlupin. He is reported to have kept on the stage for fifty
years, and never to have been excelled as an actor in farce or low comedy ; at all events, his
popularity was so great that the pieces he performed in obtained the name of *turlupinades*.

Turlupin.   Gaultier Garguille.

2. Hugues Guerin, surnamed Gaultier Garguille, was famous for his personation of ridiculous old
men and the singing of comic songs, a collection of which was published in 1631. He was also the
speaker of the prologues.

3. Robert Guerin, called Gros Guillaume, who was a coarse buffoon of extraordinary stature.

In addition to these three most celebrated actors, a fourth, named Jean Farine, another called
Jodelet, who was also the author of the comedies he played in, flourished at the same period ; a sixth,
named Jaquemin Jadot ; and a seventh, named Guillot Gorgu. All these performers, except Gros

Gros Guillaume.

Jacquemin Jadot.

Guillaume, wore masks, and always appeared each in his own particular stage costume, whatever character was assumed by them. Six are here copied from engravings of the period.

Jodelet.

Guillot Gorgu.

Underneath some of the figures are complimentary verses, describing the peculiar talent of the actor. Thus of Gros Guillaume we are told :—

> " Tel est dans l'hôtel de Bourgogne
> Gros Guillaume avec sa troigne,
> Enfariné comme un meunier ;
> Son minois et sa rhétorique
> Valent les bons mots de Regnier
> Contre l'humeur mélancolique."

Of Jaquemin Jadot it is said :—

> " Jaquemin avec sa posture,
> Sa grimace et son action
> Nazarde la perfection
> Et rend guinaude la Nature.
> On ne peut assez admirer
> Les beaux contes qu'il nous vient dire,
> Qui font qu'à force de trop rire,
> Nous sommes contraints de pleurer."

Guillot Gorgu is celebrated as a satirist and linguist :—

> " Guillot Gorgu par ses bons mots
> Et par ses discours satiriques
> Borne les niais et les sots
> Et fait aux plus savans la nique :
> Il nous entretient du Festin
> Des Romans, des métamorphoses ;
> En parlant français ou latin,
> Il dit toujours de bonnes choses."

Jodelet is praised for his manners :—

> " On peut dire de Jodelet
> Qu'il sait jouer son personnage
> Aussi bien qu'homme de son âge,
> Faisant le Maître et le Valet :
> Sa harangue est toujours polie
> Et sans avoir rien affecté :
> Par sa grande naïveté
> Il guérit la mélancolie."

As respects, however, the tragic, historical, or classical drama, which I have said I would attempt to illustrate by contemporary designs; the idea of Roman armour conceived by costumiers of the sixteenth century is fairly exemplified in the following figure, from the print published in 1551, of the triumphal entry of Henry II. and his queen, Catherine de Medicis, into Rouen, in the month of October 1550. The combination of the costume of the period with an imitation of that of ancient Rome, as exhibited in the statues of the emperors and generals which have been preserved for us, will be obvious to the reader. At the same time it would appear that a more accurate knowledge of Oriental costume existed amongst painters and sculptors, for the personators of Turks or Persians were attired with greater propriety. Take, for instance, the accompanying figure of a Turk from the same procession (see next page).

The fact may be accounted for by the circumstance that they had the advantage of frequently seeing visitors from Eastern kingdoms, in the embassies from Constantinople, Ispahan, Morocco, &c. in their national dresses.

The subsequent introduction of the peruke in the time of Charles II. and Louis XIV. rendered still more ridiculous the amalgamation of classical costume and that of the prevailing fashion.

Roman Officer and Turk. From an engraving, 1591.

Subjoined are the figures of Circe and Ulysses, from the frontispiece to a piece entitled 'Les Animaux raisonnables,' acted at the Foire de St.-Germain in 1718, in which it will be observed that the Greeks are not distinguished even conventionally from the Romans. Beside them is Mercury, from another engraving in the same collection, being one of the characters in a piece entitled 'Arlequin Thétis,' acted in 1713.

Circe and Ulysses.

Mercury.

Mademoiselle Subligny.

Mademoiselle Moreau.

Of the costume of the actresses and ballet-dancers at the end of the seventeenth century, some fine engravings were published in Paris by Mariette, Rue St.-Jacques, reduced copies of three of which I annex, representing Mesdemoiselles Subligny and Moreau dancing at the Opera, and an Italian actress, "Angélique Toscano dite Marinette," evidently the heroine in some tragedy ; also the costume

Angélique Toscano.

Costume of "Isabelle." Théâtre Français, 1682.

Asia.

Africa.

of the character of " Isabelle," the ordinary name for a young lady in the French comedies of that period. To these I add the costumes of three ladies, presumably intended to represent Asia, Africa, and America, from engravings published about the same period, as examples of the dresses assigned to allegorical personages.

At the feet of Africa in the original print is a turban, bearing out the remark of M. Quicherat, that while the grossest anachronisms were perpetrated by the French actors in the dresses they assumed for the representation of historical, classical, or mythological characters, their apparel as Turks, Persians, or other Oriental nations was comparatively sufficiently accurate. It is therefore singular that the female herself should not have been represented in a habit more characteristic of the quarter of the globe she is intended to personate, as the introduction of the turban shows the artist must have been familiar with Oriental costume. Abundant proof of this fact will be found in the frontispieces to the comic operas in the 'Théâtre de la Foire,' on which curious work I shall continue to levy contributions.

That well-abused monstrosity the hoop is said to have made its first appearance upon the French stage towards the end of the reign of Louis XIV.

America.

The actresses, we are told, who personated the heroines of tragedy, had from the time of Corneille

3 R 2

been accustomed to increase by artificial means the amplitude of their dresses, and eagerly adopted the fashion from some English ladies who visited Paris after the Peace of Utrecht.

Juno.   *Jupiter.*   *Night.*

However this may have been, there can be no doubt that the hoop petticoat was worn in its greatest extravagance on the stage, both in France and England, for the greater part of the first half

A Demon.   A Zephyr.

of the century. I have given examples of it on the English stage at pp. 404 and 406, and also of the ridiculous imitation of it in the male costume; and here are some equally incongruous and absurd from the designs of French artists, MM. Guillot and Martin, viz. "Juno," "Jupiter," [1] "Night," "a Demon," and "a Zephyr."

Addison in 'The Spectator' for Tuesday, April 3rd, 1711, makes the following remarks on the incongruity of the costume of the French Theatre in his time:—"Every actor that comes on the stage is a Beau. The Queen and heroines are so painted that they appear as ruddy and cherry-cheeked as milkmaids. The Shepherds are all embroidered, and acquit themselves at a ball better than our English dancing masters. I have seen a couple of Rivers appear in red stockings, and Neptune, instead of having his head crowned with sedges and bulrushes, making love in a fair full-bottomed periwig and a plume of feathers." The first reformers of these absurdities were Le Kain and Mdlle. Clairon, in 1755, at the suggestion of Voltaire, after violent opposition by the actresses and opera-dancers.

It is at the commencement of the eighteenth century that we suddenly discover on the French stage a group of characters previously unknown to it, brought into comic dramas of nearly every description, bearing always the same names, and, like the actors of the Hôtel de Bourgogne, wearing

Arlequin and Prince of Persia.   Mezzetin.   Cupid.   Fortune.   Arlequin.

always the same costume, no matter what the subject of the piece or in what locality the scene is laid. These characters are respectively named Pierrot, Scaramouche, Mezzetin, Arlequin, and Colombine.

It is not my province to inquire whether the two latter and most familiar personages are the lineal descendants of Mercury and Psyche, as some writers have imagined, or, according to the author of a little book published in the last century, that the more accurate tradition is that Harlequin was the son of Mercury by Iris, "Goddess of the many-coloured bow," and nursed and educated by Circe.[2] It is with the stage costume of our old acquaintances that I have alone to deal in these pages; and that of Harlequin, with which we are so familiar, first appears upon the French stage at this period. We have seen how he was attired in the reign of James I., when he was simply the servant of a mountebank, unconnected with the English drama, into which he does not appear to have been introduced before the reign of Queen Anne; but though many attempts have been made to account for the change to the peculiar and unique suit of patchwork in which we find him

[1] M. La Croix, who has engraved them, calls this figure "a King," but the thunderbolt in the right hand evidently indicates the King of Olympus, and in company with him is Juno.

[2] 'The Strange Adventures of that celebrated Genius known by the name of the Nimble-footed Harlequin.' London; no date.

at the fair of St. Germain, in the reign of Louis XIV., no satisfactory information has hitherto been afforded us. I give above a copy of the figures in a frontispiece to a piece in three acts, entitled ' La Princesse de Carizme,' acted at the fair of St. Laurent and also at the Théâtre de l'Opéra, 1718, because they represent the Prince of Persia, with Arlequin his confidant, and therefore afford an example of the Oriental costume I have alluded to; also another group from the frontispiece to ' La Ceinture de Vénus,' represented in 1715, which includes Cupid and Fortune, with Arlequin and Mezzetin, an equally popular character in early French comic opera.

The Arlequin of the French stage was not a mute, like his English successor, or a dancer; but a knavish glutton,[1] the servant and adviser generally of the lover in the drama; Colombine being the *suivante* of the young lady, a favourite name for whom was "Isabelle" (see her costume, p. 418 *ante*). Arlequin was the only one of the group who wore a mask, which was black and ugly and covered the entire face, and probably inherited from that of Turlupin. His wand or bat recalls

Pantalon. Mezzetin. Poisson as Crispin.

"the dagger of lath" with which the Vice in the old Miracles and Moralities used to belabour Beelzebub; and as that popular buffoon was ordinarily habited as a fool or jester, the party-coloured dress may have owed its origin to him also. Pierrot on the French stage was identical with the "Arlekin" of Inigo Jones, and was usually the servant of the old man of the piece, the Pantaloon of the present day, whose name, however, is of Venetian origin, and has never been included in the *dramatis personæ* of France. His name appears in the *dramatis personæ* of a comedy by Doctor Nicolo Barbieri, entitled ' L' Inavertito,' and printed at Venice in 1630. A print of that date presents us with a "Pantalon" of the old Italian theatre, but the dress has nothing in common with our modern Pantaloon (see woodcut above). But of this more hereafter. Scaramouche is also a name of Italian origin, and his dress does not appear to have been very dissimilar to that of Pierrot. That of Mezzetin, however, was peculiar to his character. It consisted of a loose jacket, and breeches of white- and red-striped calico, and a turban-shaped head-dress to match. The name

---

[1] " Poltron gourmand et fripon très célèbre." The performers of this character were instructed to accompany their dialogues by certain gestures which were called *lazzis*—the origin of the preliminary attitudes of our modern Harlequin.

of Mezzetin (Mezzetino) also occurs in the comedy above mentioned, and he is described as a merchant. An engraving of an Italian actor, one Angelo Constantini, represents him as "Mezetin" in 1659, and in 1723 he is claimed in an Italian drama for a "Bergamasco." The costume, it will be observed, greatly resembles that of Jodelet.

Another character was introduced about this time by the name of Crispin, an additional servant to the old man, and who, like the rest of the group, retained his name and dress (which was a complete suit of black, with leathern waistbelt) in every piece he played in. He was also armed with a formidable Spanish rapier. The painters and engravers of that day have preserved to us a portrait of Poisson, in his costume of Crispin, a copy of which is given above. So thoroughly was he identified with that character, that it remained for some time hereditary in his family.

The French and Italian theatres seem to have influenced each other so greatly during the latter portion of the seventeenth century that it is difficult to decide to which of them the origin of certain characters common to both stages is due.

I must therefore do my best, by strictly chronological data, to enable my readers to form their own opinion of the claims of France and Italy to be the birthplace of those popular pantomimists who have become naturalized in England, and who established a species of entertainment unknown to any other country. Of the names of Harlequin, Columbine, Pantaloon, and Clown, the earliest we meet with is that of Pantaloon. Its origin was distinctly Venetian, being a corruption of "Piante

Zanes.   Mattaccino.

Leone," the designation of the standard-bearer of the Republic; but as early as the reign of Elizabeth, in England, the appellation was used to designate an old man—"the lean and slippered pantaloon" of the sixth of Shakespere's 'Seven Ages.' About the same period (1585), we find Henry III. of France disguised as a "Pantalon Venetien" during the Carnival. In Ben Jonson's masque, 'The Vision of Delight,' A.D. 1617, "six Burratines dance with six Pantaloons," Buratin being the name of one of the grotesque characters in Venetian carnivals, and derived from that of a coarse cloth in which he was dressed. The name of Harlequin (written Arlekin) appears next also in England in another of Ben Jonson's masques, as I have already stated; but there was no such personage as Harlequin amongst the actors at the Hôtel de Bourgogne in Paris, nor as "Arlechino"

Frontispe.

The Doave.

amongst the Italian buffoons, their contemporaries. The name does not exist in Florio's 'World of Words,' 1598, nor in the list of popular masquerading characters in Italy at that period. Annexed are the figures of all that class of actors which I can find named at the end of the sixteenth century, copied from the 'Diversarum Nationum Habitus' of Pietro Bertelli, published at Padua in 1591.

Il Magnifico.

Buratin.

They are named Zanne, Mattasin, Francatripe, Buratin, Il Magnifico, and the Doctor, and obviously had their origin in the *mascarades* with which the Carnival was celebrated in Italy generally, and Venice in particular.

Il Magnifico is attired precisely as a Venetian nobleman of that period, and may be considered the typical Pantaloon of the sixteenth century, though his dress is not in conformity with the one handed down to us as that of the Pantaloon of the Italian stage, which I have already given at p. 422.

The Zanne (Zane, whence our Zany) is the only one whose costume reminds us of the "Arlekin, servant to the Mountebank," of Inigo Jones. Florio has "Zane, the name of John. Also a sillie John, a Gull, a Noddie, used also for a simple Vice, Clowne, Foole, or simple fellowe in a plaie or comedie." This is remarkable, for while it confirms my belief that in Harlequin we have a lineal descendant of the Vice of the early stage, this description of the Zane perfectly accords with that of the "Arlequin" of the French comic drama, who is a "simple fellow," and his Italian dress at the same time associates him with the Pierrot and Scaramouche of the French theatre, the old-fashioned Clown or Fool of our English pantomimes, the Jack-pudding ("sillie John"), servant to the quack doctor, the "Merry-Andrew" of the fair, and the "Mr. Merryman" of the circus, previous to the days of the celebrated Grimaldi, who introduced the present dress, restoring the scarlet cock's-comb which had first surmounted the hood, and subsequently the cap of the jester of the Middle Ages.

Mattasin, Francatripe, and the Doctor have left us no representatives; but Buratin's costume is remarkable for the slashing of his dress, his ruff, and his mask. In another engraving in the same work he is represented in a plain white jacket and trousers, like the Zanne. All we know further of him is that the character is mentioned in a masque of Ben Jonson's, as I have stated at p. 423. The female companions of these buffoons are not named, and were simply, I presume, attired in fancy dresses, preserving the Venetian style of coiffure. That curious traveller, Thomas Coryat, who visited Italy in 1608, is unfortunately more communicative respecting the costume of the Venetian playgoers than that of the players, who, he simply says, "cannot compare with us for apparell." But his description of the masks worn by a certain class of women frequenting the theatre is instructive. He tells us "they wore double maskes on their faces to the end they might not be seene : one maske reaching from the tippe of their forehead to their chinne, and under their maske another with twiskes of downy or woolly stuff, covering their noses."

Colombine is a cotemporary of the

Group of Actors of the Italian Theatre.

French Arlequin, and is generally to be met with in the Théâtre de la Foire. Watteau and his pupil Lancret, the popular painters of the first half of the eighteenth century, in their graceful pictures of masquerades and *al-fresco* entertainments, constantly introduce her in company with Arlequin and Pierrot ; and M. Paul La Croix, in his beautiful volume, 'The Eighteenth Century,' has given an engraving of the actors of the Italian Theatre, in which Colombine is a prominent object. Her dress displays in some portions the diamond-shape pattern of that peculiar to Arlequin, who is in the background, and she wears a cap and a black mask, and is represented in an attitude traditionally assumed by our Harlequin. Pierrot is, however, the principal figure in the group ; and if this really represents an Italian company, it must have been after they had taken to the performance of French dramas, on their re-establishment in Paris during the regency of the Duke of Orleans. We can, therefore, form no conclusion from this picture respecting the nationality of Columbine, while the absence of such a character in the early Italian drama is a negative proof of her having been introduced to it from the French.

Of the fusion that took place towards the end of the seventeenth century, we have abundant evidence in the publications of the period, viz. :—

'La Matrone d'Éphèse, ou Arlequin Grapignan.' Comédie en trois actes, représentée pour la première fois *par les Comédiens Italiens du Roi* dans leur Hôtel de Bourgogne, le 12 Mai 1682. Mise au Théâtre par M. D * * * *.

'Arlechino Tinto Bassa d'Algiera.' Opera seria, by Doctor Gianella. *Translated from the French.* Printed at Venice ; no date.

'Gli' Amore sfortunate de Pantalone,' 1689, in which Arlechino appears as the servant of Pantaloon.

'Arlequin Mercure Galant.' Comédie en trois actes. Mise au Théâtre par Monsieur D * * * *, et représentée pour la première fois par les Comédiens Italiens du Roi dans leur Hôtel de Bourgogne, le 22 Janvier 1682.

'Arlequin Lingère du Palais,' three acts, by Tatoniello, *partly in Italian*, at the Theatre in Paris, 4th October, 1682.

Evarista Gherardi, himself a harlequin and dramatic author, wrote his 'Histoire du Théâtre Italien, ou le Recueil général de *toutes les Comédies et Scènes françoises joué par les Comédiens Italiens du Roi*, pendant tout le temps qu'ils ont été au service,' in 1697. He commenced acting Harlequin in 1689. His only surviving comedy, 'Le Retour de la Foire de Basons,' was performed in 1695 ; but he throws no light on the origin of the character of Harlequin, or of what is more important to us in this work, the peculiar and unique costume in which he first appears on the French stage, and which has been subsequently transmitted to our times.

Having cleared the stage, to the best of my ability, of the rest of the pantomimic company, I shall devote the remainder of this portion of my task to the consideration of the conflicting theories afloat respecting Harlequin—a personage who, as Père La Rousse remarks in his 'Grande Dictionnaire Universelle,' Paris, 1866, article "Arlequin," has been the subject of what he correctly terms "une des étymologies les plus controversées."

I am not called on to enter into this controversy so far as respects the derivation of the *name* of this character, as my inquiries in these pages are properly limited to his dress ; but the two subjects are so dependent on each other, and the only facts of which we are at present in possession are apparently so irreconcilable with the theories promulgated, that I can see no way to separate them.

First, then, as to the name, which has been variously derived from almost every conceivable source. Some similar appellation, it has been asserted, was rejoiced in by a wicked Crusader, a sort of legendary Robert the Devil ; other commentators have discovered his prototype in the 'Inferno' of Dante, cap. xxx. German antiquaries have suggested derivations from Erlenking, Roi des Aunes, and "Hollen Kind," "Enfant infernal," and so on *ad infinitum.* Dismissing all these mere guesses, let us proceed to examine statements of a more substantial kind. Tradition associates Harlequin with the city of Bergamo. La Rousse, who in the article above referred to has well-nigh exhausted the subject, relates an anecdote which is so pretty and ingenious, that it is a pity it is not true. " A little boy, we are told, whose name was Arlechino, born in Bergamo, was a great favourite with his young companions. It was the custom of the citizens to give their children new clothes on the Mardi Gras of each year ; and Arlechino, having been asked by his young friends what sort of suit he was to have, answered that his parents were too poor to buy him a new one, and that he must therefore be content with what he had. The other boys thereupon agreed amongst themselves that they would each bring him a piece of the cloth of which their own suits were to be made. They did so ; but each piece differing from the other in colour, a circumstance that they had never taken into consideration, they were sadly disappointed to find their good-natured intentions fruitless. Arlechino, however, reassured them by gratefully accepting their contributions, and causing a complete suit to be made of the pieces, the different colours of which, he said, would each remind him of the friendly donor. The dress was made according to his directions, and on the Mardi Gras Arlechino skipped in it about Bergamo, delighting every one with his merry songs and smart sayings."

Now, it appears to me that one important inference may be drawn from this pretty and ingenious story. The endeavour to account for the remarkable dress of Harlequin, as it suddenly appears to us in France at the close of the seventeenth century, as surely indicates that the actual origin of it was unknown, as the drawing of Inigo Jones negatives the assertion that the costume was in existence in 1603.

Another and more plausible suggestion, namely, that Harlequin, having succeeded to the office of "the Vice" of the early stage, had inherited with the "dagger of lath" the motley habiliment of his predecessor, is not only disposed of by the same pictorial evidence, but also by the fact that the peculiar pattern of the variegated dress of Harlequin bears not a shadow of resemblance to the party-coloured habit of the Vice or Fool, which has been handed down to us completely *cap-à-pied* in the popular person of Mr. Punch, the Pulcinello of Italy and Polichinel of France, who appears in the *dramatis personæ* of the old Italian comedies in conjunction with Mezzettino, at least as early as the commencement of the eighteenth century, a period when in England he had been degraded to "a motion" and restricted to a puppet show.

As respects the name of Harlequin, the earliest derivation of it is, I believe, that of Menage, who says it was given to one of the first Italian actors who visited Paris in the reign of Henry III. in consequence of his being so much at the house and in the company of M. de Harley de Chausodon, President of the French Parliament. His comrades for that reason called him Harleyquino, or little Monsieur Harley, and this name was handed down to his successors in the particular character in which he had attained celebrity. Menage adds, "J'ay appris cette origine de Monsieur Guyot, qui m'a dit l'avoir appris de Harlequin mesme au second voyage qu'il fit en France au commencement du règne de Louis XIII. et elle a été confirmée par Monsieur Forget, Grand Maître des Eaux et Forêts d'Orléans, qui m'a dit avoir ouy Harlequin sur le Théâtre appeller Monsieur de Chausodon son parain." This alludes to an anecdote quoted by La Rousse, to the effect that the actor said to the President, "Il y a parenté entre nous au cinquième degré. Vous êtes Harley première, et je suis Harle-quint."

This is certainly very circumstantial, and the witnesses are all persons of consideration, and moreover contemporaries of the parties themselves. François Guyot was born at Angers in 1575, and died at Paris in 1658. Forget was born in 1544 : he was Secrétaire d'État during the reigns of Henry III. and Henry IV. of France, and was charged by the latter sovereign with the drawing-up of the famous Edict of Nantes, dying in 1610 ; and Menage assures us that he had his information direct from the lips of these gentlemen at a period when the actor himself was in existence, and the subject a theme of conversation.

It is most unfortunate and provoking that one link in the chain of evidence should be wanting, which would have enabled us to settle the question. Menage has omitted to furnish us with the real name of the actor who had acquired the *sobriquet* which has now become a household word with us.

The latest contribution to the mysterious biography of Harlequin is that of my lamented friend Dr. Doran, published in the forty-third volume of the 'Temple Bar' magazine, under the title of "A Dance after Harlequin." The name of Dr. Doran can never be mentioned without respect, and his opinion on all literary questions, but especially those connected with the drama, is deserving our best consideration. Rejecting contemptuously the definition of Menage, he tells us that in the year 1576 a wandering troupe of Italian players came to Paris. The manager of this strolling company was named Andreini, husband of Isabella Andreini, celebrated for her acting, for her learning, and for the honours paid to her at her funeral by the city in which she died. This company called themselves "I Gelosi," "The Jealous" (*i.e.* to please). Each performer had a stage name, and the two low comedians of the troupe, Pedrolino and Simone di Bologna, were best known by their assumed appellations; that of the former being Frenchified into Pierrot, and the latter being called Arlechino, from an old provincial Italian word signifying "a lick dish," or greedy fellow, such being one of the features of the character represented.

His dress is described, upon the same authority, to have been a patched costume of an irregular pattern. The jacket had wide side-pockets, and was tightened round the waist by a girdle, but descended like a short tunic over trousers which fitted tight to the limbs. To these were added gaiters and slippers. Arlechino was masked. He wore a cap with a hare's tail in it in lieu of a feather, and at his girdle was a wooden sword, hat, or wand.

The most unexpected and deeply-to-be-regretted death of Dr. Doran, after a few days' illness, occurred at a moment when we were in correspondence on this subject, and I was unhappily therefore deprived of the opportunity of suggesting to him that the information he relied upon respecting Simone di Bologna might be, to a certain extent, reconciled with that of Menage, which he had, I think, rather too hastily rejected *in toto.*

The Gelosi company came to Paris during the reign of Henry III., 1574-1589. This was the very period at which the young Italian actor is stated by Menage to have acquired the name of Harlequin, from his intimacy with the President of the Parliament. Now, I have already noticed the unfortunate omission by Menage of the real name of that actor, and in the absence of any proof to the contrary I am inclined to believe him to have been the identical Simone di Bologna of Dr. Doran's version. The Gelosi, we are told, returned to Italy in 1604; and as Monsieur Forget died in 1610, it is clear that the actor of whose *badinage* with the President he was an ear-witness must have been one of the Andriени company who perpetrated a bad pun on the theatrical *sobriquet* which had been *previously* bestowed on him by his companions, for the reason recorded by Menage, on the authority of these same gentlemen, who can scarcely be suspected of having invented the story. Until therefore it is proved to me that Arlechino was the name of a character in the Italian drama previous to the visit of the Gelosi to Paris, I shall continue to maintain, with the learned Père La Rousse, that "l'opinion de Menage nous paraît le plus probable."

Next as to his dress. The drawing by Inigo Jones demonstrates that the Harlequin of that period did not wear "a patched costume of irregular pattern," but the plain white jacket and trousers (*loose,* not fitting the limbs) of a Scaramouche or Pierrot; nor have I been able to find any representation of a Harlequin so attired earlier than 1645, at which date Dominique Locatelli *dit* Trivelin was a member of the Italian company then performing in Paris, and celebrated for his assumption of that character. I annex an engraving of him from a print of the period. Here we see the irregularly patched dress for the first time; but are still in the dark respecting its origin or its significance. It may be as well to remark that "Patch" was in the sixteenth century the common name for a servant. Shylock, speaking of Launcelot Gobbo, says:—

Dominique Locatelli as Arlequin.

> "The Patch is kind enough, but a huge feeder."
> *Merchant of Venice.*

And, what is perhaps more noteworthy, is the fact that Harlequin is to this day called Patch in common theatrical parlance. As far, then, as I have been hitherto able to ascertain, the alteration

A Carnival Scene.
From a MS of the 15th Century in the Ambrosian Library Milan

from irregular to geometrical patchwork must have taken place between 1645 and 1682, and I am inclined to attribute the improvement to another Dominique, who was a celebrated Harlequin in the reign of Louis XIV., and a great favourite with that monarch, who stood godfather to his eldest son, Louis. The family name of this Dominique was Biancotelli, and he came to France at the age of seventeen, in the company of Italian actors who were engaged by Cardinal Mazarin in 1657. His biography is most interesting, but I must not be tempted into even a brief sketch of it : I must confine myself to the fact of his having changed the character of Harlequin from that of a stupid lout to a witty, satirical, vivacious personage, whose graceful dancing, vocal ability, and power of imitation of the great French actors of the day made him the delight of the Court and people for nearly thirty years. As he died at Toulon in 1727, he must have long survived the alteration in the costume, if he were not indeed the inventor of it. It is singular that his successor, Evarista Gherardi, who published the ' Théâtre Italien ' in six vols. 12mo, in 1697, and made his first appearance as Harlequin the 1st of October, 1689, should make no allusion to the first assumption of a costume so unique as that in which he must have been himself attired at that date, and the inference may be fairly drawn from his silence that, it having ceased to be a novelty in 1697, he did not consider it a circumstance worth recording.

Another innovation appears to have originated with this second Dominique. His second son, *Pierre* François Biancotelli, originally intended for the Church, fell in love with the daughter of the manager of a strolling company of players, named Pasquariel, and, marrying her, followed his father's example, and instead of becoming an archbishop or a general of Jesuits took to the stage, and under the patronage of the Regent Duke of Orleans, who removed him from the Opéra Comique to his new theatre at the Hôtel de Bourgogne, "made *Pierrot* the character in which the Parisians took a never-failing delight." This anecdote, if authentic, throws a doubt on the accuracy of the assertion that Pierrot was "Frenchified" from *Pedrolino*, one of the actors in the Gelosi company in 1576, and the doubt is increased by the fact that no such name as Pierrot is to be found in the Italian drama of that date or amongst the grotesque characters of Italian carnival.

At the same time, if the first Pierrot was this younger son of the great Dominique, it gives some colour to the statement that when the father remodelled the part of Harlequin he *introduced* that of Pierrot, to which he transferred the stupidity and other characteristics of the former, assigning to it also the original plain white dress of the "Arlekin, servant of the Mountebank," which had been discarded for the patched one as early as 1645.

This, of course, is but an hypothesis, which later discoveries may prove to be untenable. Such of my readers, however, as may be interested in the controversy have here before them all the principal points of it for the first time, I believe, critically examined and chronologically arranged ; and to those who may consider that I have been unnecessarily diffuse in my commentaries on what may appear to them a trivial subject, I can only recall to them the fact that it has occupied the attention of some of the greatest scholars and most learned archæologists in Europe for many years, and has still to be satisfactorily disposed of.

I have now to notice Costume as connected with a fourth class of amusements, distinct from the *disguisements* and mummings of the fourteenth century ; the Mysteries, Moralities, and Court masques, and the regular drama which succeeded them in the sixteenth century ; or the public pageants which from the earliest period of our history have with more or less magnificence celebrated periodical festivals or occasional important events, and have terminated in this country with the annual tasteless, ridiculous, and heterogeneous hodge-podge on the 9th of November, called the Lord Mayor's Show. This fourth class is familiar to us under the title of a masquerade, and undoubtedly owes its origin to the Carnival of the Church of Rome, and probably to the peculiar mode of its celebration in Italy.

Its distinction consists in this : that whereas "the disguisements" at the Courts of our mediæval monarchs, and the masques presented for their entertainment or in which they themselves took part, were preconcerted, and limited both in their object and the number of persons concerned, a masquerade is an assemblage of guests or a promiscuous gathering of people, each of whom assumes a dress or disguise according to the fancy of the individual, and without any reference to the rest of the company.

One of the earliest representations of an entertainment of this description that I have been fortunate enough to meet with, is contained in a MS. of the fifteenth century, discovered by M. Bonnard in the Ambrosian Library at Milan, and which he has made the subject of the 63rd plate in his second volume of 'Costumes' (see chromolithograph issued with Part XXIV.).

That it depicts a scene during the Carnival there can be no doubt, as the miniature occurs on a leaf preceding the prayers prescribed to be used during Lent.

M. Bonnard in his description of it says, " Plusieurs groupes de masques circulent dans une salle." It may be questioned, however, whether, strictly speaking, the persons can be called *masques*, as, unless it be the Turk, no one appears to be masked, the faces of the females being fully displayed, and those of the men, with the exception of the Turk aforesaid, are only partially concealed by the hoods which they wear under their caps. Even the Turk himself seems to me to have simply assumed a beard, if indeed that was an assumption, as I can discern no indication of a mask in the drawing of the face, which appears perfectly natural.

Taking it however as a bal-costumé, it is nevertheless a most interesting picture of manners, and curiously corroborates my observation respecting Oriental costumes, as here is an Osmanli as well dressed as he could be at present, while the rest of the company are in fanciful or conventional habits, betraying, however, as usual, the particular characteristics of the period, *circa* 1470.

Some fifty years later, we find the remarkable passage in Hall's Chronicle which I have already quoted at p. 391, and must here repeat :—" On the daie of the Epiphanie, at night, the King with xi others were disguised after the manner of Italie, called a maske—*a thing not seen afore in England*. Thei were appareled in garmentes long and broad, wrought all with golde, with visers and cappes of gold ; and, after the banket doen, these maskers came in with thr .ix gentlemen, disguised in silke, baryng staffe torches, and desired the ladies to daunce. Some were content, and some that knew the fashion of it refused, because it was *not a thing commonly seen*. And after thei daunced and commoned together, as the fashion of the maskes is, thei toke their leave and departed, and so did the Quene and all the ladies.'"

Mr. Payne Collier, who quoted this passage in his 'Annals of the Stage' (vol. i. p. 63), observes that as the old Chronicler, who was perfectly acquainted with Court entertainments, expressly states that this mask was "a thing not seen afore in England," there must have been some difference between "a mask" and "a disguising," not now distinctly to be explained. My view of the case is, that as masks were worn in mummings and disguisings, as well as in the earliest plays and "interludes," and therefore could not have been the distinctive feature of this Italian novelty, the difference must have existed in the "manner" only of the maskers, being after that " of Italie," and which appears to have been the apparelling of a certain number of persons *all alike*, in lieu of various grotesque attire, with heads or vizors of monsters or natural animals ; a fashion which, though long known on the Continent, as we have already seen a terrible example of in the catastrophe at the Court of Charles VI. of France, I certainly have not met with any record of in England previous to the above date, after which it became a favourite pastime with Henry VIII. and his courtiers. His unexpected appearance at Cardinal Wolsey's house with a party all attired as shepherds, as related by Cavendish, and many other instances, might be quoted.

Of fancy dress balls in foreign Courts we have a representation, I presume, as early as 1463, in a painting on wood of a dance by torchlight at the Court of Burgundy of that date, in the possession of M. H. Casterman, of Tournai (Belgium). M. Paul La Croix, who has favoured us with a copy of it in his 'Manners, Customs, and Dress of the Middle Ages,' says, in this dance " each performer bore in his hand a long lighted taper, and endeavoured to prevent his neighbours from blowing it out, which each one tried to do if possible." This dance, which was in use up to the end of the sixteenth century, was generally reserved for weddings. But here, as in the illumination in the Milanese MS. of nearly the same date, we have no indication of masks ; Monsieur and Madame d'Estampes and Monsieur Philip de Hornes being merely muffled by the tippets of their hoods, similarly to the persons

DANCE BY TORCHLIGHT AT THE COURT OF PERGUENDI

(From a painting on wood, circa 1867)

in the latter drawing. "The good Duke Philip" and his Duchess are in the ordinary costume of persons of their rank, without disguise of any description ; but the dresses of the Count de Charalois and Anthony (" le Grand Bâtard ") of Burgundy appear to me to have a fanciful character about them, and, as far as I can make out, Monsieur d'Estampes is in female attire, as nearly as possible similar to that of his wife. In the absence of any explanation of the painting beyond the names of the dancers inscribed upon it, I hesitate to assign it to any particular class of entertainment. It is scarcely to be called a disguisement, it has no affinity to a masque, and the absence of vizors of any kind deprives it of all pretension to be called " a masquerade."

That masquerades, in the present acceptance of the term, had their origin in Italy, is highly probable, but their existence as early as the end of the fifteenth or beginning of the sixteenth century is not, I think, sufficiently evident. Jehan Tabouret (otherwise Thoinot Arbeau), author of a work entitled ' Orchéographie,' printed at Langres in 1588, says, " Kings and princes give dances and masquerades for amusement, and in order to afford a joyful welcome to foreign nobles ;" but he adds, " we also practise the same amusements on the celebration of marriages." It is therefore obvious to me that he is speaking of masques, and not masquerades, the former of which I have already spoken of at p. 396 ante (see also plate of Masque at the Marriage of Sir Henry Utton, who died 1596), and also those which succeeded the mediæval disguisements, and became so popular at the Court of Henry VIII. ; the first of which, we have the evidence of Hall, was, "after the manner of Italy," introduced in 1513.

The masquerade, bal-masqué, or masked ball, as a social entertainment in contradistinction to the promiscuous gathering of maskers in the streets during the Carnival in Roman Catholic countries, does not appear to have been popularized in England previously to the reign of William III.

The bal-masqué is said to have been introduced into France under the regency of Philip, Duke of Orleans. The Chevalier de Bouillon conceived the project of converting the Opera-house into a ball-room, for which he received a pension of 6000 livres ; and a Carmelite friar, named Father Sebastian, invented the means of elevating the pit to the level of the stage and lowering it at pleasure.

The first ball was given 2nd of January, 1710, and in 1711 masquerades were given, including a concert, at a room in Spring Gardens, at half-a-guinea a ticket ; " no person admitted unmasked or armed."

The particular habit with which masquerades has made us familiar is the domino. It was in the Middle Ages a sort of cowl or camail, worn in winter by the clergy in the choir, similar if not identical with the amuse, and received its appellation from the title *Dominus* which at that period was generally given to ecclesiastics in the sense of "Sir" or "Master." [1] In the sixteenth century we find it applied in France to the hooded cape worn as a disguise by Henry III. and his mignons when roaming the streets in Paris during the Carnival. This capuchon, or, as St. Simon calls it, *roquelachon* and "domino de prêtre," became subsequently a long black cloak or gown reaching to the feet, with large loose sleeves, a hood to cover the head, and a train ending in a point, which was worn by mourners at funerals, and in fact is the domino of the masquerade, now worn of all colours.

Masquerades, if not introduced, were popularized in England by the ingenuity and energy of a Swiss named John James Heidegger, the son of a clergyman at Zurich. Arriving in this country in 1708, he entered, although in the fiftieth year of his age, as a private in the Guards, and nevertheless contrived to become the "arbiter elegantiarum" of London, the fashionable world accepting him as such, and calling him "the Swiss Count." In 1709 he made 500 guineas by his designing and superintending the dresses, scenery, and decorations for Watteux's opera, ' Tamyris, Queen of Scythia,' and in 1711 he was thriving on the masquerades which he had made so much the rage, that moralists and satirists protested, and the clergy preached against them. A letter by Steele in the ' Spectator ' for Friday, March 16, in that year, contains several allusions to the dresses in vogue on such occasions, and purports to be from " the Undertaker of the Masquerade."

[1] Napoléon Landais ; Quicherat. The reader is probably familiar with the old anecdote of the Bishop of Sisteron, who, as related by Cestoile, being *in articulo mortis*, sent for his domino, "because," said he, "*beati sunt qui moriuntur in domino.*"

"SIR,—I have observed the rules of my masque so carefully in not inquiring into persons, that I cannot tell whether you were one of the company or not last Tuesday; but if you were not, and still design to come, I desire you would to your own entertainment please to admonish the town that all persons indifferently are not fit for this sort of diversion. I could wish, Sir, you could make them understand that it is a kind of acting to go in masquerade, and a man should be able to say or do things proper for the dress in which he appears. We have now and then rakes in the habit of Roman senators, and grave politicians in the dress of rakes. The misfortune of the thing is, that people dress themselves in what they have a mind to be, and not what they are fit for. There is not a girl in the town, but let her have her will in going to a masque, and she shall dress as a shepherdess. But let me beg of them to read the 'Arcadia,' or some other good romance, before they appear in any such character in my house. The last time we presented, everybody was so rashly habited, that when they came to speak to each other, a nymph with a crook had not a word to say but in the style of the pit, and a man in the habit of a philosopher was speechless, till an occasion offered of expressing himself in the refuse of the tyring-room. We had a judge that danced a minuet, with a Quaker for his partner, while half-a-dozen harlequins stood by as spectators. A Turk drank me off two bottles of wine, and a Jew eat me up half a ham of bacon. If I can bring my design to bear, and make the maskers preserve their characters in my assemblies, I hope you will allow there is a foundation laid for more elegant and improving gallantries than any the town at present affords, and consequently that you will give your approbation to the endeavours of, Sir, your most obedient servant."

The letter has no signature or address, and may be Steele's own composition, notwithstanding his statement that he found "it came from the undertaker of the masquerade;" "undertaker" being at that date the term applied to the proprietors or responsible directors of all kinds of public entertainments, in the same sense as *entrepreneur* is in French. In 1711, the "undertaker" would appear to have been Heidegger, and the question is only of interest as it affects the existence of a competitor or a predecessor of the "Swiss Count," who contrived to make £5000 a year "*and spend it*" in England, which he humorously defied anyone to do in Switzerland. If Heidegger, the "house" he speaks of must at that time have been in Spring Gardens, though no locality is mentioned by the writer, or in an earlier notice of these masquerades in No. 8 of the 'Spectator' for Friday, March 9, 1710–11.

I have now arrived, by the blessing of Providence, at the termination of this labour of love, commenced with some temerity at the advanced age of seventy-nine. I have devoted to it the greater portion of more than three years of my life; and if the perusal of it should afford to my readers but a tithe of the interest and pleasure its compilation and composition have afforded me, I can say without vanity they will not regret their trouble. Of its many imperfections I am as fully aware as my severest critic can be; but I have the satisfaction of feeling that, whatever may be its errors or shortcomings, they are not due to any neglect on my part to do the best I could to render it useful to the student and the artist, and generally satisfactory to the subscribers.

In dissenting occasionally from the opinions of some of the most eminent antiquaries, foreign as well as English, I hope I have expressed myself with due respect and consideration, and in every instance fully and fairly quoted their observations and conclusions, that my readers should be able to form their own judgment of the question at issue, and I can honestly declare that I have warped no evidence to back up a theory, or insisted on its being unassailable.[1] The experience of upwards of fifty years has beneficially enlightened me as to the extent of my own ignorance, and the principal value of this work will be in the warnings it contains against the ready assumption of long-accredited traditions as facts, upon the simple ground of their not having been hitherto doubted or contradicted.

Not the least singular proof of the darkness that still involves many important subjects treated in these volumes, is the absence of all reliable authority for the stories, more or less plausible, which have been for centuries circulated and very generally believed, respecting the origin of the most

[1] I must here express my deep regret that at the time I write one of the most highly-esteemed foreign antiquaries, M. Viollet-le-Duc, has been taken from us in the midst of his valuable labours, and before I had the opportunity of publicly acknowledging my admiration of and obligations to the exquisite illustrations contained in his works.

celebrated institutions, devices, and decorations : the Orders of the Garter and of the Golden Fleece, and their respective insignia ; the Prince of Wales's feathers, and the motto "Ich dien ;" the Collar of SS ; the mysterious letters F.E.R.T. in the collar of the Order of the Annunciation ; the badges of our Royal Family ; nay, the derivation of the word "badge" itself.

Much light also remains to be thrown on the derivation, nature, and use of various articles of wearing apparel, portions of armour and weapons of war, and which can only be obtained by the discovery of hitherto unedited contemporary documents. Many persons will, I think, be surprised to find that three hundred years have elapsed since we first heard of the familiar holiday friend of our childhood, "nimble-footed Harlequin," and that the etymology of his name and the origin of his dress are as much a matter of conjecture and controversy as ever.

The pleasant duty now alone remains to return thanks to those who have so kindly assisted me by their suggestions and information. I have already, in the course of my work, acknowledged my obligations to several ; but as I cannot thank any of them too much, I gratefully record in these concluding lines the names of Mr. Harold Dillon ; Mr. Wentworth Huyshe ; the Hon. Lewis Wingfield ; Mr. Burgess, the eminent architect ; Mr. George Scharf, Keeper of the National Portrait Gallery ; Mr. Solomon Hart, R.A., Librarian of the Royal Academy of Arts ; Mr. M'Kay, of the house of Colnaghi and Co., Pall Mall East, whose portfolios have always been most liberally open to my inspection, and selections from their valuable contents entrusted to me for reproduction ; Major Szulezwski, to whom I am indebted for much information respecting Poland ; and last, but by no means least, to my brother dramatist, Mr. Frank Marshall, whose collection of rare and curious early Italian comedies has been of important service to me in my notice of Stage costume. It is also but an act of justice to the Messrs. and Miss Murray, who, together with Miss Stone and Mr. Lambert, have so zealously and intelligently executed a considerable portion of the illustrations of this work, to say that no one who has not seen their drawings on the wood can appreciate the fidelity with which they transferred to it the particular style of each original engraver.

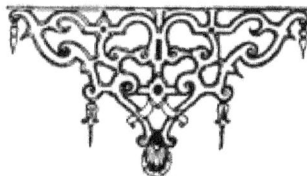

INDEX.

LONDON: PRINTED BY WILLIAM CLOWES AND SONS, STAMFORD STREET AND CHARING CROSS.

www.ingramcontent.com/pod-product-compliance
Lightning Source LLC
Chambersburg PA
CBHW022129020426
42334CB00015B/814